School
Social Work

Also available from Lyceum Books, Inc.

School Social Work

Practice, Policy, and Research

Sixth Edition

Robert Constable

Carol Rippey Massat

Shirley McDonald

John P. Flynn

LYCEUM
BOOKS, INC.

5758 S. Blackstone
Chicago, IL 60637

© Lyceum Books, Inc., 2006

Published by

LYCEUM BOOKS, INC.
5758 S. Blackstone Ave.
Chicago, Illinois 60637
773+643-1903 (Fax)
773+643-1902 (Phone)
lyceum@lyceumbooks.com
http://www.lyceumbooks.com

10 9 8 7 6 5 4 3 2 1

ISBN 0-925065-95-1

Library of Congress Cataloging-in-Publication Data

School social work : practice, policy, and research / Robert Constable ... [et al.].—6th ed.
    p. cm.
  Includes index.
  ISBN 0-925065-95-1 (alk. paper)
    1. School social work—United States.   I. Constable, Robert T.
LB3013.4.S365   2006
371.4′6—dc22
                               2005031106

Contents

Preface to the Sixth Edition

School social work is becoming essential to education throughout the world as families and communities strive to make schools safe and inclusive places for children to learn, to grow, and to flourish. Students are challenged by the complexity and risks involved in growing up today; parents and schools are equally concerned. Over the past decades the substance and process of education has had to change, as has the practice of school social work. Legislative changes, shifts in society, and the welfare system have placed additional demands on educational institutions. Schools, which often find themselves in the middle of a political battleground, must respond to the mandates of legislation and case law, as well as to the needs identified by families and communities. School social workers, from their unique positions as practitioners, are often catalysts behind creative responses to societal and community changes.

The sixth edition of *School Social Work* addresses the key issues facing schools and school social workers today. For those who want to understand the complex and diverse world of social work services within the school community, the book provides a model of role development. The model used in this book builds on the assessment; consultation, planning, coordination, and individual, group, and family intervention, which school social workers have always done well. Now focused on working with the school and its community as well, the model seeks to reconstruct the meaning of school as a safe place where families and schools can work together and manage the risks to their children's good development. Infused throughout each chapter of the book are case examples and content that exemplify the practice of school social work in all its diversity with bilingual students, immigrant children, members of minority and oppressed groups, and female students, among others.

School Social Work, sixth edition, combines traditional chronological and topical approaches to help the social worker understand the complex and diverse world of social work services within the school community. The field of social work is being constructed by many different social workers. Needs change and situations evolve, so that neither the future world of the school nor its students' needs can be typified or frozen in time. The sixth edition reflects these practical changes while retaining its productive theoretical perspective.

This edition is a product of the work of forty-two authors who collectively provide ways to get a theoretical and methodological handle on the school social worker's role. With all of the diversity in roles, there are constants and there is remarkable unity in the material. Each author addresses different aspects of an emergent role. The authors also provide updated end-of-chapter references to facilitate student's location of key source materials, and Web sites and online resources to obtain materials and information not yet in print.

Section I, History and General Perspectives in School Social Work, traces the history and evolving role of the school social worker and provides a theoretical framework for school social work practice. Constable in chapter 1 outlines the content of school social work as a specialization and traces the history of the role. This is followed by theoretical frameworks for practice in the classic chapters by Germain and Monkman. In response to the accountability movement in education and legislation, such as the No Child Left Behind Act of 2001, school social work has increased its focus on effectiveness, research, and evaluation. These issues are addressed by Flynn, Constable, and Massat, and by Sabatino, Mayer, and Timberlake. More and more, school social workers are confronted by serious confidentiality concerns, given the presence of violence in schools, communities, and families; drugs in schools and the workplace; suicidal ideation of students; self-mutilation behavior; and other sensitive issues. Two chapters address these confidentiality issues (Raines and SSWWAA).

School social workers and others develop plans and programs to meet the particular needs of each school community. This vision of practice, which continues to shape the book, can be traced to the earliest days of school social work and to its continuation through periods of fundamental changes in society and in school policy. As a result of this developed role, dealing with social dimensions and needs in the education process, schools in our age find they need the school social worker as never before. For education professionals, effectiveness has become critical. In this context an outcome-based education system is developing, characterized by common standards, flexible notions of education to meet these standards, higher standards for education professionals, and ultimately in equal educational opportunities for all. As a consequence of the emphasis on outcomes, school systems are developing systems of accountability that demand school social workers show evidence for effectiveness of their interventions. This emphasis on effectiveness calls for high professional qualifications and meshes with movements toward specialization in school social work. In accordance with the No Child Left Behind Act of 2001, states are setting standards for "highly qualified" school social workers and introducing post-masters-degree mentorships for more permanent certification as a highly qualified school professional.

Section II, Policies, Programs, and Mandates for Developing Social Services in the Schools, focuses on the framework, tools, and context for school policy development. Constable and Kordesh frame this section with their discussion of key policies that affect program policy. Hare, Rome, and Massat set out the context of central issues facing schools and school social workers in the early twenty-first century, including diversity in schools, the accountability movement in education, poverty, adolescent parenthood, violence in schools, substance abuse, school dropout, and the demands of recent legislation. Whitted, Rich, and Constable (chapter 11) and Bishop (chapter 12) lay out the key elements of special education laws that profoundly affect social work practice in schools. The tools of policy change—research, organizational analysis, needs assessment, and policy analysis—are given in chapters 13 through 16.

Policy changes often happen quickly although they usually reflect longstanding concerns. Examples of policy change and development can be found in new programs for children with special needs. The school has become the center of planning for these children. Practice adapted itself to meeting and defining the new possibilities of work with these children and families. New partnerships of parents and schools are defining new communities of concern. School communities are expecting schools to be concerned with inclusion and safety, as well as respect for individual differences. The expanded understanding of the mission, scope, and process of education has had to be shared with families if it would be successful. The social worker is in the thick of all of this, working with the principal, teachers, children, parents, and community agencies, sharing a tentative assessment and planning with others situations as they emerge in schools. The chief skills of the social worker are the ability to assess needs, to develop an appropriate school social work role to meet the emergent needs, and then to help develop an appropriate school response to these emergent conditions. Thus the social worker uses clinical skills with individual pupils and families; provides consultation, case assessment, case management, and coordination of services; works with groups; and helps develop policies and plans for concerns about safety through conflict resolution and mediation. The key to success is to develop this role in a consistent way, and not to get lost in a sea of unprocessed demands. Good practice demands an understanding, based on theory and research, of what is involved and what can be done.

Section III, Assessment, Consultation, and Planning, centers on the school social work role in assessment and consultation (chapters 17 and 20), direct work with children and families, and work with a broader school community. These tasks and skills are the basis for everything the school social worker does. To work with teachers, parents, and children is also to work with their school community context. The result is a broader assessment process, a contextual understanding based on needs assessments, action research, evaluation, consultation, policy analysis, and planning. This broader contextual awareness is crucial to the effectiveness of the school social worker in the development of programs and policies.

Cross-cultural practice, including, assessment, goal-setting and measurement, has become increasingly important for competent school social work practice. In Section III, both a broad framework and specific tools for practice are included to address these issues. In the diverse school community, an understanding of cross-cultural practice is essential. Caple and Salcido provide a framework for cross-cultural practice. The movement toward inclusion of children with disabilities in regular education has strongly affected schools across the nation. McDonald, Constable, and Holley address specific inclusion issues. Practice skills in consultation collaboration, classroom observation, adaptive behavior assessment, case study assessment, and goal setting are covered in chapters 19, 20, 21, 22, and 24.

Section IV, Practice Applications in the Schools, focuses even more strongly on current practice issues in schools. A highly sophisticated model of practice is emerging that integrates research, policy, and different forms of intervention at the school community level, such that school social work is becoming a distinct area of specialized practice. In this section of the book, chapters cover practice in the diverse conditions of schools today: personal safety of school social workers, attendance issues, case management, mental health, child welfare issues, group work, social skills training, violence in schools, crisis intervention, and mediation. Although some of these issues, such as attendance and mental health, have had historic standing in school social work practice, new legislation and increased demands for accountability have placed greater emphasis on each of these issues as specific foci for school social work practice. Throughout the world schools are becoming the main public institution for social development, carrying out missions of inclusion for those previously excluded from the opportunity for education. Schools are raising standards of learning to prepare future citizens to participate in a multinational world that is bound together by modern communication and economic and social relations. The school social worker assists economically, socially, politically, and personally marginalized children and families to participate in education, and to make the education process effective.

Acknowledgments

As the field of school social work continues to be constructed by many different social workers, we give special recognition to those who have helped construct the theory. Fondly missed, they are now with us only in their writings. Florence Poole envisioned a field of practice with practitioners guided by theory assisting the school to become a resource for children, and for children to use these school resources for their own growth. Carel Germain took a biological, ecological metaphor, a life model for social work practice, and used it to explain what social workers were doing. Marjorie Monkman, student of William E. Gordon, took Gordon's theories about building social work practice in new directions as she constructed ecological theory for school social work as a field of practice. These individuals live on in the theories they have woven, and they assist all of us in understanding the potential in the school social worker's role.

Each of us acknowledges the patience and forbearance of our spouses, children, grandchildren, friends, and colleagues, who made the endeavor possible. Our students' struggles with learning such a complex role continue to inspire us. They will take the field forward. Finally, to this we add the readers of the first, second, third, fourth, and fifth editions, now spanning over two decades, who supported us in the belief that the content is worthwhile and usable, and who urged us to further refine and develop these ideas in a sixth edition.

Robert Constable
Carol Rippey Massat
Shirley McDonald
John P. Flynn

About the Authors

Robert Constable is Professor Emeritus of social work at Loyola University Chicago. He completed his AB (Classical) at Georgetown University, his MSW degree at Loyola University, and DSW at the University of Pennsylvania with a focus on school social work. He practiced as a school social worker in Gary, Indiana, Philadelphia, Pennsylvania, and Evanston, Illinois, and in Project Head Start. Active in social work education, he has held faculty status at West Chester State University, the Jane Addams College of Social Work at the University of Illinois at Chicago, and Loyola University Chicago, and at several European universities. He organized graduate concentrations in school social work at the University of Illinois at Chicago and at Loyola University Chicago. He was co-director from 1992 through 1997 of the first social work graduate program in Lithuania at Vytautas Magnus University. Former editor of *Social Work in Education*, he is author of more than 100 publications in social work. He currently works as a social worker in private practice and continues his contribution to the literature of his profession.

Carol Rippey Massat is Associate Professor at the Jane Addams College of Social Work, University of Illinois at Chicago. She is currently editor of the *School Social Work Journal* and is the author of numerous social work publications. She serves on the Board of the Illinois Association of School Social Workers. She completed her AB (Rhetoric) at the University of Illinois at Urbana-Champaign, and her MSW at the University of Illinois at Urbana-Champaign, with a concentration in school social work. She also completed her PhD at the University of Illinois Urbana-Champaign School of Social Work. At the Jane Addams College of Social Work she has chaired the school social work concentration for many years and has taught school social work practice, policy, and research over the past fifteen years. She worked as a social worker in Decatur, Illinois, for ten years.

Shirley McDonald is Vice President of the Park/Forest Chicago Heights, Illinois, School Board and chair of the Calumet District of the National Association of Social Workers. Former editor of the *School Social Work Journal*, she has long been a leader in the field of school social work. She is Past-President of the Illinois Association of School Workers and continued to serve on the Board of the Illinois Association of School Social Workers for many years. She has retired from service as a clinical associate professor at the Jane Addams College of Social Work, University of Illinois at Chicago, where she chaired the school social work concentration for many years and where she taught school social work practice to hundreds of students over her years of service. She has been a school social worker in special education cooperatives, serving children with low-incidence disabilities and their families. She previously taught elementary school for four years, first in Chicago and then in Flossmoor, Illinois.

John P. Flynn is Professor Emeritus at Western Michigan University. He earned his MSW from University of Michigan and PhD in social welfare policy and planning from the Graduate School of Social Work, University of Denver. He has taught social welfare policy, planning, and administration at both the graduate and undergraduate levels. In addition to the many social work articles he has published, he is also author of *Social Agency Policy: Analysis and Presentation for Community Practice*, 2nd edition, Nelson-Hall, 1992.

Section One

History and General Perspectives in School Social Work

1

The Role of the School Social Worker

Robert Constable
Loyola University, Chicago

- ◆ The Purpose of School Social Work and the Purpose of Education
- ◆ An Historical Analysis of School Social Work
- ◆ Whom Does the School Social Worker Serve?
- ◆ Where Does School Social Work Take Place?
- ◆ What Does the School Social Worker Do?

School social work is a specialized area of practice within the broad field of the social work profession. School social workers bring unique knowledge and skills to the school system and the student services team. School social workers are instrumental in furthering the purpose of the schools: to provide a setting for teaching, learning, and for the attainment of competence and confidence. School social workers are hired by school districts to enhance the district's ability to meet its academic mission, especially where home, school and community collaboration is the key to achieving that mission. (School Social Work Association of America, 2005)

The family and the school are the central places for the development of children. Herein can be found the hopes for the next generation. There are often gaps in this relationship, within the school, within the family, in their relation to each other, and to the needs of students. There are gaps between aspirations and realities, between manifest need and available programs. In the dynamic, multicultural world of the child today, there are gaps between diverse cultures and what education may offer. Everywhere it is a top public priority that children develop well and that schools support that development. Nevertheless, aspirations are unfulfilled, policies fail, and effective programs fail with certain students. School social workers practice where children, families, schools, and communities encounter one another, where hopes can fail, where gaps exist, and where education can break down.

Throughout the world, schools are becoming the main public institution for social development. Schools are working to include those previously excluded from the opportunity of education. They are raising standards for educational outcomes to prepare citizens to participate in a multinational world, bound together more effectively by communication and by economic and social relations. The school social worker is becoming a useful professional to assist children who are marginalized—whether economically, socially, politically, or personally—to participate in this. Social workers work to make the education process effective and to include parents in this process.

Education has become crucial, not only for each person to cope with the demands of modern living, but also for national economic survival (Friedman, 2005). It is very serious work. As a consequence of education's enhanced mission, an outcome-based education system is developing. This system is characterized by common standards, flexible notions of education to meet these standards, and higher standards for education professionals to deal differently with different levels of need. Because children begin school with different skills, abilities, and resources, they do not begin with a level playing field, and the imposition of uniform standards to all children logically leads to shifting resources to those who are more at risk. Nevertheless outcome-driven education is a sea change that is driving education law and policy. For children with disabilities such outcome-driven education (albeit individual outcomes), together with the idea of dealing differently with different levels of need, has been established in law for thirty years.

School social workers practice in the most vulnerable parts of the educational process. And so their role can be as complex as the worlds it deals with. Practice rests on a wide range of skills, which are defined and take shape through interactive teamwork. School social workers may work one-on-one with teachers, families, and children to address individual situations and needs. They become part of joint efforts to make schools safe for everyone. In preserving the dignity and respect due any one person, the school needs to become a community of belonging and respect. Social workers work with the whole school on positive policies and educational programs, which deal with harassment of students alleged to be gay or lesbian, for example. When the school decides to implement a zero-tolerance policy, social workers are available to consult with teachers on implementation and to work with victims and perpetrators of harassment. They may help develop a crisis plan for the school with the principal, teachers' representatives, and school nurse (a crisis team). They may work with that crisis team through a disturbing and violent incident, working in different ways with individual pupils and teachers experiencing crisis and with the broader school population. They may develop mediation programs in high schools experiencing confrontations between students. The list continues through many variations.

THE PURPOSE OF SCHOOL SOCIAL WORK
AND THE PURPOSE OF EDUCATION

School social workers have long been concerned about children who may not be able to use what education has to offer. These concerns are coming to be shared by others. Over the span of a century, schools have broadened their mission and scope toward greater inclusion and toward respect for individual differences of all children. Consequently, social workers and many educators have come to share similar values. Each person possesses intrinsic worth. People have common needs. Schools and families are places where children should develop, discover their own dignity and worth, and come to realize their potential. Unfortunately, the human potential of each person is often needlessly wasted. The worlds of young people, often so full of hope, can be taken over at the same time by strange and distorted pictures, coming from many sources, of human worth and of social relations.

School social workers work with young people and their school and family environments, assisting them to accomplish tasks associated with their learning, growth, and development, and thus to come to a fuller realization of their intrinsic dignity, capability, and potential. The school social work role can be flexibly developed from this purpose and these values.

The basic focus of the school social worker is the constellation of teacher, parent, and child. The social worker must be able to relate to and work with all aspects of the child's situation, but the basic skill underlying all of this is *assessment*, a systematic way of understanding and communicating what is happening and what is possible. Building on assessment, the social worker develops a plan to assist the total constellation—teacher and students in the classroom, parents in the family, and others—to work together to support the child in the successful completion of the developmental steps that lie ahead. The basic questions are (1) What should the role of the school social worker be in this particular school community? and (2) Where are the best places to intervene—the *units of attention*—in this particular situation? Guided by the purposes and needs of education and the learning process, an effective, focused, and comprehensible school social work role can be negotiated within a school community.

Role, the key to the understanding of what the school social worker does, is a set of expected behaviors constructed by school social workers together with their school communities. In each school building, the school social worker's role is developed by social workers with others, such as the principal and the teachers. To do this, school social workers need to have a vision of what is possible, possess tools of analysis, be comfortable with the processes of negotiation, and coordinate their interventions with the life of the school.

Stories of Practice: Models of School Social Work

A Classic Example of Clinical School Social Work. A child who speaks mainly Spanish in her family has a first experience of kindergarten in a predominantly Anglo school and spends the class hiding behind the piano every day. The more the teacher tries to move her from behind the piano, the more firmly she remains; it has now become a struggle of wills between child and teacher. The school social worker first assesses the situation in a consultation conference with the teacher, and they develop a few joint strategies focusing on the child's experience in the class. They might shorten the exposure of the youngster to the class or help the teacher modify the educational focus and expectations. The youngster might get started in school with a supportive person from her own community. The teacher might help the youngster work with another child in the class who is less afraid and can be supportive. The teacher might invite the family to school to help them feel more comfortable and thus convey that feeling of comfort to the child. The social worker and teacher look for signs of the youngster's possible response. Chances are that the problem is at least partly one of language. Another possibility is that the youngster is not ready for kindergarten and should wait a bit. Or the youngster may need more detailed prekindergarten testing or different placement in school, one that accommodates her special needs. The social worker will also assist the teacher in her contacts with the parents, because in this case these contacts seem crucial.

So far the social worker has not seen the parents and may not need to. Perhaps with the social worker's consultation the teacher can manage the situation. When the teacher is open to consultation, it is the first, most effective, least intrusive, and least costly use of the social worker's time. However, in many cases, and especially in the case of a child entering school, it may be necessary to confer with the parents. Parents, especially those from a different linguistic or cultural group, may be insecure and uncertain of their role in school. They may feel strange about being involved with the school. It is of course precisely these feelings that may be conveyed to their child, so that the child fears the school and can find no way to cope with it. The school social worker, aware of these likely fears, can take a normalizing approach toward them, with the intent of helping mother and father feel at ease. The school social worker, when entering the home, is entering the world of the family. In this story, the parents gradually feel comfortable and trusting enough to discuss their real concerns. They are worried about letting the youngster go to school. They value education greatly but experience Anglo culture as distant, different, and threatening. Moreover, each parent has a different approach to discipline, and their difficulties with each other make them both feel helpless regarding some of the youngster's behavior. When the parents are in disagreement, the youngster always wins; this learned behavior is being carried to the school. The school social worker makes an assessment, jointly with the parents, of how the child is responding, what the dynamics of the home may be, and what type of agreement between parents, teacher, and child can be constructed. The school must also support the child's first steps to adapt appropriately. The school social worker's work with the parents would parallel work already done with the child's teacher. In this case, the work between the teacher and the parents may suffice. In other stories, the social worker will opt to work with the child also, building on the work already done with teacher and parents.

A School Crisis. Another school itself is in crisis. When too many things are taking place at once for the school to manage and still remain a safe environment for children or when children are having great difficulty processing a situation, a crisis happens in a school. When Christa McAuliffe, an astronaut and a teacher, died in the Challenger explosion as millions of children were watching on television, schools throughout the country seized it as a teachable moment. It was an opportunity; indeed, there was a necessity to help children process their feelings about dying and about the meanings of their lives.

In our own particular story, the school is in turmoil because of the violent death in a school bus accident of one of the children, an 8-year-old Korean girl. The school has a general plan for dealing with crises and specifically a detailed crisis manual that the school social worker helped create as a key member of the crisis team. On hearing about the death, the social worker makes an immediate assessment of the points of vulnerability in the school and meets with the school crisis team. They agree on a division of work. The principal works with the news media and community and makes an announcement to teachers and students as soon as there is a clear picture of what happened. The social worker has been in touch with the girl's family to learn what their wishes are and to assess how they are managing the crisis. The social worker agrees to work with the family, staying in touch throughout the crisis. She cancels normal appointments, except those that cannot be changed, and opens her office as a crisis center for students and teachers who want to talk about what has happened. She consults with the teacher of the student who died, and they discuss how the class is to be told. Later, people who were involved with the student or who feel the need attend a small Buddhist memorial service, and still later, students, teachers, and the family preserve the memory of the student in a more permanent way with a small peace garden in the school courtyard. School and community deal with the aftershocks of the death in a healing process that takes place over the next several years.

A Child with Special Needs. A child with a disability needs to be moved from one class to another. In the first class she is more protected but achieves less than her capabilities. Primarily, she is friends with other children with disabilities. She is moving to a class with a wide range of children with different levels of ability, where, if she feels safe and accepted, it is hoped she might achieve more. However, she will experience greater stress whatever her level of achievement.The shift is carefully planned and is based on tests that say that the student will be able to achieve in this class with some special help.The new teacher and the former teacher are fully involved in the process.The student is also fully involved, and the social worker has developed a supportive relationship with the student and with the parents.When the day comes for the move, the social worker is there in case of unforeseen difficulties.The social worker works with the teacher, parent, and child in the months following the move, until it is clear that his services are no longer needed (Welsh & Goldberg, 1979).

Consultation and Placement of Students. The social worker develops an active prevention program at a junior high school. One problem the school faces is that children are coming to the departmental structure of the junior high school from a self-contained sixth-grade class in a familiar building close to home. It is not unusual for such children to regress for a semester or more. Some never recover the achievement and feeling of safety they experienced when they had one teacher and knew the teacher and their classmates well.Through the classroom observation that is a normal part of her work in the school, the social worker gets to know the teaching styles of each of the teachers and the range of strengths each brings to his or her work with children. Before the 400 new students from feeder schools come to the junior high school in September, she reviews their records from elementary school. She places each at-risk child with a homeroom teacher who fits well with that child's needs, making certain that there are only a few children with serious problems in each classroom and a balance of children with positive social adjustments and learning skills. Referrals of children for help the following year run at about half the normal rate, and children who need more intensive help are helped earlier.

Group Work in a School. In another story, a group of seven 12-year-old boys decides in their discussions with each other that they all have problems with their fathers. They appear at the social worker's door, asking to form a group to discuss their concerns.The social worker, who is male, calls each of the parents for permission and invites them to come in to discuss the situation.The parents come in, some individually, some in a group, and the boys are seen in a group with some individual follow-up.The result in each boy is a lowering of tension in his relations with his father and a measurable improvement academically and socially. No boy needs to be seen longer than three months.

Mediation. A high school is experiencing a large number of fights between groups of students of different ethnicities over insulting language, relations with girls (or boys), and accusations of stealing, among other things.There is a particularly high level of tension around allegations of being gay or lesbian. Fights have usually been handled by the intervention of the vice principal, but this is not well accepted by the students and has resulted in escalations of punishment and students' experiencing shame and wishing revenge on the students who have shamed them and on the vice principal.The social worker and the principal develop a mediation program. Disputes between individual students are subject to mediation by a panel of specially trained students, who are selected by other students for their leadership ability and their interest in participating in the program. This program lowers tensions in the school as problems are resolved mutually, collaboratively, and without escalation, and the dignity of each student is preserved. The education program enables and encourages youngsters to deal with differences, including their own, through discussion with the social worker and with each other in a safe atmosphere. The social worker and some teachers, with the social worker's assistance, maintain contact with different coalesced groups of Hispanic, White, and African American students and with their leadership.

The work of the social worker is the work of the school, and the effectiveness of the school social worker becomes the effectiveness of education. In each example of the role of the social worker, the social worker applies the basics of the school social work role to a different set of circumstances in concert with other members of the school team, finding collaborative ways for the school and its membership to solve problems.

AN HISTORICAL ANALYSIS OF SCHOOL SOCIAL WORK

The focus of school social work has followed the historic concerns of education. The problems confronted by the education institution over its long history have ranged from old and continuing problems, accommodating large immigrant populations, discrimination against particular groups, truancy, the tragic waste of human potential in emotional disturbances of childhood, and newer problems, school disruption and safety, homelessness, drugs, the new immigrants, and AIDS. The first social workers in schools were hired in recognition of the fact that conditions, whether in the family, neighborhood, or school itself, that prevented children from learning and the school from carrying out its mandate were its legitimate concern (Allen-Meares, Washington, & Welsh, 2000; Costin, 1978). School social work would draw its legitimacy and its function from its capability to make education work for groups of children who could not otherwise participate. It has reflected in its history the evolving awareness in education, and in society, of groups of children for whom education has not been effective—the children of immigrants, the impoverished, the economically and socially oppressed, the delinquent, the disturbed, and those with disabilities. It drew its function from the needs and eventually the rights of these groups as they interfaced with the institution of education and confronted the expectation that they should achieve to their fullest potential. In each circumstance, as school social workers defined their roles, there was a match of the social work perspective, its knowledge, values, and skills, with the missions and mandates of the school.

Inclusion of All Children. During the twentieth century, schools have broadened their mission and scope toward greater inclusion and respect for individual differences of all children. The passage of compulsory school attendance laws, roughly from 1895 through 1918, marked a major shift in philosophies and policies governing American education. This would eventually become a philosophy of inclusion. Education, no longer for the elite, was for everyone a necessary part of preparation for modern life. A half-century later the U.S. Supreme Court reaffirmed that education for each child is a constitutional right, which, if available to any, must be available to all on an equal basis. The profundity of the change to education in our society is succinctly expressed in the landmark case of *Brown v. Board of Education of Topeka, Kansas* (1954):

> If education is a principal instrument in helping the child to adjust normally to this environment, it is doubtful that any child may reasonably be expected to succeed in life if he is denied the opportunity of an education. The opportunity of an education, where the state has undertaken to provide it to any, is a right, which must be made available to all on equal terms.

This belief, inherent initially in the passage of compulsory attendance laws, becomes the basis for an ever-growing extension of education to all children at risk, most recently to those with disabilities.

Respect for Individual Differences. The belief that education, if available to any, should be available equally to all, was also energized by the emergent awareness of individual differences and the need, indeed the responsibility of the school, to adapt curriculum to these differences. The initial thrust of education in a modernizing society would be to standardize curriculum, and thus the learning process, into "one best way" to learn and one set of subjects to be learned. A prescribed curriculum, standardized testing, and the grade system organized the modern school. Students had to fit into this prescribed curriculum and learning process. Their ability to do this was measured. The problem is that none of this standardization of learners, knowledge, and the learning process matches the real world of differences. Learners are different. Learning continues to be both an individual process and a relational process. Curriculum is potentially diverse. It changes as knowledge changes. For students to learn optimally, the implications of these differences demand recognition. Testing and education research recognized differences, but real change would come slowly. Learning within the norms of the grade system eventually became somewhat more individualized. Children with disabilities received individualized education programs with goals, expected learning process, and educational resources tailored to their needs. The movement to individualize education for all children in the context of standards of achievement continues to be one of the central issues in education.

Philosophies of *inclusion* and *respect for individual differences* continue to shape profoundly the practice of education and provide the basis for the role of the school social worker. The correspondence between social work values, the emergent mission of education, and the role of the school social worker is illustrated by Allen-Meares (1999) in table 1.1. The mission of education, implicit in these values, becomes the basis for school social work as it emerges through the twentieth century.

TABLE 1.1 Social Work Values

Social Work Values	Applications to Social Work in Schools
1. Recognition of the worth and dignity of each human being	1. Each pupil is valued as an individual regardless of any unique characteristic.
2. The right to self-determination or self-realization	2. Each pupil should be allowed to share in the learning process.
3. Respect for individual potential and support for an individual's aspirations to attain it	3. Individual differences (including differences in rate of learning) should be recognized; intervention should be aimed at supporting pupils' education goals.
4. The right of each individual to be different from every other and to be accorded respect for those differences	4. Each child, regardless of race and socioeconomic characteristics, has a right to equal treatment in the school.

The Beginnings of School Social Work

School social work began during the school year 1906–07 simultaneously in New York, Boston, Hartford (Costin, 1969a), and in Chicago (McCullagh, 2000). These workers were not hired by the school system but worked in the school under the sponsorship of other agencies or civic groups. In New York, it was a settlement house that sponsored the workers. Their purpose was to work between the school and communities of new immigrants, promoting understanding and communication (Lide, 1959). In Boston, the Women's Education Association sponsored "visiting teachers" who would work between the home and the school. In Hartford, Connecticut, a psychology clinic developed a program of visiting teachers to assist the psychologist in securing histories of children and implementing the clinic's treatment plans and recommendations (Lide, 1959). In Chicago, Louise Montgomery developed a social settlement type of program at the Hamline School, offering a wide range of services to its Stockyards District community (McCullagh, 2000). This unheralded experiment anticipated the much later development of school-based services for the entire community. In many ways these diverse, early programs contained in rough and in seminal form all the elements of later school social work practice. Over the following century, the diverse concerns of inclusion and recognition of individual differences, the concept of education as a relational process, and the developing mission for the schools would shape the role of the school social worker.

The First Role Definition by a School System: The Rochester Schools

In 1913 in Rochester, New York, the Board of Education hired visiting teachers for the first time. The commitment of the schools to hire visiting teachers was an acknowledgment of both the broadening mission of education and of the possibility that social workers could be part of that mission. In justifying the appointments, the Rochester Board of Education noted that in the environment of the child outside the school there are forces that often thwart the school in its endeavors to educate. The school was now broadening and individualizing its mission, attempting to meet its responsibilities for the "whole welfare of the child," and to "maximize cooperation between the home and the school" (Julius Oppenheimer, as cited in Lide, 1959).

Between School and Community: Jane Culbert

Only three years later in 1916 at the National Conference of Charities and Corrections a definition of school social work emerged in the presentation of Jane Culbert. The definition, full of the concepts of inclusion, respect for individual differences, and education as a relational process, would focus on the environment of the child and the school, rather than on the child individually. The school social worker's role was:

> interpreting to the school the child's out-of-school life; supplementing the teacher's knowledge of the child . . . so that she may be able to teach the whole child . . . assisting the school to know the life of the neighborhood, in order that it may train the children to the life to which they look forward. Secondly the visiting teacher interprets to parents the demands of the school and explains the particular demands and needs of the child. (Culbert, 1916, p. 595)

This statement of role would be developed and typified by Julius Oppenheimer as the role of school-family-community liaison (Oppenheimer, as cited in Lide, 1959). From his study of 300 case reports made by school social workers or visiting teachers he drew 32 core functions and considered this role to be primary. School social workers would aid in the reorganization of school administration and practices by supplying evidence of unfavorable conditions that underlie pupils' school difficulties and by pointing out needed changes (Allen-Meares, 2000).

From a Focus on the Environment to the "Maladjusted" Child: The Early Years

By 1920, the National Association of Visiting Teachers was organized and held its first meeting in New York City (McCullagh, 2000). Concern was expressed about the organization, administration, and role definition of visiting teachers (Allen-Meares, 2000). This organization, later the American Association of Visiting Teachers, would publish a journal, *The Bulletin*, until 1955. At that time it was merged into the newly established National Association of Social Workers. *The Bulletin* was the focus of the writing and the thinking of this emergent field of practice during these years. Influenced by the mental hygiene movement of its day, there was a gradual shift in focus from the focus on the home and school environment toward a focus on the individual schoolchild and that child's needs. Eventually this focus would shift to casework as a vehicle for working with the individual child. The shift toward casework came from the Milford Conference in 1929 (American Association of Social Workers, 1929), and later development was crystallized by the work of Edith Abbott (1942) on social work and professional education.

Fields of Practice with Casework in Common: The Milford Conference

The basic issues and the possible future direction in the maturation of social work practice and theory were laid out in the Milford Conference Report. By the end of the 1920s, a wide range of fields of practice had organized themselves around the different settings of school, hospital, court, settlement house, child welfare agency, family service agency, and so forth. Social work education followed an apprenticeship model, teaching what were perceived to be highly specialized and segmented fields of practice. The question of what all of these fields had in common became extremely important. In 1929, at the Milford Conference, the basic distinction between fields of practice, the specific practice that emerged from these fields and the generic base for practice in these fields—that is, the knowledge, values, and skills of casework—was established. This distinction was extremely important for social work education and for the field of school social work in that it allowed each field of practice to flourish and develop on a common foundation of casework. The emergent profession of social work was indeed broad and diverse. Furthermore, no theory had emerged that could do more than offer a general orientation to helping. It still was up to the learner-practitioner and supervisor to find a way to relate theory to practice. This situation would continue in various permutations of the history of social work practice theory for more than a half-century. The casework theory identified as generic would not refer to a concrete practice separable from its manifestation in different fields. There was no "generic" practice, but generic knowledge, values, and skills would be a foundation for a further differentiation of practice.

The Distinction of Generic and Specific Knowledge: Grace Marcus

The casework foundation of the 1920s and 1930s did not focus simply on individuals, as later versions did, but on persons and family units together. It was much more than a simple methodological base because it included knowledge and values. It became a conceptual foundation for practice that was "specific" to a field. Practice differentiation took place in relation to specific, identified fields, such as school social work, medical social work, psychiatric social work, child welfare, family services, and so on. Grace Marcus clarified the distinction between *generic* and *specific*:

The term generic does not apply to any actual, concrete practice of an agency or field but refers to an essential, common property of casework knowledge, ideas and skills which caseworkers of every field must command if they are to perform adequately their specific jobs. As for our other troublemaking word, "specific," it refers to the form casework takes within the particular administrative setting; it is the manifest use to which the generic store of knowledge has been put in meeting the particular purposes, problems, and conditions of the agency in dispensing its particular resources. (Marcus, 1938-39, n.p.)

The distinction was important for its ability to permit professional differentiation on a common foundation and to specify the relations of method theory, such as casework, to its manifestation in fields of practice.

A Rationale for School Social Work Practice: Florence Poole

In 1949, Florence Poole described a more developed rationale for school social work practice derived from the right of every child to an education. Pupils who could not use what the school had to offer were "children who are being denied, obscure though the cause may be, nevertheless denied because they are unable to use fully their right to an education" (Poole, 1959, p. 357). It was the school's responsibility to offer them something that would help them to benefit from an education. Education would need to change to help children who were "having some particular difficulty in participating beneficially in a school experience" (Poole, 1959, p. 357). Her rationale eventually would mark a shift in the discussion of the school social work role. School social work would be essential to the schools accomplishing their purpose:

At the present time we no longer see social work as a service appended to the schools. We see one of our most significant social institutions establishing social work as an integral part of its service, essential to the carrying out of its purpose. We recognize a clarity in the definition of the services as a social work service." (Poole, 1949, p. 454)

She saw the clarity and uniqueness of social work service as coming from the societal function of the school.

[The worker] must be able to determine which needs within the school can be appropriately met through school social work service. She must be able to develop a method of offering the service which will fit in with the general organization and structure of the school, but which is identifiable as one requiring social work knowledge and skill. She must be able to define the service and her contribution in such a way that the school personnel can accept it as a service, which contributes to the major purpose of the school. (Poole, 1949, p. 455)

Florence Poole's approach to practice was built on the parameters of the mission of the school, the knowledge and skill of social work, and the worker's professional responsibility to determine what needs to be done and to develop an appropriate program for doing it. Her conception was simultaneously freer but also more focused on the potentially rich interaction of social work methods and the mission of the school.The effect of this shift in emphasis from casework to school social work, although somewhat unnoticed at the time, was enormous.A variety of methods was now possible, governed by a complex mission and societal function of the school.The ensuing discussion of theory for school social work would become a question of the relation of methods to the needs of children and schools in the education process. It would be the basis for an emergent theoretical literature and a diversified practice.

Poole shifted the focus from the problem pupil alone, who could not adjust and adapt to the school, to a focus on pupils and schools adapting to each other in the context of every child's right to an education.The conditions that interfere with the pupil's ability to connect with the educational system are diverse. Therefore, the functions of the school social worker would be flexible and wide ranging, developed in each school by an encounter with the concrete problems and needs of the school community. There are many different definitions of what the school social worker should do as school conditions and conceptions of social work change.The elements of this encounter have remained the same over many years.

A Period of Professional Centralization

During the 1950s and the 1960s the major concern in the professional literature, in the profession, and in social work education had to do with what social workers had in common, not what made them different in different sectors of the profession. Considerable development of school social work as a field of practice had already taken place from the mid-1920s through 1955 and was the basis for the classic definitional work of Florence Poole.This growth trailed off by 1955 with the consolidation of the National Association of Social Workers (NASW). National organizations of social workers, representing different fields of practice, were merged into one single professional association. *The Bulletin* of the American Association of Visiting Teachers was merged into the new journal of the united social work profession, *Social Work*.With the loss of *The Bulletin*, school social work literature dropped off for a time.

The Transaction between Persons and Environments: Harriett Bartlett and William E. Gordon

During the late 1950s, and through the following decade, important work was done to clarify the common base of social work practice (Bartlett, 1971). Harriett Bartlett's and others' work built the foundation for a reorientation of methods and skills to a clarified professional perspective of the social worker.

Bartlett (1959, 1971) worked with William E. Gordon (1969) to elaborate the concept of the transaction between individuals and their social environments into a common base and a fundamental beginning point for social work. As the focus shifted to the person-environment transaction, it was no longer assumed that the individual was the primary object of help. The development and diffusion of group and environmental interventions and the use of a range of helping modalities in richly differentiated areas of practice would make Gordon's and Bartlett's work useful. The best summary of this work was done in the 1979 report of the Joint NASW-CSWE (Council on Social Work Education) Task Force on Specialization (hereafter Joint Task Force) of which Gordon was a member:

> The fundamental zone of social work is where people and their environment are in exchange with each other. Social work historically has focused on the transaction zone where the exchange between people and the environment which impinge on them results in changes in both. Social work intervention aims at the coping capabilities of people and the demands and resources of their environment so that the transactions between them are helpful to both. Social work's concern extends to both the dysfunctional and deficient conditions at the juncture between people and their environment, and to the opportunities there for producing growth and improving the environment. It is the duality of focus on people and their environments that distinguishes social work from other professions. (Joint NASW-CSWE Task Force, 1979)

The Beginnings of Specialization

During the late 1960s there arose a renewed interest in developing theory and practice in areas such as school social work. "Generic" approaches to practice in every field were no longer an adequate theory or practice base for the complex practice that was emerging. Differing fields, such as education and health, were demanding accountability to their goals. The survival of social work in different fields would demand this accountability to the purposes of the field. There was a gradual redevelopment of literature, journals, and regional associations of social workers in different fields of practice.

The interest in specialization led to a profession-wide discussion of this issue and the report of the Joint Task Force in 1979. The Joint Task Force developed a classic formulation. Fields of practice in social work grow from the need for mediation between persons and social institutions to meet common human needs. Practice within each field is defined by a clientele, a point of entry, a social institution with its institutional purposes, and the contribution of social work practice, its knowledge, values, and appropriateness to the institutional purpose and to common human needs. According to the Joint Task Force, these needs and their institutions would include:

- ◆ The need for physical and mental well-being—Health system
- ◆ The need to know and to learn—Education system
- ◆ The need for justice—Justice system

◆ The need for economic security—Work/public assistance systems
◆ The need for self-realization, intimacy, and relationships—Family and child welfare systems. (Joint Task Force, 1979)

In each area, the social worker works as a professional and mediates a relationship between persons and institutions.

At this time, school social work was beginning to develop its own distinct identity, methodology, theory, and organization. It had large numbers of experienced practitioners, who were encouraged to remain in direct practice by the structure and incentives of the school field. These were some of the first and strongest advocates of a movement in the mid- to late-1970s to develop practice and theory. With the development of state school social work associations, and then school social work journals, the search for some balance between what was common to all fields and what was specific to school social work began again. The issues were not always clear. Students would struggle with this balance in their attempts to match classroom theory with fieldwork.

Rethinking Casework in the Schools

During the 1960s the school social work literature reflected a broadened use of helping methods in schools and a developing interest in broader concerns affecting particular populations of students in schools. At the same time the social work profession experienced a renewed focus on social reform. The education literature, critical of the current organization of schools and the effectiveness of education, was preparing the way for school reform. Lela Costin (1969b) published a study of the importance school social workers attached to specific tasks, using a sample mainly derived from NASW members. Her findings showed a group of social workers whose description of social work mainly reflected the clinical orientation of the social work literature of the 1940s and the 1950s. Reflecting on these findings, Costin (1972) showed disappointment at what she believed was an excessively narrow conception of role, given the changing mission of the school and the potentials of practice to assist that mission. Her next step would be to develop a picture of what the school social work role should be.

Four Models for Practice: John Alderson

Following Costin's research John Alderson used a similar instrument to study school social workers in Florida with a variety of levels of professional training. In his Florida sampling, he found a much broader orientation. The workers ranked leadership and policy making either first or second in importance. Subsequently, he attempted a theoretical reconciliation of these findings with Costin's findings, and with the apparent clinical emphasis of many established school social work programs. He described four different models of school social work practice (1974). The first three of these were governed by particular intervention methods, whether by clinical theory, social change theory, or school community organization. One method would then tend to exclude the others. The *clinical* model focused mainly on changing pupils identified as having social or emotional difficulties. The *school change* model focused on changing the environment and conditions of the school. The *community school* model focused on the relation of school to its community, particularly deprived and disadvantaged communities. His final model, the *social interaction* model, was of a very different order. The move was from static conceptions to a dynamic, flexible, and changing concept of role. The focus for practice based on systems theory would be on persons and environments, pupils (in families), and schools in reciprocal interaction. Social workers would adapt their roles to this interaction. Alderson's social interaction model had followed two decades of work of William E. Gordon, Harriett Bartlett and the Committee on Social Work Practice, and the definition of a transactional, systems perspective in social work.

Seven Clusters of School Social Work Functions: Lela Costin

At about the same time, Lela Costin (1973) developed the *school community pupil relations* model, which focused on "school and community deficiencies and specific system characteristics as these interact with characteristics of pupils at various stress points in their life cycles" (p. 137). She outlined seven broad groups of functions in the school social worker's role. School social workers do (1) direct counseling with individuals, groups, and families, (2) advocacy, (3) consultation, (4) community linkage, (5) interdisciplinary team coordination, (6) needs assessment, and (7) program and policy development (Costin, 1973). With its constant relation of a diverse professional methodology to a developing school purpose, the model hearkened back to the beginnings of school social work.

Broadening Approaches to Practice

Later research in school social work (Allen-Meares, 1977) showed movement toward a model emphasizing home-school-community relations with a major focus still on problems faced by individual students. Other studies showed this broadening taking place (Anlauf-Sabatino, 1982; Chavkin, 1993; Constable, Kuzmickaite, Harrison, & Volkmann, 1999; Constable & Montgomery, 1985; Dennison, 1998; Lambert & Mullally, 1982; Timberlake, Sabatino, & Hooper, 1982). The findings can be characterized by Lambert and Mullally's (1982) pithy comment, "School social workers, at least in Ontario, do not place importance on one focus—individual change or systems change—to the exclusion of the other, but recognize the importance of both" (p. 81). The conceptual problem was not a question of one or the other, but of how to organize the methodological diversity inherent in the role. The ecological systems approach, discussed in greater detail in following chapters, was eventually to become a way of conceptually organizing the role. From a conceptual map of persons and environments in interaction in the context of education, the model would allow for variations of emphasis, related to particular situations and needs, within a common role.

School Social Work: Becoming a Specialization

During the last three decades of the twentieth century school social work became more and more a highly organized field of practice in the United States, employing a large number of practitioners and with a well-developed theoretical foundation and literature. State associations of school social workers developed from the 1970s on, so that at present thirty-one states have active professional associations of school social workers with named leadership (School Social Work Association of America [SSWAA], 2005). There are four regional associations, the Midwest School Social Work Council, the Northeast Coalition of School Social Work Associations, the Southern Council of School Social Workers, and the Western Alliance of School Social Work Organizations; and a national school social work association, the School Social Work Association of America (SSWAA). In thirty-three states there is a separate certification of school social workers by their State Departments of Education (SSWAA, 2005). There are at least 15,000 school social workers actively practicing (SSWAA, 2005). From the late 1970s on there was an increasing development of the journal and book literature in school social work. States such as Illinois and Michigan now required specialized preparation in graduate school as a precondition for certification in school social work. The observation of the coeditors over two decades in two states of specific preparation for school social work is that this preparation has significantly changed the nature of practice in the field.

Over the world school social work practice has developed in relation to each country's expectations of its schools, the problems young people encounter, and the total mix of services for young people. Despite differences, the position of the schools in the lives of young people and the aspirations of families have some similarity the world over, and there are some common dimensions to these services. A somewhat common picture of school social work is now becoming evident. At different levels of development, school social work is defining itself specifically in relation to the common concerns of the school community, region and nation, and broadly in relation to education (Huxtable & Blyth, 2002).

Emergent Issues and the Emergent Role

During the final three decades of the twentieth century the inclusive and individualizing missions of the schools expanded in response to the explication of a right to a free appropriate public education (FAPE) for children with disabilities, the school reform movement, and recent concerns around violence, peer sexual harassment, and bullying in schools.

Education is becoming *outcome-based*. Outcome-based education brings with it an emphasis on high professional qualifications to develop individualized interventions. The emphasis on high professional qualifications is meshing with movements toward specialization in school social work. In accordance with national legislation, states are setting standards for "highly qualified" school social workers and introducing postmasters-degree mentorships for more permanent certification as a highly qualified school professional (Constable & Alvarez, in press). As a consequence of the emphasis on outcomes and the demand for highly qualified education professionals, some school systems are developing evidence-based systems of accountability for professional intervention (Kratochwill & Shernoff, 2003).

These and other developments are addressed in the following sections of this book. In all of these school social work is significantly involved in the development of policies and services that affect individual children with special needs and that affect the school community as a whole. The issues that Florence Poole helped clarify are scarcely less important today. These issues are: the legal and institutional base for practice, children, parents, and the institution itself as targets for service, the interprofessional team, and the relation of all of these filtered through professional judgment to determine the resultant action taken by the worker.

WHOM DOES THE SCHOOL SOCIAL WORKER SERVE?

Society places a heavy responsibility on education not merely to teach but, with the family, to prepare children for the future, to be the vehicle for aspirations, not only for children who may conform easily to external expectations, but for every child. Responsibilities are placed on the school, on the parent, and on the child to make the educational process work so that every child who goes to school may fulfill his or her potential for growth and contribution to others. Therefore, there is concern for every child whose coping capacity may not be well matched with the demands and resources of the educational institution. At one time or other, any person could be vulnerable. In addition, certain burdens are felt by particular groups within society. Children come to school with messages from society, and sometimes from the school itself. Perhaps they feel that because of certain defining characteristics, such as gender, race, disability, ethnicity, or socioeconomic class, they could not have the same aspirations as others or that objective conditions, such as poverty, would surely prevent them from achieving their aspirations. The power of education, with many of the values that drive it, could refute these messages. School social workers could refute these messages by working with teachers, children, and families in the school community.

WHERE DOES SCHOOL SOCIAL WORK TAKE PLACE?

The School Community Context

School is conceptualized as a community of families and school personnel engaged in the educational process. The educational process is dynamic, wide ranging, and involves children, their families, and an institution called school. It is the context for school social work. School is no longer a building, or simply a collection of classrooms in which teachers and pupils work together. The school community, no longer simply bounded by geography, comprises those who engage in the educational process. As in any community, there are varied concrete roles. People fit into such communities in very different ways. Parents and families are members through their children. Teachers and other school personnel are members with a complex accountability to parents, children, and the broader community. Drawing on each person's capacities, the school social worker focuses on making the educational process work to the fullest extent. Therefore, school social workers work with parents, teachers, pupils, and administrators on behalf of vulnerable children or groups of children. The success of the process depends on the collective and individual involvement of everyone. The social worker helps the school community operate as a real community so that personal, familial, and community resources can be discovered and used to meet children's developmental needs.

As long as it was taken for granted that home would be isolated from school, one part of the role of school social work has been to span the boundary between home and school. This has taken place since the origin of school social work in the early twentieth century (Litwak & Meyer, 1966). Schools have generally operated in relative isolation from their constituent families, each protecting its functioning from "interference" from the other. This isolation is, of course, counterproductive in situations of vulnerability or difficulty. A need for someone like the school social worker to span, and even challenge, these boundaries is thus created. The traditional approach of connecting children with networks of community services has been evident from the earliest years of social work in schools. Beginning in the late 1960s, the intensified parent involvement of Project Head Start and the War on Poverty and, more recently, parent-sponsored schools have developed models of empowerment and partnership. The school is rapidly becoming the place of organization of all services to children and families.

The Societal Context

The connection of school social work to its school and community context is essential for the development of practice. The current legal and social policy context for school social work and the role of the school social worker in school policy development is discussed more fully in section II. In the United States and in certain Western European countries, there has been an erosion of state welfare systems and the supports they provide to families. As national government policies shift toward "market" approaches, a longer-term development appears to be that the protections normally associated with childhood are declining while the risks are increasing. High rates of suicide, addiction, violence to and among children, early pregnancy, AIDS, and early exposure to the job market through economic necessity are among these risks, to some extent created and in any case sustained by the laissez-faire attitude associated with the reigning free market philosophy.

Some of the risks generated by the market and the broader societal system may be buffered through strengthening of institutions at the local level, through schools and homes that work and that respect human dignity and worth. It is remarkable in the face of these problems (or perhaps because of them) that schools have continued their century-old quests, such as for greater inclusion of previously excluded groups of youngsters in the educational mainstream. The changes that have taken place in special education over the past thirty years are particularly important and are a metaphor for the possible relations between school policy and the school social worker's role. More recently, school reform experience in the United States has been bringing with it increased expectations for performance by children. Yet no progress can be made on school reform without dealing with the problems that accompany poverty and socioeconomic class: that children are at risk and will not fulfill their promise without institutional, community, and family supports (Mintzies & Hare, 1985). Data on state achievement tests in mathematics indicate dramatic differences in achievement explainable largely by the realities of poverty. Impoverished school districts working with impoverished families generally achieve at rates considerably lower than their more privileged neighbors (Biddle, 1997).

WHAT DOES THE SCHOOL SOCIAL WORKER DO?

The school social worker's role is multifaceted. There is assessment and consultation within the school team. There is direct work with children and parents individually and in groups. There is program and policy development. In 1989 a group of nineteen nationally recognized experts in school social work were asked to develop and list the tasks that entry-level school social workers would perform in their day-to-day professional roles. The result was a list of 104 tasks, evidence of the complexity of school social work. These tasks, when they were defined, fell along five job dimensions:

1. Relationships with and services to children and families,
2. Relationships with and services to teachers and school staff,
3. Services to other school personnel,
4. Community services, and
5. Administrative and professional tasks. (Nelson, 1990)

Further research on these roles, tasks, and skills found four areas of school social work to be both very important and frequently performed:

1. Consultation with others in the school system and the teamwork relationships that make consultation possible;
2. Assessment applied to a variety of different roles in direct service, in consultation, and in program development;
3. Direct work with children and parents in individual, group, and family modalities;
4. Assistance with program development in schools. (Constable, Kuzmickaite, Harrison, & Volkmann, 1999)

A key skill, the foundation of all other areas, is assessment. *Assessment* is a systematic way of understanding what is taking place in relationships in the classroom, within the family, and between the family and school, and looking for ways to make changes. The social worker looks for units of attention, places where intervention will be most effective. *Needs assessment*, a broader process, provides a basis for program development and policy formation in a school. It is often a more formal process, utilizing many of the tools of research, geared toward the development of programs and policies that meet the needs of children in school, and applying to the experiences of groups of children in school.

Role Development

Role development is the product of the interaction between what the school social worker brings to the situation, the perceptions of others, and the actual conditions of the school community. Role definitions are the joint and continuing construction of school social workers, education administrators, and others. They become reference points for practice, for policy, and for theory development, and they serve as a conceptual bridge between policy and practice. Where social workers are not the dominant profession, these conceptions interpret and validate their contributions. They regulate teamwork. General reference points for role can be found in the literature of school social work, in local education agency (LEA) expectations, and state education agency (SEA) standards. They can be found in standards developed by the NASW, the SSWAA, or other state and national associations. When these expectations are found repeatedly in practice, they set standards for professional performance. It is not usual that beginning school social workers have a great deal of influence in the initial development of their roles. Indeed, the idea of ever influencing the development of their roles in particular schools may seem foreign to their experience. However, over a longer period of time, as they learn to respond in a more differentiated way to the needs of the school community, school social workers can influence the development of their roles in particular schools. People's perceptions of a role are tested and evaluated in relation to the needs, capabilities, and social networks of a particular school and the outcome, the product that results and its influence on the experience students have of education.

The ecological systems model is a useful theoretical model to understand the school social worker's role. A system is an organized holistic unit of interdependent, transacting, and mutually influencing parts (individuals or collectivities and their subunits) within an identifiable (social-ecological) environment (Siporin, 1975). Ecology is the science of organism-environment interaction. The model leads to a view of person and environment as a unitary interacting system in which each constantly affects and shapes the other. It allows for an understanding of the relation of different methods of intervention and their theoretical bases. Behavior in the classroom may be understood better by understanding its context, its relations to other settings, and the relation of these settings to each other. As one learns to analyze the relations between systems, practice may build on this understanding. The model leads to clearer choices of where to intervene in the complexity of a system and when an intervention may be most effective.

As Carel Germain develops ecological systems theory in this edition, she uses it to clarify the dual function of social work, so we "attend to the complexities of the environment, just as we attend to the complexities of the person" (see chapter 2). She moves to a health orientation from a medical-disease metaphor and to "engaging the progressive forces in people and situational assets, and effecting the removal or environmental obstacles to growth and adaptive functioning" (chapter 2, p. 30).

Marjorie Monkman is concerned with defining and operationalizing the complex nature of transactions between persons with other persons and with the school environment. She intends to define this transaction, making it more operational, more specific for the purpose of practice and for the purpose of future research. She is doing a conceptual identification of all that goes into practice. Reflecting the thought of her teacher, William E. Gordon, she defines a transaction as a relation between a person's coping behavior and the impinging environment. The social worker assists both to accomplish a match that is good for both. Out of this she develops the characteristic focus of school social work.

Outcome-driven education brings research processes directly into the orbit of practice. John Flynn's chapter on research and evaluation outlines a research component in the school social worker's role needed for practice development. However, the practitioner cannot do this alone. New networks of practitioners, universities, professional associations, and state departments of education are needed in this move toward evidence-based practice. Chris Sabatino, Lynn Mayer, and Elizabeth Timberlake add depth to the discussion of effectiveness with a review of the research literature in school social work, and a discussion of the connections between research and practice development. The final articles on school social work and confidentiality set ethical parameters on issues the school social workers face when they work with so many different people in so many different ways. The seven-step process for dealing with dilemmas around confidentiality can become a comprehensive vehicle for weighing and deciding complex ethical issues in practice.

For specialized school social work practice one needs to understand the nature of education policy as it applies to school social work practice. The involvement with education and schooling creates a natural focus on research, policy, and program development as practice. From basic practice skills of assessment and consultation in the framework of ecological systems theory then flow a wide range of possible interventions. These are developed with teachers, pupils, families, and groups. They involve clinical practice, consultation and teamwork, coordinating and integrating services, developing inclusion plans, dealing with crisis and safety issues in the school, and developing mediation and conflict resolution, each with its own sources of theory. These and other parts of the school social work role are developed in the following chapters.

References

Abbott, E. (1942). *Social welfare and professional education*. Chicago: University of Chicago Press.

Alderson, J. (1974). Models of school social work practice. In R. Sarri & F. Maple (Eds.), *The school in the community* (pp. 57–74). Washington, DC: National Association of Social Workers.

Allen-Meares, P. (1977). Analysis of tasks in school social work. *Social Work, 22*, 196–201.

Allen-Meares, P. (1999). The contributions of social workers to schooling—revisited. In R. Constable, S. McDonald, & J. Flynn (Eds.), *School social work: Practice, policy, and research perspectives* (4th ed., pp. 24–31). Chicago: Lyceum Books.

Allen-Meares, P., Washington, R. O., & Welsh, B. L. (2000). *Social work services in schools*. Boston: Allyn & Bacon.

American Association of Social Workers. (1929). *Social casework: Generic and specific: A report on the Milford conference* (1974 reprint of 1929 edition). Washington, DC: National Association of Social Workers.

Anlauf-Sabatino, C. (1982). Consultation and school social work practice. In R. Constable & J. Flynn (Eds.), *School social work: Practice and research perspectives* (pp. 271–281). Homewood, IL: Dorsey.

Bartlett, H. (1959). The generic-specific concept in social work education and practice. In A. E. Kahn (Ed.), *Issues in American social work* (pp. 159–189). New York: Columbia University Press.

Bartlett, H. (1971). *The common base of social work practice*. New York: National Association of Social Workers.

Biddle, B. J. (1997). Foolishness, dangerous nonsense, and the real correlates of state differences in achievement. *Kappan, 79*(1), 8–13.

Brown v. Board of Education, Topeka, KS. 347 U.S. 483 (1954).

Chavkin, N. (1993). *The use of research in social work practice*. Westport, CT: Praeger.

Constable, R., & Alvarez, M. (in press). Moving into specialization in school social work. *School Social Work Journal*.

Constable, R., Kuzmickaite, D., Harrison, W. D., & Volkmann, L. (1999). The emergent role of the school social worker in Indiana. *School Social Work Journal, 24*(1), 1–14.

Constable, R., & Montgomery, E. (1985). A study of role conceptions of the school social worker. *Social Work in Education, 7*(4), 244-257.

Costin, L. (1969a). A historical review of school social work. *Social Casework, 50*, 439-453.

Costin, L. (1969b). An analysis of the tasks in school social work. *Social Service Review, 43*, 274-285.

Costin, L. (1972). Adaptations in the delivery of school social work services. *Social Casework, 53*, 350.

Costin, L. (1973). School social work practice: A new model. *Social Work, 20*(2), 135-139.

Costin, L. (1978). *Social work services in schools: Historical perspectives and current directions.* (Continuing Education Series # 8). Washington, DC: National Association of Social Workers.

Culbert, J. (1916). Visiting teachers and their activities. In *Proceedings of the National Conference on Charities and Corrections* (p. 595). Chicago: Heldman Printing.

Dennison, S. (1998). School social work roles and working conditions in a southern state. *School Social Work Journal, 23*(1), 44-54.

Friedman, T. L. (2005). It's a flat world, after all. *The New York Times.* Magazine section. Retrieved April 3, 2005, from newyorktimes.com/magazine

Gordon, W. E. (1969). Basic constructs for an integrative and generative conception of social work. In G. Hearn (Ed.), *The general systems approach: Contributions towards an holistic conception of social work* (n.p.). New York: Council on Social Work Education.

Huxtable, M., & Blyth, E. (Eds.). (2002), *School social work worldwide.* Washington, DC: National Association of Social Workers.

Joint NASW-CSWE Task Force on Specialization. (1979). *Specialization in the social work profession.* (NASW Document No. 79-310-08). Washington, DC: National Association of Social Workers.

Kratochwill, T. R., & Shernoff, E. S. (2003). *Evidence-based practice: Providing evidence-based interventions in school psychology.* WCER working paper no. 2003-13. Madison, WI: Wisconsin Center For Educational Research. Retrieved August 8, 2004, from http://www.wcer.wisc.edu

Lambert, C., & Mullally, R. (1982). School social work: The congruence of task importance and level of effort. In R. Constable & J. Flynn (Eds.), *School social work: Practice and research perspectives* (pp. 72-99). Homewood, IL: Dorsey.

Lide, P. (1959). A study of historical influences of major importance in determining the present function of the school social worker. In G. Lee (Ed.), *Helping the troubled school child* (n.p.). New York: National Association of Social Workers.

Litwak, E., & Meyer, H. (1966, June). A balance theory of coordination between bureaucratic organizations and community primary groups. *Administrative Science Quarterly, 11*, 31-58.

Marcus, G. (1938-39). The generic and specific in social work: Recent developments in our thinking. *American Association of Psychiatric Social Workers 3/4.*

McCullagh, J. (2000). School social work in Chicago: An unrecognized pioneer program. *School Social Work Journal, 25*(1), 1-14.

Mintzies, P., & Hare, I. (1985). *The human factor: A key to excellence in education.* Washington, DC: National Association of Social Workers.

Nelson, C. (1990). A job analysis of school social workers. Princeton, NJ: Educational Testing Service.

Poole, F. (1949, December). An analysis of the characteristics of the school social worker. *Social Service Review, 23*, 454-459.

Poole, F. (1959).The school social worker's contribution to the classroom teacher. In G. Lee (Ed.), *Helping the troubled school child*. New York: National Association of Social Workers.

School Social Work Association of America (SSWAA). (2005). [On-line].Available from http://www.SSWAA.org

Siporin, M. (1975). *Introduction to social work practice*. New York: Macmillan.

Timberlake, E., Sabatino, C., & Hooper, S. (1982). School social work practice and PL 94-142. In R. Constable & J. Flynn (Eds.), *School social work: Practice and research perspectives* (pp. 49-72). Homewood, IL: Dorsey.

Welsh, B., & Goldberg, G. (1979). Insuring educational success for children-at-risk placed in new learning environments. *School Social Work Quarterly, 1*(4), 271-284.

2

An Ecological Perspective on Social Work in the Schools

Carel B. Germain

- ◆ The Dual Function of Social Work
- ◆ Primary Prevention
- ◆ Influencing the School

One of the most difficult tasks for all of social work practice is to define its distinctiveness—what distinguishes the social worker from other professional helpers. In fact, this is not even a new task. In 1915 Abraham Flexner was invited to speak before the National Conference of Charities and Corrections. He was the social scientist who modernized medical education in this country, bringing it up from the depths of inadequate proprietary schools and into the universities. Because of his achievement and his resulting status in the arena of professional education, Flexner's appearance at the national conference was eagerly awaited. He would be speaking to an occupational group whose members called themselves social workers and who aspired to professional status. Imagine the consternation, then, as the speaker informed his audience that, indeed, they were not a profession nor could they reasonably aspire to becoming one because they did not have a distinctive professional knowledge base or skills that were transmissible (Flexner, 1915).

Furthermore, and this must have been the crowning blow, their only function was a mediating one for linking up their clients to other professions, and invoking their power in solving the client's problem. The impact on the audience can be sensed in the responses of those present as preserved in the conference proceedings. But the responses echoed down the years as social work continually tried to define its distinctiveness and to establish its professional sta-

CONCEPTS FOR ANALYZING RESOURCES

Resources have been identified as a major component of the environment. Resources such as family, school, hospitals, and so on, may be viewed as systems. Concepts from the general systems model are useful for conceptualizing and organizing data in the various resource systems. These concepts may be used to call our attention to the skills necessary for the worker to get in and out of a resource system. This model calls to our attention such questions as (1) For what is the major energy in the system being used? (2) Is tension in the system a productive or destructive force? (3) What effect will change in one part of the system have on the other parts? Social workers, such as those employed in schools, become parts of systems. However, although the worker is a part of the system, the worker also intervenes in the system itself as a resource for children (Monkman, 1981).

Understanding Organizations

Workers need to understand what makes organizations operate if they will be able to use the school or other social agencies as a resource. For example, organizations have a managerial structure that is generally hierarchical. Organizational structure can be best understood in relation to organizational process. Workers need to understand the informal power that can be gained either from interpersonal relationships or from assuming responsibilities, as well as power that comes from the formal structural arrangements.

A second, but no less important, process variable is communication. Communication serves a linkage function. It links various parts of the organization by information flow. This may be individual to individual, individual to group, unit to unit, and unit to the superstructure, and so on. Communication has been called the "life blood" of organizations or systems. Social workers have a particular responsibility for developing and maintaining channels of communication if they are to accomplish their own missions.

The climate of an organization has a major effect on its productivity. Climate describes expectancies and incentives and represents a property that is perceived directly or indirectly by individuals in the organization. Climate is made up of such phenomena as warmth, support, conflict, identity, reward, and risk. For social workers, climate is seen as a major quality of resources and is often a target for change.

The earlier discussion makes clear that resources are dependent variables or targets for change for social workers. Resources for clients may take a variety of meanings and may in particular be the "setting" or places of employment for social workers. Thus, it is imperative for social workers to understand the systems or organizations of which they may be a part and to know and ask the essential questions for assessing resources.

In addition, organizational systems have external environments. The exchange between an organization and its environment is essential to the tus. In particular, the casework segment devoted time, energy, and thought to developing a distinctive knowledge and value base and distinctive skills that then became confused with those of other professions on whom they were patterned, especially psychiatry. The efforts left undeveloped until the present day what might have been a truly distinctive function. Flexner's indictment of the mediating function and Mary Richmond's refusal (1917) to accept it as a social work function are particularly ironic in today's world. It is clear that what is needed in this dehumanized and depersonalized bureaucratic society is a profession that mediates between people in need—particularly the poor and other powerless groups such as children and the aged—and the institutions of society set up to serve them. Ironic, because this increasingly important function so ably performed by social work does indeed rest on an identifiable and transmissible base of knowledge, values, and skill.

In some ways, school social work followed the same historical trends of the larger professional group. Originally conceived as a response to problems of truancy created by free, compulsory public education, school social work was expected to uncover and to mitigate neighborhood and school conditions that gave rise to truancy (Costin, 1969). For many historical reasons, school social work, by the 1930s, had narrowed its focus to a casework service for children who were defined by the school as having emotional and behavioral disturbances attributable to early family experiences. The number of children thus served was necessarily small; there was little impact on adverse school structures and practices, and the service itself tended to become stigmatized.

By the 1960s and 1970s, however, schools and school social work faced new imperatives generated by new social forces. The numbers of alienated pupils and high school dropouts increased. The school's ability to teach fundamental skills to many children declined, especially those pupils whose lifestyles and languages differed from the middle-class orientation of the school. Overt conflict between communities and schools for control of educational processes increased. The pain and stress accompanying the struggle for desegregation, the worry that schools might actually be undermining the creativity and spontaneity of all pupils, and the recognition that schools solidified the inequities of social class became salient forces in the field of school social work (Rist, 1970). In addition, every profession is now under attack on issues of effectiveness, ethical practice, and accountability. Insistence on public control of all professions is mounting, and many of the consequent reforms, such as equal educational opportunities for the disabled, are long overdue. These reforms do pose new issues of formal and informal labeling, confidentiality, and even service provisions when so much time is required by the new accountability procedures and forms.

THE DUAL FUNCTION OF SOCIAL WORK

The profession's struggle for distinctiveness, which began in 1915, also influenced the development of school social work within this set of contemporary forces. William Gordon (1969) and Harriett Bartlett (1970), under the auspices of NASW, constructed a definition of social work practice that suggests social work's uniqueness lies in its location in the interface area where people's coping patterns interact with the qualities of their impinging environment. Thus, the social worker's function is to work in that interface with the person, the environment, or both, in order to secure a better match between coping needs and environmental requirements and people's coping abilities. This definition means that the social worker—in any field of practice—has a dual and simultaneous function: to strengthen people's coping patterns and their growth potential on the one hand, and to improve the quality of the impinging environment on the other. This interface position does not negate the importance of the personality and its motivational, emotional, cognitive, and sensory-perceptual elements. But neither does it overlook the complexity of the environment and its interacting physical, social, and cultural elements. Rather, it takes both into account simultaneously and seeks to improve the transactions between them. Thus the old polarity between social workers who favor social action and social workers who favor service to people can become, instead, a complementarity of two essential functions. This view of professional purpose can correct the imperfections in our commitment to the personal situation that are apparent whenever we overlook one or the other. Most often, it is the situation that is overlooked, perhaps because it is the more difficult of the two to change.

An ecological metaphor for practice can respond to this dual function in a way that the traditional medical or disease metaphor cannot do (Germain, 1979). Ecology is the science of organism-environment relations. It leads to a view of person and environment as a unitary, interacting system in which each constantly affects and shapes the other. This view directs our professional attention to the whole, so that we attend to the complexities of the environment just as we attend to the complexities of the person, developing skills for intervening with each and with their transactions. The ecological metaphor also shifts us from an illness orientation to a health orientation, and to engaging the progressive forces in people and situational assets, and effecting the removal of environmental obstacles to growth and adaptive functioning.

Most school social workers have been practicing in just this way, conceiving their social purpose to be helping children develop age-appropriate social competence, and influencing the school to be more responsive to the needs of the children. William Schwartz (1971) characterizes this as helping the children reach out to the school and helping the school reach out to the children because each needs the other. Perhaps the reason that school social workers seem to be ahead of other sectors of practice in fulfilling the distinctive dual function of social work is because the school is a real-life ecological unit, beyond the realm of metaphor or analogy. The child clearly is in intimate interaction with the school, second in intensity only to the interaction of the child and family. However, the school social worker literally is located at the interface where school and child transact, in a way that the family agency social worker or child welfare social worker, for example, can never be located with respect to the child-family transactions.

Actually, school social workers stand at the interface not only of child and school, but of family and school, and community and school. Thus, they are in a position to help child, parents, and community develop social competence and, at the same time, to help increase the school's responsiveness to the needs and aspirations of children, parents, and community. Social competence as a human attribute or achievement is tied to ideas of self-esteem and identity. It includes effectiveness with respect to knowing and deciding when to take action in the environment, as opposed to a passive orientation to life and its events and processes. It is tied also to relative autonomy from internal pressures and external demands, while maintaining relatedness to other human beings, to the world of nature, and to one's own internal needs (Germain, 1978). This appears to be a nonnormative set of ideas fitting any cultural context in any historical era, for it is the culture and the times that define the actual substance of such competence.

Robert White (1959) spoke of competence as the human being's innate drive to have an effect on the environment. Piaget referred to competence when he described how children's intellects develop through opportunities to take action on the environment, assimilating and accommodating the external into internal cognitive structures (as cited in Evans, 1973). The ego psychologists, in tracing the development of integrated ego functioning, are describing competence. Erikson's notion (1959) of school children's tasks of industry is a case in point. How children deal with the task depends, in part, on what they bring to it, on how they handled the earlier tasks of trust, autonomy, and initiative, and on what their physical states provide in health, vigor, stature, coordination, and so on. It will also depend on their cognitive, sensory-perceptual, and motivational equipment for adaptation and coping. However, and this is the value of Erikson's formulation for social work, their ability to achieve competence will also depend on the qualities of the impinging social and physical environments, particularly the family, the school, and the community. These environments must provide the growth-inducing conditions and the right stimuli at the right time and in the right amount if children are to achieve the tasks involved in establishing industry and competence. Otherwise, they may be left with residues of inferiority—social, intellectual, physical, or emotional—that may affect their ability to handle later tasks. Three examples of interface work on competence follow: First, an example from the child–school interface:

> Jim, age 13, a newcomer in a middle school, was referred to the social worker. He had no friends, rebuffed the other boys, and didn't return teachers' greetings. He often seemed angry in class, and he was failing several subjects. Yet, he had been an average student in elementary schools and had had friends and interests. During our first few interviews there was little mutuality, and I learned the meaning of patience all over again. Then one day Jim told me the family secret that his mother is an alcoholic. He was very angry with her for drinking and for the way she

treated him as a baby when she was drunk. He was afraid to make new friends and of bringing them to the house for fear he might divulge the secret. His interest in school work had all but disappeared. Mother had given Jim this permission to talk freely, which I interpreted as her call for help. I saw her alone, and with my encouragement she began attending AA. Soon Jim expressed interest in catching up at school, and we worked out a tutoring plan that seemed to go well. Yet, his teachers were not recognizing his efforts and his changed motivation and were treating him with seeming dislike and annoyance. This stimulated his anger, which then provoked their further negative responses. Jim's problems, though not caused initially by the school, were now being perpetuated by school staff. I asked the principal to call a conference in which I explained to his teachers that Jim had realistic problems in his family that were being handled. I wanted them to see that Jim had real courage in tackling his problems—first alone and now with help. He was trying hard, but marked change will require more time and patience. At the end, one teacher commented she had not really thought of Jim with such sympathy before. Jim's grades are now improving, the teachers' attitudes toward Jim and his attitudes toward them are more positive. He made several friends and was busy with them during the past four Saturdays. He also told me his mother drank only once over the last month, and my impression is that he is less involved now in his mother's behavior. His whole bearing reflects his returning self-esteem, sense of competence, and even autonomy. (Shelling, 1978)

Second, an example from the parent-school interface:

The social worker in an inner-city school in Brooklyn was concerned about poor relations between parents and the school that compounded the problems children were having in school. She persuaded the principal to turn over an unused room as a parents' drop-in lounge for those mothers bringing their small children to school each morning. She decorated it with plants and had coffee and doughnuts ready. She made each mother feel welcome and valued, and soon had a number of regulars who looked forward to the respite, the warmth, and attention given them by the school. After a bit she was able to engage two separate groups in meeting to talk to their shared needs and tasks as single parents living on limited budgets in a harsh environment. In the process, the mothers developed a mutual aid system, exchanging ideas, resources, and social support. Through social work intervention, the mothers' competence was enhanced and the school's responsiveness was increased. (Anon)

A third example is from the community-school interface:

The social worker induced the elementary school in a Hispanic neighborhood to extend its boundary beyond its doors and out into its neighborhood. It became, in effect, a community center. The parents planned family life education and ethnic programs. They held evening forums for discussion of neighborhood issues of housing, welfare, and health care. After-school recreational programs for the children were provided in the school yard, supervised by older siblings and adult volunteers. It is not surprising that this school enjoyed the full support of its community, and its children, parents, teachers, and community enjoyed a strengthened sense of competence, self-esteem, and identity. (Phillips, 1978)

PRIMARY PREVENTION

There is another implication to be derived from the school social worker's distinctive dual function. As a profession, we feel pressed to move into the arena of life itself in order to prevent problems before they arise. The school social worker's location in the child's ecological context is critical to undertaking preventive tasks. The state of our knowledge does not yet permit us to claim the same preventive success that public health professionals achieve through vaccination and sanitation measures based on known etiology. Nevertheless, we have reason to believe that emotional inoculation and life-oriented growth experiences can stave off disorganization in the child, the family, and perhaps within the community.

From an ecological perspective, all organisms use adaptive processes to change their environments and/or to change themselves in order to reach and maintain a goodness of fit. In human beings, adaptation is the active, creative use of social and cultural processes to change environments so they will conform to human needs and aspirations. Humans also actively change themselves to conform to environmental requirements and expectations through biological and psychological processes. Human beings, however, never fully achieve a goodness of fit or adaptive balance with their environments because their needs and goals forever change, environments constantly change, and also because what people do to physical and social environments is often detrimental to their own functioning (Dubos, 1968).

This evolutionary, adaptive view of people and environments lends additional support to Gordon's (1969) formulation of the social work function as strengthening adaptive potential and improving environments. It also points to the usefulness of a growing body of stress theory, which has an important bearing on primary prevention (Coelho, Hamburg, & Adams, 1974). Stress theory suggests that when the usual adaptive balance is upset by external or internal processes and events, the person and/or the environment will experience the upset as stress and will institute coping strategies to eliminate or reduce the stress or to accommodate to it. Stress and coping are mediated by age, sex, culture, physical condition, particular vulnerabilities, and previous experience. Stress is a part of living, arises from all facets of life, and is not necessarily problematic. In fact, some stress is pleasurable, is generated by desired events, or is even sought after to alleviate tedium. Stress theory suggests, however, that problematic stress must be understood as a transactional phenomenon occurring in the interface between person and environment—again the area where the school social worker is located.

Coping, too, is a transactional phenomenon located in the interface area because it depends on personality variables that are in reciprocal relation to environmental variables (Mechanic, 1974; White, 1974). For example, cognition and problem-solving skills used in coping depend on the quality and quantity of information and on the training provided by the environment of family, school, and other social institutions. Coping rests on a minimal amount of self-esteem and psychic comfort, but those qualities depend on emotional supports from the social environment. Motivation for coping depends, in part, on the incentives and rewards provided by the family, school, and community. And finally, coping requires some degree of autonomy, or having enough space and time in the physical and social environments in order to make decisions and take action. This suggests, again, that the interface area is indeed a strategic location for school social workers. Typically, they strengthen coping by supporting self-esteem and identity, rewarding motivation and coping efforts, providing information, teaching problem-solving skills, working to relieve anxiety, depression, and other threatening affects that interfere with coping, and providing opportunities for decision making and action. They also direct their efforts to reducing stress imposed on the child, the parents, or the community by the procedures or personnel of the school.

So far this discussion of adaptation, stress, and coping merely reformulates what was said earlier about the school social worker's dual function. I would now like to suggest that ideas of stress and coping bear also on issues related to the primary prevention of difficulties before they arise. In general, social work is most often engaged in secondary and tertiary prevention to prevent further disabling from already present and often entrenched problems. As a result, we often feel we are engaged also in picking up the pieces after the damage has been done and have little to do with preventing those problems in the first place. Yet, school social work is moving more and more toward primary prevention. It can also point the way for social workers in other fields of practice who are interested in primary prevention.

Primary prevention has been defined as specific actions directed at specific populations for specific purposes (Goldston, 1977). It seeks to prevent problematic stress and maladaptation and to promote adaptive functioning and positive development. To reach these goals, primary prevention engages the positive forces in individuals, families, and groups and works to change environmental properties that have an adverse effect on growth and adaptive functioning.

Knowledge of the developmental stages and tasks of the child, adult, and family, and of the environmental provisions required for those tasks, enables the school social worker to identify populations at risk. These might include, for example, children whose parents are considering or moving into separation or divorce, children experiencing the serious illness or death of a parent or sibling, or children not reaching their intellectual potential. Parental populations at risk might include single parents, unemployed parents, parents living in poverty, or socially isolated parents. School social workers frequently offer group meetings to parents of children entering school for the first time, because initial entry represents a transitional point in the life cycles of both parent and child. Thus it has potential for stress and maladaptive response.

In one such program, the social worker included the kindergarten teacher as a group member because she could provide immediate observations of the child's reactions in the classroom. Her presence also facilitated communication between parent and teacher, which could then foster mutual trust and mutual decision making and problem solving as the parents moved through the elementary grades. In this particular program, the parents who participated were engaged in planning the next year's groups and then served as their co-leaders. Thus the roles of parents changed from recipients of the program to planners, then to recruiters of other parents, eventually to group co-leaders, and thus to providers of the service now intended to reach the entire population-at-risk. (Santos, 1977, n.p.)

In a middle-class school, with bused-in children from the inner city, the school social worker—with the principal's consent—developed a project she called "Concern for Community," utilizing a team made up of a teacher and several volunteers including a retired social worker. The project involved a series of fifth-grade field trips for firsthand learning about institutions and agencies set up to meet human needs, including hospitals, adolescent group homes, and geriatric facilities. The children learned the community's layout by locating their own homes on a map in relation to the homes of the other group members and classmates. The children also met with the social worker in small groups during the school year to talk about human needs in their community and resources for meeting them. The project's objectives were to stimulate a greater concern in the children for one another, for human need, and for their shared environment, and to increase the children's sense of interdependence and mutual caring. The trips, and especially the small group experiences, were evaluated by the school as having met the objectives.[1]

Early adolescence, ages 12 to 15, is a critical period of development that involves coping with unique biological, psychological, and social demands. Because of hormonal and bodily changes, especially in girls, and sudden entry into the teen culture with its new pressures and demands, early adolescence can be a period of stress and increased vulnerability. Yet, the educational structure in many communities superimposes additional stress by the transfer from elementary school to junior high at this very time. The security achieved in a small, self-contained classroom with a single teacher can be lost in the larger population, larger campus, rotating classes, multiple teachers, and increased academic demands (Hamburg, 1974). This appears to be an appropriate population at risk for primary prevention programs by the social worker. Such programs might include meetings with teachers and administrators to educate the educators about the age-related stresses of their pupils. These would be based on the teachers' interests and work-related needs so that desired structural changes might be achieved. Anticipatory guidance groups for sixth graders,

---

1. I am indebted to Edna Bernskin, MSW, Stamford, Connecticut, for this illustration.

mutual support groups of seventh-grade teachers on how to help their students deal with demands of the transition, and mutual aid groups for parents on their shared tasks in understanding the early adolescent could also be offered (Work Group E, 1977).Although we do not know for sure, such primary prevention might contribute to reduced dropout, drug use, and pregnancy and lead to better grades, less absenteeism, and fewer court referrals. Preventive programs will need to be evaluated, particularly in the light of such real constraints as insufficient funding, insufficient staffing, and value systems that tend to resist prevention efforts as invasion of privacy.

Opportunities for preventive work will depend on the social worker's skill in establishing an ecological niche in the school, so that services are not limited to children who are referred. One social worker reported on efforts to begin relationships before problems emerge by creating an atmosphere that allows all students to confer with him about concerns and difficulties confronting many or most children, such as management of adult authority, peer group disruptions, and pressures of competition. He uses an open-door policy for children to drop in. He accepts advisory roles in student activities and participates in playground and lunchroom duties so that he can provide on-the-spot or life-space helping efforts. He suggests that this increases children's awareness of the social work service and their right to it when and where needed or desired, and without stigma (McGarrity, 1975).

INFLUENCING THE SCHOOL

Throughout this chapter, I have referred to the social worker's function as including professional responsibility to influence the school to be more responsive to the needs of child, family, or community and changing school practices that undermine self-esteem, autonomy, and competence or that add to the burden of depression, anxiety, passivity, or alienation already present. Those tasks are hard—which may explain why many social workers tend to give short shrift to the "situation side" of our person-situation commitment. Nevertheless there are two reasons for optimism: First, we are understanding our commitment better so we are more ready to accept the dual, simultaneous function. Second, real help with environmental tasks is on the way.Anderson (1974), for example, has developed a team model in school social work that has many advantages in addressing problems that affect large numbers of pupils. The team consists of the social worker, psychologist, and often the secondary counselor and nurse, and sometimes the teacher and principal, who are, in any case, included in the planning and action. A team can exert greater influence than an individual, although Anderson acknowledges there are severe difficulties in team management just as there are in medical and psychiatric settings where team practice is commonplace.

By virtue of the interface position, however, even the individual school social worker can serve as an early warning system to the school regarding undesirable consequences of its policies and procedures. This collaborative role assumes there is consensus between the school and the practitioner about what is good or bad for children, families, and communities. Where there is such consensus, efforts of the social worker to bring about change in organizational elements can be relatively easy and relatively successful. Sometimes, however, there may not be consensus—perhaps because of such issues as power, authority, prestige, competing interests, personal commitments, or fiscal and political constraints imposed by the outside environment. Assuming the advocacy role in such situations demands "influencing skills" in addition to our helping skills (Brager, 1975). Advocacy in one's own system is a delicate task because it must be done in such a way that practitioners do not alienate the very system that employs them. Social workers trying to introduce change into the organization who lose their jobs in the process are of little use to their clients. Thus, political skills of influencing are needed, including persuasion, bargaining, mediation, negotiation, and conflict management. Knowledge of a specialized kind is required in order to understand and to utilize the formal and informal systems within the school, its seats of power and decision making, channels of communication, its norms, customs, rules, and policies. Organizational theory and skills of influencing are now taught in many social work schools and in many agencies' staff development programs. They are also set forth in journal articles and books (Brager & Holloway, 1978; Germain & Gitterman, 1980; Patti & Resnick, 1972; Wax, 1968). All practitioners, however, must work at integrating them into the practice. School social workers, like many practitioners in other fields, are effective in working within the system on behalf of one child or one parent, getting the school to bend a rule, make an exception, grant a privilege here, or withhold a sanction there. This very important activity must be continued, but we must also maintain constant vigilance about the impact of the school on all its pupils and, where necessary, undertake knowledgeable, well-planned, skillfully implemented efforts to change adverse structures and practices in the school. That is the implication of the distinctive dual function of social work. It is the implication of primary prevention, and it may be today's response to Abraham Flexner.

References

Anderson, R. J. (1974). School social work: The promise of a team model. *Child Welfare, 53*, 524–530.

Bartlett, H. (1970). Seeking the strengths of social work. In *The common base of social work practice* (n.p.). New York: National Association of Social Workers.

Brager, G. (1975). *Helping vs. influencing: Some political elements of organizational change*. Paper presented at the National Conference of Social Welfare, San Francisco, CA.

Brager, G., & Holloway, S. (1978). *Changing human service organizations: Politics and practice*. New York: The Free Press.

Coehlo, G. B., Hamburg, D., & Adams, J. (Eds.). (1974). *Coping and adaptation*. New York: Basic Books.

Costin, L. B. (1969). An analysis of the tasks in school social work. *Social Service Review, 43,* 274-285.

Dubos, R. (1968). *So human an animal.* New York: Charles Scribner's.

Erikson, E. (1959). The healthy personality: Identity and the life cycle. *Psychological Issues, 1*(1), 50-100.

Evans, R. I. (1973). *Jean Piaget: The man and his ideas.* New York: E. P. Dutton.

Flexner, A. (1915). Is social work a profession? National Conference Charities and Corrections, Proceedings, 576-606.

Germain, C. (1978). General systems theory and ego psychology: An ecological perspective. *Social Service Review, 52*(4), 535-550.

Germain, C. B. (Ed.). (1979). *Social work practice: People and environments.* New York: Columbia University Press.

Germain, C. B., & Gitterman, A. (1980). *The life model of social work practice.* New York: Columbia University Press.

Goldston, S. (1977). An overview of primary prevention programming. In D. Klein and S. Goldston (Eds.), *Primary prevention: An idea whose time has come* (n.p.). (Publication No. ADM 77-447). Washington, DC: Department of Health, Education, and Welfare.

Gordon, W. E. (1969). Basic constructs for an integrative and generative conception of social work. In G. Hearn (Ed.), *The general systems approach: Contribution toward an holistic conception of social work* (n.p.). New York: Council of Social Work Education.

Hamburg, A. (1974). Early adolescence: A specific and stressful stage of the life cycle. In G. B. Coelho, D. Hamburg, & J. Adams (Eds.), *Coping and adaptation* (n.p.). New York: Basic Books.

McGarrity, M. (1975). Building early relationships in school social work. *Social Casework, 56,* 323-327.

Mechanic, D. (1974). Social structure and personal adaptation: Some neglected dimensions. In G. B. Coelho, D. Hamburg, & J. Adams (Eds.), Coping and adaptation (n.p.). New York: Basic Books.

Patti, R. J., & Resnick, H. (1972, July). Changing the agency from within. *Social Work, 48-57.*

Phillips, M. H. (1978). The community school: A partnership between school and child welfare agency. *Child Welfare, 57,* 83-92.

Richmond, M. (1917). The social caseworker's task. *National Conference of Social Work, Proceedings,* 112-115.

Rist, R. (1970). Student social class and teacher expectations: The self-fulfilling prophecy in ghetto education. *Harvard Education Review, 40,* 411-451.

Santos, R. R. (1977). Developing primary prevention programs with major community institutions. In D. Klein & S. Goldston (Eds.), *Primary prevention: An idea whose time has come* (n.p.). Washington, DC: Department of Health, Education, and Welfare.

Schwartz, W. (1971). On the use of groups in social work practice. In W. Schwartz & S. Zalba (Eds.), *The practice of group work* (n.p.). New York: Columbia University Press.

Shelling, J. (1978). Unpublished case material. The University of Connecticut School of Social Work.

Wax, J. (1968). Developing social work power in a medical organization. *Social Work, 13*(4), 62-71

White, R. (1959). Motivation reconsidered: The concept of competence. *Psychological Review 66,* 297-333.

White, R. (1974). Strategies of adaptation: An attempt at systematic description. In G. B. Coelho, D. Hamburg, & J. Adams (Eds.), *Coping and adaptation* (n.p.). New York: Basic Books.

Work Group E. (1977). Population at risk: Secondary school students. In D. Klein & S. Goldston (Eds.), *Primary prevention: An idea whose time has come* (n.p.). Washington, DC: Department of Health, Education, and Welfare.

3

The Characteristic Focus of the Social Worker in the Public Schools

Marjorie McQueen Monkman

- ◆ The Characteristic Focus of Social Work
- ◆ Ecological Perspective
- ◆ Social Work Knowledge
- ◆ T.I.E. Framework: Outcome Categories
- ◆ Concepts for Analyzing Resources
- ◆ Values
- ◆ Social Work Activities
- ◆ The Worker

Federal and state legislation and major legal decisions have given recognition to school social work services and provided an opportunity to broaden these services from the traditional roles. The recognition of school social work services in the laws and policies creates greater expectations for the worker and challenges the profession. The purpose of this chapter is to conceptualize what is the focus of school social work and what is the role of the individual worker in utilizing this focus, in developing new techniques in practice, and in demonstrating desired change.

It is hard to overestimate the importance of the individual worker's contribution to change in the practice situation. Workers carry a heavy responsibility for what they bring to the practice situation. They bring a characteristic professional focus that is both broad and unique. The worker's focus makes it possible for him or her to identify knowledge needed for intervention. The worker brings activities and skills for bringing about desired changes. The worker brings values that lead to the selection of perspective, knowledge, and action. The worker brings the contribution of charisma and personal style. It is through the social worker that the professional focus, knowledge, values, and activities impinge on the practice situation. The role of the worker is formed from these attributes as they interact with the particular structure and expectations of the setting (see figure 3.1).

FIGURE 3.1   Contributions of the Worker

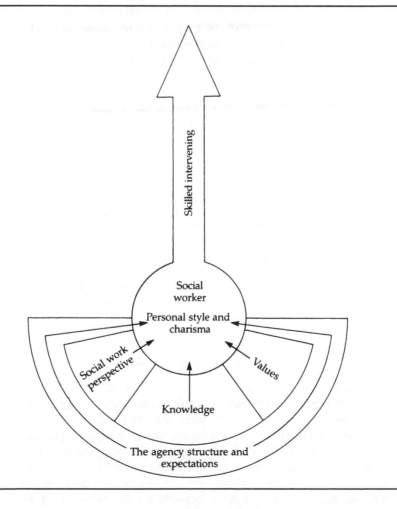

THE CHARACTERISTIC FOCUS OF SOCIAL WORK

From the beginning, the social work focus has been identified as resting on the person in the situation, a dual focus. As a result of this focus, social workers work with persons in diverse aspects of life, perhaps more than any other helping discipline. The conceptualization of the person in the situation has been enhanced for social work by the work of Harriett Bartlett (1970), William E. Gordon (1969), and others (Gitterman & Germain, 1976; Germain & Gitterman, 1980; Monkman, 1976, 1978, 1981, 1983; Monkman & Meares, 1984; Pincus & Minahan, 1972; Schwartz, 1969). These theorists have conceptualized the traditional focus in a manner that more accurately reflects the roots and multiple avenues of practice. Their approach to defining the point of intervention in social work is to emphasize phenomena at the point where the person and the environment meet. Social work interventions take place in the transactions between the coping behavior of the person and the qualities of the impinging environment. The purpose of the intervention is to bring about a better match between the person and the environment in a manner that induces growth for the person and at the same time is remediating to the environment (Gordon, 1969).

In order to understand more clearly the characteristic focus of the social worker the concepts of transactions, coping behavior, quality of the impinging environment, practice target, and outcomes of intervention need to be more clearly explicated.

Transactions

The activities at the interface may be termed transaction(s) between the individual and the environment. Transactions embody exchange in the context of action or activity. This action or activity is a combination of a person's activity and impinging environment activity; thus, exchange occurs only in the context of activity involving both person and environment. The transaction is created by the individual's coping behavior on the one hand and the activity of the impinging environment on the other (Gordon, 1969).

Coping Behavior

Coping behavior is that behavior at the surface of the human organism that is capable of being consciously directed toward the management of transactions. Coping behavior excludes the many activities that are governed by neural processes below the conscious level. It includes the broad repertoire of behavior that may be directed to the impinging environment and that potentially can be brought under conscious control. Coping behaviors include not only the behaviors directed to the environment, but also those efforts of individuals to exert some control over their behaviors—to use themselves purposively.

Coping behaviors are learned behaviors, and once learned, they become established as coping patterns. Significant repetitions in coping behavior by individuals or groups of individuals suggest coping patterns that may at times become the focus of the interventive action. Looking for these patterns in what people are experiencing and how they are responding to a set of environmental conditions takes us beyond our traditional concern for the uniqueness and integrity of each individual. If we know something about the conditions and about human coping, we can say something in some detail and substance about the response of a clientele to a social institution such as education, and from this we can develop the appropriate response of school social work. In a relationship with any one individual, we respond to that person as a unique human being and as a part of a larger collectivity. We respect and encourage the effort of an individual with disabilities to overcome adversity and/or social discrimination, but we know that some of the adversity and discrimination is shared with other persons with disabilities. This knowledge is as much a base for action as is our knowledge of his or her unique response to adversity and discrimination.

People cope with themselves as well as with the environment, and this is also learned behavior. These behaviors, as they are developed over time, incorporate expectations and feedback from the environment. The ways individuals and groups cope are related to the information they have about themselves or their environment—how they perceive self and environment. This information is patterned into a cognitive structure that directs the coping behaviors and could even direct the perception of the environment in a manner that will make it difficult to receive further information as feedback from the environment. There is a circular relation between what we usually do to cope with the environment and how we perceive things. An understanding of this relation is the crucial assessment tool. If coping behaviors and patterns are not in keeping with the environment as we perceive it, we may then examine the information and the perceptions of the coping persons. This assessment is directed toward patterns of perception and action rather than seeking some type of single cause within the individual.

Coping is an active, creative behavior that continually breaks the boundaries of "the given." Adapting is seen as a passive concept that implies that the person simply takes in the output from the environment. Some writers connect coping with stress in adapting and refer to coping as those behaviors emitted when there is stress in adapting. We would say that stress is inherent in any growing process, but that it is important to assess the degree of stress to understand the coping patterns adopted. The person is considered able to cope when he or she is dealing with the stress and "making a go of it" (Gordon, 1969).

Quality of the Impinging Environment

The other side of the transaction field is the environment. Social work practice has not confined its concern to the person in any particular situation, that is, at home, in the hospital, in school, or in any other situation. No other profession seems to follow people so extensively into their daily habitats. We have been interested in how the qualities of any of these situations interact with the coping behaviors. As in the case of the coping behaviors, Gordon (1969) gave a way of partializing the qualities of a situation. He defined the qualities of the impinging environment as those qualities at the surface of the environmental system that the person is actually in contact with, rather than "below-the-surface" structures, which are inferred to be responsible for the nature of what the human organism actually confronts.

Although emphasis on the environmental side is on the impingements, it is recognized that it is through one's knowledge of what is behind the impingements that enables the person to arrange for changes in those impingements in desired directions. It is often necessary to work for change on several levels. For example, a worker may be working with a truant child in an effort to get the child to return to school. At the same time, the worker may find that the teacher is happier with the child truant and that the administration is indifferent. Intervention may be needed at all three levels if the child is to return and remain in school (figure 3.2).

Practice Target

Transaction has been defined as activity that combines coping behaviors and the quality of the impinging environment. Through these transactions there

FIGURE 3.2   T.I.E. Framework: Transactions between Individuals and Environments

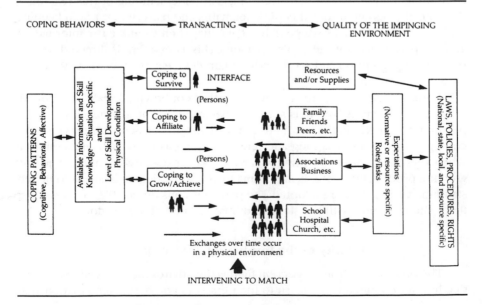

is an exchange between the components of each side. The goal of social work practice is matching, that is, bringing about a fit that makes for positive outcomes both for the person and the environment. Professional intervention for bringing about a match may include efforts to change the coping behavior, the quality of the impinging environment, or both (Gordon, 1969).

Social work is concerned with what will happen to the coping behaviors and the quality of the impinging environment as a result of the exchanges between them. The relation of coping and environment is reciprocal. Thus coping behavior and/or quality of the impinging environment could become what we are seeking to change and thus our measures of outcome or dependent variables. To the degree that activity in the transaction changes, we may predict consequent changes in either or both the coping behavior and environmental side.

ECOLOGICAL PERSPECTIVE

We are essentially operating from an ecological perspective. Ecology seeks to understand the reciprocal relation between organisms and environment: how organisms shape the environment to its needs and how this shaping enhances the life-supporting properties of the environment (Germain & Gitterman, 1980). For social work, the ecological perspective appears to fit our historical view much better than the medical or disease perspective that we seem to have adopted in past decades. The ecological perspective is essentially a perspective, a point of view, for relationships that take place in reality; it is a way of perceiving these relationships more clearly.

One of the reasons for the better fit of the ecological perspective to social work is that it is a multicausal rather than a linear causal perspective; that is, it makes possible a view of multifaceted relationships. From this perspective, our attention is called to the consequences of transactions between people and environment, but the metaphors, models, and/or theories we have previously borrowed have focused more on cause of action and have tended to be one-sided and unidirectional.

SOCIAL WORK KNOWLEDGE

A basic area of knowledge for social work is knowledge of the needs of people and how these needs are met. People individually and collectively have a need for physical well-being. These needs consist of food, shelter, and so on, which may be identified as needs for surviving. People have need for relationships, including intimacy and other forms of affiliating. People have need for growth, which may include their need to know, to learn, to develop their talents, and to experience mental and emotional well-being.

A second major area of knowledge for social work is knowledge of the institutions or societal resources that have been established to meet these needs.

We need knowledge of the major structures and processes involved in resource provision and development. This area is quite complex and includes expectations, policies, procedures, and so on.

The third major area of knowledge is knowledge of the match between these institutions and the needs of the people. From the perspective of social work, this is knowledge of the transactions and the result of these transactions for people and their environments. For example, PL 94-142 and subquently PL 105-117 (IDEA, Individuals with Disabilities Education Act) is an environmental policy change that changes societal expectations and resources for exceptional children and, in turn, affects all children. The environmental impingements that individual children experience will change as these policies change. The differences in the transactions between pupils and their teachers, peers, and even the physical structure of the school have become a part of the general experience of children. However, these children continue struggling to cope with change and new events brought on by these policies. These transactions are particularized and occur in time and space (at a particular time and in a particular place), as do all living transactions.

The Purpose of Social Work Activity

The purpose of social work activity is to improve the match between coping behaviors and the quality of the impinging environment so that the stress in these transactions is not so great that it is destructive to the coping abilities of the individual or the environment. Changes are always occurring, and people are always coping or striving to manage change. Not only is our purpose to bring a match that is not destructive but, if possible, one that makes the person better able to cope with further change and makes the environment less stressful to others.

As our focus becomes clearer, we could make the knowledge we have of transactions more explicit for social workers and other disciplines. To do this we need to develop our focus in a way that makes what we aim to change, coping behavior and the impinging environment, more explicit. Figure 3.2 illustrates the concepts we will be discussing.

T.I.E. FRAMEWORK: OUTCOME CATEGORIES

Coping Behaviors

Social workers basically deal with at least three categories of coping behaviors and three categories of the impinging environment (Monkman, 1978). This framework for dealing with the transactions between individuals and environments is called Transactions Individuals Environment (T.I.E.). Surviving, affiliating, growing, and achieving form a continuum of coping. There are then three categories of coping behaviors: (1) coping behaviors for surviving, (2) coping behaviors for affiliation, and (3) coping behaviors for growing and achieving. These categories help us set priorities for practice intervention. Coping behaviors at any point in time are affected by information from past coping experience and build themselves over time. Our first consideration is whether the client has the capacity to obtain and use the necessities for surviving, and the second, for affiliating. Both surviving and affiliating skills seem to be prerequisites to growing and achieving.

Coping behaviors for surviving are those behaviors that enable the person to obtain and use resources that make it possible to continue life or activity. To survive we need to have the capacity to obtain food, shelter, clothing, and medical treatment, and to have access to these through locomotion.

Coping behaviors for affiliating are those behaviors that enable the person to unite in a close connection to others in the environment. Subcategories of affiliating behaviors are: (1) the capacity to obtain and use personal relationships and (2) the ability to use organizations and organizational structure. Social workers would have great difficulty conceiving of a person apart from his or her social relations. Each individual experiences social relations through organizations and groups, families, schools, clubs, church, and such.

Coping behaviors for growing and achieving are those behaviors that enable the person to perform for, and to contribute to, him- or herself and others. Subcategories of coping behaviors for growing are developing and using: (1) cognitive capacities, (2) physical capacities, (3) economic capacities, and (4) emotional capacities.

Quality of the Impinging Environment

The environment can be seen as comprising: (1) resources, (2) expectations, and (3) laws and policies. The categories of the environment do not have a priority of their own. Rather, because our major value is the person, their priority gets established in the match with coping behaviors.

Resources. Resources are supplies that can be drawn on when needed or can be turned to for support. Pincus and Minahan (1972) characterized resource systems as informal, formal, and societal. Informal resource systems consist of family, neighbors, co-workers, and the like. Formal resource systems could be membership organizations or formal associations that promote the interest of the member, such as AA, Association for Retarded Citizens, and so on. Societal resource systems are structured services and service institutions, such as schools, hospitals, social security programs, courts, police agencies, and so on. Resource systems may be adequate or inadequate and provide opportunities, incentives, or limitations. In many situations, there are no resources to match the coping behaviors for surviving, affiliating, and growing.

Expectations. Expectations are the patterned performances and normative obligations that are grounded in established societal structures. Expectations can involve roles and tasks. Social workers recognize these structures and recognize that a positive role complementarity usually leads to greater mutual satisfaction and growth. However, it is not our purpose as social workers simply to help people adapt to societal roles or perform all expected tasks. Roles are the patterned, functional behaviors that are performed by the collection of persons. Examples of roles are mother, father, social worker, physician, and so on. Although these are normative patterns in our society, individuals do not always agree on the specific behaviors of a role. Roles do change, because they are socially defined and functionally oriented. Sometimes this societal change is not acceptable to the individual and creates a mismatch between coping behaviors and the environment.

The concept of task is a way of describing the pressures placed on people by various life situations. These tasks "have to do with daily living, such as growing up in the family, and also with the common traumatic situations such as bereavement, separation, illness, or financial difficulties" (Bartlett, 1970, n.p.). These tasks call for coping responses from the people involved in the situation.

Laws and Policies. Laws and policies are those binding customs or rules of conduct created by a controlling authority, such as legislation, legal decisions, and majority pressures. Subcategories of laws and policies are rights and responsibilities, procedures, sanctions, and inhibiting or restricting factors. As a category, laws and policies are seen as necessary and positive components of the environment. Yet, it is also recognized that many single laws or policies have negative effects for groups of people. Some of our policies make survival more difficult. In some cases, particularly for welfare clients, to receive assistance from welfare agencies may make affiliation almost impossible.

Expectations, laws, policies, and procedures are communicated through resources. The quality of output from a resource, such as a school, is very much affected by the state and national policies that have been adopted. The ultimate test of these policies is the match they make with coping behaviors of those persons with whom the school transacts, namely children. Thus, if these transactions are destructive to the coping behaviors of children, the procedure for implementing or the policy itself is in need of change. This is another way of saying that policy is a legitimate target for change. Social workers are often in the best position for evaluating the match between policy and coping. The classroom is an example that may make the interrelationship of the environmental categories clearer. The expectations for tasks to be accomplished in the classroom come to the child through the teacher (and others). The teacher is a resource to the child, but unless he or she is able to bring the expectations in line with the coping behaviors of the child, there is no match. In some cases, the coping behaviors are so different from the expectations that other resources are necessary. Social workers might intervene in the environment and/or in coping behaviors of schoolchildren, that is, in the resources, expectations, policies, procedures, and/or in the coping. In some situations, however, change might be indicated in all six outcome categories.

Research Evidence

An exploratory study (Monkman & Meares, 1984) using a random sample of Illinois school social workers and utilizing the focus described in this chapter (T.I.E. framework) lends evidence to the fit of this framework to practice. The data show that coping behavior and environment outcome categories were selected in approximately equal amounts. A national study using a random sample of direct practice MSWs from a variety of practice settings (Monkman, 1989) gave additional evidence that social workers' outcomes are located in the categories described in this framework.

Matching Person and Environment

The discussion to follow will be an oversimplification of the interrelation between transaction and the matching process, but it is a first step in utilizing the framework developed thus far. Two populations will be used as examples (figure 3.3).

FIGURE 3.3   The Characteristic Focus of School Social Work

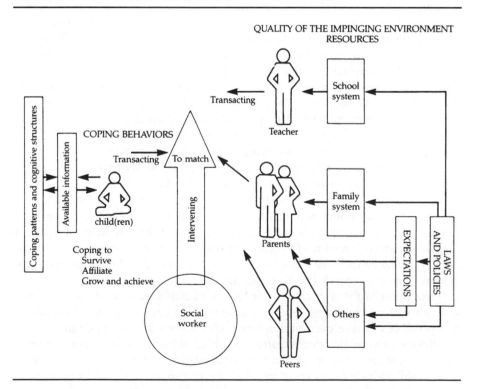

The first population to be considered comprises unmarried teenage parents. To be of help to this group it is important to consider the match between behaviors for surviving, affiliating, and growing and each of the categories on the environmental side. To give a few specific examples: placing the teenage mother on homebound instruction may enhance cognitive achievement but may be destructive to affiliation in interpersonal relationships and affiliation with society and/or organizations. The student may not be aware of laws and policies that can affect her decision to have her baby and keep her baby. Knowledge of the task of being a mother is important for both the mother and for the child.

Another population would be developmentally delayed children. Again, we are concerned with matching in all six categories. Many of the programs presently developed for developmentally delayed children are geared to maximizing cognitive development—or more specifically, academic achievement. Most of these programs do not develop affiliating or surviving skills. Very little energy is put into making a better match between the coping behaviors of the developmentally delayed child and the wide range of tasks for daily living.

It is important to remember that our outcome variables are both coping behaviors and the quality of the impinging environment. We may affect either or both. In the case of the teenage parent, the social worker may have helped to change her behavior in all three categories, as well as increasing resources. The worker may have made information about expectations, laws, and policies more available to her and may have changed some of the expectations emanating from her impinging environment; for example, the worker may have changed the demands to give up her baby or keep her baby. For the developmentally delayed child, he or she may have developed resources for increasing his or her affiliating behavior. He or she may even have measures of change in these behaviors. The worker may have helped his or her parents change their expectations so that they do not make impossible demands on the child.

Often, social work interventions include teaming with other social workers and other helping persons. For example, many growing and achieving behaviors for schoolchildren require teaming with teachers of these children. Teachers spend many more hours with children than social workers do. They have more direct opportunities to develop coping behaviors and skills in children. By teaming with teachers, social workers can increase their change possibilities for children. By bringing these two resources together, they can make a greater change in some aspect of the children's environment.

The point of these examples is to show that this framework makes it possible for us to partialize, generalize, and measure change in practice situations. It is possible to make each of these examples more explicit depending on the conditions of your practice situation. To bring about these changes a worker may, for instance, use knowledge of organizations, skills for working with groups, skills for data collecting, and skills for communicating. The worker must also determine the major critical exchanges in the transaction.

CONCEPTS FOR ANALYZING RESOURCES

Resources have been identified as a major component of the environment. Resources such as family, school, hospitals, and so on, may be viewed as systems. Concepts from the general systems model are useful for conceptualizing and organizing data in the various resource systems. These concepts may be used to call our attention to the skills necessary for the worker to get in and out of a resource system. This model calls to our attention such questions as (1) For what is the major energy in the system being used? (2) Is tension in the system a productive or destructive force? (3) What effect will change in one part of the system have on the other parts? Social workers, such as those employed in schools, become parts of systems. However, although the worker is a part of the system, the worker also intervenes in the system itself as a resource for children (Monkman, 1981).

Understanding Organizations

Workers need to understand what makes organizations operate if they will be able to use the school or other social agencies as a resource. For example, organizations have a managerial structure that is generally hierarchical. Organizational structure can be best understood in relation to organizational process. Workers need to understand the informal power that can be gained either from interpersonal relationships or from assuming responsibilities, as well as power that comes from the formal structural arrangements.

A second, but no less important, process variable is communication. Communication serves a linkage function. It links various parts of the organization by information flow. This may be individual to individual, individual to group, unit to unit, and unit to the superstructure, and so on. Communication has been called the "life blood" of organizations or systems. Social workers have a particular responsibility for developing and maintaining channels of communication if they are to accomplish their own missions.

The climate of an organization has a major effect on its productivity. Climate describes expectancies and incentives and represents a property that is perceived directly or indirectly by individuals in the organization. Climate is made up of such phenomena as warmth, support, conflict, identity, reward, and risk. For social workers, climate is seen as a major quality of resources and is often a target for change.

The earlier discussion makes clear that resources are dependent variables or targets for change for social workers. Resources for clients may take a variety of meanings and may in particular be the "setting" or places of employment for social workers. Thus, it is imperative for social workers to understand the systems or organizations of which they may be a part and to know and ask the essential questions for assessing resources.

In addition, organizational systems have external environments. The exchange between an organization and its environment is essential to the growth of the organization. Organizational environment may be thought of in two categories: (1) general environment, and (2) specific environment.

The general environment consists of conditions that must be of concern to all organizations. Examples of these would include political, economic, demographic, cultural, technological, and legal conditions. The specific environment includes other organizations with which the organization interacts frequently or particular individuals who are crucial to the organization. Examples of the specific environment of a school system are the parents of the children enrolled in the school, the local mental health center, the local child welfare services, the juvenile court, and so forth.

Social Networks

Environments are made up of networks of resources. An important, but sometimes neglected, network is the informal social network for the client: that is, peers, neighbors, friends, relatives, and so on. Each of the persons individually is an important resource for the client, but the linkage and relationship between these persons in the network are also important. Professionals are aware of the negative potential of peer influence on children. However, the positive aspects of these relationships are also useful to practice. Within these networks can be found members who serve as effective informal helpers. Knowledge of social networks and the ability to assess these in practice situations is becoming increasingly important as people become more mobile and lose continuing contact with their own roots. Mobility weakens these linkages, increases isolation and loss, and simultaneously makes network relationships more important.

Networks of Service Organizations

Social workers are often in the position of developing networks of service organizations for clients. Many of our practice situations involve a service network such as the school, family, state child welfare agency, and the courts or judicial system. Social workers are particularly concerned about the relations between these resource systems. This is a domain of social work practice. Social workers may develop and use these inter-resource linkages, establish channels of communication between these resources, and develop new resources. Thus, the school social workers are in the middle of a system, within an organizational structure, in an environment of social and environmental networks. In order to enhance the development of linkages between various human service organizations, they need to have knowledge of systems variables and organizational variables. Knowledge of the relations of change taking place in differing parts of the system, of the tendency of systems to maintain themselves, to tighten their boundaries when threatened, can make the worker much more sensitive to the necessary steps in developing linkages between agencies.

We have reviewed concepts and knowledge applicable to the environmental aspects of school social work practice. Other areas of knowledge are equally applicable. These might be (1) knowledge of normal growth and development of children and the stress in coping that accompanies different growth stages, (2) knowledge of exceptional children, (3) knowledge of various learning processes, (4) knowledge of specific resources, (5) knowledge of major policy and policy issues affecting practices in the school setting, and (6) knowledge of positive and negative transaction patterns. Certainly, the earlier discussion gives evidence of the breadth of knowledge that social workers need to bring to practice in the school setting. Although we borrow knowledge from psychology, sociology, economics, political science, education, and so on, we borrow from them in relation to our perspectives and to accomplish the purposes of social work.

VALUES

Values guide the action of social work from the preferred perspective to the preferred action. A clarification of types of values is helpful in determining the role of a specific value in practice. Siporin (1975) has defined ten different types of values; five of these are particularly useful to social work:

1. Ultimate (conceived, or absolute) value is a general, abstract formulation, such as liberty, justice, progress, self-realization, the worth of the individual.
2. Instrumental value is more specific and immediately applicable, such as acceptance of others, equality of opportunity for education, safeguarding the confidentiality of client information. This is also termed a utility value, in referring specifically to the property of things as good or beneficial because of their usefulness to an end.
3. Personal value refers to what an individual considers good and right, or what is generally so considered as right or beneficial for an individual, such as individuality, self-respect, self-reliance, privacy, self-realization.
4. Scientific value is one to which scientists commit themselves and which they believe should govern scientific behavior: rationality, objectivity, progress, critical inquiry. Society is increasingly accepting these as general social values.
5. Professional value is one to which professional people commit themselves and accept as a basis for professional behavior, such as competence, impartiality, placing a client's interest first.

The primary and ultimate value in social work seems to be that "It is good and desirable for man(kind) to fulfill his/her potential, to realize himself/herself, and to balance this with essentially equal efforts to help others fulfill their capacities and realize themselves" (Gordon, 1962, n.p.). This value represents our dual focus on people and their environment, which has characterized social work practice from its beginning. From our ultimate values follow instrumental values that guide actions in practice. An example of an instrumental value is "the right to self-determination." This instrumental value guides our practice, unless it is in conflict with our ultimate value, that is, the individual's self-determination is destructive to him- or herself or others. Knowledge is usually required to make this determination. Thus, values and knowledge are different, but interrelated, in their application to practice. Values, however, give us purpose and ethical structure in social work.

We are careful not to inflict our personal values on others, while we accept professional values as a basis for our professional behavior. Hopefully, our personal values are not in conflict with the professional and ultimate values. Yet, the professional values may not encompass all of our personal values. An example of this difference may be seen in relation to divorce. An individual worker may feel that divorce would be personally wrong, but his or her professional values would enable the worker to help clients make this decision for themselves.

It is important to remember that social work has a philosophical base and continues to require judgment as to means and ends. The judgment, however, can be made with more explicit awareness of the knowledge and value implications.

Social workers must be able to understand the differences between knowledge and values and the relationship of the two. Value refers to what persons prefer or would want to be. This preference may involve all the devotion or sacrifice of which one is capable. Knowledge denotes the picture we have built up of the world and ourselves as it is, not necessarily as we would prefer it to be. It is a picture derived from the most rigorous interpretation we are capable of giving to the most objective sense data we are able to obtain (Gordon, 1962). The future of social work may be dependent on this discrimination. That is, if a value is used as a guide in professional action when knowledge is called for, the resulting action is likely to be ineffective. If knowledge is called on when a value is needed as a guide to action, the resulting action may be destructive. Thus:

> Both outcomes greatly reduce the potential for human welfare residing in the profession's heritage of both knowledge and values. Man's ability over time to bring some aspect of the world into conformity with his preferences (realize his values) seems to be directly proportional to his ability to bring his statements and perceptions into conformity with the world as it now is (develop the relevant science). (Gordon, 1962, n.p.)

SOCIAL WORK ACTIVITIES

Social work activities involve assessing, relating, communicating, planning, implementing, and evaluating. Assessing is the bridging concept between action and knowledge and values. This does not mean to imply that assessing is a first step that occurs before any other activity. It is rather a continuous process as other data continue to be gathered. The social work perspective makes explicit the view of the phenomena into which we intervene. Knowledge gives us the most accurate picture of these phenomena that we are able to obtain in any one point in time. Values lead in the choice of perspectives, in the desire to obtain knowledge, and in the choice of action approaches. The first step in any practice situation is to assess that situation from our perspective, with our knowledge, and in relationship to our values. This step leads to change action.

In most practice situations, assessing occurs simultaneously with relating. The idea of establishing a relationship has been common in social work literature from the beginning. In more recent years, it has been discussed as a process activity that leads to an end change, resulting in the phenomena into which we intervene. At times in the past, it has been confused with an end in itself or an outcome variable. Certainly, to establish a relationship may be seen as an interim goal, but not as an outcome in the practice situation. Social work places considerable importance on the skill required to relate to the major factors involved in any practice situation, whether client or resource.

Communicating is an essential activity in practice. Most of our data is collected through communicating. To a large extent the accuracy of our data is dependent on our ability to ask questions and clarify answers. It is through communicating that we express our desire and ability to relate and to help.

Planning activities lead to "change goals" and tasks for each party involved in a practice situation. Plans need to be based on the assessment of the practice situation including the resources available to carry out these plans. Some plans include the development of other resources, as well as bringing about a match between person(s), coping behaviors, and existing resources. Planning includes time lines and criteria for assessing change, and contracts are the tools used to bridge planning and implementation.

Implementing a change plan is the activity involved in accomplishing these various tasks and goals. Implementing may involve linking people with resources, changing expectations of the client or of the resource(s), developing or changing policy, changing the procedures in a resource system, or developing new or more effective coping behaviors in person(s), and so on.

Evaluating is part of the assessing process. In the beginning, we assess where the various parts of the practice situation are and, in the end, we evaluate or assess the changes in the various parts. We also evaluate activities that the change processes have accomplished. Evaluation is an assessment of both the outcome and the process. Assessment of outcome is not possible without a perspective that makes our outcome measures clear. It is because in the past this focus has not been explicit that we have been vague and inaccurate and/or confused the relating process with an outcome measure. Assessing and evaluating are continuous processes that should be linked to our characteristic focus, knowledge, and values. Our assessing and planning processes need to be done in a manner that makes evaluation possible.

Each of these process activities involves and includes many skills. They simply serve as a way of organizing our various skill areas. While there is a beginning and an ending to the change process, the steps in this process are not mutually exclusive or linear steps. They are rather interrelated and purposeful activities that together accomplish an end result.

THE WORKER

While workers may bring the characteristic focus, knowledge, values, and actions of the profession, they also bring themselves as resources to the change process. Workers, like clients, have past experiences, information, cognitive structures or preferred views of transactions, and predictions about consequences of certain kinds of transactions. Each worker brings his or her own style of transacting. It is the responsibility of the worker to constantly change his or her perceptions in the light of new knowledge, more accurate facts from the situation, new resources, and so on.

Workers often tend to prefer particular practice activities. However, the workers' preferred skills should not blunt the awareness of what is needed in any particular situation. For example, some workers have knowledge of interventions to change coping behaviors of individuals. The specific knowledge, plus workers' preference for their individual activities, may lead to a limited practice. Various combinations of selected knowledge and individual preference may lead to a limited perspective for assessing and may lead workers to ignore the important aspects of the practice situation. Workers may fail to develop skills for working with groups, the school system, or other community resources.

Many school social workers were trained at a time when methods of practice were the major divisions of training. Workers were trained to do either casework, group work, community organization, and/or intervention at the policy or administrative level. The major method for a school social worker was casework. In more recent years, it has been recognized that there are many common activities in practice. It has also been recognized that change may be enhanced through collaboration and exchange with others who share common "change goals." It is the responsibility of practitioners to keep up with changes in knowledge and to develop their skill level to incorporate new practice activities as they develop and are tested.

There is nothing, however, in the professional methodology or activities that can subordinate the unique, personal artistic contributions that each worker brings to the helping process. Certainly, the individual's sensitive capacity to experience and express empathy and caring are valued among social workers. It is, however, the responsibility of individual workers to evaluate the effects of their individual style on any change process. It is the worker's responsibility to recognize strengths and limitations. Unique qualities and personal style must be self-conscious and disciplined, just as discipline is inherent in the definition of art itself.

We have analyzed and specified the components, characteristic focus, the knowledge, the values, and the skills that social workers contribute to the public schools. This contribution is significant and provides a response that can be uniquely useful to education in meeting the challenges of its changing mandate. In specifying the components of practice, we see the model developed as useful, both for clarification of the contribution of the social worker and as a tool for building social work knowledge, and for research testing of theory. Because the construction of a model is the first step toward measurement and testing, we would see the elements of the model as a first step toward the measurement and testing of components of social work practice, and we have developed them with that intention. For each social worker, the task of participating in the development of new knowledge is just as important as application of the characteristic focus of the profession and its knowledge, values, and skills. There is much creative work to be done. The responsibility may seem heavy, but the challenge is exciting.

References

Bartlett, H. (1970). Seeking the strengths of social work. In *The common base of social work practice* (n.p.). New York: National Association of Social Workers.

Germain, C. B., & Gitterman, A. (1980). *The life model of social work practice*. New York: Columbia University Press.

Gitterman, A., & Germain, C. (1976). Social work practice: A life model. *Social Service Review, 50*, 601–610.

Gordon, W. E. (1962, October). A critique of the working definition. *Social Work, 9*.

Gordon, W. E. (1969). Basic constructs for an integrative and generative conception of social work. In G. Hearn (Ed.), *The general systems approach: Contributions toward an holistic conception of social work* (n.p.). New York: Council on Social Work Education.

Monkman, M. M. (1976). A framework for effective social work intervention in the public schools. *School Social Work Journal, 1*(1).

Monkman, M. M. (1978). A broader, more comprehensive view of school social work practice. *School Social Work Journal, 2*(2).

Monkman, M. M. (1981). An outcome focus for differential levels of school social work practice. In *Professional issues for social workers in schools* (pp. 138–150). Conference Proceedings. Silver Spring, MD: National Association of Social Workers.

Monkman, M. M. (1983). The specialization of school social work and a model for differential levels of practice. In D.G. Miller (Ed.), *Differential levels of students support services: Including crisis remediation and prevention/developmental approaches* (n.p.). Minneapolis, MN: Department of Education.

Monkman, M. M. (1989). *A national study of outcome objectives in social work practice: Person and environment*. Unpublished.

Monkman, M. M., & Meares, P. A. (1984). An exploratory study of school social work and its fit to the T.I.E. framework. *School Social Work, 19*(1), 9–22.

Pincus, A., & Minahan, A. (1972). *Social work practice, model and method*. Itasca, IL: F. E. Peacock.

Schwartz, W. (1969). Private troubles and public issues: One social work job or two? *Social Welfare Forum*, 22–43.

Siporin, M. (1975). *Introduction to social work practice*. New York: Macmillan.

4

The Wonderland of Social Work in the Schools, or How Alice Learned to Cope

Sally G. Goren
University of Illinois at Chicago

- Systems Theory
- Visibility
- Viability
- Value

A social worker entering a school for the first time may feel a bit like Alice as she tumbled into the Rabbit Hole and landed in the long corridor, finding it lined with locked doors. Only when she discovered the means by which she could change her size and shape did she begin her adventures in Wonderland. Throughout her experience in the pages of Carroll's book, Alice used her judgment, her feelings, and her integrity to deal with the characters whom she met. This chapter will attempt to offer some guidance to the social worker who finds him- or herself in the Wonderland of a school system. The worker may initially feel that his or her district or building resembles a series of locked doors with bits of the madness of Wonderland emerging through the cracks. To function effectively, it is essential that the social worker named Alice (or Alex) learn to identify within this setting the means by which he or she can achieve that optimal effectiveness that will prove his or her value to the system and meet personal professional standards and personal needs. Therefore, an evaluation of the system will be based on some understanding of systems theory. It is this writer's belief that each social worker in a school constitutes a "miniagency" complete in one person. On such an assumption, I will examine the roles the social worker might play, the various constituencies with whom the social worker interacts, and the question of accountability.

SYSTEMS THEORY

To flesh out this view of school social work, it is important to share some common understanding of systems theory. If we view any system as a complex, adaptive organization that is continually generating, elaborating patterns of actions and interaction, we see that the school, as a system, must be understood as an entity that is greater than the sum of its parts. It has discrete properties that need to be evaluated if we are to identify the points in which social work interventions may be made to ensure the maximum effectiveness mentioned previously. To view the school as an adaptive organization supports the social worker's theoretical underpinnings in which linkage, environmental impact, and enablement of each individual's maximum development are held in high value. The systems' definition also emphasizes the interactive elements that may impede or aid goal achievement. Thus the social worker is led to identify the junctures of interactions that bridge or fragment the discrete elements within the system (Costin, 1975).

Looking further into one's own school system, it is important to estimate its openness. An open system receives input, produces output, and interacts with all the actors within and outside of the system. The interactions may not always be agreeable, but there must be the opportunity for the school, its administrators, teachers, support staff, students, parents, and community to be heard and to hear one another. An important element of a viable system is, in fact, tension. This becomes the impetus for change and growth, for negotiation, for development, and for effective, productive relationships. Another element of the open system is that of feedback (Fordor, 1976). This speaks to a communications system that generates action in response to information that is the basis for constructive change.

As an employee of the school, it is critically important that the social worker define him- or herself within the system. The opportunity to be a significant interactor rests on the social worker's ability to inform the other actors of the social work role, to accept the input from others within and outside the school, and to respond and to produce output that is designed to meet needs that have been identified. A systems' understanding speaks emphatically to the need for the social worker to be visible, viable, and valuable. I will examine next how these qualities may be evidenced within the school.

VISIBILITY

To whom is the social worker important? In what ways is the social worker significant? The answer to these questions is that the school social worker is important and significant to everyone and in every way. The social worker has an impact on any person with whom he or she interacts. To look at the possible breadth of the assignment, I examine several factors defined by Lela Costin (1972) as a guide to visibility. The effective social worker will function as:

1. Provider of direct counseling services to pupils,
2. Advocate for specific pupils or groups of pupils whose needs are underserved or unmet,
3. Consultant to administrators in their task of program development and policy change,
4. Consultant to teachers to enhance their ability to create a productive climate for maximum learning,
5. Link to community services and facilitator between the school and community in obtaining necessary services for pupils and their families,
6. Leader in coordination of interdisciplinary teams providing service to pupils, and
7. Assessor of needs of individual pupils and of the school system as related to program development.

All of these factors demand that the social worker become known to the administrators, the teachers, and pupil services personnel who function within the school or school district. The social worker also needs to create an identity with the pupils in the school and, from these contacts, with the families whose children may be the recipients of social work services. How one fleshes out his or her visibility will vary but may include:

1. Informal meetings with teachers and other school personnel over lunch or coffee, before or after the pupils are in the building;
2. Regularly scheduled conferences with administrators and with teachers with whom the social worker shares responsibility for a child's welfare;
3. Initiation of contact with community agencies to whom the social worker may refer children or families for service;
4. Explanation of services to families via attendance at meetings of the PTA or other parent groups;
5. Responsibility for presentations at in-service meetings for teachers and/ or administrators;
6. Assumption of leadership at pupil services personnel team meetings; and
7. Attendance and presentations at school board meetings.

There are many ways that the social worker's visibility may be developed and the particular manner in which this is demonstrated will depend on the social worker's understanding of the politics of the school and the district. As early in one's entry into a district as possible, one must identify the power structure. Determining that will direct the worker toward the creation of relationships that will provide him or her with the support necessary for provision of service. To attempt to work without such support from the person or persons who wield power is an exercise in frustration and a sure diminution of the effectiveness of the efforts. These remarks are not meant to imply that all workers in all settings need to be allied with the power structure, but the worker does need to identify where the power lies in order to understand how his or her work may be enhanced or inhibited. The development of successful working relationships will depend on the clinical assessment skills and the use of relationship building skills that are in the educational and employment experience of all social workers. However, it must be stated that even the most highly skilled workers may be unable to achieve an alignment with the administrative power structure in some instances. Acknowledging that there may be more frustration than gratification in such settings, the social worker may still be able to function as an advocate for children and parents, particularly when the law supports necessary services. The social worker may be a mediator between teachers and administration on behalf of individual children or particular programs. In short, the social worker retains the responsibility to carry out the interventive roles fulfilled by workers in any field of practice (Compton & Gallaway, 1994).

Visibility also implies availability. To be ready to assist a principal or nurse in handling a crisis such as child abuse is an excellent way to cement one's position in the school. To provide linkage to a neighborhood day-care center for a child whose parent has become seriously ill demonstrates the effectiveness of relationship building in the community. To educate parents regarding the symptoms of childhood depression or normal preadolescent behavior presents the social worker in an appropriate and useful educator role. To inform the school board of new legislation affecting the school and to present a plan for meeting the criteria demanded by the law again places the social worker in a position of enormous value to the school community. It is no longer possible to limit one's role to individual or group counseling of children, though only a few years ago studies indicated that many school social workers defined their responsibilities in just such limited terms (Costin, 1969). Fortunately, there has been a shift in this narrow definition, and social workers in schools are engaging in the variety of tasks that have been mentioned above (Costin, 1969). All of this leads to an examination of the viability of the school social worker.

VIABILITY

Linked to visibility is viability. Not only does the school social worker need to be seen, the social worker needs to be seen in action. Creativity is the catchword, and the ability to use oneself creatively with the interactors in the school system is imperative. No longer remaining in one's office counseling children, the worker must assess special needs of the system and develop programs to meet them. If a classroom appears to be out of control, how can the worker assist the teacher, the students, or their families? What will meet the needs of the greatest number? It might be regular consultation with the teacher or an effective education project with the class, or several small group meetings with a portion of the pupils in the classroom. Perhaps a need for systematic handling of truancy problems exists. The worker may develop a plan to meet this need in coordination with the principal or assistant principal. Families or some members of the school board may be included in the development of the plan. Time spent with community agencies may alter previous adversarial positions or simply establish a modus operandi that had not existed and which can be functional not only for the worker but also for other school personnel who identify children in need of particular services. We again see how assessment skills, organizational skills, and finally treatment skills can be applied to a school system to provide maximum learning opportunities for the pupils served by that system.

Not only might the social worker be creative in relation to direct services to pupils with specific needs; he or she can be equally creative in identifying system needs and developing programs to address them.

A social worker who noted considerable distrust and low morale among teachers in a junior high school established a series of meetings and, assuming the role of facilitator, enabled the teachers to examine some of the system problems and the impact on their work. As concerns were shared and ideas for dealing with them were explored, the suspiciousness of the teachers declined, and fruitful relationships soon developed. They admitted similar anxieties about their classroom performances and, as a unit, were able to prepare criteria for the evaluation of their work and advocate for their adoption by the administration.

In another instance, a social worker worked with a principal and pupil personnel staff to develop an enrichment program for minority first-grade students. The social worker was able to provide some research expertise that aided the program's acceptance by the school board and by the families whose children attended the school.

Since PL 94-142 was passed in 1975 (now reformulated as PL 105-117, Individuals with Disabilities Education Act, IDEA), opportunities to expand social work services in the schools have increased. The law provides funding for districts to provide new services for children with disabilities and therefore has led to the hiring of new staff and the development of creative programs to serve their target groups in ways previously not possible. In many instances, the guidelines of the law have been imaginatively and broadly interpreted in those districts that have seen the mandate as an opportunity rather than a burden. It behooves the school social worker to be in the lead in such program development and to take an active role in the execution of new programs.

Built into the law is the necessity for accountability, an ever-increasing requirement in all fields of educational and social work practice. Without minimizing the additional time this demands, and recognizing that it can be regarded as a burden for an already overworked staff, I want to emphasize that this is also a chance to dramatically detail the breadth, content, and effectiveness of social work services. The law has provided us with the impetus to devise systems that can readily indicate who we serve, how we serve them, and the time allocation the various services require. This brings us to an examination of the final V: the value of the school social worker.

VALUE

Early in this chapter I commented on the total agency concept implicit in each social worker in the schools. It is eminently clear to any reader who is employed in schools that this is true. Is it clear to teachers and administrators? As a professional working within a host setting, the requirement for interpretation of one's function is continual. This is so because the responsibilities are broad and change as needs of the school community change. Because the other professional staff are also continually changing, new staff need to be informed in order to best utilize our services. Implicit in the statement above is the responsibility of the social worker to have control of the definition of his or her role. Although it will always be defined in relation to an accurate assessment of service needs, it is the social worker who has the most intimate knowledge of his or her own skills and training, and this needs to be communicated to staff in a school setting. To expect that teachers, speech therapists, principals, psychologists, and others know what one does is to permit any and all of the staff to dictate what to do, how to do it, and when to do it. Rather than allow the job to be defined by others, it behooves a social worker entering into practice in a school to view him- or herself as that total agency with the intent of meeting the school and community needs. These needs will be addressed within the knowledge, skill, and ethics of the social work profession; therefore, it is incumbent on the social worker to have a comfortable professional identity that can be expressed soundly to delineate the functions the social worker may undertake in the setting.

Just as it is the responsibility of the worker to be visible and viable in the school building, it is even more important that the social worker, from the point of entrance into a school system, share in the control of the evaluation process. Defining one's role and the scope of the job establishes the basis on which an evaluation of the social worker will be made by the responsible administrator. If the social worker regards him- or herself as that total agency, he or she needs to think and act as administrator, supervisor, and line worker.

As an administrator, one partializes time to meet the needs of the organization. This determination of the allocation of one's resources should be cooperatively established with the school district official to whom the social worker is directly responsible. The breadth of function, client contact, and caseload management are all part of this role. In order to have realistic criteria on which one's evaluation will be based, the social worker needs to be a participant in their development. If a district has a standard evaluation form for teachers, it might need to be adapted so that it is appropriate for a social worker or else another one should be developed that will better judge the overall effect of social work services in the building. In the role of administrator, it might be well to establish regular conferences with the building principal, the special education coordinator, and/or any other administrative-level personnel who might have an impact on the worker's position. This will continuously inform them of one's work and, of course, of one's value.

There are a number of situations with which this writer is familiar where administrators avoid contact with the social worker and reluctantly have any interaction. In other districts, the principal or assistant principals are intrusively involved in the case-by-case management of the social worker. In the first-mentioned situation, administrators must be informed via some method of one's overall work. This may be achieved by memos, weekly or monthly statistical and/or case reviews, and extensive written documentation of any cases wherein issues of legal responsibility may be a factor. The reasons for avoidance may be varied, but the worker must maintain professional linkage with administration by whatever means possible. In the case of the overly involved administrator, some methods similar to those employed with the "absent" administrator may serve to satisfy the control needs of that person. If the administrator is convinced that the worker is sharing with him or her the case management issues that the administrator feels necessary to know, the worker may find him- or herself freer to pursue the tasks as they have been assessed.

There are many suggestions for management of the system in this chapter. Each may work in some situations and not in others. Many ideas have not been mentioned. Nonetheless, the message is to experiment with various means of engagement, reporting, and integration of social work services within the educational milieu. Failure of one method does not foretell failure of another, and perseverance will be rewarded in most circumstances.

As one's own supervisor, the social worker must determine individual and group needs of the pupils with whom he or she works. Judging the necessity of a referral, any indication of the need for consultation, and the type of interventive role that will most readily meet the assessed need are assists the line worker receives from a supervisor. In most school districts, the line worker must carry this dual responsibility. Some districts do provide social work supervision or consultation, some have access to psychiatric consultation, but many school social workers have no established avenue to obtain this kind of input. The need for input, feedback, and direction has led some social workers in schools to develop informal consultation groups. Without devaluing the autonomy the school social worker enjoys, the burden of such total responsibility for one's work can be shared with others. However, the significance of the responsibility should be accorded adequate valuation by the district's administration.

There is no need to review the many, varied tasks the social worker, as line worker, undertakes. There is need, however, to account for them. The importance of counting contacts with children, with parents, with teachers, and with community resources cannot be overemphasized. Adding the time to fill out necessary reports and records is imperative. This kind of statistical record will provide the basis for the evaluation of effectiveness of service. Following the time keeping is the need to demonstrate effectiveness of one's action. If the social worker has shared in the development of goals with teachers and administrators, he or she will be able to share in the evaluation of his or her service. The fact that the social worker may not be effective in every instance should not deter him or her from creating an evaluation system that will demonstrate incremental change, diagnostic reassessments, and goal renegotiations. It is important to show that service plans are related to jointly determined goals and to provide some rationale for success or failure of the plans. To reemphasize the importance of one's involvement in this evaluative process, one might consider designing a short form that could be used with any child, group, family, or teacher. The form might include goals, methods for achievement, and time spent in an effort to meet the goals.

This entire section on value may have been better titled evaluation. It is the author's contention that one's value is best understood via evaluation of one's work, and the plea is, therefore, for each school social worker to carry a major responsibility for the negotiation and creation of the criteria on which such an evaluation will be based. This is another way that one informs, educates, and indeed, determines the parameters of one's work. Control is shared, goals are shared, and power is shared. The social workers who can actively demonstrate their value will find that they have a strong advocate in the principal or other administrator, and that kind of advocacy will agitate for more social work services and, hopefully, more social workers.

To be an effective participant in the creation of an atmosphere that will enhance learning opportunities for children, the social worker in the school must use all his or her best clinical and organizational skills. The social worker must first know who and what he or she is professionally. He or she must develop respect for the work of others. Trust will grow as hopes and expectations are shared and common goals are agreed on. The social worker who creates a significant position for him- or herself in a school system will have an accurate knowledge of the system and a clear knowledge of his or her position in it. The social worker will know the loci of power, the system needs, and the style of all the interactors within the system. This assessment will be the basis for the social worker's creation of an appropriate role. The social worker in a school, in essence, is always using professional skills. Whether meeting with a child or a teacher, arranging a contractual agreement with a family service agency, or consulting with a pupil services team, the effective social worker will be actively assessing and treating.

As Alice moved through her adventures in Wonderland and the Looking Glass, she became more assertive and gained control. Alice (or Alex) in the school system will find that active involvement in all aspects of that system will be the foundation for provision of service, acceptance within the system, and professional satisfaction for a job very well done. The social worker will also be very tired at the end of each day, recognizing that he or she has indeed used him- or herself skillfully throughout every contact that he or she has had. The social worker will have been visible, viable, and of value to everyone encountered during the day at school.

References

Compton, B., & Galaway, B. (1994). *Social work processes* (5th ed.). Pacific Grove, CA: Brooks/Cole.

Costin, L. B. (1969). An analysis of the tasks of school social workers. *Social Service Review, 43,* 274-285.

Costin, L. B. (1972). Adaptations on the delivery of school social work services. *Social Casework, 53,* 348-354.

Costin, L. B. (1975). School social work practice: A new model. *Social Work, 20,* 136.

Fordor, A. (1976). Social work and system theory. *British Journal of Social Work, 6.* (Reprinted from *Social work processes* [2nd ed.], pp. 98-101, by B. Compton & B. Galaway, 1979, Homewood, IL: Dorsey.)

5

Research and Evaluation: Tools of Practice Development

John P. Flynn
Western Michigan University

Robert Constable
Loyola University Chicago

Carol Rippey Massat
University of Illinois at Chicago

- ◆ Research and Evaluation: Tools of Practice Development
- ◆ Four Approaches to Research and Evaluation
- ◆ Research and Evaluation for Policy and Program Development
- ◆ Accountability and Evidence-Based Practice
- ◆ Support for Research and Evaluation

RESEARCH AND EVALUATION: TOOLS OF PRACTICE DEVELOPMENT

Research and evaluation provide a continuum of tools for the school social worker to use for practice and policy development. The practice, programs, and policies of today's schools are driven by information and systematically collected data and interwoven with research. And so it is in this book. This chapter and chapter 13 connect with general themes in social work research to provide an overview of school social work research and evaluation methodologies. Chapter 6 discusses the relation of research and evaluation to practice effectiveness, and thus to the choice of where and how to intervene. Chapter 14 discusses needs assessment as the broadest focus of the assessment process. With an objective of developing policies, programs, or services, needs assessment focuses on the relationships among schools, communities, and specific needs of students.

Research requires specification and identification of problems, review of the literature, sampling, data collection, measurement, analysis, and reporting. Descriptive research helps to determine the size and shape or the present dimensions of a condition—what exists. Evaluation is a research method used to determine the value of a particular activity. Program or practice evaluation helps us to determine whether programs or interventions work and how they might be strengthened.

FOUR APPROACHES TO RESEARCH AND EVALUATION

Four approaches to research and evaluation methods in school social work are described here. These approaches are aimed at exploring what exists and what works. In school social work they are all aimed at improving practice and services by achieving goals and objectives aimed at supporting the educational process for children and improving the school's contribution to the life of families and the community.

Basic Research

The central objective of basic research is to establish an understanding of relationships or causality among variables. The term *basic research* does not imply that such research is simpler than other forms of research. Rather, it refers to research that is done purely to gain knowledge or understanding, as opposed to *applied research*, which has an obvious practical purpose. Basic research has been considered the province of academic or research institute personnel and few school district budgets allow for such a luxury. However, without an accumulation of findings in practice itself, there would be no basic research, so basic research is reliant on the next three categories of research.

Description

In the beginnings of any profession, activities are described through systematic observation and recording. Practice wisdom, not yet subjected to rigorous examination, is at the level of "tricks of the trade." As in a collection of best practices, the principal tasks are to describe what occurs—to observe and to record the activity, and the nature of what appears to be taking place. Hypotheses have not been sufficiently tested and supported to do much more. Practice relies on what seems to work, what has been reported in the journals, what colleagues are finding to be successful, or what emerges more and more as a hunch. These descriptive research findings are helpful to practitioners, researchers, and theorists who begin to examine systematically those hunches or intuitive interventions. Eventually theory and professional guidelines will develop. But nothing can develop without clear description of the phenomenon. It is from description that research questions can be raised.

The major topic studied in school social work has been the role of the school social worker (Allen-Meares & Lane, 1982). Until there was a better understanding of the complexity, diversity, and consistency of this role, there existed an assumption that the school social worker simply did clinical social work with children in a school, much like a school-sponsored child guidance clinic. A thirty-year tradition of research into the school social work role, beginning with Lela Costin (1969), points out a gradually broadening scope of practice with greater involvement in education. The range of utilization of the school social worker role involves consultation, multidisciplinary teamwork, assessment, direct work with children and parents, and program development (Constable, Kuzmickaite, Harrison, & Volkmann, 1999). This thirty-year trend of descriptive research would contribute to codification of school social work practice expectations and the development of theory. The role could now be described for the purposes of teaching and assessment. Existing method theories in practice, policy development, and research would be developed and related to school processes in a new configuration of role.

Codification

Codification of practice takes description a step further, identifying what is done and what works best under what conditions or at what particular times. Research and evaluation now validate systematically what exists and its relations with other conditions. In the above example a number of task analyses of school social work have pointed out that the social worker's role has shifted over time to include a broader focus. The codification of school social work practice is leading to the construction of a professional knowledge base. The accumulated and verified experiences of professionals in the field are captured, communicated, and passed on to others. Knowledge and skill for the field begin to be built cumulatively. We are currently at a codification phase in the development of school social work.

Thus there is a continuum of research. In descriptive research and codification, discussed above, the emphasis had to be placed more on what exists than on what works. Another set of approaches comprise *evaluation* and *action research*. These are geared more to what works. However, they also feed back into theory, which attempts to explain *what* and *why* something is taking place or working. Evaluation answers questions about what works in the here and now with an immediate result being an understanding of the value of the work done. Accumulated evidence of effective approaches to practice results in the eventual codification of "best" practice and the development of theory. Action research uses the research process itself as an adjunct to direct practice to engage an organization in purposeful social change.

Evaluation

Formative evaluation is evaluation aimed at examining the process of a specific program or activity. It may focus on observing or counting or categorizing the number, nature, or frequency of activities engaged in by social workers or others. It may focus on what goes into the process. Formative evaluation may examine how smoothly a new program is being implemented, and what obstacles to implementation have occurred. It may focus on what steps are usually taken to achieve a goal. It may help us determine, for example, what the social worker does with his or her time or how resources (time, money, skills) might be allocated. It may focus on the response of stakeholders to the process of developing a program and may provide feedback that shapes the direction of the program that is ultimately developed. *Summative evaluation* focuses on outcomes of social work program activity and is used by program evaluation projects and studies of service effectiveness. Outcomes are the results of professional activities, including their influence on a problem or population group. Outcome research focuses on measuring activities to determine how things are going, particularly in relation to how one (or someone) desires things to be going. Its focus is on what is preferred, focusing on "outcomes" as opposed to "outputs" or simple events.

Outcome evaluation is an important basis for the development of programs and practice. Nic Dibble (1999) offers a number of practical suggestions for outcome evaluation in school social work services. These include:

- Focus on how social work activities match the priorities of the school district;
- Determine what data already exists;
- Limit the evaluation design to the scope of what the social worker actually does in light of particular priorities;
- Involve key stakeholders in the evaluation process;
- Ensure that the variables observed are valid measures of what you wish to observe and associate with impact or outcome;
- Limit the scope of each evaluation;
- Carefully communicate one's findings with the key decision makers;
- Use the findings to improve school social work services.

In his final point, Dibble suggests that the findings may flow back to the codification of practice and the development of theory.

Single-system designs have been developed as one means of evaluating direct practice in social work. Single-system design can be used with families, groups classrooms, or any single unit of intervention. A single-system design always involves the measurement of a problem at baseline, or before intervention occurs. Then measurement occurs during intervention and when intervention is withdrawn. The simplest design is the ABA design, in which *A* stands for the period of measurement when no intervention is occurring. The letter *B* stands for a period of intervention. Single-system designs are atheoretical. They can be used to evaluate practice that uses any theoretical approach. Although single-system designs have been most commonly used in conjunction with behavioral or cognitive-behavioral interventions, they can also be used with psychodynamic approaches, various approaches to family therapy, group work, or interventions with larger systems. The key to using these designs is the focus on a single system, and the use of measurement to assess progress. Measurement can occur through direct observation of behaviors, such as observation of classroom behavior, use of paper-and-pencil measures of such constructs as self-esteem or depression through self-reports, or other systematic means of measurement. Bloom, Fischer, and Orme (2003) are an excellent source of additional information on carrying out these designs.

Action Research

Action research is a hybrid of direct practice with an orientation toward social change. The research or evaluative work includes proactively engaging others in the arena to pursue program or policy change together. The problem is often that an insufficient number of key players, decision makers, providers of services, families, and community interests are aware of or invested in a problem. The following example shows an action research process in school social work.

> I was concerned about what I perceived to be a growing problem of teasing coming close to peer sexual abuse on the school bus and in gym class. No one else seemed to recognize the problem when we discussed this in the faculty meeting. They just assumed that "boys will be boys." The outcome of our discussion was that I agreed to take an anonymous survey among seventh- and eighth-grade boys and girls. I shared the compelling results of the survey in the next meeting. The problem was undeniable, and children were getting hurt. The data also showed that boys were not the only perpetrators and girls not the only victims. After some heated discussion, the faculty agreed on a zero-tolerance policy and set up a committee, including me, to develop the policy, review it with the principal and superintendent, and present it at a future meeting.

As in this example, action research provides a relatively unbiased vehicle for planned change in a world of opinions and uncertainty. There is a need for data to inform policy, program, or practice decisions. All participants are consulted with or advised ahead of time of the methods and procedures. A consensus on the problem and the plan has to be developed.

RESEARCH AND EVALUATION FOR
POLICY AND PROGRAM DEVELOPMENT

Surveys of the role of the school social worker point out the importance of program and policy development in the role of the school social worker. These programs and policies can be targeted toward particular concerns of the school, toward groups in need or at risk, or toward the establishment and development (or survival) of social work services. Although program development takes place mainly at the local school or district level, policy development may take place in the local school, in the school district (LEA), or at the state education agency (SEA) level.

Just as individual interventions are driven by assessment and evaluation, the process of policy and program development works best when it is wedded to a more systematic process of using information gathered through research and evaluation. There are many examples of this process. A social worker new to a school does a needs assessment with the principal, the teachers, and others as part of the process of establishing her role and the direction of her services. A social worker helps develop a crisis and safety plan for the school. Another worker is concerned about bullying, teasing, and peer sexual harassment in a junior high school. He does a survey of incidents among students. When the results come in, he works with others to absorb their meaning. He helps develop a zero-tolerance policy for these damaging incidents. He participates in carrying out the policy, working with teachers, victims, perpetrators, and parents. He evaluates whether and how the policy is working. The same process can be applied to other problems and needs, such as homeless and/or hungry children, concerns about gang violence, needs in the community for an after-school program, and so on.

> At the SEA level, the issue arose whether school social work services, contracted with an outside agency, performed the same tasks and were as effective as when the social worker was in-house and a full-time school employee. There was a concrete proposal before the SEA from districts hoping to save money through contractual arrangements for social work services. Social workers from the state association of school social workers, in cooperation with the SEA and assisted by a local university, developed a statewide survey of practice. The results were discussed by the state board of education as the basis for a proposed policy regarding school social work.

Outcome-Based Education

Assessment and evaluation are engines currently driving practice in public education. An outcome-based education system is developing. There are new demands for accountability and documented evidence of the effectiveness of education and of school social work. In this climate, school social work and other school professions are finding themselves without developed data to support their interventions.

The accountability movement in education has been characterized by a series of concrete goals and efforts to measure effectiveness of all aspects of education. Goals 2000, articulated in the American Education Act, PL 103-227, was one initiative of the accountability movement. Eight goals for American education were set forth in this legislation. Former President George H.W. Bush proposed six of these goals, and former President Clinton added two more. The goals included (1) all children will arrive at school ready to learn; (2) high school graduation rate will be at least 90 percent; (3) students in grades four, eight, and twelve will demonstrate competency in subject matter; (4) American students will be first in the world in math and science achievement; (5) adults will be literate and able to compete in a global economy; (6) learning environments will be safe, disciplined, and drug free; (7) parental participation will be increased; and (8) professional development for educators will be promoted (Meares, Washington, & Welsh, 2000, p. 7). Another major step in the accountability movement has been the effort to make schools more accountable for the educational achievement of their students. This is most clearly articulated in the No Child Left Behind Act of 2001 (NCLB). This act requires annual progress toward the goal of 100 percent of students meeting state standards for academic achievement at their grade level.

ACCOUNTABILITY AND EVIDENCE-BASED PRACTICE

Simultaneous with the accountability movement in education, accountability has become increasingly critical to social work as a profession. Budget constraints have required social workers to document their worth. Both pressure from funders and ethical standards for practice have led to a focus on providing evidence that interventions are effective in assisting client systems. Currently, the concept of evidence-based practice has emerged with a dual focus on development of an empirical basis for social work practice and on practice evaluation (Gibbs, 2003).

> Evidence-based practice . . . dictates that professional judgments and behavior should be guided by two distinct, but interdependent principles. First, whenever possible, practice should be grounded on prior findings that demonstrate empirically that certain actions performed with a particular type of client or client system are likely to produce predictable, beneficial and effective results. . . . Secondly, every client system, over time, should be individually evaluated to determine the extent to which the predicted results have been attained as a direct consequence of the practitioner's actions. (Cournoyer & Powers, 2002)

The first focus of evidence-based practice is that interventions are based and practice is grounded on the known effectiveness of previous similar work. Such systematized evidence of effectiveness is now beginning to be developed, a massive endeavor, given the diversity of school social work practice. Practice evaluation is the second focus of evidence-based practice. All practice needs to be outcome oriented. School social work practice should be coordinated work between a school social worker and a client system that is guided by mutual goals, evaluated periodically, at termination of services, and following the end of services. The client system is ultimately in charge of the action, the goals, and the outcome. The practitioner, working as a coach, will use proven techniques to assist the client (system) to learn to take charge of the work and to achieve the outcome desired.

There are models to guide the individual practitioner in the use of evidence-based practice. For example, Gibbs (2003) describes how to seek evidence regarding potential interventions; how to critique the quality of that evidence; how to apply the information gained regarding effective interventions; and how to evaluate performance when an intervention is implemented. This model can be used for interventions at all systems levels, including work with children, teachers, groups, families, schools, and communities.

While evidence-based practice can be seen as a guide for individual practice, it is also a larger project than simply the work of any one individual. As problems are identified and systemized and as evidence develops, these results are fed back into practice and these understandings become the basis for a more fully developed practice. This cannot be simply a project of individual practitioners. If it is to work, it involves a complex set of relationships between universities, professional organizations, state departments of education, and individual social work practitioners, where results from practice can feed into sources of research-based knowledge and be monitored by standard setting organizations. These relationships, the knowledge base, and the organization characteristic of a specialization are only in a beginning phase.

The experiences of other school professions point out what needs to take place over the next decade. School psychologists formed an ongoing Task Force on Evidence-Based Interventions in School Psychology, which met over a number of years to address these issues. Their discussions (Kratochwill & Shernoff, 2003) point out the need for a complex network of relationships between practitioners, standard-setting organizations, and universities and the development of a wide range of collaborative research work.

According to the task force, the development of evidence-based practice demands:

1. The development of a research network of practitioners, standard setting organizations and universities;
2. A focus on particular problem areas where research has developed, and where more development is needed;
3. Differentiation of basic principles of change, underlying all interventions,[1] from specific issues of effectiveness to be further tested.

---

1. Much psychotherapy research using meta-analysis of *underlying factors*, which are generally more powerful in explaining change than a particular theoretical orientation or technique, has moved from an emphasis on symptom and technique (person as *object* of help) to an emphasis on the person as *subject* of help. Such research points out effective patterns in the relational bond: Clients need to see themselves as moving and thus actively working on a problem. Therapists should exhibit active and positive behavior in relation to tasks. The relational bond needs to be experienced as one of intimate, warm, emotionally absorbing involvement. Clients need to be able to talk about themselves in a concrete, responsive way, but attuned to their immediate inner experiences. Out of a mutual attunement to the importance of their experiences there grow shared meanings in the helping relationship. For a review of meta-analyses of thirty years of psychotherapy research, see Orlinsky, D. E., Grawe, K., & Parks, B. E. (1994). Process and outcome in psychotherapy—*noch einmal*. In A. E. Bergin & S. L. Garfield (Eds.), *Handbook of psychotherapy and behavior change*. New York: Wiley.

4. Further development of the scientist-practitioner training model;
5. Development of a typology of research into the efficacy and effectiveness of evidence-based interventions (EBIs) (Chorpita, 2003):

Type I: Efficacy studies. Efficacy studies evaluate interventions in a controlled research context.

Type II: Transportability studies. Transportability studies examine not only the degree to which intervention effects generalize from research to practice settings, but also the feasibility of implementing and the acceptability of EBIs in practice settings (Schoenwald & Hoagwood, 2001). In applied settings practitioners are faced with administrative, logistical, and ethical issues (to name just a few) that may not be part of the efficacy research agenda (Backer, Liberman, & Kuenel, 1986; Kazdin, Kratochwill, & VandenBos, 1986). Thus, transportability studies allow evaluation of the various contextual issues—such as training requirements, characteristics of the treatment provider, training resources, acceptability of treatments, cost and time efficiency, and necessary administrative supports—that facilitate or constrain the effective transport of EBI's into practice settings (e.g., Hoagwood, Burns, Kiser, Ringeisen, & Schoenwald, 2001).

Type III: Dissemination studies. Dissemination studies use intervention agents that are part of the system of services—in our case, the school. In this type of research an intervention protocol would be deployed in the school and carried out by, for example, school social workers serving either as direct intervention agents or as mediators working with consultees, such as teachers or parents. Because Type III research still involves a formal research protocol, researcher control and supervision may have an impact on the intervention and its ultimate effectiveness.

Type IV: System evaluation studies. To establish independence from the "investigator effect" present in dissemination studies, another type of research—system evaluation studies—can be undertaken. Chorpita (2003) characterized this research as involving the "final inference to be made: whether the practice elements can lead to positive outcomes where a system stands entirely on its own." (Kratochwill & Shernoff, 2003, p. 46)

Thus, assuming that groups of practitioners and researchers work together with reference to outcomes, the first steps in the development of evidence-based practice are:

- ◆ Specification of the work and the role of the school social worker with its many possibilities;
- ◆ Specification, measurement, and comparison of outcomes, beginning with qualitative and moving to quantitative data where possible;
- ◆ Systematic accumulation of comparative data on practice;
- ◆ Development of linkages of practice with universities and standard setting organizations;
- ◆ Development of systematized bodies of knowledge regarding effective interventions to feed back into practice.

In the meantime, inventories of effective practice, discussed in the next chapter, are beginning to develop. The range of possibilities in the school social worker's role is beginning to be defined. Practice models that allow for comparison, as well as data collection usable to the above enterprise, are beginning to be developed.

SUPPORT FOR RESEARCH AND EVALUATION

The field is presently faced with a dilemma. The age of accountability and current law, such as NCLB, demand that schools, social work services included, provide evidence of sound guided practice and practice/service effectiveness. Yet, the time is short. It is rare to see a line item in a school budget for any significant level of funding for research and evaluation of social work services. Even if there were resources for evaluation, which of the number of things the social worker does with presumed effectiveness should be evaluated? Providing consultation? Making assessments and contributing to the assessments of others? Running different groups? Working directly with a great variety of children presenting different problems? Developing a truancy program? Doing liaison work with outside agencies? Working with parents? Assisting in the development of programs and policies? Working with crises? Being a resource for the situations of children with disabilities? Each is a different evaluative study. On the other hand, the procedures prescribe evaluation. Nevertheless, there is a conflict between what is expected, what is possible, and what can be supported. One approach is for individual practitioners to consciously take steps to integrate research and evaluation more fully with everyday practice. Measurement can be a normal part of practice. Not all services may need evaluation, but different groups or problems may be targeted. For example, practitioners might use single-system methods. They might relate their results to other similar project or program evaluations. They would limit their efforts to what is doable. They can focus on those interventions that have promise of showing the near-term or the intermediate-term payoff. They might use existing data when possible. But then it will be equally important to connect with schools of social work, SEAs, and professional associations in a shared effort.

By examining data, school social workers can tune into the current needs of the school community. Data can be powerful and may force schools to redefine their priorities, based on the diverse views of its constituencies. The local school system's concepts of effective school social work practice and goals may be different from the community's or an individual client's view. By gathering concrete information, school social workers can know whether there is a need to respond to increased levels of teen violence, or whether issues in the world of work are affecting the school population. By systematically asking questions through the use of research methods, school social workers can be aware of different understandings on many issues, such as inclusive education for children with disabilities, or integration of school social work services with other community services using a wraparound approach. In any case, dialogue is the crucial basis for action. Beyond research and practice the key question is which goals and criteria shall govern practice and resources. This is a political, as well as substantive, scientific question.

Research and evaluation are useful tools. A habit of always examining our practice can guide it and shape it. It becomes part of our professional style. During these times, those habits may support social work practice in the schools and lead to system change. They are at the heart of sound and ethical practice.

References

Allen-Meares P., & Lane, B.A. (1982). A content analysis of school social work literature 1968-78. In R. Constable, & J. P. Flynn (Eds.), *School social work: Practice and research perspectives* (pp. 38-48). Chicago: The Dorsey Press.

Backer, T. E., Liberman, R. P., & Kuenel, T. G. (1986). Dissemination and adoption of innovative psychosocial interventions. *Journal of Consulting and Clinical Psychology, 54*(1), 111-118.

Bloom, M., Fischer, J., & Orme, J. G. (2003). *Evaluating practice: Guidelines for the accountable professional* (4th ed.). Boston: Allyn & Bacon.

Chorpita, B. F. (2003). The frontier of evidence-based practice. In A. E. Kazdin, & J. R. Weisz (Eds.), *Evidence-based psychotherapies for children and adolescents* (pp. 42-59). New York: Guilford.

Costin, L. (1969). An analysis of the tasks in school social work. *Social Service Review, 43*, 274-285.

Constable, R., Kuzmickaite, D., Harrison, W. D., & Volkmann, L. (1999). The emergent role of the school social worker in Indiana. *School Social Work Journal, 24*(1), 1-14.

Cournoyer, B. R., & Powers, G. T. (2002). Evidence-based social work: The quiet revolution continues. In A. R. Roberts, & G. Greene (Eds.), *Social workers' desk reference* (pp. 798-806). Oxford, UK: Oxford University Press.

Dibble, N. (1999). *Outcome evaluation of school social work services.* Madison: Department of Public Instruction, State of Wisconsin, Retrieved October, 2001, from http://www/dpi.state.wi.us/dpi/sspw/dlsea/pdf/outcmeval1999.PDF

Fischer, J. (1978). *Effective casework practice: An eclectic approach.* New York: McGraw-Hill.

Gibbs, L. E. (2003). *Evidence-based practice for the helping professions.* Pacific Grove, CA: Thomson.

Hoagwood, K., Burns, B. J., Kiser, L., Ringeisen, H., & Schoenwald, S. K. (2001). Evidence-based practice in child and adolescent mental health services. *Psychiatric Services, 52*, 1179-1189.

Kazdin, A. E., Kratochwill, T. R., & VandenBos, G. (1986). Beyond clinical trials: Generalizing from research to practice. *Professional Psychology: Research and Practice, 3*, 391-398.

Kratochwill, T. R., & Shernoff, E. S. (2003). *Evidence-based practice: Providing evidence-based interventions in school psychology.* WCER working paper No. 2003-13. Madison, WI: Wisconsin Center for Educational Research. Retrieved August 8, 2004, from http://www.wcer.wisc.edu

Meares, P. A., Washington, R. O., & Welsh, B. L. (2000). *Social work services in schools* (3rd ed.). Boston: Allyn & Bacon.

Orlinsky, D. E., Grawe, K., & Parks, B. E. (1994). Process and outcome in psychotherapy. In A. E. Bergin & S. L. Garfield (Eds.), *Handbook of psychotherapy and behavior change.* New York: Wiley.

Schoenwald, S. K., & Hoagwood, K. (2001). Effectiveness, transportability and dissemination of interventions: What matters when? *Psychiatric Services, 52*(9), 1190-1197.

6

The Effectiveness of School Social Work Practice

Christine Anlauf Sabatino
The Catholic University of America

Lynn Milgram Mayer
The Catholic University of America

Elizabeth March Timberlake
The Catholic University of America

◆ Incorporating the Expanding Knowledge Base into Practice
◆ Defining Outcomes
◆ Intervention Effectiveness
◆ Intervention Findings
◆ Evidence-Based Intervention and School Social Work Practice
◆ Future Directions for Effective School Social Work Practice
◆ Internet Resources

The realities of school social work practice in the twenty-first century are creating new assumptions about practice models, goals, interventions, and documentation of outcomes and consequent tasks as theory and practice are tested. This chapter reexamines the issue of practice effectiveness in school settings to:

1. Clarify expectations about practice evaluation in school social work;
2. Present criteria for locating, organizing, and assessing the information available to school social workers as a basis for developing effective school social work practice;

3. Review recent school social work outcome studies; and
4. Consider future directions for enhancing and evaluating school social work practice effectiveness.

As a field of practice and a specialization within social work, the practice of school social work resides within the processes and contexts of education. It builds on professional social work values, ethics, functions, and theoretical bases (Constable & Alvarez, in press) and uses applicable findings from other fields of social work practice and other professions. Recent school legislation has promoted an outcome-based education system (Levine, 2004). School social workers and other school-based professionals are expected to embrace the value of science in informing their intervention methods and to use evaluation as a tool in directing and legitimizing these methods (Kratochwill, Albers, & Shernoff, 2004).

Yet, for a variety of reasons, solo school social work practitioners often have difficulty meeting these expectations while functioning in the dual roles of practitioner and researcher. They cannot do this without skills in understanding and assessing the scientific data and without the concerted support of universities, professional organizations, and state and local education agencies. The demands for outcome-based practice and the realities of practice rarely coincide. For example, even though school administrators implicitly expect school social workers to document program and practice outcomes, they are unlikely to use these terms and rarely include outcome evaluation in employment descriptions for school social work positions. In addition, they rarely ask school social workers to conduct policy analyses, program evaluations, or practice evaluations. Furthermore, in order to conduct valid and reliable program and practice evaluations, school social workers need financial resources provided by school systems and other funding sources. They also need opportunities and time for collaboration with research partners and access to the developing literature on evidence-based practice in social work (Roberts & Yaeger, 2004), Internet resources, professional associations, and state departments of education.

One must first of all acknowledge the complexity of the tasks involved. Given competing expectations and responsibilities and the diversity of a school social worker's roles, it is not easy to evaluate the effectiveness of practice. Furthermore, understanding practice effectiveness in school social work is more complex than examining practice theory, methodology, and techniques. Indeed, much of the effectiveness of direct practice intervention comes from the many processes that underlie different theoretical orientations and developmental perspectives—for example, the therapeutic alliance or working relationship; client-worker agreement on problem definition, tasks, and goals; and the client's hopes and expectations (Bickman, 2002; Hubble, Duncan, & Miller, 1999; Okomoto & LeCroy, 2004; Orlinsky, Grawe, & Parks, 1994; Snyder, Michael, & Cheavens, 1999). In addition, social workers use a variety of methods to deal with the multiple problems they encounter. Many of these methods involve working with and through others in consultation and teamwork in the school, in the community, and with parents (Allen-Meares, 1994; Constable, Kuzmickaite, Harrison, & Volkmann, 1999). And so, the effectiveness of the school social worker cannot easily be isolated from the effectiveness of the total team. In the face of this complexity, outcome-based program and practice evaluations inevitably identify only a portion of what school social workers actually do and how well they do it.

In addition to comprehending the complexity of their practice, school social workers need to understand the relationship between the *efficacy* standard for evaluating interventions in controlled experimental research and the *effectiveness* standard for evaluating interventions in a real world practice context. While efficacy represents the gold standard for evaluating intervention outcomes, the translation of experimental research into effective day-to-day practice is a task to be undertaken by the entire field of professionals connected with schools: the universities, professional organizations, state education agencies, as well as school administrators and direct practitioners (Kratochwill & Shernoff, 2003; chapter 5). One danger, however, is that approaching this task with a narrowed focus on competing practice methodologies may inadvertently result in overlooking factors that research has shown to be very powerful. Examples might include the therapeutic alliance, what clients bring to the intervention, team interaction or leadership, teacher consultations, classroom climate, peer interactions, community collaboration, the influence of policy, and the importance of system maintenance as well as system change. Another danger is that the essence of the profession's way of viewing, valuing, and thinking about children in the context of their schools, homes, and communities, as well as its simultaneous dual focus on person and environment (Gordon, 1969), is neither always visible nor easily captured by traditional research methods.

INCORPORATING THE EXPANDING KNOWLEDGE BASE INTO PRACTICE

The first part of this chapter reviews some of the questions behind a concerted and ongoing effort of school social workers and researchers to review the literature. How can an expanding knowledge base be incorporated into evidence-based practice? How might school social workers measure the impact of policies, programs, administrative actions, and service practices on children's educational and personal well-being? What can work in school social work?

Beginning to answer these questions involves three steps: (1) collecting information about intervention outcomes from the literature, (2) evaluating what has been collected, and (3) organizing the material into a useable framework.

The first step involves the collection of information. Once the topic for the search is determined, computer technology can assist a review of the literature. Raines (2004) has suggested several guidelines for searching online social work abstracts and other databases. These include accessing the relevant database, limiting the search, changing the display, learning new techniques for searching, combining search terms with "or," investigating the evidence, looking for practice-related articles, narrowing the search with "and," and printing, saving, and/or e-mailing findings to one's computer.

The advent of computer technology, particularly online databases and online journals, has both facilitated and hampered the accumulation and organization of professional literature. Easier access to information has increased the availability of evidence for practice and, thereby, can have a positive impact. However, assessing the quality of the many available empirical studies, databases, and published practice guidelines remains challenging (Gilgun, 2005), since not all of the information found will be credible (Fonagy, Target, Cotrell, Philips, & Kurtz, 2002). Research needs to be evaluated by standards that match the complexity of what is being studied. Thus, the second step is evaluation of the literature utilizing the lens of research methodology for soundness and credibility.

This process of evaluating research studies and findings is presented here as a series of open-ended questions: Does the intervention work? Published articles describing randomized clinical trials with either a control or routine treatment comparison groups are clearly the scientific ideal for deciding whether an intervention works. Following this are the questions on practice effectiveness: Which treatment model works better? For whom? In real school settings, reports describing quantitative and qualitative quasi-experimental designs with focal and comparison interventions are also important in building knowledge of practice effectiveness.

In a critique of published research, the methodological rigor of each study is the primary concern (Brinberg & McGrath, 1982). The first evaluative questions may be: Is the research problem germane to school social work practice? Is the conceptual explanation of the problem clearly stated, parsimonious, feasible, and internally consistent? Internal validity involves the extent to which research findings can be attributed to the independent variables selected for study. This issue yields evaluative questions such as: Is the research method appropriate for answering the questions posed? Is the sample size adequate for answering the question? How representative is the sample? Are the variables measured by valid and reliable instruments appropriate for the research purpose? Are there multiple measures of key variables and multiple data analyses (triangulation)? Is there a control or comparison group? These kinds of questions address threats to internal validity related to history, maturation, testing, instrumentation, regression to the mean, experimental morbidity, selection bias, and interaction (Campbell & Stanley, 1963). Additional questions assess whether the research design incorporates enough difference between the focal interventions and control (or comparison) interventions to allow variance in outcome effect: Is there a large enough sample to reduce effects of individual differences and measurement reliability and remove competing variables that might influence the dependent variable? (Kerlinger & Lee, 2000). Did the experimental manipulation make a statistically significant difference and lead to clinically meaningful change?

In considering external validity, the focus is on the generalizability of the study. Evaluative questions include: Are the findings generalizable beyond the scope of the study? If the study is replicated, will the same findings occur? These questions reflect Campbell and Stanley's (1963) concerns about threats to external validity: multiple treatments, experimental condition, interactive testing, and selection interaction.

For qualitative research, the evaluation criteria focus on authenticity and trustworthiness, including credibility, transferability, dependability, and confirmability. Thus, it is critical to assess threats to authenticity (reactivity, researcher bias, and respondent bias) and internal reliability (Franklin & Ballan, 2001; Rodwell, 1998; Thyer, 2001). Evaluative questions include: Is the research question clear and congruent? Is the role of the researcher described? Are the paradigms and constructs specified? Was data collection done across a range of settings, times, and respondents? Are there comparable data collection protocols for multiple workers? Are coding and data quality checks done? Do the findings show parallelism across data sources?

Studies combining quantitative and qualitative approaches would meet the standard of achieving a balance between rigor and relevance, precision and richness, elegance and applicability, and verification and discovery. Mixed method or mixed model designs increase the breadth and scope of the study by using triangulation, complementarity, initiation, development, and expansion (Tashakkori & Teddlie, 1998).

In addition to individual studies, the process of evaluating knowledge upon which to base interventions may involve reports of statistical *meta-analyses* of multiple intervention studies targeting a focal problem in order to aggregate the findings and determine best practices (Baker & Jansen, 2000; Gilgun, 2005; Raines, 2004). In meta-analyses, practice outcome findings can be sorted according to outcome content and/or research design (quantitative, qualitative, or mixed method). The goal is to compare the aggregated findings using sophisticated statistical methodology to examine generalizability and the feasibility of replication. The results of meta-analyses, however, need to be interpreted and understood in the context of their practice applicability, distinguishing what may be efficacious in a laboratory setting and what may be effective in a real practice context.

How then can state-of-the-art knowledge about practice efficacy be translated into usable knowledge for effective practice? The lens of theory can organize the collection of methodologically sound, topical research, relevant to school social work, into a usable framework. From this identifiable framework, the literature can be synthesized into a conceptual narrative that focuses information and stimulates the development of practice models. We will review some of these theoretical frameworks, concerned about the relation between large scale and individual interventions on schools to accomplish certain objectives.

Adelman and Taylor (2000), for example, present an overarching conceptual framework for effective helping that focuses on *barriers* to student development, learning, and teaching. This framework encompasses a holistic, developmental perspective that incorporates primary prevention and early intervention programs to address the root causes of the full range of problems, from adjustment difficulties to severe and chronic conditions. They posit that, in order to overcome barriers to successful education, fundamental change in educational policies, school restructuring, and community collaboration is necessary. Their model highlights six interrelated areas: classroom-focused enabling, transition supports, student and family assistance, prevention and crisis response programs, parent and caregiver involvement, and community outreach.

Early and Vonk (2001) offer a different conceptual framework. In reviewing twenty-one outcome studies of school social work practice, they used the conceptual framework of *risk and resilience*, arguing that this framework is appropriate for school social work's preventive function. While risk refers to factors associated with the probability of a negative event or outcome, resilience refers to protective factors that promote capacity or coping abilities. On the environmental level, risk and protective factors exist in the larger environment as well as the environment of the school, neighborhood, and family. On the individual level, characteristics on the biological, psychological, social, and spiritual levels can be either risk or protective factors. The studies in this review reflect social work outcomes of decreased risk factors and augmented protective factors in youth development and psychosocial functioning. Thus, the presentation facilitates understanding of what promotes resilience or what lessens risk and, thereby, clarifies target areas for setting goals and eliminating barriers to learning.

Kratochwill et al. (2004) and the Task Force for Evidence-Based Interventions in School Psychology offer a third option for a conceptual framework. Their framework revolves around a three-tier model that encompasses *prevention* and *intervention*. The practice focus involves a continuum of prevention and intervention services based on developmental level and risk status. Services are categorized along a continuum of *universal, selected,* and *indicated* interventions.

Universal interventions include an entire student group, independent of risk status, and have goals of enhancing protective factors and preventing or minimizing future difficulties. These interventions reach approximately 80 percent of a student population. Examples include violence prevention programs or school-wide behavioral expectations. *Selective* interventions are designed to meet the needs of students who are nonresponsive to universal interventions or who display significant risk factors, perhaps 10 to 15 percent of the student population. Examples would be groups for children experiencing divorce, early intervention, transition programs, social skills groups, classroom interventions, and consultation with teachers or parents. Finally, *indicated* interventions are designed to meet the needs of the estimated 1 to 5 percent of students whose failure to respond to universal and selected interventions indicates the need for more intensive, comprehensive, and expansive services, implemented on a longer-term basis with coordinated efforts among teachers, parents, social workers, and community service providers. Examples might be students with distinguishing risk factors, delinquency, depression, or aggressive behavior.

DEFINING OUTCOMES

What is a good outcome? Or whose outcome is it anyway (Fonagy et al., 2002)? Which service programs and intervention processes are most effective in eliminating personal and environmental barriers to learning for which clients? Which children and youth need a different array of services? Do school social workers (or various team efforts) fulfill school system policy, program, and administrative directives? Which community partnerships provide the most effective service for children and families in the schools? What is the cost effectiveness of service delivery (including adequacy and efficiency)? There are three broad approaches to conceptualizing outcome and a number of possible criteria within each area:

1. *Service outcomes* document program impact and reflect the goals of the intervention, the process of the intervention delivered, and aggregate accomplishments. The measurement emphasis may be on different aspects of the service provided:

> Service availability, accessibility, and comprehensiveness;
> The intervention model itself and techniques selected;
> The processes, techniques, context, and quality of service delivery;
> The amount of intervention provided and the number of clients served; and
> The outcomes that reflect service mission and cost effectiveness.

2. *Satisfaction outcomes* document the user's contentment with the service delivered and the outcomes achieved. Satisfaction as a measure of success reflects service acceptability as well as the therapeutic relationship and is thought to correlate with client retention and change.

3. *Practice outcomes* document goal attainment or problem reduction as perceived by children, parents, teachers, school social workers, school personnel, the school system, and the community. As a measure of success, these outcomes reflect treatment processes and client changes occurring over the course of the intervention. Practice outcomes for children and parents may include in-session impact (awareness and insight, problem reduction, affect and behavior changes) and three types of postsession outcomes:

Immediate changes apparent at termination, such as symptom reduction, affect change, behavior change, and educational achievement;

Intermediate-term changes some months after termination, such as personal adaptation, psychosocial functioning, interpersonal relationships, and coping with stressors; and

Long-term improvements one year or more after termination, such as personality or other intrapsychic change.

Practice outcomes reflecting goal attainment by school and community may include environmental barrier and resource changes that are a prelude to child and parent changes; concurrent environmental changes such as school–community collaboration patterns and teacher-child interactions; and program and policy changes occurring upon consideration of aggregated case data.

INTERVENTION EFFECTIVENESS

There is a danger in focusing mainly on intervention models to the exclusion of other factors that also have profound effects on outcome. According to Hubble, Duncan, and Miller (1999), it is likely that the beneficial effects of intervention, including school social work practice models, result largely from combining four therapeutic factors, which research has identified as the principal elements accounting for client improvement:

- ◆ Client extra-therapeutic factors (strengths and needs, risk and protective factors, intrapersonal resources and deficits, interpersonal social network involvement, and reflective skills the client brings) account for 40 percent of the outcome;
- ◆ Relationship factors account for 30 percent of the outcome. These are the interpersonal connectedness and expressive attunement of the therapeutic alliance or working relationship. They include Rogers's (1957) classic core therapeutic conditions of a healing relationship—empathy, genuineness, and unconditional positive regard;
- ◆ Placebo, hope, and expectancy factors (belief that change can occur, agreement with the rationale of a treatment approach, "confidence in and mastery of a chosen method [which] ultimately works by enhancing the client's belief in the potential for healing" [Snyder, Michael, & Cheavens, 1999, p. 183]) account for 15 percent of the outcome; and
- ◆ Model-specific factors (philosophical underpinnings, rationale, theory base, format, goals, tasks, techniques, treatment processes, and anticipated outcomes) account for 15 percent.

Thus, a central question for future school social work intervention is—How do these four therapeutic factors combine with the school setting to make school social work practice unique and effective?

INTERVENTION FINDINGS

Background

In this era of accountability, mere descriptions of programs and practice models are no longer sufficient. Intervention processes and outcomes meaningful to the children, families, schools, and communities being served must be made explicitly clear (operationalized). Ideally, these school social work outcomes will grow out of the social work profession's orientation and values, target specialized school social work goals and functions, and incorporate language meaningful to the school setting's educational mission. In addition, the outcomes must also reflect the reality and complexity of the interpersonal, intrapersonal, cognitive-behavioral, and empowerment theoretical frameworks used in the person-in-environment practice models in which school social work practice is based. Much of the time, the outcomes will also need to reflect multidisciplinary team contributions to the intervention with attribution appropriately assigned to teamwork rather than to a sole practitioner.

In reviewing the professional literature produced from the 1980s through the mid-1990s, two academic review teams identified sixty-four school social work outcome studies (Bailey-Dempsey & Reid, 1996) and 228 outcome studies of mental health practices in the schools (Hoagwood & Erwin, 1997). These academic reviewers, however, judged only five studies from the first set and twelve from the second as approaching best research practices for outcome studies. That is, 17 of 292 studies approached the ideal research design for lab experiments and yielded demonstrable results. A more recent literature review (Early & Vonk, 2001) has directed attention to twenty-one controlled-outcome studies on the effectiveness of school social work interventions. This review highlighted the internal validity criteria ideally associated with outcome research and pointed toward a growing database from which social workers may draw in developing best intervention practices and policies for children. At this point in time, however, it is questionable whether reliance only on school social work outcome studies that have been judged adequate by means of experimental research design criteria provides the best yield for improving school social work practice.

Review of Outcome Studies 1998–2004

To identify outcome studies for this chapter, the authors conducted a computerized literature search of Social Work Abstracts from 1998 to 2004, using terms such as *education-school, school social work outcomes, school mental health outcomes,* and *school social work interventions.* Articles simply describing studies or client populations were excluded. This intervention-focused search yielded forty peer-reviewed journal articles by social workers that described the outcomes of both school-based social work interventions and school-based multidisciplinary mental health interventions (table 6.1). The

TABLE 6.1 Summary of Forty Selected School-Based Outcome Studies 1998–2004

Problem	Model's Conceptual Path	Ed. Level*	Goals	Attained	Authors	Date
Violence, Aggressive Behavior	cognitive/behavioral	high	• increase students' sense of environmental safety • improve attitudes toward violence • increase skills and knowledge related to coping • improve student behavior	yes yes yes yes	De Anda	1999
	cognitive/behavioral	high	• decrease disruptive classroom behavior	yes	Gerdtz	2000
	cognitive/behavioral	high	• experience more positive management and expression of anger • improve self-control	mixed mixed	Whitfield	1999
	information processing	grade	• increase knowledge about sex abuse	yes	Tutty	2000
	interpersonal, mentoring	middle	• reduce aggression of a small group	mixed	Fast et al.	2003
	ecological, mentoring	high	• evaluate the effectiveness of mentoring mothers and daughters in violent environments	mixed	Cox	2001
	ecological	high	• evaluate a school reform model in affecting violence	mixed	Corbin	2001
	ecological	high	• promote academic success in a disciplinary alternative program	mixed	Carpenter-Aeby et al.	2001
	solution/goal-oriented	grade	• achieve positive changes in behavior problems	mixed	Franklin et al.	2001
School Problems	solution/goal-oriented	high	• evaluate effectiveness of school social work as a means to solve adolescents problems in schools	yes	Young et al.	2002
	information processing	high	• change stories into healthy narratives • increase likelihood of reentering mainstream education by using narratives to promote strengths/solutions	mixed mixed	Carpenter-Aeby et al.	2000
	cognitive/behavioral	grade	• improve teacher skills for coping with behavior problems in children	mixed	Schiff et al.	2004
Academic Achievement & Attendance	solution/goal-oriented	grade	• reduce absenteeism • increase positive attitude toward school • enhance self esteem	yes yes yes	Baker et al.	2000
	solution/goal-oriented	grade	• increase assignment completion	mixed	Teall	2000

TABLE 6.1 Summary of Forty Selected School-Based Outcome Studies 1998–2004—(*Continued*)

Problem	Model's Conceptual Path	Ed. Level*	Goals	Attained	Authors	Date
	role modeling, mentoring	high	• increase school attendance	yes	Brabazon	1999
			• increase achievement	no		
	role modeling, mentoring	grade	• increase academic performance	yes	Thompson et al.	2001
	interpersonal	grade	• reduce absenteeism	yes	Grooters et al.	2002
	interpersonal, information processing	grade	• improve students' psychosocial functioning	yes	Mishna et al.	2004
			• increase understanding of learning disabilities	yes		
	information processing	grade	• assess the impact of an after-school program on academic performance	yes	Zosky et al.	2003
	interpersonal, activity-oriented	grade	• improve academic achievement	yes	Bowen	1999
			• improve behavior problems	yes		
			• increase information exchange between home and school	yes		
	behavioral	high	• increase AFDC teenagers' school attendance and completion	no	Harris et al.	2001
Drug Use Behavior	role modeling, mentoring	high	• increase sense of well-being	yes	Taylor et al.	1999
			• change reactions to situations involving drug use	yes		
	information processing	system	• prevent substance abuse	mixed	Marsiglia et al.	2000
	ecological systems	grade	• improve school climate by reducing theft, bullying	yes	Bagley et al.	1998
		high	• improve school climate, teacher morale	yes		
Peer Relations	interpersonal, activity-oriented	middle	• improve peer relationship skills	mixed	Walsh-Bowers et al.	1999
Sexual Behavior	information processing	middle	• change knowledge, beliefs about sex practices	yes	Arnold et al.	1999
	information processing	high	• prevent pregnancy and STDs	mixed	Smith et al.	2002

TABLE 6.1 Summary of Forty Selected School-Based Outcome Studies 1998–2004—*(Continued)*

Problem	Model's Conceptual Path	Ed. Level*	Goals	Attained	Authors	Date
Family Support Social Support	interpersonal	grade	• strengthen parent involvement in child's academic life to prevent academic failure	yes	Fischer	2003
	interpersonal	pre	• analyze IFSP eligibility and early intervention services for family-centeredness	yes	Sabatino	2001
	interpersonal	middle	• promote school attendance, success, and satisfaction/engagement/self-efficacy	yes	Rosenfeld et al.	2000
		high	• decreasing problem behavior	yes		
Mental Health	interpersonal	system	• promote successful transitions	yes	Walter et al.	2004
Prosocial Behavior	role modeling, mentoring	grade	• increase student prosocial behavior	yes	Bein	1999
	role modeling, mentoring	grade	• improve the functioning and empowerment of school-aged children	no	Itzhaky et al.	2001
	interpersonal, social support	pre	• assess the effects of preschool programs on life success	mixed	Caputo	2003
	cognitive/behavioral	grade	• change problem-causing behaviors	yes	Openshaw	2004
	solution/goal-oriented	high	• evaluate effectiveness of solution-focused therapy with Islamic students	mixed	Al-Garni	2004
	interpersonal	middle	• articulate feelings through verbal expression using puppets and peers	mixed	Romano	2001
	interpersonal	grade	• enhance social skills using classroom meetings	mixed	Frey	2002
	interpersonal, activity-oriented	grade	• evaluate effectiveness of a social skills intervention on problem behaviors	yes	Anderson-Butcher et al.	2003
	interpersonal, activity-oriented	high	• evaluate effectiveness of activity group therapy to advancing psychosocial growth	yes	Troester	2002

* High = high school; middle = middle school; grade = elementary school; pre = preschool; system = school system

majority of these studies used quantitative evaluative methodology. Fewer than half, however, employed comparison group or control group designs.

Of the forty outcome studies located, thirty-seven focused on clinical intervention outcomes, and three on service-related outcomes. None focused on cost outcomes or satisfaction outcomes. When these articles were analyzed by themes, patterns became apparent for the problems targeted, the models' conceptual pathways leading to change, the educational level of the targeted children, the outcome goals, and goal attainment.

The studies identified eight problem areas targeted for intervention: violence and aggressive behavior (9 studies), school behavior problems (3), academic achievement and attendance (9), drug use behavior (2), peer relations (1), sexual behavior (2), family support and social support (3), and mental health (1). Nine articles identified interventions focused on increasing strengths such as prosocial behaviors and resilience.

The intervention models are framed in six conceptual pathways highlighting change: cognitive-behavioral (6 models), information processing (6), role modeling and mentoring (5), interpersonal and activity-oriented (13), solution-focused and goal-oriented (5), and ecological systems (5).

Most of the studies targeted a particular age group: preschool (2 studies), elementary grade school (16), middle school (4), and high school (14).Two studies addressed two age groupings (middle, high–1; elementary, high–1).Two studies targeted a school system. Although some interventions targeted boys and some girls, the intervention models do not appear to be designed to address gender-specific issues or viewpoints.

These forty studies identified fifty-four outcome goals. One-third (35%) of the goals were focused on problem resolution and included: decreasing behavior problems and interpersonal violence (12 goals); and increasing positive coping skills in dealing with alcohol, drugs, violence, and sex (7 goals). Over two-fifths (45%) of the goals focused on developing strengths and included: increasing the repertoire of prosocial behaviors (12 goals); and increasing attendance and academic performance (12 goals). One-fifth (20%) of the goals were environmentally focused and included: increasing sense of environmental safety and well-being (3 goals); instituting school programs and school reforms to influence academic performance (3 goals); strengthening teaching (2 goals); and enhancing parenting in relation to their children's education (3 goals).Three-fifths (61%) of the fifty-four outcome goals were clearly attained; one-third (33%) yielded mixed results. Some (6%) were not attained.

The National Institutes of Health Review

In January 2005, the National Institutes of Health published the findings of a conference on preventing violence and related adolescent behavioral health risks through its Evidence-Based Practice Center Program.Two programs met all the criteria for effectiveness, including the gold standard of randomized clinical trials (RCT), in work with the situations of high-risk youth: functional family therapy and multisystemic therapy (National Institutes of Health, 2005; Shei-dow, Henggeler, & Schoenwald, 2003; Sexton & Alexander, 2003). Both programs included intensive, family-oriented, multisystemic approaches that were more complex interventions than focus on a youth alone. In many ways, the NIH report supports some approaches that social work practice has worked with and generally taken for granted—complex, multisystemic family interventions. Six programs addressing factors that were precursors to arrest or violence were classified as "effective with reservation"—that is, they had internal replicability but not external RCT replications. These programs included: Big Brothers Big Sisters (reduction in hitting), Multidimensional Treatment Foster Care (reduction in incarceration), Nurse Family Partnership (reduction in arrest, crime), Promoting Alternative Thinking Strategies (reduction in peer aggression), and Brief Strategic Family Therapy (reduction in conduct disorder, socialized aggression) (National Institutes of Health, 2005).

The common characteristics of these successful programs include:
◆ They were derived from sound theoretical rationales;
◆ They addressed strong risk factors;
◆ They involved long term treatments, often lasting a year and sometimes much longer;
◆ They worked intensely with those targeted for treatment, often using a clinical approach;
◆ They developed cognitive and behavioral skills;
◆ They were multimodal and multicontextual;
◆ They focused on improving social competency and other skill development strategies for targeted youths and/or their families;
◆ They were developmentally appropriate;
◆ They were not delivered in coercive institutional settings;
◆ They had the capacity for delivery with fidelity. (National Institutes of Health, 2005)

Other effective interventions included dramatically changing neighborhood environments, as in the Moving to Opportunity program. In addition, programs that increased educational attainment and decreased dropout rates were likely to have the tangential benefit of reducing violence among those who were helped (National Institutes of Health, 2005). Further, evidence suggested that the get-tough programs, boot camps, and group detention centers did not work. Indeed, there is evidence they may make the problem worse by providing an opportunity for delinquent youth to amplify negative effects on each other (National Institutes of Health, 2005).

EVIDENCE-BASED INTERVENTION AND SCHOOL SOCIAL WORK PRACTICE

Research on effective models of practice provides general orientations to be adapted to the varied situations and multiple decision points of actual practice. Roberts and Yaeger (2004) have published a seminal text on evidence-based practice that includes 103 articles on intervention. One article of note develops general intervention guidelines for promoting evidence-based, relationship-focused practice, integrating scientific method into everyday practice (Munson, 2004). Such practice would ensure that:

- An intervention could be identified by the practitioner and can be understood by the client;
- An established connection between the intervention and the problem could be articulated by the practitioner (depending on developmental level, some children can make the connection);
- The practitioner and the client could implement the intervention with reasonable effort;
- The client would have an identifiable reason/motivation to comply with the effort;
- Along with the proposed intervention, an alternate intervention could be identified by the practitioner;
- Possible outcomes (intended and unintended, positive and negative) of the intervention could be identified in advance of applying the intervention;
- The intervention could be observed and measured. (Munson, 2004, p. 255)

In this article, Munson attempted to relate the normal, finite realities of practice to the scientific method in a shared process with a client system. If evidence-based approaches truly were incorporated into practice, this would result.

FUTURE DIRECTIONS FOR EFFECTIVE
SCHOOL SOCIAL WORK PRACTICE

In the American educational system, highly skilled and committed professionals, who are guided by the latest educational policy, practice, research, and technology, provide educational and support services to millions of students. Yet, it is evident that the system is marked by serious and pervasive deficiencies in outcome quality. These service deficiencies affect children and families, school systems and school personnel, and communities, resulting in increased family stress, school failure, and community predicaments that lower quality of life and consume unnecessary resources.

To address these service deficiencies, school social workers need to begin a national dialogue that focuses on building their capacity to:

1. Develop outcome measures and reporting systems that document the quality of their practice;
2. Conceptually frame and operationalize their practice models preparatory to testing their effectiveness and facilitating replication;

3. Develop and test the effectiveness of new models with a simultaneous dual focus on both person and environment and risk and protective factors; and
4. Disseminate the findings of their research and development efforts.

Supporting these points, the *NASW Standards for School Social Work Services* (Standard 24, 2002) states, "School social workers shall be able to evaluate their practice and disseminate the findings to consumers, the local education agency, the community and the profession." For this standard to begin to strengthen school social work practice today, a common approach by school social workers to measuring the improvements in educational quality brought about by their services will be needed. An example of such a common approach is the National Quality Forum (NQF). The NQF is an association of health-care professionals whose mission is to "provide meaningful information about whether care is safe, timely, beneficial, patient centered, equitable and efficient" (NQF, 2004, p. 1). Applying the NQF goals to school social work services, a group of school social workers concerned with development of the above capacities, would:

1. Promote collaborative efforts to improve the quality of the nation's educational system through school social work performance measurement and public reporting;
2. Develop a national strategy for measuring and reporting school social work service quality;
3. Standardize school social work service performance measures so that comparable data is available across the nation (i.e., establish national voluntary consensus standards);
4. Promote home/school/community understanding and use of school social work service performance measures and other quality information; and
5. Promote and encourage the enhancement of school system capacity to evaluate and report on school social work service quality (adapted from NQF, 2004).

Priority areas for improvement of school system quality through school social work services should be established by school social workers and be accompanied by appropriate, specific goals and objectives. An initial set of priority areas might include: reducing school failure; assuring the appropriate use of regular and special education services; increasing parent involvement; increasing community collaboration and service partnerships; and expanding outcome-based research and evidence of effectiveness.

Improvements in these priority areas would require greater investment in basic research, flexible school systems, greater collaboration among stakeholders, and investment in information systems and reporting mechanisms. To set priority areas and implement a common approach to defining constructs and measuring improved educational quality requires coordination among school social workers and other stakeholders focused on shared aims and methods of accountability. It is anticipated that this approach will not only increase educational quality but also the need for school social work services.

CONCLUSION

School social work roles, along with the roles of other school-based professionals, are now more clearly defined in relation to educational processes and goals. Further, they are more precisely defined by the expectations inherent in the explicit mandates of current national laws and policies for outcome-based education and in its implied corollary of evidence-based practice in schools. As a result, school social work is now coming to the same awareness of practice and research that school psychology and counseling recognized earlier (Kratochwill, Albers, & Shernoff, 2004). That is, they are beginning to develop practice models that specify theory, method, techniques, processes, and evidence-based outcomes and facilitate replication and comparison with other models. Thus, today, a far more open, databased, and functionally based system of practice is gradually emerging.

As shown in this chapter, there are a variety of frameworks to sort the literature, identify school-related problems, and assess effective intervention outcomes. Without systematic application of critical thinking and theory-driven research, without implementation and documentation of evidence-based practice and policy, however, school social workers are at risk of failing to demonstrate their critical role in fulfilling the mission of American education and, more importantly, failing to fulfill their ethical obligation to clients.

INTERNET RESOURCES

Although school social work is only beginning to develop Internet resources, many professional organizations have ongoing commitments to maintain active Web sites about the use of evidence in practice.

Social work Web sites include:

Council on Social Work Education	www.cswe.org
Institute for the Advancement of Social Work Research	www.iaswresearch.org
National Association of Social Workers	www.naswdc.org
Society for Social Work and Research	www.sswr.org
Other Web sites include:	
American Academy of Child and Adolescent Psychiatry	www.aacap.org

American Psychological Association   www.apa.org
Division 16: School Psychology   www.sp.ebi.org
American Public Health Association   www.alpha.org
Centre for Evidence-Based Medicine   www.cebm.net
Center for Mental Health Services   www.samhsa.gov
(Substance Abuse and Mental Health
   Services Administration)
National Association of
   School Psychologists   www.nasponline.org
National Blueprints   www.colorado.edu/cspv/
                                          blueprints
National Prevention Network   www.nasadad.org/departments/
                                          prevention/prevhme1.htm
Office of Safe and Drug-Free Schools   www.ed.gov/offices/oese/sdfs
Society for Prevention Research   www.preventionresearch.org
U.S. Dept. of Education Coalition   www.exelgov.org
What Works Clearinghouse   www.w-w-c.org

In addition, Roberts and Yaeger (2004) provide a comprehensive list of Internet resources at the end of their *Evidence-Based Practice Manual.*

References

Adelman, H., & Taylor, L. (2000). Shaping the future of mental health in schools. *Psychology in the Schools, 37*, 49–60.

Al-Garni, M. (2004). Solution focused therapy: Cross cultural application to school counseling in Saudi Arabia. *Journal of School Social Work, 13*, 40–58.

Allen-Meares, P. (1994). Social work in schools: A national study. *Social Work, 39*, 560–567.

Anderson-Butcher, D., Newsome, W., & Nay, S. (2003). Social skills intervention during elementary school recess: A visual analysis. *Children and Schools, 25*, 135–146.

Arnold, E., Smith, T., Harrison, D., & Springer, D. (1999). The effects of an abstinence-based sex education program on middle school students' knowledge and beliefs. *Research on Social Work Practice, 9*, 10–24.

Bagley, C., & Pritchard, C. (1998). The reduction of problem behaviors and school exclusion in at-risk youth: An experimental study of school social work with cost-benefit analyses. *Child and Family Social Work, 3/4*, 219–226.

Bailey-Dempsey, C., & Reid, W. (1996). Intervention design and development: A case study. *Research on Social Work Practice, 6*, 208–228.

Baker, D., & Jansen, J. (2000). Using groups to reduce elementary school absenteeism. *Social Work in Education, 22*, 46–53.

Bickman, L. (2002). The death of treatment as usual: An excellent first step along a long road. *Clinical Psychology, 9*, 195–199.

Bowen, N. (1999). A role for school social workers in promoting student success through school-family partnerships. *Social Work in Education, 21*, 34–47.

Brabazon, K. (1999). Student improvement in the intergenerational work/study program. *Child & Youth Services, 20*, 51–61.

Brinberg, D., & McGrath, J. (1982). A network of validity concepts within the research process. In D. Brinberg & L. Kidder (Eds), *Forms of validity in research* (pp. 4-21). San Francisco: Jossey-Bass.

Campbell, D. T., & Stanley, J. (1963). *Experimental and quasi-experimental designs for research.* Boston: Houghton Mifflin.

Caputo, R. (2003). Head start, other preschool programs, and life success in a youth cohort. *Journal of Sociology and Social Welfare, 30,* 105-126.

Carpenter-Aeby, T., & Kurtz, P. (2000). The portfolio as a strengths-based intervention to empower chronically disruptive students in an alternative school. *Children and Schools, 22,* 217-231.

Carpenter-Aeby, T., Salloum, M., & Aeby, V. (2001). A process evaluation of school social work services in a disciplinary alternative educational program. *Children and Schools, 23,* 171-180.

Constable, R., & Alvarez, M. (in press). Moving into specialization in school social work. *School Social Work Journal.*

Constable, R., Kuzmickaite, D., Harrison, W., & Volkmann, L. (1999). The emergent role of the social worker in Indiana. *School Social Work Journal, 24,* 1-14.

Corbin, J. (2001). Addressing school violence: Using the framework of group psychotherapy to explore the impact of the school development program on school violence. *Smith College Studies in Social Work, 71,* 243-258.

Cox, A. (2001). Mentoring African American mothers and their daughters from violent environments: An approach for alternative schools. *Journal of School Social Work, 12,* 91-111.

De Anda, D. (1999). Project peace: The evaluation of a skill-based violence prevention program for high school adolescents. *Social Work in Education, 21,* 137-149.

Early, T., & Vonk, M. (2001). Effectiveness of school social work from a risk and resilience perspective. *Children and Schools, 23,* 9-31.

Fast, J., Fanelli, F., & Salen, L. (2003). How becoming mediators affects aggressive students. *Children and Schools, 25,* 161-171.

Fischer, R. (2003). School-based family support: Evidence from an exploratory field study. *Families in Society, 84,* 339-347.

Fonagy, P., Target, M., Cotrell, D., Philips, J., & Kurtz, Z. (2002). *What works for whom: A critical review of treatments for adolescents.* New York: Guilford.

Franklin, C., & Ballan, M. (2001). Reliability and validity in qualitative research. In B. Thyer (Ed.), *The handbook of social work research methods* (pp. 239-256). Thousand Oaks, CA: Sage.

Franklin, C., Biever, J., Moore, K., Clemons, D., & Scamardo, M. (2001). The effectiveness of solution-focused therapy with children in a school setting. *Research on Social Work Practice, 11,* 411-434.

Frey, A. (2002). Enhancing children's social skills through classroom meetings. *School Social Work Journal, 26,* 46-57.

Gerdtz, J. (2000). Evaluating behavioral treatment of disruptive classroom behaviors of an adolescent with autism. *Research on Social Work Practice, 10,* 98-110.

Gilgun, J. (2005). The four cornerstones of evidence-based practice in social work. *Research on Social Work Practice, 15,* 52-61.

Gordon, W. (1969). Basic concepts for an integrative and generative conception of social work. In G. Hearn (Ed.), *The general systems approach: Contributions toward an holistic conception of social work* (pp. 5-11). New York: Council on Social Work Education.

Grooters, L., & Faidley, B. (2002). Impacting early elementary school attendance: It can be done. *Journal of School Social Work, 13*, 70-90.

Harris, R., Jones, L., & Finnegan, D. (2001). Using TANF sanctions to increase high school graduation. *Journal of Sociology and Social Welfare, 28*, 211-222.

Hoagwood, K., & Erwin, H. (1997). Effectiveness of school-based mental health services for children: A 10-year review. *Journal of Child and Family Studies, 6*, 435-451.

Hubble, D., Duncan, B., & Miller, S. (1999). *The heart and soul of change.* Washington, DC: American Psychological Association.

Itzhaky, H., & Segal, O. (2001). Model of after-school treatment programs as agents of empowerment. *Journal of Family Social Work, 5*, 51-68.

Kerlinger, F., & Lee, H. (2000). *Foundations of behavioral research* (4th ed.). London: Wadsworth Thomson Learning.

Kratochwill, T., Albers, C., & Shernoff, E. (2004). School-based interventions. *Child and Adolescent Psychiatric Clinics of North America, 13*, 885-903.

Kratochwill, T., & Shernoff, E. (2003). Evidence–based practice: Promoting evidence-based interventions in school psychology. *School Psychology Quarterly, 18*, 389-408.

Levine, A. (2004). New roles, old responses. *News.* Teachers College, Columbia University. Retrieved October 15, 2004, from http://www.tc.columbia.edu/news/article.htm

Marsiglia, F., Holleran, L., & Jackson, K. (2000). Assessing the effect of external resources on school-based substance abuse prevention programs. *Social Work in Education, 22*, 145-161.

Mishna, F., & Muskat, B. (2004). School-based treatment for students with learning disabilities: A collaborative approach. *Children and Schools, 26*, 135-150.

Munson, C. (2004). Evidence-based treatment for traumatized and abused children. In A. Roberts, & K. Yeager (Eds.), *Evidence-based practice manual: Research and outcome measures in health and human services.* New York: Oxford University Press.

National Association of Social Workers. (2002). Standards for school social work services. Washington, DC: National Association of Social Workers Press.

National Institutes of Health. (2005). State of the science conference statement: Preventing violence and related health-risking social behaviors in adolescents October 13-15, 2004. Final Statement January 18, 2005. Retrieved February 24, 2005, from http:// concensus.nih.gov/ta/023/YouthViolenceFinalStatement011805.htm

National Quality Forum Mission. (2004). *National quality forum mission.* Retrieved February 13, 2005, from http//www.qualityforum.org/mission/home.htm

Okomoto, S., & LeCroy, C. (2004). Evidence-based practice and manualized treatment with children. In A. Roberts & K. Yeager (Eds.), *Evidence-based practice manual: Research and outcome measures in health and human services.* New York: Oxford University Press.

Openshaw, L. (2004). Achieving student goals by graphing student progress. *Journal of School Social Work, 13*, 9-19.

Orlinsky, D., Grawe, K., & Parks, B. (1994). Process and outcome in psychotherapy. In A. Bergin & S. Garfield (Eds.), *Handbook of psychotherapy and behavior change.* New York: Wiley.

Raines, J. (2004). Evidence-based practice in school social work: A process in perspective. *Children and Schools, 26*, 71-85.

Reid, W., & Fortune, A. (2004). Task-centered practice: An exemplar or evidence-based practice. In A. Roberts & K. Yeager (Eds.), *Evidence-based practice manual: Research and outcome measures in health and human services.* New York: Oxford University Press.

Roberts,A., & Yeager, K. (2004). *Evidence-based practice manual: Research and outcome measures in health and human services.* New York: Oxford University Press.

Rodwell, M. (1998). *Social work constructivist research.* New York: Garland.

Rogers, C. (1957).The necessary and sufficient conditions of therapeutic personality change. *Journal of Consulting Psychology, 21,* 95-103.

Romano, M. (2001). Puppets and peers in school social work. *Journal of School Social Work, 11,* 87-90.

Rosenfeld, L., Richman, J., & Bowen, G. (2000). Social support networks and school outcomes:The centrality of the teacher. *Child & Adolescent Social Work Journal, 17,* 205-226.

Sabatino, C. (2001). Family-centered sections of the IFSP and school social work participation. *Children and Schools, 23,* 241-252.

Schiff, M., & BarGil, B. (2004). Children with behavior problems: Improving elementary school teachers' skills to keep these children in class. *Children and Youth Services Review, 26,* 207-234.

Sexton,T., & Alexander, J. (2003). Functional family therapy:A mature clinical model for working with at-risk adolescents and their families. In T. Sexton, G.Weeks, & M. Robbins (Eds.), *Handbook of family therapy.* New York: Brunner-Routledge.

Sheidow,A., Henggeler, S., & Schoenwald, S. (2003). Multisystemic therapy. In T. Sexton, G. Weeks, & M. Robbins (Eds.), *Handbook of family therapy.* New York: Brunner-Routledge.

Smith, P., Buzi, R., & Weinman, M. (2002).Targeting males for teenage pregnancy prevention in a school setting. *School Social Work Journal, 27,* 23-36.

Snyder, C., Michael, S., & Cheavens, J. (1999). Hope as a psychotherapeutic foundation of common factors, placebos, and expectancies. In M. Hubble, B. Duncan, & S. Miller (Eds.), *The heart and soul of change* (pp. 179-200).Washington, DC:American Psychological Association.

Tashakkori,A., & Teddlie, C. (1998). *Mixed methodology: Combining qualitative and quantitative approaches.* Thousand Oaks, CA: Sage.

Taylor,A., Losciuto, L., Fox, M., Hilbert, S., & Sonkowsky, M. (1999).The mentoring factor: Evaluation of the Across Ages' intergenerational approach to drug abuse prevention. *Child & Youth Services, 20,* 77-99.

Teall, B. (2000). Using solution-oriented interventions in an ecological frame:A case illustration. *Social Work in Education, 22,* 54-61.

Thompson, L., & Kelly-Vance, L. (2001).The impact of mentoring on academic achievement of at-risk youth. *Children & Youth Services Review, 23,* 227-242.

Thyer, B. (2001). *The handbook of social work research methods.* Thousand Oaks, CA: Sage.

Troester, J. (2002).Working through family-based problem behavior through activity group therapy. *Clinical Social Work Journal, 30,* 419-428.

Tutty, L. (2000).What children learn from sexual abuse prevention programs: Difficult concepts and developmental issues. *Research on Social Work Practice, 10,* 275-300.

Walsh-Bowers, R., & Basso, R. (1999). Improving adolescents' peer relations through classroom creative drama:An integrated approach. *Social Work in Education, 21,* 23-32.

Walter, U., & Petr, C. (2004). Promoting successful transitions from day school to regular school environments for youths with serious emotional disorders. *Children and Schools, 26,* 175-180.

Whitfield, G. (1999). Validating school social work: An evaluation of a cognitive-behavioral approach to reduce school violence. *Research on Social Work Practice, 9,* 399-426.

Young, H., & Jung, K. (2002). A pilot project for school social work in Korea. *Journal of School Social Work, 12,* 35-46.

Zosky, D., & Crawford, L. (2003). No child left behind: An assessment of an after-school program on academic performance among low-income at risk students. *School Social Work Journal, 27,* 18-31.

7

Confidentiality in School Social Work: To Share or Not to Share

James C. Raines
Illinois State University

◆ Procedure and Principles
◆ Ethics and the Law
◆ Issues in Record Keeping

School social workers are constantly confronted with the conundrum of which student disclosures to keep confidential and which ones to divulge in the interest of school safety. Consider the three scenarios below:

> A 13-year-old girl is sexually involved with a seventeen-year-old boy. Currently, they are "only" having oral sex, but he is pressuring her to "go all the way." She reports that she's the only virgin in her peer group and that the others make fun of her. She's scared to tell her very religious parents because she's afraid they'll send her to a strict parochial school. State laws prohibit sexual contact with minors under thirteen as well as where the age difference is five or more years, so there's no legal guidance in this case.

> A 15-year-old boy reveals that he has been involved in "cutting." The wounds are all superficial and uninfected. He denies any suicidal thoughts or intent—it is merely his way of coping with feelings of numbness and existential angst about his future. He doesn't want to tell his single mother because the last time she found out she sent him to an inpatient psychiatric program. The recent research clearly differentiates cutting from suicidal attempts, so the literature warns against overreacting in such cases.

A 12-year-old boy who is angry about his poor grades and disciplinary record threatens to "blow up" the school. He doesn't have any specific plans, nor does he possess any of the skills or materials for bomb making. He doesn't want his foster parents to know because he's afraid they'll send him back to the group home where he'd be the youngest and most vulnerable kid. Unfortunately, all the necessary bomb-making information is readily available on the Internet so he could obtain it if he wanted to.

Other issues may concern alcohol and drug abuse, severe eating disorders, or mental health concerns (delusional thoughts). Each ethical dilemma is a practice problem as well. And thus the first way to deal with such dilemmas is through good practice. In each case above the youngster is telling the school social worker of concerns and fears, attempting to come to terms with them. The radical solutions proposed by the youngster are expressions of concerns that the social worker might help redirect. The listening school social worker has already clarified confidentiality and its limits in the youngster's language. They contract around helping him/her deal with an unacceptable situation. The social worker is a collaborator in the healing process. The youngster is the first place where the problem can be resolved. The social worker can help him/her in this by a simultaneous focus on the youngster and the broader situation. That might involve helping the youngster get in contact with persons who could be of help and opening some workable dialogue with parents. The social worker tells the youngster that for them to continue he/she needs to have some contact with parents. Telling the parents that the youngster has some concerns, they both know he/she will not reveal those concerns unless there is some danger or unless the youngster asks him. Contacts with others are first of all discussed with the youngster so that they can come to a joint approach. This process becomes part of the first session in one way or another and continues through the contact.

In the context of practice, illustrated above, the question of whether to reveal, what to reveal, and to whom remains central to the work of the school social worker. The position statement of the·School Social Work Association of America (SSWAA) follows this chapter. Taking these principles as a foundation, this chapter offers a procedure and principles for deciding some of the basic issues in school social work practice: whether or not to share information, how it should be shared, and how much. It also addresses the relationship between ethics and the law and provides a checklist for confidentiality (see pp. 114–15). All of the anecdotes in this chapter have used pseudonyms and minor details have been changed to protect the identities of the participants.

PROCEDURE AND PRINCIPLES

There are seven steps that school social workers can use to work through the decision about whether or not to divulge confidential student material.

Skipping or shortchanging any of these steps tends to reduce the quality of the decision.

Step 1: Know Yourself

Social workers must differentiate between their personal values and their professional values (Abramson, 1996). Sometimes these will coincide; sometimes they will conflict with each other. A helpful exercise is to list your values in a diagram with two overlapping circles. Social workers are bound by the National Association of Social Workers (NASW) Code of Ethics (Jensen, 2002). There are six core social work values in the code that become ethical principles: service, social justice, the dignity and worth of the person, the importance of human relationships, integrity, and competence. These values are normative for all professional social workers regardless of their practice settings or roles, but individual practitioners facing specific situations must apply them judiciously. This requires what Manning (1997) has termed *moral citizenship*, "the responsibility to determine right and good behavior as part of the rights and privileges social workers have as members of a community" (p. 224).

Many ethical thinkers have tended to approach problems on the basis of unchangeable principles that certain values and actions are intrinsically right or wrong (deontologists). They may hold an absolute standard of truth telling with others. Others may gauge their actions through an analysis of the goodness of their consequences (consequentialists). The latter, as relativists, would ultimately hold that the end justifies the means (Reamer, 1999). For example, they may think it is permissible to deceive the welfare system in order to obtain a livable income for clients. The most common form of the relativist approach is the utilitarian model, according to which one must weigh the costs and benefits of every decision. For example, those using a utilitarian approach may hold that both honesty and deception have risks and rewards that vary according to the situation.

A problem comes from the way the issue is often framed. The two positions reduce situations to less than what the practitioner needs to act on. They are stereotypical, somewhat oversimplistic, and ultimately radical. Social workers do need to act on the basis of principles and do need to weigh the costs and benefits of every decision. The question is how basic principles are translated into action within the complexity of any practice situation.

In the three practice cases above, each situation is already framed with differing values and consequences. By their nature they demand a more complex system of analysis, taking in more variables, including the broader context and the subjective intentions and concerns of the persons acting and ultimately applying this complex measure to each case situation. There is no way to remove action from the context of norms and values. The practice relationship is governed by expectations of society, of the profession, and of the client. The "fiduciary" relationship implies trust, which arises from vulnerability and initial inequality of power and strength, and mutual obligations (Levy, 1976). Using the physician as an example, Pellegrino and Thomasma (1981, pp. 219–220) point out that the professional needs to be competent, should respect the individual-ized nature of the transaction, and should ensure the moral agency of the client through information and informed consent. The social worker becomes a coach, and thus a moral agent, to help clients find workable directions and rela-tions with each other, to become themselves responsible agents and actors in a relational field (Constable, 1989). In the light of the inherent morality and com-plexity of the practice situation, deontological and consequentialist positions appear limited. Indeed, there is a necessary inexactness in application from the-oretical to practical. Each situation, taken on its own, demands inherently com-plex and nuanced ethical thinking, discussed in the following parts of this arti-cle. For example, the obligation of the social worker to be truthful does not mean that the social worker is obliged to tell everything he/she knows about a situation or act as judge, jury, and policeman in any situation. Taking into account the client, the social worker may give the client truthful information *in a way the client can use it.*[1] In the above cases, the key is going to be to help the *client* understand and deal with the situation, whenever possible. Taking into account the situation, the social worker has duties of protection from harm but is not obligated to enforce statutes outside his/her appropriate functions or to take responsibility for what others do, where he/she has not been involved. The social worker and a client are separate agents.

Loewenberg, Dolgoff, and Harrington (2000) recommend using an ethical principles screen by which values are rank ordered. They posit seven principles in the order in which they are listed in table 7.1.

Four caveats should be made about these principles. First, they may not be exhaustive. Social workers may decide that other values (e.g., the importance of the practitioner-client relationship) may need to be integrated with the ones stated here. Second, these are one group of authors' ideas about the correct ordering of priorities. Individual practitioners may want to reorder these to suit their own consciences. A helpful exercise may be to look at these principles individually and wrestle with one's own ranking of these principles. Third, some of the principles imply that social workers will be able to predict accurately the outcomes of their decisions. In actuality, we seldom possess 20-20 foresight. Finally, practitioners may disagree about how a particular principle is put into practice. For example, one person may feel that the least harm is accomplished by doing nothing, while another may feel that inaction is a form of tacit consent to the client's questionable behavior.

The final aspect of self-awareness relates to countertransference. Each of us probably has a proclivity to tell or not to tell. Those with the tendency to tell

---

1. While there are special applications in social work, far from not telling the truth, this is in fact a quite common virtue of ordinary life, called *tact* from the Latin word for silent.

TABLE 7.1   Ethical Principles Screen to Rank Values

Principles	Definition
1. Protection of life	Practitioners should seek to protect or prolong a person's biophysical life.
2. Equal treatment	Practitioners should treat persons in similar circumstances in a similar manner.
3. Autonomy/freedom	Practitioners should respect an individual's right to control or contribute to decisions that affect him or her.
4. Least harm	When faced with two negative outcomes, practitioners should choose the least harmful, least permanent, or most reversible option.
5. Quality of life	Practitioners should seek to promote the highest quality of life for both the individual and his or her environment.
6. Privacy & confidentiality	Practitioners should only seek to acquire relevant information and keep that material sacrosanct.
7. Truthfulness & full disclosure	Practitioners should be completely honest with their clients.

may have experienced a foreseeable harm that could have been averted if only someone had had the courage to speak out. Perhaps we were bullied, sexually harassed/assaulted, abused, or neglected. We may have suffered quietly because we lacked a champion to protect us. Social workers with a secret wish to rescue or shield others from harm will need to think twice before breaking a confidence. Those with a tendency not to tell may subconsciously equate "telling" with "tattling." As an elementary school social worker, I always explained the difference like this, "Telling is about keeping people safe; tattling is about getting people in trouble." While this distinguishes a disclosure on the basis of its purpose, the end result may feel the same: you have "ratted out" your client or "squealed" on him or her (especially if those whom you've told have a different purpose in mind). Social workers who have strong need to be liked by students will need to develop thick skin before they feel comfortable about violating student confidences.

Step 2: Analyze the Dilemma

It is helpful to obtain the answers to several questions, some of which may be deceptively complex. First, *who* are the stakeholders? Stakeholders are concerned parties with a vested interest in the outcome; they are not competing clients, as some have suggested (McWhinney, Haskins-Herkenham, & Hare,

1992; Prichard, 1999). Loewenberg, Dolgoff, and Harrington (2000) identify several participants in the social work process. *Clients* are people (or systems) who knowingly (not always voluntarily) enter into a formal, contractual, and goal-driven relationship with the social worker. One of the flaws in the NASW Code of Ethics (1999) is that it does not fully address clinical practice dilemmas in host settings. Beyond the client system (individual, family, or group), there are three other important groups in school settings. First, there are *colleagues* (other social workers, psychologists, or teachers), who also provide professional services to students. Second, there are *administrators* (superintendents, special education coordinators, principals, or deans), who have responsibility for the educational community. Finally, there are *relatives* (parents, stepparents, or foster parents), who have legal responsibility for the student. Any of these may arguably have a right to know about dangerous or destructive conduct. If any of these groups feel disregarded, they have the potential to increase the cost of confidentiality to the practitioner. These costs may include professional ostracism from colleagues, loss of promotion or position by administrators, and litigation by relatives. Thus, it would be naive to underestimate the importance of other stakeholders in the process.

Second, *which* values are in conflict? In the introductory scenarios, one of the applicable NASW values is the importance placed on human relationships. Berman-Rossi and Rossi (1990) note that confidentiality provides the basis for client self-disclosure and the sharing of intimate details. On the other hand, another NASW value is social justice. The social worker has a duty to protect both the educational community and the student. One hopes that a commitment to a third value, integrity, will help balance the conflicting demands.

Accordingly, when orienting a new child to the social work process, I usually explain that there are two rules that govern my professional behavior. Rule 1 is "Everybody is safe." Rule 2 is "Everything is confidential." I then explain that sometimes these rules conflict (e.g., if students tell me someone is hurting them or that they may hurt others). When this occurs, "Rule 1 wins." Thus, if I later feel compelled to break confidentiality, I can remind them of this prior discussion. This serves to keep the value of integrity intact.

Another set of potentially competing values is between self-determination and paternalism. A superficial reading of the NASW Code of Ethics would suggest that social workers should always choose client self-determination. This reveals a second flaw in the code: it presumes an adult-to-adult relationship that is mutual and egalitarian (Prichard, 1999). In schools, with the exception of some high school students, our clients are legal minors who cannot give informed consent for themselves. Parents or legal guardians must sign both informed consent to treatment as well as release of information forms (Jonson-Reid, 2000). While paternalism has a negative reputation, this is sometimes undeserved (Staller & Kirk, 1997). Children are both emotionally and intellectually dependent upon adults to make decisions in their best interests. Only gradually does society grant them greater control over decisions that affect them (e.g., child custody hearings, abortion, or driving privileges). What seems to be needed, especially for middle or high school students, is a procedure for *informed assent.* This differs from informed consent in that it is not legally binding but serves the clinical function of providing for some self-determination in the social work process. It is especially helpful with those cases where the child is not self-referred.

When I receive referrals for social work services, I do not assume that students have been told why they have been sent to see me. I usually tell them directly what I have heard and ask for their perspective on the situation. If treatment has been mandated, I explain what I will routinely share with others (e.g., the percentage of sessions attended out of the number scheduled; topics, not details, of what we've discussed; and a subjective impression of whether I believe they are making progress). If this is acceptable, I ask students to give their assent to treatment. Occasionally, I have had students inquire if I would lie to authorities for them. My standard answer is, "If I were to lie *for* you, you could never be sure that I would not lie *to* you." This stance, again, serves to underscore the value placed on integrity.

Step 3: Identify the Courses of Action

For any ethical quandary, there are usually at least three different courses of action and sometimes more. Given the examples that began this chapter, a social worker could decide: (1) to keep all the material confidential to maintain the primacy of the therapeutic relationship and try to help clients resolve conflicting feelings about hiding such important issues from those who care for them, (2) to divulge the confidential material to protect the student or school's well-being and try to help the client understand why such a disclosure was important, or (3) to share the ethical dilemma with the client and try to empower him or her to disclose the problem to those who need to know.

In general, the more mature the student, the more the social worker should share the ethical problem and empower the student to participate in the ethical solution. This has two benefits. First, it models the conscientious consideration of moral dilemmas. Second, it helps students to avoid seeing solutions in an either-or fashion and to find middle ground. An example will illustrate:

> Eric was a 13-year-old eighth grader with a serious marijuana problem that was affecting the completion of his schoolwork. He was the only son of two working parents, who did not provide any supervision after school until they arrived home after 6:00 p.m. He was very afraid of disappointing his parents and what measures they may take to curb his freedom. I reflected that it sounded as if he could not overcome this on his own and that he needed his family's help. I suggested that there were three ways we could handle it: (1) I could call his parents and share this with them directly while he listened; (2) I could meet with both him and his parents together to mediate between them; or (3) I could help him practice self-disclosure to his parents through role-playing. Eric worried aloud that his mother

would go "ballistic" and wanted to tell his father alone first. I compromised on this point and Eric chose to go with the second option.

Step 4: Seek Consultation

The fourth step in the decision process is to obtain outside expertise. One of the dangers in social work licensing laws is that they certify professionals for "independent practice." This tends to convey the notion that when practitioners have reached this level, they no longer need supervision or consultation from their colleagues—but nothing could be further from the truth. The NASW Code of Ethics makes it very clear that "social workers should seek the advice and counsel of colleagues whenever such consultation is in the best interests of clients" (p. 16). This consultation should be sought from colleagues with adequate expertise. Recently, Secemsky and Ahlman (2003) have provided a list of ten guidelines for choosing a supervisor, which could easily be extended to consultants as well. Social workers do not need to breach confidentiality to obtain this advice. Counsel can be sought while keeping the client's identity anonymous by only sharing the most pertinent details of a case. An example will illumine this:

> A handsome young social worker had recently begun working at a high school when he sought consultation from me about an ethical dilemma. A senior girl he'd been seeing in treatment had become increasingly interested in his personal life and he had inadvertently shared more than was wise. She asked him if he'd ever like to hang out on the weekends. While he found the girl attractive, he had no intentions of violating any boundaries and told her so. She responded that this didn't matter because after graduation, they could hook up and no one would care. Flustered and frustrated, he was now considering transferring her to another worker but was worried about clinical abandonment issues and his own reputation within the workplace. I never knew the student's name and did not need to in order to provide consultation.

Aside from clinical consultation, practitioners may also wish to obtain legal advice. It is always wise for school social workers to have their own attorney and malpractice insurance since the district or co-op's lawyers and insurance company will primarily serve the interests of those who pay their fees (Jensen, 2002). This does not mean that legal issues should be confused with ethical ones, but they do make a difference when one is considering the cost-benefit ratio.

All social workers should be familiar with the court case *Tarasoff v. Regents of the University of California* (1976). The plaintiffs were the parents of Tatiana Tarasoff, who was killed by a former boyfriend who had confided his intentions to his therapist. The university psychologist notified campus police, but they merely questioned the boyfriend, who promised to stay away from Tatiana. The therapist's supervisor recommended that no further action should be taken and ordered that the case notes be destroyed (Kopels & Kagle, 1993). The court determined that mental health professionals had a "duty to warn" when they knew or should have known that a client posed an immediate danger to a specific person or persons. In the words of the court, "The protective privilege ends where the public peril begins" (*Tarasoff*, 1976, p. 347). An example follows.

> Jose was an 8-year-old third grader who soiled his pants weekly while his estranged parents fought each other for sole custody. His mother was a recovering crack addict and his father was a recovering alcoholic. His mother had temporary custody and his father refused to pay child support, so one night she met him in the dark with an imitation gun, demanding that he pay up. He did so only to find out later that she'd used one of Jose's toys to stage the threat. He confided to me that he was so enraged about this that he was thinking of paying a heroin addict $50 to kill her while he attended an AA meeting. Deciding that he had identified a specific person, a plausible plan, and an alibi, I consulted with my supervisor and we agreed to call the police and warn the intended victim. Later on, in court, I testified that I doubted that he really meant to do it, but we couldn't take the chance given the level of his anger.

Contacting the police is not the only way to fulfill our duty to warn. Loewenberg, Dolgoff, and Harrington (2000) clarify that there are three other means as well, including warning the intended victim directly; informing others who can alert the victim to danger; or taking "whatever other steps are reasonably necessary under the circumstances" (p. 104), such as hospitalization.

Step 5: Manage the Clinical Concerns

When making decisions about confidentiality, it is essential that social workers demonstrate that they know and use the "standard of care" for dangerous clients. It is imperative that practitioners never underestimate or minimize the potential danger. This requires that we stay calm and carefully assess the client's level of risk for violent behavior. There are several areas that should be addressed. Cooper and Lesser (2002) recommend assessing: (1) the frequency of the client's violent ideas (e.g., monthly, weekly, daily, obsessively); (2) the duration of those ideas (e.g., fleeting, episodic, or sustained); (3) the concreteness of the plan (i.e., its lethality, locality, imminence, and plausibility); and (4) the extent to which preparation has begun (i.e., gathering materials and knowledge/skill for its implementation). One might also add the client's degree of emotional dysregulation (Newhill, 2003). This includes clients' emotional sensitivity (how quickly they react); emotional intensity (on a scale 1–10); and their ability to calm themselves back to a normal state. These inquiries should be considered in the context of the client's history of violence (e.g., previous attempts, fire setting, or cruelty to animals), level of impulse control, social support from family or friends, and immediate precipitating events (Center for Mental Health in Schools at UCLA, 2003). An example will illustrate.

Russell was a 15-year-old sophomore in high school with a lengthy involvement with child welfare authorities. He had been reunited with his single father, who had been through therapy and parenting classes to get Russell back from foster care. Years of abuse, however, had left Russell bitter and vengeful. He had stolen his father's vehicle and crashed it into a tree in front of the school. He vowed that when his father was old, he would get even somehow. He didn't have a plan yet, but he was determined. When his father inquired about his son's progress, I reported that Russell came regularly, was discussing his resentment about his past abuse, and that progress was slow. While Russell had a violent history and a specific target, he lacked a specific plan and there was no imminent threat.

Every student reacts differently to confrontation about a possible violation of privileged disclosure. Regardless of how well students are oriented to treatment and participate in giving informed assent, many will feel hurt, angry, and betrayed by the social worker. It is important to remain empathic and reflect both the spoken and unspoken feelings of the client (Raines, 1990), rather than become defensive about the situation. It may also be appropriate to self-disclose your own feelings of concern, worry, and sadness about the potential loss of trust (Raines, 1996). These two interventions work synergistically together to maintain the human bond between worker and client. This bond enables practitioners to engage students in introspection about *why* they revealed the information. Did they have a secret desire to be stopped, to be caught, or to be punished? Did they mean to externalize an internal conflict? All of this must be grist for the therapeutic mill.

Next, give the student as much choice as is developmentally appropriate. This does not mean, however, that social workers should shirk their ethical responsibilities. It does mean that students should be informed about what choices they have, as in Eric's case above. This gives the student a sense of ownership and control over the circumstances. One of the goals of treatment should be acceptance of responsibility for self and others (Yalom, 1980). Taking this responsibility completely out of a student's hands shortchanges this goal.

Finally, involve students in decisions made in their best interest. While Berman-Rossi and Rossi (1997) recommend that a student should be informed about team meetings on his or her behalf, students should also be invited to such meetings unless there are compelling reasons not to do so. While this may hinder some of the freewheeling discussion, it also tends to hold negativity about students in check. It also provides an opportunity to address confidential concerns immediately rather than postpone them.

Step 6: Enact the Decision

Once the dilemma has been analyzed, courses of action identified, consultation obtained, and clinical concerns managed, it would seem like the time to implement the resolution, but Loewenberg, Dolgoff, and Harrington (2000) recommend one final checklist before taking action. First, are you acting *impartially*? In other words, would you want someone to take this action if this were your child? Second, can you *generalize* this decision to similar cases? Finally, can you *justify* your decision in ways that make sense to others, including the student? If the answer to all of these is *yes*, then you are ready to act. If the answer to any of these is *no*, then more consultation should be sought.

Implementation may work as expected, but more often than not there are consequences that could not have been predicted (Robison & Reeser, 2000). Some participants (e.g., administrators) may be angry that they were not told about the problem sooner or want to punish the student for a crime he or she has not (yet) committed. Some participants (e.g., relatives) will feel embarrassed or envious that the student trusted the social worker with intimacies when they have known the child longer. Emphasize that the primary purpose is to protect people now, and applaud the student's courage for having told anyone. This will help to keep the discussion focused on protection, the present, and on the positives.

Step 7: Reflect on the Process

Mattison (2000) recommends that after the issue has been resolved, it is helpful to reexamine the process. Ask yourself the following questions: (1) To what degree did my personal values influence this decision? (2) To what extent did other participants influence my choices? (3) Were there courses of action that I failed to consider? (4) Should I have consulted other people? (5) Were there clinical concerns that I missed or underestimated? (6) In hindsight did I make the right decision? (7) What precautions (e.g., orientation or informed assent) should I take to prevent potential problems in the future?

ETHICS AND THE LAW

Too often social workers have confused the boundary between their ethical and their legal obligations. Lawsuits and subpoenas are insufficient reasons to breach confidentiality (Dickson, 1998). Another court case with which all practitioners should become familiar is *Jaffee v. Redmond* (1996). This case involved Illinois clinical social worker Karen Beyer, who refused to hand over records about her client's state of mind *after* her client killed someone in the line of duty (Nye, 1999). Beyer was held in contempt of court and the case was appealed to the U.S. Supreme Court, where the NASW filed an amicus curiae (friend of the court) brief in her defense (Supreme Court, 1996). In a 7–2 decision, the court established that client privilege extended to psychotherapists and that mental health was a public good that should be protected under the law (Lens, 2000). Social workers should not simply view themselves as agents of the state nor feel compelled to report a client's past crimes. The exception to this rule is when the crime is especially heinous because it involves vulnerable victims who are both defenseless and dependent upon others (e.g., children and the elderly).

Most states where there is licensing of social workers recognize the protection of *privileged communication*. This generally means that matters communicated by clients to social workers in their official capacity are privileged. The social worker is obligated not to disclose them, except under certain narrowly defined circumstances. For example, under the Indiana social work licensing statute (Indiana Code 25-23.6-6), in a criminal proceeding involving a homicide, a communication revealing the contemplation or commission of a crime or serious harmful act would be among these exceptions. It is important to know the privileged communication statute that governs your practice. A social worker, served with a subpoena in a child custody case, would inform the law office issuing the subpoena of this protection, citing the appropriate statutes. The attorney may not be aware of your protection. Clarifying what is your obligation to observe the law makes it then incumbent on the issuers of the subpoena to demonstrate that their request falls within the area of exceptions in the state statute. This may be quite difficult to demonstrate. On the other hand, to provide information without invoking this privilege may leave the social worker unprotected and potentially obligated to provide further information, since the information is now subject to discovery

In 1999, the NASW Delegate Assembly narrowly voted (155-133) to amend the Code of Ethics after just three years:

Privacy & Confidentiality

Social workers should protect the confidentiality of all information obtained in the course of professional service, except for compelling professional reasons. The general expectation that social workers will keep information confidential does not apply when disclosure is necessary to prevent serious, foreseeable, and imminent harm to a client or other identifiable person, [or when laws or regulations require disclosure without a client's consent]. In all instances, social workers should disclose the least amount of confidential information necessary to achieve the desired purpose; only information that is directly relevant to the purpose for which the disclosure is made should be revealed.(National Association of Social Workers, 1999, p. 10)

The revised code omitted the bracketed portion from the 1996 version, thus clearly differentiating between ethical reasons for breaching confidentiality and legal reasons for doing so. This revision was prompted by a tidal wave of state legislatures' and political agencies' creation of laws and regulations restricting the rights of gays and lesbians to adopt children; women's reproductive rights; and the rights of immigrants to obtain education, health care, and social services (Ethics, 1999). The implication of this change appears to be that, while social workers are mandated to report an imminent threat to self or others, they should not feel obligated to report someone who is merely guilty of a "status" offense, such as being a member of a sexual minority, being single and pregnant, or being an undocumented immigrant. In these cases, social workers should carefully weigh their legal mandates against their ethical obligations (Loewenberg, Dolgoff, & Harrington, 2000).

Moral conundrums, then, could be placed on a typology consisting of two dimensions: ethical issues and legal issues (figure 7.1). Such a schema results in four categories of quandaries. First, some questions are *neither ethical nor legal* issues. An example is the decision about whether social workers should disclose their feelings to clients. In general, practitioners are on safer ground when disclosing present feelings about the therapeutic process rather than disclosing personal details on their extra-therapeutic life (Raines, 1996), but this is primarily a clinical issue, rather than a moral one. Second, some quandaries, such as the ethical orientation of clients, are *only ethical* issues, not legal ones. It is wise to inform all clients (even those transferred from other workers) about one's own approach to confidentiality, but this is not a legal mandate. Third, other controversies, such as a duty to warn others of a client's potential for violence, are *both ethical and legal* issues (Kopels & Kagle, 1993). When we accept a student as one of our clients, we embark on a fiduciary relationship (Kutchins, 1991). We can violate a client's privilege only for compelling reasons. Finally, some questions, such as whether school social workers should obtain clinical licensure, are mainly *legal* issues.

> Millard was a 16-year-old who had been raised by his single mother in Brooklyn until she died from diabetes. He was then reunited with his absentee father, who lived in the Bronx. Even though I worked in Millard's old therapeutic day school, my supervisor asked me to check up on him since his previous worker had left the agency. I scheduled a home visit in Queens and found that Millard's father was a crack addict, there was no food in the apartment, and Millard had not been attending school. Millard, however, had the presence of mind to ask his father for a

FIGURE 7.1   Ethical-Legal Typology

Ethical but not legal issue	Both an ethical and a legal issue
Neither an ethical nor a legal issue	Legal but not ethical issue

note explaining that he could not care for his son. Armed with the note and a compelling case for neglect, I brought Millard back to Brooklyn and placed him in one of the agency's emergency shelters. Child welfare authorities were outraged because, in New York, separate boroughs are often separate counties and I had broken the law by crossing county lines with a minor. Fortunately, my agency stood behind my decision to remove Millard and bring him back to his old neighborhood. I successfully avoided both arrest and criminal prosecution for kidnapping.

ISSUES IN RECORD KEEPING

All social workers should be familiar with the requirements of the Family Educational Rights and Privacy Act (FERPA-PL 93-380), which guarantees parents both access and control over the dissemination of school records (Jonson-Reid, 2000). This legislation requires knowing the difference between which files are official education records and which are not. Social workers' private notes are not part of the school record, nor are sole possession files stored on a computer (School Social Work Association of America, 2001). These documents should be stored under lock and key or protected by passwords if they are on a computer. Social developmental histories, case progress notes, functional behavioral assessments, behavior intervention plans, and individualized education program documents, however, are official school records. Case progress notes should contain dates of meetings, general topics discussed, and interventions employed. They should not contain intimate details, process recordings, or clinical impressions. Thus, social workers would be wise to write these documents in a way that does not offend or obfuscate the issues for clients and their parents. Finally, there are times when practitioners may have to take extreme measures to protect their client's privacy as the following example shows.

> Maria was a recently divorced mother with whom I had weekly contact about how the domestic violence she'd experienced influenced her two boys. She was looking for work when a position opened as the head of the school cafeteria. Since she had extensive restaurant experience, she inquired if I thought it might be appropriate for her to apply for the job. I agreed but cautioned that if she was hired I may want to remove any records about our conversations from school grounds to preserve her privacy. She concurred and was offered the position. A week later I was called into the principal's office because he wanted to know why he couldn't find my social work files on this family. I replied honestly that I had put the files with my private notes under lock and key to protect both my client and the school. I used the occasion to clarify the nature of confidentiality with the principal. He was obdurate that he had to have the key as long as I worked in his school. I discussed this issue with my supervisor and my colleagues. They recounted similar stories and agreed to support me in bringing the issue to the superintendent and ultimately to the board of education. In the ensuing investigation, the principal repeated his position and was fired.

The question of what information should be shared with teachers and other members of the team is an important one. The sharing of information, often necessary for team functioning, is first of all limited to what the individual team member needs to know to carry out his/her function. A teacher, concerned about a particular child who is sleeping in class, may need to know that the child is very disturbed and saddened about things happening in the home, without knowing the details. The consultation with the teacher can be geared to helping him to help the child become a part of the class learning process, with the social worker working individually with the child, the family situation, and possibly other agencies. School social workers should inform students and parents that information gathered under the individualized education program (IEP) process *may* be shared with all members of the IEP team. However, it is the social worker's discretion in collaboration with parents and student to reveal only what is necessary for the team's functioning. This demands a good deal of judgment and discretion on the school social worker's part and it is a highly developed skill. It is very important in beginning in a school that the social worker clarify with the team the nature and limits of confidentiality, and the procedures that will be used to ensure confidentiality. In this way, situations such as the principal wanting access to the social worker's private notes can be avoided.

CONCLUSION

The ethics of social work have evolved considerably over the past one hundred years (Reamer, 1998). Hopefully, in its next incarnation the NASW Code of Ethics will pay more attention to practice conundrums with minors and involving social workers in host settings, such as schools. This process is one practitioner's viewpoint based on a review of the literature and accumulated practice wisdom. Good social workers can disagree and still be good social workers (e.g., Kopels, 1992 vs. Kardon, 1993). Legally we have a duty to warn about imminent crimes, but we do not have a duty to report past crimes. Reamer (2000) suggests that one of the ways that social workers can protect themselves is to diligently document their decision-making process. The process may ultimately be more important than the product of the decision. For this reason, I have not provided any solutions to the dilemmas that began this paper, but I offer them as discussion fodder to which this process can be applied.

Confidentiality Checklist

- ❑ I have clarified my own personal and professional values.
- ❑ I have identified the primary stakeholders in ethical issues.
- ❑ I have identified the primary competing values.
- ❑ I regularly provide an ethical orientation to new clients.
- ❑ I obtain informed consent (and informed assent) to treatment.

❑ I have identified several courses of action.
❑ I obtain clinical consultation about difficult issues.
❑ I obtain legal advice about difficult issues.
❑ I am familiar with the laws regarding the treatment and rights of minors.
❑ I carefully consider the clinical implications.
❑ I make sure the decision is impartial, generalizable, and justifiable.
❑ I review and document the process of decision making.
❑ I always keep my personal written notes in a locked file cabinet.
❑ I always use a computer password to protect private electronic files.
❑ I always write public documents in clear, unoffensive language.

References

Abramson, M. (1996). Reflections on knowing oneself ethically: Toward a working framework for social work practice. *Families in Society, 77*(4), 195-202.

Berman-Rossi, T., & Rossi, P. (1990). Confidentiality and informed consent in school social work. *Social Work in Education, 12*(3), 195-207.

Center for Mental Health in Schools at UCLA. (2003). *A technical assistance sampler on school interventions to prevent youth suicide.* Los Angeles, CA: Author. Retrieved May 19, 2003, from http://smhp.psych.ucla.edu

Constable, R. T. (1989). Relations and membership: Foundations for ethical thinking in social work. [Special issue on ethics]. *Social Thought, 15*(3/4) 53-66.

Cooper, M. G., & Lesser, J. G. (2002). *Clinical social work practice: An integrated approach.* Boston: Allyn & Bacon.

Dickson, D. T. (1998). *Confidentiality and privacy in social work.* New York: Free Press.

Ethics and reporting eyed after assembly: Left unchanged is language that requires reporting of certain acts and threats of violence (1999, November). *NASW News, 44*(10), 5.

Family Educational Rights and Privacy Act of 1974, PL 93-380, 88 Stat. 571.

Jaffee v. Redmond, 116 S. Ct. 1923 (1996).

Jensen, G. (2002, November 15). *Ethically and practically speaking: Managing your malpractice liability.* Workshop presented at Illinois State University, Normal, IL.

Jonson-Reid, M. (2000). Understanding confidentiality in school-based interagency projects. *Social Work in Education, 22*(1), 33-45.

Kardon, S. (1993). Confidentiality: A different perspective. *Social Work in Education, 15*(4), 247-249.

Kopels, S. (1992). Confidentiality and the school social worker. *Social Work in Education, 14*(4), 203-204.

Kopels, S., & Kagle, J. D. (1993). Do social workers have a duty to warn? *Social Service Review, 67*(1), 10-26.

Kutchins, H. (1991). The fiduciary relationship: The legal basis for social work responsibility to clients. *Social Work 36*(2), 106-113.

Lens, V. (2000). Protecting the confidentiality of the therapeutic relationship: Jaffee v. Redmond. *Social Work, 45*(3), 273-276.

Levy, C. S. (1976). *Social work ethics.* New York: Human Sciences Press.

Loewenberg, F., Dolgoff, R., & Harrington, D. (2000). *Ethical decisions for social work practice* (6th ed.). Itasca, IL: F. E. Peacock.

Manning, S. S. (1997). The social worker as moral citizen: Ethics in action. *Social Work, 42*(3), 223-230.

Mattison, M. (2000). Ethical decision making: The person in the process. *Social Work, 45*(3), 201-212.

McWhinney, M., Haskins-Herkenham, D., & Hare, I. (1992). NASW Commission on Education position statement: The school social worker and confidentiality. *School Social Work Journal, 17*(1), 38-46.

National Association of Social Workers. (1999). *Code of Ethics of the National Association of Social Workers* (revised). Washington, DC: Author.

Pellegrino, E. D., & Thomasma, D. T. (1981). *A philosophical basis of medical practice*. New York: Oxford University Press.

Prichard, D. C. (1999). Breaking confidence: When silence kills. *Reflections, 5*(2), 43-51.

Raines, J. C. (1990). Empathy in clinical social work. *Clinical Social Work Journal, 18*(1), 57-72.

Raines, J. C. (1996). Self-disclosure in clinical social work. *Clinical Social Work Journal, 24*(4), 357-375

Reamer, F. G. (1998). The evolution of social work ethics. *Social Work, 43*(6), 488-500.

Reamer, F. G. (1999). *Social work values and ethics* (2nd ed.). New York: Columbia University Press.

Reamer, F. G. (2000). The social work ethics audit: A risk-management strategy. *Social Work, 45*(4), 355-366.

Robison, W., & Reeser, L. C. (2000). *Ethical decision making in social work*. Boston: Allyn and Bacon.

School Social Work Association of America. (2001). *Position statement: School social workers and confidentiality*. Northlake, IL: Author. Retrieved April 7, 2003, from http://www.sswaa.org

Secemsky, V. O., & Ahlman, C. (2003). Proposed guidelines for school social workers seeking clinical supervision: How to choose a supervisor. *School Social Work Journal, 27*(2), 79-88.

Staller, K. M., & Kirk, S. A. (1997). Unjust freedom: The ethics of client self-determination in runaway youth shelters. *Child and Adolescent Social Work Journal, 14*(3), 223-242.

Supreme Court upholds social work privilege: Majority of seven cites NASW legal brief. (1996, September). *NASW News, 41*(8), 1, 10.

Tarasoff v. Regents of the University of California, 551 P. 2d 334 (1976).

Yalom, I. D. (1980). *Existential psychotherapy*. New York: Basic Books.

8

School Social Workers and Confidentiality

Position Statement of the School Social Work Association of America

Adopted March 15, 2001

Standards of practice for school social workers require that adequate safeguards for the privacy and confidentiality of information be maintained.[1,2] Confidentiality is an underlying principle of school social work and is essential to the establishment of an atmosphere of confidence and trust between professionals and the individuals they serve.

Information is communicated to school social workers by students and families with the expectation that these communications will remain confidential. An assurance of confidentiality promotes the free disclosure of information necessary for effective treatment.

ETHICAL AND LEGAL RESPONSIBILITIES

Direct Services

Providing services to students in the school setting requires a careful balance between legal and ethical responsibilities. School social workers must be conversant with federal, state, and local laws and policies governing confidentiality. School social workers must follow the guidelines established by the state and school district in which they work, recognizing that these guidelines may differ from those governing private practice.

---

1. Standard 14, NASW Commission on Education. (1992). *NASW standards for school social work services, 1992.* Washington, DC: NASW.
2. NASW Commission on Education. *Position statement: The social worker and confidentiality.* Washington, DC: NASW.

Most states recognize that communications between social worker and client are privileged[3]; however, this privilege is not absolute. School social workers as members of a team of professionals may be confronted with situations where disclosure of information is critical to providing assistance to the student and family. It is the school social worker's obligation to obtain informed consent, that is, explain the limitations of confidentiality to the student and family, prior to service delivery.

Information should be shared with other school personnel only on a need-to-know basis and only for compelling professional reasons. Prior to sharing confidential information, school social workers should evaluate the responsibility to and the welfare of the student. The responsibility to maintain confidentiality must be weighed against the responsibility to the family and to the school community. However, the focus should always be on what is best for the student.

School social workers must be conversant with affirmative reporting requirements. All states now require school professionals to report suspected cases of child abuse and neglect. School social workers should be aware of school board policies and should ensure that such policies safeguard confidentiality of the reporting individual.

School social workers should familiarize themselves with school board policies and state and local laws governing reporting requirements for students who are HIV-positive or have AIDS. School social workers should also be aware of state statutes providing confidentiality to minor students who seek treatment for sexually transmitted diseases, information about and access to birth control, and pregnancy-related health care and counseling.

Therapists, including social workers, are under an affirmative duty to warn if there is clear and present danger to the student or another identified individual.[4] The social worker must warn any individual threatened by the student and must take steps to ensure the safety of a student who threatens suicide.

In all instances school social workers must weigh the consequences of sharing information and must assume responsibility for their decisions.

Written Material

School social workers must be conversant with federal, state, and local laws and policies regarding confidentiality and access to education records. Education records are all records that contain information directly related to a student and that are maintained by an education agency or institution.[5] Parents have the

---

3. Privileged communications are statements made by persons in a protected relationship, which are legally protected from disclosure on the witness stand. The privilege is exercised by the client and the extent of the privilege is governed by state statutes. H. C. Black. (1979). *Black's law dictionary* (5th ed.).

4. Tarasoff v. Regents of the Univ. of Calif., 17 Cal. 3d 425, 1551 P.2d 334 (1976).

5. The Family Education Rights and Privacy Act (FERPA), 20 U.S.C. 1232g; Individuals with Disabilities Education Act(IDEA), 20 U.S.C. 1400 (1997).

right to inspect and review education records. Social workers' personal notes kept for use by only those individuals are not considered education records and are confidential.

School social workers should inform students and parents that information gathered under the individualized education program (IEP) process may be shared with all members of the IEP team. The team, which includes other school personnel and the parents, may use the social history compiled by the school social worker in making decisions about the student's educational program and placement.[6]

Documents maintained on a computer become education records if shared orally with another staff person. Sole possession records maintained on a computer are not considered part of the education record and are confidential. School social workers may also be aware that other staff members or computer technicians may have access to school-owned equipment. Saving sole possession records to an individual diskette and securing that diskette may provide greater assurance of confidentiality.

Confidential records should be transmitted by facsimile only when absolutely necessary. Such reports should include a notation indicating that the material is confidential and is for professional use by only the designated recipient. The notation also should indicate that review, dissemination, distribution, or copying of the facsimile is prohibited.

Conclusion

The school social worker must carefully weigh the decision whether to preserve the confidentiality of information or share the information, using the best interests of the student as a guide. Those decisions must be informed by federal, state, and local laws and policies, as well as the professional ethics of the school social worker.

---

6. IDEA 1412(a)(4).

Section Two

Policies, Programs, and Mandates for Developing Social Services in the Schools

9

Policies, Programs, and Mandates for Developing Social Services in the Schools

Robert Constable
Loyola University, Chicago

Richard S. Kordesh
Bluehouse Institute, Inc.
Oak Park, IL

- ◆ Policy and Program Development for School Social Workers
- ◆ Developments that Shape School Social Work
- ◆ From Civil Rights to School Programs: Children with Disabilities
- ◆ The Educational Rights of Children with Disabilities
- ◆ Principles and Models of Responsive, Family-Centered School Community Services
- ◆ Implications of Reform Movements for School Social Workers

POLICY AND PROGRAM DEVELOPMENT FOR SCHOOL SOCIAL WORKERS

School social work has been shaped by the interaction of two narratives. First is the narrative of *social work* with its professional purposes, its values, its paradigm of the transactions of persons with their environments, and its methods developed over a century of practice, theory, and research development. Second, there is the narrative of *schools*: developing greater inclusiveness, beginning to adapt themselves to individual differences, yet seeking to meet the demands of a multinational economy for high levels of education for individual and national survival. While progress is being made toward universal basic education, there are obstacles that prevent many children from having access to education and from using it well. School social work, developing throughout the world because the demands on education have amplified, seeks to deal with these obstacles (Huxtable & Blyth, 2002). Internationally, there is an increasingly level playing field provided by information technologies, and in every country economic survival is related to education (Friedman, 2005). Education has become the key to social development (Midgeley, 1997). With greater demands for educational achievement, American school reform is shifting toward outcome-based education, higher standards for school personnel, and greater accountability for effective practice. For school social workers, state education agencies (SEAs) are beginning to require specialized preparation prior to employment and a period of performance assessment as a school social worker afterwards (Constable & Alvarez, in press). There is a movement toward national certification of school social workers (Alvarez & Harrington, 2004).

Section II focuses on *policy and program development* in school social work. The relationship between school social work practice and education continues through the concrete development of social policies and programs that allow educational institutions to achieve their purposes. These policies and programs are formulated in a context of societal and professional values, through institutional structure, and through a developing and growing body of law. They are implemented, and may be developed, in the local school community. They are manifested through the practice of the myriad professionals in a school in their daily encounters with students and through the concrete organization of the school itself. Thus, the concrete organizational and economic realities of the school reflect the merging of law, public expectations, and what is humanly and organizationally possible. There is usually a gap between the aspirations of policy and the actualities of practice. However, even the identification of gaps implies an awareness of needs and a possible direction for change. The awareness of a gap is an important spur to change; it may be prophetic of the future.

The role of the school social worker is shifting and broadening from a focus on individual children to one that includes participation in program and policy development at the local school and community level. This broader role demands, in addition to clinical skills, a deepened understanding of the school as an organization, of policy analysis, and of research geared to program development and evaluation. To the traditional assessment of the relations of vulnerable children to their educational and family environments is added *needs assessment*. Needs assessment is the focus on the relationship between school community systems and needs of specific populations of students for policies, programs, or services. A major tool in policy and program development at the school community level, needs assessment is discussed later in this section and throughout the book. In this section of the book, we review policies, programs, and mandates for social work services in the schools. We review the relations between these contexts for practice and the school social worker's role. Finally, continuing the focus on research, several chapters discuss the research and analytic skills needed for school social work policy development.

For school social workers, policy development needs to take place in the state education agency (SEA) as well as in the school community. However, social policy has traditionally been pictured as national policy, far from the vital areas where much of school social work policy is developed. And so, there can be a disconnect between theory and practice. Traditionally, policies are pictured as developing through federal, state, and local statutory, regulatory, and case law (court decisions) that take place *from the top down*. But this is only one part of policy and program development in school social work. At the federal and state level, laws and policies may prescribe and suggest common goals and means. However, it is up to the grassroots level, the level of implementation, the level of the school community, the local education agency (LEA), and the local school to develop ways to carry them out.

Although policy is always embedded in practice, practice theory usually has been pictured as developing in a separate orbit. When this connection is not acknowledged, there appears to be little basis for a real practitioner role in policy development. When there is no possibility of changing the contexts that shape it, practice becomes less effective. Furthermore, the limits of policies that prescribe but do not implement are becoming all too clear. Any such policy's success depends on the real environment of service and the capabilities of those implementing it. Some policies exist mainly on paper because no one has found a way to implement them successfully. Others may even work against their initial purposes. For example, a national dress code for schools would be unlikely to be helpful to local schools. Regional variation, local and school commitment to "school colors," and other factors would render such a policy useless, if imposed nationally. However, many schools have found dress codes that meet their specific needs in addressing gang control, issues of class, and school solidarity.

School social workers participate in policy and program development, particularly in the small community of the schools where practice itself often creates policy. There are really two necessary directions of policy development—from the *top down* and from the *bottom up*. Policies may originate from grassroots programs that resonate with needs and empower consumers to take action on these needs. Initiatives may develop as experiments from points where need and service are defined. In developing programs to meet the needs of the school community, school social workers are both developing and implementing policies. School social workers are well situated to have access to both levels.

For school social workers, the common thread in all of this is a need to understand the language and theory of policy as well as of practice. For example, it is part of their role to help develop and implement crisis plans as members of the school crisis team, and a crisis plan is both policy and practice. Social workers work with teachers, parents, and pupils to create solutions to include youngsters with disabilities in general education classes. In all of these, school social workers and the school team develop programs that make policy possible. Since social workers work in the most difficult areas of education, their role inevitably is an innovative one that goes beyond the "givens" of the institution or the situation. The distance from such innovation to policy and program development is not great. The two directions of policy, from the top down and from the bottom up, are beginning to mesh, particularly in recent legislation and school reform initiatives. It is important that school social workers see policy and program development as their participation in the school's active response in its own community to societal conditions and to mandates. When school social workers have the freedom to develop their role, the school can become more responsive to societal and community conditions, as they inevitably affect the educational process (Meenaghan & Gibbons, 2000; Meenaghan & Kilty, 1994).

DEVELOPMENTS THAT SHAPE SCHOOL SOCIAL WORK

The role of the school social worker is being shaped by ten current developments in education and society, discussed in this and in subsequent sections:

1. American education is growing socially and culturally diverse.
2. School reform is moving toward common, measured expectations of what students should achieve and thus toward outcome-based education.
3. Systems of accountability for effective education are developing.
4. There is growing awareness of complex student needs that prevent achievement.
5. Ambitious goals of reform on the federal, state, and local education levels are often confounded by the inability of many schools and pupils to achieve them.
6. Children with disabilities are demanding implementation of their right to a free appropriate public education and to inclusion in the education process.
7. School communities are being defined as communities of service, resources, and safety for all children and families (particularly for families at risk).
8. Relations of federal, state, and local involvement in education are shifting. The SEA is gaining great importance mediating between federal and LEA levels of policy development and implementation.
9. School social workers are beginning to assist in the development of policy at all levels from the local school, the district, the state, and the national level. They understand that their involvement is essential to their survival.

10. The movement toward specific educational prerequisites for school social work certification at the state level, toward a national specialty credential, and toward postdegree performance assessment is also a move toward specialized practice.

This development brings together the streams of practice methods, policy, and research into a role that would assist children, families, and school personnel with social tasks and transactions in the process of education. These developments will be discussed in the context of recent school reform and service initiatives taking place within the school community, some of these from the top down; others come from the bottom up.

Reform Principles: Their Diverse Origins

Problems of social fragmentation, increased risks, and "savage inequalities" in education have energized a variety of efforts at social and educational reform converging on the schools and on families. For many children the education process is fragmented and ineffective. Youngsters coming from difficult family and social situations seem hardly ready for the challenge of the more rigorous curriculum imagined by school reform movements. A host of data identify many family structures that are unable to carry out effective socialization of children. The consequent changes in public policy reflect a strikingly consistent reform agenda reshaping diverse arenas: education, child welfare, juvenile delinquency prevention, community development, and others. They have heightened the need for new working models of service coordination in schools and are combining with local forces to create an expanding new frontier for human service delivery.

The reforms in policy that are leading to the development of human services in schools emanate from a variety of legislative and administrative actions. A major current vehicle for school reform at the national level is the reauthorization of the Elementary and Secondary Education Act, PL 107-110, the No Child Left Behind Act (NCLB), described in greater detail in the following chapter. The act, coming out of concerns for student achievement from international comparisons, makes schools and students accountable for outcomes. Briefly, specific student outcomes to be attained by the schools and their students are now mandated by states. Statewide tests have been implemented to assess whether students are meeting those standards. Although some evidence suggests that high-stakes testing will lead to better performance (Carnoy & Loeb, 2002), leaders in general education and in special education are pointing out the need for further data and midcourse corrections to ensure that the law's promise is fulfilled (Hess & Finn, 2004; Sharpe & Hawes, 2004; Ysseldyke et al., 2004). To make this work there will be a need for shifts in funding according to what children need to meet state standards (Levine, 2004) and supplemental services for students having difficulty (Hess & Finn,

2004). Furthermore, developing the "highly qualified" teachers and education personnel needed to implement a system of individual assessment and flexible educational methods to reach these common goals would require SEAs to raise the bar for certification of teachers and other education personnel. These will have a profound effect on school social work. According to Art Levine (2004) in a widely quoted essay from Teachers College, Columbia University, the implications of revolutionary changes are only beginning to be felt.

- ◆ Education has become one of the most powerful engines driving economies and determining individual and national success (Friedman, 2005).
- ◆ In the United States the schools were told to raise achievement and intellectual skills to the highest levels in history for all students. The states mandated this by adopting higher standards for promotion and graduation, outcomes, testing, and certification accountability.
- ◆ Schooling needed to be redesigned, and to shift its focus from process to outcomes. The historically standardized processes would need to become variable and the traditionally variable outcomes would have to become standardized. The emphasis would have to shift from teaching to learning. The focus would have to change from the teacher to the student.
- ◆ The teacher and administrator forces had to be redeveloped. The country needed millions of new teachers and administrators to quickly replace most of the current teacher and administrator corps. And it needed more able teachers and administrators to achieve the higher standards (Levine, 2004).

Although it is schools that are being held accountable for achieving outcomes, they are still generated by families and communities together. The school social worker can serve as an anchor for a strong family and community perspective in a school, even as professional educators and school boards must focus on the educational process, on their outcomes, and on preparation of their staff.

FROM CIVIL RIGHTS TO LOCAL SCHOOL PROGRAMS: CHILDREN WITH DISABILITIES

The implementation of the Education for all Handicapped Children Act (later amended as the Individuals with Disabilities Education Act [IDEA]) provides an excellent example of successful movement from a general federal policy to the locality. This legislation first articulated the rights of children with disabilities to a *free appropriate public education* (FAPE) in 1975. The direction was continued and developed in subsequent amendments. Most recently the reauthorization of this act, now the Individuals with Disabilities Education

Improvement Act of 2004[1] (IDEA 2004), aligned many of the principles of IDEA with NCLB. At the national level, the process of policy development and implementation moves from court cases, which originally articulated FAPE, through the legislative branches to laws signed by the president, and then to regulations published by the Department of Education in the *Federal Register*, possibly one to two years after the law has been passed. From that point on, the SEAs develop their own education plans and regulations to comply with the law. This process takes time. Thus, it may take three years from its signing in 2004 before regulations and state plans at the SEA level become the context for educational policy development at the LEA and school levels. Each level interfaces with each other in an elaborate and sometimes discordant dance. At the same time, court cases continue to challenge and redefine a body of law in particular arenas.

It is very important for school social workers to understand the basic principles behind the legislation and policies and to be able to access information about this constantly changing picture. School social workers have learned to become increasingly sophisticated in their involvement with policy development and implementation as experts, as members of professional associations, and as citizens. In states where school social workers have been well organized, sophisticated, and active in policy development, the practice has flourished. In this book, the current policies are discussed in chapter 10. The current law from the U.S. Code and from applicable court decisions is discussed in chapter 11. Law and policies applied to Early Intervention (age 0–3) and Early Childhood Education (3–5) are discussed in chapter 12. As regulations and policies develop, these will appear in subsequent editions of this book. However, readers will need to access appropriate Internet sites to get developing versions of the law and its regulations.

THE EDUCATIONAL RIGHTS OF CHILDREN WITH DISABILITIES

Over the past thirty years, laws and policies for children with disabilities have been developed, moving from the federal level to the SEA to the LEA. Responsible over thirty years for profound changes in schools, these laws and policies, powered by a civil right, have become a model for an activist federal role in education (Turnbull & Turnbull, 1998). From the beginning, school social work had something to offer and found itself at the center of the decision-making and procedural safeguards for children with disabilities. The extension of these rights to the area of early childhood in 1986 further opened the opportunity for early intervention with families as well as with children. Finally, the Regular Education Initiative (REI) encouraged movement back into the regular

---

1. See http://edworkforce.house.gov/issues/108th/education/idea/1350confsummary.htm for a summary of H.R.1350 (IDEIA). Also see www.copaa.org for a line-by-line comparison by Jess Butler of the wording of IDEA and IDEIA.

classroom for youngsters with mild disabilities. Although the focus of this legislation has been on children with special needs, the thrust toward involvement with regular education is a trend that inevitably involves all children and the school as a whole.

In 1970-72, two court decisions were made that were destined to revolutionize the delivery of services to pupils with disabilities in schools. The effects of these decisions would reverberate for many years and they would change the fundamental nature of social services to children in schools. These decisions, *Pennsylvania Association of Retarded Children (PARC) v. Commonwealth of Pennsylvania* and *Mills v. Board of Education of the District of Columbia*, each contributed to the revolution by defining the concept of rights of persons with disabilities to an appropriate education and to access to the same opportunities enjoyed in our society by children without disabilities. These court decisions acknowledged a set of civil rights for persons with disabilities and sketched out the boundaries in giving shape to those rights. With these constitutional rights now defined by court decisions, the laws had to catch up with the definitions coming from the decisions. In the years following those decisions, laws were passed, such as the Vocational Rehabilitation Act of 1973, the Education of All Handicapped Children Act (PL 94-142), its current incarnations being the Individuals with Disabilities Education Act (IDEA; PL 105-17) and the Individuals with Disabilities Education Improvement Act of 2004 (IDEA 2004; H.R. 1350). These laws defined the rights more precisely and set down the mechanisms for enforcement. Without the precision of definition provided by laws and regulations, the decade following the court decisions would have been chaotic in education.

By the end of the decade and the beginning of the 1980s, there gradually emerged a refined body of court decisions, laws, ensuing regulations, Office of Special Education policies, and Office of Civil Rights findings. These have defined what is now an irreversible direction toward the enforcement of the rights of people with disabilities. The right to a FAPE was to consist of more than equal access to education or even compensatory education. For people with disabilities, neither opportunities nor objectives could be the same as for students without disabilities. The new concept of the right to an education was to encompass, as Weintraub and Abeson (1976) clarified, "equal access to differing resources for differing objectives" (pp. 7-13).

Two major federal district court decisions dominate the many right-to-education decisions of this period and illustrate the definitive change taking place: *PARC v. Commonwealth of Pennsylvania* and *Mills v. Board of Education*. The *PARC* case was taken on behalf of thirteen school-age children with developmental disabilities placed in state institutions and the class of all other children with developmental disabilities in the state. These children had been denied free access to public education opportunity by public policy as expressed in law, policies, and practices of the state education agency and school districts throughout the state that would postpone, terminate, or deny children with developmental disabilities access to a publicly supported education, including a public school program, tuition or tuition maintenance, and homebound instruction. The order struck down sections of the state school code and set dates by which the plaintiff children and all other children with developmental disabilities in the state were to be reevaluated and provided a publicly supported education. Local districts that provided programs of preschool education were required to provide the same for children with developmental disabilities. Furthermore, the court urged that these children be educated in a program most like that provided to children without disabilities.

Mills v. Board of Education followed *PARC* by several months and was basically similar except that a wider range of disabilities was represented, and some of the children were residing at home. As in *PARC*, the court ordered that the plaintiffs and all others of the class receive a publicly supported education; the decision also specified that the plaintiffs were entitled to due process of law prior to any change in educational program. The District of Columbia Board of Education failed to comply with the court order, stating that it did not have the necessary financial resources—to divert money from regular education programs would deprive children without disabilities of their rights. The court was not persuaded by that contention. The school has an obligation to provide a free public education to these exceptional children. Failure to provide this education could not be excused by the claim that there are insufficient funds. "The inadequacies of the District of Columbia public school system cannot be permitted to bear more heavily on the 'exceptional' or disabled child than on the normal child" (*Mills v. Board of Education*). The resultant court order, which was quite comprehensive, could be summarized under two basic sections: (1) A declaration of the constitutional right of all children, regardless of any exceptional condition or disability, to a publicly supported education, and (2) A declaration that the defendant's rules, policies, and practices, which excluded children without a provision for adequate and immediate alternative educational services, and the absence of prior hearing and review of placement procedures denied the plaintiffs and class rights of due process and equal protection of the law.

With these two cases, the rights of children with disabilities to free and appropriate public education and many of the procedural safeguards that were to find their way into later legislation and regulations were already manifest. Shortly following the court decisions, two closely related laws were to clarify further the rights of children with disabilities to an education. The first, Section 504 of the Vocational Rehabilitation Act of 1973, prohibited discrimination based on disability in programs and activities receiving federal financial assistance. The second, the Education for All Handicapped Children Act, further defined the right to a free appropriate public education for all children with disabilities from kindergarten to age twenty-one. The latter also provided for education in the least restrictive environment (LRE) and spelled out the accountability and procedural safeguards that would ensure this right. A recent clarification of these rights can be found in the Individuals with Disabilities Education Act (IDEA) of 1997 and IDEA 2004. States that request funding under this law must file a state plan that ensures that the state will comply with the requirements set forth in the legislation. The Office of Special Education and Rehabilitative Services reviews these state plans and conducts on-site visits to determine whether educational programs comply with the law. Furthermore, all states that accept federal funds for any educational purpose must comply with Section 504 of the Vocational Rehabilitation Act of 1973. Section 504 is somewhat broader in its coverage, covering students who may be physically ill and have a disability but do not have an educational disability. They may need special accommodations, "aids and services," but not "special education and related services" as specified in IDEA. A state may decide to reject funding under IDEA but must still comply with Section 504 unless the state decides to reject all federal educational funds (this has not occurred). The Office of Civil Rights enforces Section 504 by investigating complaints and coordinating compliance reviews.

The Individuals with Disabilities Education Improvement Act of 2004 (IDEA 2004) retains much of the FAPE framework discussed above and aligns IDEA with NCLB. However, the changes of this act, as they work their way into regulations, may be far reaching. The civil right to FAPE continues to be built on a nondiscriminatory evaluation, defined in an individualized educational program (IEP) and protected by procedural safeguards. However, whenever possible and appropriate, the same academic achievement goals that govern general education would be applied to the more individualized goals and processes of special education. The civil right is secured by adherence to procedural safeguards, but also in a substantive way, whenever appropriate, to the same academic expectations governing general education. Parental involvement is strengthened considerably. The relationship of national policy making to the SEA is clarified. The national level sets firm guidelines for SEAs to develop specific plans to meet the criteria. Finally, NCLB expects the SEA to develop a system that defines and assesses the qualifications of every education professional, including school social workers, and this system is extended to special education. These latter provisions will have profound effects on school social work (Constable & Alvarez, in press).

PRINCIPLES AND MODELS OF RESPONSIVE, FAMILY-CENTERED SCHOOL COMMUNITY SERVICES

Families, Schools, and Communities

Through the remaining parts of this section, we will examine the implications for the school social worker of school reform from the ground up. In the face of growing societal complexity and fragmentation, family and community structures can deteriorate and become less capable of providing a good, socializing context for children. When family or community structures deteriorate, there is a tendency for social institutions such as schools to take over family functions. This often has negative consequences. The solution is neither in isolated family structures, nor in a school's attempts to compensate for family dysfunctionality.

The answer lies in family-school relationships that preserve the integrity of both and build a community of care. In the late 1980s and 1990s, schools had been rapidly creating new program centers as well as community building efforts intended to make education institutions hospitable to families and embed schools in comprehensive community revitalization projects. This is continuing to develop in the form of family-centered school community services. Social workers work with these, participating in efforts to develop the school community and to help families take back their functions. Schools are becoming the major vehicle for the provision of services in the community to children and their families. Virtually every field of human services is creating new programs in schools, at least partly at the behest of a reform agenda. Federal policies, such as empowerment zones and enterprise communities, seek to make school-based services part of the neighborhood revitalization process (U.S. Department of Housing and Urban Development and U.S. Department of Agriculture, 1994). Some of the same reform principles are reshaping long-standing programs such as Head Start. With the support of federal Head Start State Collaboration Grants, states are studying strategies for creating more seamless linkages between local Head Start programs and kindergartens in public schools. Relocating Head Start classrooms into schools and linking them with other school-based preschool programs are among the strategies.

Many school reform strategies are leading to the placement of human services in educational facilities. For example, federal goals for education reform espouse the routine objective of having "every child ready to learn" by the time he or she reaches kindergarten; this objective has been used to justify many new preschool initiatives in schools. The goal of making schools safer has prompted more juvenile delinquency and prevention initiatives to be based in schools (McGroder, Crouter, & Kordesh, 1994). The goal of increasing the job readiness of students has led to more integration of employment training and job counseling into the formal curriculum and in school-to-work programs. Moreover, health clinics and substance abuse prevention programs are increasingly repositioned into schools because they are seen as supportive of a healthy education setting.

The principles reflected in the human service reforms essentially seek to break down barriers between categorical programs; they seek to make formal service systems more responsive to families, communities, and diverse cultures (Adam & Nelson, 1995; Bruner, Both, & Marzke, 1996; National Commission for Children, 1991). The theme of integration of education, health, and social welfare services reverberates through local, state, and national dialogues. Social work practitioners will find the principles familiar:

1. Services are to be designed and delivered with respect for the diverse cultures of clients, or, to use a predominant term in reform language, "customers.""Culturally competent" practices are required by policies to ensure that human services help recipients utilize the strengths in their cultural traditions and institutions.

2. Services are to empower families to take active roles in the design, implementation, and evaluation of programs that serve them.

3. Services are to prevent problems from occurring, rather than to only respond to problems after the fact.

4. Services are to be accessible to people in the neighborhoods where they live.

5. Services are to be linked in comprehensive strategies, drawing on multifaceted resources from mental health, health, economic development, delinquency prevention, and other traditionally separate fields.

6. Services are to conduct assessments and provide interventions that address the problems and resources of whole families, rather than individuals only.

7. Services are to emphasize the strengths, or "assets," of the communities in which they are located, rather than stressing the deviance and deficiencies that might be present.

Locally based school reforms often dovetail with these principles. Like human services, schools also seek to improve their culturally appropriate practices. A vast array of methods for involving families in schools is being tested. More schools are experimenting with programs that keep them open into the evenings, on weekends, and during summers, allowing them to function as community centers for a wide range of populations with a wide range of services, rather than only as sites for classroom-based teaching. In short, schools and human services are reaching for many of the same goals. These shared aspirations have called forth new institutional models for school-based services.

These ideas are also very much at the heart of school social work practice as it has developed from the beginning. In 1906, the University of Chicago Settlement House and the Chicago Public Schools sponsored the work of Louise Montgomery at Hamline School in the "Back-of-the-Yards" neighborhood to "make the public schools a center of social and education activity" (McDowell & Bass, as cited in McCullagh, 2000, p. 3). As a self-identified social worker, Montgomery had a triple focus. Her project would reach out to parents of Hamline's schoolchildren, alumni, and others. It would develop social, cultural, and recreational activities for children and adults. Men, women, and children of all ages participated in lectures, travel talks, social gatherings, plays, and choruses by the schoolchildren. After-school clubs for children involved cooking, sewing, music, stories, books, pictures, gardening, and school dramas. Throughout 1906 Montgomery arranged for and made assessments on the health and social circumstances of 208 children performing below grade level. Assembling and reporting these data with an eye to the promotion of social change, Montgomery detailed their social and medical conditions. She proposed that the school had an obligation to know the living conditions of each schoolchild. She demonstrated that poverty or wage insufficiency was the primary problem that led to inadequate nutrition, inadequate housing, and in turn, large numbers of children below grade performance for their age (Montgomery, as cited in McCullagh, 2000).

Models for School-Based Services

Among the more widely used models for creating school-based services are family centers, complex prevention initiatives, and brokered service networks. Increasingly, community leaders see the utilization of such models as a step toward the eventual establishment of *full-service schools* (Dryfoos, 1994). Family centers create places in schools for whole families to receive services, to deliver mutual support to one another, and to deepen the involvement of parents in the school itself. Complex prevention initiatives take advantage of the fact that the school provides the best setting in which to reach the greatest numbers of children who are at risk of failure or have serious health or social problems. Brokered service networks, such as those established by Communities in Schools, reposition human services into schools in order to keep children in school and to allow teachers to focus on basic education.

Family Centers. Utilizing funds from federal early childhood programs as well as family support funds, many states have made the family center a leading tool in the implementation of human service reform (Dupper & Poertner, 1997). Schools have often been the preferred sites for the creation of such centers. The centers hold several advantages. They allow for considerable expansion of the productive roles of parents in schools, as well as for service delivery. They facilitate one-stop shopping—the co-location of diverse services in one setting. They encourage a focus on the whole family. Pennsylvania is one of the states that has directed considerable investment into the family center model. Other states, most notably Florida, Kentucky, Maryland, and Tennessee, have also made family centers central to their school reform and human service system reform efforts. The Kentucky centers have received very favorable evaluations (Pennsylvania Children's Cabinet, 1994; Southern Regional Education Board, 2001). Since 1989, Pennsylvania has provided funding and training to new family centers serving all of its sixty-four counties. The majority of the family centers are based in public elementary schools. The centers are operated by local nonprofit organizations, usually those that already exist in their localities.

The Pennsylvania Department of Public Welfare describes the family center as a "process, a philosophy, and a place." The *process* refers to the collaborative, egalitarian decision-making it establishes between parents, service providers, and administrators. The *philosophy* stresses prevention, cultural competence, and bolstering of natural, helping relationships among families. The shared *place* buttresses a sense of community and ownership among families, staff, and other stakeholders. The Commonwealth of Pennsylvania requires that each center be designed through intensive collaboration among parents, community leaders, service providers, local government representatives, and school representatives. The deliberations struggle to balance the goal of creating programs that the families themselves define as necessary with the goal of staying within the legally prescribed terms of various funding sources. This balancing of family preferences with policy objectives requires considerable flexibility on the part of state administrators, local program managers, and school officials.

This balance is illustrated by the outreach programs that many family centers offer to parents of young children. Most of the centers operate as a core program a family-visiting service structured on the Parents as Teachers (PAT) model for parenting education. The program trains parents, usually mothers from the surrounding neighborhoods, to become certified in the PAT curriculum. Each "family educator" then begins building a caseload of up to twenty-five families with children under the age of three years. Home visits take place about twice a month. Visits cover many aspects of early child development. The family educator seeks to build a trusting relationship with parents and children, which hopefully will lead them to come to the center for family-to-family groups and seminars and even to participate in governing board meetings. Moreover, because the center is also supposed to structure community forums on broader school and neighborhood issues, educators and other center staff hope that families who visit the center will also feel more empowered to become involved in community activities.

The PAT model on its own is a straightforward expression of many early childhood policies, including the Child Care and Development Block Grant (Child Care and Development Block Grant, 1990). Thus the Commonwealth of Pennsylvania would have no trouble justifying the use of public funds to support it. Participation in the center is often triggered by family visiting or by meeting with families in the center. This participation can generate requests from parents that the center undertake initiatives that might not dovetail so closely with regulations in existing funding streams. They might request that the center become involved in community crime prevention or community development, activities whose funding might not normally be earmarked for family centers. Its philosophy requires the family center to respond to such preferences, even when doing so will challenge it to undertake initiatives with organizations, such as an economic development corporation, with whom it is not accustomed to working. It might lead staff members to stretch their job descriptions to the point where they need to learn skills they do not initially possess. They might get involved in community organizing or public advocacy. Parents might seek a program for which there is not an obvious funding source among those currently allocated to family centers, such as teen dance classes.

The family center's process demands that it evolve over time into an institution that expresses the visions and the cultures of the families in the surrounding neighborhood. Thus, in addition to the challenges it presents to staff, it can also present challenges to the school. Often the center will stimulate new activities—community meetings or after-school recreation—that might not have been anticipated by the principal or school board when they initially signed on to the concept of a school-based family center. It might expand the presence of new cultural groups whose families traditionally had not been visible in the school.

Because it is well suited to adopt reform principles, the family center has become one of the favorite tools for instituting these principles in human services. The elementary school is, in important respects, a site well suited for a family center. The school is already "owned" by the entire community, rather than sitting under the control of a particular cultural group or income group. The school constitutes a "normalized" site for services. There usually is not any label of deviance or dependency associated with attending the public school. It is the single best place to reach most of a community's children and, through them, their families. It offers advantages for setting up one-stop shopping. It can facilitate a more intensive integration of educational goals with human services goals, an integration especially important to children in vulnerable families.

Complex Prevention Initiatives. Whereas a family center represents a relatively autonomous new institution in a school, another type of initiative—a complex prevention initiative—constitutes a more complex and multifaceted partnership among different individuals and institutions. Such a partnership seeks to involve formal and informal resources from within the school and outside of the school in mutually reinforcing, risk-focused prevention strategies. It is a major new approach to bringing human services into school settings.

A good example of a risk-focused prevention framework is the Communities That Care (CTC) model (Hawkins & Catalano, 1992). CTC is fast becoming a widely used model for community risk assessments and community resource assessments (Developmental Research and Programs, 1995). It structures a multitiered method for community participation. Moreover, it offers many "best-practice" examples of promising prevention strategies that a community can integrate into a school-based, as well as a community-based, project. In addition, it has received considerable funding support from foundations, states, and the U.S. Department of Justice.

CTC recommends that a locality form two participatory bodies. The first body is a "key leaders" group composed of the school superintendent, the mayor, a few major agency directors, and top leaders from government, business, and perhaps local foundations. This group commits various institutions to the process. The second group advocated by CTC is the "community policy board." This broadly representative body includes neighborhood residents, parents, agency professionals, community activists, principals, teachers, and often youth. The community policy board meets regularly to oversee and help conduct the risk assessment and resource assessment. It also devises the prevention strategies that will respond to findings from the assessments. The key leaders group and the community policy board work together to garner the resources necessary to implement the strategies.

The CTC risk and resource assessments build schools directly into the process. For instance, the risk assessment gathers data on nineteen risk factors that can raise the likelihood of children and youth getting involved in harmful behaviors (dropping out, teen pregnancy, juvenile crime, substance abuse, and violence). Four of the risk factors focus directly on the school environment. Many of the other risk factors pertain to family, community, and individual characteristics that can also be related indirectly to conditions in the school. School-based risk factors include "early and persistent antisocial behavior," "lack of commitment to school," and others. Schools and the services they offer are prominent among the community's assets studied by the resource assessment. Resources include formal and informal institutions, programs, practices, and people who, in the view of risk-focused prevention, constitute the real and potential "buffers" between youth and the risk factors.

After the community policy board reviews data from the risk and resource assessments, it selects (usually) three to five of what it considers to be the locality's highest or most serious risk priorities for complementary strategies for risk prevention. Many such multifaceted projects take place wholly or partly in schools. For example, a project might focus on risk factors exhibited in elementary schools. Failure rates in third and fourth grades might be of concern. Suspension rates for violence or acting out in classrooms might also be rising. In such a case, a prevention initiative might include tutoring for the third and fourth graders by older, successful students; anger management seminars; a gang prevention project; and perhaps a parent support group to reinforce the positive roles of parents in each of these areas. Such an initiative would be typical of the kind of school-based projects that are proliferating rapidly because of CTC and other prevention models.

Complex prevention initiatives reflect many of the same reform principles espoused by the family centers. The resource assessment delves into the culturally based institutions and practices that might be drawn on to counteract the presence of particular risk factors. The risk assessment is comprehensive and requires comprehensive strategies. It is a type of community-based research or needs assessment. The family, as well as the school, is viewed as a critical institution for prevention. In addition, the community policy board creates opportunities for families and residents to participate meaningfully in all phases of the process.

Brokered Service Networks. A third trend affecting schools through human service reform is the establishment of brokered service networks. Brokered service networks, although they are not as tightly coordinated as complex prevention initiatives, also reposition community resources into schools. Many schools engage in such brokering through their own personnel. However, some organizations, most prominently Communities in Schools, Inc., work with schools and communities to help facilitate this repositioning. Communities in

Schools, Inc., based in Alexandria, Virginia, has affiliates in many cities in the United States, England, and Canada. Virtually all of them see the task of repositioning human services and other community resources into schools as central to their missions.

The Chicago affiliate presents a prominent and straightforward example of how to create brokered service networks. It works closely with thirty-five public schools in Chicago and is adding fifteen new schools per year. Chicago Communities in Schools' (CCIS) mission statement reads as follows: "CCIS repositions existing community resources into school sites to help young people successfully learn, stay in school, and prepare for life" (Chicago Communities in Schools, 1998). It repositions these resources through a finely honed process of negotiation with the school, brokering between the school and other community institutions, coordination within the school, and assessment. In order to work with CCIS, a school must demonstrate commitment to the process by designating a "site coordinator" who will work with the CCIS staff person, the agency coordinator, on a regular basis. Site coordinators must be full-time regular staff. Often they are assistant principals, school social workers, or counselors who can make significant time commitments to working with CCIS and the resources they help bring to the school.

The process begins with a team of staff and volunteers from the school designating the ten most important issues with which it needs help if the team is to make a substantial improvement in the educational environment. The issues that have surfaced across the thirty-five schools vary considerably. However, among the most prevalent concerns are supporting parents, preventing gang development, and responding to health needs. Once the top issues are identified, the CCIS agency coordinator (a full-time CCIS staff member who works with up to seven different schools) begins to search for, and negotiate with, organizations or individuals who can deliver the needed services at the school. CCIS does not pay the entities, which move into schools. Rather, it emphasizes the advantages to the organizations of positioning some of their services into these new settings.

An example of a school that has made substantial use of the CCIS brokering service is Victor Herbert School on Chicago's West Side. Thirteen providers working in this school have included:

American Red Cross: workshops on HIV/AIDS awareness,
Bobby E. Wright Mental Health Clinic: culturally centered problem solving, life skills, and conflict resolution,
Chicago Police Department: conflict resolution, safety, violence, and gang prevention,
Cook County Children's Hospital: health services for students and families,
Cook Country Sheriff's Department: drug awareness and gang awareness programs,
Hartgrove Hospital: group and individual counseling,

Junior Achievement: entrepreneurial curriculum,
Sinai Community Institute: life skills, healthy decision making, and self-
    esteem, and
Software for Success: computer-aided reading skills program.

Provider lists can grow and change as the school revisits its needs with CCIS in an annual contract review and assessment.

Once the staff are in the school, CCIS staff also helps to coordinate the repositioned resources. This is not the intensively managed collaboration required by a comprehensive prevention initiative; rather it is more an effort to ensure that providers know one another, that schedules are synchronized, that duplication is avoided, and that agencies can cooperate with one another when the need arises. CCIS's goal is for each school eventually to be able to undertake the brokering and coordinating on its own. Thus, CCIS staff pay close attention to developing a skilled, committed, and stable leadership base at the school. It is critical that the site coordinator develop the leadership capacity to maintain, build, and evaluate the networks of providers working in his or her school. CCIS has received considerable financial support from foundations and corporations because what it does is seen as advancing school reform and human service reform. It advances school reform partly by opening up new relationships between schools and communities. It advances human service reform by making services more accessible to children and families and by encouraging cross-agency teamwork. It brings more of the community's resources to bear on keeping children in school and by helping them to address social and health problems that can place them at higher risk of school failure.

Full-Service Schools. The full-service school goes well beyond family centers, prevention initiatives, and networks to fully transform the school into a comprehensive service center. Throughout the country, community agencies are locating programs in school buildings, mainly in low-income urban and rural areas. Close to 1,500 comprehensive school-based clinics have been identified, and many more are in the planning stage. Hundreds of family resource centers provide other support services, including parent education, Headstart, after-school child care, case management, meals, crisis intervention, and whatever else is needed by parents and young children (Dryfoos, 1994). Joy G. Dryfoos proposes a model for the full-service school. Her vision of the full-service school puts the best of school reform together with all other services that children, youth, and families need. Most of these can be located in a school building. The educational mandate places responsibility on the school system to reorganize and innovate. The charge to community agencies is to bring the following into the school: health, mental health, employment services, child care, parent education, case management, recreation, cultural events, welfare, community policing, and whatever else may fit into the picture. The result is a new seamless institution, a community-oriented school with a joint governance structure that allows maximum responsiveness to the community, as well as accessibility and continuity for those most in need of services (Dryfoos, 1994).

A few schools can claim to have achieved the full-service status. Dryfoos describes how a middle school in the Washington Heights section of New York City teamed with the Children's Aid Society to create a full-scale settlement house in the school. Other schools are reaching for the comprehensiveness and strong community base that this school has established. In fact, a number of schools in New York City, such as the Beacons Schools and others, see themselves as "community schools." These are schools through which neighborhoods mobilize their resources not only to improve education, and not merely to provide services. Community schools seek to serve as the nerve centers for comprehensive neighborhood revitalization. Community schools and full-service schools exhibit the distance the movement can go to integrate human services, community development, and education. As the momentum to bring more services into educational facilities grows, more schools are beginning to measure up as full-service schools.

IMPLICATIONS OF REFORM MOVEMENTS FOR SCHOOL SOCIAL WORKERS

The inclusion in education of children with disabilities is an example of effective *top-down* reform, successful however because it is a civil right and because there was some level of support at the SEA and LEA levels. Whether educational policy is made through regulations or through the courts, the effect of such policies and the direction taken by the courts in interpreting IDEA and Section 504 are becoming fairly clear. It is crucial to analyze the effects of these provisions on school social work practice, on delivery of services to children with disabilities, and on the school itself as it has traditionally conceived of its mission. However, the larger and related question is one of implementation. How might schools absorb the changes in their traditional mission? How may the current service delivery system adapt to the current reality of entitlement to services through the schools? What models of school social work practice emerge from these mandates, which cover areas where school social workers have been serving for nearly a century? What role might school social work play in the implementation of services to children based on educational rights?

The development of school-based services is a reform that comes from the school community and state levels. The first implication of these developments for social workers is the creation of a changing boundary between the school and the community. When the school is a service center for the community, its traditional boundaries shift to include the entire community with a very different range of ages and needs. Education inevitably becomes redefined. Although the school is the natural place for such a center of services, as at Hamline School, this is still a radical change. The history of American education points out that it will take schooling a considerable amount of time to absorb these changes. The school social worker, much more familiar with the broader community and its concerns, is in a most important position to make the concept work. Given this broadening of the school's identity into a community-wide service institution, school social workers, with their generalist practice perspectives, might be best positioned among school-based professionals to play leading roles in implementation of these reforms. Such leadership might entail school community needs assessments, monitoring policy changes in human services that would support new school-based services, facilitating planning groups to establish new school-based collaboratives, or utilizing the increased supports in policies to expand the generalist approaches in their own practice.

Along with the changing boundaries, the school also must deal with the inherent diversity of the communities it may encompass. Schools have often been the places where ethnic and class differences found some resolution. The increased importance of school as a central resource for families may also make the potential for conflict greater.

The key to effectiveness of the programs will rest on whether they successfully assist and empower families. Such programs should be resources to help families develop the internal capacities needed to carry out their roles effectively. However, as history and experience attest, in the face of a weakened family structure, a program might further weaken families by attempting to "manage" their problems. The language and theory of practice and policy need to address these issues so that families remain in charge of their domains and partner with schools in a broadened education mission. This is discussed in greater detail in chapters 12, 27, and 30.

School reforms and human service reforms are creating considerable diversification in the roles families can play in schools. School social workers seeking to empower families to play more meaningful and productive roles in their children's education as well as in service delivery will find new opportunities to do so. Family centers constitute new institutional bases for parents in schools, allowing for better communication with school-based professionals as well as with one another. They make it easier to carry out family-centered, as opposed to merely student-centered, practice. They create a legitimate base from which families can support one another, a process that group practice skills of social work can help facilitate.

The role of the social worker, responding to community demands, could on the other hand become more limited, with different types of social workers doing different things. The school social work role could be reduced, simplified, and adapted so that it could be managed by a less well-prepared (and less expensive) practitioner. The role could become deprofessionalized, if school social workers do not adapt and develop their roles to meet these challenges at a high level of service or if universities do not prepare students appropriately. On the other hand, the history of school social work has been one of active response and engagement with changing conditions, such as the educational rights of children with disabilities. There is no reason to assume that they will not rise to this challenge as well.

Changes in the expectations of schools and in school structure are profoundly influencing the purposes and functions of school social work. Furthermore, as the school social worker becomes more deeply involved with consultation on issues that have implications not simply for single cases, but for entire school districts, an understanding of the roots of policy development in the schools is essential. Even now, in many locales the knowledge and skills of school social work and its understanding of the school clientele are proving useful to the policy development process. Further development will depend on the commitment of school social workers to seeing policy development as a natural direction of practice and to preparing themselves for this role.

References

Adam, P., & Nelson, K. (1995). *Reinventing human services: Community- and family-centered practice.* New York: Aldine de Gruyter.

Alvarez, M. E., & Harrington, C. (2004). A pressing need for acceptance of an advanced national school social work certification. *School Social Work Journal, 29*(1), 18–27.

Bruner, C., Both, D., & Marzke, C. (1996). *Steps along an uncertain path: State initiatives promoting comprehensive, community-based reform.* Des Moines, IA: National Center for Service Integration.

Carnoy, M., & Loeb, S. (2002). Does external accountability affect student outcomes—A cross-state analysis. *Educational evaluation and policy analysis, 24*(4), 305–331.

Chicago Communities in Schools, Inc. (1997). *Service provider guide book for Victor Herbert School, school year 1997–98.* Chicago: Author.

Chicago Communities in Schools, Inc. (1998). *Connections.* Chicago: Author.

Child Care and Development Block Grant, PL 101-508. Enacted as part of the Omnibus Budget and Reconciliation Act of 1990.

Developmental Research and Programs, Inc. (1995). *Communities that care: A comprehensive prevention program-team handbook,* Seattle, WA: Author.

Dryfoos, J. G. (1994). *Full-service schools.* San Francisco: Jossey-Bass.

Dupper, D. R., & Poertner, J. (1997). Public schools and the revitalization of impoverished communities: School-linked family resource centers. *Social Work, 42,* 415–422.

Friedman, T. L. (2005). It's a flat world, after all. *The New York Times.* Magazine section. Retrieved April 3, 2005, from newyorktimes.com/ magazine.

Hawkins, J. D., & Catalano, R. E. (1992). *Communities that care.* San Francisco: Jossey-Bass.

Hess, F. M., & Finn, C. E., Jr. (2004, September). Inflating the life rafts of NCLB: Making public school choice and supplemental services work for students in troubled schools. *Phi Delta Kappan, 86*(1), 34–40, 57–58.

Huxtable, M., & Blyth, E. (2002). *School social work worldwide.* Washington, DC: National Association of Social Work Press.

Individuals with Disabilities Education Act, PL 105-17. U.S.C. 11401 et seq.

Levine, A. (2004). *New rules, old responses.* Teachers College, Columbia University. Retrieved October 15, 2004, from http://www.tc.columbia.edu/news/article.htm?id=4741

McCullagh, J. G. (2000). School social work in Chicago: An unrecognized pioneer program. *School Social Work Journal, 25*(1), 1–5.

McGroder, S. M., Crouter, A. C., & Kordesh, R. S. (1994). *Schools and communities: Emerging collaborations for serving adolescents and their families.* University Park, PA: PRIDE Project and Graduate School of Public Policy and Administration.

Meenaghan, T., & Gibbons, W. E. (2000). *Generalist practice in larger settings: Knowledge and skill concepts.* Chicago: Lyceum Books.

Meenaghan, T., & Kilty, K. (1994). *Policy analysis and research technology.* Chicago: Lyceum Books.

Mills v. Board of Education of the District of Columbia, 458 G. Supp. 866 (DDC, 1972).

National Commission for Children. (1991). *Beyond rhetoric: A new American agenda for children and families.* Washington, DC: U.S. Government Printing Office.

Parents as Teachers. 9374 Olive Boulevard, St. Louis, MO 63132.

Pennsylvania Association of Retarded Children (PARC) v. Commonwealth of Pennsylvania, 334 F. Supp. 1257 (E.D. Pa. 1971).

Pennsylvania Children's Cabinet. (1994). *A blueprint for the future of Pennsylvania's children and families.* Harrisburg, PA: Author.

Southern Regional Education Board. (2001). *Helping families to help students: Kentucky's family resources and youth service centers.* Atlanta, GA: Author.

Turnbull, H. R., & Turnbull, A. P. (1998). *Free appropriate public education: The law and children with disabilities* (5th ed.). Denver: Love Publishing.

U.S. Department of Housing and Urban Development and U.S. Department of Agriculture. (1994). *Building communities: Together. Empowerment zones and enterprise communities application guide.* Washington, DC: Author.

Vocational Rehabilitation Act of 1973. 29 U.S.C. 794.

Weintraub, F. J., & Abeson, A. (1976). New education policies for the handicapped: The quiet revolution. In F. Weintraub, A. Abeson, J. Ballard, & M. LaVor (Eds.), *Public policy and the education of exceptional children* (pp. 7-13). Washington, DC: Council for Exceptional Children.

Ysseldyke, J., Nelson, J. R., Christenson, S., Johnson, D. R., Dennison, A., Triezenberg, H., et al. (2004). What we know and need to know about the consequences of high-stakes testing for students with disabilities. *Exceptional Children, 71*(1), 75-94.

10

The Developing Social, Political, and Economic Context for School Social Work

Isadora Hare
Rockville, MD

Sunny Harris Rome
George Mason University

Carol Rippey Massat
University of Illinois at Chicago

- ◆ Does the Education System Really Prepare Students?
- ◆ School Reform and National Goals
- ◆ Demographic, Psychological, and Socioeconomic Factors Influencing Achievement and Schooling
- ◆ Federal, State, and Local Responses
- ◆ The State Education Agency (SEA) and the Local Education Agency (LEA)
- ◆ Local Initiatives in Education: Social Services and Health Care
- ◆ The Role of School Social Workers in a Changing World

Since its inception a century ago, school social work's content and direction have been influenced by the social environment, by conditions and events within society, and the educational system. Schools play an integral role in preparing our youth to become healthy, creative, and productive adults, workers, and citizens. Because public schools are designed to serve all children, they inevitably reflect events and trends in society at large. Schools are a microcosm of the larger society in which they function. The United States is a vast, complex, pluralistic society. In a free market democracy, economic success and citizen participation at all levels of government are prime national goals. The extent to which the education system prepares the upcoming generation to achieve these goals in the new global economy is a matter of deep concern. For the United States, this concern has been the source of almost a quarter-century of school reform. The events of September 11, 2001, accelerated some of these trends, particularly school safety and awareness of the school community. Lela Costin (1987) wrote that the essential purpose of school is "to provide a setting for teaching and learning in which all children can prepare themselves for the world they now live in and the world they will face in the future" (p. 538). Reflecting all of the realities of this dynamic environment, school social work is at the center of an intricate transactional field of forces (Germain, 1987). This field includes demographic, social, economic, and political forces, to which schools respond with both conservative and innovative strategies.

DOES THE EDUCATION SYSTEM REALLY PREPARE STUDENTS?

One of the most hotly debated questions in education is whether our system prepares the upcoming generation to achieve in the global economy. There has been an increased focus, now over several decades of discussion of school reform, on setting high standards for student achievement. Testing is now mandated for all states (No Child Left Behind Act of 2001), but it is still difficult to compare the results, since each state is allowed to set its own standard and to develop its own testing system. Thus, the most commonly used national standards are performance on SAT and ACT exams, which are taken only by college-bound high school juniors and seniors. Currently, 21 million students take the SAT and 2 million students take the ACT in the United States annually. More than 90 percent of U.S. colleges and universities require the SAT or ACT, despite the low ability of these tests to predict college performance. The test, is however, used as common measure to equalize the problem of different grading patterns in different schools (Black, 2005). SAT scores have stabilized after edging up for the past ten years. Members of minority groups have increased their scores since 2003 (Rafferty, 2004).

The need for reform has been accentuated by the performance of U.S. students on international tests. The 2004 results of the Program for International Assessment (PISA) indicated that the United States ranked twenty-fourth of twenty-nine member nations of the Organization for Economic Development (OECD) on performance of 15-year-olds in math. Since the last assessment three years earlier, student scores had fallen below those of Hungary, Poland, and Spain. The Trends in International Mathematics and Science Study (TIMSS) evaluates students in fourth and eighth grade and tested half a million students in forty-one countries in thirty languages. These included some chief U.S. trading partners and economic competitors, such as Canada, Germany, Hong Kong, Japan, Korea, and Singapore. On this test, U.S. students tested in 2003 had improved over the previous four years, and the gap between White and Black student scores had become smaller. This gap, which was closing in the 1970s and 1980s, saw no improvement in the 1990s. The TIMSS 2003 figures indicate that scores for U.S. students have remained stable since 1995 (Bybee, & Stage, 2005). Bybee and Stage suggest that these results are because "U.S. schools emphasize the acquisition of information at the expense of problem-solving and the acquisition of knowledge" (p. 4), and "the United States, in its effort to close the achievement gap, has emphasized basic knowledge to help underachievers rather than ensuring that all students learn challenging material" (p. 4). The United States educational system continues to require change, from teacher training to creating a more challenging curriculum for all students.

SCHOOL REFORM AND NATIONAL GOALS

During the 1980s, national reports drew attention to serious problems in American education. These concerns and responses to them culminated in the adoption of laws and public policies geared to education reform. In 1994, Goals 2000: Educate America Act (PL 103-227) put into place eight national educational goals, six of which had already been adopted by the nation's governors in 1989. These goals were the precursor to the No Child Left Behind Act of 2001 (NCLB), a sweeping educational reform act that focused on the achievement of educational goals for all children in the United States. President George W. Bush was able to obtain bipartisan support for NCLB in part because of wide support for the educational goals that were set for the nation in the 1990s. Thus, in the first decade of the second millennium, these national educational goals, although unachieved, remain important in education policy:

Goal 1: Readiness: By the year 2000, all children in America will start school ready to learn. Objectives include ensuring access to high quality and developmentally appropriate preschool programs for all disadvantaged and disabled children, facilitating parent involvement in education and providing the training and support required to perform this function, and supplementing education with nutrition and health care.

Goal 2: School Completion: By the year 2000, the high school graduation rate will increase to at least 90 percent. Objectives include reducing the dropout rate and eliminating the gap in high school graduation rates between students from minority backgrounds and their nonminority counterparts.

Goal 3: Student Achievement and Citizenship: By the year 2000, all students will leave grades 4, 8, and 12 having demonstrated competency over challenging subject matter including English, mathematics, science, foreign language, civics and government, economics, arts, history, and geography, and every school in America will ensure that all students learn to use their minds well, so that they may be prepared for responsible citizenship, further learning, and productive employment in our modern economy.

Goal 4: Teacher Education and Professional Development: By the year 2000, the nation's teaching force will have access to programs for the continued improvement of their professional skills and the opportunity to acquire the knowledge and skills needed to instruct and prepare all American students for the next century.

Goal 5: Mathematics and Science: By the year 2000, United States students will be first in the world in mathematics and science achievement.

Goal 6: Adult Literacy and Lifelong Learning: By the year 2000, every adult American will be literate and will possess the knowledge and skills necessary to compete in a global economy and exercise the rights and responsibilities of citizenship.

Goal 7: Safe, Disciplined, and Drug-Free Schools: By the year 2000, every school in the United States will be free of drugs, violence, and the unauthorized presence of firearms and alcohol and will offer a disciplined environment conducive to learning. The U.S. Department of Education created the Office of Safe and Drug-Free Schools in order to implement this goal. It continues to carry out this goal and is accessible to school social workers at the Web site http://www.ed.gov/about/offices/list/osdfs/index.html

Goal 8: Parental Participation: By the year 2000, every school will promote partnerships that will increase parental involvement and participation in promoting the social, emotional, and academic growth of children. Objectives of this goal include developing policies and programs for increasing partnerships that respond to the varying needs of parents and the home, including parents of children who are low-income, or bilingual, or parents of children with disabilities, and engaging parents and families in a partnership that supports the academic work of children at home and shared educational decision making at school (National Education Goals Panel, 1997).

The goals embody several important themes that are reflected in current educational policies. One is an emphasis on high standards of student academic achievement (goals 2–6). Another is the recognition that nonacademic, psychosocial factors also influence educational outcomes and must be addressed if high standards are to be reached and maintained. These factors influence school readiness, parental involvement in schools, and the ability to stay in school and not drop out (goals 1, 2, 7, and 8). They also reflect an emergent relationship between the federal and state levels on education policy (and goals) and funding. Their lack of achievement by the year 2000 does not diminish their continuing importance. It only highlights the work remaining. Indeed, the problem may not be in the system itself as much as in the relation between the system and the conditions children bring with them to school (Mintzies & Hare, 1985).

DEMOGRAPHIC, PSYCHOSOCIAL, AND SOCIOECONOMIC FACTORS INFLUENCING ACHIEVEMENT AND SCHOOLING

Demographics

Factors outside the school represent key influences on outcomes within school reform. These factors, rightly understood, are directly related to school social work. One of these factors is school demographics. Currently, these demographics reveal a dense, complex, diverse, and multicultural picture. In 2003, 25 percent of the population was under age 18 (U. S. Census Bureau, 2005). The extent and nature of population diversity is changing rapidly. The United States is currently experiencing its second great wave of immigration, this time not from Europe, but from the economically developing worlds of Asia and Latin America (Booth, 1998).

> Between 1970 and 2000, the share of foreign-born U.S. residents from Europe dropped from 62 percent to 15 percent. Over the same period, the share of the foreign-born from Asia grew from 9 percent to 25 percent, and the share from Latin America increased from 19 percent to 51 percent. (U.S. Census Bureau, 2000, p. 17-1)

The foreign born population in the United States has grown from a low of 10 million in 1970 to 20 million in 2000 (U.S. Census Bureau, 2000). Overall, about 15.9 percent of the United States population is made up of foreign-born children, compared to 28 percent of the total population that are native-born children. However, in states like New Mexico, California, and Texas, the number of children under age 18 who are African American, Latino, Asian and Pacific Islanders, and Native American together far exceed the number of White children. For example, in 2002 in California the percentage of White young adults was 36 percent, with 64 percent being members of minority groups (Larsen, 2003; Annie E. Casey Foundation, 2004). As of 2002, 49 percent of American children were non-White or Hispanic (Fields, 2002). In some urban areas, it is common to have thirty-five differing linguistic groups in an elementary school with approximately 200 children.

Poverty

In spite of enormous wealth in the United States, the child poverty rate is among the highest in the developed world. One study, which examined child poverty rates in seventeen developed countries, indicates that the child poverty rate in the United States is 50 percent higher than the next highest country. The child poverty rate for the country as a whole has hovered at or above 20 percent for more than a decade (Annie E. Casey Foundation, 2004). Currently the number of children in poverty is increasing, with 37 percent of all American children living near or below the poverty line. The rates are even more alarming for infants and minority children, with 42 percent of infants, 58 percent of African American children, and 62 percent of Latino children living below or near the poverty line (Fellmeth, 2005). According to the U.S. Census Bureau, children tend to be more economically advantaged if they are born to parents with a college degree. Children living in households with two married parents are far less likely to live in poverty than children living in female-headed families: 15 percent compared to 65 percent in 2002 (Fields, 2002).

Childhood poverty has both immediate and lasting negative effects. Children who are poor are more likely to have difficulty in school, to become teen parents, and, as adults, to earn less and be unemployed more (Federal Interagency Forum on Child and Family Statistics, 1997). The gap between children living in poverty and their counterparts is greatly accentuated by the enormous differences in the role government plays in alleviating child poverty. Education and welfare funding, for example, show dramatic inequalities. Poor children often go to school in school districts that are impoverished and less able to provide.

Substance Abuse

Recently, illicit drug use among all students has continued to decline but remains a significant concern. The Monitoring the Future project, conducted by the University of Michigan's Institute for Social Research, began in 1975 and has monitored adolescent drug use since that time. In 2003, they surveyed 48,500 eighth-, tenth- and twelfth-grade students across the country. At that time they found that the use of ecstasy, marijuana, methamphetamines, and LSD had declined across all three grades. Amphetamine and tranquilizer use declined among tenth and twelfth graders. Use of other drugs remained steady. Those include heroin, narcotics other than heroin, crack and powder cocaine, and "club drugs." They found an increase in use for several drugs, including Vicodin, inhalants, and oxycontin. Factors that continue to make adolescent drug use a problem include the continuing introduction of new drugs or new forms of older drugs. Licit drug use continues to be troubling, with 54 percent of U.S. twelfth graders having tried cigarettes and 77 percent having consumed alcohol. Although the decline in use of specific drugs is encouraging, it is quite troubling that 51 percent of American teenagers have tried an illicit drug before completing high school, and the decline in use of a number of drugs by eighth graders has halted or slowed (Johnston, O'Malley, Bachman, & Schulenberg, 2004).

Teen Sex and Pregnancy

There is a close association between teen parenthood and school factors. Child Trends, Inc. (1997) has identified four risk factors for teen births: (1) early school failure, (2) early behavior problems, (3) family dysfunction, and (4) poverty. In contrast, involvements in school activities after the birth of the first child, receipt of a high school diploma, or even a GED were strongly associated with postponing a second teen birth. Most U.S. adolescents begin having sexual intercourse in their mid- to late teens. Sixty-two percent of young women and 61 percent of twelfth graders have had intercourse, compared with 35 percent of women and 55 percent of men in the early 1970s. These figures have declined, however, since 1991, when 66.7 percent of twelfth graders had experienced sexual intercourse at least once. Although the likelihood of having intercourse increases steadily throughout the teen years, 18 percent of adolescents (almost one in five) do not have intercourse during their teen years (Alan Guttmacher Institute, 1996). The teen birthrate has declined steadily since 1991. In 1996 it was 61.8 per 1,000 young women aged 15 to 19 years, while the rate has declined to 41.7 births per 1,000 young women aged 15 to 19 in 2003. In 2003, around 840,000 teens between the ages of 15 and 19 became pregnant. This figure has steadily declined, since a high of 117 per 1,000 in 1990 (National Campaign to Prevent Teen Pregnancy, 2005). The proportion of girls aged 15 through 19 who obtained an abortion the previous year increased from 2.3 percent in 1973 to 2.9 percent in 1996, with a high of 4.4 percent in 1986. Similarly, from the decade of the 1980s through 1995 the proportion of teen pregnancies resulting in birth increased from 48 percent to 55 percent (USDHHS-ASPE, 2000). In 2000, the percentage of live births resulting from pregnancy among 15- to 19-year-olds remained at 55 percent; the percentage of pregnancies resulting in legal abortions declined to 30 percent, and miscarriages were estimated at 14 percent (Alan Guttmacher Institute, 2005). Although birth rates for black teens fell 42 percent between 1991 and 2002, and birth rates for Hispanic teens fell 20 percent between 1991 and 2002, they remain higher than for other groups (National Campaign to Prevent Teen Pregnancy, 2005).

Child Abuse and Neglect

In 2003, child protective service agencies identified approximately 906,000 abused or neglected children. Nationwide, the rate of victimization of children was approximately 12.4 per 1,000 children under age 18. This has dropped from 13.4 children per 1,000 in 1990. More than 60 percent of these were victims of child neglect, with 20 percent suffering from physical abuse, 10 percent from sexual abuse, and 5 percent from emotional maltreatment. About 17 percent were affected by "other" types of maltreatment as defined by various state laws (U.S. Department of Health and Human Services, 2005). Children from birth to age 3 were most frequently the victims of child maltreatment, and girls were more likely to be victimized than were boys. In 2003, 1,500 children died as a result of child abuse or neglect. Of those children who died, 35.6 percent had suffered neglect only, almost 30 percent suffered from physical abuse only, while 28.9 percent suffered multiple forms of maltreatment. Psychological mal-treatment resulted in 6.7 percent of the deaths, and sexual abuse resulted in 0.4 percent of the deaths (U.S. Department of Health and Human Services, 2005).

Youth Violence

Although violent crime among youth is declining, violence continues to be a serious threat to child well-being and school functioning. Violent crime increased during the late 1980s. However, from 1994 to 2003 rates of victim-ization among adolescents fell to 51.6 per 1,000 for youths aged 12 to 15 and 53 per 1,000 for youths aged 16 to 19. These rates are about half those found in 1994 (Child Trends Data Bank, 2005). Among all persons aged 15 to 24, homi-cide is the second leading cause of death, and suicide is the third leading cause of death (United States Census Bureau, 2001). African American males are at par-ticular risk of homicide. Homicide is the leading cause of death for African Amer-ican men aged 15 to 24. The rate rose almost 200 percent between 1985 and 1991 (46.5 to 134.6 per 100,000) (Resnick et. al., 1997; U.S. Department of Health and Human Services, 1999). In 1998, the suicide rate for white males 15 to 19 was nearly twice the rate for white females (USDHHS-ASPE, 2000). Although suicide is still highest among whites, the rate of suicide is highest for American Indian youth.

> Of youth ages 7-17 who committed suicide between 1981 and 1998, 17,954 were White (86%), 1,958 were Black (9%), 443 were American Indian (2%), and 415 were Asian (2%). Because White youth were 80% of the juvenile population during this period, they were overrepresented in juvenile suicides. More specifically, the suicide rate for White juveniles (31 per 1 million) averaged nearly twice the rates for Black juveniles and Asian juveniles (both at 18 per 1 million). However, the sui-cide rate for American Indian juveniles (57 per 1 million) was almost twice the rate for White juveniles. (Snyder & Swann, 2004)

In 2001, 18 percent of youth reported that they had been threatened or injured at school during the previous year. Astor, Meyer, Benbenishty, Marachir, and Rosemond (2005) report that "between 1992 and 1996, the annual average rate of victimization for teachers was 76 incidents per 1,000 teachers" (p. 19). Astor et al. also report that 35 percent of school social workers were assaulted or threatened in a given year. He reported that most of the experiences involved attacks by students (77%), parents (49%), or gang members (11%) (Youth Violence Project, 2003). In March 1998, the White House released sur-vey results that reported that one in ten American public schools experienced serious violent crimes such as rape or robbery in the past year (Associated Press, 1998). The prevalence was higher at large schools and at schools in urban areas. However, the violent crime rate has been consistently declining in public schools, with a 2001 rate of 6 per 1,000 students as compared to the 1994 rate of 13 incidents per 1,000 students aged 12 to 18 (Youth Violence Project, 2003).

A Spectrum of Violent Behaviors in School. Despite widespread con-cerns about youth violence, only about 0.5 percent of all youth homicides and suicides occurred in school (U.S. Dept. of Education, 1998, as cited in Dwyer, Osher, & Hoffman, 2000). Nevertheless, incidents of violence in schools have led children to question whether they can be safe. The issue of safety in schools is now getting considerable attention from education professionals and parents (Dwyer, Osher, & Warger, 1998). These efforts have major implications for social work. The concern to make schools safe has become a major policy goal at fed-eral, state, and local levels. Schools have been working on safety and developing crisis plans now as a matter of course.

Examining the roots of violence in schools and among young people in gen-eral exposes a spectrum of violent behaviors. Bullying or harassment, once taken for granted as part of "growing up," are now seen as violent behaviors, seri-ously hurtful in themselves, and totally unacceptable. If left alone, they can lead to greater violence or to suicide. Schools and school personnel who knowingly fail to respond to harmful conditions, such as peer sexual harassment, are made responsible and can be liable (*Davis v. Monroe County Board of Education*, 1996; *Nabozny v. Podlesny*, 1996). Not only is this spectrum of violence dan-gerous and harmful to its victims and perpetrators, the fact is that nothing can succeed in a school when members of the community feel unsafe. Hunter and Schaecher (1995), discussing lesbian and gay youths who experience harass-ment, pointed out that "teachers and administrators bear responsibility for (the students') lack of learning ... because students are forced to concentrate on sur-viving in the school system, rather than on their studies" (p. 1058). At this point social workers customarily work with others in the school community to cre-ate a safe school environment (see chapter 36), to develop conflict resolution and mediation programs (see chapter 38), and to assist in the provision of school-based crisis intervention for traumatic events (see chapter 37). The prob-lem of the spectrum of violence is first of all a problem of the school commu-nity, of its policies and procedures, of who is included, and how differences are managed. Only then is it also a problem of victims, perpetrators, and their membership in the school community.

Bullying and Sexual Harassment. Bullying and harassment were ignored for years as simply part of the experience of growing up. A reexamina-tion of both points out that for children perceived as "different," schools can be toxic places. In Norway and Sweden public concern about bullying was aroused when several student suicides followed experiences of chronic bullying. Other countries, such as Japan and Korea, have identified school bullying as one of their chief concerns. Studies done on bullying involving 150,000 Norwegian and Swedish students found rates of 15 percent of schoolchildren involved in bully–victim problems. When these studies were done in parts of the United States, the prevalence rates for bullying were at least as high or higher. More than 25 percent of North Carolina 10-year-olds, girls and boys, report being bul-lied several times or more during the past three months (Olweus, Limber, &

Mihalic, 1999). The National Crime Victimization Survey found that bullying is one form of violence that has been on the rise. According to their survey, in 2001, 8 percent of students reported being bullied in the previous six months, compared to 5 percent in 1999 (U. S. Bureau of Criminal Justice, 2003).

Peer sexual harassment is experienced by even larger numbers of young people, boys and girls alike. It appears to be an indicator of a larger problem of interpersonal violence in schools. In a study published in 1993 by the American Association of University Women (AAUW), 1,600 high school students were asked whether they had experienced any of a list of things that would be considered sexual harassment. These might involve comments or actions demeaning to another's sexuality or sexual orientation, or some sort of unwanted sexual imposition, such as pulling clothing off or down. The results of this study showed 80 percent of students, boys as well as girls, reported being sexually harassed. Of those harassed, 79 percent stated it was by a peer (AAUW, 1993) In a similar study among 342 urban high school students, Fineran and Bennett (1999) found 84 percent of students experiencing sexual harassment (87% of females and 79% of males). Seventy-five percent of students reported perpetrating sexual harassment, boys at twice the rate for girls.

Students who identify themselves as gay or lesbian often have the most difficult experience. Among 1,800 high school students in an anonymous survey taken in a Northern California school district, about 6 percent said they were gay, lesbian, or bisexual, and 13 percent were uncertain about their sexual orientation (Lock & Steiner, 1999). In the AAUW (1993) study cited above, 53 percent of students harassed reported being harassed by students of the same sex. Eighty-six percent of all students reported that being labeled gay or lesbian would create the most distress in them. This was particularly true among boys. A 1989 USDHHS report suggested gay and lesbian youths are two to three times more likely to commit suicide than other youths. Other studies estimate up to 40 percent of gay, lesbian, and bisexual youths attempt suicide. The risk of suicide appears to become greater with greater disclosure of sexual orientation (Hershberger, Pilkington, & D'Augelli, 1997). This vulnerable population needs the full range of social services from policy and program development through individual intervention. However, most of all, every school must be made safe for each person in it.

Dropouts

Goal 2 of the National Education Goals aimed to increase the high school graduation rate to at least 90 percent by the year 2000. This has not taken place. In 2001, 86.5 percent of students completed a high school education. The completion rate has increased gradually since 1972, when it was 82.8 percent. Across different states, there is considerable variability, ranging from 90.1 percent in North Dakota to 65 percent in Louisiana. Although gaps between

White and Black student completion rates narrowed in the 1970s and 1980s, no improvement has occurred since that time. In 2001, 91 percent of Whites completed high school; 85.6 percent of Black students completed high school, and 65.7 percent of Hispanic students graduated (Kaufman, Alt, & Chapman, 2004).

Parent Participation

Parent participation "in promoting the social, emotional, and academic growth of children" is an important factor in academic achievement. Schools cannot educate children, particularly vulnerable children, without the cooperation of families (Walberg & Lai, 1999). Recent studies provide substantial evidence of the importance of "parental connectedness" in providing protection against a range of risk behaviors. Such "connectedness" involves frequency of activities of children with parents, perceived caring, and high expectations of school performance (Resnick et al., 1997). Goal 8 envisaged that state policies would assist school districts and schools to establish programs for partnerships that respond to and support the varying needs of children; their academic work promotes shared educational decision making. Parents for their part are charged with the responsibility of holding schools and teachers to high standards of accountability (National Education Goals Panel, 1997).

In this context a low level of parental involvement is cause for concern. In 1996, parental attendance at parent-teacher conferences decreased from 84 percent in elementary schools to 47 percent in middle schools. Forty-one percent of elementary and middle schools reported that parental input is considered when making policy decisions in three or more areas. Although 62 percent of parents of students in grades 3 through 12 reported that they participated in two or more activities in their child's school, this percentage dropped from 73 to 53 percent between the elementary and high school grades. A report issued by the U.S. Department of Education in October 1997 showed that it is not merely contact between fathers and children that is important. Rather it is "active participation in their children's lives through involvement in their schools that makes a difference in school outcomes" (Nord, Brimhall, & West, 1997, p. xi). Schools are finding that they need a more active outreach to get this involvement, particularly among lower income and vulnerable families.

FEDERAL, STATE, AND LOCAL RESPONSES

Historically the federal government has attempted to promote student achievement by addressing the needs of children challenged by adverse physical, social, and economic conditions. It has become more active in education by beginning to develop laws and standards and to fund some school reform efforts.

Head Start

Head Start provides learning activities for economically disadvantaged preschool children, comprehensive health care services, and social services including community outreach, referrals, family needs assessments, and crisis intervention. It also promotes parental involvement in the educational process. The Head Start program, begun in 1965, is being implemented in approximately 20,050 community-based nonprofit organizations and school systems (Administration for Children and Families [ACF], 2005). Despite acknowledged effectiveness and widespread bipartisan support, the program has never been funded at a high enough level to reach all eligible children (Ginsburg, 1995). The 1994 amendments to Head Start (PL 103-252) contained new performance standards, along with quality assurance measures designed to identify and aid deficient grantees. It also established a new Early Head Start program, expanding the program's benefits to families with children under age 3 and to pregnant women. Services include early education in and out of the home, home visits, parent education, comprehensive health and nutrition services, case management, and peer support for parents (ACF, 2005).

Individuals with Disabilities Education Improvement of Act 2004 (IDEA 2004)

The Individuals with Disabilities Education Act (IDEA), first entitled the Education for All Handicapped Children Act, and most recently reauthorized as IDEA 2004, defines the constitutional right of all children with disabilities to a *free appropriate public education in the least restrictive environment.* This very important legislation and the consequent role of the school social worker is discussed in greater detail in chapters 9, 11, and 12. It provides a model for the relation of policy development at the federal, state, and local school level. It also provides a model for the possible relation between policy development and the school social worker's role. IDEA 2004, in effect July 2005, contains a number of changes from IDEA '97. It strongly reflects the scientifically based philosophy of NCLB. It requires school personnel and special education teachers to be "highly qualified." LEAs are required to provide professional development for all school staff in order that they may deliver "scientifically based academic instruction and behavioral interventions." "Adequate yearly progress," a key NCLB term, is one of the goals for the performance of children with disabilities. IDEA 2004 strongly emphasizes inclusion of all children in regular state and district-wide assessments and requires that alternate assessments be aligned with the state's "challenging academic content standards." IDEA 2004 states that to the extent possible special education and related services provided to the child should be based on peer-reviewed research. Concepts included in IDEA 2004 stress the importance of maintaining high academic achievement standards, clear definition of expected results, in objective, measurable terms, coordination of services, and availability of qualified personnel.

IDEA 2004 also reflects a shift in attitude toward parents. This is reflected in a broadening of the definition of *parent* to include foster parents, kinship caregivers, and surrogate parents. In addition, there is a stronger emphasis on requirements of local school districts to provide special education services for children whose parents have placed them in private schools and on requiring states to provide Child Find and similar activities for children in parentally enrolled private schools. IDEA 2004 also takes a stand on requiring families to medicate children by prohibiting SEAs and LEAs from requiring a child to obtain a prescription for a substance covered by the Controlled Substances Act (21 U.S.C. 801).

IDEA 2004 also made changes in procedures related to eligibility for special education, development of IEPs, and reevaluations. It removes the requirement that tests be conducted in the child's native language. The wording of this requirement is changed to "Assessments . . . are provided and administered in the language and form most likely to yield accurate information about what the child knows and can do academically, developmentally and functionally, unless it is not feasible to do so." IDEA 2004 states that, when determining whether a child has a specific learning disability, LEAs do not have to take into consideration severe discrepancy between achievement and intellectual ability in oral expression, listening comprehension, written expression, basic reading skill, mathematical calculation, or mathematical reading. When discussing evaluation for eligibility for special education, the legislation also removes the language regarding "present levels of performance" and changes the wording to "present levels of academic achievement and related developmental needs of the child."

IDEA 2004 makes some changes that affect the development of IEPs. It removes the requirement for benchmarks and or short-term objectives to be part of an IEP, except for children with disabilities who take alternate assessments aligned to alternate achievement standards. For all other children with an IEP, the requirement is for a statement of measurable annual academic and functional goals. For children who take alternate assessments, an explanation of why the alternate assessment is necessary and why the selected assessment is appropriate for the child is required. Mandatory attendance at IEP meetings may be somewhat altered by the provision that a member of the IEP team shall not be required to attend an IEP meeting if parents and the LEA agree it is unnecessary. Similarly, after an annual IEP meeting has been held, parents and the LEA may then agree not to convene a later IEP meeting to make changes. Instead, they may agree to develop a written document to amend the current IEP. IDEA 2004 also provides for alternative methods of carrying out IEP meetings, including conference calls and videoconferences. It provides for multi-year IEP demonstration projects to be made through grants to states who apply. A reevaluation must occur every three years unless the parent and the LEA agree it is unnecessary. This changes the requirement for reevaluation of a child every three years to reevaluation *if* the LEA determines such a need or if a child's parents or teachers request it. For potential due process proceedings, IDEA 2004 adds a mandatory resolution session to occur within fifteen days of a complaint.

In IDEA 2004, when there is consideration of disciplinary actions, the school district's burden to prove that behavior was not a manifestation of a child's disability has been removed. Similarly, if parents have refused evaluation of a child for eligibility for special education, the LEA is not deemed to have knowledge of a disability.

Elementary and Secondary Education Act Reauthorization: No Child Left Behind Act

The Elementary and Secondary Education Act (ESEA) was originally enacted in 1965. Its primary aim, through Title I, was to assist states in providing compensatory education to low-income, educationally disadvantaged children. The Improving America's Schools Act of 1994 (PL 103-382) amended ESEA to emphasize the need for children in Title I programs to attain the same high standards of performance demanded of students in the general population. Services were extended to teen parents, migratory children, to neglected or delinquent youth in state institutions, and to community day programs. There were also new opportunities for schools to operate school-wide programs (serving all children in high-poverty schools), participation of private-school students, and coordination of education with health and social services. In its other titles ESEA (1994) provided grants for a wide range of other categorical needs, such as professional development of school staff, character education, and civic education.

The 2001 ESEA reauthorization, the No Child Left Behind Act (NCLB), was signed into law on January 5, 2002, by President George W. Bush. The act is considered the most sweeping reform of ESEA since its enactment. Its title is consistent with the language of the national goals. Extending the reform agenda of the 1989 Governor's Conference, it embodied the four basic principles of President George W. Bush's education reform plan: stronger accountability for results, expanded flexibility and local control, expanded options for parents, and an emphasis on teaching methods that have been proven to work, such as through the teaching of reading and the improvement of teacher training. It extended the Title I program and increased federal funding for education. There would be an annual assessment of student progress in reading and in math through testing of students in grades three through eight, beginning in the 2004–05 school year. These results, when disaggregated by school, by district, by state, by race, and by gender, were expected to create an accountability system, an annual "report card" on school performance and on statewide progress. If a school is identified as "failing" over a number of years, parents would be allowed to transfer their child. There is money available for supplemental services for children in failing schools, for reading programs, and for charter schools. Other parts of the bill are geared to enhancing the flexibility of LEAs in developing their own programs and policies. ESEA money, for example, could be transferred to different related programs without separate approval (House-Senate Education Conference Report, 2001). In contrast to strictly regulated categorical programs of previous ESEAs, the focus is on outcomes and increased flexibility for SEAs and LEAs. Counseling and school social work services are supported. The act recommended a ratio of one school social worker to eight hundred students (Mandlawitz, 2002).

The ultimate impact of this legislation can only be assessed in the coming years. It promises to make a profound shift in the federal–state–local relations in American education. In some ways, the LEA and the school community behind it become even more important. There is a delicate balancing act with the SEA and the federal government. School social workers might have an opportunity to help students and their families to deal with some of the source conditions behind underachievement. The possible empowerment of parents and local school communities and the development of community resources may be particularly important for school social workers in communities where schools are failing. On the other hand, without developing programs of assistance to students and their families, the development of high-stakes accountability systems might have negative results. The symptoms rather than underlying problems would have been addressed. The dangers of grade retention and dropout are now even greater for nonachieving youngsters. Some states have tended to shift nonachievers into special education, avoiding their count within the general education population. Schools that have succeeded in these systems have done so through the promotion of intensive learning, professional development for teachers, and targeted supports for students. They looked at how particular students were learning and supported them with adaptive education strategies (Darling-Hammond, 2002).

THE STATE EDUCATION AGENCY (SEA) AND THE LOCAL EDUCATION AGENCY (LEA)

Devolution from the Federal to the State Level

The emergent federal–state relationship "devolves" a certain amount of discretion to the state education agencies (SEA). In the Individuals with Disabilities Education Act (IDEA) and the No Child Left Behind Act of 2001, the federal level remains active in setting general goals and standards, and to some extent in funding them. SEAs, in turn, set standards for achievement of pupils in the local school districts (LEAs) and they develop statewide testing. They develop regulations and procedures to conform to national standards, such as in the area of education of children with disabilities. States have adopted a variety of strategies to improve local education, including developing statewide testing programs; increasing efforts to prepare students for jobs; recruiting better educators; promoting more family, community, and business involvement; making schools safer; and increasing access to computers. States have adopted statewide standards for student learning, and statewide testing systems (Darling-Hammond, 2002). As these and other innovations are implemented, state and local governments will be facing additional challenges brought about by devolution. The Personal Responsibility and Work Opportunity Reconciliation Act of 1996 (PL 104-193), which is known as the Welfare Reform Act, for example, gives states the primary responsibility for meeting the needs of low-income children and families. This includes making key decisions about welfare benefit levels, eligibility criteria, work requirements, time limits on receipt of assistance, and exemptions. Some states have, in turn, passed this responsibility on to their individual counties.

Despite the increased activism of the SEA, the LEA remains the point of origin for the actual policies governing pupils and school personnel. In the United States, education is locally controlled: there are almost 93,000 schools in approximately 14,000 school districts, all of which jealously guard their independence and decision-making power (U.S. Department of Education, 2004). Working hand in hand at both the LEA and the SEA levels, school social workers have learned that professional survival depends on their influence on school policies.

State Reform: School Finance

Another area of intense activity, intended to address one of the primary barriers to student achievement, has been the area of school finance. The exact nature of the relationship between educational spending and student achievement is a matter of some controversy (Biddle, 1997). Yet it is undeniable that financial resources contribute in important ways to our educational system to maximize student success. Even more than family poverty, schools with high concentrations of poverty are associated with adverse student outcomes (Kennedy, Jung, & Orland, 1986, as cited in Terman & Behrman, 1997). High rates of poverty and low rates of school funding conspire to affect student achievement in areas such as science and math (Biddle, 1997). This is particularly acute in urban school districts where the cost of educating children is highest. Resource discrepancies affect the entire educational climate, including the quality of buildings and facilities, equipment and technology, curriculum materials, availability of gifted and talented or extended-day programs, teacher salaries, teacher training, and teacher-student ratios (Biddle, 1997). Teachers in high-poverty schools report more student misbehavior, disruption, weapons, and violence; more absenteeism, and less parental involvement in education. Racial and ethnic minority students are more likely to attend high-poverty schools and thus are particularly disadvantaged by resource discrepancies (Smith, Young, Bae, Choy, & Alsalam, 1997).

The major questions are whether this arrangement is fair to all students and whether there is an acceptable remedy. The U.S. Supreme Court rejected the notion of a constitutional right to equality of education (*San Antonio Indepen-*

dent School District v. Rodriguez, 1973), thrusting the issue of equity to states and to their constitutions. Courts in over forty states have reviewed the question of whether, considering a school finance arrangement largely dependent on property taxes, their own educational systems are in accord with their state constitutions. The lawsuits would focus on the adequacy of educational opportunity or the equity of resource distribution. Many of these challenges have been successful. These lawsuits continue to serve as catalysts for states to examine, refine, and, in some cases, redesign their school financing schemes, but the results are inevitably uneven.

Sources of Funds

Historically, education was financed almost exclusively by local property taxes. Over time, this system became increasingly inequitable, with wealthier districts enjoying the dual advantages of a larger tax base and fewer school-age children among whom the proceeds must be spread. After the Depression, state governments dramatically increased their contributions. Drawing on state income and sales taxes, they now match local government in their overall share of education spending (Howell & Miller, 1997). On average, schools receive 46 percent of their funding from state funds and 37 percent from local governments (CBIA Education Foundation, 2005). This typically supports priorities including curriculum materials, special education, reduced class size, facilities improvement, teacher training, and textbook acquisition (Monk, Pijanowski, & Hussain, 1997).

The federal financial contribution to education, though well publicized, remains quite small at approximately 8.2 percent (CBIA Education Foundation, 2005). It takes the form of categorical assistance to aid schools in meeting the needs of specific populations of children, such as those with disabilities or the economically disadvantaged (Howell & Miller, 1997). On a national average, elementary and secondary schools receive approximately half of all locally generated taxes. Yet individual states vary considerably in the degree to which they rely on federal, state, and local funding. Data from 1995–96 show Hawaii, for example, drawing 8.1 percent of its educational budget from federal funds, 90 percent from state funds, and only about 2 percent from local funds. New Hampshire, on the other hand, uses 5.1 percent federal funds, 49 percent state funds, and 46 percent local funds. Mississippi shows the greatest reliance on federal funds, at 15 percent (U.S. Census Bureau, 2003). As a general rule, wealthier states and districts derive more of their educational budgets from local taxes, while poorer states and districts rely more heavily on state and federal funds. Some states are also turning to new sources of revenue, including proceeds from lotteries, private payments, contributions, or corporate sponsorships. The allocation of educational dollars is very similar across jurisdictions. Typically, 60 to 65 percent is spent on instruction; 11 percent goes to administration; 10 percent to facilities operation and maintenance; 9 percent to transportation and food services; 7 percent to student services, including health, attendance, guidance counseling, speech and other special education services, and school social work services (Monk et al., 1997).

Discrepancies in Spending

Although overall spending per pupil has increased over time in the United States, discrepancies in school funding—between states, between districts within a state, and between schools within a single district—can be staggering. For example, although the average national per pupil expenditure in 2000–2001 was $8,589, New Jersey spent an average of $12,485 per pupil, while Utah spent an average of only $5,578 per pupil (National Center for Education Statistics, 2003). At one time, in Texas and California, the highest-spending school districts had average per pupil expenditures that were more than ten times those of the lowest-spending district (Guthrie, 1997).

The story told by these numbers is complicated by the fact that equity is a difficult concept to define. The nation's 14,000 school districts vary tremendously in both size and composition; some have concentrations of students who are considerably more costly to educate because of poverty, disability, mobility, or limited English proficiency. For example, the state of Washington reports that it costs 18 percent more to educate a student with limited English proficiency than the average per pupil expenditure (Bergeson, Mayo, Wise, Gomez, Malagon, & Bylsma, 2000). In terms of students with disabilities, although some federal assistance is provided through IDEA, it covers only about 19 percent of the actual costs of educating these children (Samuels, 2005). Per pupil expenditures for students who receive special education services are 1.91 times greater than costs to educate students without disabilities. For students with multiple disabilities, costs are 3.1 times higher than for a regular education student. If students are placed in nonpublic schools or other agencies, the cost rises to 3.9 times that of a regular education student (Chambers, Skolnik, & Perez, 2003). This has a particularly strong impact on schools with high concentrations of children in poverty, because poor children are more likely to be diagnosed as having a disability (Terman & Behrman, 1997).

Legal Remedies

Since the mid-1960s, courts in many states have entertained lawsuits based on the inequitable distribution of resources across school districts. Arizona was the first state in which the court found the school finance system unconstitutional because it failed to provide equitably for the construction and maintenance of school buildings. Other states where the state's school financing scheme was found in violation of the state constitution include Arkansas, California, Connecticut, New Jersey, Washington, West Virginia, Wyoming, Kentucky, Montana, New Jersey, Texas, Arizona, Massachusetts, and Tennessee. Litigation around school finance continues in Florida, Louisiana, New Hampshire, North

Carolina, Pennsylvania, South Carolina, and Virginia. One case has resulted in a single school district (Los Angeles Unified) agreeing to equalize spending across its 564 individual schools (Augenblick, Myers, & Anderson, 1997). In the vast majority of cases, states have attempted to remedy financing inequities by increasing their overall educational budgets and targeting the increased resources to low-spending districts. This way, they are able to avoid taking resources away from higher-spending districts. In most cases, budgets are being enlarged by increasing the state's contribution, and by requiring an increased local contribution or rewarding school districts that make a strong local tax effort.

Kentucky, whose entire system of public schools was declared unconstitutional in 1989, totally revamped its financing scheme. It introduced a system whereby the projected cost of educating students includes a differential reflecting special educational needs (pupil weighting). It capped the amount that districts would be permitted to raise locally. It supplemented local taxes raised above a certain base amount so that efforts by poorer districts would net the same amount as efforts by wealthier districts. It created new categorical grants for high-priority activities. Moreover, it increased the state contribution by increasing the sales tax. These and other innovations have reduced by 55 percent the relationship between a school district's wealth and the amount its students receive (Adams, 1997). In the early 1990s, Michigan took the bold step of completely abolishing its property tax, which had provided two-thirds of the state's educational budget. Instead, it increased the state sales tax. The bulk of its school financing now comes from state, rather than district, coffers (Center for Education Reform, 1997).

LOCAL INITIATIVES IN EDUCATION: SOCIAL SERVICES AND HEALTH CARE

There have been a plethora of changes in the educational, health care, and social services sectors, and these are influencing the practice of school social work. Schools are experimenting with various innovations in pursuit of better educational outcomes. New models of delivering a variety of services to children and families are emerging, most of these at the local level. School systems at the state and local levels are introducing a variety of nontraditional measures in the hope that these will raise student standards of achievement. Charter schools and vouchers, for example, are both designed to increase parental choice. Other examples include contracting with private, for-profit corporations, single-sex classes, and school uniforms.

Charter Schools

Finn (1994) defined charter schools as "independent public schools, often run by a group of teachers or parents, innovative or traditional in content, and free from most regulations and external controls" (p. 30). Most charter schools emphasize a particular academic philosophy ranging from back to basics to newer pedagogical approaches. Charter schools are regulated at the state level and face a number of complex financial, governance, regulatory, and management challenges (Koppich, 1997). Minnesota was the first state to enact charter school legislation in 1991. As of March 1998, twenty-nine states and the District of Columbia had charter school laws. There are now 1,010 charter schools nationwide, with the largest number of charter schools in Arizona (207), California (133), and Michigan (135). Another 535 charter schools are distributed across the other forty-seven states (National Center for Education Statistics, 2002).

Voucher Programs

Koppich (1997) defines vouchers as "government payments to households, redeemable only for tuition payments at authorized private schools" (p. 105). Vouchers are extremely controversial because private schools can select which students they will accept, thereby potentially leaving only the most disadvantaged or disabled students in the public schools. It is also unclear whether vouchers to faith-sponsored schools violate the constitutional requirement of separation of church and state. Eighty-two percent of private schools are religiously affiliated.

Contracting for Services or Privatization

This involves the use of public education funds to purchase services from for-profit or not-for-profit organizations in the private sector. The most controversial form involves hiring for-profit firms to manage entire public schools. A private firm, Minnesota-based Education Alternatives Incorporated (EAI), contracted with the city of Baltimore in 1992 to operate nine public schools, but the contract was canceled after three-and-a-half years of its expected five-year period. EAI also operated schools in Hartford, Connecticut, and Dade County, Florida, but thus far these schools have not demonstrated improvements in academic results. Another national for-profit firm, the Edison Project, is managing schools in twenty states and claims positive results (Edison Schools, 2005).

School-Linked Services

The emergence of new models of delivering health and social services to children and families is also changing the context of school social work (Franklin & Streeter, 1995). In January 1994 more than fifty national organizations concerned with the well-being of children, youth, and families gathered in Washington, DC, and reached a consensus regarding principles for developing integrated service systems. Such systems should be community based, school linked, family centered, culturally competent, comprehensive, and prevention focused. They should also feature ongoing needs assessment and program evaluation and should be collaborative in nature, merging categorical funding streams for most efficient service delivery to families and children. Usually called school-linked services, these models are discussed in some detail in chapter 9 and chapter 30. They were developed in response to two forces. First was the recognition that many students were at risk of educational failure because of complex economic, social, and psychological problems (National Commission on Children, 1991). Second was the concern that services to children and families in general are insufficient. The delivery system is fragmented, difficult to access, confusing, and uncoordinated. In school-linked comprehensive strategies, schools are no longer isolated providers of a single component-education for children and youth. They are active partners in a broader effort. As partners, schools have increased cooperation, communication, and interaction with parents, community groups, service providers and agencies, local policymakers, and other stakeholders (U.S. Department Education, 1996).

There are many models of school-linked services based at the local school level. Some are called full-service schools (Dryfoos, 1994); others are called family resource centers, or one-stop shopping centers (Hare, 1995). Another model is the school-based health center. Once considered controversial, these centers, first established in Dallas, Texas, and St. Paul, Minnesota, in the 1970s, now total 1,500 in forty-five states and Washington, DC. The centers provide comprehensive physical and mental health services to underserved youth in high schools (41%), middle schools (12%), combined middle-high (5%), elementary schools (30%), combined elementary and middle (7%), and combined K–12 (5%) (National Assembly on School-Based Health Care, 2000). These various models of school-linked services provide both an opportunity and a challenge to school social workers. Often they bring social workers and other professionals from community agencies, both public and private, into the schools. Ironically, problems of communication and coordination have arisen between practitioners hired by outside agencies and those employed by the school. School social workers must be proactive in overcoming such problems because they are "strategically placed to act as bridges connecting agencies and schools, to provide a glue factor in collaborative work" (Pennekamp, 1992; University of California at Los Angeles, 1996, p. 126).

Changes in Health Care

School social work is increasingly affected by developments in the health care delivery system. Many poor children in the United States lack health insurance. Medicaid (Title XIX of the Social Security Act) funding for students living in poverty is being used in many school systems to finance certain social work services. These would be parts of the early and periodic screening, diagnosis, and treatment or the targeted case management provisions of the Medicaid law (Farrow & Joe, 1992). This requires that school social workers have clinical credentials to enable them to be recognized as providers of Medicaid-funded services. These developments are causing social work services in schools to evolve in different and challenging ways.

THE ROLE OF SCHOOL SOCIAL WORKERS IN A CHANGING WORLD

Implications for Social Workers

All the developments described above reflect a shift in school policy development to the local level, a belief even that "a substantial part of budgeting, decision making, and accountability should occur at the level of individual schools, rather than at the school district level" (Guthrie, 1997, p. 37). Whether school social work survives and flourishes in this environment will depend on whether school social workers can articulate the connection between the social, the personal, and the education process.

School social workers are school employees paid for by educational dollars. They must project their image not only as providers of clinical services to individual students and their families, but also as informed change agents with contributions to make to crafting policies and programs in the LEA. They must be able to define their contribution to the educational mission of the school. They must assist in translating education policies emanating from various levels—federal, state, or local—into effective, outcome-oriented programs in individual school buildings. New service models require that they enhance their team-building skills, both with other school professionals and also with other social workers and members of other disciplines entering the school from the community. They must learn the skills required for collaboration and services integration. They must learn to become experts in community and school needs assessments.

References

Adams, J. E. (1997). School finance policy and students' opportunities to learn: Kentucky's experience. *Future of Children: Financing Schools, 7*(3), 79–95.

Administration for Children and Families (ACF). (2005). *Head Start: Fact sheet.* Retrieved March 24, 2005, from http://www.acf.hhs.gov/programs/hsb/research/2005.htm

Alan Guttmacher Institute. (1996). *Teen sex and pregnancy: Facts in brief.* New York: Author.

Alan Guttmacher Institute. (2005). *U.S. teenage pregnancy statistics with comparative statistics for women aged 20–24.* Retrieved March 23, 2005, from http:www.agi-usa.org/pubs

American Association of University Women (AAUW). (1993). *Hostile hallways: The AAUW survey on sexual harassment in America's schools* (Research Report No. 923012). Washington, DC: Harris/Scholastic Research.

Annie E. Casey Foundation. (2004). *Kids count data book: State profiles of child well-being 2004.* Baltimore: Author.

Associated Press. (1998, March 20). Study: Violence hits 10% of public schools. *Washington Post,* p. A3.

Astor, R.A., Meyer, H.A., Benbenishty, R., Marachi, R., & Rosemond, M. (2005). School safety interventions: Best practices and programs. *Children & Schools, 27*(1), 17–32.

Augenblick, J. G., Myers J. L., & Anderson, A. B. (1997). Equity and adequacy in school funding. *Future of Children: Financing Schools, 7*(3), 63–78.

Bergeson, T., Mayo, C. L., Wise, B. J., Gomez, R., Malagon, H., & Bylsma, P. (2000). Educating limited English-proficient students in Washington State. Olympia, WA: Washington Office of the State Superintendent of Public Instruction. (Eric Document Reproduction Service No. Ed 451311).

Biddle, B. J. (1997). Foolishness, dangerous nonsense, and real correlates of state differences in achievement. *Phi Delta Kappan, 79*(1), 9–13.

Black, S. (2005). Acing the exam. *The American School Board Journal, 192*, 35–39.

Booth, W. (1998, February 22). One nation indivisible: Is it history? Soon, no single group will comprise majority. *Washington Post*, pp. A1, A18–19.

Bybee, R. W., & Stage, E. (2005). No country left behind. *Issues in Science & Technology, 21*(2), 69–76.

CBIA Education Foundation. (2005). 10 facts about K–12 education funding. Retrieved March 26, 2005, from http://www.cbia.com/ed/NCLB/10facts.htm

Center for Education Reform. (1997). *Education reform nationwide: State by state summary*. Available from: http://edreform.com/pubs/stxsts97.htm

Chambers, J. G., Skolnik, J., & Perez, M. (2003). *Total expenditures for students with disabilities, 1999–2000*. Palo Alto, CA: American Institute for Research in the Behavioral Sciences. (Eric Document No. Ed 481398).

Child Trends Data Bank. (2005). *Violent crime victimization*. Retrieved March 24, 2005, from http://www.childtrendsdatabank.org/indicators/71ViolentVictimization.cfm

Child Trends, Inc. (1997). *Facts at a glance*. Washington, DC: Author.

Costin, L.B. (1987). School social work. In A. Minahan (Ed.), *Encyclopedia of social work* (18th ed., pp. 538–545). Silver Spring, MD: National Association of Social Workers.

Darling-Hammond, L. (2002). What's at stake in high stakes testing? *Brown University Child and Adolescent Behavior Letter 18*(1), 1, 3.

Davis v. Monroe County Board of Education, 74 F. 3d 1186 (11th Cir. 1996).

Dryfoos, J. (1994). *Full service schools: A revolution in health and social services for children, youth, and families*. New York: Jossey-Bass.

Dwyer, K., Osher, D., & Hoffman, C. C. (2000). Creating responsive schools: Contextualizing early warning, timely response. *Exceptional Children, 66*(3), 347–365.

Dwyer, K., Osher, D., & Warger, C. (1998). *Early warning, timely response: A guide to safe schools*. Washington, DC: U.S. Dept. of Education.

Edison Schools. (n.d). Retrieved March 28, 2005, from http://www.edisonproject.com/design/d23.html

Farrow, F., & Joe, T. (1992). Financing school linked integrate services. *Future of Children: School-Linked Services, 2*(1), 56–57.

Federal Interagency Forum on Child and Family Statistics. (1997). *America's children: Key national indicators of well-being*. Washington, DC: Author.

Fellmeth, R. (2005). Child poverty in the United States. *Human Rights: Journal of the Section of Individual Rights and Responsibilities, 32*(1), 2–5.

Fineran, S., & Bennett, L. (1999). Peer sexual harassment and the social worker's response. In R.T. Constable, S. McDonald, & J. Flynn. (Eds.), *School social work: Practice, policy and research perspectives* (4th ed., pp. 459–477) Chicago: Lyceum Books.

Fields, J. S. (2002). Children's living arrangements and characteristics: March 2002. Retrieved March 23, 2005, from http://www.census.gov

Finn, C. E. (1994, October). What to do about education 2: The schools. *Commentary,* 30-37.

Franklin, C., & Streeter, C. L. (1995). School reform: Linking public schools with human services. *Social Work, 40,* 773-782.

Germain, C. B. (1987). Social work services in schools [Book review]. *Social Casework, 68,* 510-511.

Ginsburg, L. (1995). *Social work almanac* (2nd ed.). Washington, DC: National Association of Social Workers Press.

Goals 2000: Education America Act. PL 103-227.

Guthrie, J. W. (1997). School finance: Fifty years of expansion. *Future of Children: Financing Schools, 7*(3), 24-38.

Hare, I. (1995). School-linked, integrated services. In R. L. Edwards & J. G. Hopps (Eds.), *Encyclopedia of social work* (19th ed., vol. 3, pp. 2100-2109). Washington, DC: National Association of Social Workers Press.

Head Start Reauthorization of 1994, PL 103-252.

Hershberger, S. L., Pilkington, N. W., & D'Augelli, A. R. (1997). Predictors of suicide attempts among gay, lesbian and bisexual youth. *Journal of Adolescent Research 12*(4), 477-497.

House-Senate Education Conference Report. (2001, December 11). *No child left behind.* Washington, DC: U.S. Department of Education.

Howell, P. L., & Miller, B. B. (1997). Sources of funding for schools. *Future of Children: Financing Schools, 7*(3), 39-50.

Hunter, J., & Schaecher, R. (1995). Gay and lesbian adolescents. In R. L. Edwards (Ed.), *Encyclopedia of social work* (19th ed., pp. 1055-1063). Washington, DC: National Association of Social Workers Press.

Individuals with Disabilities Education Act, PL 105-17 (20 U.S.C. 343, 1400-1491).

Johnston, L. D., O'Malley, P. M., Bachman, J. G., & Schulenberg, J. E. (2004). *Monitoring the future: National results on drug use: Overview of key findings, 2003* (NIH Publication No. 04-5506). Bethesda, MD: National Institute on Drug Abuse.

Kaufman, P., Alt., M. N., & Chapman, C. (2004). *Dropout rates in the United States: 2001.* [NCES 2005-046]. Washington, DC: National Center for Education Statistics.

Koppich, J. E. (1997). Considering non-traditional alternatives: Charters, private contracts, and vouchers. *Future of Children: Financing Schools, 7*(3), 96-111.

Larsen, L. J. (2003). *The foreign-born population in the United States: 2003.* Retrieved March 23, 2005, from http://www.census.gov

Lock, J., & Steiner, H. (1999). Gay lesbian and bisexual youth risks for emotional physical and social problems: Results from a community-based survey. *Journal of the American Academy of Child and Adolescent Psychiatry, 38*(3), 297-304.

Mandlawitz, M. (2002). Government relations report. *School Social Workers Association of America Mini Bell,* 1-3.

Mintzies, P,. & Hare, I. (1985). *The human factor: A key to excellence in education.* Washington, DC: National Association of Social Workers Press.

Monk, D. H., Pijanowski, J. C., & Hussain, S. (1997). How and where the education dollar is spent. *Future of Children: Financing Schools, 7*(3), 51-62.

Nabozny v. Podlesny, 92 F.3d 446 (7th Cir. 1996).

National Assembly on School-Based Health Care. (2000). *Creating access to care for children and youth: School-based health center census 1998-99.* Washington DC: Author.

National Campaign to Prevent Teenage Pregnancy. (2005). *Teen birth rates in the United States, 1940-2003*. Retrieved March 24, 2005, from http://www.Teenpregnancy.org

National Center for Education Statistics. (2001). *Dropout rate in the United States: 2001*. Retrieved March 24, 2005, from http://www.nces.ed.gov/pubsearch/pubsinfo.asp?pubid=2005046

National Center for Education Statistics. (2002). *Number and percentage distribution of charter schools and students, and percentage of charter schools and students by school origin status, by selected school characteristics: 1999-2000*. Retrieved March 28, 2005, from http://nces.ed.gov/programs/digest/d02/tables/PDF/table100.pdf

National Center for Education Statistics. (2003). *Total and current expenditures per pupil in fall enrollment in public elementary and secondary education, by function and state or jurisdiction: 2000-01*. Retrieved March 26, 2005, from http://nces.ed.gov/programs/digest/d03/tables/dt168.asp

National Center for Education Statistics. (2003). *The condition of education: Societal support for learning*. Washington, DC: Author.

National Commission on Children. (1991). *Beyond rhetoric: A new American agenda for children and families*. Washington, DC: Author.

Nord, C. W., Brimhall, D. A., & West, J. (1999). *Fathers' involvement in their children's schools* (NCES 98-09). Washington, DC: U.S. Department of Education, National Center for Education Statistics.

Olweus, D., Limber, S., & Mihalic, S. F. (1999). *Blueprints for violence prevention. Book nine: Bullying prevention program*. Boulder, CO: Center for the Study and Prevention of Violence.

Pennekamp, M. (1992). Toward school-linked and school-based human services for children and families. *Social Work in Education, 14*, 125-130.

Personal Responsibility and Work Opportunity Reconciliation Act of 1996, PL 104-193.

Rafferty, I. (2004). ACT and SAT scores remain stable in 2004. *Chronicle of Higher Education, 51*(30), A-36.

Resnick, M. D., Bearman, P. S., Blum, R. W., Bauman, K. E., Harris, K. M., Jones, J., et al. (1997). Protecting adolescents from harm: Findings from the National Longitudinal Study of Adolescent Health. *Journal of the American Medical Association, 278*, 823-832.

San Antonio Independent School District v. Rodrigues, 411 U.S. 1 (1973).

Samuels, C. A. (2005). District "bills" government on special education costs. *Education Week, 24*, 31.

Smith, T. M., Young, B. A., Bae, Y., Choy, S. P., & Alsalam, N. (1997). *The condition of education 1997* (NCES 97-3888). Washington, DC: U.S. Department of Education, National Center for Education Statistics.

Snyder, H. N., & Swahn, M. H. (2004). *Juvenile suicides: 1991-1998*. Washington, DC: Office of Juvenile Justice and Delinquency Prevention. Retrieved June 3, 2005, from http://ncjrs.org/html/ojjdp/196978/contents.html

Terman. D. L., & Behrman, R. E. (1997). Financing schools: Analysis and recommendations. *Future of Children: Financing Schools, 7*(3), 4-23.

U.S. Census Bureau. (2005). *Annual estimates of the resident population by selected age groups for the United States and States July, 2003*. Retrieved March 23, 2005, from http://www.census.gov

U.S. Census Bureau. (2000). *Adding diversity from abroad: The foreign born population, 2000*. Retrieved March 23, 2005, from http://www.census.gov

U.S. Census Bureau. (2001). *Deaths and death rates by leading cause of death: 2001.* Retrieved March 24, 2005, from http://www.census.gov/prod/2004pubs/04statab/ vitstat.pdf

United States Bureau of Criminal Justice, Bureau of Justice Statistics. (2003). *Indicators of school crime and safety.* [NCES No. 2004-004]. Washington, DC: Author.

U.S. Census Bureau. (2003). *Public education finances.* Washington DC: Author.

U.S. Department of Education. (2004). *Results agenda.* Washington DC: Author.

U.S. Department of Education. (1996). *Putting the pieces together: Comprehensive school-linked strategies for children and families.* Washington, DC: Author.

U.S. Department of Education. (1998). *Early warning, timely response: A guide to safe schools. Press report: Frequently asked questions.* Washington, DC: Author. (ERIC Document Reproduction Service No. ED418372).

U.S. Department of Health and Human Services, Administration for Children and Families. (2005). *Child maltreatment, 2003.* Washington DC: U.S. Government Printing Office.

U.S. Department of Health and Human Services. (1999). *The surgeon general's call to action to prevent suicide, 1999.* Washington, DC: Author.

U.S. Department of Health and Human Services (USDHHS). (1989). *Prevention and interventions in youth suicide.* Rockville, MD: Author.

U.S. Department of Health and Human Services, Office of the Assistant Secretary for Planning and Evaluation (USDHHS-ASPE). (2000). *Trends in the well-being of America's children and youth: 2000.* Washington, DC: U.S. Government Printing Office

Walberg, H. J., & Lai, J. (1999). Meta-analytic effects for policy. In G. J. Cizek (Ed.), *Handbook of educational policy* (pp. 418–454). San Diego, CA: Academic.

Wren, C. S. (1997, December 21). Survey suggests leveling off in use of drugs by students. *New York Times,* p. 24.

Youth Violence Project. (2003). *Violence in schools.* Retrieved March 24, 2005, from http://youthviolence.edschool.virginia.edu/violence-in-schools/national statistics.html

11

Educational Mandates for Children with Disabilities: School Policies, Case Law, and the School Social Worker

Brooke R. Whitted
Whitted and Cleary LLC

Malcolm C. Rich

Robert Constable
Loyola University, Chicago

- ◆ What Are the Educational Rights of Children with Disabilities?
- ◆ How Does the Special Education System Work?
- ◆ What Is the Role of the Local School System (LEA)?
- ◆ Who Is the Child with Disabilities?
- ◆ What Are Social Work Services in the Schools?
- ◆ What Is an Individualized Education Program (IEP)?
- ◆ What Is Special Education?
- ◆ What Are Related Services?
- ◆ What Services Must the School Provide?
- ◆ What Is Placement in the Least Restrictive Environment?
- ◆ What Are Placement Procedures?
- ◆ Can Students with Disabilities Be Suspended or Expelled?
- ◆ What Are Provisions for Mediation and for an Impartial Due Process Hearing?
- ◆ What Are Due Process and Judicial Review?

This chapter is one of several in the book that focus on the implementation for school social workers of the mandate to provide a free appropriate public education (FAPE) to children with disabilities. Here we provide an overview of the current law and its interpretation in court decisions. Chapter 9 focuses on the court decisions that defined the right. Chapter 12 focuses on clinical and educational program development for preschool children with disabilities. Section III will discuss the assessment process, least restrictive environment and inclusion, the social developmental study, and the individualized education program.

The Individuals with Disabilities Education Act (IDEA) and its accompanying regulations require that every state and the District of Columbia ensure FAPE is available to all children with disabilities. The education of unserved or underserved children with disabilities has a clear priority over the education of children already receiving services. Such services must be provided to all qualifying children with disabilities. A student must generally be able to benefit from appropriate services. There is no financial needs test. The act is heavily parent/guardian oriented and requires states to maximize parental involvement in educational decision making every step of the way. Parents of pupils with disabilities or the schools may invoke a formal administrative system for the resolution of disputes. Throughout this system, detailed steps of identification, evaluation, determination of eligibility, planning, service, and administrative appeals are set forth. The school social worker, as a school staff member, is an important figure throughout. School social workers, who inevitably work with children with disabilities and the special education system, need a working knowledge of the requirements of the act.

WHAT ARE THE EDUCATIONAL RIGHTS OF
CHILDREN WITH DISABILITIES?

Over a period of twenty-five years a cumulative body of law, court decisions, and policies has developed in relation to the educational rights of children with disabilities to a FAPE. These became summarized in IDEA and its amendments, such as PL 105-117, signed into law June 4, 1997, and now PL 108-446, the Individuals with Disabilities Education Improvement Act (IDEA-2004), signed into law on December 3, 2004. When we refer to the law, we are referring to legal principles in the law, codified in 20 United States Code, sections 1401-1468 (cited as 20 U.S.C. 1401-1468). When we refer to regulations, we are referring to 34 Code of Federal Regulations parts 300 and following (here cited as 34 C.F.R. 300 ff). These are frequently updated as the law and its regulations develop and can be found in any law library or on the Internet. In reading this chapter you may also wish to consult the footnotes for more detailed explanations of the law and case precedents. For the school social worker in the United States, the contents of this book furnish a general update on the most recent provisions of the law through 2004. It is important for social workers in the

United States to be familiar with this evolving body of law and its updates in order to design school social work roles that help the school respond to these mandates. As this book went to press, the most recent Individuals with Disabilities Education Improvement Act of 2004 (IDEA-2004) had not yet been integrated into the current U.S. Code (20 U.S.C.) or the Code of Federal Regulations (43 CFR). The law can be accessed in summary form at http://edworkforce. house.gov/issues/108th/education/idea/1350confsummary.htm. The bill itself is available from the Web site of the Council of Parent Attorneys and Advocates (COPAA) at www.copaa.org in a line-by-line comparison with IDEA prepared by Jess Butler for COPAA. When the new law and regulations are integrated into 20 U.S.C. and 43 CFR, you would find them in or close to the sections of the law or regulations cited in this chapter.

For the international reader, practicing in a different legal orbit, it is important to see the relation of law to school policy and from this to the school social worker's role. The difference in the U.S. legal tradition is the absence of a national education ministry, actively managing local schools. Instead, on the national level the emphasis is on law and policy development with different levels of policy and implementation at the state (SEA) and local (LEA) school levels. In every locality the legal context for schooling needs to be taken into account to develop the school social worker's role. An important part of this role is influencing the development of the school social worker's legal, organizational, and program context. A large part of the law deals with the protection of vulnerable groups. In any society it is out of this legal framework, as well as the educational mission of the school, that the school social worker's role is constructed.

In the face of some neglect of children with disabilities prior to 1968, the rights of children to a FAPE have had considerable development in the United States. Turnbull and Turnbull (1998) summarize this tradition, continuing through IDEA 1997 and IDEA 2004, in the form of six rights:

1. The right to attend school—the principle of *zero reject*. Each school-age person with a disability has the right to be educated in a system of FAPE. Agencies and professionals may not expel or suspend students for certain behaviors or without following certain procedures; they may not exclude students on the basis that they are incapable of learning; and they may not limit the access of students to school on the basis of their having contagious diseases.

2. The right to a fair appraisal of their strengths and needs—the principle of *nondiscriminatory evaluation*. Socioeconomic status, language, and other factors need to be discounted and must not bias the student's evaluation; agencies and professionals must obtain an accurate, nonbiased portrait of each student. Decisions need to be based on facts, not simply categories: on what students are doing and are capable of doing, in relation to behavioral outcomes individualized for the student. The resulting education would remedy the student's impairments and build on strengths.

3. The right to a *beneficial experience* in school—the principle of free appropriate public education—means that schools must individualize each

student's education, provide needed related services, engage in a fair process for determining what is appropriate for each student, and ensure that the student's education indeed confers a benefit. Education should have a positive outcome for each student. The emphasis of this discussion is not simply on provision of access to education but on adapting the system and on building capacities in the person with a disability so that certain results are attained.

4. The right to be *included* in the general education curriculum and other activities. The principle means that the schools must include the student in the general education program and may not remove a student from it unless the student cannot benefit from being in that program, even after the provision of supplementary aids and services and necessary related services.

5. The right to be treated fairly. The principle of *procedural due process* means that the school must provide certain kinds of information (notice and access to records) to students, special protection when natural parents are unavailable (surrogate parents), and access to a fair hearing process.

6. The right to be included in the decision-making process. The principle of *parent and student participation* means the schools must structure decision-making processes (including policy decisions on a statewide level) in such a way that parents and students have opportunities to affect meaningfully the education the students are receiving. A related principle of enhanced accountability to pupils and parents is moving in the direction of report cards related to individualized goals and educational programs.[1]

Building on this concept of educational rights, the term *free appropriate public education* means special education and related services that:

1. Have been provided at public expense, under public supervision and direction, and without charge;
2. Meet the standards of the state educational agency and secondary school educational agency;
3. Include an appropriate preschool, elementary, or secondary school education in the state involved; and
4. Are provided in conformity with a student's individualized education program. (20 U.S.C. 1401[8])

HOW DOES THE SPECIAL EDUCATION SYSTEM WORK?

It is important to understand the impact of laws, court decisions, and policies on state and local educational systems. To respect the rights of children with disabilities to a FAPE and to qualify for federal financial assistance under IDEA, a state must demonstrate that it "has in effect a policy that assures all handicapped children the right to a free appropriate, public education" (26 U.S.C. 412[l]). That policy must be written in the form of a "state plan" and is

---

1. Turnbull, H. R., and Turnbull, A. P., *Free appropriate public education: The law and children with disabilities* (pp. 273-274). Denver: Love.

subject to reapproval every three years by the U.S. Department of Education.[2] Children receiving no education are to have priority over those receiving some form of education (20 U.S.C. 1412[3]). Children with disabilities must be educated to the maximum extent appropriate with children who are not disabled. This is called the least restrictive environment mandate (20 U.S.C. 1412[5]). The FAPE required by IDEA must be tailored to the unique needs of each child through a document called an individualized education program (IEP), prepared at a formal meeting between a qualified representative of the local education agency (LEA), the child's teacher, the child's parents or guardian, and, where appropriate, the child.[3] Parental involvement and consultation in this process must be maximized.[4] IDEA also imposes on the states detailed procedural requirements, that is, a set of rules outlining exactly how the educational rights of children with disabilities are to be protected. The rights of parents to consent to the provision or termination of special education services, to question the decisions of educational personnel, and to invoke a highly specific administrative hearing process are all outlined in IDEA (20 U.S.C. 1415 et seq). Parents may request mediation or an impartial due process hearing to appeal virtually any educational decision.[5] Any party dissatisfied with the results of the initial due process hearing may request and receive an impartial review by the state agency[6] and if not satisfied with that review, may then go to court.[7]

---

2. 20 U.S.C. 1412; 20 U.S.C. 1413. The state plan describes the goals, programs, and timetables under which the state intends to educate children with disabilities within its borders.

3. 20 U.S.C. 1401 (18). The IEP must include at the minimum statements of present levels of educational performance, how the child's disability affects involvement and progress in the general curriculum, annual goals, short-term instructional objectives, specific services to be provided to the child, the extent to which the pupil will be able to be educated with nondisabled students, the projected date of initiation and anticipated duration of services, a statement of needed transition services, and various criteria for evaluating progress. 20 U.S.C. 1412(3), 1412(5), 1401(1), (19). IDEA 2004 projects an alternate assessment for pupils who cannot participate in the regular (grade level) assessment. Short-term objectives will be required only for pupils having an alternate assessment (H.R. 1350, 614(a) (2) A,B).

4. *Board of Education of the Hendrick Hudson Central School District, Westchester County, et al. v. Amy Rowley et al.*, U.S. 176, 73 L. Ed.2d 690, 102 S. Ct. 3034 (1982). Excluding parents from the process has, pursuant to Rowley, often been held by courts to be a "fatal flaw" committed by educators. *Spielberg v. Henrico County*, E.H.L.R. 441:178. E.H.L.R. refers to Education of the Handicapped Law Review (hereafter E.H.L.R.) (Washington, DC: CRR Publishing).

5. 20 U.S.C. 1415(b)(1)(D) and (E). Complaints can be brought "about any matter relating to" the child's evaluation and education.

6. Mayson by *Mayson v. Teague*, 749 F.2d 652 (1984).

7. 20 U.S.C. 1415(b)(2) and (c), 20 U.S.C. 11415(e)(2). A party may go to either state or federal court. Recently, plaintiffs filing in state court have been "removed" by the school district to the federal district court. This is only a good strategy where a state board of education seeks removal, as these entities are protected by Eleventh Amendment sovereign immunity, while local school districts are not protected. *Dellmuth v. Muth*, 109 S. Ct. 2397 (1989), *Gary A. v. New Trier High School District and the Illinois State Board of Education*, 796 F.2d 940 (1986.)

Although IDEA leaves to the states many details concerning development and implementation of particular programs, it imposes substantial requirements to be followed in the discharge of the states' responsibilities. Noncompliance with federal procedural requirements may be sanctioned by the withholding of federal dollars flowing to the offending agency.[8] For example, a state's educational system might be investigated by the U.S. Department of Education for failing to educate children in the least restrictive environment. Such a failure would be evidenced by a pattern of educating children with physical disabilities in separate facilities even though the children in question may have no problems other than the physical ones that challenge them. The federal law requires that education of children with disabilities be, to the maximum extent appropriate, with children without disabilities. The failure of a particular state to meet this requirement raises a risk of sanctions.

WHAT IS THE ROLE OF THE LOCAL SCHOOL SYSTEM (LEA)?

The law ultimately obligates the LEA to provide a FAPE with related services to all children with disabilities. The federal legal mandate requires the local school district to be the "agency of last resort" for the provision of specialized services to this population of children. Other child-serving agencies might engage in interagency squabbles concerning who should pay for or provide services. LEAs and the respective state boards of education are not able to engage in such fingerpointing.[9] Under the Illinois school code, for example, special education services not provided by another agency must be provided by the LEA or the state board of education.[10] Thus the educational sector—even in a time of shrinking resources—is and has been a consistent source of dollars for children's services.

WHO IS THE CHILD WITH DISABILITIES?

IDEA defines *a child with a disability*:

as a child evaluated . . . as having mental retardation, a hearing impairment including deafness, speech or language impairment, a visual impairment including blindness, a serious emotional disturbance, . . . an orthopedic impairment, autism, traumatic brain injury, other health impairment, a specific learning disability, deaf-blindness, or multiple disabilities, and who because of these impairments needs special education and related services. (34 C.F.R. 300.7)

---

8. 20 U.S.C. 1414(b)(2)(A). Noncompliance may also be sanctioned by judicial review. U.S.C. 1416.

9. *Parks v. Pavkovic*, 753 F.2d 1397 (7th. Cir. 1985). In the district court opinion, Judge Prentice Marshall said that such fingerpointing was one of the most heinous violations of federal law he could imagine.

10. Ill. Rev. State. Ch. 122 [14-8.02].

Eligibility runs from birth to age twenty-one. The key to eligibility is having a listed disability and needing special education and related services. Having a disability implies difficulty in dealing with one's environment and indeed with the very programs and supports intended to help. The purpose of IDEA cannot be achieved without a profession, such as school social work, that focuses on child, family, and learning environment, each in relation to the other, and that views the child as a whole.

WHAT ARE SOCIAL WORK SERVICES IN THE SCHOOLS?

Social work services in schools include:

1. Preparing a social or developmental history on a child identified as possibly having disabilities,
2. Group and individual counseling with the child and family,
3. Working with those problems in a child's living situation (home, school, and community) that affect the child's adjustment in school,
4. Mobilizing school and community resources to enable the child to learn as effectively as possible in his or her educational program, and
5. Assisting in developing positive behavioral intervention strategies. (34 C.F.R. 300.24 [13]; 20 U.S.C. 1402 [29])

Social work addresses the fit between schooling and the needs of children with disabilities and their parents. A particular group of children who experience difficulties in school, and usually need social work assistance, are those who are emotionally disturbed. Emotional disturbance is a condition exhibiting one or more of the following characteristics over a long period of time and to a marked degree, which adversely affects educational performance:

An inability to learn which cannot be explained by intellectual, sensory, or health factors;

An inability to build or maintain satisfactory interpersonal relationships with peers and teachers;

Inappropriate types of behavior or feelings under normal circumstances;

A general pervasive mood of unhappiness or depression;

A tendency to develop physical symptoms or fears associated with personal or school problems. (34 C.F.R. 300.7 [9])

WHAT IS AN INDIVIDUALIZED EDUCATION PROGRAM (IEP)?

The IEP is the blueprint for all that happens in the education of a child with disabilities. It is a series of guidelines for educators to follow in conferring educational benefit and a useful document for parents to follow in determining whether those benefits are being made available. School districts must write an

IEP before they can provide services (20 U.S.C. 1401 [18]). IDEA is quite detailed in its specification of the contents of this document (20 U.S.C. 1401 [19]).All IEPs must be reviewed at least every year.A new IEP needs to be written at least every three years.[11] Parents or guardians are always entitled to question IEPs through the due process procedures (20 U.S.C. 1414 [a][5]). Many state boards of education publish manuals on how to write an IEP, and all states have organizations and resource centers to assist parents and guardians in understanding the process of writing an IEP. The input of the social worker during the drafting of the IEP often has a substantial effect on the recommendations made, and social work services are often among the crucial "related services" in the IEP. School districts sometimes list their recommendations for the pupil prior to drafting an IEP. This is a significant procedural error. IDEA requires the IEP to be written first, on the logical assumption that recommendations for a particular educational setting and specific services cannot possibly be made until the needs of the child are determined.When recommendations are made before the IEP is drafted, this is sometimes a good indicator that school authorities are simply offering the program they have available, rather than creating a customized program to meet all of the needs of the child. It is legally improper and a violation of IDEA for recommendations to be based on administrative convenience, costs, waiting lists, or any factor other than the needs of the child with disabilities in question.[12]

The parent or guardian of a child covered by IDEA must be given prior notice whenever the school district proposes a change in the educational placement of a child, or a change in its provision of a FAPE for the child (20 U.S.C. 1415 [b][1][c]).This notice must, at the minimum, contain a complete description of available procedural safeguards, an official explanation for the change being proposed, and the reasons why other less restrictive options were rejected (20 U.S.C. 1415 [b][1][d]). The consent of a parent or guardian is required for the initiation or termination of educational benefits (34 C.F.R. 300.505). It is good practice to secure this consent for a reevaluation and/or change of the program.The parent has the right to ask for revisions in the child's IEP (34 C.F.R. 300.350). Notification of proposed changes, regardless of their magnitude, is required in all instances under IDEA because the right to demand a hearing is always vested in the parent or guardian who disagrees with the changes (20 U.S.C. 1415 [b][1][E] to [d]). "Complete failure" to implement an IEP has been held to constitute a change in the child's educational placement, as well as a failure to provide a FAPE.[13] An IEP is not, however, a contract, nor is it a guarantee that the child will achieve the results contemplated.

---

11. IDEA-2004 now recommends this take place at least once every three years "unless the parent and LEA agree that a reevaluation is unnecessary" (H.B. 1350 614 [a][2] A, B).

12. *Timothy W. and Cynthia v. Rochester, N.H., School District*, EHLR 441:393. 875 F.2d 954 (1989).

13. *Lunceford v. District of Columbia Board of Education*, 7455 F.2d 157, 1582 (D.C. Cir. 1984).

WHAT IS SPECIAL EDUCATION?

Special education and related services are defined individually for each pupil by a multidisciplinary team, that is, in each particular situation and for each child. The team, which must include the parents, prepares the resulting IEP. The need for special education and related services is a key to the definition of the child with a disability. Thus because of that disability and based on a complete, multifaceted, nondiscriminatory assessment (hereafter assessment), there is a need for special education and related services. According to IDEA, special education means specially designed instruction, at no cost to the parent, to meet the unique needs of a child with a disability. This includes classroom instruction, instruction in physical education, home instruction, and instruction in hospitals and institutions (34 C.F.R. 300.26).

WHAT ARE RELATED SERVICES?

Related services means transportation and such developmental, corrective, and other supportive services as are required to assist a child with a disability to benefit from special education. The term includes such services as transportation, speech pathology and audiology, psychological services, physical and occupational therapy, recreation, early identification and assessment of disabilities in children, counseling services, and medical services for diagnostic or evaluation purposes. It also includes school health services,[14] social work services in schools, and parent counseling and training (34 C.F.R. 300.24).

WHAT SERVICES MUST THE SCHOOL PROVIDE?

The LEA is obligated to provide the special education and related services (or for certain other children the "supplementary aids and services") required so that the pupil can attain the objectives stated in the IEP. The components of an IEP are special education, related services, supplementary aids and services, program modifications, and personal support. These are to benefit the student so that he or she may:

1. Advance appropriately toward attaining the annual goals,
2. Be involved and progress in the general curriculum and participate in extracurricular activities and other nonacademic activities, and

---

14. Except nondiagnostic medical services, such as ongoing medical treatment. The federal government says medical services are defined by who must provide the services, not by the specific service. If a particular nondiagnostic medical service can be provided only by a physician, the LEA need not cover it as a related service. 20 U.S.C. 1401(17); also see *Kelly McNair v. Oak Hills Local School District*, E.H.L.R. 441:381 (6th Cir. 1988-89), in which the court held that special transportation need not be provided to a deaf child because the need for it was not related to her disabling condition. The statute specifically required a connection between the related service and the unique needs of the child.

3. Be educated and participate with other children with disabilities and nondisabled children in those extracurricular and nonacademic activities. (20 U.S.C. 1414 [d][1][a][3])

The mandate for use of related services is broad, going beyond special education to include what is necessary for the child to participate in general education and extracurricular activities.

Social Work Services

Under IDEA the educational sector is required to pay for related services, which would include any services required to assist a child to benefit from special education. A key issue has been what level of related services is necessary for a child to "benefit" from special education. The *Rowley* case involved a hearing-impaired girl who understood only about half of what was occurring in class. Nevertheless, Amy Rowley received As and Bs because of her high intelligence.[15] Her parents wanted the school to provide a full-time sign language interpreter to attend class with her, but the Supreme Court held that the student was not so entitled, as she was already receiving an "educational benefit" without the interpreter.

Rowley generally is used by schools to back up the argument that they are not required to provide the "best" education—only an education that is minimally appropriate and available. Social workers should likewise be aware that the recommendations contained in their reports should address services necessary to minimally enable the child to benefit from educational programming. For instance, some depressed students may need nonmedical psychotherapy to attend to instructional tasks. In some cases such psychotherapy has been held to be a related service that must be provided by the schools.[16] The distinction between a fundable service and a nonfundable service turns on whether mental health services, psychotherapy, or social work services (as they are defined earlier) would assist a particular student to benefit from special education. In a number of decisions the courts further defined a "service-benefit" standard.[17]

---

15. *Rowley,* 458 U.S. at 184.

16. *Max M. v. Thompson,* 592 F. Supp. 1450 (1984). This student's neurotic anxieties prevented him from attending school, and the school social worker, among others, recommended psychotherapy. The school district did not provide the therapy. The parents paid for two years of treatment and then asked for reimbursement from the district. The court held that the school was responsible for the services to the extent that a nonphysician could provide them. The district, then, had to reimburse parents for the equivalent of psychologist-provided therapy, a lower amount than the actual cost, since a psychiatrist had been the therapist. See also *In the Matter of "A" Family,* 602 P.2d 157 (S.C. Mont.), which held family therapy to be a related service; and *Gary B. v. Cronin,* 625 F.2d 563, n. 15: "While psychotherapy may be related to mental health, it may also be required before a child can derive any benefit from education."

17. See *Papacoda v. Connecticut,* 528 F. Supp. 68 (D. Conn. 1981). *Vander Malle v. Ambach,* 673 F.2d 49 (2nd Cir. 1982), further proceedings 667 F. Supp. 1015 (S.D.N.Y. 1987). *Mrs. B. v. Milford Board of Education,* 103 F.3d 1114 (2nd Cir. 1997).

The standard involves evaluating two criteria: (1) whether the program is designed to improve the student's educational performance, and (2) whether the program is based on the student's classification as having an emotional disturbance.[18]

Psychotherapy

On the other hand, in another decision it was held that the service-benefit standard for determining whether psychotherapy is a related service is overly broad and inordinately encompassing. When the justification of the services is only psychological improvement, the LEA is not responsible for providing mental health services to the student.[19] It must be clearly demonstrated that social work services would assist students to benefit from special education. In school social work the general language for demonstrating this is found in the previous definition of school social work services. For many years, school social workers have defined their practice in relation to education in both practice and in theory, as the present book will attest. Further court decisions will clarify these boundaries.

Children Unable to Benefit from Education

There are several thousand children in the United States so lacking in brain capacity that they are unable to benefit from any educational services, no matter how elementary they are.[20] The U.S. Supreme Court has declined to review a hotly contested case in which a child "lacking any cortex" was held to be entitled to related services even though he was unlikely to benefit from services.[21] The *Timothy W.* case originated in Rochester, New Hampshire, where the school district argued that providing any services to such a hopelessly disabled child would be a waste of tax dollars better spent on less disabled children.[22] In their pleadings to the Court, the attorneys for the schools, astonished by the decision of the appellate court, said that such decisions requiring school personnel to provide services to children who cannot benefit from any services "may have

---

18. See also the discussion of these points in Turnbull and Turnbull, pp. 161–164.

19. *Clovis Unified School District v. California Office of Admin. Hearings*, 903 F.2d 635 (9th Cir. 1990).

20. R. Rothstein, Educational rights of severely and profoundly handicapped children, *Nebraska Law Review* 61 (1982): 586. See also *Parks v. Pavkovic*, 753 F.2d at 1405, in which the Court speculated about what type of child might not ever be able to benefit and concluded that such a child would have to be in a coma.

21. E.H.L.R. 441:393; *Timothy W. and Cynthia W. v. Rochester, N.H. School District*, E.H.L.R. Summary and Analysis, pp. 265-266 (December 1989). Federal appellate court citation: 875 F.2d 954 (1989); U.S. District Court citation: E.H.L.R. 509:141 (1987). See also article by B. R. Whitted, Educational benefits after *Timothy W.:* Where do we go from here? *Illinois Administrators of Special Education Newsletter,* Winter 1990.

22. 875 F.2d at 954.

unfortunate consequences for families of uneducable children because [they] raise false hopes, which in turn often lead to bitterness and disillusionment" and ultimately to intensive family therapy or marital counseling.[23] The U.S. Supreme Court will not, however, "read in" any exceptions to IDEA that are not present—and no exception was drawn for so-called uneducable children with disabilities.[24]

If a child needs a residential setting in order to benefit from education, the schools must pay for such a setting, and there can be no charges to the parents or guardian.[25] If other agencies are active and are able to pay part of the cost, such payments are allowed as long as such agencies do not charge the parent.[26] When a school district writes an IEP stating that another agency is to provide some of the services, the school district is still the "agency of last resort," and parents may rightfully turn to the schools for recompense.[27]

A well-known U.S. Supreme Court case has held that clean intermittent catheterization (CIC) is a related service.[28] Amber Tatro needed CIC several times daily in order to stay in class and to benefit from educational services. In *Tatro* the schools argued that CIC was a medical service and therefore not a related service. The U.S. Supreme Court did not agree, noting that CIC was not exclusively within the province of physicians and could be administered easily by the school nurse. The school district was required to provide this service.

WHAT IS PLACEMENT IN THE LEAST RESTRICTIVE ENVIRONMENT?

One further principle, that of *least restrictive environment*, governs the all-important placement process. This principle is defined in the law as follows:

> To the maximum extent appropriate, children with disabilities . . . are educated with children who are nondisabled, and that special classes, separate schooling, or other removal of children with disabilities from the regular education environment occurs only if the nature or severity of the disability is such that education in regular classes with the use of supplementary aids and services cannot be achieved satisfactorily. (20 U.S.C. 1412 [a][5][A])

---

23. *Petition for Writ of Certiorari to the United States Supreme Court of Rochester NH School Dist. v. Timothy W. and Cynthia W.*, E.H.L.R. Summary and Analysis, 226 (November 1989).

24. *Honig v. Doe*, 484 U.S. 305, 108 S. Ct. 592 (1988). Note that the Supreme Court, in refusing to review a decision, does not in the process issue an opinion covering its reasons. The citation in this note refers to the Court's tendency to read IDEA rigidly, and in *Honig*, it refused to read in a dangerousness exception to the principle that restricts exclusion of pupils with disabilities from school.

25. *Parks v. Pavkovic*, 753 F.2d 11397 (7th Cir. 1985), cert. denied at 473 U.S. 906 (1985). Interprets 34 C.F.R. 300.302, among other regulatory provisions.

26. See, the Disabled Children's Program of the Social Security Act, 42 U.S.C. 1382 et seq.

27. *Kattan v. District of Columbia*, E.H.L.R. 441:207.

28. *Amber Tatro et al. v. Irving (Tx.) Independent School District et al.*, 4568 U.S. 883 (1984).

This principle is extremely important in achieving the general purposes of IDEA. Related services in the IEP (including the school social worker's contribution) are intended to assist the pupil to advance appropriately toward attaining his or her annual goals, to be involved and progress in the general curriculum, to participate in extracurricular and other nonacademic activities, and to be educated and to participate with other children with disabilities and nondisabled children in the general curriculum. The principle of inclusion presumes that the child with disabilities should participate in the general curriculum. It requires the IEP to explain the extent, if any, to which the child will not participate with children without disabilities in regular classes and in extracurricular and other nonacademic activities (20 U.S.C. 1414).

However, the term *inclusion* is not to be found anywhere in the IDEA legal mandate. In recent years, some advocates have said that the special education system is not working, and that to benefit from educational services, students must be "fully included" in the mainstream. Many have gone so far as to present this concept as a "part of the law" and to tell parents this new law says they must cooperate in the full mainstreaming of their children. Nothing could be further from the truth. The law governing the least restrictive environment has not changed and merely requires that to the maximum extent appropriate, children with disabilities should be educated with children without disabilities. Although there is a presumption that the child with disabilities should participate in the general curriculum when appropriate, no federal law has ever mandated "full inclusion" without consideration of educational needs. Inclusion as such, discussed in chapter 23, is often a matter of state policy. Federal law requires all school districts to make available a full continuum of alternatives from the least restrictive (such as complete mainstreaming with one resource period per day) to most restrictive (private residential placement). Part of the school social worker's role in these cases is to work with pupil, parents, and the school to construct this environment.

WHAT ARE PLACEMENT PROCEDURES?

Placement procedures make the connection between the assessment and the IEP. Disabilities are inevitably connected with social functioning in one way or another. If assessments are to be complete, multifaceted, and nondiscriminatory, as the law prescribes, the school social worker should participate in most assessments. In some school districts the social worker is the person responsible for the social developmental study of the child. The social worker's understanding of the child's current adaptation to home and school environments, the child's previous developmental steps, and the culture and functioning of the family is essential to any assessment. In the same vein, the annual goals for the child, the corresponding educational program, and related services, as developed in the IEP, often explicitly involve tasks for the social worker with the child, with the family, and with education professionals. In the process of interpreting evaluation data and planning an IEP, the multidisciplinary team needs to:

1. Draw on information from a variety of sources, including adaptive and achievement tests, teacher recommendations, physical condition, social or cultural background, and adaptive behavior;
2. Ensure that information obtained from all of these sources is documented and carefully considered;
3. If a child needs special education and related services, an IEP must be developed for the child. (34 C.F.R. 300.535)

CAN STUDENTS WITH DISABILITIES BE SUSPENDED OR EXPELLED?

On January 20, 1988, the U.S. Supreme Court issued its opinion in *Honig v. Doe*.[29] This strongly worded case set forth guidelines that educators have actively and hotly debated ever since. Two California cases related to *Honig* involved violent, acting-out pupils who were suspended "indefinitely" and later expelled under the California statute that allowed indefinite suspensions. The school district's attorneys argued, when the cases finally reached the judicial level, that Congress could not possibly have intended that the schools be required to keep serving dangerous, emotionally disturbed pupils, when staff members and other students were at peril. The Court held that Congress "very much meant to strip schools of the unilateral authority they had traditionally employed to exclude disabled students, particularly emotionally disturbed students, from schools."[30] The U.S. Supreme Court, in this case, demonstrated clearly its reluctance to read into IDEA meanings never expressed by Congress.

The net effect of this case is that a school may not remove a pupil with a disability from school for behavior that is a manifestation of the disabling condition without the consent of the parents.[31] If the parents refuse to consent to a relocation of the child, the school's only recourse is to have its attorneys file a petition in a court of proper jurisdiction to obtain the permission of a judge. School authorities may contend that the behavior is "unrelated" to the disabling condition, but such contentions, as a basis for expulsion or exclusion, leave edu-

---

29. *Honig v. Doe*, 484 U.S. 305, 108 S. Ct. 592 (1988), interpreting the "stay put" provision of the Education of the Handicapped Act, 20 U.S.C. 1415(e)(3). The authors strongly recommend that social work students read this case in its entirety. *Honig* is a powerful tool for advocates of special education, and a thorough knowledge of the procedures set forth by the Supreme Court is crucial.

30. 484 U.S. at 321.

31. If the LEA, the parent, and relevant members of the IEP team determine that the conduct was a manifestation of the child's disability, PL 108-446 (IDEA 2004) requires that the IEP team conduct a functional behavioral assessment and implement a behavioral intervention plan (see chapters 19 and 24). Except for special circumstances outlined above in the text, the child is returned to the original placement (H.R.1350, Sec 615[k][1][F]).

cators on very unstable legal ground.[32] Almost invariably, a court will determine that the exclusion is a "change of placement" pursued outside the mandatory multidisciplinary process and therefore in violation of federal law. The Supreme Court has clearly expressed its feeling that allowing schools to suspend pupils who are dangerous to themselves and others for up to ten days cumulatively per school year gives educational authorities sufficient time to seek parental consent, negotiate alternatives, or go to court. The 1997 amendments to IDEA have created certain circumstances (students bringing guns to school, etc.) where the school may go beyond the ten-day limit, possibly up to forty-five days.[33]

Social workers should become familiar with the basic law of suspension and expulsion of pupils with disabilities, because they may find themselves in the position of mediating disputes between schools and families of disabled students.[34] Moreover, social workers are commonly called as experts in due process hearings for the purpose of establishing whether the behavior in question is or is not related to the pupil's disabling condition. Finally, current law relating to suspension and expulsion is a powerful tool for families of the disabled to persuade school authorities to consider more restrictive alternatives for the child, such as private extended-day school programs or residential placement, when appropriate.

WHAT ARE PROVISIONS FOR MEDIATION AND FOR AN IMPARTIAL DUE PROCESS HEARING?

It is not surprising that there could be differences between parents and others on the multidisciplinary team over a possible recommended placement for a child. In these circumstances the due process protection of the Fifth and the Fourteenth Amendments to the United States Constitution demands more formal procedures. After all, a civil right is being defined. It was the intent of the framers of PL 105-17 that parents and educators be encouraged to "work out

---

32. Yell, M. L. (1990) *Honig v. Doe*: The Supreme Court addresses the suspension and expulsion of handicapped students, *Exceptional Children 56*, 69; also see Yell, M. L. (1990) The use of corporal punishment, suspension, expulsion, and time out with behavioral disordered students in public schools; legal considerations, *Journal of Behavior Disorders, 15*, 2.

33. IDEA 2004 adds "serious bodily injury upon another person" to the list of behaviors that can lead to a forty-five-calendar-day removal. If a student with a disability engages in behavior leading to serious bodily injury of another person while on the school premises, the school can place the student in an alternative education setting for up to forty-five days.

34. For further information on mediation, see Gallant, C. B. (1980). Mediation: A unique due process procedure which utilizes social skills. In R. J. Anderson, M. Freeman, and R. L. Edwards (Eds.), *School social work and PL 94-142: The Education for All Handicapped Act.* (Washington, DC: National Association of Social Workers). Most of the mediation systems have been quite effective. Frequently, social workers are called upon to act as impartial mediators as well as to utilize their skills in facilitating communication between the school and family.

their differences by using nonadversarial means" (*Congressional Record*, May 12, 1997, p. S4298). The IDEA 1997 and IDEA 2004 amendments prescribe a two-step process to resolve disputes prior to taking them to the courts. The first step is mediation. The second step is the impartial due process hearing. In most cases, it is only after these steps have been taken, and the issue is still unresolved, that the case would go to court.

Mediation is a voluntary process conducted by a "qualified and impartial mediator who is trained in effective mediation techniques" (20 U.S.C. 1415 [e]). Mediation cannot be used to deny or delay a parent's right to an impartial due process hearing. The state education agency usually has a list of approved mediators and would carry the cost of the mediation process. Any agreement reached by the parties to the dispute would be set forth in a written mediation agreement. Discussions in the mediation process are confidential and cannot be used as evidence in subsequent due process hearings or civil proceedings. Both parties may be required to sign a confidentiality pledge prior to the mediation process (20 U.S.C. 1415 [e][A through G]).

The *impartial due process hearing* is conducted by either the state education agency or the LEA, although not by an employee involved with the education of the child. It is a somewhat more formal process than mediation. Any evaluation completed in relation to the pupil must be disclosed at least five days prior to the hearing. There are procedural safeguards: the right to be accompanied or advised by counsel and by experts, the right to present evidence and confront and to cross-examine and to compel the attendance of witnesses, the right to a verbatim record, and the right to written findings of fact and decisions. If the hearing is conducted by the LEA, its outcome may be appealed to the state education agency, where another hearing may take place. If the problem is not resolved at this point, it may be brought to court (20 U.S.C. 1415 [f] [g]). During due process hearings the child's placement would remain the same unless he or she has not been admitted to public school. In the latter case the child would be, with the parents' permission, placed in the public school until the completion of the proceedings.

WHAT ARE DUE PROCESS AND JUDICIAL REVIEW?

Once the second review is completed, any party dissatisfied with the result may appeal it to either state or federal court (20 U.S.C. 1415 [e][2]) by filing a lawsuit against the other party, requesting appropriate relief.[35] It is important to

---

35. A practical note: If the district loses, there is a fair degree of reluctance on the part of the school boards to proceed with a lawsuit. One reason is that the child usually has to be sued as a "necessary party." Another reason is expense. Insurance carriers for districts resist providing coverage for these matters, so a school board must vote to proceed knowing that the district will expend precious local dollars with no hope of recoupment if the district loses. Finally, even if the district wins on the administrative level, if it is sued by the parents, the insurance carrier will resist cover-

note that the "stay put" provision operates while all proceedings are taking place (20 U.S.C. 1415 [e][3]).This provision requires that the child remain in his or her then-current placement during such time as due process proceedings are pending. During this time, the district must pay for all educational services in the then-current placement. When certain behaviors occur, the school may place the student in an alternative education setting for up to forty-five calendar days. In these instances, the stay-put placement is this alternative setting.

The *Burlington* case clearly provides that even if the parent loses at each stage of the process, the district cannot obtain reimbursement from the parent.[36] The stay-put provision is thus a powerful tool for parents if proceedings commence when the pupil is in an educational setting that satisfies the parents. Most commonly, the child will be in a school-funded residential placement while the district seeks to return him or her to a less restrictive setting. If the parents request due process at this point, the child must remain in the residential setting at district expense during the pendency of all proceedings, through and including appellate court review.

Conversely, when the current placement is one that the parents feel is not appropriate, the stay-put provision operates to the benefit of the school district. In this instance, the parents' goal is to effect an alternative placement that they and their experts feel is more appropriate than the current setting, whereas the school district usually seeks to maintain the status quo.The school district continues to pay the cost of the child's educational placement, regardless of who requests due process.[37] For younger pupils entering school for the first time, the

---

age for any reimbursement costs or Protection Act attorney fees, since these are not "damages." *Tonya K. v. Chicago Public Schools et al.*, 551 F. Supp. 1107 (1988).The greatest pressure on a district for settlement, then, is at the end point of the administrative proceedings. The IDEA 2004 allows a prevailing school district to recover their reasonable attorney's fees if a court determines that the parents' action in filing a due-process action is "frivolous, unreasonable or without foundation." Courts can also levy a fee against the parents if their action is deemed to have been brought for an improper purpose, such as "to harass, to cause unnecessary delay, or to needlessly increase the cost of litigation."When parents prevail they may be able to recover their attorney's fees, but some federal courts have ruled that parents who prevail through private settlement agreements with school districts are not entitled to attorney's fees. On the other hand, under the IDEA 2004 the prevailing party, whether parent or school district will be able to collect the cost of attorney's fees (H.R. 1350, sec. 615 [I][3][B]).

36. See *Burlington School Committee v. Department of Education*, 471 U.S. 359 (1985).There have been instances, however, where school districts have sought reimbursement. In November 2003, for example, a federal district court in Illinois ruled in favor of the parents in an action where the school district was seeking to be reimbursed for transportation costs under stay-put (*Aaron M.v.Yomtoob*, 38 EHLR 122 [2003]). In the court's ruling, allowing school districts reimbursement of monies during stay-put periods would have a chilling effect on parents exercising their rights under the school law.

37. Note here that it is not just parents who can request due process. Schools sometimes seek to provide a service that the parents oppose. For instance, the district may want to place the child in a classroom for the retarded, while the parents may feel that their child is not retarded, but learning disabled.The parents' refusal to consent to the "MR" placement may be met with the district's

"current" placement is interpreted by most states to be the setting in which the child would be placed in the absence of any disability. For a student with disabilities transferring from one school district to another, the current placement is determined by the student's most recent IEP.

Legislation and case law on the civil right to a FAPE for children with disabilities have created new structures of service for these children. The social worker's services are framed in a developing body of law. It is important to understand that this law is not simply a set of procedures. It places a mandate on the school district and on the social worker to provide services that will enable children with disabilities and their families to survive in an initially unequal struggle. Here the language of the law can be translated into the language of service. The more familiar social workers are with both languages, the more able they will be to translate them into services that can redress this inequality.

---

request for due process. From a liability point of view, this is the only alternative for districts in such a position. Parents are frequently unable to accept that their child is so low functioning. The social worker may be called upon to assist the parents in working through their shame and guilt, among other feelings.

12

Family-Centered Services to Infants and Toddlers with or at Risk for Disabilities: IDEA 2004, Part C

Kathleen Kirk Bishop
Wheelock College

◆ Historical Perspective
◆ Mandate versus Choice of Services
◆ Analyses of Selected Aspects of the Law
◆ Requirements for a Statewide System
◆ Developing Best Practice Models
◆ Part C's Continuing Impact

This chapter on Part C of the Individuals with Disabilities Education Improvement Act of 2004 (IDEA 2004) has a threefold purpose. It presents a brief summary of key parts of the law with the greatest relevance for social work education and practice. It suggests areas where social workers can assume practice and leadership roles in the continued interpretation and implementation of the law, and it seeks to describe and highlight best social work practice with infants, toddlers, and their families.

HISTORICAL PERSPECTIVE

Part C continues to pose challenges to professionals and families to go beyond their traditional roles and to work collaboratively with one another, in health, education, social services, mental health, and other public and private agencies (Bishop, 1987). The precursor to IDEA 2004's Part C was signed into law by Congress in 1986 as PL 99-457, Part H. Part H signaled a new concern for the health and well-being of infants and young children at risk for/with disabilities and their families. It created a discretionary program to help states plan and implement statewide, comprehensive, coordinated, multidisciplinary, interagency systems of early intervention services for all eligible infants and toddlers from birth to 3 years and their families.

Perhaps the most unique and groundbreaking aspect of this legislation was the initiation of a paradigm shift in the way professionals would provide services to families. This paradigm shift is represented mostly clearly by the requirement that an individualized family service plan (IFSP) be developed, rather than the more traditional individualized educational program (IEP). The requirement for an IFSP recognizes that families are essential partners in all aspects of the care of their children. Thus any IFSP that is developed requires professionals to collaborate with families in the planning, design, and implementation of service systems. The requirement encourages interprofessional and collaborative practices, recognizes and supports the strengths of families, and encourages the delivery of services in the natural environments of infants and toddlers. All social workers who work with the birth-to-3-years age group of children and their families are essential partners in the implementation of this legislation, whether they are in hospitals, early intervention programs, schools, child care and after school programs, or public and private child welfare agencies.

MANDATE VERSUS CHOICE OF SERVICES

IDEA 2004 provides formula funding on a voluntary basis for all states to fully implement a comprehensive, multidisciplinary, interagency, statewide system of early intervention services for infants and toddlers with disabilities and their families. States are not required to participate in the program. In addition, they are not required to include infants and toddlers at risk for developmental delay in the state definition of whom they will serve. What this means is that some states may, and have, excluded *at-risk* groups from their definition of the population to be served, and some states may choose not to accept the funds and implement the program.

For social workers Part C is a moral mandate. It is legislation that can be used to leverage services to historically underrepresented populations, particularly minority, low-income, inner-city, and rural populations. It is also legislation that can be used to support states that have higher-than-average populations of infants and toddlers with high infant mortality rates and high rates of children living in poverty. There is a major emphasis on prevention. Thus, social workers must use their advocacy skills to implement Part C and to make sure that infants and toddlers who live in poverty or with disabilities have the same opportunities for health and well-being as all infants and toddlers.

ANALYSES OF SELECTED ASPECTS OF THE LAW

This discussion is limited to selected aspects of IDEA 2004 in relation to infants and toddlers at risk of disabilities. A developed discussion of educational mandates and policies of Part C can also be found in chapters 9, 11, 17, and 24. This section explores several key components of the law and the regulations: who will be served, early intervention services, requirements for a statewide system, procedural safeguards, the individualized family service plan (IFSP), and service coordination. These components of the law have major implications for social work practice.

It is important to understand the philosophy of this act, as it was originally authorized and subsequently revised. Perhaps the philosophy is best reflected in the fact that the word *families* is mentioned at least thirty-one times in the original 1986 legislation. The family focus continues in subsequent versions. The opening policy statement of the current law sets its major focus on families and on prevention[1] (sec. 631 [a]):

> Congress finds that there is an urgent and substantial need to enhance the capacity of families to meet the special needs of infants and toddlers with disabilities, to minimize developmental delay, and to recognize the significant brain development that occurs during a child's first three years of life. (sec. 631(a))

The focus on families signals a change in philosophy for early childhood intervention services from child centered to family centered. Services to infants and toddlers with disabilities are to be provided within the context of their families and other natural environments.

This family-centered philosophy recognizes the family as the central presence and support in the child's life, while service systems and personnel change. It suggests recognition, respect, and support for the crucial role that family members play in the daily care and nurture of their children. It directs professionals to work as partners with families in securing the best possible early intervention services for their children. The principles of family-centered services and family-professional collaboration guide social workers as they participate in the implementation of all aspects of Part C services, whether one is working directly with children and families or developing policy, programs,

---

1. Quotes from the law have adapted its technical language to the needs of the text. For exact quotes see 20 U.S.C. 1400 et seq in the appropriate section.

practice guidelines, and/or evaluation strategies. In whatever arena social workers participate, families' voices and experience are to be central in all aspects of providing services, resources, and supports.

Who Will Be Served?

In the context of the law, infants and toddlers with disabilities are defined as children under 3 years of age who need early intervention services because they are experiencing delays in cognitive, physical, communication, social or emotional development, or adaptive development, or they may have a diagnosed physical or mental condition that has a high probability of resulting in developmental delay. Beyond this, developmental delay takes the meaning given such terms by the state. Each state is required to adopt a definition of developmental delay, as comprehensive or as restrictive as it wishes. The *at-risk* infant or toddler means an individual less than 3 years of age who would be at risk of experiencing a substantial developmental delay if early intervention services were not provided to the individual (sec. 632[1]). Defining risk and developmental delay remains a pressing challenge for each state and for children and their families. Eligibility in such categories could include children who are biologically, socially, emotionally, medically, or environmentally at risk.

Early Intervention Services

The term *early intervention services* means developmental services that are designed to meet the developmental needs of an infant or toddler with a disability *as identified by the IFSP team* (sec. 632[4][C]) in any of the above areas as defined by the state. These services need to meet the standards of the state in which the services are provided. Services are diverse, reflecting the complex needs at this age level. They include:

1. Family training, counseling, and home visits;
2. Special instruction;
3. Speech pathology and audiology services, and sign language and cued language services;
4. Occupational therapy;
5. Physical therapy;
6. Psychological services;
7. Service coordination services;
8. Medical services only for diagnostic and evaluation purposes;
9. Early identification, screening, and assessment services;
10. Health services necessary to enable the infant or toddler to benefit from other early intervention services;
11. Social work services;
12. Vision services;

13. Assistive technology devices and assistive technology services;
14. Transportation and related costs that are necessary to enable an infant or toddler and the infant's or toddler's family to receive services. (sec. 632[4][C-E])

These services need to conform with the IFSP. They need to be provided in natural environments, including the home and community settings in which children without disabilities participate (sec. 632[4][E]).

REQUIREMENTS FOR A STATEWIDE SYSTEM

It is up to each state to develop the early intervention system that best suits its needs. In general, a statewide system of coordinated, comprehensive, multidisciplinary, interagency programs providing appropriate early intervention services to these children would include the following components:

1. A rigorous definition of the term "developmentally delayed" that will be used by the state in carrying out programs;
2. A policy that ensures that appropriate early intervention services are available to all infants and toddlers with disabilities and their families, including American Indian infants and toddlers and their families residing on reservations geographically located in the state;
3. A timely, comprehensive, multidisciplinary evaluation of the functioning of each infant or toddler to assist appropriately in their development;
4. An IFSP including coordination of services;
5. A comprehensive child-find system, including a system for making referrals to service providers;
6. A public awareness program focusing on early identification of infants and toddlers with disabilities
7. A central directory that includes early intervention services, resources and experts available in the state, and research and demonstration projects being conducted;
8. A comprehensive system of personnel development and standards for training;
9. Procedural safeguards;
10. A state interagency coordinating council; and
11. Policies and procedures to ensure that to the maximum extent appropriate early intervention services are provided in natural environments. (from sec 635 [a][1-16])

Members of the State Interagency Coordinating Council are appointed by the governor. In making these appointments the governor should ensure that the membership reasonably represents the population of the state. The composition should include at least 20 percent parents of infants or toddlers with disabilities, and at least 20 percent providers of early intervention services. In addition, members of state agencies, Head Start, the state legislature, and professional education would be involved.

The law delegates an important policy agenda to the council. It advises and assists the "lead agency" (determined in each state) in the identification of sources of support for early intervention programs. It deals with the assignment of financial responsibility to the appropriate agency, and the promotion of interagency agreements. It assists the lead agency in the preparation of applications and amendments to policies. It advises and assists the state education agency regarding the transitions of toddlers with disabilities to preschool and other appropriate services. It prepares and submits an annual report to the governor on the status of early intervention programs within the state (sec. 641 [a-e]).

The Individualized Family Service Plan (IFSP)

The IFSP is the key document governing provision and evaluation of services to individual children and their families. As such, it models family involvement in planning and in family-centered and collaborative practice. Revolutionary in its conception, it addresses in a single plan the child and family as a unit, regardless of who delivers and who pays for the services. It reflects family-professional collaboration that honors the wishes of the family. It is first of all a family-directed assessment of the resources, priorities, and concerns of the family. Building on this, it identifies the resources, supports, and services necessary to enhance the family's capacity to meet the developmental needs of the infant or toddler. The IFSP requires collaboration with the family on the identification of major outcomes expected for the child and family, and building on that, a clear and specific statement of the services to be provided to the infant or toddler and the family. Although there may be a tendency to see the IFSP as another form of an individualized education program (IEP), it is important to conceptualize the IFSP differently. The IFSP is not an IEP with a couple of family goals added, nor is it a group of plans from a variety of agencies located in a single folder labeled "IFSP."

The components of the IFSP are described in chapter 24. A major goal of the IFSP is to ensure that the family is an integral part of the plan from the beginning of its development to the end of its implementation. For school social workers, whose orientation would put them in a leadership position in this process, these requirements translate into the need for family-centered communication and interventions. There is a considerable body of literature pertaining to the value of family-centered approaches to children and families. Many programs emphasize the importance of being family centered. However, families and professionals continue to report difficulties in translating the family-centered philosophy into concrete actions. Some concrete examples of best practices in constructing the IFSP include: (1) collaborative agenda development for IFSP meetings, (2) openness to holding meetings in places and at times that are convenient for the family, and (3) use of language that is strengths based, respectful of families, and easily understandable by all participants.

Service Coordination

Service coordination is an active, ongoing process and requires the coordinator to carry out the following responsibilities:

Assisting parents of eligible children in gaining access to early intervention services and other services identified in the IFSP,

Coordinating the provision of early intervention services, such as ongoing pediatric care,

Facilitating the timely delivery of services, and

Continuously seeking appropriate services and situations necessary to benefit the development of the child.

The law states that the IFSP must identify the service coordinator from the profession most immediately relevant to the infant's or toddler's and family's needs (or the person who is otherwise qualified to carry out all applicable responsibilities) (sec. 636 [d][7]). This person will be responsible for the implementation of the plan and coordination of services with other agencies and persons. The kinds of specific service coordination activities that are included are activities that are very familiar to social workers. These would be: coordinating evaluations and assessments; ensuring the development, review, and evaluation of the IFSP; assisting families in finding service providers; ensuring that services are delivered in the natural environments for infants and toddlers and as close to home as possible; helping families access advocacy services; and, finally, facilitating the development of a transition plan to preschool services.

These service coordination activities recognize the multidisciplinary, collaborative, interagency nature of the services that are required for this population of children and families. They emphasize the importance of the coordination function necessary to integrate and implement the services effectively. Although the law suggests that the service coordinator come from the profession most immediately relevant to the infant's or toddler's or family's needs, in reality several factors are of critical importance in the choice of a service coordinator. She will need to be responsible for the implementation of the IFSP. She should be someone with whom families are comfortable working. She should believe in and support families as experts on the care of their child. She should have experience using a collaborative process with families and other professionals. She should see families as full members of the team. She should have the skills and experience to coordinate services with other agencies and providers.

School social workers have long experience in liaison with other agencies, and with case management and coordination of services (see chapter 30). They are a natural choice to assist families with service coordination activities. For social workers, the service coordination functions and activities described in the laws and regulations are natural and expected components of social work services (Kisthardt, 1997; Rose, 1992). Social work as a profession traditionally has supported the values of client self-determination and participation in the development of plans for service, including privileging the voice of families and advocating for structural and systemic change. They are recognized in many settings as the link between clients and community services and resources

Procedural Safeguards

Inclusion of a program or service in a statewide system demands procedural safeguards. The following are minimal procedural safeguards expected by the law (sec. 639). Infants, toddlers, and families have the right to:

1. Timely administrative resolution of complaints. Any party, aggrieved by the outcome of an administrative complaint, has the right to bring a civil action relating to the complaint in any state court of competent jurisdiction or in federal district court;
2. The right to confidentiality of personally identifiable information, including the right of parents to written notice of and consent to the exchange of such information among agencies consistent with federal and state law;
3. The right of the parents to accept or decline any particular early intervention service without jeopardizing other services;
4. Parents have the opportunity to examine records relating to assessment, screening, eligibility determinations, and the development and implementation of the IFSP;
5. Procedures to protect the rights of wards of the state, including the assignment of an individual to act as a surrogate for the parents;
6. Written prior notice to the parent of the infant or toddler when changes in the identification, evaluation, or placement of the infant or toddler are contemplated;
7. Parents should be fully informed in the parents' native language of any contemplated changes unless it clearly is not feasible to do so; and
8. Parents may use mediation for some exceptions to policies or procedures. (sec. 639 [a][1-8])

In the course of any proceedings or action regarding the placement, the infant or toddler would continue to receive the appropriate early intervention services currently being provided, unless the state agency and the parents otherwise agree (sec. 639[a][8][b]).

Practice Implications for Social Workers

Before discussing particular approaches to practice, social workers who are practicing with infants and toddlers with or at risk for disabilities and their families must first examine their own values, biases, culture, attitudes, and beliefs about families. This examination must include their own family of origin, extended family history, and their practice history. The examination and work on self must be continuous throughout one's practice life.

As we move toward identifying best practice in the twenty-first century, it is imperative that we develop practice models that are responsive to the rapidly increasing numbers of children from racial minorities in the U.S. population. By the year 2010, one of every four children will be a child of color (Chan, 1991). These children are also the largest at-risk group for disabilities associated with poverty. Lack of maternal prenatal care, poor prenatal nutrition, and inadequate health care for poor children themselves (Schorr, 1989) all contribute to risk of disability.

Social workers have a long history of concern for families (Germain, 1968; Hartman & Laird, 1983; Richmond, 1917) and the environments in which they live and work. Family-centered practice is a model of social work practice that locates the family in the center of the unit of attention or field of action (Germain, 1968). As conceptualized within the *life model* of social work practice (Germain & Gitterman, 1980), the domain of family-centered social work practice is in the transactions between families and their environments. Within the past ten years, new theories and new ways of conceptualizing and contextualizing the issues and challenges for children and families within their social environment have emerged. These approaches include empowerment (Cochran, 1992; Pinderhughes, 1995), strengths-based practice (Weick & Saleebey, 1995), social constructionism (Laird, 1995), narrative therapy (White, 1995), collaboration with families (Bishop, Woll, & Arango, 1993), and partnership with communities (Bishop, Taylor, & Arango, 1997; Delgado, 2000; Ewalt, Freeman, & Poole, 1998) and with multiple organizations and systems (Gray, 1989). Services should be developed and delivered in a culturally appropriate and responsive manner (Fong & Furato, 2001; Rounds, Weil, & Bishop, 1994). The intent of the law dovetails with social work's concern to secure social justice and human rights for those families most oppressed and marginalized by issues of poverty, racism, and "ableism." Newer expectations provide new opportunities to apply these emerging approaches to early intervention services for infants and toddlers most at risk or with a disability.

DEVELOPING BEST PRACTICE MODELS

The following social work practice approaches lend themselves to the spirit and the requirements of the legislation to provide early intervention services to infants, toddlers, and their families. Families have reported that these are the approaches that are most respectful for their children and themselves (Bishop et al., 1993). It is within a partnership with social workers and other professionals that they can work most effectively to achieve their goals for their child and for their family (Bishop et al., 1997). Helping families identify their priorities and connecting them to appropriate services will increase the likelihood that they and their child will receive the early intervention services they want and need. These practice approaches have the following characteristics: family centered, community based, culturally competent, interprofessional, and coordinated.

A social worker who uses *family-centered practice* approaches views the family and its members as people with strengths, honors the expertise and experience of the family, and works with the family as a full partner and decision maker. The social worker should not be making assumptions about what the family wants and needs to care for their child with a disability. Instead, the social worker should explore with each family their priorities and concerns, what resources and supports they have, and what the family wants and needs in order to provide the best care to their children. Such approaches and questions, which transfer power and decision making to the family, will require new ways of doing business for schools, child care centers, after-school programs, and all agencies serving young children and their families. If such agencies value families and aspire to deliver services in a family-centered manner, it will mean changes such as flexible service hours and examining the agency menu of services and asking families to help define what is missing and what is unnecessary. Where teams are in place to do evaluations of infants and young children, family members must be welcomed as part of the team and integral to all aspects of the assessment, intervention, and evaluation processes. Such practice approaches move us from viewing families as dysfunctional, from blaming families for their child's problems, and from rescuing children from their families. They move to strengths- and empowerment-based models that view family members as people with strengths and resources, as people with expert knowledge about their children, and as crucial partners in all aspects of their child's care.

A social worker who uses *community-based practice* approaches works with families to understand the natural environments in which they live, work, and play as a family. Using an ecological approach and the ecomap tool, the social worker will need to work with the family to understand where their sources of strength and support are, and what community resources they are currently using with their child. This exploration includes natural systems of support for the family, such as extended family, church relationships, local storekeepers, neighborhood social networks at playgrounds, child care centers, and the like. Most families want their services delivered as close to home as possible, and in the context of a community of support. (For a fuller discussion of community-based practice see Delgado, 2000; Ewalt et al., 1998).

A social worker who uses *culturally appropriate practice* approaches (Lum, 2003), will need to ask families to be their teachers and/or to suggest other community members who might be willing to help the social worker and other members of the team understand the cultural norms and values associated with providing help. Families will need to be given opportunities to teach team members about their particular culture and what are acceptable cultural practices in relation to the disability. In addition, the role of religion and spirituality in relation to cultural practices may also need to be explored. Team recommendations will need to be adapted to fit the family's unique notions of supports, services, and resources.

The social worker providing services to very young children and their families is often working with many providers from a variety of disciplines, as well as paraprofessionals, and will need to be skilled at *interprofessional collaborative practice* approaches. No single provider, no single agency, and very few communities can provide all the services families with infants and toddlers with disabilities need. "Collaboration with families and other(s) is a necessity and an obligation of professional leadership" (Corrigan & Bishop, 1997, p. 149). Families face a confusing array of services, troubled child services, and family health insurance programs. They want and need professionals who can work together, overcome turf battles, share resources, and use team building and collaboration skills to help their child and family. Social workers have these skills and can forge partnerships between families and the professionals who provide their services, so that they are offered in the most family-friendly and effective manner.

A social worker must be skilled in *service coordination practice* approaches. Service coordination involves using family-centered, community-based, and interprofessional collaborative approaches as an active and ongoing process to meet the infant's or toddler's and the family's needs and priorities. It is the service coordination element that translates the individual family service plan from a paper document to a series of services and activities that are focused on providing the early intervention services that the child needs and includes supporting the family to achieve their goals for their child. Social workers have a special responsibility to this population of children and families. Infancy and toddlerhood are critical and vulnerable times in the lives of children, times of rapid growth and change. They are critical and vulnerable times for families too. Families who have infants and toddlers with disabilities face the additional challenges of responding to the unique needs of their child with a disability. Social workers are skilled at providing the appropriate services and supports that the family and their child require.

The following suggestions provide some examples of how social workers can fulfill their responsibilities as providers and advocates for early intervention services that reflect a family-centered, community-based, culturally responsive, and coordinated approach. Such practice needs to develop and model family–professional partnerships (Bishop et al., 1993) in all aspects of service provision, especially in the development of an IFSP and the provision of case management services. It needs to ensure that family support services are available to all families who desire them, including such services as respite care, sibling support, grandparents' support, family-to-family support, and fathers' groups. It needs to provide services to families that reflect the principle of normalization, as close to home as possible and in the families' natural environments. It needs to support a family's participation in all meetings that concern their child and family using planning instruments, such as IFSPs, in partnership with families and other service providers. It needs to advocate for services that are accessible, flexible, culturally sensitive, and responsive to the diversity of family desires and styles (Rounds et al., 1994). It needs to assist other professionals in understanding the cultural and social experience of the child in the family and community (Clark, 1989) and facilitate collaboration between and among service providers and agencies in the family's local community.

In order to support this type of practice, state- and community-wide models for practice with infants and toddlers and their families need to be developed. School social workers need to connect with the contact person at the designated lead agency in the state and collaborate in statewide efforts to develop best practices. The following tasks, among others, are particularly important as these models are developed and implemented:

- ◆ To work on confidentiality procedures that will ensure maximum protection of families while facilitating information sharing that will benefit families and protect them from duplicative procedures and services;
- ◆ To develop collaborative training programs in which families and professionals have opportunities to educate each other;
- ◆ To advocate for the necessary financial resources to facilitate full implementation of the law, particularly including serving at-risk infants and toddlers.

PART C'S CONTINUING IMPACT

Since 1986, service systems in education, social services, health, and mental health have become more complex. They have continued to grow and expand in a manner that makes it increasingly difficult to provide family-centered, community-based, culturally responsive services in a coordinated and seamless manner. New parents of an infant or toddler with a disability face this complexity and disarray in services at a point when they may have the least time and energy to find services for their child and themselves.

With Part C acting as a catalyst for change, there has been considerable leadership from federal agencies, particularly the Maternal and Child Health Bureau's Programs for Children with Special Health Care Needs (Brewer, McPherson, Magrab, & Hutchins, 1989). In January 1994, more than fifty national organizations concerned with the well-being of children, youth, and families, including the National Association of Social Workers, American Academy of Pediatrics, and National Education Association, developed a set of principles that would pave the way for unprecedented collaboration among essential services at the local, state, and federal levels (American Academy of Pediatrics, 1994). The Federal Interagency Coordinating Council has also provided leadership by using family-professional collaborative processes and developing materials that describe and encourage family-centered, community-based, culturally appropriate early intervention services. At about the same time, the National Commission on Leadership in Interprofessional Education (NCLIE) was founded to promote interprofessional collaborative practices and training. Its purpose was:

> Through a family/professional partnership, the Commission will support the preparation of a new generation of interprofessionally oriented leaders in health education and practice, who possess the knowledge, skills, and values to practice in new community-based integrated service delivery systems. (NCLIE, 1995)

More recently, the social work accrediting body, the Council on Social Work Education (CSWE), has begun to study issues of certification, licensing, and accreditation for interprofessional practice. The accreditation standards passed by the CSWE Commission on Accreditation in 2001 include interprofessional practice as part of the content for social work practice. In December 2001, the Maternal and Child Health Bureau, Division of Programs for Children with Special Health Needs and Their Families, in concert with the 2010 Goals for the Nation, launched a ten-year Action Plan to Achieve Community-Based Service Systems for Children and Youth with Special Health Care Needs and Their Families. This ten-year action plan reaffirms the need to work in partnership with families in their local communities to achieve appropriate care and to support all children with or at risk for a disability, and for their families. Families have been active leaders and participants in all of these developments. They continue through organizations, such as Family Voices and Parent-to-Parent, to influence Congress and federal, state, and community agencies. Their object is to fulfill the promise of Part C and encourage full funding for the family-directed provision of early intervention services.

Although much of this emphasis on interprofessional education and practice (Kane, 1975, 1982) is not new to social work education and practice, the emphasis on a family-professional partnership in the planning, implementation, and evaluation of services is new (Bishop et al., 1993). Families are now recognized as having critical knowledge and experience about the care of their children and are viewed as equal partners on the team. Part C has been instrumental in the implementation of this philosophy of care.

The emphasis on the provision of services in the natural environments of infants and toddlers coincides with a rededication to the concept of community as an important source of supports and resources for children and their families. This new era of community renewal has dramatically changed the role of social workers in community practice. Social workers once again have assumed the role of change agent. Today, greater emphasis is placed on encouraging community members to participate and assume leadership roles in all phases of community capacity development. (Ewalt et al., 1998, p. xi).

In summary, social workers have a leadership role and need to make a major contribution to this process. They collaborate with families in the development and implementation of early intervention services that reflect a family's concerns and desires for their child with a disability as well as the needs of the child. They can advocate for systemic changes that support families' efforts to be successful with their children, regardless of their social, cultural, political, and economic status in society. In addition, social workers have a role to play in assisting other professionals in understanding the values, knowledge, and skills needed to work with families in a family-centered manner. The social worker's responsibility requires action in four areas:

1. Family-centered services and supports to infants, toddlers, and their families;
2. Service coordination activities in partnership with families, providers, agencies, and communities;
3. Service system change activities; and
4. Legislative advocacy.

Social workers should be actively engaged in partnership with parent/family leaders and parent/family organizations, with local and state legislators, with federal and state health, educational, social services, and mental health service systems to develop family-oriented services to this population and best practices at state and community levels. At stake is the possibility that all infants and toddlers at risk or with disabilities may be supported to grow, develop, and learn to their full potential. It is the right thing to do, and it helps ensure human rights and social justice (Finn & Jacobson, 2003) for these young children and their families.

Web sites

The following Web sites will allow the interested reader to follow conversations among family and parents' groups as they monitor the changes in the law, their projected responses, and other areas of interest. In some cases these Web sites are not limited to Part C but are useful in understanding the current issues for families.

Fv-talk@yahoogroups.com
Groups@yahoo.com/group/FV-talk/
Familypartners@yahoogroups.com
www.Isi.ku.edu/isi/internal/guidelines

References

American Academy of Pediatrics. (1994). *Principles to link by: Integrating education, health and human services for children, youth, and families: Systems that are community-based and school-linked*. (Final report). Available from the American Academy of Pediatrics, 601 Thirteenth Street, NW, Suite 400 North, Washington, DC 20005.

Bishop, K. K. (1987).The new law and the role of social workers. *Early Childhood, 3*(2), 6-7.

Bishop, K. K., Rounds, K., & Weil, M. (1993). PL 99-457:The preparation of social workers for practice with infants and toddlers with handicapping conditions and their families. *Journal of Social Work Education, 29*(1), 36-45.

Bishop, K. K.,Taylor, M. S., & Arango, P. (Eds.). (1997). *Partnerships at work: Lessons learned from programs and practices of families, professionals and communities.* Burlington: University of Vermont, Department of Social Work (available through K. K. Bishop, Division of Social Work,Wheelock College, Boston, MA).

Bishop, K. K.,Woll, J., & Arango, P. (1993). *Family/professional collaboration for children with special health needs and their families.* Burlington: University of Vermont, Department of Social Work (available through the National Maternal and Child Health Clearinghouse,Arlington,VA).

Brewer, E. J., McPherson, M., Magrab, P. R., & Hutchins,V. L. (1989). Family-centered, community-based, coordinated care for children with special health care needs. *Pediatrics, 83*(6), 1055-1060.

Chan, K. (1991). Social work with ethnic minorities: Practice issues and potentials. *Journal of Multicultural Social Work, 1*(1), 29-39.

Clark, J. (1989, January 17). *Proposed roles and mission for professionals working with handicapped infants and their families.* Unpublished comments, Iowa State Board of Education.

Cochran, M. (1992). Parent empowerment: Developing a conceptual framework. *Family Sciences Review, 5,* 3-21.

Corrigan, D., & Bishop, K. K. (1997). Creating family-centered integrated service systems and interprofessional educational programs to implement them. *Social Work in Education, 19*(3), 149-163.

Delgado, M. (2000). *Community social work practice in an urban context.* New York: Oxford University Press.

Ewalt, P. L., Freeman, E. M., & Poole, D. L. (Eds.). (1998). Community building: Renewal, well-being, and shared responsibility.Washington, DC: National Association of Social Workers Press.

Finn, J. L., & Jacobson, M. (2003). *Just practice:A social justice approach to social work.* Peosta, Iowa: Eddie Bowers Publishing Co.

Fong, R., & Furato, S. (Eds.). (2001). *Culturally competent practice: Skills, interventions and evaluations.* Boston:Allyn & Bacon.

Germain, C. B. (1968). Social study: Past and future. *Social Casework, 49,* 403-409.

Germain, C. B., & Gitterman,A. (1980). *The life model of social work practice.* New York: Columbia University Press.

Gray, B. (1989). *Collaborating: Finding common ground for multiparty problems.* San Francisco: Jossey-Bass.

Hartman,A., & Laird, J. (1983). Family-centered social work practice. New York: Free Press.

Kane, R.A. (1975). *Interprofessional teamwork.* Syracuse, NY: Syracuse University School of Social Work.

Kane, R.A. (1982). Lessons for social work from the medical model:A viewpoint for practice. *Social Work, 27*(4), 315-321.

Kisthardt,W. (1997).The strengths model of case management: Principles and helping functions. In D. Saleebey (Ed.), *The strengths perspective in social work practice* (n.p.). New York: Longman.

Laird, J. (1995). Family-centered practice in the postmodern era. *Families in Society, 76*(1), 150–162.

Lum, D. (Ed). (2003). *Culturally competent practice: A framework for understanding diverse groups and justice issues* (2nd ed.). Pacific Grove, CA: Brooks/Cole.

National Commission on Leadership in Interprofessional Education (NCLIE). (1995). Executive board minutes. Unpublished.

Pinderhughes, E. (1995). Empowering diverse populations: Family practice in the 21st century. *Families in Society, 76*(3), 131–140.

Richmond, M. (1917). *Social diagnosis.* New York: Russell Sage Foundation.

Rose, S. (1992). *Case management and social work practice.* New York: Longman.

Rounds, K., Weil, M. O., & Bishop, K. K. (1994). Practice with culturally diverse families of infants and toddlers with handicapping conditions. *Families in Society, 75*(1), 3–15.

Schorr, L. B. (1989). *Within our reach: Breaking the cycle of disadvantage.* New York: Anchor Books.

Weick, A., & Saleebey, D. (1995). Supporting family strengths: Orienting policy and practice toward the 21st century. *Families in Society, 75*(1), 141–149.

White, M. (1995). *Reauthoring lives: Interviews and essays.* Adelaide, Australia: Dulwich Centre Publications.

13

Conducting and Using Research in the Schools: Practitioners as Agents for Change

Nancy Farwell
University of Washington

Sung Sil Lee Sohng
University of Washington

- ◆ Research in Schools
- ◆ Applications of School-Based Research
- ◆ Connecting to Unrecognized Constituencies
- ◆ Improving Home-School-Community Partnerships
- ◆ Promoting Inclusion and Involvement
- ◆ Beginning Your Research
- ◆ Low-Cost, Straightforward Methods

School-based practitioners seek practical knowledge to help students, schools, families, and communities improve educational experience, processes, and outcomes in authentic ways. As schools become key public institutions fostering social and economic development, educational systems face increased demands to respond to the changing nature of a knowledge-based economy. New trends have brought profound changes for education, notably the increasing requirements that schools provide knowledge and skills linked to economic production needs. Entrepreneurial ideas concerned with profit and micro-focused knowledge could clash with broad and humanistic understandings of our world. Increasingly, school restructuring, accountability, testing, standardization, and measurement of educational activities have been framed as solutions to both social and educational problems (Lipman, 2004). Changes in the world economy require educational administrators and practitioners to examine closely the interlinked imperatives of productivity, accountability, and community in the processes and management of public education (Boyd, 1999). Under conditions of increasing social, economic, and political inequalities, inclusion is ever more crucial to the mission of public education, ensuring that those who have been marginalized or excluded have the opportunity to participate fully. Practitioner researchers are uniquely situated to work collaboratively within the interconnected networks of students, families, communities, and educational institutions to facilitate these changes.

These ideas are basic to the research process. As a practitioner-researcher, one views oneself as having the potential to build knowledge, an act of learning as well as a form of professional practice. Information is everywhere. One must learn to be attentive to information that sheds light on issues and processes that can promote creative and collaborative ways of identifying and addressing changing needs, challenges, and opportunities. Being a practitioner-researcher also means that one becomes disciplined—one learns to account for one's reasons for gathering information, for structuring questions in particular ways, for how one gathers information, and how one uses it.

This chapter demystifies a process generally considered the exclusive domain of professionally trained researchers. It suggests low-cost research approaches that can be carried out by school-based practitioners. Practitioner research is a unique genre of research. *Experimental* researchers strive for valid and reliable measures to ensure generalizability of their results; *naturalistic* researchers seek trustworthiness and authenticity to uncover the social rules for the situations they describe. In contrast, *practitioner-researchers* seek to understand the individuals, actions, policies, and events in their work environment to make professional decisions. As practitioner-researchers, school social workers participate in improving educational outcomes for students, restructuring schools and influencing curriculum, developing on-site prevention programs, involving students in networks of community-based supports, and fostering social and political change to ensure that schools become more inclusive. Practitioner research reaches both within and beyond educational institutions to facilitate collaborative efforts with communities and families to support students' social development needs and contributes to the social work knowledge base.

A number of concurrent forces have advanced the growth and legitimacy of practitioner research. First, the conduct of research has been linked to the professionalization of social work practice. Second, following the postmodern challenge of "objective truth," narratives, self-studies, cases, biographical methods, vignettes, and other writings as well as oral histories have been recognized as potentially significant sources for the knowledge base (Chamberlayne, Bornat, & Wengraf, 2000; Harold, Palmiter, Lynch, & Freedman-Doan, 1995; Holland, 1991; Josselson, 1996; Martin, 1995). Third, the interest in practitioner research has also increased in response to the movement to create reflective, critical practitioners (Altrichter, Posch, & Somekh, 1993; Jay, 2003; Pearlmutter, 2002). Fourth, educational reformers have recognized that the success of reform is dependent on an understanding of the context in which reform is to be implemented. Using inquiry processes such as action research, practitioners can bridge the gulf between policies and the actuality of everyday lives, adapting the reforms to suit particular work situations (Armstrong & Moore, 2004). Emphases on the complex interrelated contextual factors that are the reality of students' lives as well as the interconnections of these with educational processes and outcomes have since the 1970s fueled a shift to qualitative research methods in education (Hammersley, 2000). Practitioner research can also underscore the importance of connective pedagogies that flexibly link individual learning styles and needs with the curriculum as well as with relationships, values, and experiences in the wider community (Corbett, 2001; Simpson, 2004). Finally, the work of Paolo Freire (1973) and others (Carr, 1995; Hick, 1997; Noffke & Stevenson, 1995; Sohng, 1996) has forged a link between practitioner research and critical pedagogical thought. Practitioner inquiry and other forms of action research are seen as emancipatory tools to help practitioners to become aware of the often hidden hierarchical institutional structures that govern their work.

Following an introductory discussion of research in the schools, we consider a range of alternative applications and discuss their relevance for the school-based practitioner. We outline guidelines for initiating research, and we identify several low-cost methods for gathering data and using research.

RESEARCH IN SCHOOLS

The impact of the research explosion on local schools is well known to practitioners, showing itself in constantly growing paperwork requirements. School personnel at all levels spend much of their time completing forms and reports, usually providing data for research conducted elsewhere. The bulk of research, evaluation, and data-gathering efforts in the schools is a response to federal and state legislative mandates. Legislative bodies demand strict accounting for the funds they appropriate and impose heavy reporting and evaluation requirements. Legislation may also mandate regulations for what is "legitimate" research. For example, the No Child Left Behind Act stipulates that the majority of research funded under federal law utilize experimental designs and methods, randomized control groups, and models of causality (Lather, 2004; NCLB, 2001).

Such methodological requirements could make research the domain of academics, whose specialized language and methods are assumed to be necessary conditions for scientific validity. In fact, the use of complex statistical methods often limits the communication of research results, shutting out practitioners and the public. All too often esoteric language and methods are worn as a badge of expertise and rationalized as necessary for scientific precision. Local school personnel, parents, and community members are rarely involved in designing the research, assessing research products, or suggesting applications. More often, these potential partners are considered instruments for achieving organizational objectives. They are, in this sense, passive receivers of information and objects of administrative control. Furthermore, even the most rigorous research, designed from afar, may yield statistically significant findings that have little practical application.

APPLICATIONS OF SCHOOL-BASED RESEARCH

If externally driven research is so often irrelevant to practice, as suggested above, then why should the practitioner be concerned with research at all? There are compelling reasons, both defensive and affirmative, for school social workers and others to conduct their own research. First of all, this is the age of accountability. Implementation of performance-based accountability systems can bring about complex reactions in school systems. Externally imposed performance-based accountability systems are rarely adequate for producing significant changes in program delivery at individual schools, beyond an emphasis on test performance (Elmore, 2001). Practitioner-based research can support a bottom-up change process, warding off top-down bureaucratic measures, and supporting a collegial form of accountability. Student engagement and learning are nested within complex contextual family and community networks that practitioner-based research can help illuminate. Educational reforms emphasize working toward institutionalization of cooperative principles as the focus of school renewal (Board on Children, Youth and Families, 2003; Holy, 1991). Studies of educational innovations suggest that involving the local school community in research helps mobilize the capacity for internal regeneration of policies and strategies for school-driven improvement (Broussard, 2003; Herr, 1995; Jones, 1991; Sirotnik, 1989). Rather than being passive consumers or clients, parents and community members can become active partners in the collaborative network (Armstrong & Moore, 2004).

Because school personnel spend their working lives with students, they are in an excellent position to identify educational issues firsthand. They are interested in what works and are sensitive to the practical constraints of school settings in ways that outside researchers may not be. The utilitarian, participatory, and localized nature of school-based research significantly reduces the gap between the discovery of what works and practical applications of this knowledge (deMarrais, 2004; Elliot, 1991; Hammersley, 2000). School-based research is the antithesis of externally generated and externally imposed change. Just as administrators and policy makers use research as a political resource, school social workers can do the same. Teachers, school social workers, psychologists, and others can use research to ward off new programs and requirements that are unfeasible, impractical, or harmful to students. On the other hand, they can use research in a positive way to gain support for new program initiatives, to demonstrate the effectiveness of their services, to obtain additional resources, or to find out what kinds of interventions work best. School social workers can use research to move beyond traditional clinical roles to enlarge the arena of practice. Research can be used as an adjunct to consultation and as a way of demonstrating the potential of a more ecological social work role.

Fostering Collaborative Practice

School social workers are in an especially advantageous position to develop collaborative school-based research. Collaborative, interdisciplinary efforts highlight the social worker's expertise and recognition of the profession's unique competencies, moving the social worker from the periphery to a central role (Stevens, 1999). The profession has long been interested in effecting change through the empowerment, participation, and action of the people involved. The collaborative approach to research calls on interactive skills, cultural sensitivity, group decision making, and mediation and conflict management skills necessary for negotiation among diverse constituents and interests. This kind of collaborative research is characterized by (1) participation in problem posing; (2) practitioner participation in data gathering that answers questions relevant to his or her concerns; and (3) collaboration among members of the school community as a "critical community." Here, research is aimed at generating data that can guide and direct planned change. It involves observation, assessment, interviewing, reading, analyzing reports and documents, and writing findings. These skills are already within the behavioral repertoire of school social workers. We will review how to do it. However, first we examine some of the uses and potential benefits of practitioner-initiated, school-based research.

Developing Multicultural Resources

Consciousness of multiple realities lies at the heart of postmodern thinking. Schools must incorporate diverse voices into their communities and their curricula, with particular attention to those who have been silenced (Banks, 1996; Sleeter, 1996). For example, a social worker at a predominantly White school noted that students of color continued to drop out at a high rate. She formed a multiethnic team in collaboration with an administrator and a teacher to conduct an action research project examining the experiences of students of color at the school. The project helped focus attention on the larger institutional processes that silenced and privatized students' experiences of exclusion and alienation (Herr, 1995). The key concept in this endeavor is the deliberate, thoughtful development of research that illuminates the diversity of perspectives and interests. School-based research can offer a promising vehicle for assessing cultural diversity in curriculum, classroom, and school practices, and improving the campus climate for a diverse student body.

To make the case for new multicultural resources, you might begin by taking a look at how the composition of the student population at your school has changed over the years. To get an overall picture, you might examine student characteristics over the past ten years, comparing two different years for which you can get good demographic data. In considering diversity at your school, you should also familiarize yourself with both official and informal institutional policies and procedures, academic programs, and instructional support. Have these policies and programs kept pace with the changing student population? Are they being implemented fairly and effectively? A social worker in a large urban school district received many complaints from parents that their English-speaking children were placed in English as a Second Language (ESL) classes for no apparent reason other than assumptions about their language abilities because they had Latino surnames. Similarly, bicultural instructional assistants in another district noted that East African children were being placed inappropriately in special education classes, instead of in ESL classes. Social workers in these instances can collaborate with teachers, instructional aides, and assessment personnel in a self-study to investigate processes within the school, such as assessment and placement of students in remedial, special education, and ESL classes. Such processes may be affected by student ethnicity, immigration status, age, or gender. Combined with an analysis of changing demographics, policies, and available resources, this self-study can make the case for in-service training for staff and improved bilingual-bicultural resources such as student mentoring, tutoring, and support programs.

CONNECTING TO UNRECOGNIZED CONSTITUENCIES

The constituent base of multicultural education in this society consists of disenfranchised people, particularly parents and children of color and/or of low-income backgrounds; immigrants and refugees; children who are disabled; and youth who identify themselves as gay, or lesbian, as well as their parents. However, in many arenas of multicultural activity, the professionals sometimes act as if they were the constituents. Professionals can certainly be allies, but they need to recognize their power and their self-interest, which may lead them to shape multicultural education to fit their own needs. A growing literature on multicultural education is directed toward professionals, often substituting for dialog between school personnel and community people (Sleeter, 1996). Research redirected toward parents and community activists from diverse groups can serve as an empowering resource for those who are often unheard and uninvolved. A community needs assessment (see chapter 15), for example, provides an instrument whereby community members can make their educational needs known, expressing an action agenda for school change (Delgado-Gaitan, 1993; Williams, 1989).

IMPROVING HOME-SCHOOL-COMMUNITY PARTNERSHIPS

School social workers are in a good position to facilitate the involvement of family members in their children's education, a critical factor in student and family success (Broussard, 2003). Practitioner research can provide avenues for the involvement of immigrant and refugee parents and other marginalized families in the schools through parent support groups (Delgado-Gaitan, 2001), multicultural policy advocacy groups, facilitation of direct parent–school communication, and ensuring that the school provides a welcoming environment for families (Witherspoon, 2002). Practitioners concerned about community violence and personal safety of students can use action research to assess the impact of local programs such as Neighborhood Watch in protecting youth from violence as they walk to and from school. Such research can identify methods of retaining students who live in potentially dangerous neighborhoods (Salcido et al, 2002). Collaboration with public housing and community-based youth programs can be an excellent means for the practitioner-researcher to understand and address student concerns regarding contradictions between their self-perceived strengths and obstacles in their "real life" community contexts and the norms and missions of mainstream institutions such as the schools (Gran-O'Donnell, Farwell, Spigner et al., 2001).

PROMOTING INCLUSION AND INVOLVEMENT

Creating and sustaining inclusive education involves the school social worker as cultural agent, one who is in a position to both assist and resist the contradictions that exist in the transmission of dominant culture in the schools (Blair, 2002). Practitioner research can be instrumental in promoting an agenda for inclusion, through the process itself, as well as by transforming school culture, curriculum, practices, and community relationships. Action research involving students of color or other marginalized populations, such as gay and lesbian youth, can be designed to educate the school community about diversity and homophobia, encouraging student engagement through activism and advocacy (Herr, 1995; Peters, 2003). For example, students of First Nations from West Seattle High School formed a community of inquiry to examine the use of Native American mascots, nicknames, and logos within the public school system and their impact on Native American youth cultural identities. Supported by the school social worker and the Native American community, they identified sixty-five schools in Washington State that have Indian mascots or logos. Their research indicated that Indian imagery within schools not only disrespects Native Americans by buying into historical stereotypes and caricatures but also perpetuates cultural ignorance and insensitivity within what is purported to be a supportive learning environment. The students who were originally "interviewees" became collaborators in a passionate change process, leading the campaign to change racist school practices and the school environment (Beeson,

2002).Another example is a Community Youth Mapping project carried out by Latino and Southeast Asian students in Seattle. This project was supervised by one of the authors and a school social work intern in collaboration with key, community-based social service agencies in 2003. Youth mapping provided a guided forum for youth to identify and critically examine assets and deficits in their community, find ways to build on the assets, and articulate actions to the deficits.

Demonstrating the Effectiveness of Services

As practitioners, we generally know, or think we know, the effectiveness of the services we provide. We sometimes assume that because we are professionals, others should take us at our word when we make claims about the need for and benefits of our services. However, in the absence of convincing evidence, such claims can be dismissed by others as self-serving.

> One school social worker, for example, was valued by the principals and teachers of the schools she served for her effectiveness in handling crisis situations— episodes of students acting out, students' threatening violent and destructive behavior, and confrontations between students and teachers. She was frequently called on to handle emergencies. She felt that this disruption of her regular work schedule was well worth the price, because her availability to handle crises gave her the credibility needed to get into the schools to do some of the more routine work. However, her crisis work was not officially recognized. It was not part of her job description, nor did her superiors know how much time it took or how much the principals appreciated it. Had she taken the time to document the number of such cases per month, to describe the circumstances and outcomes, and to record the feedback from the students and teachers, she could have used these data to gain official acknowledgment of an enlarged work role. She might also have gained greater insights into her work, recognition of her contribution, additional resources or decreased demands, or authorization for training school personnel in crisis intervention. As it stood, her work was appreciated by many but unacknowledged and unrewarded by administrators.

Fostering Collegial Accountability

School-based research conducted by practitioners on practical concerns can foster a greater congruence between research and practice and help to demystify the research process. It can also contribute to building greater collegial, shared accountability.

> Let us assume, for example, that a social worker and a group of teachers have developed an alternative tutorial strategy, adding adult helpers to the classroom to work with a group of students, rather than taking these students out of class for remedial instruction. The team wants to examine the effect of this experiment. The results would be measured by outcomes such as the students' progress,

increase/decrease of tutoring time spent with each student, and the students' and teachers' assessment of the new procedures. Here, the purpose of research does not necessarily require rigorous research procedures but calls for collegial problem identification and problem solving.

The process of observing students and gathering data may also be an occasion for the team to examine and reflect on their interaction and behaviors with students. By having the opportunity to experience and experiment with the research process, the team members may gain an increased appreciation of research and come to demand more of themselves, for example, to be more parsimonious and specific in the data they collect, and more clear about learning objectives.

Establishing the Need for New Services

Arguments for the establishment of new services are all the more persuasive when supported by research data.

Let us assume, for example, that the social worker and teachers feel that there is a need for a school breakfast program. School administrators resist this, concerned about the cost as well as the administrative problems of implementing a program for which there may be little constituent demand. In the absence of any other compelling reasons, administrators can easily deflect teachers' and social workers' requests for the program. When the request is accompanied by data showing the support from the students and parents, the number of children who come to school without breakfast, well-documented reports of behavioral problems and the lack of attentiveness of such children, information on effects of nutritional deficits on learning, and data on the costs of the program, the request would be more seriously considered.

In another example, the social worker is concerned about reports of bullying across multiple age groups on and near the school grounds and advocates for the implementation of an anti-bullying/conflict resolution curriculum. The principal discourages this, due to lack of funds and concerns about workload. The social worker surveys parents, children, and teachers about the school climate and documents serious instances of bullying experienced by a significant percentage of children. This is then identified as a priority area for intervention, and the principal adopts a curriculum used in other district schools, with support from the Parent Teacher Association.

Establishing the Need for Additional Resources

School personnel are constantly seeking increased resources or reduced workloads to accomplish their work in keeping with professional standards. Administrators hear such requests so often that they are routinely discounted. Administrators like to sidestep conflicts between professional standards or official policy requirements and the limited resources available to meet them.

This forces the practitioner to reconcile conflicting demands as best he or she can. For example, with the requirements of the Individuals with Disabilities Education Act (IDEA), school social workers, psychologists, special class teachers, and other educational specialists are often expected to carry out their regular work while accommodating time-consuming and cumbersome assessment and paperwork requirements for increased numbers of children. Administrators, themselves caught between federal and state requirements and limited resources, often thrust the problem downward, leaving it to school-based personnel to figure out how best to meet the new demands. School personnel work harder, take paperwork home with them, forgo planning and preparation time, or routinize work tasks. A more proactive approach would be to conduct team-based data gathering, documenting carefully the time required to perform specific tasks, thereby demonstrating the impossibility of completing them without sacrificing quality and deferring other responsibilities. Furthermore, the group involved in such data gathering and analysis can identify ways to reduce duplication and redundancy and can recommend new procedures more relevant to the school community.

Testing New Programs or Procedures

Often administrators develop new procedures in response to mandates from Congress, the state legislature, or the local school board. This top-down approach often results in new requirements being imposed with insufficient sensitivity to actual conditions within the schools. School-based personnel cope as best they can. However, it makes more sense to test new programs and procedures before they are implemented throughout the system. As an advocate for and participant in pilot tests, school social workers can expand their role while indirectly contributing to the empowerment of all school-based staff.

Illuminating Practices Normally Hidden from View

In all organizations, schools being no exception, there generally are some practices tacitly accepted but at variance with official policy and not openly discussed. Research offers a way of bringing such practices out into the open by guaranteeing anonymity and confidentiality, thereby depersonalizing what may be very emotional issues. Examples include disciplinary practices, cultural sensitivity, discrimination, or concerns about student-to-student sexual harassment and harassment of gay and lesbian students. Teachers may be reluctant to discuss their own practices because they may violate official policy or because of the divisive nature of an issue. Such emotion-laden issues may be driven underground and beyond the scope of discussion. An anonymous survey might elicit responses that would never be brought out in open discussion and could serve to bring to the attention of administrators practices of which they might otherwise not know.

A favorite method of politicians to avoid taking action is to call for a study of the issues. Although outright opposition to an undesirable policy may be viewed by the administration as insubordination, proposing a study is a more constructive and conciliatory step that is harder for recalcitrant administrators to oppose. If, in fact, a study is undertaken, the results may help resolve differences about implementing a proposed policy.

BEGINNING YOUR RESEARCH

We have discussed a number of ways in which research can be used to enhance the role of the school social worker and to support organizational change initiated from below. We turn now to the more difficult question of how to do it. In this section, we offer guidelines for getting started and suggest ways to augment limited resources. The concluding section provides a discussion of readily available data sources and methods of conducting research that do not require special research training.

Questions for Focus

The most important part of research is your thinking process prior to doing something, and during the research process. Here are six questions to help you put your research process together. When you work through these questions, you end up with a research design.

- ◆ What do you want and need to know? Why do you want to know this? Right from the start you'll have to be clear about how you'll use the information you collect.
- ◆ What do you already know? Answering this question lets you make use of the information you already have, or that is available in the published literature.
- ◆ Where do you go to find out? Where are the answers to your questions? Are you going to ask people? Are you going to review reports and documents?
- ◆ Whom do you ask? If you're going to ask people to give you information, whom are you going to ask? If you need certain documents, where are you going to find them?
- ◆ What kind of information do you need? Do you need descriptive information? Do you need some numbers? Do you need stories? Do you need information that tells you what others think?
- ◆ Do you need help? What kind of help do you need? Advice about the topic? Help with research tools? Help in deciding whom to interview? Help with language translation or interpretation? Help from colleagues, students, parents, and supervisors?

Answering these questions will help you make decisions about what research tools to develop.

Be Clear about Objectives

The first step in contemplating any research is clarity of objectives, both political and substantive. What are the specific group or organizational goals to be accomplished by undertaking the research? Will these objectives be realized if the research is carried out? What are the costs in terms of both resources and possibly strained relations? If, for example, the objective is to encourage the implementation of a free breakfast program, would research findings in fact bring about that result?

It is important to distinguish between fairly broad goals and more specific objectives. A frequent error of practitioner-researchers is to undertake a study with only vague objectives, hoping to make some sense out of the findings later. This approach is time consuming and wasteful for researcher and participants alike. For example, in approaching the issue of discipline, one could try to find out about teacher, student, and parent attitudes as well as actual practices in the schools. However, if current practices are the focus of concern, that is what should be studied. If teachers' support for a particular policy is at issue, then their attitudes and opinions may be a more appropriate focus. The objectives, framed as precisely as possible, should determine the direction of the research, not vice versa.

Don't Try for Too Much

When thinking in research terms, everything becomes a potential subject of research. One must guard against being overly ambitious and be realistic about the adequacy of the resources available to do the job. If one is planning to do a study without additional help, how much time can realistically be spent? Will this be sufficient to complete the study? One should estimate the time needed to accomplish each specific step. Even if it can be done, are the results likely to be worth the effort? If the answer to the latter two questions is no, then the research should not be undertaken.

Involve Others at an Early Stage

There are two reasons to involve others at the early stage of a project. First, some might feel slighted, and justifiably so, if asked to join a project after the major directions have already been decided by others. Second, and more important, the contributions of others enlarge the scope of issues considered and provide an essential source of new ideas. On the one hand, group process may complicate the orderly achievement of objectives, and groups are subject to groupthink, which may constrain the consideration of alternatives. On the other hand, research aimed at changing current practices should be undertaken with a view of building constituencies of support to help implement the findings.

Ask for Help

One way of extending available resources is to get additional help. This might mean seeking release time or volunteer assistance from colleagues and students. If the research objective is to bring about change, the greatest possible involvement of both colleagues and school community is desirable. Additional resources are available outside the school system. These include academics, student researchers, retired teacher associations, PTAs, community organizations, and advocacy groups. Advocacy groups have their own particular interest in practices within the schools, although their advocacy position may itself increase suspicions of administrators. Academics are often interested in consulting on practical issues and may even be willing to undertake the research themselves if offered an interesting research issue and access to a site. University students are often available from a number of academic disciplines—social work, education, psychology, sociology, political science, and public administration—to carry out research that satisfies their practicum requirements under academic supervision.

LOW-COST, STRAIGHTFORWARD METHODS

Most social research is an extension of logical processes used in everyday life. In shopping for new clothes, getting estimates for car repair or home improvement, or planning a vacation, the customary first step is to gather data on the reliability of the seller, the quality of the merchandise or service, its availability, and price. Prior to the data-gathering stage, there may be some assessment of the need and ability to pay. Similarly, when contemplating research in the work setting, a first step is to specify the objectives of the research and then develop a research plan. This involves a determination of the information needed, its availability, the methods required to obtain it, and the relative costs of time, materials, and other resources. At this point, you may also wish to review documents, data, and literature that are relevant to your research questions.

Use of Readily Available Data

There are several research approaches that require a minimum of time, some of which may be undertaken using readily available data. Although it is generally desirable to enlist the support of administrators and colleagues in undertaking research, there occasionally may be situations in which some administrators are threatened by the proposed research and withhold permission or seek in other ways to block it. In such instances, it is still possible to gather data using records and documents that are public information. Perhaps the most straightforward kind of research involves the analysis of existing data.

Schools are constantly compiling reams of data on every conceivable activity. Much of this information is funneled to state and federal agencies to meet reporting requirements but is not necessarily analyzed for local administrative purposes. Examples include aggregate data on pupil characteristics, family income, attendance, grades, achievement test scores, the numbers receiving free lunches, the incidence of visual or dental problems, the prevalence of handicapping conditions, the numbers in special classes or programs, the incidence of problems requiring disciplinary action, and so forth. Other data are available with respect to class size and caseloads of social workers and other educational specialists. Frequently, when caseload sizes are examined in relation to the performance requirements, a discrepancy between expectations and the reality of the workload is immediately apparent. The fact that a class for children with special needs contains fifteen children of differing ages and levels of ability and is taught by one teacher with no aide offers prima facie evidence of a resource deficiency.

Use of Public Documents

Another invaluable source of information is the school district's budget. The budget is a planning document that paints a good picture of what the district actually does and what its priorities are, as represented by the commitment of resources. An examination of the budget permits a comparison of the stated objectives with the actual allocation of resources to achieve those objectives. Other public documents that may shed light on local practices are federal and state laws, administrative codes and regulations, court decisions, state agency policy and procedural statements, and state and local education agency reports. (Increasingly, such documents and data are available on the World Wide Web. See chapter 15.) A reading of the state or federal requirements may reveal a discrepancy between these requirements and local practices. Some administrators intentionally keep information about the specific state and federal requirements from those school personnel who must implement them. Knowledge of deliberate violations of law can give school-based staff a powerful tool for advocating change. School practices with regard to discipline, suspensions, expulsions, and the notification and involvement of parents in placing children in special programs may be at variance with the law and/or district policy. If so, a range of interventions can encourage change, all the way from judicious questioning to encouraging advocacy groups to file suit.

Calculations of Costs and Procedural Practices

Another powerful kind of analysis is estimating the costs of procedures and practices. For example, it is a humbling exercise to calculate the cost of a single meeting in relation to its objectives and results. When one counts the dollar value of the participants' time, the costs can be quite substantial. Certain reporting requirements are costly, yet the costs are rarely calculated. In processing paperwork, one must consider both the actual cost of completing the forms and reports as well as other hidden costs. These hidden costs include the costs of printing the forms, moving the paper through the organization, handling and storing it, and the time of those who must read it, comment on, and analyze it. Cost comparisons of alternative procedures can be used to support one alternative rather than another.

Seeking out Library, Web, and Other Agency Resources, Records, and Research

Chances are good that most problems have been encountered elsewhere and subjected to some kind of analysis or research. Therefore, a good starting point in any research activity is the library and the Web. A review of the literature is a critical starting point for any research you plan to do. Reviewing the literature establishes what is already known on the topic and is the basis for the research focus. The existing literature can suggest methods for carrying out the research. Published measures and questionnaires can make the job a lot easier by providing an established means of collecting data. The key is to familiarize oneself with the literature before finalizing any research questions or design. You may find that your question can be answered primarily through looking at existing studies, rather than by collecting original data.

When reviewing the literature, it is important to examine the most recent studies, especially since they will generally include summaries of earlier work in their review of the literature. However, classic studies must not be ignored. Often these classics can be identified by examining the reference lists of the articles you find when a particular author or study is repeatedly cited. This would indicate that their work is significant in the field and should be read. For example, someone who is interested in studying the role of the school social worker would not ignore the work of Lela Costin or Paula Allen-Meares in this area (see chapter 1).

University librarians are generally helpful in locating studies and reports. There are a number of excellent computerized reference files that can produce a list of titles and abstracts on specific subjects at nominal cost. Some excellent databases that can assist in a literature search are the Educational Resources Information Center (ERIC), PsycINFO, EBSCO Host, and others available at libraries or through an Internet search engine. Many of these databases, obtained through libraries, include online, full-text copies of articles in major journals. Access may be limited to patrons of libraries that have purchased access to these resources. However, gaining access through a local university, or through your university alumni association, makes these resources available to the practitioner. Partnering with a university faculty member or graduate student, or a professional association, can make these resources more accessible to the school social worker.

Academic specialists in schools of education and social work and departments of psychology and sociology may be familiar with specific bodies of literature and be willing to share their expertise with practitioners. For just about any problem that can occur in a public school setting, there are likely to be some interested specialists. In addition to academic departments of universities, educational specialists are found in the federal Department of Education, in state departments of education, in contract research firms, and on the staffs of interest groups such as state chapters of Children's Defense Fund, Council for Exceptional Children, National Association of School Boards, Council of Chief State School Officers, National Association of Social Workers (NASW), National Alliance for the Mentally Ill (NAMI), state school social work associations, and so on. A few phone calls or a visit to organizational Web sites are generally sufficient to access such networks and learn what work has already been done in a specific problem area. For example, if one is investigating student discipline, the Children's Defense Fund may be able to provide a number of references to completed studies, summaries of legal opinions and pertinent laws, and suggestions about model programs. The state teachers' union may maintain a research staff and have access to information on many school issues. Newspaper articles provide another source of data about school policies. In larger cities, local newspapers often have reporters who specialize in educational concerns and who develop expertise in particular educational areas. The papers themselves frequently maintain clipping files, as does the school administration. This is an important documentary record that should not be overlooked. The school board minutes are available to the public and also supply a documentary record of actions taken and contemplated.

Methods for Gathering New Data

Other methods for gathering data about school activities include surveys, structured observation, interviews, action research, and online databases. Questionnaires are advantageous for gathering information that safeguards anonymity and providing a structured format for analysis of responses. The disadvantages are that they restrict the amount of data that can be gathered and analyzed, and questionnaire responses may be at variance with actual behavior. Face-to-face interviews offer an opportunity to gather information in greater depth. The interviewer can probe, ask additional questions, and clarify responses. Furthermore, some structure may be maintained through an interview schedule, a listing of topics, or questions. Structured observations are those in which there is some purposeful gathering of data according to predetermined categories. Observational techniques can become very sophisticated and complicated, as with the use of interaction scales to record information about who initiates and responds in a group meeting or in a class. More straightforward, simple observational methods will usually suffice. For example, the methods described in chapter 21 for use in classroom observation are readily adaptable to research purposes. Very simple categorization and computations will sometimes reveal profound meanings. Sometimes it is possible to enlist others in making observations. For example, all school social workers may agree to keep records of certain activities or to record observations of meetings in which they participate for subsequent analysis.

Letting the Facts Speak for Themselves: Compiling Data and Preparing Reports

A final stage in the process is the compilation of data and the preparation of a report or position paper. The format will depend on the purpose of the research and the objectives sought. If one is attempting to block the initiation of a new policy or procedure, the report would necessarily differ from that used in attempting to compare two alternative procedures, neither of which is particularly preferred. Those guidelines offered earlier for initiating the research will also serve in planning the report—one should be clear about objectives, avoid being overly ambitious, keep it simple, involve others, and seek the help of those with expert knowledge. In writing the report, one should avoid pejorative language, cast the findings in objective or neutral terms, and let the facts make the argument. Brevity and clarity are the watchwords. Graphic programs and materials, music, and multimedia sources enhance research presentations. Using technology can make dry materials interesting, colorful, and appealing. Dissemination of research reports to the constituent communities through community centers and local organizations is important to enlist their involvement with the school.

The following example illustrates a collaborative practitioner research effort utilizing a number of the methods and resources described above:

> A school social worker observed that communications between staff and parents of incoming refugee and immigrant children were often strained and incomplete. Using existing school data and public documents, she noted the increasing diversity within the school population. She then initiated informal conversations with newcomer parents, who explained that, although they were concerned about their children's education and well-being at school, there were many barriers to participation in parent-teacher conferences, and to discussing educational and disciplinary concerns. These barriers were linguistic, cultural, and logistical—for example, timing of appointments, adequate notification of activities at the school, differing cultural expectations on the part of both parents and teachers, need for language interpretation, and transportation. It was also apparent that, even with the presence of bilingual classes, ESL teachers, students, and bilingual instructional aides, school personnel envisioned "family" within a narrow construction of mainstream, educated, middle-class, English-speaking parents. The practitioner brought these concerns to a course on empowerment practice with refugees and immigrants taught by one of the authors. For her course project, the practitioner developed a participatory action research project in collaboration with staff at a local agency serving refugees and immigrants, and with an intern who worked

with school-age youth at a local multiethnic service organization. Through interviews with parents and school personnel, focus groups with parents and youth, and meetings with agency staff and parents, the research team developed a needs statement and designed a parent advocate project to help bridge the gap between newcomer families and schools. The research team further informed the project by reviewing the educational and social work literature, searching for model interventions that had been effective in other school districts working on similar issues. They also sought the expertise of parents who had successfully involved themselves in the schools, and school personnel and staff at other refugee service agencies. They thus brought together multifaceted resources with which to facilitate the problem solving and creative work of the project participants. The team successfully submitted a proposal for funds for a three-year project to form and mentor parent advocate groups. The practitioner-researcher as an agent of change successfully mobilized family and community collaboration to improve children's educational experiences by building mutual cultural understanding and better school-family-community relationships.

Research is too important to be left entirely to researchers. This chapter shows some of the ways practitioners can conduct and use research and, in the process, enhance their practice roles. Perhaps the most difficult step is getting started, particularly in view of the widely held perception that the proper conduct of research requires expertise that comes only from years of specialized training and experience. Such a view effectively rules out many of the more relevant applications of research in schools. However, as shown in this chapter, the school-based practitioner can rescue research from researchers and, by so doing, assume a more affirmative role in fostering collaboration, making space for diverse perspectives, and shaping school policy.

References

Altrichter, H., Posch, P., & Somekh, B. (1993). *Teachers investigate their work: An introduction to the methods of action research*. New York: Routledge.

Armstrong, F., & Moore, M. (2004). Action research: Developing inclusive practice and transforming cultures. In F. Armstrong & M. Moore (Eds.), *Action research for inclusive education: Changing places, changing practices, changing minds* (pp. 1–16). London: Routledge/Falmer.

Banks, J. (Ed.). (1996). *Multicultural education, transformative knowledge and action*. New York: Teachers College, Columbia University.

Beeson, J. (2002, May). We are not your mascot. *Colors North West*, 12–14.

Blair, K. (2002). School social work, the transmission of culture, and gender roles in schools. *Social Work, 21*(1), 21–33.

Board on Children, Youth and Families, Division of Behavioral and Social Sciences and Education (BCYF) (2003). *Engaging schools: Fostering high school students' motivation to learn*. Washington, DC: The National Academies Press. Retrieved Jan. 24, 2005, from http://www.nap.edu/books/0309084350/html/.

Boyd, W. L. (1999). Environmental pressures, management imperatives, and competing paradigms in educational administration. *Educational Management & Administration, 27*(3), 283–298.

Broussard, C. A. (2003). Facilitating home-school partnerships for multiethnic families: School social workers collaborating for success. *Children & Schools, 25*(4), 211–222.

Carr, W. (1995). *For education: Towards critical educational inquiry*. Bristol, PA: Open University Press.

Chamberlayne, P., Bornat, J., & Wengraf, T. (2000). *The turn to biographical methods in social science: Comparative issues and examples.* London: Routledge.

Corbett, J. (2001). *Supporting inclusive education: A connective pedagogy.* London: Routledge/Falmer.

Delgado-Gaitan, C. (1993). Researching change and changing the researcher. *Harvard Educational Review, 63*(4), 389–411.

Delgado-Gaitan, C. (2001). *The power of community: Mobilizing for family and schooling.* Lanham, MD: Rowman & Littlefield.

deMarrais, K. (2004). Elegant communications: Sharing qualitative research with communities, colleagues, and critics. *Qualitative Inquiry, 10*(2), 281–297.

Elliott, J. (1991). *Action research for educational change.* Milton Keynes, UK: Open University Press.

Elmore, R. F., & Furman, S. H. (2001). Research finds the false assumption of accountability. *Education Digest, 67*(4), 9–14.

Freire, P. (1973). *Education for critical consciousness.* New York: Seabury Press.

Gran-O'Donnell, S., Farwell, N., Spigner, C., Nguyen, C., Ciske, S., Young, T., et al. (2001). *Perspectives of multicultural youth on community building: A participatory approach.* Unpublished manuscript.

Hammersley, M. (2000). Evidence-based practice in education and the contribution of educational research. In L. Trinder & S. Reynolds (Eds.), *Evidence-based practice: A critical appraisal* (pp. 163–183). London: Sage.

Harold, R. D., Palmiter, M. L., Lynch, S. A., & Freedman-Doan, C. R. (1995). Life stories: A practice-based research technique. *Journal of Sociology and Social Welfare, 22*, 23–44.

Herr, K. (1995). Action research as empowering practice. *Journal of Progressive Human Services, 6*(2), 45–58.

Hick, S. (1997). Participatory research: An approach for structural social workers. *Journal of Progressive Human Services, 8*(2), 63–78.

Holland, T. P. (1991). Narrative, knowledge and professional practice. *Social Thought, 17*(1), 32–40.

Holy, P. (1991). From action research to collaborative inquiry: The processing of an innovation. In O. Zuber-Skerritt (Ed.), *Action research for change and development* (pp. 36–56). Brookfield, VA: Gower Publishing.

Jay, J. (2003). *Quality teaching: Reflection as the heart of practice.* Lanham, MD: The Scarecrow Press, Inc.

Jones, J. (1991). Action research in facilitating change in institutional practice. In O. Zuber-Skerritt (Ed.), *Action research for change and development* (pp. 207–223). Brookfield, VA: Gower Publishing.

Josselson, R. (1996). *Ethics and process in the narrative study of lives.* Thousand Oaks, CA: Sage.

Lather, P. (2004). This *IS* your father's paradigm: Government intrusion and the case of qualitative research in education. *Qualitative Inquiry, 10*(1), 15–34.

Lipman, P. (2004). *High stakes education: Inequality, globalization, and urban school reform.* New York: Routledge/Falmer.

Martin, R. (1995). *Oral history in social work: Research, assessment, and intervention.* Thousand Oaks, CA: Sage.

No Child Left Behind Act of 2001, PL 107-110, 115 Stat.1425(2002), pp.1596-98. Retrieved January 25, 2005, from www.ed.gov/policy/elsec/leg/esea02/107-110 pdf.

Noffke, S., & Stevenson, S. (1995). *Educational action research: Becoming practically critical.* New York: Teachers College Press.

Pearlmutter, S. (2002). Achieving political practice: Integrating individual need and social action. *Journal of Progressive Human Services, 13*(1), 31-51.

Peters, A. (2003). Isolation or inclusion: Creating safe spaces for lesbian and gay youth. *Families in Society, 84*(3), 331-337.

Salcido, R., Ornelas, V., & Garcia, J. (2002). A neighborhood watch program for inner-city school children. *Children and Schools, 24*(3), 175-187.

Simpson, L. (2004). Students who challenge: Reducing barriers to inclusion. In F. Armstrong & M. Moore (Eds.), *Action research for inclusive education: Changing places, changing practices, changing minds.* London: Routledge/Falmer.

Sirotnik, K. A. (1989). The school as the center of change. In T. J. Sergiovanni & J. H. Moore (Eds.), *Schooling for tomorrow: Directing reforms to issues that count* (pp. 89-113). Boston: Allyn & Bacon.

Sleeter, C. (1996). *Multicultural education as social activism.* Albany: State University of New York.

Sohng, S. (1996). Participatory research and community organizing. *Journal of Sociology and Social Welfare, 23*(4), 77-97.

Stevens, J. (1999). Creating collaborative partnerships: Clinical intervention research in an inner-city school. *Social Work in Education, 21*(3), 151-162.

Williams, M. R. (1989). *Neighborhood organizing for urban school reform.* New York: Teachers College Press.

Witherspoon, R. (2002). The involvement of African American families and communities in education: Whose responsibility is it? In S. Denbo & L. Beaulieu (Eds.), *Improving schools for African American students: A reader for educational leaders* (pp. 181-191). Springfield, IL: Charles C. Thomas.

14

School Social Work: Organizational Perspectives

Edward J. Pawlak
Western Michigan University

Linwood Cousins
University of North Carolina, Charlotte

◆ People-Processing and People-Changing Perspectives
◆ Formal Organizational Structure
◆ Informal Structure and Relations
◆ The School as an Organizational Culture
◆ Imaginization: Metaphorical Perspectives of Schools
◆ Managing Organizational Change

Schools are organizational entities that have structures, processes, policies, and cultures. These factors affect school officials, teachers, staff, students, and their families. Accordingly, school social workers have responsibility to understand and influence these factors—especially on behalf of students and families who are clients. School social workers cannot understand and influence what they cannot see. Therefore, they must use several organizational lenses—conceptual frameworks—to discern organizational structures, processes, policies, and culture. A review of all organizational frameworks would take us far afield, thus we have selected those that we believe are particularly useful to school social workers.

PEOPLE-PROCESSING AND PEOPLE-CHANGING PERSPECTIVES

Hasenfeld (1983) analyzes human service organizations as entities that rely on people-processing and people-changing operations. As applied to schools, these perspectives direct attention to several processing tasks (Lauffer, 1984): (1) assessing and classifying student attributes, qualifications, and circumstances to decide eligibility for particular programs of study, special services and benefits, or participation in athletics and other extracurricular activity; (2) exploring those attributes, qualifications, and circumstances to decide appropriate program and benefit alternatives; (3) selecting among the alternatives; and (4) referring or placing the student in a curriculum or program, or providing a benefit. The key elements that a school social worker must address are organizational decision making, school modes of operation, patterns of processing and changing students, and whether these patterns are appropriately or inappropriately different among students with particular attributes.

School social workers can use people-processing and -changing perspectives to explore several questions. What are the rules and procedures used by school officials and faculty in transactions with students? Are these rules and procedures applied equitably among students who, for example, face discipline, suspension, or expulsion? What are the consequences experienced by students of decisions made or not made by school officials or teachers? Examples would be a decision to refer or not to refer for testing or to special services; a decision to place a student on one academic track rather than another; a decision to not sponsor "Saturday School" as a form of in-school suspension for students who are truant or have behavioral problems. Do students with particular characteristics experience different and less favorable school career paths (e.g., low-income vs. upper-income students, girls vs. boys, White students vs. minority students)? Are students with particular characteristics screened in or out of particular programs (e.g., what kinds of students with what kinds of behavior in the primary grades are more likely to be screened into the early identification program)? Are some groups of students often inappropriately classified? Are students with particular characteristics or circumstances likely to have favorable or unfavorable labels? Do students with particular attributes have equal access to school curricula, programs, and activities? Is stigma attached to participation in some school programs and activities? Which teachers or staff members are working with which students? These and other questions can be raised about the school's processing operations and how decisions about teachers, staff, and students are reached.

The answers to these questions might lead school social workers to engage in one or more types of intervention (Jansson, 1994). There is (1) policy sensitive practice: alerting a parent to his or her rights at an upcoming individual educational program (IEP) meeting; (2) policy-related practice, which would involve informing a principal that a student who was qualified for a program was excluded; and (3) policy practice, which would involve advocating to elementary school administrators a change in school policy by which some students with behavioral problems are disciplined by removal from class and placement on "the bench" in the main office.

FORMAL ORGANIZATIONAL STRUCTURE

Formal structure refers to official, established patterns in an organization. Several dimensions are used to describe the formal structure of organizations: formalization, standardization, centralization/decentralization, horizontal, and vertical complexity (Hall, 1996). These dimensions can be manipulated or altered such that aspects of the organization or its programs can be designed to be more or less formalized, standardized, centralized, or complex. Variations in organizational and program structure lead to variations in consequences (positive or negative) for school administrators, teachers, students, and parents. Although some school organizational and program structures are not accessible to and manipulable by school social workers, some are. Practitioners have a responsibility to figure out which ones are and try to alter them. Some illustrations are provided next.

Formalization refers to the degree to which rules, policies, and procedures that govern behavior in the organization are officially codified and set forth in writing. Examples of this would be rules governing how IEP meetings should be conducted, criteria governing discipline of students, guidelines for conducting locker searches, and protocols for recording and reporting unexcused absences. Formalization prescribes behavior and usually reduces discretion (e.g., in a particular school district, principals may suspend students, but only the superintendent can expel a student). However, formalization may legitimate discretion (e.g., in one school district a school social worker is charged to help children in their roles as students but may provide counseling to parents if such assistance will facilitate the child's school adjustment).

Standardization is a type of formalization in which organizations carry out uniform ways of dealing with uniform situations; rules or definitions are established that cover a particular set of circumstances and apply invariably. For example, schools have standardized forms and practices to record student absences and report them to parents, and school officials often follow a steplike protocol in which the frequency and intensity of interventions vary as absences increase.

Each of these concepts can be used to analyze several aspects of a school's formal structure. Such analyses are useful for several reasons. Formalization and standardization can be functional if they reduce role ambiguity; document rights, duties, and expectations; and hold school officials, staff, teachers, students, or parents accountable. For example, formal structures that entitle students and parents to appeal a counselor's assigned program of study promote due process, fairness, and opportunity to negotiate and champion academic preferences, which may also ease strong feelings. The lack of due process is likely to cast school administrators and teachers as authoritarian and arbitrary officials. Such perceptions held by students and parents may contribute to strained relationships and lead to student behavioral problems, or parental defamation of the school in the community. Formalization and standardization may eliminate or constrain arbitrariness and may promote equitable treatment and equal opportunity for programs, services, or benefits. Standardization may promote consistency among staff members who have similar decision-making or processing tasks.

Formalization and standardization can be dysfunctional if they promote "bureaupathologies" such as "red tape," inflexibility, devotion to method, and discourage innovation and appropriate discretion (Patti, 1982). When school rules and procedures are contested, a school social worker might ask if they have been formalized or are they informal and a matter of convention (e.g., experienced teachers have probably heard a student or parent say: "Where does it say that students can't do that?"). Formalization and standardization may be dysfunctional when they lead to routinization or ritualistic behavior, but the situation calls instead for individualizing the interpretation and implementation of a policy. For example, some states have a zero tolerance for weapons in the school with severe penalties such as automatic expulsion from school for an academic year—no exceptions. A 4th-grade student in a small town school brought a knife to school to cut brownies for her classmates. Her behavior came under the stipulations of the law, and she was barred from school. Some proponents were concerned that a precedent might be set if an exception was made, whereas others advocated that an exception does not drive out the rule. The student was suspended for a week after the superintendent and school board reviewed her case, and the incident was used to educate the school community about zero tolerance.

Centralization refers to the concentration of power, authority, and decision making at the top of the organization. As applied to a school district or system, centralization refers to the board, superintendent, or what is commonly known as "the central office" or "central administration." As applied to a particular school building, centralization refers to the principal, assistant principal, and office staff. Decentralization refers to the distribution of power, authority, and decision making down through the organization. As applied to the school district or system, decentralization refers to arrangements such as regional offices or centers, or the delegation of some functions to local school principals and faculty. As applied to a particular school building, decentralization refers to the delegation of some functions to individual teachers, faculty committees, parent-teacher advisory councils, or teacher-student workgroups. Within a particular school building, principals can make decisions about discipline, suspension, and access to services, or they can involve staff and parents in developing guidelines for such decisions or rely on a faculty advisory committee. Whatever the case may be, school social workers must first learn what is concentrated or distributed before they can engage in organizational change.

Centralized and decentralized structures can be functional or dysfunctional. For example, centralizing decisions regarding expulsion in the superintendent's office is functional, because dismissal has profound consequences for the student and could lead to litigation; decentralizing decisions to local school officials regarding which students should be referred for school social work services is functional, because the predominant needs of students vary from school to school. Generally speaking, centralization of authority, power, and decision making may be functional when schools have to manage boundary relationships with the external environment (e.g., the press, police, juvenile court, community advocacy groups), when scarce resources have to be rationed and carefully allocated, or when there are threats to the school (e.g., protests, litigation, complaints). Decentralization enables teachers, students, or their parents to gain ownership of policies and programs and increases the likelihood of their legitimacy and successful implementation. For example, a decentralized decision-making structure, such as a joint faculty-student committee on student conduct, might promote student ownership of the code of conduct, whereas a centralized top-down imposition of the code might generate resistance. Decentralization is also suited to managing change and uncertainty at the front lines of the organization and promotes bottom-up innovation and adaptation (Wagoner, 1994).

Horizontal complexity refers to the type and degree of organizational segmentation, such as departmentalization, and specialization of positions, roles, jobs, or duties. The degree of specialization and departmentalization can be functional or dysfunctional. High specialization sometimes leads to fragmented and uncoordinated delivery of services, but it also might contribute to efficiency and the availability of high levels of expertise. Sometimes school social workers have to run interference for students and parents who are overwhelmed with their problems and the bureaucratic maze of services.

Vertical complexity refers to the number of levels in the hierarchy from the top to the bottom of the organization. Vertical complexity may be functional or dysfunctional from the standpoint of a school social worker or parent interested in promoting change. If a change proposal has to traverse many hierarchical levels for approval, the structure may not be functional; if officials are accessible and there are few levels between the top and the bottom, organizational change may be more easily influenced.

Some aspects of formal structure are often depicted in pyramidal organizational charts or tables of organization that identify hierarchical relationships, preferred communication paths, and the complexity of the organization in terms of the different divisions, specializations, departments, or programs. However, these traditional organizational charts are being replaced by circle diagrams that partially overlap or are drawn in concentric fashion to depict interdependencies, collaboration, and participation in decision making among organizational units (Tropman, 1989). Linear, rational approaches to horizontal and vertical coordination in organizations are being supplanted by flatter organizations, negotiated political orders, fluid and dynamic structures, and combinations of loose and tight coupling among organizational units (Fennell, 1994). A variety of geometric shapes and diagrams are used to graphically depict these nontraditional organizational structures and relationships (Mintzberg, 1983).

As school social workers begin their assignments in a new school, they should devote time to comprehending the school's horizontal and vertical complexity, or its negotiated political order, often found in school manuals or handbooks. If such documentation is not available, school social workers are advised to be observant, check out the arrangements with opinion leaders, and map the structure or negotiated order for themselves. Such understanding is important because school social workers are required to integrate, coordinate, link, and communicate with different departments, units, positions, or roles in the school's structure. The role of school social worker gives practitioners legitimate, unique access to most if not all segments and roles within schools—structural mobility. Thus, school social workers must figure out their niche in the school and which individuals in which positions might facilitate or hinder work with officials, teachers, students, and families.

INFORMAL STRUCTURE AND RELATIONS

People in schools—in fact, in all organizations—develop social relationships that are not prescribed by organizational officials. These social relationships evolve into patterned group processes and social structures that are known as "informal organizations," or "informal structures and relations." These social relationships are informal in that they are unofficial, not mandated, and not planned. Informal structure is rarely, if ever, documented (so don't ask your principal for a copy of the school's informal organization chart, because it doesn't exist, but as we will point out shortly, you can draw one on your own).

There are four types of informal structure: affectional, communication, decision making, and power. These structures are not mutually exclusive, and the same participants may be involved in all structures but in different ways. Affectional structure refers to patterns of social relationships based on friendship, mutual attraction, similar interests, common experiences—for whatever reason, people like each other and spend time together when it is not formally required by the organization. Affectional structure manifests itself in several ways: two or more staff members frequently have coffee breaks or lunch together, sit next to each other at meetings, attend professional conferences together, play volleyball together after school, or socialize off-the-job. Communication structure refers to patterns of social interaction among staff members based on giving and getting information, opinions, viewpoints, or feelings (even when they are not within an affectional structure). Some common metaphors for communication structure include "the rumor mill," "the grapevine," "the talk on the street," "leaks," and "inside information" or "inside track." Informal communication structure can be detected by observing who talks with whom after a controversy or a staff meeting. Who are the confidants, the listeners? Whom do teachers depend on to figure out and report "what's going on?" Decision-making structure refers to patterns of social interaction among school personnel based on the solicitation or provision of analysis, insights, and advice leading up to a decision. Decision-making structure can be detected by observing who consults with whom during deliberations (e.g., Is there a small group of experienced teachers who are often consulted "on the side" by the principal? Do particular teachers meet informally before a meeting in an attempt to sway opinion prior to a formal meeting?). Power structure refers to patterns of social interaction based on ability to influence. There are four types of power: referent, expertise, reward, and coercive (French & Raven, 1968). A teacher may have referent power because she is liked, and another may have expertise power because she is a respected English instructor. Some teachers have reward power because they support colleagues and praise them for their contributions, and others have coercive power because they have years of experience, they are abrasive, and colleagues are intimidated by them.

School social workers must strive to discern informal structure, because they will inevitably become a part of it, and they may have to work with or against it. School social workers must figure out who is included in which informal groups. Who is the "power behind the throne?" Who are the quiet "shakers and movers?" Who has the "ear of the administration" and who is "wired in?" Who really runs this place? Who are the insiders and outsiders? Is there an inner circle?

If mapping relevant informal structures and relations is essential or desirable, school social workers can easily do so with a formal organization chart and highlighters of different colors. Let's assume that the school has an organizational chart in which each school official's, staff member's, and teacher's name and position is posted within its own rectangular box. Let's assume that an assistant principal and two teachers are an affectional group, and the principal relies on the school secretary and head of the physical plant to "keep their ears to the ground and keep her posted on goings-on." Different colored highlighters can be used to visually map these two informal structures. Such mapping may help demystify the complex informal operational structure and relations within a school and their congruence with formal structure.

Several factors contribute to the development and maintenance of informal structure and relations. These are (1) the characteristics or attributes of individuals, such as gender, race, age, and religion;(2) common life experiences (e.g., among teachers and staff-single parenthood, caring for an adult parent, attendance at the same university); (3) shared values and interests (e.g., conservative orientation, quilting, or fishing); (4) common memberships in organizations external to the school (e.g., a church, a political party); and (5) sharing a common fate such as working under an authoritarian, domineering principal. When informal structure is detected, school social workers should try to determine the factors that bond members together.

Informal structures not only involve administrators, teachers, and staff in varying combinations but may include students and parents. Teachers sometimes have "favorites," both parents and students. Some students and parents are insiders because they have high participation rates in school activities; some students, teachers, and parent volunteers are involved in the ski club or play basketball together in the school gym on Sunday afternoon. Students detect informal structure and have names for some aspects of it—teacher's pets, brown-nosers, suck-ups, grungies, preppies, and nerds.

Informal structure serves several functions in organizations: (1) it provides informal linkages between departments, positions, and roles (e.g., the school social worker and attendance officer worked together in another school district); (2) it sometimes compensates for problems in the formal structure (e.g., when a school principal was of little help to teachers who had to manage classroom behavior problems, they turned to a tenured experienced teacher for assistance); (3) it socializes and orients new school personnel and students to life in the organization—what are the "dos and don'ts?"; (4) it provides a network for the circulation of information; (5) it provides social support and alleviates stress and frustration; and (6) it meets interpersonal and associational needs. In examining a school's informal structure, school social workers should try to figure out the functions that it serves and determine whether it supports or undermines the students served.

THE SCHOOL AS AN ORGANIZATIONAL CULTURE

The organizational culture of a school affects all school functions. This fact is particularly relevant to social workers who practice in schools where there is difficulty in understanding the mutual influence and effect on intraschool relationships of social and academic processes occurring between schools and society at large. Posing several questions brings the issues into focus: What is the nature of organizational culture in schools? Why is this information important to social workers? What do social workers need to know about organizational culture in schools to function effectively?

What is cultural about the organization of schools? Culture can be defined as the beliefs, values, traditions, and attitudes that are the basis of the frames of reference or meanings people use to organize reality and direct their behavioral actions. In deciphering the culture in how schools work as organizations, two pathways are important.

Schools are transmitters of dominant cultural standards, norms, and values emanating from society at large. Dominant cultural norms are infused into schools through federal regulations, state and local boards of education, and universities as institutions for knowledge development and training. These institutions define, design, and organize academic material that becomes a part of the educational and social activities that have to be administered in a school. For example, the selection and enforcement of reading, writing, and arithmetic curricula, as well as the methods to teach these subjects, are artifacts of Western cultural beliefs about learning and socialization, rather than a universal fact of human nature.

Interpersonal transactions occurring between students and teachers or staff provide another pathway for culture to permeate schools as organizations. Culture operates in schools in this way by providing a blueprint for the meaning and interpretation of acceptable and unacceptable behavior, attitudes, emotions, and beliefs. For example, students generally understand that when they enter the classroom, the teacher is in charge. The teacher makes the rules and enforces them. He or she decides who can talk and when. In addition, when a student violates rules, the consequences generally fit the sanctioned norms in school. As such, culture in schools manifests in an organized way various frames of reference or meanings associated with compliance and violations of official policies and regulations.

Both pathways of culture in the organization of schools are alike in reflecting varying degrees of influence by dominant culture norms in society at large. When there is a high degree of compatibility and homogeneity among students and school officials, there is likely to be less conflict within the organizational milieu of the school. However, such compatibility and homogeneity in schools have never been fully the case for nonwhite groups (e.g., African Americans, Native Americans, Hispanics) and are becoming even less the case because of the increasing ethnic, religious, and economic diversity of groups residing in the United States.

School social workers must be abreast of the influence and impact of organizational culture through dominant beliefs, values, attitudes, and behaviors that are embedded in the customs, traditions, and notions of common sense forming the basis of administrative policy and regulations in schools. For example, social workers should examine disciplinary and evaluative activities occurring between social workers and students, between students and staff, and among parents, staff, and social workers. When observing disciplinary activities in school, social workers can ask themselves the following questions:

- Do the infractions that led to disciplinary action reflect commonly held beliefs, values, and attitudes between the student and school official about the rule or standard that has been violated?
- When there is a lack of commonality, are the differences labeled dysfunctional rather than as variations in how people understand the multiple meanings of the rules and standards being enforced?

These questions are especially important to consider when the outcomes are detrimental to the social, emotional, and academic well-being of students.

Understanding and Action

What do social workers need to know to understand and effectively engage in situations in which dominant cultural frames of reference that organize schools do not work? We refer to cases in which the organizational culture of a school is not held together by common frames of reference and therefore leaves students, teachers, and staff acting, thinking, and feeling incompatible and alienated. For example, many African Americans have experienced strain in relation to dominant cultural norms in school and have responded with resistance. Many African Americans have questioned the relevance of the subjects taught in school to their plight as a stigmatized group. Being able to read, write, and do arithmetic have not directly led to less racial discrimination and increased economic and political liberation. Mastery of these academic subjects can help, but not always. In this context, when frames of reference operating in the organizational culture of a school are juxtaposed, compliance and noncompliance are better understood.

Another example is the kind of etiquette required in classroom interactions among students and between students and teachers. Many, but certainly not all, African Americans have been socialized in environments that value a high degree of expressiveness and animation through language and the body in communicating with people. However, classroom etiquette generally requires that students sit still when speaking, stay in their seats, only address the teacher, and so forth. When students do not or cannot comply with these social and behavioral norms, they are punished or labeled dysfunctional.

Social workers must understand that organizational cultures contain meaningful processes manifested in terms of beliefs, values, attitudes, and behaviors that comprise frames of reference. Among minority and majority groups, meanings and frames are influenced by, among other things, historical and contemporary experiences in the Unites States and beyond. Minorities specifically tend to experience school norms as extensions of the social, economic, and political inequality they experience in U.S. society. Many studies have documented this, coupled with the finding that such relational strain between minorities and school staff influences the academic performance of the students and the evaluations of students by teachers and staff (Gibson & Ogbu, 1991; Spindler, 1997). Consider that social workers tend to perform evaluations and assessments that serve as the basis of various forms of psychological, social, and educational intervention with students in school. These activities serve an important social and cultural function for schools and society at large. This predicament requires social workers to understand the complicity of their roles and activities in enforcing dominant, and often oppressive, societal norms that function as parts of the organizational culture in schools. The full extent of what is meant here is more acutely realized in schools with significant numbers of minority students or students from low-income backgrounds.

What commonly happens, for example, is that social workers interact with school staff who believe unquestionably that academic processes and contexts are free of culture or cultural bias. Noncompliance and low academic performance, in their view, reflect psychosocial dysfunction and cognitive or intellectual abnormality, respectively. School personnel and even some social workers may have difficulty seeing beyond the seemingly natural and just plain common-sense processes of most social and academic aspects of schooling. Taking these processes for granted, however, is partially a product of the blinding nature of a dominant culture. Taken as a whole in a contemporary context, these beliefs, traditions, and notions of common sense form parts of a frame of reference that maintains currently dominant organizational cultures in school and widespread social, economic, and political inequality in society. They have contributed to (1) racism or the belief that minorities fail in school because of their inferiority as a people, and (2) beliefs that minority students simply need to persevere in their work and tolerate or overcome their feelings and perceptions of being treated inequitably by assimilating to or accommodating dominant cultural norms.

Social workers can do something about this. They can individually engage in accessible levels of the organizational culture of the school and collectively engage in advocacy, public education, and political action. Individual engagement begins with asking and answering the questions raised earlier: What are the beliefs, values, attitudes, and behavior that form the basis of social and academic compliance and noncompliance by students? Answers to such questions can lead to interactions with students and staff in which one is not only guided by the surface or manifest understandings of disagreements between students and teachers, but also by the underlying or latent meanings that are the cultural foundation of such incompatibilities. The next step is to conduct educational, social, and psychological interventions that reach both levels of the problem without leaving students and teachers with understandings that limit them to a traditional arsenal of labels, diagnoses, and other disciplinary actions and reactions.

The second application as a social worker is a matter of scale. That is, the focus is on those legislative and academic policy practices that provide unidimensional approaches to education in the first place. Activities in these domains require social workers to participate in advocacy and public education through community dialogues and political actions that directly or indirectly address official policy-making bodies. School staff meetings, board meetings, state legislatures, and tracking federal bills in consort with NASW's lobbying arm are excellent sites of practice.

In conclusion, the understandings and actions regarding the organizational culture of schools proposed in this discussion offer a way in which social workers can become transformative professionals. We can begin by understanding and refusing the notion that academic and social functions in schools are neutral transactions in organizational culture. Acting as such, social workers contribute to the realization of the overall interdependence between U.S. institutions such as schools, as well as social, economic, political, and cultural processes in society at large.

IMAGINIZATION: METAPHORICAL PERSPECTIVES OF SCHOOLS

Imaginization is the name for organizational assessment and development as created and practiced by Gareth Morgan, an academician and consultant

(Morgan, 1993). Imaginization, the word, is the result of the fusion of the concepts of imagination and organization. Imaginization, the concept, refers to the creative use of metaphor to interpret and shape organizational life and develop shared understandings of organizational structure, processes, roles, and culture. Metaphors enable "new ways of thinking about management styles, organizational design, approaches to planning and change, and basic products and services" (Morgan, 1993, p. 265). One imaginizes by invoking metaphorical images to frame and reframe organizational situations in new ways: "We don't teach in a school; we teach in a military organization with a principal who acts like General Patton." "Faculty and students are like an extended family." "The school is an oasis in a community beleaguered by gang fighting, drug dealing, inadequate housing, with many single parents hanging on by their fingernails." School cultures are often characterized through metaphors: "The teachers approach their work as if it were a calling, not just a job." "The only time you see those teachers move is when it's time to go home, and they usually beat the students out the door." Metaphors send a strong metamessage that influences student and parental attitudes and behavior toward the school.

These examples reveal how the process of imaginization begins—with metaphorical characterization and images that serve as the point of departure for assessing the organization. Imaginization is not codified in behaviorally specific steps such that one could mechanically follow them. Metaphorical language is used to describe the basic protocol of imaginization: "Get inside." "Adopt the role of a learner." "Map the terrain." "Identify key themes and interpretations" (to produce an evolving "reading" of the situation). "Confirm, refute, and reformulate throughout." The method is exploratory yet deliberative; it is free flowing yet anchored in organizational realities; it is directive yet participative; it is subjective, yet objective. Nevertheless, there is sufficient structure and direction in the method for open, venturesome practitioners to begin imaginizing (Pawlak, 1994).

The fundamental processes of imaginization are not foreign to social workers. We intuitively rely on metaphor in our everyday organizational lives to "read into" and characterize what is going on. However, we seldom "play out" the "readings" to use them as heuristic devices to analyze and solve problems. School social workers will find imaginization congruent with their professional values and education. The process has a primacy of orientation toward organizational members' definition of the situation, ownership of organizational problems, and responsibility for change (Pawlak, 1994).

Images of schools through metaphor development have been used to study school climate and environment. Grady, Fisher, and Fraser (1996) developed a questionnaire to gain "insight into teachers' mental images of their school as it is and as they think it should be" (p. 51). The questionnaire was used in a workshop with teachers who were led through four steps that can be adapted by school social workers to assess their schools:

1. Identify several most favored and least favored images of the school.
2. Identify positive and negative aspects of these favored and nonfavored images.
3. Identify assumptions/beliefs/values/philosophies which underpin these favored and non-favored images.
4. Identify exemplars of language, rituals, ceremonies, stories, heroes, schedules, decision-making/delegating/accountability processes and so on which ought to be fostered in the school in light of the exercise. (Grady, Fisher, & Fraser, 1996, p. 51)

As an exercise, formulate a metaphor about your school. Run with it. Where does it take you? What does it reveal about the school as an organization? What corrective action or change is suggested by the metaphor? What are the factors that might facilitate or hinder change? This delightful approach provides a refreshing counterpoint to traditional yet essential approaches to organizational analysis.

Thus far we have presented several conceptual frameworks that we believe are useful in understanding and analyzing schools as organizations: schools as people-processing and -changing organizations; schools as formal and informal structures; schools as cultures; and schools viewed from metaphorical perspectives. Each framework enables school social workers to understand schools from different organizational viewpoints. We believe an eclectic approach is essential. No one perspective is adequate to penetrate the complexities of schools as organizations. If the application of one framework does not yield insight into organizational problems, then another should be tried.

School social workers are not interested in organizational analysis for its own sake. The results of organizational analysis must be transformed into change efforts. In the final section of this chapter, we offer some general guidelines for introducing and managing change. Detailed discussions of organizational change models, strategies, tactics, and development abound in the literature (Bailey, 1992; Brager & Holloway, 1992; Burbach & Crockett, 1994; Flynn, 1995; Gottfredson, 1987; Holloway & Brager, 1985; Mulkeen & Cooper, 1992; Netting, Kettner, & McMurtry, 1993; Pawlak, 1998; Smithmier, 1996).

MANAGING ORGANIZATIONAL CHANGE

Organizational analysis yields insights or findings about organizational conditions or problems. These insights and findings are essential to the planning and implementation of change efforts. The following guides are offered as one way to approach changing schools from within.

1. Describe the organizational problem, condition, or opportunity for change. What are the features of the problem or change opportunity? How is the problem distributed in the school? What are the key groups affected by the problem?

2. What factors contribute to or sustain the condition or problem? What factors brought about the change opportunity at this time?
3. What is the goal of the change you propose? What are the reasons for changes?
4. Identify the key persons, groups, roles, positions, or units affected by the proposed change.
5. What are the sunk costs in the status quo? There are two kinds of sunk costs—financial and psychological investments (e.g., "this program is my baby"). What are the likely sources of resistance to change, the degree of resistance, and how might resistance be expressed (Patti, 1980)?
6. Identify possible approaches to change and possible positive and negative effects.
7. Think through the change that you want to introduce by anticipating potential adverse consequences and how they might be overcome. (Don't make your chess moves one at a time.)
8. Anticipate the reactions of school officials, staff, teachers, students, or parents.
9. Explore these matters with trusted colleagues and ask for ideas.
10. What resources, time, support, or training are needed to implement change?
11. Develop a plan to influence change and a workplan to implement change so that influential persons can envision the feasibility of change. Strive to develop shared ownership of the change proposal and process.

School social workers have a primacy of orientation toward helping students and their families through individual or group counseling, and often such approaches are appropriate. However, when organizational conditions contribute to or sustain student problems, helpful interventions on behalf of students must be directed at the school as an organization. The roles and status of school social workers, as well as their professional education, enable them to take holistic perspectives and to legitimately engage the many different units, roles, and personnel within schools. School social workers have more opportunities to leverage change than they might realize. Carpe diem.

References

Bailey, D. (1992). Organizational change in a public school system: The synergism of two approaches. *Social Work in Education, 14*(2), 94–105.

Brager, G., & Holloway, S. (1992). Assessing prospects for organizational change: The uses of force field analysis. *Administration in Social Work, 16*(3-4), 15–28.

Burbach, H. J., & Crockett, M. (1994). The learning organization as a prototype for the next generation of schools. *Planning and Change, 25*(3-4), 173–179.

Fennell, H. A. (1994). Organizational linkages: Expanding the existing metaphor. *Journal of Educational Administration, 32*(1), 23–33.

Flynn, J. P. (1995). Social justice in social agencies. In R. L. Edwards & J. G. Hopps (Eds.), *The encyclopedia of social work* (19th ed., pp. 2173-2179). New York: NASW Press.

French, J. R. P., & Raven, B. (1968). The bases of social power. In D. Cartwright & A. Zander (Eds.), *Group dynamics* (3rd ed., pp. 215-235). New York: Harper & Row.

Gibson, M., & Ogbu, J. (1991). *Minority status and schooling: A comparative study of immigrant and involuntary minorities.* New York: Garland.

Gottfredson, D. C. (1987). An evaluation of an organization development approach to reducing school disorder. *Evaluation Review, 11*(6), 739-763.

Grady, N. B., Fisher, D. L., & Fraser, B. J. (1996). Images of school through metaphor development and validation of a questionnaire. *Journal of Educational Administration, 34*(2), 41-53.

Hall, R. (1996). *Organizations: Structure, process, and outcomes* (6th ed.), Englewood Cliffs, NJ: Prentice Hall.

Hasenfeld, Y. (1983). *Human service organizations.* Englewood Cliffs, NJ: Prentice Hall.

Holloway, S., & Brager, G. (1985). Implicit negotiations and organizational practice. *Administration in Social Work, 9*(2), 15-24.

Jansson, B. (1994). *Social welfare policy: From theory to practice* (2nd ed.). Belmont, CA: Brooks/Cole.

Lauffer, A. (1984). *Understanding your agency* (2nd ed.). Beverly Hills, CA: Sage.

Mintzberg, H. (1983). *Structure in fives: Designing effective organizations.* Englewood Cliffs, NJ: Prentice Hall.

Morgan, G. (1993). *Imaginization: The art of creative management.* New York: Sage.

Mulkeen, T. A., & Cooper, B. S. (1992). Implications of preparing school administrators for knowledge work organizations: A case study. *Journal of Educational Administration, 30*(1), 17-28.

Netting, E. F., Kettner, P. M., & McMurtry, S. L. (1993). *Social work macropractice.* New York: Longman.

Patti, R. (1980). Organizational resistance and change: The view from below. In H. Resnick & R. Patti (Eds.), Change from within (pp. 114-131). New York: Haworth.

Patti, R. (1982). Analyzing agency structures. In M. Austin & J. Hershey (Eds.), *Handbook on mental health administration* (pp. 137-162). San Francisco, CA: Jossey-Bass.

Pawlak, E. J. (1994). [Review of the book Imaginization: The art of creative management.] *Administration in Social Work, 18*(4), 132-134.

Pawlak, E. J. (1998). Organizational tinkering. In B. Compton & B. Galaway (Eds.), *Social work processes* (4th ed, n.p.). New York: Allyn & Bacon.

Smithmier, A. (1996). Schools and community-based collaboration: Multiple resistances and structural realities. *Planning and Change, 27*(1/2), 15-29.

Spindler, G. (Ed.), (1997). *Education and cultural process: Anthropological approaches.* Prospect Heights, IL: Waveland Press.

Tropman, J. E. (1989). The organizational circle: A new approach to drawing an organizational chart. *Administration in Social Work, 13*(1), 35-44.

Wagoner, R. V. (1994). Changing school governance: A case for decentralized management. *Planning and Change, 25*(3-4), 206-218.

15

Conducting a Needs Assessment in a School Setting

Lyndell R. Bleyer
Western Michigan University

Kathryn Joiner
Western Michigan University

WHAT IS NEEDS ASSESSMENT?

The ability to conduct a needs assessment is a crucial skill in school social work. It provides a systematic means of gathering data about a problem experienced by more than a few students in the school. It provides a broader context for the problems that students are experiencing. It provides a data-based means of communicating about this broader context in a way that school administrators, teachers, and community members can understand. It provides school social workers with a powerful, data-based means of customizing their roles to fit the needs of a particular school or district.

A *human need* is any identifiable condition that limits a person in meeting his or her full potential. Human needs are usually expressed in social, economic, or health-related terms. From a research perspective they are frequently qualitative statements. Needs of individuals may be aggregated to express similar needs in quantified terms (United Way of America, 1999).

A *needs assessment* is a data-gathering and planning activity to inform decision making. The data describe the characteristics, achievements, knowledge, behaviors, desires, needs, and/or opinions of a group of persons or an entire community. Many have attempted to define human need in a more specific way than the previous definition. These definitions have ranged from Erikson's (1968) eight critical stages of development to Maslow's concept of motivation based on a hierarchy of needs (Maslow, 1970). J. A. Ponsioen (1962) stated that every society's first duty is to take care of the basic survival needs of its citizens, which include biological, emotional, social, and spiritual aspects. According to this view, each society must establish a level below which no person must fall. These levels vary from society to society and change over time within the same society. Therefore, *need* is a normative concept involving value judgments and is greatly influenced by social, political, and economic conditions. For example, in the early 1950s a family was considered fortunate if it had a television. Today, a student whose family does not have a computer might be considered academically disadvantaged.

WHY CONDUCT A NEEDS ASSESSMENT?

The data obtained through a needs assessment process are used to:
◆ Help understand the nature of a problem, its characteristics, magnitude, or consequences;
◆ Provide clues about causes and possible interventions;
◆ Compare students with other students or other schools;
◆ Identify and monitor trends (academic achievement, graduation rates, etc.);
◆ Document a need to be included in the problem statement of a grant proposal;
◆ Convince school officials that a problem exists that warrants the allocation of resources;
◆ Demonstrate the need for programs threatened by budget cuts;
◆ Document the support for new programs or interventions;
◆ Determine if and where additional resources are needed;
◆ Provide information to assist with planning or developing new services/ programs; and
◆ Influence legislation.

A needs assessment can be as simple as examining existing data. It can be as complex as a multiyear, multiphase study involving strategies to collect new data, through questionnaires or holding community forums. Designing and administering surveys is time consuming and expensive. It is generally wise to

first explore and use existing data before considering any type of new data col-
lection.Analyzing existing data can be very effective, and schools generally have
a wealth of data on hand. Data are collected on attendance, test scores, demographic characteristics, free lunch eligibility, enrollment in specific programs,
grades, results of standardized tests, and many other issues.

Types of Data

◆ *Characteristics* describe the group or population being studied and
   include ascribed features such as age, gender, race, and achieved characteristics like family income, poverty status, highest grade completed, and
   so on.
◆ *Counts and rates* provide data on the incidence and prevalence of conditions. For instance, the teen birthrate incidence is a measure of the
   number of births to teenage mothers compared to the number of female
   teenagers. Prevalence is the number of cases in a given population at a
   point in time, such as the number of teen suicides that occurred during
   a particular period in your community (Simons & Jablonski, 1990).
◆ *Knowledge* might include math proficiency, reading comprehension levels, standardized test scores, street smarts, and so on.
◆ *Beliefs and opinions* range all the way from thoughts about one's self,
   such as self-esteem, to views about behavior, such as moral or cultural
   values, and stereotypes about others, such as gender or ethnic stereotypes.
◆ *Behaviors* might include frequency of talking out in class, the duration
   of study time, eating habits, use of alcohol, participation in sports, number of hours worked per week by full-time students, absences, number
   of students suspended or expelled by reason, and so on. Normative
   behaviors fall within culturally expected/acceptable ranges.
◆ *Desires* are what people want (or think they want) but don't have,
   whereas needs can encompass things missing that are self-perceived or
   perceived by others. Needs might be determined by directly asking the
   intended audience, observed, or inferred from available data; whereas
   desires and opinions are usually gathered directly from questions on a
   survey and/or are gathered through observation, interviews, focus
   groups, or community forums.

PLANNING YOUR NEEDS ASSESSMENT

Determining What You Need to Know

The first step is determining what you need to know, and then deciding
what information is needed to make an informed decision. The second step is
determining the best source, balancing accuracy and reliability against cost and

time constraints. Often as you begin to explore doing a needs assessment, the list of questions to be answered keeps growing. To expedite the process, make a checklist and decide which data are critical to your goal, which data would be helpful to clarifying issues, which would be interesting to have, and which will not add any insight to the problem being studied. As part of your checklist, include a source column. This may help you narrow your choices. Remember to look at existing data first, before gathering new data.

For example, if a school district wants to know if a school breakfast program is a worthwhile pursuit, extensive research has already been done nationally, indicating that behavior and academic performance of most students improve in school systems where breakfast programs have been established. So what would be studied is not the relationship between breakfast and performance, but rather the need for a breakfast program in a particular school district.

The information needed is: (1) what percentage of students currently do not eat a nutritious breakfast, (2) how many children would be eligible for a subsidized breakfast program, and (3) for those children not eligible, but not having a nutritious breakfast, how many parents would buy into a breakfast program? Other factors influencing academic performance might also be interesting to study such as adequacy of sleep and parental involvement in study habits. Table 15.1 provides a grid to help frame the data needed, sources, methods of data collection, and level of usefulness.

To answer these questions, you might employ two tactics. First, have students keep a breakfast log or journal for three weeks in which they record everything they ate for breakfast each morning. To be effective, the students should update their journal as soon as possible after arriving at school (homeroom or first class of the day). These journals would be analyzed, using a nutritional guide, to give positive points for healthy foods consumed. If a question at the end of the journal asked if the student was eligible for free or reduced-price lunches and/or Medicaid, that would answer the eligibility question. If a survey were developed for parents, it would also ask about eligibility, and for those not eligible, whether the parent would like nutritious breakfasts to be available for purchase. Don't forget to ask each family the grade level of the students in their family—just in case your school system can only phase in a new program a few schools at a time.

Once the data are summarized, the school district can then look at need (students not currently eating nutritious breakfasts) and examine the cost of starting a breakfast program (the number of students eligible for free and reduced-price meals, and the number of students for whom parents are willing to pay). Eliminating barriers to participation is important too. Schools that use a prepaid meal card that does not distinguish between family-paid and subsidized meals have had the greatest success in getting eligible students to participate in meal programs without the stigma of being identified by peers as low income.

TABLE 15.1 Types of Data or Questions and Associated Sources or Methods

Type of Data or Questions	Source and Method	Essential	Helpful	Interesting	No Use
Breakfast's impact on learning—does it make a difference?	Literature review, e.g., Nutrition & Learning www.nal.usda.gov/fnic/service/learnpub.htm	✓			
How many of our students eat a nutritious breakfast?	Students and/or parents via log, diary, or question	✓			
What are eligibility guidelines for subsidies?	U.S. Dept. of Health & Human Serv.; census		✓		
How many of our school's students are eligible?	School records: i.e., now eligible for free milk or lunch subsidy; census data on poverty		✓		
Are there any differences in achievement between:	*Grades and test scores plus:*				
Our students who do and don't eat breakfast?	students &/or parents, teacher observation	✓			
Our students who get <7 vs. >7 hours sleep?	students &/or parents log/diary, teacher observation			✓	
Our students with parental review of homework?	parent signature on homework or not			✓	

Your school may have other topics that need answers. Some examples of information that may be useful in planning school services or child-related programs are the following:

- The number of children living in your community and the percentage of the total population that those children represent;
- Children living in poverty;
- Homeless children (number using shelters and doubled-up with other families);
- Mobility/transience or the number and percentage of students who attend the same school in June that they attended in September;
- Children with disabilities or special needs by type;

- Children living in single-parent families or families in which both parents work outside the home;
- The reported incidence of violent, serious, and misdemeanor juvenile crimes;
- The services and resources already available to meet the specific need you are addressing.

A thorough analysis could also look at other factors that might influence performance, such as amount of sleep, family income (access to reading materials, access to a home computer, educational toys, etc.), and parental involvement such as regular parental review of homework, and encouragement of reading in the home.

Build a Base of Support by Getting Others Involved

Discuss the project with school administrators, teachers, parents, and student representatives to develop a clear idea of the purpose of the needs assessment and what you hope to learn or achieve. One way to encourage cooperation among all the concerned parties is to form a small committee to help you formulate an action plan. In addition to promoting ownership of the project, involving others in the planning stage is a good way to make sure you haven't overlooked important details. Having the scope of the activity agreed on by a majority of those involved will reduce hurdles.

Write a Proposal or Plan

After you have determined the scope of the needs assessment, develop a written plan. In the proposal, include the following:
- Methodology of the needs assessment;
- Tasks to be performed and by whom;
- Projected time line. Don't set short deadlines. Give yourself enough time to collect data, review it, and produce a well-written summary;
- Budget for the project. Base this on the activities and time needed to carry them out. In addition to personnel, other expenses might include copying of questionnaires and summary reports, computer time, phone, postage, and resource materials.

In writing your plan, be realistic about whether or not you have the time and the expertise to carry out all elements of the project. Keep in mind the impact school breaks will have on your project. It may be that you will want to perform certain tasks but will need to engage additional help from other professionals to perform certain functions. If there are colleges or universities close by, you may be able to work out a plan for a graduate-level or upper-level undergraduate class to take on all or portions of your study as their semester project. Many colleges and universities have research centers that provide technical assistance and consultation to nonprofit organizations at cost. Large corporations may have research staff that they are willing to loan for committee work or consultation. If you intend to carry out the needs assessment yourself, consider whether you will need or can get release time.

IMPLEMENTING THE ASSESSMENT

Accurate information is key to successful planning. Having reliable data can help you make your point and persuade others. Think of the group or groups that will be the beneficiaries of the needs assessment and also think of the groups that will be potential funding sources or will make the decision to allocate resources to address the need. Gather data with both audiences in mind.

> You are concerned about the need for enhanced substance abuse prevention education. You provide a number of statistics from existing data (see Youth Risk Behavior Surveillance System, Centers for Disease Control below) regarding substance use and abuse. These could be: the age at which children begin to smoke, use drugs and alcohol; the number of teenagers and young adults who smoke or use alcohol; gender differences in who uses drugs; changes in use/abuse patterns over time; the number of automobile crashes attributed to substance abuse by age of driver, etc. Some data may only be readily available at state or national levels. You may cite the data as found, or you could provide a rough estimation of local incidence by applying state or national rates to local populations. In addition, you may gather local incidents and estimates from key observers. You might use an anonymous questionnaire with the caution that the information could be under- or overstated.

Gathering Existing Data

Be sure to make use of your own organization. Most school districts have data on absences, suspensions, number repeating a grade, standardized test scores, student turnover (migration in and out of school district or building), immunization records, and so on. Also check with the regional or intermediate school district and the state department of education. Local libraries possess a wealth of data. If materials are not available at your library, the librarian may be able to assist with interlibrary loans, searches of other libraries' catalogs, and computer searches of various databases, including educational associations, census data, and federal and state resources. A local college or university library may provide access to the most current literature.

◆ Do a literature review or search to find out what other studies or data exist.

◆ Establish a profile of the student population affected by the problem.

◆ Describe your organizational structure, goals, and objectives.

◆ List programs, services, and resources currently in place to meet the need.

Identify sources of existing data (see list at end of chapter for additional ideas and resources).

Federal—U.S. Census Bureau, Dept. of Education, Dept. of Health and Human Services, and other federal agencies

State—Dept. of Education, Dept. of Public Health, state data centers, state human service leagues, special interest/lobby groups, and so on.

Local—Public, college, and university libraries; police or public safety departments; chambers of commerce; school boards; technical consulting with local universities; and computer-based/Internet searches. Many hospitals maintain medical libraries that may be open to the public.

Other national—Children's Defense Fund, Child Welfare League of America, and many nonprofit foundations that fund programs and research about children and teens.

Your organization—Other potential sources of data include teacher and guidance counselor records, evaluation forms and reports done for accreditation reviews, and standardized test scores.

Gathering New Data

Exhaust existing sources of data before determining if you need to collect any new data. If you determine that you need additional data that can only be gathered firsthand, several methods are possible: (1) observation, (2) focus groups, (3) key informant interviews, and (4) use of surveys.

The following methods might be used to collect data for your project:

Observation—The classroom observation methods outlined in chapter 21 can also be adapted for your needs assessment. Observation involves counting the frequency of events, their duration, the context of schooling, or interactions between persons. Observation of behavior is often the clearest method of measurement available. An example of data gathered through observation would be to count the number of aggressive behaviors during passing periods in a high school. To do so, it would be necessary to clearly define aggressive behavior and to develop codes for behavior that are exhaustive and mutually exclusive. Piloting the coding scheme with more than one observer and then checking for interrater reliability is helpful in developing your observation method.

Focus groups—These small informal groups, led by a facilitator, gather information from audiences who fill out a questionnaire (teachers, students, parents, school administrators). You usually have a script or a short questionnaire to serve as a guide; however, the advantage of a focus group is that people build on the ideas of others (brainstorm, think tank), and therefore, the group may explore ideas that you or the committee never anticipated. The groups need to be audiotaped or transcribed or careful notes made of responses.

Key informant interviews—Key informants are persons in a position to know or be aware of the problem you are studying. They may include the same people you would invite to a focus group (teachers, administrators, parents, other professionals, and/or students). A questionnaire is used, but the format enables the interviewer to follow up and clarify responses as well as explore areas that were not on the original questionnaire. This procedure is best when there are a limited number of issues to be discussed, a limited number of people to interview, and there are interviewers available who are well trained not to be judgmental or to allow their own opinions to influence the outcome.

Using existing instruments—If an appropriate instrument or questionnaire already exists and has been tested, it may be the best use of time to obtain permission to use that instrument. Instruments may be found in the review of the literature or through searches of collections of measures.

Designing new survey/questionnaire instruments (mail, phone, or in-person interviews and focus group scripts)—Surveys may be used with in-person or phone interviews or can be distributed by mail or at meetings or other gatherings. If you decide to design a new instrument, develop your questions with data analysis and output in mind. Try to make it as easy as possible for respondents to answer. Keep in mind that a large number of open-ended questions requiring the person to write answers (rather than circle answers on a provided list) will add considerable time to your data analysis process as you will have to categorize and then synthesize these responses. However, if you don't want to lead or limit the respondent by providing checklists or multiple-choice answers, an in-person or telephone interview, in which the interviewer reads the questions, but not the checklist of answers, is often a good compromise.

If time permits, pilot test your questionnaire on a small group (12 to 30 people) to help you anticipate the range of responses for checklists, and to see if some questions are too ambiguous or poorly worded. At the very least, have the person who will analyze the data look at the questionnaire from the perspective of data analysis. The ideal situation is to envision the type of data you want in a report, then build a good questionnaire that addresses those topics.

Suggestions for Getting the Most Out of Each Method

Focus groups—Carefully identify those you want included to be as representative as possible and reduce bias or skewing. Schedule in advance. Hold the sessions at a location convenient for those who will be attending. Offer an incentive for attending (food, beverages, on-site child care for those with young children, drawing for a prize or gift certificate). Have someone experienced lead the focus group. If possible, tape-record your sessions so you won't have to concentrate on note taking and have a backup tape recorder.

Key informant interviews—Schedule the interviews in advance and have your questions prepared. Let those being interviewed know how long the interview will take and stick to that time frame.

Mailed survey—Allow adequate time for the return mail, and possibly time to do follow-up if your initial response rate is low. Including a business-reply envelope or stamped self-addressed reply envelope will increase your response rate. This tends to be the least expensive method. However, response rates are lower in this method than other methods, unless you offer an incentive or have a hot topic on which people want to express their opinion.

Phone survey—Try to schedule your phone calls at the most likely time to reach your specific population. For example, schedule interviews during the day for stay-at-home moms or retirees, evenings for working parents. This method tends to be expensive, unless you have volunteers, such as PTA members, to make the calls. Phone interviewers must be trained so that they ask the questions and record answers in a standard format. You will need approximately ten phone numbers for every three surveys you hope to complete, and this is if you attempt each phone number at least three times on different days and different times. It takes approximately six nights with twelve interviewers to complete 300 to 350 four-page questionnaires.

In-person survey—Use interviewers who are friendly and outgoing. Keep the questions short so those being interviewed don't have to remember long sentences or lists of things. Use 3 x 5 cards for answer scales, which can be handed to the person (i.e., 1 = strongly agree, 5 = strongly disagree). Carry out the surveys at a time when those you want to reach aren't rushed. Pick your interview location carefully. Example: If you want to talk to students, a good place might be a quiet room located near a study hall or the library. Bad timing for students would be during midterm or final exams.

ANALYZING YOUR DATA

Unless your study is funded by a major foundation or a federal or state agency, which requires detailed documentation, you may be able to analyze your data by looking primarily at the frequency or prevalence of conditions. How many students are not eating a nutritional breakfast more than three times a week? How many students come from families with incomes below the poverty level? How many parents attend parent-teacher conferences? You may examine the frequency of opinions, such as: How many parents believe their children are receiving a strong foundation in the three Rs? How many parents feel it is important to review their child's homework?

If, however, you need to provide more extensive data analysis, many of today's computerized software packages will provide you with an assortment of statistical measures and tests that are appropriate for various types of data. If you feel your data-analysis skills are rusty, consider using a consultant to provide this level of analysis for you. Remember, it's important for the consultant to review your data-collection methodology, including the questionnaire, before you begin collecting data. Contact local colleges and universities for consultants within educational leadership, social work, statistics, and other disciplines that specialize in research.

Your data can be hand tabulated (under 50 respondents), entered into a spreadsheet, such as Excel (50 to 500 respondents), or entered into and analyzed by a statistical analysis software package such as SPSS (Statistical Package for Social Sciences), SAS (Statistical Analysis System), or other software packages. It depends on the size of the sample and the resources available to you.

Tips on Using Excel

For small sample sizes (50 to 500 respondents), you may manually enter the responses in Excel and calculate totals and percentages for each question or set of answers. The easiest way to get clean results is to enter each survey (subject, student, parent, or respondent) as a separate row. Enter each answer as a separate column. Then simply sum or total each column to get the frequency or number who answered yes or no, strongly agree, etc., to each question. Table 15.2 represents the results of a few questions from ten surveys.

TABLE 15.2   Example Format for Data Entry and Analysis Using Excel Spreadsheet

ID	Eat Nutritious Breakfast 3x/Wk		Eligible for Free Lunch		Important for me to review my child's homework				
	Yes	No	Yes	No	Strongly Agree	Agree Somewhat	Undecided	Disagree Somewhat	Strongly Disagree
270	1		1		1				
271		1		1		1			
272	1			1			1		
273	1			1				1	
274		1	1				1		
275		1	1			1			
276		1		1	1				
277		1	1			1			
278	1			1		1			
279		1	1				1		
Total	4	6	5	5	2	4	3	1	0
%	40.0%	60.0%	50.0%	50.0%	20.0%	40.0%	30.0%	10.0%	0.0%

Another tip is to freeze the column headings. In that way as you enter more and more rows of data, the headings will remain at the top of the page, helping ensure that you are entering the data for the matching question. To freeze columns in Excel, place your cursor in the first row that has data (just under the heading and to the right of the first ID number. ID numbers are important for going back and finding data entry errors or tracing inconsistent answers back to a survey. Write the ID number on the survey as you begin to enter each questionnaire in the Excel file.

One drawback of using Excel is that you have to block or highlight all the data in your rows before sorting data. If you sort without highlighting all the data, it sorts just that column and the tie or relationship to the rest of the questions for each individual is lost.

Optical Scanning

For larger samples (over 500 respondents), you may want to consider using an optical scan form for questionnaire responses. With this method, answer sheets are optically scanned instead of typed manually into a computer file. The optical scan format for data gathering and analysis generally saves time and money with large size samples. Customized scan forms, which allow the respondent to read the question and mark their answer next to each question, have the highest degree of accuracy. However, the minimum fee for printing customized forms is likely to be $1,000, making it more cost efficient for surveys involving 500 or more respondents.

If your school has a software program that scans and produces results for teacher-designed student tests and quizzes, especially multiple-choice style questions, you may be able to adapt your questionnaire to use that software. Make sure such use does not violate the software's purchase agreement.

REPORTING YOUR FINDINGS

This is a critical element to the success of your needs assessment. Present your results in a manner that is easy to understand. Do not lose sight of your audience. Focus your attention on the specific issue you have been studying and use your data to show that the changes you are proposing will make a difference. If you want to convince your audience that there are programs or services that are effective, you should cite examples of successful programs or efforts.

Lengthy narratives are often not the best way to report your findings. You may find that a simple summary accompanied by charts, graphs, or tables showing your data in easy-to-interpret formats is the best way to present the results. Table 15.3 illustrates one method of displaying standardized test scores. The key statistic is the percentage of students with satisfactory test scores. School districts evaluate strengths and weaknesses in their curricula by looking at these

TABLE 15.3   Comparing Our School with State Proficiency Test Scores

Percentage of Students with Satisfactory Proficiency Test Scores: 2003–2004

Grade Level	4th		7th		11th	
Geographic Area	State	ZPS	State	ZPS	State	ZPS
Reading	47.5%	48.5%	44.2%	46.2%	43.5%	44.5%
Math	49.9%	50.2%	46.8%	48.4%	33.0%	32.7%
Science	70.0%	70.0%	61.9%	63.5%	58.1%	57.5%

State = State-wide average. ZPS = Average for our local public school
SOURCE: Fictitious Educational Assessment Program: 2003–2004

data over time. Comparing your own school or school district with others in your county or state provides a measure of where your district stands in relation to others.

Graphical Presentation

Sometimes it is easier to get a point across by providing the data in a graphic format (figure 15.1). For example, the difference in family income is very different for single-parent households in which the parent is a male or a female. Instead of wading through paragraphs of narrative, the reader can see at a glance how dramatically different economic circumstances can be for children living with two parents versus a single, female parent.

FIGURE 15.1   Impact of Family Type on Family Income

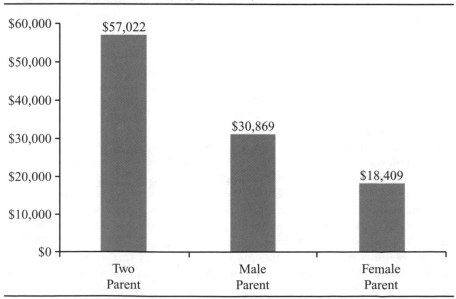

SOURCE: http://www.census.gov/hhes/income/histinc.html 8/9/2000

Summary

Needs assessment is a systematic data collection and analysis process. Its purposes are: (1) to discover and identify the resources the community is lacking in relation to generally accepted standards, and (2) to transmit that information to those who make resource allocation decisions. The choice of data collection methods will depend on several factors, including: availability of existing data, the topic of need being explored, and time and cost constraints. Using existing data will help conserve time and funds. Using focus groups and/or key informants will provide information on the level of support and help rank needs by your audience's opinion of their importance. Questionnaires, although more costly and time intensive, enable you to directly measure the desires, beliefs, knowledge, and opinions of your intended beneficiaries and benefactors.

SOURCES FOR DATA AND OTHER RESOURCES

The Internet has a wealth of information, including results of studies, how-to guides, and data. Many reports are available on the World Wide Web, and some can be downloaded. Often the reports are in Adobe or PDF format. You can download the Adobe Reader software at the census.gov site and also at many of the sites that publish reports in the Adobe format. If you do not have a computer with a Web browser, try your school library or computer lab, your community's public library, or a local college or university computer center. Some of the federal, state, and private sources have data down to the local county level, as well as state and federal levels.

STATE GOVERNMENT RESOURCES

Education Agencies

U.S. Department of Education (relevant department for your state). School demographics, enrollment http://firstgov.gov/Citizen/Topics/ Education_Training.html

State Government—Substitute the name of your state in the example that follows. Michigan, State Government http://www.michigan.gov/

FEDERAL GOVERNMENT RESOURCES

General Sources

Federal Government—Official Web portal and starting point for any federal agency or department inquiry http://firstgov.gov

National Contact Center (This is a centralized service that will help the caller find any type of national data.) (800) 333-4636 toll-free between 8 a.m. and 8 p.m. eastern time, Monday through Friday, except federal holidays. Staff will answer your question or get you to someone who can. Recorded information on frequently requested subjects is available around the clock.

U.S. Census Bureau Customer Services. Bureau of the Census, Washington, DC 20233-8300. 301. 457.4100. Customer services has phone numbers for the following data sources:

Depository Libraries—1,400 libraries (college and public) that have selected publications and some computer files on CD-ROM from the U.S. Government Printing Office and Census Bureau

State Data Centers—usually state government agencies (and assorted affiliates—often state universities) with data services. Centers receive Census Bureau data for their areas and make them available to the public. Found in all states.

U.S. Census Bureau Publications

2000 Census of Population Reports, Characteristics of the Population. (There are several different volumes in this series: General Social & Economic Characteristics; Detailed Population Characteristics; Living Arrangements of Children and Adults, Household & Family Characteristics.)

Income, Poverty and Health Insurance in the United States: 2003 (P60-226). http://www.census.gov/hhes/www/income03.html

Money, Income and Poverty Status in the United States.(2002). The population census is conducted once every ten years. The education and economic data for the census. http://www.census.gov/prod/www/abs/money.html

County and City Data Book: 2000—provides selected characteristics about counties and cities above 50,000 in population.

Statistical Abstract of the United States: 2004–2005. National Technical Information Service. Available at http://www.census.gov/prod/www/statistical-abstract-04.html

Demographic data via the Census Bureau http://www.census.gov

U.S. Department of Health & Human Services YouthInfo Web site http://www.acf.dhhs.gov/programs/fysb/youthinfo/index.htm

Centers for Disease Control *Youth Risk Behavior Surveillance System.* This Web site provides the national and state percentages of students by gender and grade level that self-report engaging in risk-taking behavior such as cigarette use, social drinking, binge drinking, use of drugs, seat-belt use, riding with a driver who is drunk, suicidal ideation and attempts, being the victim of bullying, intimidation or violence at school, getting into a physical fight, carrying a weapon, etc.) http://www.cdc.gov/HealthyYouth/yrbs/index.htm

Library of Congress http://www.loc.gov/

Native American, Indian, and Alaskan Native Health Service http://www.ihs.gov/

National Center for Education Statistics *Education Statistics at a Glance* brings together data from several NCES sources including: The Condition of Education, Indicators of School Crime and Safety, Projections of Education Statistics, and Youth Indicators, as well as *Digest of Education Statistics* (gives per pupil expenditures). http://nces.ed. gov/edstats/

Office of Minority Health Resource Center http://www.omhrc.gov/

USA Services Links to Federal government sites, including Pueblo Publications. http://fic.info.gov/

The White House Social Statistics Briefing Room http://www.whitehouse. gov/fsbr/ssbr.html Assessments and Evaluation

PRIVATE AND NONPROFIT RESOURCES

The University of Maryland *Practical Assessment Research and Evaluation* (PARE) http://pareonline.net/

The United Way of America Outcome Evaluation Measures http://www. unitedway.org/outcomes/

Child Advocacy, Data and Publications

Center for the Future of Children. The Woodrow Wilson School of Public and International Affairs at Princeton University and the Brookings Institution. Several examples of publications produced by the Center include: *Children and Computer Technology, When School Is Out, Home Visiting: Program Evaluations, Protecting Children from Abuse and Neglect, School Readiness: Closing Racial and Ethnic Gaps* (15(1), Spring 2005). http://www.futureofchildren.org/

Center for Schools and Communities, 275 Grandview Ave Suite 200, Camp Hill, PA 17011 Tel: 717.763.1661. Committed to improving outcomes for children and families through training, technical assistance, program evaluation, research, and resource development. http://www. center-school.org/

Children's Defense Fund, 25 E Street N.W., Washington, DC 20001 Tel: 202.662.3652. The State of America's Children Yearbook 2004. http:// www.childrensdefense.org/

Council of Chief State School Officers, One Massachusetts Avenue, N.W., Suite 700, Washington, DC 20001-1431 Tel: 202.336.7000. http:// www.ccsso.org/

Communities In Schools National, 277 South Washington Street, Suite 210, Alexandria, VA 22314 Tel: 703.519.8999/800 CIS 4KIDS. Communities In Schools (CIS) works to help students stay in school, learn, and prepare for a successful future. It sponsors a network that serves over 1,000 schools around the country. http://www.cisnet.org/

Harvard Family Research Project. Cambridge, MA 02138. Online publications: http://www.gse.harvard.edu/hfrp/

Kids Count. National Statistics for all 50 states, updated annually by Annie E. Casey Foundation. http://www.aecf.org/kidscount/There may also be a Kids Count for your state that provides more detailed county-level information. Example: Kids Count in Michigan: Data Book 2004: County profiles of child well-being. (Produced annually). Michigan League for Human Services. 1115 S. Pennsylvania Ave, Suite 202, Lansing, MI 48912. 517.487.5436. http://www.milhs.org

National Association for the Education of Young Children (NAEYC) leads and consolidates the efforts of individuals and groups working to achieve healthy development and constructive education for all young children. Primary attention is devoted to assuring the provision of high-quality early childhood programs for young children. http://www.naeyc.org/

National Campaign To Prevent Teen Pregnancy works to prevent teen pregnancy by supporting values and stimulating actions that are consistent with a pregnancy-free adolescence. Its goal is to reduce the teen pregnancy rate by one-third by the year 2005. http://www.teen pregnancy.org/

National Dropout Prevention Network provides linkages to and among educators, communities, researchers, parents, and the private sector to find solutions to the common goal of preventing and recovering dropouts. http://www.dropoutprevention.org/

National Foundation for the Improvement of Education. The National Education Association 1201 16th Street, NW, Washington, DC 20036. Tel: 202-822-7840 http://www.nfie.org/

United Way of America. 701 N. Fairfax St., Alexandria, VA 22314. 703.836. 7100. http://national.unitedway.org

Youth Crime Watch (violence prevention programs) http://www.ycwa. org/

References

Erikson, E. H. (1968). *Identity, youth and crisis* (1994 reissue edition). New York: W.W. Norton.

Hick, S., & McNutt, J. (2002). *Advocacy, activism, and the Internet: Community organization and social policy*. Chicago: Lyceum Books.

Maslow, A. H. (1970). *Motivation and personality*. New York: Harper & Row.

Ponsioen, J. A. (1962). *Social welfare policy: contributions to theory.* The Institute of Social Studies, Vol. 3. The Hague, the Netherlands: Mouton & Co.

Simons, J., & Jablonski, D. (1990). *An advocate's guide to using data.* Washington, DC: Children's Defense Fund.

United Way of America. (1999). *Community status reports and targeted community interventions: Drawing a distinction.* Alexandria, VA: United Way of America.

U.S. Census Bureau. (2004). *Current population survey, 2004: Annual social and economic supplement.* Washington, DC: Author.

16

School Policy Development and the School Social Worker

John P. Flynn
Western Michigan University

- ◆ Policy Defined
- ◆ Policy Analysis—Why Bother?
- ◆ Functioning in the Policy Space
- ◆ A Framework for Policy Analysis
- ◆ The Analysis of Existing Policy in a School System (with Proposed Changes)

The responsibility for shaping educationally based policy is clearly shifting downward (hierarchically speaking) from the national to the state and local levels. There is a shift in certain areas, such as children with disabilities, away from closely regulated national standards and guidelines and toward encouragement of some state and local discretion in design of programs and services for students and families. The task of education is to draw on a range of competencies to facilitate the process and to minimize barriers to learning. The school social worker is in a unique position to make valuable contributions to the opportunities afforded by this shift. The school social worker has an extensive repertoire of skills to contribute that comes from the profession's base in both clinical and direct services as well as its resources in policy, planning, and administration of human services. Social work's forte is the development and maintenance of functional linkages in human systems, a logical necessity for school systems aimed at educating the whole child and engaging families and community services. With education being defined increasingly as engagement with the whole person-in-environment, social work experiences and skills bring unique perspectives and competencies to the team and to the school system.

The school social worker initiates, shapes, modifies, and applies organizational or school system policy in a number of ways. These opportunities lie in the ability to conceptualize, organize, and communicate systematic analysis of policies and the skill in knowing how and when to advocate for a policy's implementation. This is true for an existing policy, revision of a dysfunctional policy, or in proposing and effectively communicating new policy options that meet student, family, and organizational needs. These policies can positively or negatively affect students and particularly vulnerable or troubled students at risk. Depending on the content and implementation of such policies, opportunities or resources can be made available or taken away from students.

POLICY DEFINED

Policy might be said to undergird all that is legitimate and sanctioned in organizations such as a school system. Dollars are not spent unless there is adequate authority in *budget policy*. Individuals are only free to act in ways that are commensurate with *building policies*. Teachers are free to improvise with instructional methods, so long as those approaches are within *curriculum policy*. And so forth. These phrases are commonplace in schools and their corollaries can be found in any organization. But what is policy?

First, policy, defined in its most general terms in the social welfare context, refers to those principles that give expression to valued ends and provide direction for appropriate action. That is, policy announces value preferences and provides a (verbal or nonverbal) statement of the broadest expectations and boundaries of intent and action. Some examples might be found in general institutional or organizational preambles, in mission statements, or in the annual performance objectives of a department such as a special education unit. These might be broad statements of intent that speak to equality, fair play and fair treatment, equal opportunity, or open enrollment, for example. Each of these concepts is a statement of principle, indicates valued ends, and suggests a range of actions to be taken to achieve desired ends. On the other hand, policy statements may be specific, rather than general, as with requirements for eligibility, specification of parental rights or obligations, or expectations of staff performance.

Second, policy increases or reduces the number of probable outcomes that are possible in social interaction. Policy limits choices and opportunities and narrows the range of possible action. This is what is meant by the "stochastic nature" of social policy. When the expectations of behavior are not clear, the limits are boundless, and the environment becomes unpredictable and, at times, even chaotic. On the other hand, clarification through policy (assuming it is monitored and implemented) creates a powerful way to communicate the values intended by the organization. Policy that is effectively implemented can make order out of chaos and increase the likelihood that behavior will be directed toward desired ends. Policy makes the outcomes of a social process much more predictable—people know (generally speaking) how to behave, what is expected of them, and what the likely outcome is to be when policies are clearly stated, implemented, and outcomes are monitored. Policy channels and influences human behavior. One example would be a school system's requirements on earliest age of entry into the school system. Others would be policy statements limiting the size and nature of any object that may be perceived as a weapon brought into a school building, or rules around who is welcome in the school building and under what conditions. These all limit the range and number of possible outcomes. Consequently, policy is a means whereby influence is exercised over the participants in the school system and over those in the school's significant environment(s).

Third, these policies may be embodied in formal policy statements or in the informal action of school staff. Common illustrations of formal policy might be rules and regulations, board resolutions, or administrative directives from a central office. Informal policy could be exemplified in the behavior or professional actions of school staff (such as a social worker's willingness to extend herself to do home visits, the teacher's availability to meet with parents after hours, or the principal's acceptance of certain errant behaviors and total rejection of others). The important point here is that these examples (i.e., both formal and informal manifestations of policy) are all illustrations of valued ends that give rise to personal desired actions as exemplified by school personnel.

Some would argue that policy is not "policy" unless it is formally ratified by some legitimate body or office. However, that characterization applies only to formal policy that has been properly legitimated or sanctioned by those who have the right to take action. On the contrary, the fact cannot be denied that individuals and groups in social systems, schools included, establish policies by their own choices and behaviors within or in spite of formal policy boundaries. School personnel do this through their conscious and unconscious choices and preferences in interactions among themselves, with students and their families, or with other organizations in the community.

Consequently, the school social worker must be aware of the power inherent in implementing or even creating policy within the school system. Policy is a tool that cannot be neglected and must be used appropriately. This is why the school social worker should have facility in the use of that tool in conducting a systematic analysis of policy affecting everyday practice of the profession and be prepared to make that contribution to the team.

POLICY ANALYSIS—WHY BOTHER?

The ability to make or apply policy is the ability to influence the behavior of others. The ability to have power over another person or situation, to influence the probabilities of outcomes just discussed, carries no small ethical obligation. Consequently, it is absolutely essential for the social worker in the schools to be aware of this power, just as much as the ethical obligation of being able to conduct a technically sound behavioral assessment or to assist a parent in making an informed decision. Development of skills in policy analysis can enable the social worker to examine the efficacy of a particular system-level or building-level policy, can assist in offering credible arguments for change, and can provide a framework to offering constructive or creative proposals for new policy. To appreciate the reality of this power, the school social worker must: (1) recognize what a particular policy is or could otherwise be, (2) be aware of how policy does or could influence a situation, and (3) understand the fact that policy is both formal or informal in its impact on stakeholders in the school environment. A clear understanding of these aspects of policy in a school system is fundamental in fulfilling the social worker's membership in the professional team in the school.

FUNCTIONING IN THE POLICY SPACE

The social worker in the schools has a unique opportunity to function as both a policy practitioner and a policy analyst. That is, the social worker applies school policy in bringing services to the student/family or in bringing the student/family to the services. This role of providing linkage is an aspect of practice that makes the school social worker unique among team members. Social workers, given their assignment in schools, are in a position to observe and assess the utility or disutility of many policies (and their resultant procedures) from many sides due to that linkage position. In other words, the social worker in a school system or in a particular building has the opportunity to occupy a "policy space" in the course of providing services to students and/or families and in working within the school system. Consequently, direct practice and the delivery of services are intricately interwoven with opportunities for policy analysis. By way of illustration, perhaps a school system has particular guidelines on eligibility for special educational services. There is likely some latitude left to the discretion of school staff (i.e., the policy space) on how the criteria shall be met (such as what documents must be offered or available to determine eligibility) or how the eligibility data will be prepared and presented. The social worker has the opportunity to assist the classroom teacher and other ancillary personnel as well as the family to come to a productive decision for a child. At the same time, important information is generated concerning the adequacy of policies and procedures governing decision making on special education placements. On the clinical level, the nature and style of the social worker may color or shape the policy space. The social worker may or may not take an active or supportive role in developing the information for an eligibility claim or in monitoring any resultant plans agreed to by the parents and the school system. In other words, the school social worker has opportunity to create her or his own "minipolicies" over time, as does the service team to which the social worker may be attached. Informed policy determines how and in what manner professional decisions are systematically or routinely carried out. Stated another way, school social workers and their team colleagues have tremendous discretionary power in many situations and their decisions and their behaviors speak loudly of principles that give expression to valued ends and provide direction for appropriate action.

The school social worker has many opportunities to monitor, implement, modify, or promote school policy. In the first instance, it is essential for the analyst to realize the difference between policy that authorizes an action, program, or procedure as opposed to the actual implementation of that policy. The social worker as policy monitor is in a position to identify disparities between authorization or enactment of a policy. Any failures or shortcomings of policy implementation can be brought to light through thorough analysis and credible argument for change. The social worker can also use the analysis for other policy roles, such as acting as a policy expert on external policy mandates, by acting as a constructive critic in voicing the policy options to be found in existing or proposed school policy, by serving as a conduit or sounding board for students or families on the impact of school policies, or by becoming a policy change agent within the school system itself or with the external environment (e.g., mental health agencies) regarding administrative or operational procedures in enacting school policy. Taken together, these roles provide a constellation of policy-relevant activities that compose the role of the social worker as a policy practitioner in the school. Nevertheless, whether one is fulfilling the role of policy monitor, expert, constructive critic, conduit/sounding board, or policy change agent, it is absolutely necessary that the role is supported by sound systematic analysis of the policy driving the professional activity. Such analysis supplies credibility to what is advocated by the social worker and lends to the power of any recommendations that might be accepted or implemented by others.

A FRAMEWORK FOR POLICY ANALYSIS

A disciplined and well-prepared professional person sets forth his or her theoretical perspective and plan of intervention prior to taking action. That is, professionals don't just "come off the wall," as the saying goes. A true professional is aware of what theoretical model is to be used and what techniques are to be employed before taking action. This is obvious to the clinical practitioner, who can easily identify what theory or model she might be employing in working with a client. The need for conscious choice of assessment tools or policy analysis is no less important for those doing such analyses. This chapter will set forth suggested elements for the analysis of the content and process of policy and will provide illustrations by using examples relevant to social work services in the schools. This framework is an abridged version of one provided in detail in Flynn (1992). A number of examples and illustrations may be found in that publication. An additional approach may be found in a publication by Jansson (1999).

The elements for analysis are grouped into five categories and may generate different information depending on whether the policy under analysis is:

1. Currently in place as a formal policy.
2. A proposed policy.
3. A proposed revision of an existing policy.
4. An operational reality or informal policy.

The five categories are:

1. Identify the policy problem, the policy goals(s), and the policy statement (as written or published and/or as might be inferred from behavior).
2. Assess current and anticipated system functioning due to present policy or because of any proposed policy.
3. Determine the implications for selected values embedded or implied in the policy.
4. Establish the feasibility of the policy and resources needed for the desired outcomes of the policy.
5. Provide recommendations for wording and action of the new or revised policy.

These categories are relevant to examining the substantive content of a policy or the process by which a policy is implemented or has been developed. In real life, one may not need to examine every element of each category or all content and all processes. In all instances, however, it is necessary to examine the values implied in the policy as stated or as proposed.

THE ANALYSIS OF EXISTING POLICY IN A SCHOOL SYSTEM (WITH PROPOSED CHANGES)

In the following pages of this chapter, a hypothetical policy statement (i.e., a policy established by a fictitious school system, called "Middleville Schools") will be used throughout to provide a basis for illustrating the elements of an analysis of policy. The reader could, of course, speculate about the use of these analytic elements on any particular existing policy or any policy that might be proposed for analysis or adoption. For heuristic purposes, we will assume that Middleville Schools has heard some concern in the community about the extent to which parents and guardians are properly involved in matters concerning their children. There is some question whether anyone other than school personnel is welcome.

A hallmark of any analytic framework is to set forth, in advance, the elements or characteristics of any phenomenon that will be studied or subjected to analysis. The reader will see that our first task is to identify the actual policy statement involving the policy under question, followed by groupings of explicitly stated elements that will be examined.

A. Identify the Policy Problem, the Policy Goal(s), and the Policy Statement. What Is the Problem, the Goal(s) Desired, and How Is/Would the Policy Be Stated?

Meaningful participation of parents in their own children's school experience and in the overall life of the school itself is often stated as a goal and a desirable condition in many school systems. This is often pursued by support for formal teacher-parent organization (e.g., PTA or PTO), systematic use of volunteer parents in the classroom, augmenting a school's technical/professional resources by involving particularly talented parents, and so forth. The goal, in those instances, is generally to weld the interdependence of school and families or school and community in some instances. The goal may also be to maximize the use of resources in the school's environment. Other situations involve parents in decision making, such as handling of disciplinary measures for a particular student or in placement planning and individualized service plans for special educational services. Although there has been some feedback from the community that parents are not adequately represented, the Middleville School Board does have the following policy in place:

> In all instances involving disciplinary action for a student and those events considering a student's placement in a special educational program, the parents or legal guardian of such student will be informed, consulted and actively participate in the decision process and any resultant determination. (October 12, 2001)

In this instance, the policy is formally stated, rather than being merely an informal but prevailing expectation, and is formally legitimated by the school board. As will be noted later in our analysis, formalization and legitimation may not necessarily mean that the policy is promulgated and enforced.

1. Base(s) of Legitimacy of the Policy and Source or Location. Is the location of the policy within or external to the school system? Who provides the right to take action and where is that documented (i.e., in written form where it can be easily documented or in the repetitive or patterned behavior of significant actors observed in the system)? The policy has clearly been legitimated (i.e., the right to take action has been established) by the Middleville School Board. In fact, the documentation is available in writing and dated in board minutes. Furthermore, additional legitimacy is obtained in state and federal guidelines regarding parental participation in development of individualized service plan processes for special education evaluation and placement decisions. Parental notification (though not necessarily parental participation) is also required by state regulation involving a child's suspension or expulsion.

2. The Targets and/or Clients of Concern. Who is the object of change and whose interests will be served by the policy? The *target* of a policy may be seen as that element in whom desired behavior is being sought. In this sense, the target of the policy may be seen as all staff of the school system and the parents as well since it is clear that the assurance of participation is both a right and a responsibility across the board. All parties are obligated to behave in ways that parents are significantly involved.

On the face of it, every policy is presumed to benefit the client, and "the client" is widely assumed to be the customer, the guest, or the citizen, or in this case the student or the parent. However, if one assumes that the client is truly that element (i.e., person or persons) on whose behalf the goal is being sought, then the school system itself, or its staff, could also be seen as a beneficiary or a client in a number of ways. First, assurance of parental participation allows the school system to satisfy state and federal requirements and, consequently, obtain outside funding, serving then the interests of the system as a whole. On the other hand, such a policy surely serves the interest of those parents who might otherwise find it difficult to participate in a meaningful way in key decisions affecting their children. This policy legitimates parental entry.

3. The Factors of Eligibility. Who is or what will be included or covered in the policy and under what conditions? Any one claim to eligibility under this policy is rather vague. For example, the policy states that "In all instances . . . the parents or legal guardian . . . shall be informed." The policy gives no direction or suggestion as to whether "all instances" includes the first incident or first formal action or even the first informal discussion of the propriety of taking action. On the other hand, one could logically conclude that parental participation was mandated only when formal consideration of action was first considered or when final decisions are on the table. Some of this same vagueness can be said regarding the policy's wording regarding "will be informed, consulted, and actively participate in the decision." Consequently, the policy is vague and weak in this area and certainly provides a good example of the utility of having policy guidelines. Guidelines may be thought of as less formal, less restrictive signposts or suggested ways to operationalize policy so that the policy is consistently applied. Guidelines are not generally published in formal policy and are generally developed after a policy has been established. The analyst may need to determine whether such guidelines exist and whether they are adequate.

4. The Effect upon System Maintenance, Change, or Control. What is the intended and/or unintended effect upon issues of maintenance, change, or control within or for the school system? Who has vested interest(s) in the policy's initiation or continuation? It would appear on the face of it that the intent of the policy is to bring about system change. The presumption is that parental participation has been inadequate and is desirable.

A question here is whether parental/guardian participation is actually the norm in this school system or whether there is some misperception about the policy's implementation. One would have to examine the data on actual levels of participation of parents. For example, one needs to know the rate of participation at the present time in the various buildings, grade levels, and neighborhoods in the entire school district to determine if there are any differential rates of participation. Moreover, those rates might have to be examined both before and after enactment of the policy to observe any change in participation rates. Another aspect of examining change would also be to observe or document the behavior of school staff. Are various staff groups any more or less conscientious in fostering parental participation? Analysis of these data may offer some suggestion whether or not the policy serves the purpose of social control of staff or parents or both in bringing about desired participation within the system as a whole.

5. *Explicit or Implicit Theories.* What theoretical foundation gave rise to or supports the policy? The fundamental theoretical foundation of parental participation can be found in basic democratic theory that citizens have the right and responsibility to fully participate in decisions affecting their own (or their children's) lives. Furthermore, the policy is entirely in concert with common and case law regarding the primacy of parental responsibility for the welfare of children. Hence, this criterion is, generally speaking, unassailable as a policy feature.

There may be some significant actors within the school system who hold the theoretical or philosophical view that participation beyond the school's walls by others in the community (including members of the family) actually broadens and enriches the educational process and aids in individualized planning. On the other hand, some may view parental participation in "professional affairs" as an unnecessary burden. Those persons should also be identified, and their positions and influence should be examined, and the resultant information may also have implications for the change or control questions raised above.

6. *Topography of the Policy System.* Can you "map the terrain" of who is involved in this system? What offices or units are logically included as being affected by this policy as it stands or as any changes might be proposed? Who might constitute a viable "action system" to provide support for or opposition to such a policy? Who are some of the key participants? If one were to sketch out a conceptual map, there would be a number of relevant actors. The map would certainly include the building principal(s), the classroom teachers involved, any special education personnel having professional knowledge of a particular situation, perhaps other community agencies also providing services relevant to a student and the parent or guardian. It would be necessary, then, to examine the information on the actual range and variety of opportunities for participation. Are there potential advocacy groups involved? Are certain staff groupings or certain building principals especially interested in or opposed to investing in this issue?

7. *Contemporary or Antecedent Issues.* What are some of the issues embedded in this particular policy within or around the school system that should be considered? Are there other relevant past events that explain the existence of this policy or how the policy was developed or stated? It would be very important to identify any prior incidents related to the conditions covered by the policy (e.g., children bringing weapons to the school, controversial disciplinary actions, the general and actual practice—or lack of consistency, on the

other hand—in involving parents/guardians in individualized service planning, etc.).There may be some historical "baggage" that gave rise to the policy's adoption. It may have been hastily crafted; or it may have been carefully considered and debated.

There may also be contemporary issues that place this issue on the system's agenda. For example, perhaps there are other issues in the community also involving matters of informed consent of parents or alleged arbitrary decisions being made by public officials in other arenas, such as adolescents gaining access to health care without parental knowledge or counseling services being provided to students without parental approval. These factors may suggest something about the potential for amending the policy or how firm a base of support the policy has in its present form.

B. Assessment of Current and Anticipated System Functioning

To some extent we have already moved into the domain of the second set of elements. In real life, it is impossible to deal with human systems in linear fashion. Real-life interaction is circular and iterative. However, this second set of the elements emphasizes an assessment of the current structural state of a system. Consequently, the following elements or questions involve:

1. The State of Communication and System Boundaries. What is the nature of communication and interaction between key elements in the system as a result of this policy? For policy to be effective and to achieve power to bring about predictable behavior, policy must be clearly published and implemented. Do families actually have clear and frequent communication with, from, and to the school? Do the boundaries between home and school, in general, seem permeable or impermeable? That is, is there generally a free flow of interaction or communication between home and school, or are the barriers and gates firm and protected? It is essential to determine the extent to which publication and implementation of this policy has actually occurred.Then, too, have divisional- and departmental-level administrators and supervisors adequately monitored the implementation of this policy? Has the communication been unilateral by way of mere policy pronouncements from above? Rather, has communication been bilateral in that those who manage and supervise staff have engaged in practical discussions with those staff implementing in order to get corrective feedback?

From a practical point of view, have parents been informed sufficiently in advance so that their participation is reasonably convenient? Have professional staff appropriately assisted parents or guardians to be adequately prepared for whatever participation might be needed? In this particular policy, the parent would need to become familiar with the decision process and the range of options available in advance, in coming to decision about an individualized educational plan for a student, for example. Do staff assist them in meeting the spirit and intent of this policy? In the case of pending disciplinary action by the school, do staff assist parents in joining the school in productive problem solving or, instead, is the parent brought in only to be informed of decisions already made?

It is useful to examine the direction of the feedback by observing whether any difficulties encountered by staff in achieving full participation have been taken into account in changing the policy or in developing guidelines. This might have been done by examining staff experience with the policy or in the allocation of more resources in achieving the policy goal. For example, have the boundaries between home and school been altered through increased funding for staff transportation for home visits or by publishing informational materials that familiarize parents with basic information on procedures?

It is sometimes instructive to identify key system points for communication. Are there various groups that have opportunity to influence one another concerning this policy? Are there any particular bargaining, negotiating, or any collaborative groups or coalitions likely to be forming because of this policy? Do psychologists, speech therapists, and social workers tend to have a position on informing and including parents that differs from most building principles, or do those groups work together on this?

Here it might be beneficial to see if any advocacy groups have communicated their interests in this matter, for example when the rate of expulsions or suspensions appears to weigh more heavily on a particular neighborhood or segment of the community. Do these groups tend to bring their concerns to staff who work at the implementation level or do they tend to bring their concerns about the policy directly to the board at public meetings?

It could also be instructive to examine the school's general posture on parental participation at times other than special education or disciplinary action. Some examples might be the school's overall use of parent volunteers in the classroom, logistical support given by the school system for parent-teacher organizations, or other ways in which the school might give the metamessage that parents/guardians are welcome or unwelcome. In practical terms, how frequently do the home and the school come into interaction in this school system?

2. Authority, Influence, and Leadership. What authority, exercise of power, or leadership is given to or needed to effect this policy? Who holds power and who actually can or does exercise that power? Assuming that the policy is functioning effectively, by whose or what authority and influence is the policy held to the line? Is the system's superintendent involved and aggressive? Is there monitoring by that office? On the other hand, is there actually little support but for the outreach initiatives of staff at the lowest levels? Could it be that the policy is failing due to lack of support at the departmental level(s) or due to the lack of cooperation by many building principals? On the other hand, are building principals generally advocates for meaningful parental involvement, but are service staff lax in taking initiatives to involve parents or guardians in any meaningful way? In any case, why is this happening? One might examine the extent or manner in which the system's administrative leaders in the persons of departmental directors, program heads, coordinators, or other significant actors play roles in leadership in implementation of this policy.

3. Strains and Constraints. What effect does the policy have upon tension, variety, and entropy (i.e., the tendency toward disorder or the inability to do work in a system) within the system? Is it dysfunctional or functional? Some variety and variability in human systems is good. Groups and organizations thrive on sustainable variety, school systems included. In fact, it might be argued that the greater variety of inputs into the educational process, input from the home included, the stronger the overall educational process. However, when tension is not managed and variety leads to chaos or a school's response is no longer predictable, then entropy sets in. That is, the system has less functional order and has less ability to do its work. Remember that the main purpose of policy is to give order and/or direction.

Some forms of tension are caused by strains in the system that (at least theoretically) can be corrected. Some examples in this instance might be inadequate numbers of service-level staff, overworked teachers with classes that are too large, principals having responsibility for too many buildings, and so forth. The greater the variety of more points of view provided by parents contributes more information for decisions about children, but it also adds to the quantum of information that staff have to deal with. In addition, when policy is published but not implemented, it may sometimes be due to its lacking support of guidelines giving direction to system personnel. A well-intended but unimplemented policy can be minimized or become practically nonexistent in this instance.

Other factors may be more in the form of constraints, defined here as those barriers that cannot be moved (except under unusual circumstances) because they are part of the nature of the phenomenon. In a school system, constraint may be found in the existence of labor agreements, such as a limiting definition on the length of the work day (though this factor is sometimes erroneously used as an excuse for inaction). Another example might be due to lack of adequate physical facilities to accommodate some meetings, though this factor could be more of a short-term barrier, given newly assigned resources in the future.

4. Resistance to Change. How salient is this policy (i.e., how many groups or other issues does this policy affect or cut across boundaries)? What are the issues, forces, or factors that might give resistance to or mitigate against change as a result of the policy? A key question here is how many different groupings or categories does this policy affect? The likely answer is that this is a very salient policy in that regard. The superintendent and the school board are very much in touch with a variety of publics that likely see themselves as stakeholders who should have a meaningful say in the system. There are currently nonprofit foundations interested in fostering family and community participation in local schools. State and federal statutory regulations require such participation in certain circumstances. In addition, some school personnel value broad participation highly, as suggested earlier. Consequently, there would appear to be very high probability of leverage here to promote a salient issue.

The next level of questions, then, is where any resistance or counterresistance to policy implementation or change might exist within specific pockets or positions of school personnel. Is implementation of this policy in competition for financial resources with other needs in the system? Moreover, there should be some examination of whether particular segments of the community do not or cannot fully cooperate in seizing their opportunities to participate. Some examples of the latter grouping might be those who have been alienated by school experiences in the past, those who are limited due to inadequate transportation available, those who lack adequate substitute child care, or those who are limited by language barriers. Implementation of the policy may require allocation of new or altered resources to reach out to those parents.

In terms of bringing about system change for the policy, it is essential to determine where or to whom (i.e., what person or office) any informal and formal presentations of analysis and recommendations might best be brought forward. Might it be at the lowest level nearest the problem (i.e., using the principle of subsidiarity), such as a department having the most direct dealings with parents and families? Might it be in open discussions, such as at board meetings? Which point of entry is likely to have the greatest leverage, or the ability to engender meaningful discussion and change?

5. Feedback Devices. What channels exist that provide for information that guides the system toward corrective action based upon the policy's outputs? Good policy has built-in mechanisms for providing self-corrective feedback. Although we have had some discussion regarding feedback, this characteristic of policy needs additional attention. Some policy statements include a provision for assignment of monitoring to a particular position or office within the organization. Some "sunset" laws, those that purposely expire at a time specified before continuation legislation is again considered, are an excellent example of a built-in feedback mechanism. Furthermore, both positive and negative feedback should be systematically sought. Middleville School's policy on participation is lacking in this regard. There is no suggestion in the policy statement itself that such feedback is desired or required. Hence, this policy analysis will likely recommend, in its summary analysis, that appropriate feedback devices must be established.

6. Impact upon the System's Dynamic Adaptation. To what extent does the policy enhance the system's ability to be more adaptive and self-corrective? Organizations must alter their forms over time in order to survive. This is what is meant by "dynamic adaptation." However, lacking the feedback mechanism just noted, there is nothing to suggest that the parental participation policy has any impact on the system's ability for dynamic adaptation. Although Middleville Schools may be very dynamic in their forward movement, there is no evidence found in this particular policy.

7. *Environmental Impact.* What impact is there (or will there be) in the general educational climate because of the policy being in existence? It is reasonable to assume that this policy would engender more positive feelings in the community, not only for parents and guardians of the system's students but for the broader community as well. After all, such a policy communicates the meta-message that "this system is an open system." The school is open to the community, so to speak. Input is welcome. In fact, a parent's being informed and fully participating could easily be interpreted as also welcoming any of those who might appropriately inform and advocate for a particular student, parent, guardian, and/or family in given problem-solving situations. Other community agencies might well perceive that there are open doors to this school system.

C. Determine Implications for Selected Values

The third category of elements involves an assessment of the congruence of the policy and its implementation with selected values. The word *selected* is carefully chosen here because who is to say what set of values should be brought to the analysis? First, since the values of adequacy, effectiveness, and efficiency are so much a part of U.S. folklore, it would be foolish not to include these values. Second, inasmuch as this text is for and about the practice of social work, the framework has drawn heavily on the Code of Ethics of the National Association of Social Workers (NASW, 1996). Hence, the inclusion of the values of social justice, self-determination, identity, individualization, nonjudgmental attitude, and confidentiality. Consequently, the following elements and questions should be considered and involve:

1. *Adequacy.* To what extent is the goal achieved when/if the policy is carried out, both in terms of "coverage" for individuals and for the system as a whole? The elements of adequacy, effectiveness, and efficiency are often uttered together in popular analysis as if the phrase provides a mantra for responsible citizenship. However, each of these elements differ in the sense of what is examined and expected. *Adequacy* is defined here in terms of the question given earlier: Adequacy is the extent to which a goal is achieved if the policy is carried out. Furthermore, adequacy may be thought of as "horizontal" or as the degree or extent to which all those who were meant to be "covered" are covered. In this instance, are all parents/guardians found to be included when it comes to participation in designated decisions? On the other hand, adequacy may be "vertical," or the extent to which particular targets or clients or individuals were/are affected. Here, the question is whether only certain socioeconomic segments in the community receive different support in their participation, or whether only certain types of decisions receive differential parental attention by the school, such as placement for gifted children's planning, or for special education, or only for participation in the Parent-Teacher Organization. The issue with adequacy is coverage, who is covered, and how sufficient that coverage is.

2. Effectiveness. To what extent is there a logical connection, if any, between the means or techniques employed by the policy and the policy goal that is to be achieved? *Effectiveness* is related to what most people generally consider the *outcome* and its relation to what means were employed to obtain that outcome. In this instance, one must examine the means or methods whereby Middleville School personnel went about ensuring and obtaining full participation as mandated by the policy. As just noted, the presence and impact on specific target populations might be examined in this regard. Although suggested pure cause-and-effect relationships are rarely documented in social phenomenon, correlations between methods employed and participatory outcomes would likely be valid.

3. Efficiency. To what degree are the means employed in goal achievement maximized with the use of the minimum amount of necessary resources? The useful concept of *efficiency* has recently been clouded by the contemporary contest between the pervasive dialogue on "managed *care*" versus "managed *cost*." In that debate, the emphasis is either on efficiency in cost or on level of effort. Efficiency as an evaluative concept that refers to the degree to which the means employed in achieving the goal are maximized (i.e., used judiciously) and are employed while using the minimum amount of necessary resources. Put another way, did the job get done while using the minimum amount of effort or cost?

This criterion suggests that the analyst should examine costs to both the parents/guardians and the school system as well as the benefits to both the parents/guardians and the school system. This analysis would likely be highly speculative in nature but worth the effort in determining how and to whom and to what extent any recommendations for action might be shaped. Furthermore, such analysis is likely to suggest both tangible and intangible costs and benefits that are likely to be difficult to concretize. Many of the costs could easily be psychological or social in nature. Nevertheless, this is a very important part of the analysis, and the analyst will have to be creative. We would likely have to operationalize such concepts as time, effort, satisfaction, improvement, the quality of relationships, commitment, sharing, and even the concept of *participation* itself.

4. Impact on Rights, Statuses, and Social Issues. What is the policy's impact on individual, group, or organizational rights and statuses, particularly in terms of equity, equality, and fairness? These elements are at the center of this analysis, because examination of these values and their presence or absence in the policy or its implementation are likely to shed light on much of the rest of the analysis. Policy can vitally affect a person's or a group's status and position in any social system, including a school system. Policy and its implementation can affirm proper rights and obligations, duties and responsibilities, prerogatives or privileges, or rewards or punishments. Aside from food and shelter, these are factors that heavily sustain life itself. This policy on parent/guardian participation surely assigns status and rights to some members of the community, whether the policy is operationalized adequately and whether it is enforced. A real test at the level of application may be found, however, in the extent to which people are treated equitably, equally, and fairly.

Equity may be defined as the extent to which people in similar circumstances are treated similarly. This is not to be confused with *equality*, in which people are treated the same in all circumstances. The policy analyst should try to determine whether all people were informed of the policy and that all parents and guardians were given the same opportunity to participate. That would be evidence of essential equal treatment. At the same time, it should be determined whether the principle of equity prevailed in that children and families with differential situations needed differential treatment to achieve reasonably similar results as others. This would entail, for example, aggressive outreach to some; additional time before coming to joint decisions for others; possible inclusion of additional aides, advocates, or spokespersons for some; and so forth. Achievement of both equity and equality is more likely to give evidence that the policy was implemented with fairness.

Fairness is concerned with whether people or situations were dealt with in a manner that is reasonable and just because of application of the policy. Consequently, evidence of carefully considered decisions, jointly arrived at, in an open process without arbitrary rules is likely to promote just or fair treatment. The analyst should look for evidence of realization of this value or be prepared to provide rewording for the policy or a set of guidelines that would honor such outcomes.

5. Self-Determination. Does the policy honor the right of citizens to a voice in the determination of those matters that vitally affect themselves? Surely self-determination is likely to be honored if the issues involved in justice and fairness are also to be achieved. Self-determination does not provide one with a unilateral right to establish the rules of conduct or the rights of choice beyond what is the generally acceptable in a social contract. A central question here is whether the school system "takes over" for the family by unilaterally making decisions that should properly be made by or shared with the family.

6. Identity. What effect does this policy have on the self-image of the beneficiary (client) or the target of the policy and on the need for and right to human dignity? This criterion speaks to the extent to which the policy or its application allows the receiver of the policy's intent to accept its impact with dignity. That is, human dignity should not be reduced by unreasonable and inappropriate policy directives. The purpose of policy is to support and enhance human interaction, not to demean any of its members. On the face of it, one might assume that the mere fact of inclusion in important decision-making processes would respect and enhance one's sense of identity. However, to gather data for this part of the task, the analyst will likely have to gather personal opinions from past, current, and nonparticipating and participating parents and guardians. The views of third party observers could also be of value.

7. *Individualization and the Nonjudgmental Attitude.* To what extent is the need for individuals (or groups or organizations) to be treated in terms of their unique nature, needs, and qualities recognized by the policy? This criterion is akin to the question of the policy's impact on identity. The emphasis in this criterion is focused more on the means and/or manner by which the system carries out its implementation of the policy, whereas identity speaks more to the outcome effect on the target person(s) who presumably are the beneficiaries of the policy.

Individualization speaks to the need for individuals or groups to be treated in terms of their unique nature, needs, and qualities. The nonjudgmental attitude speaks to the quality of behavior or demeanor of those who carry the policy out as representatives of the school system.

Here, one would want to examine whether the policy is put into practice by person-to-person contact by informing families of the parents'/guardians' rights and opportunities or, instead, by merely informing families by memo or referring to school system policies in general. It could also be worthwhile to see how and whether participation as a concept is presented, such as whether it is characterized as a pro forma requirement or an inconvenience to the staff or whether it is a positive opportunity to share or collaborate in a child's school experience.

8. *The GRADES Test.* What are the implications of this policy for matters of Gender, Race, Age, Disability, Ethnicity, or Socioeconomic Status? It can reasonably be said that most school personnel are not racist, or sexist, or guilty of a number of isms, at least in terms of their conscious intentions and behaviors. Nevertheless, as patterns of behavior are established and routines set in, it is easy for the collective behavior of organizations and individuals to become institutionalized. Consequently, it is absolutely essential that the policy analyst consciously and explicitly press the analysis against a number of very similar questions. The question would go something like: "Given what has been observed, or given what might take place in the implementation of this policy, what implications are there for those of any particular gender or sexual orientation?" Or "for persons of any particular racial identity or for people of color?" Or "for any particular age group?" Or "for any person with a disability?" Or "for people of any particular ethnic group?" Or "for those of any particular socioeconomic status?" Here is where you can do more than give lip service to advocating for those who might be disadvantaged by policy because of their GRADES identity.

In our fictitious policy in the imaginary Middleville School system, could it be that the task (and perhaps even burden) of participation will more likely fall on female caretakers? It is widely known that mothers, for example, are generally more active in relating to schools than fathers. An example would be mothers' attendance at conferences regarding their children. Could this mean that more aggressive efforts have to be made to involve males in the home-school collaboration, for example?

Or how about the fact that there are increasing numbers of grandparents now raising their grandchildren? It is possible that grandparents may be less familiar with the culture of current school systems and even school buildings because it has been some time since they, themselves, may have been active with the schools. Perhaps different assumptions may have to be made regarding what needs to be communicated to grandparents or how the school might be perceived by those family situations.

Then there are those families in which one person's disability is sometimes a limiting factor in the extent to which they can freely participate in a whole range of activities in the community, including the schools. Perhaps there are special needs for transportation for the person who might otherwise visit the school, or perhaps an inordinate number of visits to the home are needed as a substitute for some of the conferences on-site at the school. Perhaps a disability of a family member would require that respite care is needed to facilitate a family caregiver's visits to the school. These are just a few possibilities that could be considered in the policy analysis.

Then there is the question of any implications for the ethnic identity of the family. In carrying out the policy, are all staff adequately sensitive to unique subcultural factors such as those families in which only the male has authority to speak with those who might "intrude" on the family? Or how about those families in which any formal institution from the outside is seen as a manifestation of authority—to be feared or to be obeyed or to be revered?

Finally, what might seem the most obvious is often overlooked: the socioeconomic status of the family and what opportunities might have to be forgone due to lack of supports available to the "average" family. This would include considerations of the availability of a telephone, transportation, general good health, availability of clothing in which a family member feels comfortable in public, access to substitute child care, and so forth.

The main point in the GRADES test is that not all people have equal ability to enjoy what is offered to them, even with a sound and positively motivated social policy. Consequently, the professional person who is really committed to responding to the unique needs of individuals must consider that fact, not only in professional clinical practice and service, but in any adequate policy analysis and policy implementation.

D. Establish Feasibility and Resources Needed for the Desired Outcomes

The fourth set of elements in the framework involves an assessment of the feasibility and availability of resources necessary to implement the policy. There are obviously a myriad of possible considerations but we will limit our framework to the following:

1. Technical Capacity. What particular technology, skills, and/or talents are available to the school system internally or externally to achieve the goal?

Does that technology consist of people or equipment? Implementation of our sample policy would require very little hardware. Surely there could be some support needed in terms of distribution of newsletters, the use of advertising media, keeping mailing lists and phone lists up to date, and so forth. However, this policy is more likely to focus on considerations of people power.

People are resources in an organization. Foremost would be some assessment of the attitudes and commitment of administrators and service staff toward assertive implementation of this policy. If the assessment is positive or affirmative, then the need would be primarily to facilitate and provide support. If the assessment is negative or questionable, it may require in-service training or a different approach to supervision and performance evaluation of administrative and staff functioning. In situations wherein it is particularly difficult to obtain cooperation of parents or guardians from certain groups or areas of the system, outside consultation may be needed from those who have also faced this problem but have experienced successful outcomes.

2. Finances. Are the financial resources available or likely to become available? Use of staff time, whether in training, retraining, or even in reallocation of staff resources devoted to the goals of most any set of policy priorities, can be seen as a financial cost. An obvious cost of aggressive outreach is a likely increase in reimbursable travel time for staff, or possibly a decrease in alternative reimbursable services provided by that same staff. It is important to the analyst to try to determine, if only speculatively, what the real cost might be to focus or refocus staff direction on implementing this policy. At the same time, one must try to also estimate the opportunity cost of not implementing the policy by not appropriately involving the targets of the policy. There may be long-term and broader systemic costs that have a financial price tag. Psychological costs must also be considered, such as impact on morale, stress, and/or community relations.

3. Time. To what extent is time a resource or a hindrance in achieving the policy goal? There appears to be no obvious implication for time as a factor in this policy in terms of any urgency for implementation. As just noted, there is an implication for the reallocation of use of staff time. If the school system has a history of excluding parental/guardian participation, the policy surely will demand more time of families. Time is a resource for families as well as for organizations. Consequently, there could be an increased demand on family resources in pursuit of a common mission, the adequate educational experience.

4. Rationality. In the final analysis, to what extent is or will the policy be perceived as being rational? Does the policy, as conceived, forge a link between the perceived problem and its logical solution? It is hard to think of an argument for not perceiving this policy as being rational, unless one might have a narrow or erroneous view of what constitutes efficiency in use of staff time. As noted previously, the concept of assuming full participation of people in affairs having personal implications in their lives is rooted in basic democratic theory.

However, there might be those who would argue from a philosophical point of view that the purpose of the school is to teach, and that teaching is perceived only as a technical function performed only by those technically prepared in a particular way. However, this view is surely not prevalent today.

  5. Power of the Policy. To what extent is the policy actually likely to shape or alter the behavior of those intended? Finally, one must question the extent to which this policy will actually have an impact on those for whom it is intended. This is the ultimate measure of the power of the policy. Will it actually shape the administration's or the staff's patterns of behavior in fostering and effectively using the benefits of more complete family participation? Will the policy actually do anything to increase or enhance the frequency and/or quality of participation by parents or guardians? Are there any sanctions related to compliance to bring about the desired outcomes?

  On the face of it, "participation," being "informed," being "consulted," "decision process," and "determination" are words and phrases with a positive valence. Few people could be frightened or rejecting of the concepts and values generally implied. Put another way, who could argue with these concepts or the construct created by bringing these concepts together in a policy statement? On the other hand, participation by family members can be rewarded but surely not punished. Regarding staff, however, certain incentives and disincentives can be tied to their support for this policy.

E. Provide Recommendations

  The fifth and final step of the analysis is, of course, to provide a clear and cogent statement of recommendations for (1) wording of the policy (if any changes), and (2) key action elements. This statement should focus on both the strengths and weaknesses or any factors peculiar to the issue and those factors suggested by the data generated by the analysis. In this context, there are a number of considerations for communicating or conveying a policy analysis and any recommended action. For your convenience, the original policy is restated again:

> In all instances involving disciplinary action for a student and those events considering a student's placement in a special educational program, the parents or legal guardian of such student will be informed, consulted, and actively participate in the decision process and any resultant determination. (October 12, 2001)

Any resistance to this policy would likely be negative criticism of those portions of the policy statement that are vague or poorly operationalized. Here are some of the issues:

  1. The policy refers to "all instances" involving disciplinary action. One questions whether this is appropriate. Surely there could be classroom situations that are best handled within the classroom and, in some instances,

those events could be shared with parents/guardians later if appropriate. Perhaps there are some minor infractions of school building rules that, given the opportunity to build positive rapport between, say, the principal and the student, it would be best to handle more informally.

Consequently, the analyst may suggest a rewording to something on the order of "all instances involving disciplinary action in which suspension, expulsion, or removal of a student's privileges" to replace "involving disciplinary action."

2. Perhaps the reference to "special educational program" might not be interpreted the same by many in the community. This term serves as jargon for many within the system and most often refers to those with learning and behavioral difficulties, but to others it might include reference to programs for gifted children.

The analyst might suggest substitute language of "in programs other than the student's regular classroom or curriculum schedule" to replace the phrase "in a special educational program."

3. Presuming that the school board is committed to its goals of family participation, it is important to build a feedback mechanism directly into the policy statement rather than leaving this matter up to development of adequate guidelines or through the good intentions of school personnel. Consequently, the policy statement could include: "Implementation of this policy shall be monitored regularly by the Assistant Superintendent for Community Affairs and progress reports will be provided quarterly to the Board of Education."

4. Perhaps the most difficult concepts to operationalize in the policy statement have to do with "will be informed, consulted, and actively participate in the decision process and any resultant determination." Experience would suggest that these policy provisions are not likely to be satisfied or clarified by mere words in one reworded policy statement. This is where development of more explicit policy guidelines would be appropriate. Guidelines are not part of the actual policy statement but are necessary statements of intent and behavior that are necessary to achieve the intent of the policy. The following guidelines could be considered as suggestions for action elements and content:

   a. "Drafting of any recommendations should clearly include active participation of parents and guardians of children currently enrolled in the school system. Special consideration should be given to soliciting input from both individuals who have been active in and may be assumed to represent any parent-teacher organization and any individual(s) who is/are not generally attached to any organized group associated with the school."

   b. "The issue of 'informed' should include development of guidclines that will specify organizational behaviors that will give evidence of a person being informed. Such activities could include being presented with written procedures on review of a student's status and performance, specification of types of issues and procedures for appeal, participants' right to be accompanied by advocates of choice, opportunity for dialogue with staff for purposes of clarification, and so forth. These alternatives should be considered in any drafting of guidelines."

c. "The question of operationalizing 'consulted' should speak to the manner and frequency with which contact should be initiated and pursued by school personnel. This would include fostering participation by both postal and telephone invitations and/or personal visits to the home, allowing sufficient advance notice, and convenience in time and place of meetings, and the like."

d " 'Actively participate' will, of course, be up to the participant to determine as to its extent and nature. However, the school could develop guidelines that communicate a valuing of family members in giving suggestions, comments, or statements of preference. It should be noted in writing (and not solely reliance on nonverbal behavior of staff) that family members' input is not only necessary but valued."

e. "Reference to 'resultant determination' could be clarified through guidelines and will be dependent on the type and nature of the decision or problem dealt with. For example, issues of disciplinary action may require reference to legal limitations or mandates of state law, as in the instance of weapons or drugs being brought into a school building. Such matters may require certain written commitments by both the school and the parent. In the case of special programming for a particular student's unique needs, some agreements may be informal and a monitoring process agreed on. In other instances, there may need to be an official "sign off" by both the school and the parent/guardian so as to satisfy mandatory regulations or funding and reimbursement considerations and to otherwise formalize agreements."

f. "Development and promulgation of guidelines should be mandated within the policy statement and the office responsible for that task should be specified."

Given this analysis and the changes just suggested, the modified policy to be recommended to the superintendent for ultimate consideration by the board would be:

In all instances of (1) suspension, expulsion, or removal of a student's privileges for a student, and (2) those events considering a student's placement in programs other than the student's regular classroom schedule, the parents or legal guardian of such student will be informed, consulted, and actively participate in the decision process and any resultant determination. Implementation of this policy shall be monitored regularly by the Assistant Superintendent for Community

Affairs and progress reports will be provided quarterly to the Board of Education. Guidelines necessary for implementation of this policy shall be developed and promulgated by <date specified>" (Amended: New Date).

Additional Proposed Action

Other actions in support of our hypothetical Middleville Schools example for support of the policy changes have been introduced in the course of the analysis earlier. To summarize, these action aspects (in additional to analytical tasks) should include:

1. Obtain the endorsement of all key administrative or service departments within the school system, as appropriate, for the policy changes.
2. Establish liaison with community advisory and advocacy groups, such as the Association of Retarded Citizens, the Council for Exceptional Children, and the like.
3. Participate in any in-service training for teachers and other ancillary service staff to adequately prepare them and to prepare parents in advance for effective participation.
4. Obtain directives pertaining to the policy in writing.
5. Review such directives and policies, where possible, with new staff and new families as part of orientation routines.
6. Facilitate, support, initiate, and encourage all those who embrace the policy and its purposes.

Fair Warning to Conscientious People

The foregoing is merely an illustration of how an analytic framework might be used. It is not an instruction book. An analytic framework merely gives a list of possible considerations. This chapter has added a few possible mind teasers to those considerations to offer illustrations if this approach is to be used. In real life, the process is not so linear. It is, instead, circular with a lot of back-and-forth filling. In addition, in real life one is not able to gather information for each element nor is it necessary to do so. Furthermore, any analytic framework should serve primarily as an instigator that merely stimulates further creative thought for the imaginative professional trying to take responsibility for constructive criticism.

A Few Final Words about Presentation of Policy Analyses

Effective analyses of policy are not hidden under a bushel basket. They need to see the light of day, of course, because they are done to be communicated. Such analyses are performed to teach, inform, or persuade. Consequently, policy analysis can be seen as fundamentally and honestly a political act, even under the most disciplined and objectively driven circumstances. Although the topic of how to communicate one's policy analysis is a topic in and of itself, there are a few generalities that can be stated to serve as reminders. These are provided here in the form of a list that will hopefully, in each case, suggest further exploration:

1. The form and style, written or oral, should be comfortable and clearly not a repetition of the laborious manner that we have just completed. The manner should be objective and surely not attacking of any individual or group.
2. The content must be accurate and informative; the reader or listener must be assured that the analysis has contributed to his or her understanding and increased confidence in understanding the issues.
3. The analysis should show working familiarity of all the relevant antecedent and contemporary issues impinging on the policy choice.
4. Argument must be balanced, with the analysis identifying potential pros and cons or arguments for and against key choices to be made.
5. Speculation must be offered on the probable impact of key choices.
6. The presentation must select language that keeps the reader or listener target groups in mind and helps those targets to have a clear mental picture of what is being communicated. This is best done by clearly labeling sections, numbering key points or choices, and by providing clear and concise summaries.
7. Lastly, the presentation must be consistent with professional values and ethics. Special emphasis must be given to accuracy of information and being free of attempts at manipulation.

A comprehensive policy analysis, communicated with these considerations in mind, will add to the credibility of the analyst as well as to the analysis that is provided.

References

Flynn, J. (1992). *Social agency policy: Analysis and presentation for community practice* (2nd ed.). Chicago: Nelson-Hall.

Jansson, B. S. (1999). *Becoming an effective policy advocate: From policy practice to social justice*. Pacific Grove, CA: Brooks/Cole.

National Association of Social Workers. (1996). *Code of ethics*. Washington, DC: Author.

Section Three

Assessment, Consultation, and Planning

17

Assessment, Multidisciplinary Teamwork, and Consultation: Foundations for Role Development

Robert Constable
Loyola University, Chicago

Galen Thomas
Southern Illinois University

- ◆ Assessment in School Social Work
- ◆ Needs Assessment of a School Community
- ◆ Multidisciplinary Teamwork
- ◆ Consultation
- ◆ How Do Assessment, Teamwork, and Consultation Work? (and How Do They Work Together?)
- ◆ New Developments in General and Special Education: An Outcome-Oriented, Strengths-Based Service Delivery Approach
- ◆ Positive Behavior Intervention and Support (PBIS)

This section is focused on the related processes of assessment, multidisciplinary teamwork, and consultation. These processes deal with decision making. This decision making often takes place as a process with the principal and with the team. The process of *needs assessment* with the principal and with the multidisciplinary team could determine the school social worker's role. In this way, school social workers can tailor their role to meet the emergent and particular needs of the school. The nature of a student's situation and of the team demands multiple perspectives. Assessment of the classroom learning environment and its dynamics is linked to consultation with teachers and other team members, to functional behavior assessments, to positive behavioral interventions and support (PBIS), and to the social worker's work with particular students and their families. Finally, there is comprehensive case study assessment (CSA) of a particular student's situation.

ASSESSMENT IN SCHOOL SOCIAL WORK

At one time education was predominantly defined by standard curricula at each grade level. Some students fit into this system, but many did not. This changed in special education with the development of individualized curricula, geared to the student's individual needs. When education is driven by the goals of each student, methods of education can become flexible, individualized, and dependent on an individualized assessment. Such an assessment process demands more of the multidisciplinary team, and the school social worker has an important role in this process. In general education the development of outcome-based education and the movement toward common standards for students could have similar consequences. The teacher would eventually become the diagnostician of student learning styles, the prescriptor of the best means for each student to master the skills and knowledge that constitute common standards, and the assessor of student progress (Levine, 2004). The school social worker, now a specialist, would assist in these assessments, working between the team, the student, and the family to individualize these processes to the needs of the students.

Assessment in school social work is a systematic way of understanding and communicating what is happening in the pupil's relations within the classroom, within the family, and between family and school. It provides a basis for deciding the places where interventions will be most effective. The school social worker has access to major sectors of life activity of individual pupils, teachers, and parents and this access allows for a practice approach that emphasizes interaction with the individual and with these important sectors. The ecological systems perspective allows the social worker to understand transactions with the environment and to make institutional and psychosocial assessments that address the complex transactions of persons with their environments. The relation of education to the psychosocial tasks of child and family gives focus and definition to assessment, clarifies the possible unit(s) of attention, and develops the consequent role of the school social worker.

The focus of assessment is on strengths as well as problems. The social worker looks for strengths and resources in the situation and in its participants in the face of processes, which without intervention can lead to deterioration and deficit. What are the possibilities for changes in the relations, tasks, and expectations in the classroom, in the home, and in the child's patterns of learning to cope? From this unique vantage point, the worker assists teachers and parents to discover their own personal repertoire of ways to assist the child's coping. Taking strengths into account, assessment also focuses on conditions in the person, the environment, and in their transactions that may be causing difficulty. What support systems or services might make it possible for persons to survive, to cope, to form satisfactory interpersonal relationships, and to experience an increased level of success in the community and family environment? The answers will depend on these persons' needs and capacities, how they are coping with their environment, and how their environment responds to them.

Assessment and intervention have their own logical sequences. Strengths-based and rooted in systems theory, they are all about possibilities for change. They move from the outside in, from the environment to the person interacting and coping. Assuming a natural process—with the relational connections inherent and necessary to the education process—the social worker helps this process take place and helps pupils, teachers, and parents to deal with obstacles. In different circumstances and with a better understanding of the pupil's needs, teachers and parents might modify their own educational approaches and expectations. When important adults change their approach, sometimes the pupil responds without further intervention. At other times, the social worker helps the pupil to respond differently to what are often small changes in the classroom and the family. At the same time, the social worker assists parents and teachers to respond to the pupil's efforts at coping.

NEEDS ASSESSMENT OF A SCHOOL COMMUNITY

The broadest assessment of the school and its community is *needs assessment*. This type of assessment, described in greater detail in chapter 15, is an assessment of the *context* for the problems individual students and groups are experiencing in school. Needs assessments provide a systematic means of gathering data about a problem experienced by more than one student. A needs assessment focuses on relationships among the school, the community, the family, and student needs. The purpose of a needs assessment is to inform development of policies, programs, or services for schools. Needs assessments provide data that parents, teachers, administrators, and community members can understand. With these data, social workers can tailor their roles to fit the needs of their particular school and community. A good example of this is the need to develop a safety plan in every school. This process, discussed in greater detail in chapters 36 and 37, involves the social worker in the school's and the community's attempt to develop a rapid and appropriate *response* to a situation where children are potentially at risk and to develop longer term supports for grieving and healing processes.

In the following example a social worker did a needs assessment as she started her new job in a school:

> As the first school social worker in a school district, my responsibilities were to be focused in a new elementary school (grades 2–5) enrolling more than 700 children. The new school had consolidated several old smaller schools. The children were from diverse communities and backgrounds. Additional pressure was presented by new families moving in from outside the region due to the availability of jobs at a new industrial plant. One of my first challenges was to determine what my role would be in this situation and how I would set priorities on my time. I decided I did not have enough information to set priorities on my services. I needed information on the perspectives of other members of the school community, especially the teachers. With administrative approval I developed a brief needs assessment form and distributed it to the teachers. This one-page form offered some possible areas of concern from which they could indicate priorities and concerns as well as space to identify specific issues not listed. This questionnaire was based on listening to teachers in the teachers lounge as well as in initial conversations with the principal and some key informant teachers. The feedback I received told me that teachers were concerned about several issues: (1) There was a general lack of civility among pupils, resulting in frequent fights on the playground and in the lunchroom; (2) There was a lack of parent involvement, especially with parents who were new to the district; and (3) Some students appeared particularly in need of individual help. After the initial needs assessment, I discussed priorities with the principal. My first goals emerged: to help restore civility in the school; to develop special services for specific pupils who were out of control; and to get parents involved. I started by assuming responsibility for a supervised recess program for students who were referred by their teachers. Here I showed social skills videos, had pupils role play appropriate behaviors, and focused on skill development activities. I kept data on the number of repeat offenders. The school would punish repeat offenders by preventing them from socializing with peers. I was able to demonstrate that there were relatively low numbers of students who were "abusing" the fact that I used the time of supervised recess to teach skills. Later we developed a peer mediation program and a student assistance program (SAP). Students could voluntarily request peer mediation for interpersonal conflicts. Teachers could refer pupils who were having difficulty for consultation with the SAP team before deciding whether a referral to special education was necessary.
>
> On the basis of the needs assessment information, which I continued to collect, I initiated several new programs over the year, including:
>
> A peer mediation program—a local law school provided training for student peer mediators;
> A parent survey, distributed to all parents with children in the school;
> Three parent workshops during the year based on the parent survey;
> A student assistance program to provide early prevention and interventions for students experiencing problems;

Whole classroom lessons for topics such as conflict resolution, offered to teachers
   at their request;
A small minigrant for family-centered services. The grant funded parent
   workshops, bought materials, and supported students attending an after-
   school tutorial program.

I have been continually assessing the impact of these programs through data collection as well as informal feedback from teachers and students. This information
keeps administrators informed and helps us to make adjustments in services
offered. It was important to document the impact of the programs, because there
were some skeptics who preferred more punitive interventions with students.
Later I provided consultation with the district, so that the SAP approach and peer
mediation programs have been expanded through the high school level. Most
recently the superintendent told me of her plans to add another social work position, now at the high school level to develop these and other programs.

The Comprehensive Social Work Assessment

The comprehensive school social work assessment differs from the use of
assessment instruments by the school psychologist for establishing intelligence and academic achievement. The school social work assessment has a
broader focus than these and as such must be qualitative in nature. Although
qualitative as a whole, the assessment can include quantitative findings. The
assessment aspires to a depth and personalized understanding that goes
beyond comparison of the person's attributes to a larger population of individuals. Qualitative assessments rely on credibility and dependability of the
information presented, rather than being normed by a comparison to a broader
population. Credibility and dependability are strengthened by the confirmation of multiple sources of information gathered from multiple settings inside
and outside of school. There are multiple respondents (parent, teacher, and student). There are multiple methodologies to gather information: interviews with
parents, teachers, and the student; observations in various settings (classes,
playground, the home, and the community); formal instruments; and records
from school and community providers can be used as well. With all these
methodologies, the focus is always on the dynamics of relationships, and not
simply on the particular individual. It seeks areas of strengths for the student,
family, and school personnel rather than just identifying areas of deficit (see
Jordan & Franklin, 1995).

Assessment of a Classroom Learning Environment and Its Dynamics

In a school the classroom learning environment is a central context for
assessment. Teaching is a challenging and intense job. Since the pupil's need is
also to some extent the teacher's need, assisting the teacher is always central to
this process. It is the first step in intervention. The school social worker
responds to concerns expressed by a teacher by gathering information, often

observing the class, providing consultation, and developing a plan with the teacher. The goal is to help the teacher to find a perspective and a way to deal with the challenging situation and to review other possibilities for intervention when necessary. These may be direct work with the parents or the pupil. When there is a possibility for a special education referral, *prereferral intervention* with the teacher by the team is recommended. This is a team-based, preventive, problem-solving approach with the teacher prior to taking the step of a formal referral. Together with the teacher, they review the situation, hypothesize causes to explain the student's difficulties, and develop strategies to remediate those difficulties (Buck, Polloway, Smith-Thomas, & Cook, 2003). This discussion of assessment of the classroom learning environment is expanded in chapters 19, 20, and 21. For children with special needs, teamwork and consultation are expected and prescribed by law and regulations. These processes are described in greater detail in chapter 20 on consultation, in chapter 19 on the social developmental study, in chapter 21 on classroom observation, in chapter 24 on the individualized education program, and throughout the book.

MULTIDISCIPLINARY TEAMWORK

Schools are increasingly oriented to teamwork as their responsibilities become more complex. Teamwork involves working through other persons and other persons working through you. Good teamwork is an antidote for inevitable dysfunctionality in the often stressful and sometimes competitive world of school professionals. Teams balance their common goals with differences in expertise. As schools deal with increasingly complex expectations, collaborative teams and teaming processes gradually have come to be seen as the means to define problems and develop solutions through face-to-face interaction. Skills can be exchanged. Thinking processes can change, and more novel solutions can be generated. Interdependent decision making and problem solving rest on small group interpersonal skills of trust building, communication, leadership, creative problem solving, decision making, and conflict management (Thousand & Villa, 1992).

A *multidisciplinary, problem-solving team* is defined as a number of individual members of the school community, each of whom possesses particular knowledge and skills, who come together to share their expertise with one another for a common purpose (c.f. Toseland, Palmer-Ganeles, & Chapman, 1986). Teams don't just happen; they are constructed by their members in the context of particular expectations. Collaborative teams and teamwork processes are major instruments of substantive school change. Collaborative decision making implies shared ownership of problems and solutions, the sharing of skills, a different level of thinking processes, and the ability to persist in working at difficult tasks. It opens the way toward attainment of group goals (Thousand & Villa, 1992). On the team there are five components of decision making and action critical to its success. Members of the collaborative team agree to:

1. Coordinate their work to pursue common, publicly agreed-on goals,
2. Believe that all team members have unique and needed expertise,
3. Value each member's input equally,
4. Distribute leadership among all the members of the group, and
5. Collaborate with others, using face-to-face interaction on a frequent basis assuming interdependence and individual accountability. (Thousand & Villa, 1992)

There are a number of problems experienced when teams attempt to share expertise for a common purpose. The team needs to find a way to balance the power and perspectives of its members toward a genuine sharing of resources (Tiefenthal, 1980). It also needs to maintain its objectives or change them systematically when necessary. It needs to maintain its appropriate authority structure. The problem of professional differences and "territory" is complicated by some overlap of responsibilities and functions among the roles of the social worker, psychologist, and counselor on the school team (Agresta, 2004; Radin & Welsh, 1984). Each has particular strengths to contribute. At the local school level, teams define their roles differently according to the district policy, according to the perceived needs of clientele, and according to the capabilities of their members. School social workers need to negotiate aspects of their roles with the team and with the school principal. Other team members may have a very limited understanding of social work training and expertise.

The roles and relations of team members are also defined in a general way at the state education agency (SEA) level. At the SEA level the stakes are high. Social workers have learned that if they are not active in these deliberations at the state level, they can lose at the local level as well. There is constant vigilance of professional associations over their territory. There is often conflict between the SEA's interest in defining and delimiting (or broadly expanding) certain pupil personnel functions and the local education agency's (LEA's) definitions and interests. Professional rivalries and political realities may mask and legitimatize themselves as a constant concern for administrative efficiency.

Professional Boundaries and Distorted Power Arrangements

The team's effectiveness is built on its ability to utilize its members' differing perspectives and skills. There needs to be a shared understanding of roles. Distorted power arrangements on the team can limit a team's potential effectiveness. Professional boundaries within the team can be too high. Members can spend considerable energy protecting their territory to the exclusion of their common purposes. In contrast, excessively low boundaries can lead to mediocrity and at worst to chaos. For example, if the social worker is limited to only gathering information from the family, this would severely restrict her ability to gain a full perspective on the interpersonal dynamics occurring at school. However, if team members do not take responsibility for reaching consensus on solutions, their work will be unproductive.

Teams are constantly working out their balance of relationships. Social workers can't do an assessment or even effectively enter the team without an understanding of the capabilities and skills of each team member, and an understanding of the agreements team members have arrived at to regulate their contributions. Often team members have difficulty translating their specialty into something the team (or even the pupil and family) can use. The social worker, as a functional generalist, works across the multispecialty and multicultural worlds of schools, agencies, and homes. This skill often results in the social worker assuming a leadership role, such as serving as the coordinator of the team.

In special education, with its more prescriptive legal framework, the team process is more formalized. The minimum team composition is governed by regulation. To this core team could be added an expanded team, the various other experts who are called in, as needed (Thousand & Villa, 1992). For example, parents (or parent surrogates) of children with disabilities are expected to be invited to take part in team deliberations around their child (34 CFR 300 121[a]). Assessment is then developed in the context of the multidisciplinary team's efforts to assist pupils in the educational process and individualize plans based on what the school can offer.

CONSULTATION

Research points out that consultation is perhaps the most important tool of the school social worker (Allen-Meares, 1994; Anlauf-Sabatino, 1982; Constable, Kuzmickaite, Harrison, & Volkmann, 1999; Nelson, 1990). If teamwork involves the act of sharing perspectives and skills in the interests of a common purpose, consultation is the art of assisting others to become more effective in dealing with complex problems. Consultation, discussed in greater detail in chapter 20, presumes good teamwork. Team membership is the best path to the development of a trusting consultative relationship. Assessment is a key component of consultation and teamwork. Applied to the pupil, the family, the classroom, and the resources of the team, assessment is done as a joint and shared problem-solving process.

HOW DO ASSESSMENT, TEAMWORK, AND CONSULTATION WORK? (AND HOW DO THEY WORK TOGETHER?)

To see how assessment, teamwork, and consultation work, let us examine typical cases in general and special education.

Hakim was a very sad first grader. He had few friends and seemed dazed in class. He would play with pencils and other supplies on his desk while the teacher talked. The teacher noticed him making "strange random noises, deliberate hums and grunts" in class as he did his work. When it came time for him to work independently, he had to ask the teacher to repeat the directions. His need for constant adult attention made the teacher, with a class of twenty-eight 6-year-olds, feel desperate. "Fix him please." On the other hand, he was working at grade level. His art, which he loved, revealed close family connections, houses and yards, and his brothers playing soccer with him. The teacher had made no effort to contact the family. Hakim was the youngest of a large and close Assyrian family. His brothers, two uncles, two cousins, his grandmother, and his parents all lived together with him. His father worked long hours. The parents were bilingual, but Assyrian was spoken in the home. He was very bonded to his mother. His mother was shy, uncertain whether she should be involved with the school, and somewhat overprotective. She talked about her own difficulties in school and with the language. The social worker observed Hakim in class, contacted the family, and set up ongoing communication between the mother and the teacher. The assessment revealed a shy, somewhat immature first grader dealing with a different language and culture. His noises in class were Hakim talking to himself in Assyrian. The teacher felt helpless with his differences and what they seemed to mean. She had little information about the situation and was becoming impatient with him. Hakim perceived her impatience and was reacting to it. The mother, herself uncertain in a different culture, was reacting to Hakim's stories of school with her own defensiveness. Although the social worker contacted the mother and developed a relationship, much of her work was with the teacher. The social worker provided cultural information. Working with the strengths of the teacher, she helped her to be more confident with Hakim and his parents, to provide appropriate attention, and set appropriate goals with Hakim. When she did this and took a strengths-based approach to involve the family, Hakim responded positively, gradually becoming more confident with the teacher in class. He began to share his unique sense of humor with others.

Here the cultural situation reinforced Hakim's shyness, the mother's uncertainty, and the teacher's impatience and feelings of helplessness. As a team member, the social worker assessed the situation and worked through the teacher, provided information and support, and helped build a connection between the family and the school. Once contact had been made with the family, the teacher could handle the situation with the social worker's ongoing consultation and availability in case of emergency. To work apart from or in competition with the teacher in this case would have been dysfunctional and self-defeating.

Special Education

The right to a free appropriate public education (FAPE) for the child with disabilities demands a more formalized assessment process (a complete multi-faceted nondiscriminatory evaluation) and an individualized education program (IEP) for educational placement of the child with disabilities. Multidisciplinary teamwork is mandated in special education as part of this process. The team should at least include the parents of the child, a regular education teacher, a school administrator, and a person to interpret the results of testing (34 CFR 300.344). The parents are expected to be equal participants along with school personnel in developing, reviewing, and revising the IEP for their child (34 CFR

Appendix A, Question 5). School social workers are often members of this team. Their services are defined in the federal regulations to include:

1. Preparing a social or developmental history on a child with a disability;
2. Group and individual counseling with the child and family;
3. Working in partnership with parents and others on those problems in a child's living situation (home, school, and community) that affect the child's adjustment in school;
4. Mobilizing school and community resources to enable the child to learn as effectively as possible in his or her educational program; and
5. Assisting in developing positive behavioral intervention strategies. (34 CFR 300.24[b][13])

The same principles in general education of respecting others' different competence and functions apply to special education with the additional procedural safeguards meant to protect a constitutional right. Two somewhat typical case examples of social work assessment, teamwork, and consultation in special education follow:

> Steve was a 10-year-old African American boy who had received special education services since early childhood and was placed in a special classroom for children with behavior disorders/emotional disturbances. He had been in four schools before his father died three years ago. His mother's confusing and disruptive lifestyle finally brought his maternal grandmother to take permanent custody of him the year following his father's death. In the evaluation two years ago, he was reported to have serious learning problems. He appeared to be angry in school, easily frustrated, and distractible, and had very low self esteem, but the assessment had not taken into account the turbulence and confusion of his living situation. His current teacher saw none of the previous problems. He was not a slow worker and was no longer easily frustrated. Grandmother, who came to school for the first time when invited by the social worker, confirmed a picture of a boy who, after a turbulent period in his other schools, was gradually adjusting to his new home and school, although he was shy in the neighborhood. The team noted that the previous, out-of-date, and narrowly focused assessment had taken on a life of its own but no longer reflected Steve's current situation. In any case, a reevaluation was essential. Based on the reevaluation, a plan for Steve's placement in a general education class with supports was developed. The social worker helped Steve manage the transition to general education, provided consultation to the new teacher, and continued to provide support to the grandmother and to Steve as needed.

> Brian was a 15-year-old placed in math and reading classes for youth with learning disabilities in his high school. He was neatly dressed and well groomed. Both parents saw him as truthful, neat, responsible, adultlike, and perfectionistic. He interacted well with his parents but tended to withdraw when faced with something unpleasant. His history was of mixed school achievement. Sometimes he did very poorly, but in both seventh and eighth grades he made the junior high school honor roll. Nevertheless, there was no reevaluation of his situation or recommen-

dations for changes. In his sophomore year Brian stopped working almost entirely and refused to participate in any activity, including taking tests. He was nondisruptive, but passively resistant in the classroom. He refused to engage with the social worker. Despite the implications of his learning disability, teachers took his lack of cooperation personally. There was a pervasive negative tone in their discussion of him and in correspondence sent home. Brian saw this as his power struggle with his teachers. They were thinking of punishing him by having him drop driver education. This is the only class he enjoyed and demonstrated achievement. Parents sensed the teachers' attitudes and felt alienated from them and from the school. Their only weak hope was that he would pass sophomore year before he dropped out. If he did that, they would reward him with a pickup truck. His father had himself dropped out in tenth grade. The social worker worked with his teachers to defuse their power struggle with Brian. He worked with the parents to develop more appropriate expectations and rewards. He developed a transition plan with Brian and the family in case Brian did drop out this year, and he worked with Brian on Brian's own educational and vocational goals.

As in the case of Hakim in general education, and Steve and Brian in special education, the assessment, teamwork, and consultation processes are interrelated and crucial to the success of these cases. In both special education cases, the earlier reviews appear to have been either missing or perfunctory. However, the faulty assessment began to take on a life of its own. The team needed to rethink its approaches and make sense of both situations. There needed to be a broader, strengths-based assessment. The social worker found herself working between the student, the parents, and the team. As a prerequisite to working in special education, the social worker needed to translate terms, such as "reevaluation," "complete, multifaceted nondiscriminatory assessment," "parent participation," and "transition planning" into skilled social work practice. The social worker was able to use an understanding of the regulations governing special education to assist the student. Further work with the student and family, discussed in the next section, is dependent on assessment and the decision-making processes within the team, as well as with the parents and with the student.

NEW DEVELOPMENTS IN GENERAL AND SPECIAL EDUCATION: AN OUTCOME-ORIENTED, STRENGTHS-BASED SERVICE DELIVERY APPROACH

The approaches prescribed in the laws of special education, detailed here and elsewhere in this book, have created profound changes in the entitlements of children with disabilities to a free appropriate public education. Assessment, however, can still be based on a *deficit* approach, leading inevitably to categorizing the pupil and to placement outside of general education. Based on their own research into educational outcomes, critics of the current system (Skrtic, 1991; Ysseldyke, Algozzine, & Thurlow, 2000) pointed out seven problems with this deficit approach:

- ◆ Eligibility for services is determined by identifying deviant characteristics that permit the labeling of disability;
- ◆ Services are delivered through categorical programs, such as those for learning disability, emotional disorder, and so on;
- ◆ The role of regular education personnel becomes to refer problem students to other experts; referral usually means removal, and so a perverse incentive is created to identify and refer problem students (Algozzine & Ysseldyke, 1981; Ysseldyke, 1983).
- ◆ Assessment and diagnosis use standard criteria for disability; the issue becomes not what may be affecting the behavior or what the student needs to do better (functional assessment), but whether he or she fits into a predetermined class;
- ◆ The least restrictive environment (often a stressful environment for the teacher and student) proves difficult to implement, and therefore students tend to be segregated in special classes or separate resource rooms;
- ◆ The special education system disproportionately enrolls minority students; and
- ◆ The majority of students receiving special education services continue to receive separate instruction until they graduate or drop out of school.

In many ways the problems present in the cases of Steve and Brian exemplify some of these concerns with the deficit approach. Students tend to be caught in categories. Strengths can be ignored because of this categorization. Power struggles develop. Members of the team might stay within their specialties and lose the student and the meaning of the situation. Students feel they are trapped in special education no matter what they do. Parents, particularly minority parents or parents of high school pupils, can be left out. These concerns have led to an approach that focuses on strengths, on outcomes, and on collaboration.

Assessment

Assessment in an outcome-oriented, strengths-based, collaborative service delivery approach places a strong emphasis on direct observation in the natural environment (classroom, playground). *Functional behavior assessments* are often made of the student's academic and behavioral performance. The key questions in functional behavior assessments are: How is the student currently performing? How does the student respond to interventions suggested by the problem-solving team? and What is the relation between students, educational environments, and their behavior? The helping process is based on strengths-based problem solving. This builds on the resources of the teacher, the student, the parents, and the resources of other personnel in a manner similar to the social work theoretical models discussed in this book. Services are flexible in terms of who provides the services, where services are provided, and the amount of services provided. *Eligibility*, the decision whether a referral for special education is needed, is based how the student responds to an identified concern or problem, and to change efforts of the teacher, the student, the parents, and others, or whether change is resisted. Regular educators and special educators work collaboratively to support the student's and the teachers' work in the regular class.

Interventions

The assessment, teamwork, and consultation demanded by this approach have to be extremely sophisticated. The functions of the team (now the problem-solving team) shift from the older multidisciplinary team tasks—referral, testing, and placement—to an ongoing, dynamic, problem-solving focus. Instead of following a deficit model that focuses on dysfunction in the pupil alone, the team looks for combinations of factors, as in the previous social work assessment and intervention examples. It follows an *interaction* model, examining and responding to the combination of student × curriculum × instructional environment × family × community systems. This encourages a holistic focus, rather than just assessing/testing for student deficits. Interventions are identified based on needs in the student/school curriculum/instructional/family/peer group/community environment, rather than simply delivering services to the student after a disability label has been identified. This approach is very compatible with the ecological systems model developed in this book, but without proper supports, it could fail or, if misused, become an excuse for limiting services, developing inexpensive services, or not delivering services at all. Further testing of this approach will be an opportunity for social workers to develop a helping role in a context that would be most compatible with their theoretical and value orientations.

POSITIVE BEHAVIOR INTERVENTION AND SUPPORT (PBIS)

The identification and implementation of positive behavior interventions with students who display behavior problems is clearly mandated in IDEA. The school social worker is specifically identified as one of the professionals who are expected to assist in this process. The regular education teacher is also identified as an important contributor to identifying positive interventions that may be effective in decreasing negative behaviors and/or increasing positive behaviors. Individual behavior intervention plans, building on a functional behavior analysis, for students who display behavior problems are developed further in chapters 19 and 24.

The development of school-wide systems of positive interventions has been encouraged through a variety of federal initiatives: safe and drug-free schools, IDEA, character education, and so on. At this point, there is an expectation in the law that positive behavior interventions and supports (PBIS) should be a part of every general and special education teacher's repertoire of skills. The PBIS model proposes proactive strategies to define, teach, and support appropriate student behaviors. This emphasis has resulted in coordinated and research-supported efforts for all school personnel to participate in positively focused school-wide discipline models. The goal is to prevent school discipline problems through *system-wide* interventions that focus on increasing positive behavior of all students rather than using traditional punitive efforts directed toward students who engage in rule-breaking behavior.

> The school administrator, school social worker, and other members of the school planning team decided to adopt a PBIS model. After attending a training session, the school social worker began providing whole-class presentations on prosocial topics each month. The teachers were provided possible activities to use during the month to reinforce the lesson presented. School-wide monitoring of specific behaviors permitted reinforcement of positive goals through recognition ceremonies and "celebrations" for class and individual accomplishments. Families were included through a variety of techniques: a newsletter explaining the goals of the program, things that families could do to encourage the positive behaviors to occur at home, and invitations to participate in some of the recognition ceremonies held at the school. All of these efforts contributed to a positive learning environment and promote prosocial behaviors for all students, not just those with IEPs.

CONCLUSION

Recent research on the school social work role (Allen-Meares, 1994; Constable et al., 1999) has pointed out the overarching importance of assessment, multidisciplinary teamwork, and consultation. Because these affect how others in the school will work with children, they have a broader impact than the social worker's direct intervention with individuals and groups of students and their families. The emphases on teamwork and functional assessment, emerging from laws, policies, and regulations for children with disabilities, have long been a familiar part of school social work practice. Section III develops these related themes of assessment, teamwork, and consultation as the foundations for policy, program development, and intervention with children and their families in the school community.

PBIS Resources

PBIS is in its infancy. Nevertheless there are a number of resources that track this developing and changing field (Zuna & McDougall, 2004):

www. pbis.org from the Office of Special Education Programs (OSEP) of the Department of Education.

www.nichcy.org from the National Information Center for Children and Youth with Disabilities.

www.beachcenter.org from the Beach Center on Disability.

www. apbsinternational.org an organization dedicated to positive behavior support. Members receive newsletters and a subscription to the *Journal of Positive Behavior Interventions.*

Journal of Applied Behavior Analysis, University of Kansas.

Carr, E. G., Levin, L., McConnachie, G., Carlson, J. I., Kemp, D. C., & Smith, C. E. (1994). *Communication-based interventions for problem behavior: A user's guide for positive change.* Baltimore: Paul H. Brookes.

Koegel, L. K., Koegel, R. L., & Dunlap, G. (Eds). (1996). *Positive behavioral support: Including people with difficult behavior in the community.* Baltimore: Paul H. Brookes.

Luiselli, J. K., & Cameron, M. J. (Eds). (1998). *Antecedent control: Innovative approaches to behavioral support.* Baltimore: Paul H. Brookes.

Repp, A. C., & Horner, R. H. (1999). *Functional analysis of problem behavior: From effective assessment to effective support.* Belmont, CA: Wadsworth.

References

Agresta, J. (2004). Professional role perceptions of school social workers, psychologists and counselors. *Children and Schools., 26*(3), 151-164.

Allen-Meares, P. (1994). Social work services in schools: A national study of entry-level tasks. *Social Work, 39,* 28-34.

Algozzine, B. A., & Ysseldyke, J. E. (1981). Special education services for normal students: Better safe than sorry? *Exceptional Children, 48,* 238-243.

Anlauf-Sabatino, C. (1982). Consultation and school social work practice. In R. T. Constable & J. P. Flynn (Eds.), *School social work: Practice and research perspectives.* Homewood, IL: Dorsey.

Buck, G. H., Polloway, E. A., Smith-Thomas, A., & Cook, K. W. (2003). Prereferral intervention processes: A survey of state practices. *Exceptional Children, 69*(3), 349-360.

Constable, R., Kuzmickaite, D., Harrison, W. D., & Volkmann, L. (1999). The emergent role of the school social worker in Indiana. *School Social Work Journal, 24*(1), 1-14.

Jordan, C., & Franklin, C. (1995). *Clinical assessment for social workers: Quantitative and qualitative methods.* Chicago: Lyceum Books.

Levine, A. (2004). New rules, old responses. *News,* Teachers College, Columbia University, Retrieved October, 2001, from http://www.tc.columbia.edu/news/article/.htm?id=4741

Nelson, C. (1990). *A job analysis of school social workers.* Princeton, NJ: Educational Testing Service.

Radin, N., & Welsh, B. (1984). Social work, psychology and counseling in the schools. *Social Work, 24*(1), 28-33.

Skrtic, T. M. (1991). *Behind special education: A critical analysis of professional culture and school organization.* Denver, CO: Love Publishing.

Thousand, J. S., & Villa, R. A. (1992). Collaborative teams: A powerful tool in school restructuring. In R. A. Villa, J. S. Thousand, W. Stainback, & S. Stainback (Eds.), *Restructuring for caring and effective education* (pp. 73-107). Baltimore: Paul H. Brookes.

Tiefenthal, M. (1980). Multidisciplinary teams. In R. T. Constable & M. Tiefenthal (Eds.), *The school social worker and the handicapped child: Making PL 94-142 work* (pp. 21-24). Dekalb: Illinois Regional Resource Center.

Toseland, R. W., Palmer-Ganales, J., & Chapman, D. (1986). Teamwork in psychiatric settings. *Social Work, 31*(4), 46-52.

Ysseldyke, J. E. (1983). Current practices in making psychoeducational decisions about learning disabled students. *Journal of Learning Disabilities, 16,* 226-233.

Ysseldyke, J. E., Algozzine, B. A, & Thurlow, M. L. (2000). *Critical issues in special education.* Boston: Houghton-Mifflin.

Zuna, N. & McDougall, D. (2004). Using positive behavioral support to manage avoidance of academic tasks. *Teaching Exceptional Children, 37*(1), 18-25.

18

A Framework for Cross-Cultural Practice in School Settings

Frances Smalls Caple
University of Southern California

Ramon M. Salcido
University of Southern California

- ◆ Culturally Competent Practice
- ◆ Understanding Culture through Perspective Building
- ◆ The Role of Social Worker-Learner
- ◆ Understanding Acculturation and Cultural Exchange
- ◆ A Framework for Culturally Competent Practice
- ◆ Systems Assessment
- ◆ Family Assessment and Engagement
- ◆ Skills of Cross-Cultural Practice
- ◆ Planning and Service Delivery

This chapter focuses on how school social workers might be better prepared for and therefore more effectively deliver culturally competent practice. Many young people and their families occupy subordinate positions in societies throughout the world, often dominated (colonized) by the social and economic power, privilege, and prestige of other groups. Subordination of so-called

Some material from this chapter was originally published in Caple, F. S., Salcido, R., & di Cecco, J. (1995). Engaging effectively with culturally diverse families and children. *Social Work in Education, 17*, 159–170. Used with permission of the National Association of Social Workers.

minority populations (Longres, 1991; Taylor, 1994) arises most typically when powerful members of the dominant group hold in low esteem some characteristic such as race, gender, ethnicity, or religion (Taylor, 1994). When this attitude is translated into discriminatory or prejudicial actions, the subordinated persons are often placed at a distinct disadvantage in regard to the achievement of life goals. On the other hand, the importance of education for national and personal survival has led to the growth throughout the world of school policies that aspire to: (1) *raise* the quality of education to an international standard; (2) *include* previously marginalized populations who never had equal access to a good education; and (3) *individualize* the educational process to accommodate disabilities, personal differences, and ways of learning. Women in Afghanistan, tribal groups in South Africa, Russian children in Lithuania, Gypsies in Romania, children of migrant workers, homeless families, families facing racial discrimination in the United States, and many others continue to be marginalized throughout the world. For children who are members of such populations, school can become a battleground for personal survival.

CULTURALLY COMPETENT PRACTICE

Culturally competent school social work practice (NASW, 2001) has grown from the need to connect previously marginalized people to the education process, to develop just conditions in the school community, to assist in the individualization of education, and to counter negative beliefs about human capability (Huxtable & Blyth, 2002). Indeed, school social work derives its legitimacy from the fact that there is still a struggle and that special efforts need to be made to make education work for people who have experienced social marginalization. In this process the school social worker has multiple roles working with different systems: individual pupils, parents, and teachers (microsystem); the *nexus,* the connections between all of these in an educational process in a school community (mesosystem); and the *mix* of laws, policies, and cultural beliefs and the broader systems that affect every school community (macrosystem). In this context, the examples given in this chapter connect more broadly with international processes.

Social workers live in and are a part of society and are therefore subject to the class values, attitudes, and norms predominant within that society (Weaver, 1999). These norms may have also served to subordinate members of different cultural groups. The content of any social worker's perspective for working with culturally diverse clients is drawn from values and beliefs as well as from specialized knowledge and skills. In the absence of a way of organizing acquired knowledge into culturally competent practice, one's perspective may become biased in different ways. In the process of becoming a social worker, one needs to develop *cultural competence.*

Cultural competence refers to the process by which individuals and systems respond respectfully and effectively to people of diverse cultures, languages, classes, races, genders, sexual orientations, ethnic backgrounds, religions, and other diversity factors. Culturally competent school social workers recognize, affirm, and value the worth of individuals, families, and communities and protect and preserve their dignity. Cultural competence is a lifelong process for social workers, who will always encounter diverse clients and new situations in their practice (NASW, 2001). It requires social workers to recognize the strengths that exist in all cultures and to struggle with ethical dilemmas arising from value conflicts or special needs of diverse clients (NASW, 2001). True cultural competence goes far beyond the individual social worker. School social workers help school community systems develop capacities to become more culturally competent by: (1) valuing diversity; (2) developing the capacity for cultural self-assessment; (3) developing understandings of the dynamics inherent when cultures interact; (4) institutionalizing cultural knowledge; and (5) developing programs and services that reflect an understanding of diversity between and within cultures (NASW, 2001).

From the perspective of this chapter, the school is a center of cultural development for children and for the developing community. It must become safe for learning and development for all children and for their families. For this to succeed there must be a belief that there is real, community ownership by everyone of the process of education and what school stands for. School communities all over the world are dealing with ethnic and cultural differences and the tensions and fears that often arise from these differences. School social workers join with educational administrators, teachers, and parents to build a school community that may be *different* from its surroundings in its norms of nonviolent resolution of differences, respect for others, their values and life ways, and the respect for self that accompanies this respect for others in a safe community. School social workers are concerned about social justice in the school community. And so, they engage in actions to correct and change unfair situations, discrimination, and actions that hurt others because of differences due to race, ethnicity, gender, sexuality, religion, or any other aspect of persons that may make them culturally different. One important problem in the United States and throughout the world is the issue of racial and ethnic tension in schools. This issue is addressed by school social workers in the following two real-life examples:

> In the United States, Rita McGary, a high school social worker in a suburb of Washington, DC, worked with a multiethnic population of Native Americans, various Hispanic cultures, various Asian cultures, African Americans, and various White cultures. It was a situation of racial and ethnic tension. She developed mediation systems and conflict resolution and worked with six different cultural groups in separate forums to build group solidarity and resolve problems within and between groups in a context of respect (McGary, 1987).

> In post-Soviet Lithuania, Daiva Kuzmickaitc, a school social worker, worked in a conflicted school. The school culture, reflecting Soviet times, was somewhat

artificial and full of conflicts and hopelessness. There were serious problems experienced between and among majority Lithuanian, and the Polish and Russian minority students. No one expected these groups to befriend each other. The school itself and its students felt disconnected from the realities of post-Soviet Lithuania and the economic competition of an emergent multinational world. Students were in a bubble prior to their entrance into very different economic and social realities; however, in some ways they knew the harsh world they lived in, and they reflected these realities in their relationships with each other. Teachers, trained to impose harsh discipline and to shame their students into submission, were uncertain in the face of an emergent Lithuania. The school social worker worked with others to guide a process of cultural change within the school community. She worked with the principal and with teachers to develop policies that fit the emergent Lithuanian cultural realities. She developed group programs for students to find different ways to work out problems themselves, with their own resources. She assisted teachers in finding new ways of relating to the needs of their students. She worked with diverse families and with children who were having difficulty with this process as well.[1]

Throughout the world, schools exist whose students are primarily from minority or vulnerable populations. In these cases, schools may serve both as places of safety and of transaction with the larger society. The following example illustrates this process:

In South Africa, Miriam Mabetoa, a school social worker, worked in a rural Black homeland. Although tribal differences have meaning, there are no other ethnic groups in the school. Students and residents of this homeland feel left out of an urban society. The painful national history of racism, together with rural-urban issues, is experienced through lowered expectations and hopelessness. The school, built by the labor of homeland residents and parents, tries to be a place of development and hope. Here the broader society is partially experienced; however, the greater problems are truancy and dropouts, and the combination of hopelessness and economic realities behind these problems. The school social worker's model of practice focused on school-community development and then helping individuals and groups of students and parents find a part for themselves in this reconstructed community that offers hope (Mabetoa, 1996).

In each case the school social worker assisted in the building of a safe school community where differences are respected, resolved, and indeed the basis for growth and development of the whole school community.

UNDERSTANDING CULTURE THROUGH PERSPECTIVE BUILDING

Social workers seeking cultural competence soon realize the impossibility of acquiring specific knowledge about every racially, ethnically, or otherwise diverse client. We have identified four principles as essential for developing a

---

1. The example is taken from R. Constable's field liaison work in Lithuania in 1994.

generic perspective for culturally competent practice in the United States and in many other countries in this developing multinational and multicultural world:

1. In a developing, multicultural world, cultures are complex; there is no single American culture;
2. Diversity is to be acknowledged and valued;
3. Members of each cultural group are diverse; and
4. Acculturation is a dynamic process.

Historical and Theoretical Views

In U.S. culture the school has been both a center of development and of conflict throughout its multiethnic history. Over a century it has struggled with different levels of success and failure to develop an inclusive community where there is some avowal of respect for individual differences. For young families it is becoming more of a center of development. Problems of violence experienced in the community, issues of harassment, intimidation, and bullying have brought about a needed focus on developing a culture of safety and respect for differences. Legislation and case law have mandated desegregation and thus the interaction of diverse groups in schools. The focus on cross-cultural practice appears to have been influenced by several historical developments within the United States as a whole, within the public schools in particular, and within the social work profession itself. Although these factors are varied and complex, some observational reflection on history can be important in assisting school social workers to think about their practice and follow through with effective assessment of needs and plans for change.

The United States has always been a culturally diverse country even though it has often functioned as if it were a single culture. Legislation, public policies, and procedures were drawn on the order of the dominant groups who held elected or appointed offices and who shaped those laws and policies. The United States was settled by peoples from all countries of the world, whether they came free and voluntarily, were enticed by the possibility of economic gains, or were enslaved or indentured and came involuntarily. The earliest settlements in the northern colonies were often voluntarily formed according to the country of origin of the residents. The ethnic communities of modern cities reflect a similar continuing pattern of members of groups tending to band together. One reason for such community and neighborhood formation is obvious: it allows for the greatest preservation of those things held dear and most familiar by the people who settle there—those things that help identify who they are as a people—the customs, values, and beliefs that comprise their culture.

The pattern of community growth and development in the southern colonies was more racially oriented. The earliest settlement included Black immigrants brought involuntarily as slaves. Legal mandates for segregation of the races followed the Emancipation Proclamation. Settlements in the West included immigrants from Mexico and from Asian countries. Native Americans were restricted to reservations established by treaties between the various Indian nations and the U.S. government. Altogether, these early patterns resulted in highly segregated communities, whether they were formed involuntarily or voluntarily. Chow (1999) noted, for example, that the "isolated, residentially segregated Chinatowns developed as mechanisms of self-protection against the racism, exclusion, and oppression experienced by early Chinese immigrants" (p. 71). With the advent of public education for all children, the highly valued neighborhood school was thus similarly segregated on racial and ethnic cultural lines. Southern schools were segregated by laws that prohibited the mixing of racial groups.

For the last half century, the country has struggled to keep up with rapid changes brought about by federal and state orders to desegregate public schools and public facilities, based on the historic Supreme Court decision *Brown v. Board of Education, Topeka, Kansas,* 1954. The nature of racially and ethnically isolated neighborhoods meant that school buses became one vehicle of desegregation. In the aftermath of all efforts, some U.S. schools became more racially mixed than they had ever been, while significant numbers of African American and Latino students still attend schools that almost exclusively enroll one ethnic group. In addition, immigrants seeking personal gain and refugees from war-torn countries joined what was often referred to as the "melting pot." The relative ease and various means of transportation in this country enable constant migration within its borders, and the populations of many states reflect constant shifts in their demographic mix. The United States is becoming more diverse (Weaver, 1999), largely through immigration. At the same time, the ever-present diversity in the United States is becoming more obvious with the disruption of barriers as to where residents live, work, and attend school. Recent population figures from the 2000 U.S. Census (U.S. Bureau of the Census, 2001) show increases in minority group numbers when compared to the 1990s figures. The 2000 Census population counts show increases for Hispanic groups from 9 percent to 12.5 percent; Blacks from 12.1 percent to 12.3 percent; and Asian/Pacific Islanders from 2.92 percent to 3.7 percent. By contrast, the White population (excluding Hispanics) showed a decrease from 71.3 percent to 62.6 percent, suggesting an opposite trend. In addition, the projected figures (as reported by Booth, 1998) for 2050 show Hispanics to be 25 percent, Blacks about 14 percent, and Asian/Pacific Islanders at 8 percent, indicating a continued upward trend. The White population is projected to be about 53 percent of the population in 2050. These trends clearly suggest a need for understanding of cultural diversity today and in the future.

These figures reflect a marked difference from figures reported of actual immigration at the turn of the twentieth century. Between 1890 and 1920, there were approximately 18 million immigrants, including Catholics and Jews, who came to the United States from Ireland, Germany, Italy, and Eastern Europe. This was the largest entry of immigrants in the country's history. The second wave of a large number of immigrants, occurring at the close of the twentieth century, included great numbers of persons from economically developing worlds of Asia and Latin America (Booth, 1998). Already in states such as New Mexico, California, and Texas, the numbers of children under age 18 years who are African American, Latino, Asian and Pacific Islanders, and Native American together far exceed the number of White children (Annie E. Casey Foundation, 1997). In some urban areas, it is not unusual to have 35 different linguistic groups in an elementary school with approximately 200 children.

The European immigration sparked the notion of America as "the 'melting pot,' a place where many cultures were blended to create a strong American identity" (Pryor, 1992, p. 153). Because the English language was one vehicle for binding people together, schools became the place for teaching the language as well as "transmitting the knowledge and values needed for successful social functioning" (Pryor, 1992, p. 153). The social work profession as a whole and school social work practice in particular emerged during this same time, "assisting in the process of assimilating and acculturating immigrants" (Pryor, 1992, p. 154) to become citizens. The development of a multicultural economy in the later years of the twentieth century made schooling even more important for personal and national survival.

The notion of a melting pot—a single American culture with a single set of common values, customs and beliefs—was challenged during the 1960s when much debate and demonstrations were carried out to affirm and actualize the civil rights of oppressed people, notably African American people in southern states (Pryor, 1992).

Despite challenges to the melting pot metaphor, there continue to be strong efforts to retain an expectation of conformity to a single American culture. A newer metaphor that also attempts to reflect a unified American culture refers to U.S. culture as a "salad bowl"—one where diverse elements become a part of an integral whole while still retaining their special qualities. In this world picture, the entire salad bowl is the single U.S. culture, which has a unifying set of meanings, purposes, and global values such as "all (people) are created equal" and there is "liberty and justice for all." Yet, there is visual confirmation and clear acknowledgment that each element is unlike any other and is able to have and retain its individual set of meanings and purposes even as it participates in making the whole what it is. There may be no need for metaphors of either kind, when there is greater refinement of the knowledge, understanding, and acceptance of the cultural diversity that exists in the United States. The distinct diversity of each person's system, and of the various groups to which persons belong, is to be acknowledged and valued as providing real and potential sources of strength for the person's overall functioning and well-being.

THE ROLE OF SOCIAL WORKER-LEARNER

There is no single profile that fits all members of any specific cultural group. The most direct and accurate source of data concerning cultural realities is the person one is working with, in the context of the school culture and its values. Reliance on the worker's general, acquired knowledge of how Americans behave or how the members of a given ethnic group behave is insufficient. The social worker must be willing to assume the role of social worker-learner (Green, 1999). Specifically the social worker must begin immediately to explore directly with members of the school community, and in the context of their cultural values and lifestyles, the meaning of life events and presenting problems, any history of past or current oppression, and the person's relative acculturation to the dominant culture. In the emerging transcultural world assessment becomes a set of strategies, developed by Helen Brown Miller (Constable & Lee, 2004, p. 107), which provide guideposts to discern both differences and commonalities across cultures.

- Consider all clients as individual persons first, then as members of a specific ethnic group.
- Never assume that a person's ethnic identity tells you everything about his or her cultural values or patterns of behavior.
- Treat all "facts" you have heard or read about cultural values and traits as hypotheses, to be tested anew with each client; turn facts into questions.
- Remember that all members of minority groups in this society are at least bicultural; they have had to integrate two value systems that are often in conflict, and these conflicts may override any specific cultural content.
- Some aspects of a client's cultural history, values, and lifestyle are relevant to your work with a client; others may simply be interesting to you as a professional; do not prejudge what areas are relevant.
- Identify strengths in the client's cultural orientation that can be built upon; assist the client in identifying areas that create social or psychological conflict related to biculturalism; seek to reduce dissonance in those areas.
- Know your own attitudes about cultural pluralism, particularly whether you tend to promote assimilation into the dominant societal values or to stress the maintenance of traditional cultural beliefs and practices.
- Engage your client actively in the process of learning what cultural content should be considered.
- Keep in mind that there are no substitutes for good clinical skills, empathy, caring, and a sense of humor.

UNDERSTANDING ACCULTURATION AND CULTURAL EXCHANGE

There is no single American culture and little likelihood that there ever will be, and furthermore, there is diversity among members of each cultural group, which is to be acknowledged and valued. How, then, do diverse members of a society coexist, and how can school social workers understand and incorporate their knowledge into effective cross-cultural practice? In actuality, some understanding of the dynamic process of acculturation as ongoing to some greater or lesser extent throughout the life span in individuals and groups can be helpful in this task. In a dynamic sense, acculturation means a process in which either we are constantly "adapting to or borrowing traits from (other) cultures" or "cultures (are merging) as a result of prolonged contact" (*Merriam-Webster's Collegiate Dictionary*, 2000, p. 8). Changes occur as members of a multicultural society transact in extended contact or have extended exposure to other cultural groups, as through the media. This phenomenon is most easily seen in cross-cultural adoption of hairstyles, clothing, music, foods, and selected rituals. The understanding and appreciation of such cultural exchanges are vital for the promotion of professional competence in cross-cultural practice.

This life-span phenomenon is especially true for children throughout their school years. Although some family cultures are similar to that of the school, each child will make some adaptive shifts from one system to the other. Thus, it is common for families to report different child behavior at home than reported by school personnel. In addition, immigrant children may be at a different level of acculturation to dominant U.S. culture than their parents, and this fact may require special attention in the engagement and ongoing treatment process.

Most schoolchildren will make such shifts between family and school cultures without much difficulty; the child perceives the norms of the school and behaves accordingly. The greater the incongruity between the personal culture of the individual and the culture of the system in which interaction occurs, the more dynamic the process of acculturation becomes. The potential for conflicts is particularly high when the cultural imperatives of one group are ignored or openly dismissed as irrelevant in person-environment transactions. The social worker should be prepared to recognize, assess, and negotiate resolution of such conflicts. One approach to conflict resolution would include the facilitation of an accurate perception of cultural differences and the open sharing of cultural beliefs and norms by all parties engaged in the social work process.

The dynamic processes of acculturation may be even more keenly observed in situations where there are recent immigrants, migrants from other locales, or where there are specially designed plans for integration that bring students from diverse neighborhoods to a more distant school. The social worker is well advised to anticipate cultural conflicts and to prepare some preventive planning and strategies to attenuate potential problems.

A FRAMEWORK FOR CULTURALLY COMPETENT PRACTICE

Overview

School social work, as specialized practice, brings together interventions at the micro-, meso-, and macrosystem levels and uses a variety of skills so that the entire school community strives to make education work for all children. This is especially important for children in danger of exclusion from effective participation in this process. In a variety of chapters dealing with direct and indirect intervention, practice, policy development, and research, this book develops an integration of theory, supporting the role as it is carried out in schools. At the *microsystem* level, the social worker focuses attention on the biopsychosocial-educational needs of the child and family. Those actions that take place within the school itself are considered *mesosystem* interventions because the social worker is typically a part of and working within that system. *Macrosystem* interventions are those undertaken on behalf of schoolchildren and their families with larger systems such as a neighborhood and community organizations and would include efforts to influence local, state, and national policy and budget developments.

There are a number of major issues that American schools face and that relate directly to their own diversity. The first issue is a long-standing one of overrepresentation of minority children in special education (Hosp & Reschly, 2004). The second issue is the achievement gap on standardized tests between minority and nonminority students (Barton, 2003). Some of these issues may have to do with difficult conditions many minority children face. Other parts may indicate that, from one small action to another, the system itself is sorting out children from kindergarten on and is systematically failing to recognize inherent capabilities and ways of learning until it is too late. A third issue is that of racial tension in schools (Goldsmith, 2004; Hawley, 2004; Stearns, 2004). School social workers can address these problems through intervention at all levels, including school-wide interventions. In the previous example from a multiethnic high school in the United States, a social worker combines group work and community development, working with different subgroups in conflict. She helps each to develop internal supports and participates in their education, developing conflict resolution and mediation processes to manage intergroup tensions (McGary, 1987). Various chapters of this book present examples of theory and practice of school community needs assessment, consultation, collaboration, inclusive education, coordination of services, family involvement, social skills groups, development of mediation, school responsiveness to risks and violence, and safety programs—all of which can deal with aspects of conflict and racial/ethnic tension. However, the issue is often ignored. In the absence of a way to address the issue it becomes embedded in the fabric of the school, so that both students and staff experience aspects of racial/ethnic tension.

Basic Assumptions and Perspectives

Schools in the United States have always reflected some degree of diversity. Every person has some cultural uniqueness that places him or her in a category apart from everyone else. And so, all social work practice is multicultural (Thornton & Garrett, 1995). The basic knowledge, values, and skills of the profession provide a solid foundation for building a framework for such practice. (see Compton & Galaway, 1999; Hepworth, Rooney, & Larsen, 2002; Woods & Hollis, 2000.) The social worker, armed with the paradigm of person in transaction with the environment, a concept broadened by practice theorists in the ecological perspective (Germain & Gitterman, 1980; chapter 2 and chapter 3), begins with a perspective of establishing a transactional relationship. With the open-system paradigm comes the expectation that clients have key expertise on their situations and that all participants in the service transaction will be influenced to some extent by the others. With a de-emphasis on experts solving problems, the social worker now assists participants in finding workable solutions together. The social work relationship is marked by empathy and caring concern; social workers will demonstrate nonjudgmental acceptance and expectation; clients will be aided as far as possible to exercise their rights of self-determination (Compton & Galaway, 1999). When the social worker genuinely demonstrates a nonjudgmental attitude toward clients, the distinct diversity of each client system is also acknowledged. The acknowledgment of differences can provide real strength for the client's overall functioning and well-being. Value dilemmas will arise, but the social worker would recognize and address these in ways that do not harm client systems.

Learning the nature and meaning of the client's or a group's life situation is of key importance. It is when the culture of the client system is markedly different from that most familiar to the social worker that social workers may have the greatest challenges meeting the ideals of the profession. Not only may the worker's own values, beliefs, and patterns of behavior be inherently different from those of the client, but the client's life experiences within society may not be sufficiently understood by the worker to allow real empathy. However, effective cross-cultural work is more than "skin deep." Within the United States, so much emphasis is placed on race and ethnicity that it is often believed that when the worker and the client are of the same race, all will be well. Even when the social worker and client system have great similarities, there are also inevitable differences. During a consultation session with another social worker, a White school social worker openly expressed her concerns about her difficulty in understanding and working with poor White clients. In that instance, there were cultural issues other than race or ethnicity to consider, such as class, regional origins, neighborhood norms, and so on.

SYSTEMS ASSESSMENT

Practice in school settings makes an assessment of the entire ecosystem and intervenes at the most appropriate points in the system to effect desired change. The focus of treatment ultimately is to improve the goodness of fit between the client and others in the ecosystem, including the social worker. The effectiveness of problem solving depends as well on the worker's understanding of and sensitivity to the client's cultural beliefs, lifestyle, and social support systems. Assessments and interventions may be directed toward a variety of units of attention: the family, specific members of the family, the teacher, or others in the ecosystem. A primary emphasis of treatment is to empower client systems (pupils and their families) and to intervene in other parts of the ecosystem that create barriers to empowerment. And so, the worker who uses the ecosystems framework assumes various roles—enabler, facilitator, coordinator, mediator, and teacher—as he or she moves across system boundaries in dealing with the transactions between the client system and the school ecosystem.

The School Social Worker

One of the essential components of effective cross-cultural practice is each social worker's ongoing examination and assessment of one's own cultural beliefs and values, and how personal biases may impact the social work process (Weaver, 1999). Another part of this process would include working to understand and accept one's own cultural identity. Beginning to think about this activity can evoke surprising responses for the social worker who may not have thought about his or her racial or ethnic culture. In open forum in a university setting, White students have sometimes commented that they have no ethnicity; that they had given no thought to their "culture," per se. A part of the ensuing discussion included the observation that the White person had grown up in the United States and simply had not had to consider his race or ethnicity at any time in his life. In other discussion, there were notions expressed that "ethnicity" was a reference just for "persons of color." Whatever the social worker's cultural identification, it is important that the self-assessment be open and honest. Therefore, it is vital to have a safe place to review attitudes and value conflicts that routinely arise. It could be helpful to begin by making lists, such as "I will/may have difficulty working with (name: race, ethnicity, religion, sexual orientation. . . .)," then identifying and reviewing the nature of the anticipated difficulty. The importance of this work is emphasized by Allen-Meares and Burman (1999), who noted that "with the development of self-awareness and cultural competency, biases and discriminatory practices shaped by socialization processes and erroneous beliefs can be recognized and altered, replaced with a focus on client strengths, abilities, and resources" (p. 50).

The School Site/System

Assessment also includes the manner and degree to which the school site and system as a whole demonstrates its attitudes about cultural diversity. In what ways are all children welcomed, their cultures acknowledged and valued? Are first-time enrollments facilitated or made difficult to a point where children are not permitted to attend until all records are in place? How are behavior problems handled? Are proportionately more or fewer children from certain racial or ethnic groups referred for suspension, or for special education evaluation? Are parents welcomed and treated with respect in nonstereotypical ways? A subtle but telling expression of stereotyped behavior from a school:

An African American family responded to their child's elementary school with resentment when a letter from the school regarding their child's academic performance was addressed to the mother only. The information card on file had contained the father's name as well, and a notation that both parents resided at the home. The family felt that the father had been totally ignored and that they had been stereotyped as a "Black single-mother household." Their feelings of resentment needed to be addressed before the real work of problem solving could begin.

The Community System

Cross-cultural knowledge and skill also include becoming familiar with the client community, a part of every needs assessment of a social worker coming into a new school and working out a service plan. One skill includes using available census data and other computerized sources to develop a community profile as to boundaries of the census tract served by the school, recent changes in and the current racial/ethnic characteristics of the community, and other information, such as poverty rates and housing ownership. Is the immediate school neighborhood the primary or only census tract for the students? Are students from other neighborhoods permitted or mandated to attend this particular school? How are such students transported? Can they easily participate in after-school activities? Are there culturally competent community support systems conveniently available in the school or home community to address identified needs?

The community profile enables the school social worker to prepare a cultural map. This can be a useful tool, especially if the social worker lives outside the school's boundaries. The cultural map serves to identify and record the cultural resources of a community (Green, 1999) and thereby link services with the community. Culturally sensitive organizations and services often have been developed within the ethnic community to meet the needs and promote the strengths of Latinos, African Americans, Asian Americans, and Native Americans (Chow, 1999; Gutierrez, Ortega, & Suarez, 1990). The information documented in the cultural map would include culturally sensitive organizations, such as: (1) racial/ethnic service providers, (2) faith-based organizations, (3) volunteer networks, (4) full range of other community organizations, and (5) small community businesses that provide information and referrals. The skills developed in cultural mapping replicate a small community study and facilitate gaining entry into the community.

School Policies in the Meso- and Macrosystem

Cross-cultural practice that focuses on social justice would encourage critical assessment of structural inequalities that create unjust and oppressive conditions. However, a recent study by Ornelas (2004) showed that most of the social work activities of both professionals and interns were for the benefit of the organization and not necessarily to correct unfair policies. There was little evidence of involvement in developing policy or organizational changes that might address issues such as the achievement gap or overrepresentation of minority students in special education. What is needed is an understanding and support for advocacy. Advocacy is practice that emphasizes policy development and that seeks to assist powerless groups to develop and improve their situations (Jansson, 1999). Advocates work with others to make school services and policies more responsive to children and their families, communities, and diverse cultures, emphasizing cultural strengths and assets in the development of services and programs.

Advocacy can begin with applied research and needs assessment. How are school policies and programs working to meet needs? There needs first of all to be an understanding of the legal and political systems and the federal, state, and local codes, policies, and procedures governing both general and special education, which profoundly impact the state and local education systems. These are discussed in chapters 9, 10, 11, and 12.

Some aspects of how the school community mesosystem actually operates can be addressed through research and evaluation as tools of practice development (chapters 5 and 13), organizational analysis (chapter 14), and needs assessment (chapter 15). Among questions the school social worker might use to assess performance are: What are the numbers and nature of suspensions and expulsions at the school site? What is the demographic profile of students and staff in the school? Is there a match between race and ethnicity of teachers and students? Does racial/ethnic tension exist in the school? Are informal patterns of segregation occurring in the school, for example, in nonstructured settings? What are the numbers and nature of assignments to special education classes or special schools? Is there appropriate parental involvement in decision-making processes for such assignments? Is there a higher rate of problems for particular groups than is reflected among all pupils in the school? Are there appropriate processes and procedures to ensure the safety and equal educational opportunity for everyone?

These various levels of assessment of the entire school community ecosystem enable the school social worker to intervene at the most appropriate points in the system to effect desired change, and enhance the potential cross-cultural work with and on behalf of the school child and his or her family. Building on such assessments, the processes and tools of policy development are discussed in chapter 16. Strategies to ensure social justice could include a range of advocacy activity from regular reminders of stated policies in planning sessions, consultation, and workshops with teachers and administrators to more remedial measures designed to correct observed inequities. Given that the school social worker is a part of the school system itself, it is important that tactics and strategies be carefully planned so as to maximize the likelihood of effective change.

FAMILY ASSESSMENT AND ENGAGEMENT

Cultural assessment of the child and family requires that the school social worker be open and willing to learn from the client, and to use that knowledge on the client's behalf. In every culture, there exist some expectations and codes of behavior around areas of discipline, time, health, and religious beliefs. A worker's understanding of what these values are, where they fall on a value continuum of traditional to modern, and how they interface with behavioral expectations of the education system regarding children's learning is a key element of cross-cultural practice in school settings.

People from diverse racial and ethnic groups have experienced different forms of oppression and racism in their interactions with the majority culture. Placing these concerns into a cross-cultural perspective involves exploring the client's historical experiences with the majority culture and, if applicable, with migration and immigration. This history may include movement both within the United States and across foreign borders. In this connection, there may be historical conflicts among or between certain cultural groups that will need to be explored, especially as settlement in new areas brings youth and their families in direct contact with other cultural groups they may have sought to avoid in their former communities.

Ethnography offers a useful set of principles to guide the process of cultural assessment of the child and family (Thornton & Garrett, 1995). Such an approach is critical because *all* practice has some cross-cultural elements; it would be impossible for a social worker to know everything about a particular culture. Furthermore, it is not sufficient to categorize a client as belonging to one or more cultural groups and assume—or stereotype—experiences, behaviors, and needs. The values and lifestyles of individuals are highly personal and are best known by the client. It is within that cultural context that the social worker comes to understand the meaning of life events and presenting problems, any history of past or current oppression, and the client's relative acculturation to the dominant culture. Thornton and Garrett (1995) described the application of ethnographic research to multicultural practice and noted three assessment tools: the open-ended interview, direct observations, and document analysis.

The purpose of the *open-ended interview* is to understand clients and their points of view (Thornton & Garrett, 1995). Questions that elicit a personal narrative and discussion are used in this process. Whatever background information the school social worker has can be used to begin. Then, as responses come from the client, new open-ended questions may become obvious to continue and to broaden the social worker's understanding. For example, recent immigrants might be asked: How did you come to move to this place? What was life like in your original country (home town)? In what ways is life different here? An interview with a family whose child has been referred because of frequent absences might be asked other global questions. Throughout this process, the social worker learns "to be slow to assess and cautious to generalize, understanding that information relevant to one client may not transfer to another" (Thornton & Garrett, 1995, p. 69).

The second skill from ethnography is *observation*, which can occur in home visits, at community events, or interviews. These observations would be objectively documented and would particularly include foods, activities, communication patterns, interactions, relationships, schedules, dress, and roles (Thornton & Garrett, 1995). School social workers whose clients are predominantly of a specific racial/ethnic or religious group may seek immersion experiences, such as extended visits to the clients' country of origin or frequent visits to neighborhood restaurants or other eateries that cater to local residents, churches, synagogues or mosques, community centers, and community celebrations such as parades, ballgames, and picnics. In some areas, local television stations devoted to ethnic/racial and religious broadcasting provide other less direct sources of observations.

Finally, *documents analysis* that can promote cultural understanding includes study of popular and professional literature written about and/or by persons identified as part of the cultural group, as well as any available descriptive information generated by community and government groups (Thornton & Garrett, 1995). In addition, given the earlier patterns of settlement and resettlement of many culturally diverse groups, historical documents, such as the history of African slaves in the United States, the Emancipation Proclamation, treaties with Native American nations, and federal Indian policies can be helpful in understanding the landmarks in their memories of oppression and racism or liberation experienced by a particular group (Weaver, 1999).

SKILLS OF CROSS-CULTURAL PRACTICE

The social worker needs to understand and be able to:
- Take the perspective of the other in building relationships and coming to common ground, as well as valuing differences;
- Assist students and teachers to do this through individual and through group work;
- Assist particular groups and individuals to build their own identity in ways that also regard the identities and needs of others;
- Assist in the formulation, development, and the implementation of respectful school policies and practices;
- Assist in building a school community of safety and respect where conflicts and differences are resolved in a creative way; and
- Engage in multiple forms of practice, intervening at different system levels (microsystem, mesosystem and macrosystem levels) to promote respect for cultural differences and address issues of a safe and civil community.

To do this the social worker initially must develop skills of assessment based on a transcultural perspective, alive to the different experiences of others and other groups. He shares this perspective with others in the school—teachers and students and parents—as appropriate. Together, but with many difficulties along the way, they attempt to build a common school culture of respect, appreciation, and valuing of diversity. The development extends to school policies and procedures and, of course, to every aspect of the school social worker's role. In every society, each with its own inherent racism, with fears of others and fears of difference, this is a challenge. It is implicit in the expectation that the school be a center of cultural development for children and for the community. The school cannot simply reflect the attitudes of its surroundings; it will inevitably reflect these tensions. However, in any case, it must aspire to something better.

Caple, Salcido, and di Cecco (1995) identified some common basic skills for cross-cultural practice in the engagement stage. Early in initial contacts, it is important to spend some time simply getting to know the client, making appropriate introductions, and exchanging small talk. In this activity, the school social worker begins to convey the empathic caring and concern so vital for establishing a trusting relationship in the cross-cultural practice. The ethnographic interview process could be helpful in highlighting the importance the school social worker places on getting to know and understand who the client is as a person, notwithstanding the nature of the presenting problem. Obviously if the presenting problem involves a crisis or is heavily charged with conflict and expressions of anger from the client, the ethnographic questions would be postponed to a later, more appropriate time in the engagement process.

Interaction between practitioner and client may also be influenced by parents' perceptions of the roles of the worker. In the countries of origin of some immigrant clients, the social work role is not known, and some of these clients may view the practitioner as a government agent. Therefore, the task of the practitioner is to explain his professional role and the function of the services he can provide (Caple et al., 1995).

Other basic skills described by the authors of this chapter are:

1. *Relationship-Building Skills.* The building of the worker-client relationship is the next task after observing courtesy protocols. Our observation in working with parents is that minority parents often feel powerless to express their needs to professionals if they feel the practitioner will not "hear" them. Thus, an important part of establishing rapport is being an effective listener and demonstrating attention and interest in the client's communications. The practitioner's use of facilitation skills can demonstrate to clients a desire to truly listen. Chamberlain et al. (1985) defined facilitation as short utterances used by the practitioner to prompt the client to continue talking. Ivey and Authier (1978) suggested nodding the head, using phrases such as "mm hmm" and "tell

me more," and repeating one or two words spoken by the client as approaches to promote a continuing conversation. These behaviors convey interest and acceptance.

2. *Communication Skills.* Effective cross-cultural practice requires effectiveness not only in listening and facilitation, but also in spoken communication. Ivey and Authier (1978) proposed that one way the effective practitioner can engage in culturally appropriate behavior is by generating a broad array of selective communication skills including, open- and closed-ended questions, paraphrasing, reflection of feelings, and summarization. Ivey's (1977) work on cross-cultural skill development (microcounseling) sets the groundwork for developing universal cross-cultural communication skills. After using paraphrasing, reflection of feelings, and summarization, the practitioner then repeats the information she has gathered and specifically asks the client if the information is accurate. In our model, we conceptualize this validation step as a "cultural check."

3. *Understanding the Client's Definition of the Problem.* Definitions of problems are culture specific and complex. Sue and Zane (1987) argued that defining a problem is a culturally bound activity. Members of a particular cultural group may not agree with the definition of a problem provided by members of the dominant culture (Gold & Bogo, 1992) or persons perceived by the client as representing the dominant culture. Green (1999) noted that it is critical to recognize how the client views the problem. Pedersen (1988) explained that each person perceives the world from his or her own cultural point of view, and one skill practitioners can use is to perceive the problem from the client's cultural point of view. The nature of the client's worldviews and values interacts with the behavioral norms that the client has adopted (Mokuau & Shimizu, 1991).

4. *Promoting Social Belonging; Without Belonging There Is No Survival.* People live, not simply in their own worlds, but in networks and in communities of belonging. There is a well-known Korean proverb: "As a fish must live in water, so people must live in a society where they find acceptance "(Constable & Lee, 2004, p. 115). Both an understanding of social connectedness and belonging and an ability to promote and develop it are crucial for every level of transcultural practice. In Rita McGary's example in a suburb of Washington, DC, a large part of her work had to do with developing intergroup connections, so that the groups could communicate and work out problems with other groups and with the school community. In Miriam Mabetoa's example, the students felt great solidarity with each other and with their teachers, but not with the national government and the prevailing economic necessities, which demanded migration and loss of this solidarity for economic survival. In Daiva Kuzmickaite's example, students had to develop real solidarity with each other, parents with the school, and teachers with each other. They never had this solidarity in the previous system and had to learn it anew. In short a whole school community had to be re-created, something her visionary principal did perceive as the essence of the school social worker's role in the emergent, new Lithuania.

The problems or issues discussed need to be well identified and conceptualized by the client. The school social worker should ask parents or family units what the problem means to them, their family, and their culture. Various cultures have developed their own indigenous models of service, help-seeking behaviors, and belief systems. The school social worker must have or seek knowledge of the array of culturally specific imperatives and responses available in a particular school's ecosystem to understand the client's cultural definition of the problem. These cultural perceptions may then lead to a decision to work with the entire extended family, respected community leaders, and other natural helpers (Morales & Salcido, 1995).

PLANNING AND SERVICE DELIVERY

Planning for effective service delivery is activated only after a broad-based assessment. There may be urgent needs arising from a crisis situation, however, in general the plan is made and put into action after the cultural assessment is incorporated with other assessment of the presenting problem. Parents and, to the extent possible, the child are engaged as active members—partners—in the planning and service delivery process, as they were in the assessment phase. For example, no real purpose will be served by referring a client to a worker-determined resource that the client does not value or agree will be helpful. The design of the service plan is consistent with the ecosystems perspective where strengths are promoted and reinforced. The social worker assumes various roles—consultant, enabler, facilitator, advocate, broker, coordinator, mediator, collaborator, counselor, or case manager—as he engages any or all parts of the client's ecosystem (Caple et al., 1995; Gutierrez, Yeakley, & Ortega, 2000).

The social worker's role within the school is vitally important in promoting culturally appropriate attention to the needs of individual students as well as for groups of children. Through roles as consultant, collaborator, and teacher, the school social worker imparts information and translates to teachers and administrators the meaning of behaviors that may have cultural links or inferences. In-service training may be a contribution the social worker can make to enhance the cultural competence of the school as a whole. Parents may be asked to participate in all activities directed to improving the cultural competence of the system.

The social worker as advocate would use information gathered in the assessment of the school to promote systems changes that would be culturally responsive to identified needs.

Within the community, the social worker as cultural broker develops linkages with cultural community agencies that may be effective resources for the child and family. Included in the broker role are the skills of coordination and collaboration. Clients who have special language needs will require particular attention on referral to ensure effective outcomes. Linking non-English-speaking clients to bilingual professionals or bilingual services is another form of cultural brokering.

There are occasions in cross-cultural practice when the school social worker may need an interpreter to manage linguistic or cultural communication. Care should be taken in using members of the extended family or others in the client's social network for professional work of counseling and gathering sensitive information. In the general planning for cross-cultural practice in a school and community, the community profile and cultural maps drawn during the needs assessment phase should include notations of where cultural and language interpreters may be located. (For a fuller discussion of the use of interpreters in cross-cultural practice, see Caple et al., 1995, pp. 165–167.)

CONCLUSION

Competence in cross-cultural social work will only come through continued practice. The open learner who makes errors in calculations and processes can review these—ideally directly with the client—or with one's supervisor or consultant, or at least in self-reflection, with a view of correcting those errors or refining one's skills for the next time. A sense of humor helps. Clients who observe the social worker as genuinely seeking to understand and meet the client when he or she is working with them are very likely to be willing to overlook errors of that kind. Like all practice, whether including a new set of principles and considerations or sharpening skills used before, there is a developmental continuum. For cross-cultural practice, it begins with awareness and sensitivity to the needs of others and emerges as beginning and growing competence. As values and knowledge are honed into effective practice these skills can be applied at micro, meso, and macro levels for effective interventions and social change.

References

Allen-Meares, P., & Burman, S. (1999). Cross-cultural therapeutic relationships: Entering the world of African Americans. *Journal of Social Work Practice, 13*(1), 49–57.

Annie E. Casey Foundation. (1997). *Kids count data book: State profiles of child well-being 1997.* Baltimore: Author.

Barton, P. (2003). Parsing the achievement gap: Baselines for tracking progress. Princeton, NJ: Educational Testing Service. (ERIC Document Reproduction Service No. ED482932)

Booth, W. (1998, February). One nation, indivisible: Is it history? *The Washington Post, 22.A,* pp. 18–19.

Caple, F. S., Salcido, R. M., & di Cecco, J. (1995). Engaging effectively with culturally diverse families and children. *Social Work in Education, 17,* 159–170.

Chamberlain, P., Davis, J. P., Forgatch, M. S., Frey, J., Patterson, G. R., Ray J., et al. (1985). *The therapy process code: A multidimensional system for observing therapist and client interactions.* Eugene: Oregon Social Learning Center.

Chow, J. (1999). Multiservice centers in Chinese American immigrant communities: Practice principles and challenges. *Social Work, 44*(1), 70–81.

Compton, B. R., & Galaway, B. (1999). *Social work processes* (6th ed.). Pacific Grove, CA: Brooks/Cole.

Constable, R., & Lee, D. B. (2004). *Social work with families: Content and process.* Chicago: Lyceum Books.

Germain, C. B., & Gitterman, A. (1980). *The life model of social work practice: Advances in theory & practice.* New York: Columbia University Press.

Gold, N., & Bogo, M. (1992). Social work research in a multicultural society: Challenges and approaches. *Journal of Multicultural Social Work, 2*(4), 7-22.

Goldsmith, P. A. (2004). Schools' role in shaping race relations: Evidence on friendliness and conflict. *Social Problems, 51*(4), 587-613.

Green, J. (1999). *Cultural awareness in the human services: A multiethnic approach* (3rd ed.). Boston: Allyn & Bacon.

Gutierrez, L., Ortega, R. M., & Suarez, Z. E. (1990). Self-help and the Latino community. In T. Powell (Ed.), *Working with self-help* (pp. 221-236). Silver Spring, MD: National Association of Social Workers.

Gutierrez, L, Yeakley, A., & Ortega, R. (2000). Educating students for social work with Latinos: Issues for the new millennium. *Journal of Social Work Education, 36*(3), 541-555.

Hawley, W. D. (2004). Who knew? Integrated schools can benefit all students. *Education Week, 23*(34), 41.

Hepworth, D. H., Rooney, R. H., & Larsen, J. A. (2002). *Direct social work practice: Theory and skills* (6th ed.). Pacific Grove, CA: Brooks/Cole-Thomson Learning.

Hosp, J. L., & Reschly, D. J. (2003). Referral rates for intervention or assessment: A meta-analysis of racial differences. *The Journal of Special Education, 37*(2), 67-80.

Huxtable, M., & Blyth, E. (2002). *School social work worldwide.* Washington, DC: National Association of Social Workers Press.

Ivey, A. (1977). Cultural expertise: Toward systematic outcome criteria in counseling and psychological education. *Personnel and Guidance Journal, 55*, 296-302.

Ivey, A., & Authier, J. (1978). *Microcounseling.* Springfield, IL: Charles C. Thomas.

Jansson, B. S. (1999). *Becoming an effective policy advocate: From policy to social justice.* Pacific Grove, CA: Brooks/Cole Publishing Company.

Longres, J. (1991). Toward a status model of ethnic-sensitive practice. *Journal of Multicultural Social Work, 1*(1), 41-56.

Mabetoa, M. (1996). *An indigenised school social work model for rural communities in Bophuthatswana.* Unpublished PhD dissertation, University of Witwatersrand.

McGary, R. (1987). Student forums: Addressing racial conflict in a high school. *Social Work in Education, 9*(3), 159-168.

Merriam-Webster's Collegiate Dictionary (10th ed.). (2000). Springfield, MA: Merriam-Webster.

Miller, H. B. (1995). Personal communication.

Mokuau, N., & Shimizu, D. (1991). *Handbook of social services for Asian and Pacific Islanders.* New York: Greenwood Press.

Morales, A. T., & Salcido, R. (1995). Social work practice with Mexican Americans. In A. T. Morales & B. W. Sheafor (Eds.), *Social work: A profession of many faces* (7th ed.), pp. 527-552). Boston: Allyn & Bacon.

NASW (National Association of Social Workers). (2001). *NASW standards for cultural competence in social work practice.* Retrieved February 9, 2004, from http://www.social workers.org/practice/standards/cultural_competence.asp

Ornelas, V. (2004). *Examining characteristics of school social work macro practice: The academic preparation of MSW students.* Unpublished doctoral dissertation, University of Southern California.

Pedersen, R. (1988). *A handbook for developing multicultural awareness.* Alexandria, VA: American Association for Counseling and Development.

Pryor, C. B. (1992). Integrating immigrants into American schools. *Social Work, 14*(3), 153-159.

Stearns, E. (2004). Interracial friendliness and the social organization of schools. *Youth & Society, 35*(4), 395-420.

Sue, S., & Zane, N. (1987). The role of culture and cultural techniques in psychotherapy. *American Psychologist, 42*, 37-45.

Taylor, R. (1994). Minority families in America: An introduction. In R. L. Taylor (Ed.), *Minority families in the United States: A multicultural perspective* (pp. 1-16). Englewood Cliffs, NJ: Prentice Hall.

Thornton, S., & Garrett, K. J. (1995). Ethnography as a bridge to multicultural practice. *Journal of Social Work Education, 31*(1), 67-74.

U.S. Bureau of the Census. (2001). *Census 2000 summary file 1 PHC-T-9. Population by race and Hispanic or Latino origin for the United States 2000.* Washington, DC: U.S. Government Printing Office.

Weaver, H. N. (1999). Indigenous people and social work profession: Defining culturally competent services. *Social Work, 44*(3), 217-225.

Woods, M. E., & Hollis, F. (2000). *Casework: A psychosocial therapy* (5th ed.). New York: McGraw-Hill.

19

Assessment of the Learning Environment, Case Study Assessment, and Functional Behavior Analyses

Galen Thomas
Southern Illinois University

Marguerite Tiefenthal

Rita Charak

Robert Constable
Loyola University, Chicago

- ◆ Ongoing Assessment and Decision Making
- ◆ The Case Study Assessment (CSA) and the Social Development Study (SDS)
- ◆ Special Education Assessments

ONGOING ASSESSMENT AND DECISION MAKING

Assessment is a systematic way of understanding what is happening in the pupil's relations within the classroom, within the family, with peers, and between family and school. It provides a basis for deciding which interventions will be most effective. Thus, it is an individualized effort to identify and evaluate the interrelations of problems, people, and situations (Siporin, 1975). The objective of assessment is effective intervention with a system that is itself in process. Assessment is more than a one-time, required procedure, or a formal evaluation. It is a continuous, ongoing process in which school social workers engage as they work with students, their families, school personnel, and community agencies. Its power is its focus on the identification of strengths in individuals and systems rather than on deficits alone. It is geared toward collective decision-making processes potentially involving the social worker, the parent, the pupil, and the team. It is geared toward the process of assisting persons in a situation to take initiatives and resolve problems. The social worker's decision about which intervention to use comes from integrating data and drawing conclusions about the interrelated factors contributing to the problem(s) and the potential effectiveness of various interventions. Because assessments are individualized, the amount of data collected will vary according to the purpose and context of the assessment. The worker needs to develop a systematic way to gather and evaluate information, sifting out significant details from a potentially vast universe of information available.

Assessment of the Dynamics of the Learning Environment

Assessment of the complex dynamics of learning environments, especially the classroom environment, is essential to any understanding of a pupil in school. Information is gathered through observations and conversations that occur throughout the workday. Through sensitivity to signs of potential problems with individual students as well as indications of more general systemwide problems, the social worker is able to take a proactive approach to identify issues that need to be addressed either individually or through a broader base of team effort. This information is shared with others who function as part of the decision-making process. Prior to their work in school, social workers should have a good general understanding of human development, family interaction and relationships of the child in the community context, and of group dynamics.

On this foundation school social workers need to develop an understanding of group dynamics within a classroom, and of the impact of teaching styles and classroom group composition on pupil behavior and the learning process. The understanding of the classroom is an interactive understanding, which comes from direct observation and from the teacher's account. Consider a situation where children may feel fearful, unsafe, or challenged by their peers. If the teacher feels uncertain or unequipped to deal with the problem, the behavior of one child may become "contagious" to others. Perhaps an overwhelmed teacher is unwittingly fanning the flames of general out-of-control behavior with a fearful or excessively rigid response. Perhaps the legitimate need to clamp down on an out-of-control situation overlooks the needs of other children in the class. By providing an objective, strengths-based perspective through classroom observation and consultation with the teacher, the social worker may help the teacher identify more effective solutions for managing the classroom.

The first prerequisite to any person's effective functioning in any group is safety. Nothing else can be done without the belief that one is safe, that one's personhood and dignity will be respected. Both teachers and students need safety. This is so important that a person's energies will be deflected by safety concerns before investing in anything else. A classroom or school environment that does not value each person's contribution, that permits bullying, scapegoating, or other abusive behavior will hardly be able to do much other than cope with its own toxic surroundings. In addition to outlawing bullying, the school community must work at developing a climate of acceptance and positive value for each person. Effective schools present learning and social processes to which all students can connect. The atmosphere of productive work, respect, and comfortable order is noticeable immediately when one enters the building or classroom. Leadership is clear and uncontested. The climate is safe and orderly. There is an emphasis on basic skills and continuous assessment of pupil progress. There are high expectations for achievement (Finn, 1984; Purkey & Smith, 1983). In the effective school or classroom these are taken for granted by the students and faculty, but they are not accidental. They are the result of a good deal of work over a number of years by the school leadership, and by teachers, students, and community. When something upsets this equilibrium, the school community (or classroom) may go into a crisis mode, but it can be a productive crisis as members work together to restore the lost (and remembered) equilibrium.

Assessments of the learning environment start with observation and concrete description. To learn assessment of the learning environment it is best to begin by taking a student the teacher has some concern about and a classroom where you are welcome to observe unobtrusively. Forms for observation, such as the ones in chapter 21, are useful ways to begin to find the patterns and sequences of the student's interaction with learning tasks, the teacher, and other students. To look further for patterns and sequences, a good model to follow is the Antecedent-Behavior-Consequences (ABC) model. Here you, as an observer, record in anecdotal form in each instance of (A) significant antecedent events, (B) the behavior of concern, and (C) the immediate and longer-term consequences of the behavior. From repeated observations and interviews with the teacher and parents, you can begin to map out the *times* and *conditions* the student *did* or *did not* exhibit the particular behavior of concern (Raines, 2002; Repp & Horner, 1999). You can then begin to develop some hypotheses about the possible *functions* or purposes of the behavior. Hypotheses are plausible explanations of the function of the behavior that predict the general conditions under which the behavior is most likely to occur as well as the possible consequences that serve to maintain the behavior (Raines, 2002). The key is to develop a conceptual language for nonacademic, developmental learning, such as illustrated in the sampler of developmental (functional) learning objectives in table 24.1 in chapter 24. With this approach, you can begin to explain classroom behavior and develop a positive behavior intervention plan, changing the antecedents and/or consequences of the behavior and/or assisting students to develop skills to deal with certain situations.

Functions of Behavior. Normally students are expected to behave in class in ways that address the tasks of one's own learning and do not interfere with the learning of others. When students are off task or interfere with others, it is assumed that their behaviors may serve functions of *seeking attention* from the teacher or others in the class, *communicating their needs* to teacher or peers, or *avoiding academic tasks* (Zuna & McDougall, 2004). These functions cover motivations for a wide range of behavior and are a good beginning. Raines (2002) goes further to suggest needs from the perspective of normal development: for autonomy, individuation and control, for self-esteem, to regulate stimulation, and to set some structure in what may be perceived as an unstructured environment. Other functions of behavior, maladaptive and less amenable to immediate change, may be needs to repeat a learned scapegoat role, to create safety from imagined threats, to display grandiose invulnerability, to be punished, to have revenge, or to derive pleasure from the discomfort of others (Raines, 2002).

Antecedents in the Classroom. Each classroom is different, reflecting the teacher's preferred style and the composition of the classroom group. To begin to understand these differences we need to consider:

1. The number of students in the classroom;
2. The resources available to address problems;
3. The amount of freedom a teacher has to individualize and modify curriculum or select alternative behavior management techniques;
4. The amount of time to individualize for one student's needs;
5. The degree of pressure placed on teachers for accountability through state and district "high-stakes" testing and the effect of that on the learning process;
6. The group composition and atmosphere of the class: How many "prosocial" students? How many students with difficulties? How much time is available "on task"? How much distraction is there?
7. The teacher's preferred style and repertoire of teaching approaches to respond to a situation or to the needs of particular students.

Details about the classroom environment that can be significant to the student can include seating arrangement, the lighting, window location, noise from outside the room, total number of students in the room, number of interesting items hanging around the room, and so on. Class size, class structure, number of discipline problems, student-to-teacher ratios, classroom management rules, direction and frequency of teacher attention, and the number of opportunities for students to respond academically all affect student learning (Roberts, 1995). Teachers teach in different ways.. Where do teachers position themselves in proximity to the student? Are modifications made to individualize material to students who are having difficulties? Does the teacher appear confident dealing with issues of discipline? Although these are potentially politically sensitive issues, they are important considerations in reviewing student learning and behavior problems.

We cannot really advocate for an individual student without advocacy for the teacher's needs, and without empathy for the teacher's reality. Without some understanding of the pressures on teachers, social workers will have difficulty developing a working relationship with them or even gaining their acceptance of the assessment information. Understanding the learning environment demands that we first understand the realities a particular teacher is facing. Teachers have different styles that can be effective with certain types of students. Some teachers are very comfortable with their firmness and can work compassionately with students needing limits. Others do better with youngsters by using patience, warmth, and nonpossessive concern. Experienced teachers often can call on a variety of approaches to a situation, especially if they can analyze it objectively. However, each of us responds to every situation within the framework and limits of ourselves as persons. It is important for school social workers to practice with teachers the same attitudes they typically are trained to use with students and parents. They should exhibit a nonjudgmental attitude, start where the teacher is, exercise positive regard, and assume teachers are doing their best given the amount of support they have, available resources, and the extent of their experience.

An understanding of the pupil's perspective often comes with experience, from the teacher's account, and from observation, but there is hardly a substitute for the learning contained in a direct interview with the pupil. In the interview, the social worker can explore whether personal or family factors are supporting, assisting, discouraging, or distracting the student. Perhaps a student could be motivated by a different tangible or social reward other than the ones currently available in the classroom. Sometimes a child needs glasses, warm clothes and shoes, a medical exam, a hearing test, or a welcoming friend in a new and frightening environment. Teachers are often more receptive to trying alternatives when they understand that problems are either more complex than initially perceived, or that *they* can make some impact on what they see as an initially impossible situation. The small steps of progress that they see are in reality very important. The social worker often needs to reframe the student in positive terms to the teacher. The child is not simply being oppositional or lazy. Both the teacher and the social worker need to give up the idea of a quick, mechanically smooth solution to the problem. Solutions eventually do emerge with trial and error, persistent support, time, patience, and appropriate engagement with the problem and the people involved in it.

Prereferral Interventions

The Individuals with Disabilities Education Act (IDEA) encourages prereferral intervention. It specifically mandates that eligibility as a student with emotional disabilities requires that the student has had the characteristics over an extended period of time and the behavior has persisted even after attempts at intervention have been made. It emphasizes the need for school-wide approaches and early intervention services to reduce the need to label children as disabled. Documentation of efforts to work with the student through the identification of appropriate functional areas of learning and Goal Attainment Scaling (see chapter 24) are critically important from a compliance standpoint as well as for practical reasons.

When students are experiencing nonacademic difficulties and are not showing clearly identifiable disabling conditions, it is appropriate for teachers to seek consultation with the team of colleagues who are designated to assist in reviewing possible interventions to support positive changes in student performance and/or the school social worker. The support team will often review interventions already attempted, conduct a functional assessment of the student's behavior, and monitor student response to interventions over a designated period. As a general rule of thumb, at least three interventions should be attempted to achieve objectives over the course of six weeks. If the student shows progress on the objectives, even though not "cured," the team has to make a decision. On the one hand there is progress and more time and further interventions could be tried rather than proceeding with the referral for special education assessment. On the other hand there could be pressure to "get on with the referral," because the minimum time has been expended. If there is progress, the need to maintain the student in the least restrictive environment would support going with the progress. However, this will not be successful without discussion and the commitment of everyone: the student, the parents, and the teacher(s).

THE CASE STUDY ASSESSMENT (CSA) AND THE
SOCIAL DEVELOPMENTAL STUDY (SDS)

Purpose and Definition

Assessment brings everything together by creating a picture of how pupils function in a learning situation, with their families, and with their peers in their school and in the larger community. *Case Study Assessment* (CSA) is a more formal assessment process in which school social workers participate. The CSA is a compilation and analysis of information concerning those life experiences of the child, both past and present, that pertain to the pupil's problems in school. It provides a comprehensive baseline of the pupil's personal and social functioning as well as identifying significant environmental realities and assisting with planning interventions. One major purpose of the CSA is to assist the team, the parents, and the pupil in understanding the pupil's life circumstances as they relate to school performance or behavior. A second major purpose is to assist parents and school personnel to develop the most suitable educational environment and to intervene in a way that would be most helpful to the optimum learning and development of the child. The CSA includes information from many sources, including the student, parents/foster parents, teachers, other school personnel, involved agency personnel, and other significant people outside the school, such as extended family or other caretakers. Each is significant in developing a profile of the student's current social and developmental functioning. When the CSA is used as part of the evaluation for services for a child with a disability, it should include an assessment of the pupil's adaptive behaviors, discussed later in this chapter and in chapter 22.

Although the CSA is sometimes referred to as the *social history*, a tool often used by social workers to understand client dynamics, the CSA has additional components that make it more comprehensive than a social history. The CSA includes a basic description of the following:

1. The pupil,
2. The pupil's current social functioning and the presenting problem,
3. Observations in classroom(s) as well as other less structured school environments,
4. An individual interview with the pupil,
5. The pupil's sociocultural background,
6. Any events or stressors possibly contributing to the problem,
7. Other significant life experiences, and
8. Current abilities of the pupil.

The CSA is an assessment of the whole child in his or her environment. It focuses on identified strengths as well as areas in need of support. It brings into focus the developmental systems and ecological factors that affect the child's learning and behavioral patterns. By involving the family in this information gathering, the school social worker can begin a cooperative working relationship between parents or guardian and the school that may not have been present earlier. A relationship can be established through which emotional support, counseling, information about community resources, and legal rights can be discussed, and the mediation of significant differences between home and school can begin. The relationship with the family formed by the social worker when compiling a CSA can continue through the development and implementation of an educational plan. Even if it is a brief contact, this relationship frequently can have a positive impact on the parents or guardians, helping them to address feelings of anxiety or alienation from their child's educational experience. During this process the social worker needs to help parents gain an understanding of the implications of the assessment for their child's long-range educational needs. Giving parents or guardians the chance to vent frustration, anger, or fear of the future for their child is time well spent. In a few cases this may lead to more than one meeting, but it will pay off later when active parent or guardian cooperation will be necessary for the success of the child.

Components of a Case Study Assessment

The CSA assembles the evaluations done by the school social worker into a single written statement. With the addition of professional judgment, the foundations for the social worker's recommendations emerge. We outline nine components that contribute to the gathering of information for a CSA:

1. Pupil interview(s),
2. Parent interview(s),
3. Social history and current functioning,
4. Socioeconomic and cultural background,
5. Assessment of the pupil's learning environment,
6. Observation of the pupil in the school (in classrooms, in individualized tasks, in a structured group, in the playground) and ideally in the home environment),
7. Consultation with the pupil's current and (preferably) previous teachers,
8. Review of student files (grades, discipline, achievement testing),
9. Consultation with other staff and agencies when necessary.

Although the potential wealth of descriptive information gathered through this process may go beyond the scope of one's assessment focus, only information directly pertinent to the child's educational progress that does not breach the confidentiality of the parent or child may be included in the written report. As a useful concrete framework, we can outline eight components of the CSA:

I. Identifying Information.

A. The child's name, birth date, school, grade, and teacher
B. Each family member's name, age, relationship to the child, educational background, occupation, employment, address, and marital status
C. Names of other persons living in the home and their relationship to the child
D. Race/ethnicity of the family
E. Brief impression of the child at your initial meeting

II. Reasons for Referral.

A. The stated reasons for the referral and any specific questions that should be addressed

   B. The problem (the child's learning or behavior) as described by the teacher, parent, or others

   C. What has been done to try to correct the situation (should include at least three significant interventions)?

   D. What were the immediate precipitating events that prompted the referral?

   E. A checklist of specific behaviors that interfere with the learning process

III. Sources of Information. A list of dates and sources of data obtained should include, but not be limited to, the following:

   A. Home visit(s) or alternative modes of interviewing parents, guardians, or other relatives

   B. Social worker's or other's interview(s) with the child

   C. Review of school records

   D. Outside evaluations

   E. Observations of the student ideally in various settings, but at least in the classroom and one unstructured situation, for example, recess

IV. Developmental History. Developmental milestones may be significant and can include problems that occurred during pregnancy, delivery, or any unusual conditions at birth. This information conveys an understanding of the child over time to determine whether development is progressing appropriately. Developmental history from infancy forward should include tolerance of frustration, sources of frustration, and what parental coping strategies have been employed. Emotional development includes the ability to successfully get needs met and to develop satisfying age-appropriate relationships. Lucco's (1991) tables of developmental evaluation provide an excellent developmentally informed guide for this phase of assessment. In addition, for a child between ages 3 and 5, the social-developmental profile may include an assessment of the following:

Infancy to 5 years of age

   A. Degree of independence

   B. Quality of and types of interpersonal relationships experienced

   C. Self-image

   D. Adaptability

   E. Play behavior

Children 5 years and older

   A. Level of independence

   B. Interpersonal relationships, including quality of
      1. Peer interactions
      2. Adult interactions
      3. Range and intensity of play activity

   C. Self-image

    D. Self-awareness

    E. Self-esteem

    F. Self-confidence

    G. Coping and effectiveness in social situations

    H. Sensitivity to others

    I. Adaptability and appropriate persistence

    J. Problem-solving abilities

The CSA can include any traumas, hospitalizations, accidents, health problems or chronic conditions, disabilities, unusual problems, or chronic need for medication, if relevant to the child's educational functioning. The reasons for absences from school need to be considered. The child's stamina, energy level, and length of attention span in specific situations or times of day can be significant. The child's physical appearance and conduct while in the company of the social worker should be noted. This information can form the basis for an evaluation of the child's strengths and areas of need. It will be useful for the team, particularly if the information provides a different perspective on the youngster.

    V. School History. The school history for young children begins with day care, nursery school, preschool, and early childhood classes and experiences. Increasingly children experience group learning and day-care facilities from infancy forward. This section should include a chronological account of informal and formal learning experiences, including their changes and interruptions and the progress or lack of progress the child has made to date. School records are quite useful. For an experienced school social worker often a cumulative record gives a clear indication of the issues and directions in the pupil's life, learning patterns, and what appears to work and not work. The record would reveal attendance patterns, progress rates, special instructional assistance, testing results, and remarks of teachers. Teacher's remarks should be interpreted cautiously, but they often reveal what the pupil's behavior may have brought out in others, as well as insights into the pupil's progress at different periods. Parents frequently recall the pupil's difficulties making transitions, and their own difficulties, and significant changes, problems, and traumatic experiences that have affected their child's learning progress over the years. The parents' attitudes toward early learning situations, their involvement with their child's learning, and their expectations of the school are all important data. The school history includes a current classroom observation.

    VI. Cultural Background, Family History, and Current Issues. The assessment of cultural background is done to determine how the child's culture or background affects his or her ability to function in school as well as whether the school and community are responding appropriately. All children have a cultural background. It includes an identification of the family's ethnicity and primary language spoken in the home, the degree of English-speaking proficiency, the usual mode of communication (spoken, sign, etc.) utilized by the student and the family, and the family's socioeconomic status relative to the community. In a dynamic sense how do the family and the student process the meanings from their culture and from the broader culture? Children's understanding of their cultural background may include ethnic customs, special observances, and unique dress or food not shared by others their age, but also how they come to experience the larger society. An appropriate assessment might read in part:

> Ranjit's family is of East Indian origin, and they observe Sikh traditions. They currently reside in a community with about 25 percent minority population; however, only one other family is of East Indian background, also of Sikh tradition. Fluent in English and in their own language, both of Ranjit's parents come from professional families in India. Economically, Ranjit's family seems to be about average in this solidly middle-class community. Though the family is close knit, they feel well respected and comfortable with their neighbors. Ranjit only speaks English and in many ways appears more adapted to the culture of his peers than to the culture of his parents.

In addition, this section may include information specific to this family's history or dynamics—for example, length of marriage, separations, divorces, deaths, remarriages, moves, transfers, changes in child care, presence or absence of various family members, and other significant events. Observations of the child's role in the family, family expectations, opportunities for friends outside of school, and sense of humor can all contribute to understanding the child as a person in the environment. The atmosphere within the family (which may be temporarily in crisis) should be noted, along with the family's methods and abilities, individually and as a unit, to cope with stressful situations. Because, as previously mentioned, some of this information may be highly sensitive and confidential, an agreed-to substitute statement may be needed, such as, "Some current difficulties in the home make consistent parental support difficult at this time." Because the focus is on the pupil's functioning, the impact of the situation on the pupil's functioning is more important than what actually happened.

VII. Current Functioning. Sensitivity of family members to the child's problem and the family's ability, time, temperament, and willingness to be helpful are important. The parents' view of the child's personality, the interrelationships between family members, the family's interests, activities, hobbies, and leisure activities all give clues to possible recommendations to help the child. Special attention is given to a child's interests at home, how he or she seems to learn best, areas of giftedness, hobbies, and special opportunities the child has for learning. Any maladaptive tendencies toward temper tantrums, fears, impulsivity, enuresis, sleep disturbances, stealing, or other difficulties should be noted.

VIII. Evaluation, Summary, Conclusions, and Recommendations. The final part of the CSA is a concise summary of the meaningful information, including how these experiences affect the child's educational progress. This forms the basis for the social worker's recommendations regarding the educational needs of the child, the best learning environment, parent counseling,

available school-based services, and further diagnostic evaluations. Specific recommendations about how parents can be helpful and supportive are appropriate. Because the CSA is a diagnostic tool and is often essential in assessing
severity of emotional problems and mental retardation, the data must be carefully collected and evaluated to ensure its accurate contribution to a differential diagnosis.

IX. Signature. The CSA ends with the name and professional qualification
of the writer (Susan Smith, MSW and/or LCSW) and the date of completion of
the document.

Confidentiality is a frequent concern in writing a CSA. The social worker
may be given sensitive information that has a direct bearing on the pupil's problem, but it may be inappropriate to share the information with other school personnel. "Sometimes social data is very personal and its potential prejudicial
effect may outweigh its diagnostic values" (Byrne, Hare, Hooper, Morse, &
Sabatino, 1977, p. 52). One approach to this problem is to ensure the parents
early in the initial interview that this confidential information will not be shared
with the school unless the parents give their permission or unless withholding
it would endanger the health or welfare of the child. One procedure in keeping
with this approach is to prepare the study in the form in which it will be presented and give the parent(s) the opportunity to read it and correct factual inac-
curacies. This procedure gives the parents concrete emotional assurance that
confidentiality will be honored and adds trust to the social worker-parent relationship. Often the social worker and parent can collaborate on wording that
will convey concern without revealing sensitive details. In rare cases, information to which the parents object may need to be included. Such information is
included only if it is accurate and critical to decisions to be made about the
child's educational needs.

SPECIAL EDUCATION ASSESSMENTS

The CSA is sometimes called a *Social Developmental Study* (SDS) when it
evaluates a student's possible eligibility for special education services. The SDS
is the social worker's contribution to the complete, multifaceted nondiscriminatory evaluation of the student's needs as required by law. This complete evaluation becomes the basis for the team's planning for and with pupils with special needs through development of individualized education programs (IEPs).
The school social worker needs to ensure that the SDS addresses cultural, environmental, and familial influences on the student's behavior and learning. It
should contain an *adaptive behavior assessment* of the youngster's behavior
patterns and functional abilities both in and outside of the learning environment. In the case of youngsters with discipline problems, it may need to contain
a *functional behavior assessment*, the basis for a *behavioral intervention plan*.

The SDS is an analysis and synthesis of the information gathered from various sources into a concise presentation of those life experiences of the child,

both past and present, that pertain to the child's educational experiences. It contains all of the components of the traditional CSA together with an adaptive behavior assessment and, for pupils experiencing disciplinary problems, a functional behavior assessment. The SDS provides information to the team that can guard against inappropriate labeling or placement of a child. Such inappropriate placement is more likely to occur when test scores and school performance evaluations are the *only* data used. The inclusion of developmental and ecological information provides a more complete view of the child and expands the range of possibilities appropriate to address the needs of the child (see Bronfenbrenner, 1979; Hobbs, 1976). The SDS is written in educational language (behavioral descriptions, not psychological diagnoses) and should not include the social worker's recommendations for interventions that address the stated concerns. These will be developed later at the team meeting and by the entire team. Thus, specific identification of a special education category or recommendations for placement are not appropriate. A special education category designation, such as behavior disordered, learning disabled, and so forth, is the result of the compilation of the findings of the full multidisciplinary team, including the parents, as an outcome of the multidisciplinary conference. Only when the child's learning needs have been identified from a variety of different perspectives in the meeting can the multidisciplinary team determine the most appropriate and least restrictive environment (or placement) in which these needs can be met.

The Adaptive Behavior Assessment

A simplified definition of *adaptive behavior* is the effectiveness with which the individual functions independently and meets culturally imposed standards of personal and social responsibility. The concept of adaptation historically has been used to differentiate a person's general functioning from his or her measured intellectual functioning (IQ) and was used before the term adaptive behavior was adopted. Assessing children's levels of adaptive behavior is a significant step toward two important objectives: (1) that children from minority and culturally diverse groups are not overrepresented in special education designations as a result of cultural influences rather than true disabilities, and (2) that children of all ages and cultural backgrounds are appropriately diagnosed and placed. Adaptive behavior assessments are discussed in greater detail in chapter 22.

Informal Adaptive Behavior Assessments. The social worker, a generalist and an expert in family patterns and cultural differences, is often identified as the professional responsible for conducting this assessment. Adaptive behavior information is typically gathered either through paper-and pencil instruments or qualitatively and informally through observations and interviews. It is useful to understand the informal, qualitative assessment, as well as the formal, quantitative assessment discussed in chapter 22. Informal, qualitative assessments compare the child's functioning in the classroom with his or her functioning out of the classroom: at home, in the community, and during external school activities. The areas of functioning, outlined in table 19.1, include *independent functioning, personal responsibility,* and *social responsibility.* When addressing independent functioning, the informal, qualitative assessment will answer the question, "Does he or she have (or can he or she acquire) the necessary skills in each area?" When addressing the child's personal responsibility, the assessment will answer the question, "Does he or she use the skills in each behavior setting?" When addressing social responsibility, the question to be answered is, "Does he or she use the skill appropriately, that is, in the appropriate place, at the appropriate time?" Table 19.1 presents a conceptual model that may be used in acquiring this information systematically. The child's age and sociocultural background are, of course, essential ingredients in such an informal, qualitative assessment, as they are in formal assessments.

In any case, the key element in the SDS is the social worker's analysis and synthesis of significant information from a variety of sources using multiple methodologies. This requires going well beyond the computer-generated reports produced by some assessment instruments. If the computer-generated report is used as a part of the SDS, the social worker needs to be prepared to explain and defend it. To do this, it is important to see the fit of the adaptive behavior assessment into the total social work assessment scheme. While formal instruments are very popular with school districts, the computerized report that is automatically generated by some of the instruments, even if it may look professional in its presentation of data, is not a substitute for a comprehensive

TABLE 19.1   Informal Adaptive Behavior Assessment: A Conceptual Model

Environmental Settings	Areas of Functioning		
	Independent Functioning	Personal Responsibility	Social Responsibility
Academic school: subject areas *Nonacademic school:* playground, halls, gym, to and from school and classes *Out-of-school:* home, neighborhood, peers, parents, other adults	Does he/she have/can he/she acquire the necessary skills?	Does he/she use the skills?	Does he/she use the skills appropriately (time and place)?

All criteria must be appropriate to the age of the child and to the sociocultural setting.

SOURCE: Suggested design by George Batsche, director, School Psychology Program, Eastern Illinois University, NASW Workshop on Adaptive Behavior, March 1981.

social work assessment. Sometimes formal instruments are not available or appropriate. Sometimes their rigid format is not adapted to the situation or misses what the social worker has learned about the pupil's functioning, the cultural background, or environmental conditions in other parts of the assessment. And so, even if a formal instrument is used, the social worker may need to add to the findings or discuss them further with qualifications.

The Functional Behavior Assessment

When IDEA was reauthorized in 1997 and 2004, it specified that when disciplinary action is being considered, students who receive special education services are to be provided with some additional procedural safeguards. A multidisciplinary team in the school is directed to conduct a functional behavior assessment of certain behaviors of concern of the student. This in turn assists in developing a behavioral intervention plan for (and with) the student. The assessment is based on:

◆ An objective, detailed, and behaviorally specific definition or description of the behaviors of concern;
◆ A description of the frequency, duration, intensity, and severity of the behaviors of concern and the settings in which the behaviors occur;
◆ A description of other environmental variables that may affect the behavior (e.g., medication, medical conditions, sleep, diet, schedule, social factors, etc.);
◆ An examination and review of the known communicative behavior and the functional and practical intent of the behavior;
◆ A description of environmental modifications made to change the target behavior; and
◆ An identification of appropriate behaviors that could serve as functional alternatives to the target behavior. (see Clark, 2001)

In any case the key questions in functional behavior assessments are the following: How is the student currently performing? and How does the student respond to interventions suggested by the problem-solving team? The focus is on gathering systematic information not only on the student but also on the factors in the school, home, and community settings that may be contributing to the difficulties. Analysis of the functional behavior assessment focuses on understanding:

◆ The purpose and function of the behaviors of concern;
◆ The factors/conditions that may precipitate these behaviors;
◆ The person's social, emotional, and behavioral functioning in relation to expectations;
◆ The development of interventions;
◆ The identification of needed supports; and
◆ The identification of desired behavior(s) that could serve as functional alternatives (see Clark, 2001).

There is a beginning guide to the development of a functional behavior assessment in the earlier discussion of assessment of the dynamics of the learning environment in this chapter. There is also a good sampler of developmental learning objectives in chapter 24 (table 24.1). Using these principles and this language, the school social worker can contribute to the team's mapping of the *functions* of a targeted behavior, and the *antecedents* and *consequences* of the behavior.

In many ways the functional behavior assessment is not very different from the way social workers ordinarily think, except that it is quite behaviorally specific. It does not explicitly compare or classify the pupil in relation to an abstract norm of the behavior of other pupils (often the problem with normed, paper-and-pencil evaluative instruments). Rather it begins where the pupil is, looks at what may trigger a behavior and what might be workable next steps and goals for social participation. What antecedent conditions might possibly trigger the behavior? What functional payoff might there have been for the student? What did he get or avoid? Multiple methods should be used to gather the information—interviews, observations, checklists, and so on. This process would then result in the development of a *behavioral intervention plan* (BIP) with interventions linked to the functional assessment.

The Behavioral Intervention Plan (BIP)

The BIP should have measurable goals and objectives, and a clear description of how to help the student increase positive behaviors rather than simply trying to reduce the undesirable behaviors. As such, it is the responsibility of the entire team, and in particular the teacher, who may have the most contact with the student. It is not simply something the social worker does. It is an integral part of teamwork and consultation. Social workers may assist in the construction of the plan. In its implementation, they may have responsibilities in skill development and in modifying antecedent conditions and consequences. Building on the ABC functional behavior analysis, described earlier in this chapter, a plan would specify:

- ◆ Needs for development: motivation, behavior, social skills, self-image (see figures 24.1 and ff.);
- ◆ Antecedent conditions (these might be modified);
- ◆ Consequences (these might be modified).

Antecedent conditions that could be modified might include: task or instructional modifications, incorporation of student interests, "chunking" or reducing assignments, use of advance organizers, peer tutors or models, student choices, instruction in alternative forms of communication, or limitation of homework to tasks that the student has mastered, shared power, alternating tasks, increased supervision, decreased sensory input, or decreased classroom overcrowding (Raines, 2002; Zuna & McDougall, 2004). It may involve a short, daily check-in with the social worker, as in the case of Alan (chapter 26). It may involve a group program at the YMCA that indirectly teaches social skills. Consequences that could be modified might include: ignoring or redirecting mildly inappropriate behavior, providing incentives, or noticing and reinforcing appropriate behavior (Raines, 2002). Auxiliary supports may include parent training, family therapy, couples counseling, psychiatric referral for medication, outpatient child therapy, case coordination with other agencies, or youth programs at local YMCAs (Raines, 2002). Under different circumstances they may either be antecedents or consequences. Finally, the BIP would have a list of responsible participants and resources to access. Evaluation can take place by comparing a measure of the initial target behavior with a later period.

CONCLUSION

Social workers have traditionally used observation and interviews as their basic tools for gathering information for assessing the dynamics of persons in their environments, preparing social histories, and conducting needs assessments. This chapter has addressed the application of these skills in the school environment. This chapter has also presented an introduction to some of the additional tools that are necessary for the school social worker to be of service to school personnel, students, and families. Conducting assessments of the learning environment is essential if we are to move beyond just being focused on the student as the recipient of services. Being prepared to assist in conducting functional assessments of behavior will be essential for not only meeting the needs of students, but also for demonstrating the social worker's ability to help schools meet the mandates that are being placed on them. Fortunately, functional assessments are very close to the analysis of person-environment relations social workers have always done, now applied to the educational setting. Gaining some experience with adaptive behavior assessment and being able to do either informal, qualitative assessments or use formal instruments will require going beyond the traditional generalist skills provided in graduate schools of social work. However, the results can give additional credibility to the clinical impressions gained through the interviews and observations. This is especially important when we are being called on to assist in special education decisions about a student's possible eligibility for additional services. Our role is essential for ensuring environmental and familial factors are taken into consideration as well as helping parents be aware of their rights.

References

Bronfenbrenner, U. (1979). *The ecology of human development*. Cambridge, MA: Harvard University Press.

Byrne, J. L., Hare, I., Hooper, S. N., Morse, B. J., & Sabatino, C. A. (1977). The role of a social history in special education evaluation. In R. J. Anderson, M. Freeman, & R. L. Edwards (Eds.), *School social work and PL 94-142: The Education for All Handicapped Act* (pp. 47–55). Washington, DC: National Association of Social Workers.

Clark, J. (2001). Functional behavioral assessment and behavioral intervention plans: Implementing the student discipline provisions of IDEA '97. *NASW school social work hot topics*. Washington, DC: National Association of Social Workers. Available at http://www.naswdc.org/sections/SSW/hottopics/schalark.htm

Finn, C. E. Jr. (1984). Toward strategic independence: Nine commandments for enhancing school effectiveness. *Phi Delta Kappan, 65*(8), 513-524.

Hobbs, N. (Ed.). (1976). *Issues in the classification of children*. San Francisco: Jossey-Bass.

Lucco, A. A. (1991). Assessment of the school-age child. *Families in Society: The Journal of Contemporary Human Services, 81*(5), 394-407.

Purkey, S. C., & Smith, M. S. (1983). Effective schools: A review. *The Elementary School Journal, 83*(4), 427-452.

Raines, J. C. (2002). Brainstorming hypotheses for functional behavior assessment: The link to effective behavioral intervention plans. *School Social Work Journal, 26*(2), 30-45.

Repp, A. C., & Horner, R. H. (1999). *Functional analysis of problem behavior: From effective assessment to effective support*. Belmont, CA: Wadsworth.

Roberts, M. (1995). Best practices in assessing environmental factors that impact student performance. In A. Thomas & J. Grimes (Eds.), *Best practices in school psychology* (pp. 679-688). Washington, DC: National Association of School Psychologists.

Siporin, M. (1975). *Introduction to social work practice*. New York: Macmillan.

Zuna, N., & McDougall, D. (2004). Using positive behavioral support to manage avoidance of academic tasks. *Teaching Exceptional Children, 37*(1), 18-24.

20

Collaboration and Consultation: Professional Alliances for Children, Families, and Schools

Christine Anlauf Sabatino

The Catholic University of America

- ◆ Collaboration: Integration of Services across Professional Boundaries
- ◆ The Knowledge Base of Consultation
- ◆ Practice Models: Goals, Objectives, Skills, and Techniques
- ◆ Stages of Consultation
- ◆ Challenges for School Social Work Consultants
- ◆ A Model of Mental Health Consultation for School Social Workers
- ◆ A Case Example of Mental Health Consultation
- ◆ A Case Example for Multiple Consultation Models

Collaboration and consultation are two practice methods for incorporating the professional insights of school personnel and community agencies to improve the quality of school-based assessment and intervention services. The objective of this chapter is to provide school social workers with conceptual frameworks to guide their collaboration and consultation practice using current and classical concepts and theory. Principles for successful collaboration are identified and described. Further, several typologies of collaboration practice relevant to schools and communities are presented. Consultation literature is synthesized in relation to theory, practice, and research from a variety of professions. Six models of consultation are identified, including the major goals, objectives, skills, and techniques for each. One model is presented in greater detail because it provides the school social worker with an empirically derived and theoretically derived framework for quickly sorting, understanding, and addressing classroom teachers' informal and formal comments about their students. Finally, the chapter offers case examples for analysis and discussion that capture real-life problems that might be handled by multiple consultation approaches.

COLLABORATION: INTEGRATION OF SERVICES
ACROSS PROFESSIONAL BOUNDARIES

Collaboration is a broad term that carries a variety of meanings including teamwork, partnership, group effort, association, alliance, relationship, and cooperation. It is not consistently linked with any particular theoretical framework or associated with specific concepts for assessment or intervention. Rather, the term is used as a descriptor in conjunction with work with various fields of practice, populations, problems, or therapeutic methods (see Roberts & Greene, 2002). As collaboration is becoming more important for school social workers, Tourse and Mooney (1999) have edited a text for social workers and educators, which includes materials that address students, families, the school system, and the community.

Barker (2003) defines professional social work collaboration as the procedure in which two or more professionals work together to serve a given client. In other words, collaboration is a course of action in which various participants work together to achieve a common goal by pooling their knowledge, skills, and resources (Abramson & Rosenthal, 1995). In the schools, it is based on the premise that no one discipline can meet the diverse needs of today's student body because countless factors contribute to students' school success. Indeed, the school system by itself is often unable to meet the needs of some students, but through collaboration it accomplishes collectively what cannot be achieved separately (Graham & Barter, 1999). Pooling school staff expertise and promoting community partnerships is emerging as a highly effective service strategy in pupil services (Dryfoos & Maguire, 2002).

Collaboration challenges isolated professional and organizational work efforts and shifts multidisciplinary work from discrete policies and procedures to holistic student well-being. It requires service delivery systems that create inclusive and flexible processes that break through categorical program approaches (Mizrahi & Rosenthal, 2001). Collaboration challenges professionals to go beyond their traditional roles. It also contributes to the growth and well-being of the participants. The process enhances professional capabilities because collaborators understand that the world is more complex than the one that lies within their professional boundaries and functions. Participants have more opportunities to deal with the entire context and process of a problem. The problem-solving efforts undertaken and the service delivery systems implemented through collaboration capture these understandings and act in response to them.

Bridging traditional professional and organizational boundaries for collaboration is a complex process. Successful interdisciplinary and interorganizational work does not magically emerge because collaborators gather around an issue. Collaboration, if it is to succeed, requires that the participants develop relationships of trust. It requires a common view of what is in the best interest of the student and his or her family.

Collaborative decision making means the team shares ownership of problems and solutions, shares skills, uses different thinking processes, and has the flexibility to work on different aspects of a complex task. It opens the way toward attainment of group goals (Thousand & Villa, 1992). Gallessich (1982) and Lopez, Torres, and Norwood (1998) offer the following guidelines, which may be applied to build effective collaboration among school teams and community stakeholders.

1. *Structure.* Each member brings professional discipline, knowledge, values, and skills to the team. Efforts to blend interprofessional strategies may give rise to fear that one's own profession will get washed out or that there will be turf battles. The underlying philosophy of collaboration calls for various disciplines to plan to act together. In some instances this requires revisions in policy, job descriptions, leadership structure, and accountability requirements. These types of changes often bring about a different work culture. Roles and assignments must be agreed upon and explicated. Goals and methods must be clarified. Unresolved conflicts will generally result in high tension.

2. *Openness.* A culture of trust between collaborators is necessary to develop and maintain flexible collaboration. This trust requires recognizing each other's competencies, trusting each other's communications, and relying on each other's work. Mutual respect and understanding of each other's professional values and service orientation are preconditions to successful work.

3. *Self-examination.* Collaborators must commit to systematically reviewing and studying their own processes. Successes and accomplishments as well as failures require review and exploration. These efforts ensure accountability because it is one thing to conceptualize collaboration and another to implement it.

4. *Heterogeneity.* The inclusion of different professions with different styles and perspectives strengthens collaboration through joint planning, and shared decision-making. It supports the school's mission, maximizes resources, and generates new paradigms for assessment, service, referral, and follow-up. The heterogeneity of a collaborative work group must not be so great that it interferes with the structure, openness, and processes of the group. Blending and meshing different professional values and philosophies, however, guards against excessive specialization and fragmentation.

Lopez, Torres, and Norwood (1998) use these same principles but delineate them as three levels of collaborative competencies. *Intrapersonal competence* is the routine personal reflection and self-awareness wherein one acknowledges one's own beliefs, values, and thoughts about collaborative practice. *Interpersonal competence* is the development, maintenance, and nurturing of collaborative relationships with mutual respect and appreciation as the central features (Kapp, 2000). *Interprofessional competence* encompasses the skills of group process and includes a shared vision, awareness of professional differences, and respect for collective power (Bronstein, 2003).

Anderson-Butcher and Ashton (2004) describe a variety of collaborative frameworks that are employed to specifically address different types of student needs. *Intraorganizational* collaboration refers to the interactions and communications among school personnel in a specific school setting. These efforts provide direction and strategies to promote positive student outcomes. Familiar examples include school-wide prevention programs, prereferral services, special education teamwork, Section 504, Title I, and alternative language teams (Mishna & Muskat, 2004). *Interagency collaboration* exists when agencies with different mission statements develop formal agreements to work toward a common purpose or goal. These usually consist of the school and local public and private social service, health, mental health, and early intervention programs. The overarching goal of an interagency collaboration is to provide outreach and support in the service of positive youth development. Community-based interagency councils developed in conjunction with Early Intervention programs are an example of interagency collaboration (Mizrahi & Rosenthal, 2001). *Interprofessional collaboration* involves two or more professionals working together to help a particular student and his/her family. This usually occurs when there are co-occurring conditions that might bring about school failure. The interrelationship of the problems requires comprehensive, integrated, individualized and supportive services. Examples of interprofessional collaboration include full-service schools, school-linked services, after-school youth development programs, and collaborative partnerships between universities and school systems (Dryfoos & Maguire, 2002; Jozefowicz-Simbeni & Allen-Meares, 2002). *Family-centered collaboration* is born out of the belief that parents are full-time partners with professionals in deciding what types of services meet their priorities, resources, and concerns. Parents have the capacity to implement case management components of service plans and to serve as liaison between the school and community agencies. Family-centered collaboration is strengths-based and empowering (Lynn & McKay, 2001). *Community collaboration* involves all stakeholders to improve children's learning. It is inclusive and diverse, providing the opportunity for all stakeholders to learn from one another. Sometimes community collaboration takes the form of *locality development* to bring about overall citizen participation in issues; other times it takes the form of *social planning*, wherein problem analysis and problem solving are data driven. In both cases, the overarching goal is to strengthen the community to resolve the problems they identify as barriers to youth development and school success (Altshuler, 2003).

THE KNOWLEDGE BASE OF CONSULTATION

History and Definition

Consultation is an indirect method of professional social work that helps others become more effective in dealing with their complex work-related problems. Consultation has evolved into one of the most significant forms of intervention in school social work practice. Its scope has widened from expert clinical assessment of a child's psychosocial functioning for special education evaluations to the current concerns with the relationships and processes in the broader social environments of the classroom, the school, and the community that promote student well-being and supportive school environments. The range of consultation services offered by school social workers has expanded to include education and training, behavioral and mental health consultation, program and organization development consultation, and interagency collaboration for service coordination and community planning.

The relationship between school social work practice and consultation has been traced back as far as the turn of the twentieth century (Oppenheimer, 1925). It has been historically identified in the literature as an enduring and valued school social work task (Allen-Meares, 1994; Allen-Meares, Washington, & Welsh, 2000; Boyle-Del Rio, Carson, & Hailbeck, 2000; Carr, 1976; Constable, Kuzmickaite, Harrison, & Volkmann, 1999; Costin, 1969; Meares, 1977; Meares, 1982; Timberlake, Sabatino, & Hooper, 1982).

Consultation is defined as an interactional process that takes place between a help-giver and a help-seeker. The help-seeker is experiencing difficulties in performing professional functions with a client, group, or organization. Although there are a variety of approaches to consultation, there is common agreement that all have the following characteristics: (1) It is a problem-solving process; (2) It takes place between a professional consultant and a consultee who has responsibility for service delivery; (3) It is a voluntary relationship; (4) The objective is to solve a work-related problem of the consultee; (5) The consultant and the consultee share in solving the problem; and (6) Consultation helps the consultee become better prepared to deal with similar problems in the future (Caplan & Caplan, 1993; Kadushin, 1977; Meyers, Parson, & Martin, 1979; Zischka & Fox, 1985).

Another way to define consultation is to contrast it with supervision and education. In a supervisory relationship, the supervisor holds a position of authority in the hierarchical institutional structure that requires an ongoing relationship of an evaluative nature with the consultee. In an educational relationship, there is a curriculum, which must be imparted during the learning process that is developed apart from the consultation process. Consultation by its very nature excludes positional authority and a priori educational objectives. It is contracted for on a time-limited basis. The consultant and the consultee have a co-equal relationship. Both are responsible for professional activities and knowledge development. The consultant does not bring an agenda, but one develops through an exploration of the consultee's needs and the consultant's expertise.

According to Caplan (1970), consultation is a specialized method of intervention. It employs information and concepts that are often unknown, unfamiliar, or unclear to most professionals. It has a specific knowledge base with distinct principles and concepts to guide consultation methods. Training and certification in one's own profession does not translate into competence in consultation knowledge and skills. Further, helping others with their work problems is a much more complex process than working directly with one's own work-related problems. Specialized preparation is needed so that one understands the consultation process, consultation phases, different models of consultation, and the unique functions of the consultant's role.

Role of Federal Government and Contributions of Allied Professions

School social workers and mental health workers have traditionally utilized consultation as an expected part of their role. In 1963 the federal government became a major catalyst in the development of consultation theory, practice, and research with the signing of the Mental Retardation Facilities and Community Mental Health Centers Construction Act, PL 88-164. This statute mandated the provision of mental health consultation and education by publicly funded community mental health centers. The National Institute of Mental Health furthered the intellectual base of this method of intervention when it established the Mental Health Study Center. The center developed a series of monographs and supported publications on mental health consultation. The purpose of these monographs was: to assist community mental health centers in the planning, development, and evaluation of consultation; to provide technical resources to universities in developing consultation training programs; and to stimulate research on the impact of consultation (Grady, Gibson, & Trickett, 1981; Mannino, 1969; Mannino & MacLennan, 1978; Mannino, MacLennan, & Shore, 1975; Mannino & Shore, 1971; Mannino & Shore, 1979; Mannino, Tricket, Shore, Kidder, & Levin, 1986; McClung & Stunden, 1970). This body of work remains one of the richest original sources of professional consultation knowledge to date.

Current consultation literature now has a very eclectic knowledge base. Each of the allied helping professions, such as social work (Kadushin, 1977; Rapoport, 1963; Reiman, 1992), psychiatry (Caplan, 1970; Caplan & Caplan, 1993), psychology (Brown, Pryzwansky, & Schulte, 2001; Erchul & Martens, 2002), school psychology (Conoley & Conoley, 1992; Gutkin & Carlson, 2001; Parsons, 1996), school counseling (Dinkmeyer & Carlson, 2001), and early childhood education (Carslon, Splete, & Kern, 1975; Donahue, Falk, & Provet, 2000) have published texts on the theory and practice of consultation. Further, there is a growing literature that documents the need for professional associations to provide continuing education, training, and professional development programs (Allen & Blackston, 2003; Berkovitz & Sinclair, 2001; Bramlett, Murphy, Johnson, Wallingsford, & Hall, 2002; Fowler & Harrison, 2001; Luellen, 2000; Martens & Ardoin, 2002; Sterling-Turner, Watson, & Moore, 2002; Wesley, 2002; Wesley, Buysee, & Keyes, 2000; Wilczynski, Mandal, & Fusilier, 2000). Seminal works and current research on consultation are found in the professional literature for the various school disciplines (Dinkmeyer & Carlson, 2001; Dougherty, 2000; Erchul & Martens, 2002; Hughes, 2000). Special issues of professional journals are devoted to consultation. (see, for example, *Child and Adolescent Psychiatric Clinics of North America*, January 2001, or *School Psychology Quarterly*, Summer 1998). Retrospective reviews analyze consultation literature by the decades (Berlin, 2001).

Indeed, consultation literature in the allied helping professions is now classified according to specific *types* of consultation (Alpert & Meyers, 1983). These are: behavioral consultation (Sheridan, Eagle, Cowan, & Mickelson, 2001; Wilkinson, 1999), mental health consultation (Berlin, 2001; Bostic & Rauch, 1999; Bostic & Bagnell, 2001), program consultation (Kerr, 2001; Lusky & Hayes, 2001), and organization consultation (Blake & Mouton, 1983; McDowell, 1999; Packard, 2001; Schein, 1999; Sperry, Kahn, & Heidel, 1994; Wilson & Lubin, 1997). The issues of culture and ethnicity are two important recent additions to the literature (Fischer et al., 2002; Goldstein & Harris, 2000; Henning-Stout & Meyers, 2000; Ingraham, 2000; Rogers, 2000; Sheridan, 2000; Annotated Bibliography, 2000).

PRACTICE MODELS: GOALS, OBJECTIVES, SKILLS, AND TECHNIQUES

There are a number of theoretical frameworks for different models of consultation. Behavior theory, systems theory, organizational development theory, group theory, psycho-educational theory, family systems theory, and psychodynamic theory all have been used as a foundation for various practice models. *The Profession and Practice of Consultation* (Gallessich, 1982) remains a classic text that provides a comprehensive survey of various consultation approaches that analyzes each using specific dimensions. Information applicable to one dimension of a model naturally leads to the other dimensions of the model to build an internally consistent and specific consultation approach. Clarifying one's thinking on a few of these dimensions helps lead the practitioner toward or away from other types of consultation. The dimensions are the following:

- ◆ The conceptualization or formulation of the problem,
- ◆ The overall or broad goal of consultation,
- ◆ The major methods used by the consultant,
- ◆ The consultant's assumption about change,
- ◆ The consultant's role or source of power, and
- ◆ The underlying value of the model.

Gallessich compares and contrasts six different types of consultation models using these dimensions. A brief synopsis of each is presented here in order to assist school social work consultants to select the most appropriate consultation model for the presenting problem.

1. *Education and Training Consultation.* In the education and training consultation model, the assessed problem is the consultee's lack of technological knowledge, information, or skills. The consultant's goal is to provide the needed knowledge, information, or skill. Methods used may include lectures, multimedia presentations, learning materials, structured laboratory experiences, small-group discussion, modeling, and feedback measures. The consultant assumes that the consultee changes through cognitive learning. The consultant is viewed as an expert who values the growing fields of information and technology services to sustain the future of a group organization, agency, or program. This model assumes that, in a school, the administrators have conferred with the faculty and reached mutual agreement that staff may benefit from the proposed education and training.

When the client base for the school system literally grows and develops during their school years, there is limitless subject matter for education and training programs. The breadth of issues that may confound educational progress is endless. Education and training programs are an important and familiar way to impart new information that supports the teaching-learning process. These programs let school personnel see the vast amount of information available to assist them in their roles and tasks. Dupper (2002) offers a framework for consideration when conducting a needs assessment for staff development. Programs might revolve around students' externalizing behaviors such as classroom behavior problems, bullying, peer harassment, suspension, and expulsion. Internalizing behaviors that might puzzle a teacher include anxiety, loneliness, grief, and depression. Social problems, categories of vulnerable students, cultural diversity issues, and parent involvement are other topics that lend themselves to education and training. After the tragedies of Columbine and Red Lake, school leaders frequently spoke about the professionals brought to the schools to provide information and support. Professional development and training programs are vital to successful classroom climates, the school organization, and administrative structures (Gottlieb & Polirstok, 2005). Further, the literature now documents the value and effectiveness of preservice and in-service training (Agresta, 2004; Bartels & Mortenson, 2002; Boyle-Del Rio, Carlson, & Hailbeck, (2000); Curtis, Hunley, & Grier, 2002; Davis, 2003; Rosenberg, 2001; Sawka, McCurdy, & Mannella, 2002; Watckins, Crosby, Pearson, & Jeremy, 2002).

2. *Clinical Consultation.* The clinical consultation model reflects medical assumptions. The need, due to the consultee's lack of technical expertise in the identified problem area, is for an expert diagnosis and authoritative recommen-

dation regarding a client's disease or dysfunction. The consultant's goal is limited to the diagnosis and amelioration of a particular set of problems in order to restore normal social functioning or remediate symptoms in a case situation. The methods include diagnosis, prescription, and treatment. It is assumed that the diagnosis is outside the consultee's range of competencies; therefore, the consultant's expertise is essential for providing knowledge to bring about change. The consultant may be collegial or directive in relating to the consultee, but in either case, the consultant values the healthy functioning of the client. This model assumes that, in a school situation, the student's problem is so complex it requires a specialist for evaluation, disposition, and management.

School social workers always use clinical consultation as one of their professional roles in the schools system when they conduct the psychosocial evaluation for special education evaluations and for prereferral interventions. Here school social workers are viewed as the team member with expertise in psychosocial-spiritual factors that must be ruled in or ruled out for a specific learning problem. Given resource problems and the importance of finding workable solutions, where a more restrictive environment is less necessary, prereferral intervention processes are becoming more and more important. However, there are many issues other than those related to special education in which the school social worker might offer expertise (Jackson & White, 2000; Buck, Polloway, Smith-Thomas, & Cox, 2003).

3. *Mental Health Consultation.* In the mental health consultation model, the problem is defined as the consultee's need for knowledge, skill, self-confidence, or objectivity. The consultant's goal is to increase competencies and strengthen the consultee's professional functioning, with improvement in the client as a side effect. Although methods differ for each of these four problem categories, all use education, facilitation, and support. The model assumes that the consultee has the capacity to solve the work problem with cognitive and emotional support. The consultant brings many sources of power to the role and becomes a model teacher, resource, collaborator, and encourager. The consultant's primary underlying value is the infusion of mental health concepts and principles as a form of mental health intervention. This model assumes that there is administrative sanction and support that provides the consultant and the consultee with the necessary time to analyze the identified problem and plan and implement interventions.

The President's New Freedom Commission on Mental Health Executive Report (2003) identifies six goals for transforming mental health in America. Goal 4, entitled *Early Mental Health Screening, Assessment, and Referral to Services are Common Practice*, is critical to school social work practice. This goal specifically addresses the promotion of mental health in young children and calls for improvement and expansion in school mental health programs. This goal has been partially implemented by the U.S. Department of Health and Human Services, Health Resources and Services Administration, Maternal and

Child Health Bureau, Division of Child, Adolescent and Family Health, and the Substance Abuse and Mental Health Services Administration Center for Mental Health Services. They have funded two national centers to conduct research, training, technical assistance, and networking. The Center for School Mental Health Assistance at the University of Maryland School of Medicine (2005) and the University of California, Los Angeles, School Mental Health Project, Center for Mental Health in Schools (2005) are advancing effective school-based mental health programs. Each center offers an extensive reference list related to mental health in the schools. The challenge for social workers is to publish their findings related to school mental health theory, practice, and research because most of the references found at the centers are by other professions who serve the school population (See *Children & Schools*, Special Issue: Mental Health in the Schools, January 2001; Lynn, McKay, & Atkins, 2003).

4. *Behavioral Consultation.* In the behavioral consultation model, the problem is formulated in terms of dysfunctional behavior. The goal is to reduce or eliminate undesirable behaviors and replace or increase the frequency of desired behavior. The method used is the systematic application of cognitive-behavioral learning principles. It is similar to methods of clinical consultation with its case-centered focus on the methods of diagnosis, prescription, and treatment. The method involves the following elements: the problem is defined in behavioral terms; behaviors are observed and recorded; antecedents and consequences are analyzed; and reinforcement contingencies are designed and implemented. When this takes place, the consultant withdraws and the consultee assumes responsibility for the client's behavioral management program. The model assumes that change is possible with the consultant's empirical and rational expertise, which is the consultant's source of power. The behavioral consultation model places great value on technology and the scientific method. It assumes that the teacher is willing to collaborate with the consultant in the recording of observed behaviors, implementation of behavior modification strategies, evaluation of behavior changes, and integration of a new behavioral management program in the appropriate setting.

Today behavioral consultation is a common strategy used in the schools to provide treatment and support to an increasing number of students with behavioral challenges that interfere with their learning (Wilkinson, 2003). It has taken on far greater importance since Congress revised the Individuals with Disabilities Education Act, 1997, and mandated the development of functional behavioral assessments (Raines, 2002). In fact, recent literature is replete with materials that document its use for individual students, classroom-wide interventions, home-school partnerships, and whole school programs (Cowan & Sheridan, 2003; Lewis & Newcomer, 2002; Luiselli, 2002; Metzler, Biglan, Rusby, & Sprague, 2001; Noell, Duhon, Gatti, & Connell, 2002). The federal government also has underscored the worth of behavioral interventions through the United States.

The Department of Education, Office of Special Education Programs, Technical Assistance Center on Positive Interventions & Supports (2005) offers technical assistance guides, literature searches, online articles, and school-wide positive behavior support literature. Again, the challenge is for social workers to publish their practice and research prospective in this area of consultation.

5. *Program Consultation.* Program consultation formulates the problem in terms of a lack of expertise needed to successfully carry out specialized services designed to benefit a target population. Methods used vary considerably due to the diversity of programs. Generally, they include some or all of the following progression: needs are assessed, specific goals are delineated, and methods to achieve identified goals are selected. Then resources are identified, benefits assessed, and constituencies identified. Administrative procedures are established. Staffing needs and funding guidelines are determined. Later, outcomes are evaluated and new programs are integrated with existing services and programs. The consultant assumes that theory and research is the foundation for changes made to alter or develop a program. The consultant is viewed as an expert who values the scientific approach to program planning or supports the values reflected in the program.

Although program development is traditionally the role of school administrators, recent surveys of school social work roles validate that program development is a vital component of practice (Agresta, 2004; Boyle-Del Rio, Carlson, & Laibeck, 2000;Constable, Kuzmickaite, Harrison, & Volkmann, 1999). Peer mediation is an excellent example of programs developed by school social workers to serve general education populations. Further, research has found that some federally mandated programs are not in compliance when school social workers are not present for the assessment and intervention plans (Sabatino, 2001). School social workers must expand their thinking and view themselves as program planners who intend to influence education based on policies that drive program development.

6. *Organizational Consultation.* Problems in the organizational consultation model may fall into several domains. These are technology, structural, managerial, and human relations. The goal is to increase organizational productivity and morale. The methods used by organizational consultants vary widely depending on the domain of concern. In some instances, teams composed of consultants with certain specialties are used. Consultants assume that change is brought about by empirical knowledge and reeducation. The consultant's authority comes from expert knowledge. In addition, the consultee usually identifies with the consultant's area of expertise and the consultant's role performance. Organizational consultants base their models on the values inherent in technological information and human development services. As with education and training consultation, this model assumes that members of the organization agree that the services of a consultant are of value.

Organizational consultation is a new role for school social workers (Packard, 2001). However, there are reviews of the literature and outcome studies that document that organizational consultation yields robust effects (Matheny & Simmerman, 2001; Reddy, Barboza-Whitehead, Files, & Rubel,

2000). School social workers are well situated to provide organizational consultation given their ecological approach with the assumption that students and their families are embedded in social and environmental contexts. With this knowledge, they are capable of introducing strategic change for the entire school organization (Mishna & Muskat, 2004).

There are some efforts in place to integrate these six consultation models along common dimensions and shape them to fit the needs of the situation. Curtis and Zins (1981) offer another framework for sifting consultation theory and practice to select an appropriate consultation practice model. They ask the following questions: What should be changed? (value orientation), For whom is change intended? (target), Through whom is change brought about? (operational level), How will change take place? (consultative methods), and What is the style of interpersonal interaction between the consultant and the consultee? (consultant role). Gallessich (1982) would vary these questions by focusing on the *problem definition,* the *goal* of consultation, the *target* of change, the requisite *skills* and *techniques*, and the *role* of the consultant. Both of these models emphasize a common *process* of consultation, matching the *type* of consultation to the *needs* of the situation.

STAGES OF CONSULTATION

Regardless of the theoretical base or type of consultation one chooses to use in practice, all models of consultation have a common set of stages or phases. Gallessich (1982) identifies the following phases of the consultation process. Each stage needs to be explored in relation to both the school social work consultant's and the consultee's roles and responsibilities. Each stage may have several subphases, and there is fluidity among the stages. The value of identifying these stages is that it gives the consultant and the consultee a common framework for reference and discussion if the consultation process becomes unproductive, thereby helping the consultation to remain focused. Each of the phases is presented with a series of questions extrapolated from Gallessich and adapted to reflect the needs of schools in developing appropriate consultation service.

1. **Preliminary exploration**
   ◆ What are the school's needs?
   ◆ What are the consultant's qualifications regarding these needs?
   ◆ Is there a satisfactory fit between the consultant and the consultee?
   ◆ Are there any value conflicts among the parties?
2. **Negotiation of a contract**
   ◆ What are the terms for working together?
   ◆ Is this a formal or legal contract?
   ◆ Is this an informal or oral contract?
   ◆ Does the contract include consultation goals, length of contract, consultant responsibilities, school responsibilities, consultant's role, and evaluation or termination procedures?

3. **Entry**
   - Where will consultation take place?
   - What physical, social, or psychological barriers to entry are encountered?
   - What school dynamics might be a barrier to being trusted and accepted in this school system? What tensions arise in the course of building a relationship with the consultee?
4. **Diagnosis of problems or needs assessment**
   - Do the consultant and consultee collaborate in data collection?
   - Is assessment seen as an ongoing activity?
   - Has the entire context for consultation been scanned or is the assessment narrowly focused on the presenting problem?
   - Have hard data and soft data been used?
   - Has more than one theoretical perspective been used to sort and analyze the problem? Is further data gathering required?
5. **Goal setting**
   - Who has proposed the goal(s)?
   - Have the merits of a number of goals been evaluated?
   - Are there realistic solutions to the problem?
   - If not, is the consultant prepared to terminate the consultation?
   - Can the goals be reached by the school staff without consultation?
   - How urgent is it to achieve a goal?
   - How successful might this goal be?
   - How feasible is a goal?
   - What is the cost of this goal in time and money?
6. **Exploration and selection of alternative consultation approaches**
   - What is the best method for achieving the goal?
   - Have alternative methods been generated and examined?
   - Is there a clear definition of the objective?
   - Is there a clear plan of action to reach the objective?
   - What problems are anticipated?
   - Which school personnel are responsible for which actions?
   - Have the consultant's role, function, and responsibility been delineated from those of the consultee?
7. **Implementation of intervention**
   - Does implementation involve the consultant?
8. **Evaluation of outcomes**
   - To what degree have the goal(s) been achieved?
   - Is evaluation one of the consultant's functions?
   - What factors contributed to the positive and the negative outcomes?
   - Is the evaluation informal and anecdotal?
   - Is the evaluation formal and quantifiable?
   - Has the consultant's performance been evaluated?

9. **Institutionalization of changes**
   - ◆ Have new procedures or behaviors been incorporated to become standard practice?
   - ◆ Does this change require additional training and monitoring?
   - ◆ Does this change require that incentives be institutionalized?
10. **Termination of consultation**
   - ◆ What are the criteria for termination?
   - ◆ What are the emotional reactions surrounding the termination?
   - ◆ Will termination occur through a series of steps?
   - ◆ Are there follow-up plans to termination?

These stages and processes may not unfold in an orderly and sequential pattern. They will vary and be specific to each consultation contract (Tindel, Parker, & Hasbrouck, 1992).

CHALLENGES FOR SCHOOL SOCIAL WORK CONSULTANTS

The interpersonal relationships established during these phases are crucial to the success of the consultation services. It is important for the consultee to feel comfortable, accepted, and respected. The consultant may help to establish this atmosphere by being trustworthy, accepting, respectful, nonjudgmental, and collegial. Throughout the consultation process, it is important to remember that it takes time for a consultee to build a relationship, to understand what consultation is, and to learn how to use it. The consultee needs to learn how to present relevant information, what kind of help to expect from the consultant, and what the consultant has to offer. Sometimes the consultee will have a hidden agenda in consultation. The consultant might be invited into a conflict as an "expert" to support one viewpoint. The consultant might be expected to share the emotional burden of making a difficult decision, or to enable someone to abdicate responsibility for a difficult problem. Sometimes there is a wish to substitute consultation services for clinical, programmatic, or organizational efforts. In any case, there may need to be several preliminary meetings if the consultee is to understand the processes and use them effectively.

It is important that the consultee understand what consultation is and how it is to be used. Caplan and Caplan (1993) note that what is labeled as "resistance" may only be a lack of professional preparation for consultation. Or it may signal the belief that asking for consultation is an admission of professional incompetence. To overcome these barriers, the consultee may be reminded that problems often are complicated and confusing and that the request for consultation services is a sign of professional competence. No significant problem can be managed hurriedly. It is important to distinguish consultation from therapy. In consultation, material is discussed that is often delicate in nature, personal to the consultee, and risky to share with others. In order to meet the agreed-upon goal of solving work-related problems, it is not appropriate for the consultant to interpret or reflect unconscious or personnel material or to foster the development of a therapeutic relationship. In fact, these traditional elements of psychodynamic intervention distract the consultant and the consultee from their central task of focusing on the presenting problem.

In a school setting the consultation relationship is a *coordinate* relationship wherein two differently prepared professionals concentrate on helping students reap the full benefit of their education. The faculty and school system are entirely competent and retain full authority and responsibility. They are free to accept or reject the consultant's ideas and recommendations. It is best to avoid advice giving and jargon. These imply some level of ignorance on the part of the consultee. They may be seen as a devaluation of the consultee's abilities. To reinforce this coordinate relationship, it is important to develop a joint language for communicating with each other about work-related difficulties by exploring the semantic meanings of the consultee's narrative (Saleeby, 1994) and by using language that is understandable and acceptable to him or her. The nature of the concepts communicated must fit the culture of the school and teacher (Caplan & Caplan, 1993). The goal is to enable the teacher or school system to deepen the understanding of those aspects of the presenting problem that are puzzling.

A MODEL OF MENTAL HEALTH CONSULTATION FOR SCHOOL SOCIAL WORKERS

A practice model contains rules for practitioners in defining and assessing target problems and delineating sequences of interventions to be used in attempts to alleviate problems (Reid, 1979). A model organizes discrete principles, methods, and procedures into coherent strategies. Models are bridges between theory and practice, the translation of theory into how-to-do-it descriptions of activities.

The following *mental health consultation* model has been adapted for school social workers from Caplan and Caplan (1993). It is a research-based and practice-based model that has been significantly effective for providing remedial and preventive services within private and public school systems (Sabatino, 1986). Specifically, this model builds on one of Caplan's four specific categories of mental health consultation, *consultee-centered case consultation*. The author has found that the theory and practice of consultee-centered mental health consultation may be easily applied to school social work consultation. Further, the paradigm is easy to teach in staff development workshops to groups of school social workers.

According to Caplan's theory, there are four reasons why a teacher might have a problem with a student: need for *knowledge*, need for *skill*, need for *self-confidence*, and need for *objectivity* (Caplan, 1970). These four reasons provide the core concepts of the model.

1. *Need for Knowledge.* The school social work consultant is able to assess the need for knowledge when, due to lack of specific psychosocial knowledge or the issues involved, the teacher misunderstands or draws erroneous

conclusions about a student's puzzling behavior. In some instances, the teacher possesses the professional knowledge necessary to understand the situation but does not see its relevance or application to this particular child and problem. Interventions consist of imparting missing general information or sharing specialized expertise in an area. Caplan takes the position that the need for knowledge should be the least frequent reason for consultation because the consultee is a trained professional. In a regular classroom setting, however, the teacher's primary training is in elementary or secondary education. Sometimes teachers are lacking in complex theoretical knowledge about the cognitive, emotional, social, or interactional processes that accompany a child's problem in the teaching-learning process. Other times a specific problem arises that would rarely be part of a teacher's training or expertise. It is inevitable that teachers will be confronted with experiences for which they received no professional education or training. Psychological, social, and interactional processes related to a child's presenting problem are not a routine part of teacher education. In such instances, the task of the consultant is to impart the missing information in the most economical manner. This may call for continued individual consultation but also lends itself to in-service workshops that disseminate information more broadly and may benefit the entire faculty and administration.

2. *Need for Skill.* Sometimes the consultant will become aware that the teacher possesses the requisite professional knowledge to understand the presenting problem but does not possess the ability to apply appropriate skill to solve it. It is one thing to discern cognitively the difficulty, but quite another matter to call forth and exercise the appropriate problem-solving skill. The main task for the consultant is to explore with the teacher how he or she might develop skill. The teacher might invoke the assistance of colleagues, the principal, or a specialist. By offering to supervise or model skill development there is a risk that the school social work consultant may threaten the collegial relationship and be perceived to be violating the norms of the role. Sometimes the skill necessary is fairly obvious, and it is a matter of support for the teacher's efforts to acquire it. At other times, the social work consultant may want to suggest to the teacher that he or she review the case with the principal or another teacher who can assist in developing techniques of intervention. In some instances, however, the social worker is the ideal staff person for skill development. For example, the Individual Family Service Plan, required for families of young children, calls for assessment of family priorities, resources, and concerns. In many school districts, teachers who often lack basic family interviewing skills are expected to assist in the development of this. Tasks such as interviewing families and helping them to identify their views of their children's developmental delay are very challenging. The social worker, as a team member, might assist the teacher to do this.

3. *Need for Self-Confidence.* There are instances when the teacher does demonstrate adequate psychosocial knowledge and skill performance but does

not use it because of personal insecurities or lack of self-confidence. This problem may be detected in the teacher's tentativeness and uncertainty, or worse, in feelings of incompetence and worthlessness. In this case, the consultant listens to the teacher describe how the situation was handled and provides support for these work efforts. Another intervention centers on assisting the teacher to seek out experienced faculty members who have had similar experiences and, thereby, engender the very powerful support of the "all in the same boat" phenomenon.

A heartrending illustration of this concept occurs when a student suddenly dies. One often hears teachers recount catastrophic losses they have suffered, where they were when it occurred, how they reacted, what they thought, how they felt, what was helpful, and what was not helpful. In many cases, their students experience the same range of reactions. In the immediate aftermath of this type of catastrophe, however, teachers often are very reticent to use their personal knowledge and experience as a support base for their class. Bringing together the teachers in a group offers them a way to gain confidence in using themselves effectively to help students express their feelings and perceptions and to mourn.

4. *Need for Objectivity.* Lack of objectivity is defined as the teacher's loss of professional focus by becoming too close or too distant from the child or the family. When this occurs, conscious or unconscious factors invade the teacher's role functioning, distort perception, and cloud judgment. Five causes for loss of objectivity are (1) direct personal involvement, (2) simple identification, (3) transference, (4) characterological distortions, and (5) theme interference (Caplan, 1970; Caplan & Caplan, 1993). *Direct personal involvement* takes place when the teacher's professional relationship evolves into a personal relationship. The teacher receives personal satisfaction rather than professional satisfaction in relation to the child. The task of the consultant is to help the teacher control the expression of personal needs in the workplace and develop professional goals and a professional identity. Modeling empathy while maintaining appropriate distance is one technique of intervention to be used. Another is to recount a similar experience the consultant has had in mastering personal feelings. When it is not feasible to discuss directly the teacher's over-involvement and the difficulties that come from that, the problem can be reversed and reframed. What would the teacher do if the child or family might wish to have a personal relationship with him or her to the exclusion of classmates? It may be easier to discuss the ramification of a direct personal relationship in this way.

When the teacher describes a problem in such a way that one person is perceived in glowing positive terms and the other person is perceived in derogatory, stereotypic terms, a tendency toward *overidentification* with a pupil might be evident. One might expect the teacher to possess some similar characteristics or experiences to the person seen in sympathetic terms (Caplan, 1970; Caplan & Caplan, 1993). The same process can also result in excessively *negative or hopeless characterizations* of the subject. The task of the consultant is to weaken the identification by having the teacher reanalyze the data about the entire situation. As this process unfolds, the consultant helps the teacher to see the actors as separate and unique people rather than extensions of the teacher. *Transference* problems occur when the teacher imposes a preordained set of attitudes, perceptions, or expectations derived from the teacher's own life experiences that block an objective assessment and work with the child and family. The danger is that the teacher will use the child to act out or resolve the teacher's own unconscious conflicts or fantasy. One way to detect this problem is the teacher's paucity of data to support assertions made about the child. The consultant identifies the conflict that has stimulated the teacher's transference reaction then asks the teacher to observe the child more closely in this area of conflict. Sometimes the newly collected observational data will help the teacher identify the conflict. In other cases, the best the consultant can do is to offer emotional support, allow the teacher to vent feelings, and steer the teacher toward more appropriate outlets for the conflict.

The concept of *theme interference* refers to a teacher's temporary ineffectualness in a limited segment of the work field when suddenly confronted by a situation that is confusing and upsetting. Caplan and Caplan (1993, p. 122) postulate that an unresolved life experience or a fantasy persists in the consultee's "preconscious or unconscious as an emotionally toned cognitive constellation ... a theme." A major component of the theme is its repetitive quality that links an initial category to an inevitable outcome. The teacher is reminded of an unresolved conflict and associates it with the current situation. This condition is perceived to lead to one particular outcome, usually involving pain and suffering. For example, a teacher may say, "Immigrant children whose parents do not learn English [initial category] will not succeed in school [inevitable outcome]." One intervention technique to use with theme interference is to influence the teacher to change his or her perceptions about the child so as to remove the initial category. This "unlinking" frees the child from the inevitable outcome. An unintended consequence of the technique, however, may be the consultee's displacement of the conflict onto another child. To avoid this problem the consultant can use a technique called *theme interference reduction*. The consultant accepts the placement of the child in the initial category but, through examination of the specifics of the child's case, influences the teacher to see that the inevitable outcome is only one of several possible outcomes for the child. In fact, the data often suggest a different outcome.

In all professions, some members have serious psychiatric problems that Caplan and Caplan (1993, p. 119) label "characterological distortions of perception and behavior." The work-related difficulty is largely due to the teacher's own mental health problems. The task of the consultant is to support the teacher's defense structure and lower anxiety so that the teacher maintains an optimal level of professional functioning. The goal is to help the teacher maintain control over impulses, fantasies, and regression and develop appropriate role boundaries.

A CASE EXAMPLE OF MENTAL HEALTH CONSULTATION

Tommy is a third-grade student who came from out of state to Parkside School this September. He is a very anxious little boy who is distracted easily by others as well as by his own thoughts and activities. He has attention deficit disorder, asthma, and a moderate learning disability with speech and language impairment. When he feels stress, he becomes enuretic, something that has happened fairly regularly in his new classroom. His strengths are that he is very friendly and verbal. He wants very much to please the adults in his life. He is embarrassed by his enuresis and reports that he does not become aware of it until it is too late. Tommy's family situation is presently more stable than it has ever been. He lives with his adoptive parents and his biological sister, Janice, a year older. His adoptive parents are very invested in Tommy and Janice. The children were removed from their birth parents for neglect and possible abuse. They were subsequently placed with three foster parents before being placed with their current adoptive family. It was determined that, while in foster care, Janice was sexually abused by the birth father, and it was suspected that this also happened to Tommy. They were legally adopted last year, after which the family moved to another state in order to terminate all contact with the birth parents, who had become threatening. Tommy's mother reports that he needs considerable reassurance and praise. The family has consulted with an allergist and a urologist, and no physical cause for his enuresis has been found. The problem comes and goes, becoming more apparent when major life changes occur, such as moving and starting school.

Tommy's teacher, Julie Brown, is very distressed by his enuresis. She felt that he was doing this to get back at her for disciplining him in the classroom because "it only seems to happen when he's having a bad day." The more she thought about Tommy's behavior and what she felt were the reasons for it, the more she would focus on him. Then the incidents increased, confirming her suspicions. She referred him to the team, asking that he be placed in a self-contained class for emotionally disturbed children because of his difficulty in maintaining attention and his enuresis. She is an inexperienced teacher, not directly hostile to consultation and interested in help from the social worker with Tommy. She didn't think changing her teaching style would make much of a difference with Tommy, and she wanted the "expert" social worker either to give her a "quick fix" for Tommy's problem or remove him from her class. If this quick fix didn't work, the social worker sensed that she would withdraw even more from constructive involvement with Tommy and push hard for placement.

Intervention. The team assessed that Tommy was doing quite well, considering his history and delicate clinical situation. He might have the capability eventually to deal with his classroom environment under different circumstances. It was worth a try. The team perceived the circular classroom interaction with his teacher. His behavior confirmed the teacher's beliefs. The teacher's negative focus resulted in increased anxiety and problematic behaviors on Tommy's part. In order to stave off placement in a more restrictive environment, the team would offer weekly consultation with the social worker and others on the team and develop with Tommy a classroom behavior modification program with positive reinforcement. Tommy agreed to be responsible for marking a chart on his desk every half-hour when he went to the bathroom whether he felt urgency or not. The parents were willingly involved with this program, supported it, and agreed to do it at home as well. His desire to please adults, for praise, and his discomfort with the problem were powerful reinforcements.

Ms. Brown would be open to some help through consultation, if it could be a positive experience for her. On the other hand, the social worker assessed that, for the reinforcement program to work and for Tommy to be able to remain in a less restrictive environment, Ms. B. needed help in the areas of knowledge, skill, self-confidence, and objectivity. In the realm of knowledge, she needed to understand that many children, even at Tommy's age, do have enuresis in response to stress, but with help many could learn to manage their response to stress. She needed to understand, without going into great detail, that Tommy was doing quite well for what he had experienced. It was his *fear* of losing control of his bodily functions that could trigger a loss of control. The reinforcement program was demanding on her; it was hard for her to focus on teaching and on Tommy at the same time. Using more experienced teachers and normalizing Ms. B's frustration, the team encouraged her to develop skill to manage the program without focusing excessively on Tommy. The team's noncritical, strengths-based approach, together with Tommy's ultimate response, eventually helped Ms. B to draw on her own teaching experience and feel confident that *she* could help Tommy manage. Finally she began to reframe her picture of Tommy, eventually decreasing her belief that he was getting back at her. Taking a nonblaming, problem-solving approach with Ms. B and validating her frustration, together they identified classroom situations that might trigger Tommy's response. She began to see the complexity of the situation and looked at it in a different way. She began to decouple Tommy from her initial perceptions. In the two-and-a-half weeks that the intervention was put in place, Tommy did respond. Incidents of enuresis in school greatly decreased. Tommy's mother reported some progress at home, however, consistent monitoring is difficult due to the parents' work schedules.

The case example, which is real and altered only for confidentiality, is useful. All of Caplan's needs were present and can be traced through the consultation process. There was good will on everyone's part, although it could be quickly lost if the situation were managed poorly, and one person, whether teacher, Tommy, or parents, was made a scapegoat for the inevitable problems. The plan was effective and did work. It is a good example of mental health consultation. Can you identify teachers in your school who may have similar needs in particular situations? How would you work with them? What would be your plan?

Consultation theory is at an early stage of development and many situations are even more complex and difficult than Tommy's. Often there are more complex problems in the school to be dealt with. Some school situations can be difficult, continuous and unyielding, because neither the school social worker nor teacher has the power to change certain conditions. The social worker may have to align with the teacher and administration and work on these problems so that little by little and over a number of years some of these difficult continuing, even unyielding, situations may get better. The following case example points out the complexity of the collaboration consultation situation. How would you conceptualize the following case and manage it?

A CASE EXAMPLE FOR MULTIPLE CONSULTATION MODELS

You are the school social worker at Washington-Lee High School (W&L), which has an enrollment of 1500 students. W&L is located in a large metropolitan community in the mid-Atlantic region, where employment revolves around federal and state government, the military, tourism, national corporations, and private businesses. The high school offers a rigorous academic curriculum that includes many advanced placement courses and the International Baccalaureate Program; however, parents of "students in the middle" have expressed concern about the lack of attention and resources for their children. The school is academically ranked 15 of 150 high schools in the region. At the same time, 37 percent of the student body is eligible for reduced or free lunch. Many of these students are first-generation immigrants from Central America, although the school population is evenly divided among African Americans, Asians, Whites, and Hispanics, with no one group in the majority.

You are a member of the multidisciplinary special education evaluation team. The principal often asks you to help with issues that arise in the high school that are not related to your clinical assessment role. The faculty perceives you as a valuable member of the professional school community and seeks your input on a range of issues. This year you have been asked to serve on the school's cultural diversity committee.

Cas is a 14-year-old freshman. He has been referred to you by his English teacher for academic and behavioral problems. He has great difficulty with term paper assignments and struggles with any form of written expression. In class, Cas has taken the role of class clown and often avoids using class time to draft his papers and, in fact, disrupts the others during this time. In meeting with Cas and his family, you learn the following: Mr. and Mrs. Choudry emigrated from India to the United States ten years ago with their two children. Cas has a younger sister, Sala, who is 12 years old and in the seventh grade. The father is a successful professional, and the mother has remained at home to care for the children. The family has an economically stable, middle-class lifestyle. They have lived in the same neighborhood for the last six years, where they have been well accepted and integrated into a predominately White community. The children have attended private elementary and middle schools in the community. Cas enrolled in the local public school high school, where he hoped to become a member of the cross country team and to compete in regional meets because he is a gifted long distance runner. In the eighth grade, Cas's academic work began to slip. He failed one of the sections of the standards of learning test mandated by the state department of education and required special classes to pass the exam. At the end of the first quarter in high school, he received failing grades in English and History, two Cs and one B. Though Cas entered high school with some of the same classmates from the private middle school he attended, he found himself now being excluded by them. Cas injured his knee at the beginning of the school year and was unable to try out for any fall sports teams. According to his parents, Cas has begun to hang around with the wrong crowd, and they are worried that, in addition to poor academic performance, Cas may get into drugs or into trouble with the law. He refuses to attend religious services with his family. This is very painful for Mr. and Mrs. Choudry, who strongly believe that religion is a central feature of one's daily life activities. Sala is performing well academically, but her mother has noticed that she is no longer invited over to friends as much as she used to be, nor is she inviting classmates to their house. Mr. and Mrs. Choudry do not understand what is happening or how to make things better for their children (Plionis and Sabatino, 1998).

This vignette provides the school social worker with a variety of consultation opportunities. Clinical consultation is required, if Cas is referred for a special education evaluation. Behavior consultation might be useful in changing Cas's classroom actions and mental health consultation might be helpful in expanding the teacher's understanding of Cas's bicultural experiences during adolescent development. Honoring ethnic, racial, and cultural differences among the student population might call for program consultation through the school's cultural diversity committee, while responding to the "students in the middle" might call for organizational consultation at the school system level. Further, there might be the need for interagency collaboration to bring various resources from the community, such as the recreation department, the career center, and private businesses, into the school for enrichment programs and after-school activities. What other consultation models do you think might be applied to this case vignette? Which would be more important, and which less important as you approached this situation?

CONCLUSION

In this age of evidence-based practice, we must document school social work effectiveness. Collaboration and consultation are well-established methods of delivering professional services to students, families, schools, and the communities. The materials presented in this chapter offer a rich conceptual and empirical foundation to guide practice and research in collaboration and consultation.

References

Abramson, J. S., & Rosenthal, B. B. (1995). Interdisciplinary and interorganizational collaboration. In R. L. Edwards and J. G. Hopps (Eds.), *Encyclopedia of social work* (19th ed., Vol. 2; pp. 1479–1489). Washington, DC: National Association of Social Workers Press.

Agresta, J. (2004). Professional role perceptions of school social workers, psychologists, and counselors. *Children & Schools, 26*(3), 151–163.

Allen, S., & Blackston, A. (2003). Training preservice teachers in collaborative problem solving: An investigation of the impact on teacher and student behavior change in real-world settings. *School Psychology Quarterly, 18*(1), 22–51.

Allen-Meares, P. (1994). Social work services in schools: A national study of entry-level tasks. *Social Work, 39*, 560–565.

Allen-Meares, P., Washington, R. O., & Welsh, B. (2000). *Social work services in schools* (3rd ed). Boston: Allyn and Bacon.

Alpert, J. L., & Meyers, J. (1983). *Training in consultation: Perspectives from mental health, behavioral, and organizational consultation.* Springfield, IL: C. C. Thomas.

Altshuler, S. (2003). From barriers to successful collaboration: Public schools and child welfare working together. *Social Work, 48*(1), 52–63.

Anderson-Butcher, D., & Ashton, D. (2004). Innovative models of collaboration to serve children, youths, families and communities. *Children & Schools, 26*(1), 39–54.

Annotated bibliography for the mini-series on multicultural and cross-cultural consultation in schools. (2000). *School Psychology Review, 29*(3), 426–28.

Barker, R. (2003). *The social work dictionary* (5th ed.). Washington, DC: National Association of Social Workers Press.

Bartels, S., & Mortenson, B. (2002). Instructional consultation in middle schools: Description of an approach to training teaches to facilitate middle school teams. *Special Services in the Schools, 18*(1), 1–21.

Berkovitz, I. H., & Sinclair, E. (2001). Training program in school consultation. *Child & Adolescent Psychiatric Clinics of North America, 10*(1), 83–92.

Berlin, I. N. (2001). A retrospective view of school mental health consultation. *Child & Adolescent Psychiatric Clinics of North America, 10*(1), 25–31.

Blake, R., & Mouton, J. S. (1983). *Consultation: A handbook for individual and organization development* (2nd ed.). Reading, MA: Addison-Wesley.

Bostic, J. Q., & Bagnell, A. (2001). Psychiatric school consultation: An organizing framework and empowering techniques. *Child & Adolescent Psychiatric Clinics of North America, 10*(1), 1–12.

Bostic J. Q., & Rauch, P. K. (1999). The 3 R's of school consultation. *Journal of American Academy of Child & Adolescent Psychiatry, 38*(3), 339–341.

Boyle-Del Rio, S., Carlson, R., & Hailbeck, L. (2000). School personnel's perception of the school social worker's role. *School Social Work Journal, 25*(1), 59–76.

Bramlett, R., Murphy, J., Johnson, J., Wallingsford, L, & Hall, J. (2002). Contemporary practices in school psychology: A national survey of roles and referral problems. *Psychology in the Schools, 39*(3), 327–335.

Bronstein, L. (2003). A model for interdisciplinary collaboration. *Social Work, 48*(3), 297–306.

Brown, D., Pryzwansky, W. B., & Schulte, A. C. (2001). *Psychological consultation: Introduction to theory and practice* (5th ed.). Boston: Allyn & Bacon.

Buck, G., Polloway, E., Smith-Thomas, A., & Cox, K. W. (2003). Prereferral intervention processes: A survey of state practices. *Exceptional Children, 69*(3), 349–360.

Caplan, G. (1970). *The theory and practice of mental health consultation.* New York: Basic Books.

Caplan, G., & Caplan, R. (1993). *Mental health consultation and collaboration.* New York: Jossey-Bass.

Carr, L. D. (1976). *Report on survey of social work services in schools.* Washington, DC: National Association of Social Workers. Mimeograph.

Carlson, J., Splete, H., & Kern, R. (Eds.). (1975). *The consulting process.* Washington, DC: American Personnel and Guidance Association.

Conoley, J. C., & Conoley, C. (1992). *School consultation: Practice and training* (2nd ed.). Boston: Allyn and Bacon.

Constable, R., Kuzmickaite, D., Harrison, W. D., & Volkmann, L. (1999). The emergent role of the school social worker in Indiana. *School Social Work Journal, 24*(1), 1-14.

Costin, L. B. (1969). A historical review of school social work. *Social Casework, 50*(8), 439-453.

Cowan, R., & Sheridan, S. (2003). Investigating the acceptability of behavioral interventions in applied conjoint behavioral consultation: Moving from analog conditions to naturalistic settings. *School Psychology Quarterly, 18*(1), 1-21.

Curtis, M. J., & Zins, J. E. (Eds.). (1981). *The theory and practice of school consultation.* Springfield, IL: Thomas.

Curtis, M., Hunley, S., & Grier, J. E. (2002). Relationships among the professional practices and demographic characteristics of school psychologists. *School Psychology Review, 31*(1), 30-42.

Davis, K. (2003). Teaching a course in school-based consultation. *Counselor Education and Supervision, 42*(4), 275-82.

Dinkmeyer, D.C., & Carlson, J. (2001). *Consultation: Creating school-based interventions* (2nd ed.). Philadelphia: Brunner-Routledge.

Donahue, P. J., Falk, B., & Provet, A. G.(2000). *Mental health consultation in early childhood.* Baltimore: Paul H. Brookes Publications.

Dougherty, A. M. (2000). *Psychological consultation and collaboration in school and community settings* (3rd ed.). Australia: Brooks/Cole.

Dryfoos, J., & Maguire, S. (2002). *Inside full-services community schools.* Thousand Oaks, CA: Corwin Press.

Dupper, D. (2002). *School social work: Skills and interventions for effective practice.* Hoboken, NJ: John Wiley & Sons.

Erchul, W. P., & Martens, B. K. (2002). *School consultation: Conceptual and empirical bases of practice* (2nd ed.). New York: Kluwer Academic/Plenum.

Fischer, D., Hoagwood, K., Boyce, C., Duster, T., Frank, D., Grisso, T., et al. (2002). Research ethics for mental health science involving ethnic minority children and youths. *American Psychologist, 54*(12), 1024-1040.

Fowler, E., & Harrison, P. (2001). Continuing professional development needs and activities of school psychologist. *Psychology in the Schools, 38*(1), 75-88.

Gallessich, J. (1982). *The profession and practice of consultation.* San Francisco: Jossey-Bass.

Goldstein, G., & Harris, K. (2000). Consultant practices in two heterogeneous Latino schools. *School Psychology Review, 29*(3), 369-377.

Gottlieb, J., & Polirstok, S. (2005). Program to reduce behavior infractions and referrals to special education. *Children & Schools, 27*(1), 53-57.

Grady, M.A., Gibson, J. J., & Trickett, E. J. (1981). *Mental health consultation, theory practice, and research 1973-78. An annotated reference guide.* (DHHS Publication No. ADM 81-948). Rockville, MD: National Institute of Mental Health.

Graham, J. R., & Barter, K. (1999). Collaboration: A social work practice method. *Families in Society, 80*, 6-13.

Gutkin, T., & Carlson, J. (2001). *Consultation: Creating school-based interventions* (2nd ed.). Florence, KY: Brunner-Routledge.

Henning-Stout, M., & Meyers, J. (2000). Consultation and human diversity: First things first. *School Psychology Review, 29*(3), 419–425.

Hughes, N. (2000). The essential role of theory in the science of treating children: Beyond empirically supported treatments. *Journal of School Psychology, 38*(4), 301–330.

Ingraham, C. (2000). Consultation through a multicultural lens: Multicultural and cross-cultural consultation in schools. *School Psychology Review, 29*(3), 320–343.

Jackson, S., & White, J. (2000). Referrals to the school counselor: A qualitative study. *Professional School Counseling, 3*(4), 277–286.

Jozefowicz-Simbeni, D., & Allen-Meares, P. (2002). Poverty and schools: Intervention and resource building through school-linked services. *Children & Schools, 24*(2), 123–136.

Kadushin, A. (1977). *Consultation in social work.* New York: Columbia University Press.

Kapp, S. (2000). Defining, promoting and improving a model of school social work: The development of a tool for collaboration. *School Social Work Journal, 24*(2), 21–41.

Kerr, M. M. (2001). High school consultation. *Child & Adolescent Psychiatric Clinics of North America, 10*(1), 105–115.

Lewis, T., & Newcomer, L. (2002). Examining the efficacy of school-based consultation: Recommendations for improving outcomes. *Child & Family Behavior Therapy, 24*(1–2), 165–181.

Lopez, S. A., Torres, A., & Norwood, P. (1998). Building partnerships: A successful collaborative experience between social work and education. *Social Work in Education, 20*(3), 165–176.

Luellen, W. (2000). An examination of consultation training in National Association of School Psychology approved programs and its relationship to professional practice. *Dissertation Abstracts, 61*(4-A), 1308.

Luiselli, J. (2002). Focus, scope, and practice of behavioral consultation to public schools. *Child & Family Behavior Therapy, 24*(1–2), 5–21.

Lusky, M. B., & Hayes, R. L. (2001). Collaborative consultation and program evaluation. *Journal of Counseling & Development, 79*(1), 26–38.

Lynn, C., & McKay M. (2001). Promoting parent-school involvement through collaborative practice models. *School Social Work Journal, 26*(1), 1–14.

Lynn, C., McKay, M., & Atkins, M. (2003). School social work: Meeting the mental health needs of students through collaboration with teachers. *Children & Schools, 25*(4), 197–209.

Mannino, F. V. (1969). *Consultation in mental health and related fields: A reference guide.* (PHS Publication No. 1920). Rockville, MD: NIMH.

Mannino, F. V., & MacLennan, B. W. (1978). *Monitoring and evaluating mental health consultation and education services.* (DHEW Publication No. ADM 77-550). Rockville, MD. NIMH.

Mannino, F. V., MacLennan, B. W., & Shore, M. F. (1975). *The practice of mental health consultation.* (DHEW Publication No. ADM 74-112). Rockville MD.

Mannino, F. V., & Shore, M. F. (1971). *Consultation Research in Mental Health and Related Fields: A critical Review of the Literature.* (PHS Publication No. 2122). Rockville, MD. NIMH.

Mannino, V. F., & Shore, M. F. (1979). Evaluation of consultation: Problems and prospects. *New Directions for Mental Health Services, 3*, 99–114.

Mannino, F V., Trickett, E., Shore, M., Kidder, M. G., & Levin, G. (1986). *Handbook of mental health consultation.* DHHS Publication No. ADM 86-1446). Rockville, MD. NIMH.

Martens, B., & Adroin, S. (2002). Training school psychologists in behavior support consultation. *Child & Family Behavior Therapy, 24*(1-2), 147-163.

Matheny, A., & Zimmerman, T. (2001). The application of family systems theory to organizational consultation: A content analysis. *American Journal of Family Therapy, 29*(5), 421-433.

McClung, F., & Stunden, A. (1970). *Mental health consultation to programs for children.* (PHS Publication No. 2066). Rockville, MD. NIMH

McDowell, T. (1999). Systems consultation and Head Start: An alternative to traditional family therapy. *Journal of Marital & Family Therapy, 25*(2), 155-168.

Meares, P.A. (1977). Analysis of tasks in school social work. *Social Work, 22*(3), 196-201.

Meares, P.A. (1982). A content analysis of school social work literature, 1968-1978. In R.T. Constable and J.P. Flynn (Eds.), *School social work: Practice and research perspectives* (pp. 38-41). Homewood, IL: Dorsey.

Metzler, C., Miglan, A., Rusby, J., & Sprague J. (2001). Evaluation of a comprehensive behavior management program to improve school-wide positive behavior support. *Education and Treatment of Children, 24*(4), 448-479.

Meyers, J., Parsons, R. D., & Martin, R. (1979). *Mental health consultation in the schools.* San Francisco: Jossey-Bass.

Mishna, F., & Muskat, B. (2004). School-based group treatment for students with learning disabilities: A collaborative approach. *Children & Schools, 26*(3), 135-150.

Mizrahi, T., & Rosenthal, B. (2001). Complexities of coalition building: Leaders' successes, strategies, struggles, and solutions. *Social Work, 4*(1), 63-78.

Noell, G., Duhon, G., Gatti, S., & Connell, J., (2002). Consultation, follow-up, and implementation of behavior management interventions in general education. *School Psychology Review, 31*(2), 217-234.

New Freedom Commission on Mental Health. (2003). *Executive report.* Washington, DC: Author.

Oppenheimer, J. J. (1925). *The visiting teacher movement with special reference to administrative relationships* (2nd ed.). New York: Joint Committee on Methods of Preventing Delinquency.

Packard, T. (2001). Enhancing site-based governance through organization development: A new role for school social workers. *Children and Schools, 23*(2), 101-113.

Parsons, R. P. (1996). *The skilled consultant: A systemic approach to the theory and practice of consultation.* Boston: Allyn and Bacon.

Plionis, E., & Sabatino, C. (1998). *Personal communication.* Washington, DC: The Catholic University of America.

Raines, J. (2002). Brainstorming hypotheses for functional behavior assessment: The link to effective behavioral intervention plans. *School Social Work Journal, 26*(2), 30-45.

Rapoport, L. (Ed.). (1963). *Consultation in social work practice.* New York: National Association of Social Workers.

Reddy, L.A., Barboza-Whitehead, S., Files, T., & Rubel, E. (2000). Clinical focus of consultation outcome research with children and adolescents. *Special Services in the Schools, 16*(1-2), 1-22.

Reid, W. J. (1979). The model development dissertation. *Social Service Research, 3*(2), 215-225.

Reiman D. W. (1992). *Strategies in social work consultation: From theory to practice in the mental health field.* New York: Longman

Roberts, R., & Greene, G. (2002). *Social workers' desk reference.* New York: Oxford University Press.

Rogers, M. R. (2000). Examining the cultural context of consultation. *School Psychology Review, 29*(3), 414–418.

Rosenberg, M. (2001). Intro to program descriptions. *Teacher Education and Special Education, 24*(3), 262.

Sabatino, C. A. (1986). The effects of school social work consultation on teacher perception and role conflict–role ambiguity in relationship to students with social adjustment problems. *Dissertation Abstracts International, 46*(1), 2443.

Sabatino, C. A. (2001). Family-centered sections of the IFSP and school social work participation. *Children & Schools, 23*(4), 241–251.

Saleeby, D. (1994). Culture, theory, and narrative: The intersection of meanings in practice. *Social Work, 39*(4), 351–359.

Sawka, K., McCurdy, B., & Mannella, M. (2002). Strengthening emotional support services: An empirically based model for training eaches of students with behavior disorders. *Journal of Emotional and Behavioral Disorders, 10*(4), 223–232.

Schein, E. H. (1999). *Process consultation revisited: Building the helping relationship.* Reading, MA: Addison-Wesley Publishing.

Sheridan, S. M. (2000). Considerations of multiculturalism and diversity in behavioral consultation with parents and teachers. *School Psychology Review, 29*(3), 344–353.

Sheridan, S. M., Eagle, J. W., Cowan, R. J., & Mickelson, W. (2001). The effects of conjoint behavior consultation: Results of a 4-year investigation. *Journal of School Psychology, 39*(5), 361–385.

Sperry, L., Kahn, J. P., & Heidel, S. H. (1994). Workplace mental health consultation: A primer of organizational and occupational psychiatry. *General Hospital Psychiatry, 16*(2), 103–11.

Sterling-Turner, H., Watson, T. S., & Moore, J. W. (2002). The effects of direct training and treatment integrity on treatment outcomes in school consultation. *Schools Psychology Quarterly, 17*(1), 47–77.

Thousand, J. S., & Villa, R. A. (1992). Collaborative teams: A powerful tool in school restructuring. In R. A Villa, J. S Thousand, W. Stainback, & S. Stainbeck (Eds.), *Restructuring for caring and effective education* (pp. 73–107). Baltimore: Paul H. Brookes.

Timberlake, E. M., Sabatino, C. A., & Hooper, S. N. (1982). School social work practice and PL 94-142. In R. T. Constable and J. P. Flynn (Eds.), *School social work: Practice and research perspectives* (pp. 49–71). Homewood, IL: Dorsey.

Tindel, G., Parker, R., & Hasbrouck, J. (1992). The construct validity of stages and activities in the consultation process. *Journal of Educational & Psychological Consultation, 3*(2), 99–118.

Tourse, R. W. C., & Mooney, J. F. (Eds.). (1999). *Collaborative practice: School and human service partnerships.* Westport, CT: Praeger.

University of Maryland, School of Medicine, Center for School Mental Health Assistance. (2005). Retrieved August 14, 2005, from http://csmha.umaryland.edu

University of California, Los Angeles, School Mental Health Project, Center for Mental Health in Schools (2005). Retrieved August 14, 2005, from http://www.smhp.psych.ucla.edu

U.S. Department of Education, Office of Special Education Programs, Technical Assistance Center on Positive Behavioral Interventions and Supports (2005). Available from http://www.pbis.org

Watkins, M., Crosby, E., & Pearson, J. (2001). Role of the school psychologist: Perceptions of school staff. *School Psychology International, 22*(1), 64–73.

Wesley, P. (2002). Early intervention consultants in the classroom: Simple steps for building strong collaboration. *Young Children, 57*(4), 30–34.

Wesley, P. W., Buysse, V., & Keyes, L. (2000). Comfort zone revisited: Child characterisitics and professional comfort with consultation. *Journal of Early Intervention, 23*(2), 106-115.

Wilczynski, S. M., Mandal, R. L., & Usuilier, I. (2000). Bridges and barriers in behavioral consultation. *Psychology in the Schools, 37*(6), 495-504.

Wilkinson, L. A. (1999). School-based behavioral consultation: Delivering treatment for children with externalizing behavior problems. *Dissertation Abstracts International, 59*(7-A), 2350.

Wilkinson, L. A (2003). Using behavioral consultation to reduce challenging behavior in the classroom. *Preventing School Failure, 47*(3), 100-105.

Wilson, C. D., & Lubin, B. (1997). *Research on professional consultation and consultation for organizational change.* Westport, CT: Greenwood Press.

Zischka, P. C., & Fox, R. (1985). Consultation as a function of school social work. *Social Work in Education, 7*(2), 69-79.

21

Classroom Observation

Carol Rippey Massat
University of Illinois at Chicago

David Sanders

- ◆ Teaching Styles and Classroom Dynamics
- ◆ The Sanders Classroom Observation Form
- ◆ Recording Event Sampling
- ◆ Observing Multiple Students
- ◆ Observing Teacher Pupil Interactions

Classroom observation is a key assessment tool of the school social worker. School social workers cannot understand a student's educational experience until they understand the concrete interaction that takes place between teacher and child in the context of a class group. When this is understood, assessment becomes faster and more effective, and positive consultation with teachers becomes possible.

TEACHING STYLES AND CLASSROOM DYNAMICS

The experienced school social worker knows that differences in *teaching style* can profoundly affect students' development and learning. Each teacher develops a personal teaching style, compatible with his or her personality, that generally works for certain kinds of students. Some teachers, for example, have a no-nonsense, limit-setting style that lets students know exactly where they stand. Other teachers are less directive, more accepting of differences, but less clear about their expectations. These styles will have different effects on students. At best, the students who do well with one style may do less well with another. Good, experienced teachers may have more than one style, indeed a repertoire of teaching styles to match the needs of different students. They may vary their styles with certain students without undermining their effectiveness with the rest of the class. They may keep students on task in different ways, use other members of the class group to help a student, or manipulate rewards in different ways.

An experienced school social worker also gets to know *classroom dynamics.* Having some formal preparation in group dynamics, the social worker learns to apply this knowledge to the classroom. Just as teachers are different, so is each class different in the dynamics of interaction between its members and the effect of these dynamics on individual students. Group contagion among students with certain behavior problems is particularly challenging to the teacher and dangerous for the educational process. Frequently teachers have no formal training in dealing with the dynamics of the class as a group, and so the problem is particularly disabling.

Understanding how teaching styles and classroom dynamics interact, the social worker needs to examine both in relation to individual students, who may be less responsive to a particular teaching style, or who may become negative targets of classroom dynamics. This examination is a prelude to a more developed understanding of alternative ways of working with classroom dynamics or the needs of individual students.

To acquire this skill, the school social worker needs to spend many hours unobtrusively observing classes. The teacher's permission to do this must be received. Teachers will grant permission willingly only if they see the observation as supportive and helpful to them, as a part of team problem solving, or as a part of a consultative relationship in which teacher and social worker put their heads together to help a student and to assist the teacher to be helpful. Some teachers will resist having school social workers in their classes. Social workers often find themselves beginning with the more personally secure members of the teaching faculty until their confidence and positive reputation increase. As the social worker begins to understand teaching styles and classroom dynamics through observation, work with teachers and students will go more quickly.

The school social worker needs an objective way of understanding the often complex interactions in a classroom and their effects on individual students. The instruments described in this chapter provide ways to measure the behavior of individual students in a classroom context. They provide a useful foundation for a report to the multidisciplinary team but also can be an excellent vehicle for consultation with teachers, helping them match their repertoire of teaching skills to the needs of the classroom situation and the individual students at the same time.

Classroom observations are also used by school social workers when evaluating children with dysfunctional classroom behaviors for eligibility to receive special services, when assisting physicians who are diagnosing attention deficit disorders or measuring the effectiveness of a treatment plan, and when documenting the results of a specific classroom intervention strategy. It is important to know how the target student compares to a particular criterion: for example, he was "aggressive" three times more often than the average student in the room, or his "on-task" performance went from 58 percent to 82 percent after he began a medication regime, or his "off-task" behavior dropped from 32 percent to 18 percent after a new classroom management plan was implemented. This kind of precise information gives practitioners confidence in their decisions and helps them make good decisions.

But classroom observations do not usually produce this kind of precision or uniformity. Typically, an observer—most often a school psychologist, social worker, administrator, or supervisor—arranges to visit a classroom, sits in as unobtrusive a position as possible, observes as long as her schedule permits, and then departs with notes to assess what has happened. The ensuing staffing report goes something like this: "He appeared to be off task much of the time. He fidgeted around a lot in his seat and fiddled with objects in his desk. He got up and moved around the room quite a bit and bothered his neighbor many times. He was certainly more active than the rest of the students."

This format has served well enough, usually because of the integrity of the participants and the needs of the process, but mostly because there are few alternatives. Where this anecdotal and essentially casual approach fails is in its objectivity, reliability, and precision.

This approach is not objective because it allows the observer too much latitude, either intended, coincidental, or subliminal: What, precisely, is "off-task" behavior? How are "fidgeting" and "bothering others" interpreted? And is the observer too much influenced by peripheral issues that may distort the conclusion? For instance, is he or she under pressure from administrators to "do something" with a troublesome student? Is the observer's relationship with the classroom teacher too close, or strained? No matter how mature and professional we think we are, we often respond, sometimes unwittingly, to subtle and disquieting pressures. And in the absence of an objective and standardized observation procedure, they are often difficult to resist.

And reliability? Can the observation process be duplicated, either by new personnel or by the same professional at another time and place, with enough consistency and uniformity to produce meaningful results that can be fairly compared? Criteria for such classroom behaviors as "fidgeting," "bothering others," and being "off task" were mentioned earlier as examples that can have various meanings. This lack of a common reference base can result in misleading conclusions and poor understanding of critical classroom behaviors. Can we expect decision makers to have any faith in our conclusions when our methods are so varied and haphazard?

And precision is totally lacking. How much more "off task" was Jane than Astrid? Was it enough to be significant? And how much more "on task" is Tommy after starting his medication? A lot? Quite a bit? These terms are not helpful and do not build confidence. To ameliorate the present state of confusion and uncertainty with this important diagnostic tool, and to give it some uniformity, consistency, and definition, this chapter suggests an observational procedure.

THE SANDERS CLASSROOM OBSERVATION FORM

The procedure itself is nothing more than the well-established, universally accepted timed-interval technique. But to provide a framework for collecting, organizing, standardizing, and presenting the data, the classroom observation form is introduced (figure 21.1).

The first line of the form has spaces for all pertinent identifying information: the student's name, grade, teacher, school, and the date. Next, the legend gives brief explanations of the four critical student behaviors that will be observed (*on task; off task, passive; off task, active; off task, severe*), as well as two important observations about the classroom (*group on task; transitions*). Starting time, finishing time, notation interval, and observer's identification are noted on the next line.

Conduct the process as follows: First, complete all preliminary consultations with the teacher, administrator, parent, or physician to legitimize the observation. Then, confer again with the classroom teacher to set a date and time, and during these conferences emphasize that you will be measuring time on task and that lessons should be presented as usual and the classroom management plan followed—no special changes should be made just for the observation.

Tell the teacher that you will be observing two students: the target student and a sample student. The sample student should be of the same sex and selected at random from the seating chart. Allow the teacher to veto your selection if he feels the student you have chosen has similar symptoms (e.g., there are often several students in a classroom with attention deficit disorders). After selecting the sample student, decide on a place from which to observe. You should be comfortable and as unobtrusive as possible, and you will need to be in a position to see their facial expressions (you will need all the cues you can get to analyze their behavior).

You will need two classroom observation forms: one for the target student and one for the sample student. Fold the target student's at the top arrows (with the identifying information folded under) and place it over the sample student's at the bottom arrows so that you can easily make entries under "class" and "student" for both. You need to keep the target student's form on top because you will be making frequent notes in the spaces below.

You need to decide on a time interval to record your observations. The more data you collect, the more reliable your conclusion will be, provided of course the data are good. The most comfortable time interval is thirty seconds. This requires a notation every fifteen seconds: one for the target student, then one for the sample student, alternately. At fifteen-second intervals the pace is lively but still manageable, unless you fall behind with your note taking. This interval also allows you to complete the form's one hundred spaces in fifty minutes; this is a good time period for most classrooms, and you can always return for more information later, if needed—and it makes the math calculations easy.

FIGURE 21.1   Classroom Observation Form

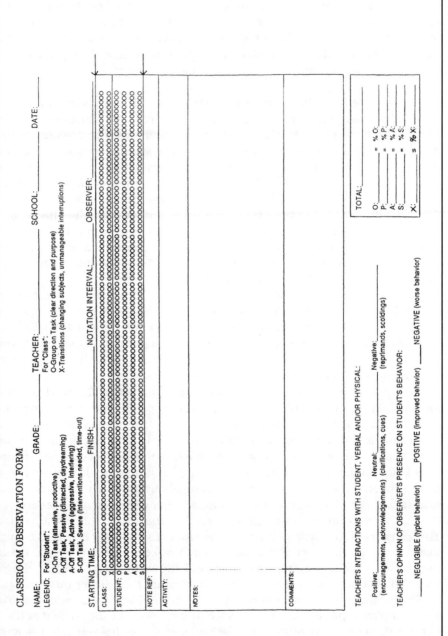

SOURCE: © 1990 David Sanders, LCSW.

Position your timepiece where you can watch the seconds go by. At the minute, observe the target student for a few seconds, make a decision about his or her behavior, then mark the form. At the quarter-minute, do the same for the sample student, and mark his or her form. Then, at the half-minute, go back to the target student. Every fifteen seconds you will be observing either the target student or the sample student, alternating between them, analyzing and categorizing their behavior into one of the four categories mentioned earlier:

1. *On task (attentive, productive).* This is the "O" line under "student." All clues tell you that the student is attending to the given task. Obvious clues, such as thoughtful engagement in completing the assignments or responding to a discussion question, are easy to assess, but others, such as apparent daydreaming or looking about the room, can be misinterpreted. Contextual information will help you make a good decision here. None of your decisions will be isolated from the ones you made thirty seconds earlier; if the student has established a pattern of listening and participating in a discussion, then his sudden, daydreamlike appearance is probably due to his trying to recall the correct response to the question. You will never know, of course, but acknowledging habits and patterns will help you make the best decision possible at each observation interval when the clues are not obvious.

2. *Off task, passive (distracted, daydreaming).* This is the "P" line. All clues here tell you that the student is detached from the given task and has little interest in completing it—the student's mind is somewhere else. Obvious clues are looking about absentmindedly, playing with things in or on the desk, having an unusual preoccupation with his or her thumb, and so forth. The same cautions apply here as for the previous category.

3. *Off task, active (aggressive, interfering).* This is the "A" line. This behavior is usually easy to identify because it is likely to be obvious, at least to you. It often escapes the teacher's attention because the student may be quite clever concealing it until the teacher's back is turned or the student is busy helping other students. Common behaviors that fall under this category are whispering or talking with neighbors; aggravations, teasing, or otherwise disrupting a classmate's attention; being out of seat or moving about the room without permission; talking out, silliness, throwing things, or other classroom disruptions.

4. *Off task, severe (interventions needed, time-out).* This is the "S" line. This category is for those times when the student's behavior is severe enough that the teacher has to confront the student, invoke a time-out, or give a negative consequence to preserve enough control and authority to continue the lesson. As mentioned earlier, it is important to reassure the teacher that you want to observe the student under normal classroom conditions and under the management plan in place. Some teachers feel you need to see the student at his or her worst, so they will allow unruly behavior to go unchecked, but it is more important to see how the student responds to the teacher's classroom methods.

The line for "class" (above the "student" line) is there to record any disruptions in the classroom routine, because only students with exceptional self-discipline and control can remain "on task" when the teacher is distracted. If the task is well defined and the directions are clear, note the "O" line, but when there is an interruption of the lesson and the teacher is preoccupied (such as when the principal interrupts to confer with the teacher, or during transitions to new subjects), note the "X" line. (You will save time by noting the "O" line once and then noting the "X"s only as they occur because there are usually few of them.)

This division of classroom behaviors into four basic categories will suffice for nearly all behaviors you will witness. When you have made your observation and categorized the behavior, darken the circle on the line corresponding to its code letter at the interval. If necessary, you can also make other supplemental notations on the form using the following guidelines:

◆ The line for "note ref" is used to refer to an explanation in the "notes." You may want to describe in detail a particular student behavior so you can refer to it later during your report. These spaces are provided to organize those observations. For example, during one interval you see the student poking his neighbor with a pencil. At that moment you would darken the circle on the "A" line, and in the "note ref" space below it you would jot down a reference number (1, 2, etc.) Then in the space for "notes," you would write, "1. jabbed neighbor with pencil." Usually these details are only important to note for the target student.

◆ The "activity" line is important because it provides a reminder of what the classroom activity was during the observation. But more important, it sometimes gives clues about how students react differently to various teaching methods and learning activities. For instance, it may reveal that the student maintained good attention during a cut-and-paste activity but lost all interest during a classroom discussion, or that the student was on task when doing desk work but became very active during a small-group activity. This kind of information is helpful when planning intervention strategies.

◆ The "comments" space is good for general comments on the observation period and physical classroom features, as well as any unusual events that occurred to minimize or alter the legitimacy of the conclusion.

◆ There is space at the bottom of the form to tally the teacher's interactions with the target student. Positive interactions are clearly encouraging and rewarding. "Good job, Billy." "That's exactly right, Sally." Neutral interactions are informative, inquisitive: "Did you bring your note back, John?" "It's time to put your book away, Doris." Negative interactions are usually reprimands or warnings: "I told you to sit down!" "Put that back in your desk!" Be aware that "interactions" are not just verbal; also count physical interactions (looks, smiles, frowns) when you observe them.

Try to note all interactions you witness, not just the ones that occur during an observation interval.

This information is important for two reasons: first, it reveals the frequency, or lack of, such interactions; second, it reveals the nature (positive, neutral, or negative) of such interactions. This will be helpful when discussing strategies for amelioration, because if positive interactions are infrequent, then a legitimate recommendation can be made to increase them, but if they are frequent, then the teacher can be commended and valuable time can be spent brainstorming other strategies.

The final notation to record is whether the student's behavior during the observation period was typical. Some students love to "perform" for guests while others seem unaware of visitors in the room. When naturally curious students ask, "What are you doing here?" probably the best response is simply to say, "I'm here to visit for a while and I promised Ms. Jones I wouldn't talk to anyone." Check with the teacher on this final question and mark the teacher's response; if the behavior appeared to be much different than typical, you will have to make a decision about how valid the results are.

The table in the lower right-hand corner is to summarize the data you observed and to record the final percentages. As mentioned earlier, this will be easy when all one hundred spaces are used because the calculations can be done quickly; otherwise, a pocket calculator will be useful to speed things up. Because it would be unfair to penalize a student for general class transitions and interruptions, observations made when the class "X" line is noted are overridden and calculated as an "X" percentage.

Another difficult time to assess is when students finish their work and are not sure what to do next. For instance, should the sample student be marked "off task" when he or she completes the work and has nothing to do while the target student is still working on the assignment? Typically, this is when students begin to talk with their neighbors and "active" behaviors begin, even for otherwise compliant students. Most teachers anticipate this with clear directions about what to do when work is finished, but not all. It might be wise to bring this to the teacher's attention before the observation begins. Your previous experiences will be your best guide. Figure 21.2 is an example of a completed classroom observation form.

RECORDING EVENT SAMPLING

Another type of observation is *event sampling* (Boehm & Weinberg, 1987). Event sampling records observations of behaviors each time they occur. Event sampling often involves behaviors that occur infrequently. Time sampling, or observing within a limited time frame, may not capture these behaviors. The school social worker may ask teachers or parents to do event sampling in a given day. Event sampling may be used to record completion of homework,

FIGURE 21.2 Classroom Observation Form

CLASSROOM OBSERVATION FORM

NAME: Billy Student   GRADE: 3   TEACHER: Jones   SCHOOL: Castle Hill   DATE: 9-26-97

LEGEND: For "Student":
- O-On Task (attentive, productive)
- P-Off Task, Passive (distracted, daydreaming)
- A-Off Task, Active (aggressive, interfering)
- S-Off Task, Severe (interventions needed, time-out)

For "Class":
- O-On Task (clear direction and purpose)
- O-Group on Task (clear direction and purpose)
- X-Transitions (changing subjects, unmanageable interruptions)

STARTING TIME: 9:10   FINISH: 10:00   NOTATION INTERVAL: 30 sec   OBSERVER: Smith

ACTIVITY:
| reading (vocabulary) | math (telling time) | math pages (work in group) |

NOTES:
1. distracted (daydreaming symptoms)
2. distracted (playing with pencils) (crayons)
3. whispering to neighbor
4. called on for answer, didn't know
5. out of seat
6. reprimand (back to desk)
7. reprimand (back to work)
8. bothering neighbor
9. time-out

COMMENTS: teacher gave clear directions; tasks were well defined; teacher encouraged on-task behavior; time-out given for "bothering others"; interruption at 9:47 when specialist conferred with teacher.

TEACHER'S INTERACTIONS WITH STUDENT, VERBAL AND/OR PHYSICAL:

Positive: IIII (4)   Neutral: IIII IIII (11)   Negative: II (2)
(encouragements, acknowledgements)   (clarifications, cues)   (reprimands, scoldings)

TEACHER'S OPINION OF OBSERVER'S PRESENCE ON STUDENT'S BEHAVIOR:

X NEGLIGIBLE (typical behavior)   ____ POSITIVE (improved behavior)   ____ NEGATIVE (worse behavior)

TOTAL: 100

O: 47	= % O: 47.9%
P: 26	= % P: 26.9%
A: 16	= % A: 16.9%
S: 7	= % S: 7%
X: 4	= % X: 4%

completion of in-class assignments, or whether a child completes an activity without assistance.A format for an individual child's event sample may be a simple grid, such as tables 21.1 and 21.2.

TABLE 21.1   Event Sample for Individual Child: School Behaviors

Date	Time	Completed spelling	Completed math	Completed language arts

TABLE 21.2   Event Sample for Individual Child: Home Behaviors

Date	Got dressed independently	Got to bus on time independently	Completed homework	Packed all home-work in backpack

Event sampling can also be used by a school social worker to record the acquisition of skills for a group of children or a classroom. For example, the school social worker might record when each child in a social skills group demonstrates a new skill for the first time.Table 21.3 demonstrates an example of a recording format for such an application.

TABLE 21.3   Social Skills Group Skill Acquisition

Child	Greets others	Starts conversation	Requests a behavior change appropriately	Independently makes "I" statements	Takes turn in the group

OBSERVING MULTIPLE STUDENTS

The school social worker may wish to observe the behavior of multiple students in a classroom, or all of the students. In doing so, it is important to have in mind no more than 10 codes for behavior, since trying to recall more than ten codes is difficult to impossible (Medley & Mitzel, 1963). Each code must reflect an exhaustive and mutually exclusive category of behavior, which means that categories cannot overlap and each category must include all the possibilities. Because observing thirty students at a time is unrealistic, it may be useful to observe students in sequence, during a five-minute observation period, and then repeat this process to count the number of behaviors observed in a classroom during a thirty minute period. Table 21.4 is an example of a recording format for this type of observation. For this example, each child in each cluster would be observed in turn for ten seconds. Observations for that child would be recorded, and then this process would be repeated for each time sequence.

TABLE 21.4   Observing Classroom Patterns of Social Behavior

Setting: Social Studies Class, Mr. Smith's fourth grade

Time Period: 9:00 am–9:40 am

Environmental Notes: Classroom is set up with desks in clusters of four. There is a total of six clusters. The class is studying the topic of Jane Addams and the settlement house movement, and each cluster is working on a group project to construct a diorama of Hull House.

Codes: 1 = talking to peer, 2 = listening to peer, 3 = direct aggressive behavior toward peer, 4 = indirect aggressive behavior toward peer, 5 = working, hands on, mutually with peer, 6 = ignoring peer

Child	Time Period								Total
	9:00	9:05	9:10	9:15	9:20	9:25	9:30	9:35	

OBSERVING TEACHER-PUPIL INTERACTIONS

According to Boehm and Weinberg (1987), the Flanders system for *observing teacher-pupil interactions* is the foundation for most current systems of teacher-pupil observations. Flanders categorizes behaviors into ten categories, (Simon & Boyer, 1970, as cited in Boehm & Weinberg, 1987), as shown in table 21.5.

In using the Flanders system, "the observer makes a notation for every change in category and also records one category number at least every three seconds, whether there is a category change or not (Boehm & Weinberg, p. 81). The recording format could simply record the setting, activity, date, and time and then sequentially list the category codes of the interactions that were

TABLE 21.5   Flanders's Categories for Classroom Behavior

Teacher/Student	Category Number	Description
Teacher Talk	1	Accepts pupils's feelings
	2	Prasises or encourages pupils
	2	Accepts pupils' ideas
	4	Asks questions
	5	Lectures
	6	Gives directions
	7	Criticizes or justifies authority
Student Talk	8	Student talk—narrow response
	9	Student talk—broad response
	10	Silence or noise

observed during that time period. The Flanders system is helpful for observing classroom patterns of teacher-student communication and may be helpful in completing a functional behavioral analysis. By observing patterns of teacher-student behaviors, it is likely that the school social worker can identify antecedents and consequences of student behavior in a systematic way.

CONCLUSION

By using standard procedures for classroom observations, social workers and diagnosticians will be able to give intelligent, reliable, precise information about a student's classroom behavior, specifically about time on task. They will be able to present this information in percentages, an easily understood and readily accessible format. Percentages make comparisons with previous observations practical and allow baselines to be established for future comparisons. Observers will be able to repeat the process in a standardized format, which will enhance uniformity and reliability, and they will be able to share these results with other practitioners with the confidence only consistency provides.

References

Boehm, A. E., & Weinberg, R. A. (1987). *The classroom observer: Developing observation skills in early childhood settings*. New York: Teachers College Press.

Medley, D. M., & Mitzel, H. E. (1963). Measuring classroom behavior by systematic observation. In N. L. Gage (Ed.), *Handbook of research in teaching* (pp. 247–328). Chicago: Rand McNally.

Simon, A., & Boyer, E. G. (Eds). (1970). *Mirrors for behavior: An anthology of classroom observation instruments*. Philadelphia: Research for Better Schools.

22

The Assessment of Adaptive Behavior

Richard Van Acker
University of Illinois at Chicago

- ◆ Why Social Workers Do Adaptive Behavior Assessments
- ◆ Defining Adaptive Behavior
- ◆ The Assessment of Adaptive Behavior
- ◆ Reasons for Assessing Adaptive Behavior
- ◆ Common Measures Used in the Assessment of Adaptive Behavior
- ◆ Problems with Current Assessment Measures of Adaptive Behavior

For many years, social workers, psychologists, educators, and others have attempted to identify and measure accurately those behaviors related to competence that distinguish individuals as they interact with their physical and social environments (see Kelly, 1927), that is, assess their adaptive behavior (Schmidt & Salvia, 1984). Adaptive behavior assessments fall into two major types: formal and informal. This chapter will discuss primarily the formal, usually semistructured interview style of assessment. Informal adaptive behavior assessment is discussed in chapter 19. Understanding how individuals adapt themselves to the requirements of their physical and social environment is the goal of many of our social sciences. The ability to function effectively across a range of adaptive skill areas is essential for personal success and adjustment in life. Maximizing adaptive behavior skills for individuals with physical, mental, or emotional challenges is often a goal for social work intervention. Thus, the construct of adaptive behavior is becoming increasingly important in the identification and treatment of individuals with various disabilities, such as cognitive impairments, emotional disturbance, and mental impairments. The American Association on Mental Deficiency (AAMD), formerly the AAMR (AAMD and AAMR will be used interchangeably in this chapter, depending on the date of the citation), is the international leader in the conceptualization, definition, and classification of mental retardation. This organization has included adaptive behavior as a critical factor in defining mental retardation since the late 1950s (Heber, 1959, 1961).

WHY SOCIAL WORKERS DO ADAPTIVE BEHAVIOR ASSESSMENTS

Social workers have assessed people's functioning in their various environments throughout the history of the profession. Assessments are made in comparison to others in the same cohort, controlling for age, gender, ethnicity, community, environment, socioeconomic status, and any perceived or suspected disabilities, as well as other defining characteristics. For most people, functional abilities are relatively stable across various settings, however, for some there is significant variation. Describing this variability is an essential component of a social developmental study and is identified as the adaptive behavior assessment. It is important that in school settings the social worker take responsibility for adaptive behavior assessments, for three reasons:

1. Social workers are well trained in the interviewing process.
2. The professional focus of social work is the functioning of persons in an environment. The central theme of social work practice is improving the fit between the person and the environment.
3. Finally, one of the fundamental concepts, and indeed requirements, of the Individuals with Disabilities Education Act (IDEA, PL 105-17) is the multidisciplinary approach to assessment and decision making in determining each referred student's learning needs.

Thus, both through training and theoretical framework, the adaptive behavior assessment falls well within the professional responsibility of the social worker.

DEFINING ADAPTIVE BEHAVIOR

Over the past three decades, there has been much discussion and frequent professional disagreement regarding what specifically constitutes adaptive behavior (Clausen, 1967; Gresham, MacMillan, & Siperstein, 1995; Halpern, 1968; McGrew & Bruininks, 1989, 1990; Zigler, Balla, & Hadapp, 1984). At this time, there is no single definition of adaptive behavior that is universally agreed on in the professional community (MacMillan, Gresham, & Siperstein, 1992; 1995). Adaptive behavior reflects the ability to meet the immediate physical and social demands of the environment as well as prepare for probable future environments. Adaptive behaviors are those that allow the individual to live successfully, avoid life-threatening dangers, and interact with the physical and social environment in a manner that is safe. Effective adaptive behavior skills will allow a person to thrive and to find acceptance within his/her social environment.

What behaviors or skills are important to measure when assessing adaptive behavior? The current AAMD definition for mental retardation, which is perhaps the most widely held, identifies ten critical adaptive skill areas: (1) communication, (2) self-care, (3) home living, (4) social skills, (5) community use, (6) self-direction, (7) health and safety, (8) functional academics, (9) leisure, and (10) work (American Association on Mental Retardation [AAMR], 1992). One major criterion for the identification of mental retardation calls for limitations in two or more of these adaptive skill areas (AAMR, 1992).

This is a rather comprehensive list of adaptive skill areas that includes behaviors that are difficult to assess reliably given the current status of our measures. One can conclude that adaptive behavior is an inherently developmental and social construct and that these skills change over time and are defined at least in part by interpersonal, environmental, and societal expectations.

Adaptive Behavior as a Function of Age

The age of the target individual must be considered when assessing adaptive behavior. When assessing adaptive behavior, the person completing the measure must take care to be sensitive to the realities of child development. As most assessment measures call for the respondent to rate the frequency with which the target individual displays a given behavior (e.g., usually, sometimes, never, or seldom), knowledge of what is developmentally appropriate is assumed. Only a subset of the ten adaptive skill areas identified by the AAMD may be relevant at a given age. For example, when one is assessing early elementary-age students, the skills related to work will be significantly less important than issues related to functional academics, communication, and self-care (Gresham et al., 1995; Reschly, 1987). The nature of the expectations placed on the individual for the display of adaptive behavior changes dramatically over the life span. As children grow, assessment of adaptive behavior targets learned behavior. We expect young children to communicate socially with others and to demonstrate social skills as they play together. We anticipate that children will demonstrate increased independence in self-care (e.g., dressing, feeding), community use (e.g., mobility in their neighborhood), self-direction, and engagement in leisure time activities as they mature. With adolescence come expectations for eventual transition into the adult world of work.

Adaptive Behavior as a Function of Cultural Expectations

Cultural awareness and sensitivity play a critical role in the assessment of adaptive behavior. Culture, by definition, affects the display of language, behavior, and beliefs. For example, some cultures support personal independence and individual achievement more so than others. The age at which children are expected to display specific behaviors related to self-care, self-direction, and independent community use differ dramatically across cultures. The respondent must be aware of the cultural expectations of the individual being assessed. Moreover, the validity of the score obtained will depend on the similarity or difference of the person being assessed to those individuals included within the normative sample of the measure being employed. That is, if the target individual differs significantly in level of acculturation from those individuals used to norm a particular measure, the score should be interpreted with great care.

Adaptive Behavior as a Function of the Environment

Successful adaptation requires a good "person-environment fit." The individual's capabilities must match the environmental demands. The concept of environment in the assessment of adaptive behavior includes those specific settings in which the individual functions, in particular the home, school, work, and community environments. What is considered adaptive in one environment may prove maladaptive in another. A behavior that proves adaptive in a rural setting may have quite a different outcome in an urban setting. For example, as children mature, greater independence and greater self-directed mobility within and between neighborhoods in the community are expected. For many children growing up in the inner cities of our large urban centers, such mobility might significantly increase the personal danger to which these children are exposed. Movement through rival gang territories can lead to confrontation, assault, and death. Therefore, increased mobility and independence could be viewed as maladaptive in some contexts.

The Assessment of Maladaptive Behaviors

The inclusion of maladaptive behavior in measures of adaptive behavior often increases the confusion and difficulty in the interpretation of findings. Like adaptive behavior, maladaptive behavior suffers from a lack of a clear and agreed-on definition. For obvious reasons, the identification of maladaptive behavior is important in its own right. The relation of adaptive to maladaptive behavior, however, is not that of behaviors at opposite ends of a continuum. In fact, these behaviors can appear to exist quite independently of one another. An individual can display both adaptive and maladaptive behavior in the same area. For example, many individuals who practice many acts of great care in the area of health and safety (e.g., good diet and exercise) also will engage in significant levels of substance abuse (e.g., smoking and alcohol consumption). Moreover, the absence of maladaptive behavior does not imply the presence of adaptive behavior.

THE ASSESSMENT OF ADAPTIVE BEHAVIOR

Adaptive behavior is measured across multiple environmental settings using typical, everyday functioning rather than optimal performance. Adaptive behaviors are those that are performed regularly (habitually and customarily), spontaneously, and without prompting or assistance from others. When assessing adaptive behavior, we are not interested in what the target individual can do (ability), but rather what the individual typically does (performance). This is an important and often misunderstood distinction. Often individuals who have the knowledge and skills necessary to perform a given response however fail to do so routinely in their everyday interactions with their environment. For example, a student might know how to solve a given social problem (e.g., peer conflict) in an acceptable fashion (e.g., verbally expressing his feelings in a calm manner). However, when confronted with a peer conflict, the student might routinely respond with aggression. The assessment of his adaptive behavior is not aimed at the discovery of his potential response (verbal problem solving), but rather at a measure of his typical response (aggression). Behaviors are rated as performed regularly (habitually and customarily). Moreover, behaviors must be displayed spontaneously without prompting or assistance from others.

Adaptive behavior information may be gathered either through a standardized measure or through observations and interviews as a more qualitative assessment. IDEA does not specify that standardized measures are required to make an adaptive behavior assessment. Informal adaptive behavior assessments can bring an understanding of the effect of environmental conditions and cultural background on behavior, as well as the school social worker's professional judgment. Informal or qualitative assessments can be used to assess a child's functioning in the classroom and compare this to his or her functioning in other settings. The child's age and sociocultural background are, of course, essential ingredients in such an informal assessment, as they are in formal assessments. Areas of functioning include independent functioning, personal responsibility, and social responsibility. For each of these areas, the school social worker needs to determine whether the child has necessary skills to function at his/her grade level.

Adaptive behavior is most often assessed using a formal, standardized instrument. The report comes from an interview with a third person (respondent) and this in turn generates a standardized rating of a target individual. Rather than employing systematic observation of the behavior of the target individual, the examiner relies on the cumulative observations of a respondent who is familiar with the target individual. This method of assessment is susceptible to various types of limitations, errors, and biases. The respondents are limited to those behaviors they have had the opportunity to observe. Often different respondents will observe individuals in only a limited number of contexts (e.g., the school classroom, the lunchroom, the home setting). Students will often display quite different behavior in these various contexts. Thus, assessments provided by different respondents can report significantly divergent results.

There also is a concern that respondents can differ significantly in their awareness and/or tolerance for some behaviors. Most assessments of adaptive behavior ask respondents to rate on a scale the frequency or seriousness of various behaviors with an underlying assumption that respondents will employ a similar standard. Thus, there is an assumption that one respondent's "sometimes" is assumed to differ from another respondents "usually." This may not be a safe assumption.

Another problem results from the method used to calculate the target individual's scores (subscale, domain, and composite scores). These scores are obtained by assigning numbers (e.g., 0, 1, or 2) to the various ratings and manipulating these numbers mathematically. Remember, what are really being added are subjective ratings (e.g., a "sometimes" + a "usually" + a "seldom" = _____). This should be kept in mind as one interprets the results of any assessment.

Another concern with the traditional approach to assessing adaptive behavior is that the individual being assessed may conceal important behaviors from the respondent, perhaps due to cultural demands, fear of consequences, or other personal agendas. Thus, the respondent may not report the presence of a potentially important adaptive or maladaptive behavior; or a respondent might be less than truthful when completing an assessment. This is especially true if the respondent has a stake in the outcome. For example, parents might be more willing to give their child the benefit of the doubt or provide responses based on ability rather than typical performance if they are concerned that their child might be classified as mentally retarded or emotionally disturbed. On the other hand, a teacher might be inclined to magnify the frequency or magnitude of a maladaptive behavior if it will increase the likelihood of removing a particularly challenging child from the classroom setting.

Given these potential limitations, errors, and biases, the examiner is advised to seek information and assessments of adaptive behavior from multiple people across a variety of settings within which the target individual interacts. The goal of multiple measurements of adaptive behavior is the identification of patterns in responding and the development of a reliable understanding of the target individual's adaptive and maladaptive behavior. As mentioned previously, however, multiple ratings by third parties can often produce significantly disparate profiles for the target individual. One procedure recommended in the 1992 AAMR manual for reconciling disagreements among third-party respondents in assessing adaptive behavior and reducing error is to average ratings. Most measures of adaptive behavior are designed to be administered individually, that is, each respondent is to complete the measure independently. Thus, to assess a child's adaptive behavior in the school, a given measure might be completed by two or three relevant teachers independent of one another. The teachers are not to discuss the child and then provide a response that constitutes the consensus of the group. The same is true for assessments by parents.

Each should complete an independent rating of the child. Specifically, the 1992 AAMR manual states: "The use of at least two raters to score an individual on the same scale and derivation of an average of the results will increase the validity of the results" (p. 43). This statement has come under considerable attack as being psychometrically incorrect (Gresham et al., 1995). The averaging of two disparate scores does nothing to reduce measurement error and does not assist in the achievement of consensus. Perhaps a better strategy involves collecting additional data, such as additional third-party ratings, direct observational data, and anecdotal records and engaging in a triangulation of the data to identify consistent patterns of behavior. One has to keep in mind that disparate ratings do not necessarily indicate error but could signal the differential behavior of an individual in various settings and/or similar settings with different people (respondents).

REASONS FOR ASSESSING ADAPTIVE BEHAVIOR

There are a number of reasons for assessing adaptive behavior. One of the most frequently used reasons involves the identification or clarification of an individual's skills and deficits when attempting to determine if a disability exists. As mentioned earlier, the AAMR (1992) definition of mental retardation states:

> Mental retardation refers to substantial limitations in present functioning. It is characterized by significantly subaverage intellectual functioning, existing concurrently with related limitations in two or more of the following applicable adaptive skill areas: communication, self-care, home living, social skills, community use, self-direction, health and safety, functional academics, leisure, and work. Mental retardation manifests before age 18. (p. 1)

In response to this definition, federal regulations and state school codes began to require that adaptive behavior be assessed before a pupil could be considered eligible for special education services under the category of mental retardation or cognitive impairment. Adaptive behavior also is typically assessed for students being considered for other types of disabilities. For example, when the possibility of an emotional disturbance is being explored, an assessment of adaptive and maladaptive behavior is frequently recommended.

Another reason for assessing adaptive behavior relates to program planning. The reauthorization of the Individuals with Disabilities Education Act in 1997 specified the need to develop educational objectives and behavior management plans for students with disabilities whose behavior interferes with their own learning or that of others. Thus, the assessment of both adaptive and maladaptive behavior has an increased level of importance in the identification of target behaviors. This legislation also specifies increased responsibility in the development of educational objectives to promote the transition of students with disabilities into the workplace. Again, the assessment of adaptive behavior can play an important role in the identification of appropriate goals and objectives.

COMMON MEASURES USED IN THE
ASSESSMENT OF ADAPTIVE BEHAVIOR

In the next section of this chapter, a number of the most frequently used measures of adaptive behavior are reviewed (table 22.1). The 1992 AAMR manual clearly states that a valid determination of adaptive skills requires the use

TABLE 22.1 Common Measures of Adaptive Behavior

Measure (Authors)	Age Range	Informant	Type of Measure
AAMD Adaptive Behavior Scale: Interview (Nihira, Leland, & Lambert, 1993)	18–79 years	Staff member or other professional	Interview questionnaire
AAMD Adaptive Behavior Scale: School 2 (Nihira, Leland, & Lambert, 1993)	3–21 years	Teacher	Interview questionnaire
Adaptive Behavior Inventory (Brown & Leigh, 1986)	6 years to 18 years, 11 months	Teacher	Interview questionnaire
Scales of Independent Behavior-Revised (Bruininks, Woodcock, Weatherman, & Hill, 1996)	3 months to 90 years	Parent, teacher, or significant other	Interview checklist
Vineland Adaptive Behavior Scales-Interview Edition (Sparrow, Balla, & Cicchetti, 1984a, 1984b)	Birth to 18 years, 11 months	Parent or significant other	Interview
Vineland Adaptive Behavior Scales-Classroom Edition ((Sparrow, Balla, & Cicchetti, 1984a, 1984b)	3 years to 12 years, 11 months	Teacher	Checklist

"of an adaptive skill assessment to evaluate the person's adaptive skill profile on an appropriately normed and standardized instrument" (p. 25). The purpose of this section, therefore, is to familiarize the reader with some of these measures and to point out some of the important features related to scoring the measure, the normative samples available for interpretation, and critical psychometric properties of the measure. This information should help the reader select the appropriate measure for a specific need and aid in the interpretation of results.

AAMD Adaptive Behavior Scales (ABS)

As an organization, the AAMR has developed its own rating scale, titled Adaptive Behavior Scales (ABS), which correlates with the ten behaviors they identify as crucial. The revised ABS are composed of a school edition—The AAMR Adaptive Behavior Scale-School 2 (ABS-S2) (Nihira, Leland, & Lambert, 1993); and a Residential and Community edition—the AAMR Adaptive Behavior Scale: Residential and Community Scale, 2nd edition. Both are individually administered measures. The school edition is designed for children and youth ages 3 to 21 years, while the residential and community version is normed for individuals aged 18 to 79. The ABS has undergone numerous revisions since first introduced in 1969. The latest versions comprise items selected from previous editions based on the items' interrater reliability and their ability to discriminate among various levels of adaptation.

The Residential and Community version of the ABS was standardized on 4,103 individuals with developmental disabilities stratified on living arrangements (living at home, small group home, community-based residence, and large institution). Sample members represented individuals from forty-six states and the District of Columbia and were predominantly between the ages of 18 and 39. The norm sample was generally representative of the nation as a whole with regard to race, ethnicity, and geographical region.

Adaptive Behavior Inventory

The Adaptive Behavior Inventory (ABI; Brown & Leigh, 1986) is an individually administered, norm-referenced measure to assess the behavior of students who range in age from 6 to 18 years. The typical respondent when using the ABI is the target student's classroom teacher or other professional with whom the child frequently interacts. The ABI is specifically developed to explore the adaptive behavior skills of a given target individual. Both a full-scale and a short form (sometimes referred to as a "screening" instrument) of the ABI are available.

Two distinct samples were used to develop norms for the ABI. One sample was made up of students with mental retardation from special education programs or residential facilities. The second norm sample included students representing the general U.S. population. The methods used to identify participants for these samples are poorly described, and much of the information needed to evaluate the quality of the norm samples is not provided in the test manual.

Scales of Independent Behavior-Revised

The Scales of Independent Behavior-Revised (SIB-R; Bruininks, Woodcock, Weatherman, & Hill, 1996) is an individually administered measure to be used with individuals aged 3 months through 90 years. There are three forms of the SIB available: the full-scale form, the short form, and the early development form. The short form of the SIB-R is intended to serve as a screening device and consists of 40 items selected from the 259 items of the full-scale version. The early development form has been developed to assess "the development of preschoolers and the adaptive skills of youths or adults with serious disabilities" (Bruininks et al., 1996, p. 16). The SIB-R is specifically intended to be used to assess independent functioning within various settings such as the home, school, community, or workplace. The SIB-R lends itself well to purposes such as the establishment of appropriate instructional goals, making placement decisions, and evaluating program outcomes. This measure is frequently employed for both clinical and research purposes.

The SIB-R is normed on a sample of 2,182 individuals ranging in age from three months to ninety years of age. Norms are a composite of those established for the first edition of this measure (N = 1,764) and a separate standardization conducted for the revised edition (N = 418). The sample approximates the population as specified in the 1990 U.S. census in terms of gender, race, and community size.

Vineland Adaptive Behavior Scales (VABS)

The Vineland Adaptive Behavior Scales (VABS) result from a significant revision and update of the Vineland Social Maturity Scale (VSMS; Doll, 1935, 1965), which was completed in 1984. The VABS is administered individually and is completed by a respondent familiar with the target individual. There are three separate forms of the VABS, each with its own technical manual. Two of the forms are termed interview editions: the expanded form (Sparrow, Balla, & Cicchetti, 1984a) and the survey form (Sparrow, Balla, & Cicchetti, 1984b). The survey form includes fewer items than the expanded interview form and consequently requires less administration time. Interviews are conducted in a semistructured format with the interviewer asking questions in her own words to probe the respondent about the target individual's functioning (rather than simply reading the interview items). When the interviewer has gathered enough information about a given skill area, she rates the individual on the scale's items. Thus, the VABS requires that the interviewer gain familiarity with the instrument before administering it and provides a manual with a good deal of data about scoring the items. The interview forms of the VABS are designed for assessment of children from birth to 18 years. The third form of the VABS provides a classroom edition of the measure (Harrison, 1985). This printed survey is completed by the student's teacher and requires approximately twenty minutes. This edition is suitable for children ages 3 to 12 years.

Depending on the form employed, a variety of norming groups were employed for the VABS. The interview editions were standardized with a national sample of 3,000 individuals ranging in age from newborn to 18 years, 11 months. The classroom edition was normed on 1,984 children between the ages of 3 and 12 years, 11 months. These samples were selected to represent the population of the United States as described by the 1980 Census with respect to racial/ethnic group. The sample was unrepresentative with regard to geographical region (underrepresenting the north central region), community size (underrepresenting the rural communities), and parental education (overrepresenting of parents with a college education). A supplementary sample of individuals with disabilities was employed also for the interview editions. This sample included individuals with mental retardation, emotional disturbance, visual impairment, and hearing impairment. These supplementary norms are not described very well but must be employed when exploring the maladaptive behavior domain (Part 2).

PROBLEMS WITH CURRENT ASSESSMENT MEASURES OF ADAPTIVE BEHAVIOR

A number of concerns should be acknowledged related to our current efforts at assessing adaptive behavior. To date, relatively few adaptive behavior scales have adequate national norms and sufficient psychometric qualities to warrant use in diagnostic and placement decisions (Gresham et al., 1995; Kamphaus, 1987).

The Ability to Assess Potential Adaptive Behavior Domains

The AAMR definition specifies ten adaptive skill areas that should be considered when attempting to assess a child suspected of displaying cognitive impairments. Again, these ten adaptive skill areas are: (1) communication, (2) self-care, (3) home living, (4) social skills, (5) community use, (6) self-direction, (7) health and safety, (8) functional academics, (9) leisure, and (10) work. The 1992 definition specifies, "if two or more adaptive skill limitations fall substantially below the average level of functioning (as determined by either formal comparison to a normative sample or through professional judgment), then the individual would meet this second criterion for a diagnosis of mental retardation" (p. 49). In 1985, Holman and Bruininks conducted a content classification analysis of thirteen adaptive behavior scales. They identified forty-five content areas and concluded that these scales vary markedly in content coverage. For the most part, each of the adaptive behavior scales currently available appears to measure a general personal independence factor. None of these measures, however, provides a comprehensive coverage of potential adaptive behavior domains (McGrew & Bruininks, 1989).

SUMMARY

The assessment of adaptive behavior is an increasingly important activity for teachers, social workers, and psychologists. When assessing adaptive behavior, the examiner is generally interested in how well a target individual meets the needs of his or her physical and social environment. Does the individual function well enough not to represent a significant risk to self or others? Unfortunately, there is a lack of agreement as to exactly which behaviors need to be assessed. Adaptive behavior is greatly influenced by societal expectations. The developmental level and cultural heritage of the individual must be taken into consideration when assessing adaptive behavior.

Adaptive behavior is usually not measured directly, but rather through information provided by a third-party respondent familiar with the target individual. When assessing adaptive behavior, one is interested in what the target individual does on a regular basis (not on what the individual can demonstrate under optimal conditions). The assessment of adaptive behavior suffers from a lack of adequate measures. There is a lack of reliability across many of the subscales in the various measures that results in serious error measurement. Moreover, the norms available are often inadequate.

Care must be taken when selecting measures for assessing adaptive behavior. Examiners may wish to select scales, or subscales, from any number of measures to maximize the validity and reliability of the results. When conducting an assessment of adaptive behavior, seek multiple respondents who are very familiar with the target individual. Look for patterns of behavior displayed in the target individual as reported across respondents. When behavior varies across respondents the evaluator attempts to identify elements in the contexts assessed that might affect behavior. The ultimate goal of an assessment of adaptive behavior is to identify both the strengths and deficits displayed by an individual as she interacts with the world. With care and understanding of the potentials as well as the limitations of current measures of adaptive behavior, one can proceed to identify possible areas of both adaptive and maladaptive behavior.

References

American Association on Mental Retardation (AAMR). (1992). *Mental retardation: Definition, classification, and systems of supports* (9th ed.). Washington, DC: Author.

Brown, L., & Leigh, J. (1986). *Adaptive behavior inventory manual.* Austin, TX: Pro-Ed.

Bruininks, R., Woodcock, R., Weatherman, R., & Hill, B. (1996). *Scales of independent behavior, revised, comprehensive manual.* Chicago, IL: Riverside Publishing Company.

Clausen, J. (1967). Mental deficiency: Development of a concept. *American Journal of Mental Deficiency, 71,* 727-745.

Doll, E. A. (1935). A genetic scale of maturity. *The American Journal of Orthopsychiatry 5,* 180-188.

Doll, E. A. (1965). *Vineland social maturity scale* (rev. ed.). Minneapolis, MN: American Guidance Service.

Gresham, F. M., MacMillan, D. L., & Siperstein, G. N. (1995). Critical analysis of the 1992 AAMR definition: Implications for school psychology. *School Psychology Quarterly, 10,* 1-19.

Halpern, A. (1968). A note on Clausen's call for a psychometric definition of mental deficiency. *American Journal of Mental Deficiency, 72,* 948-949.

Harrison, P. (1985) *Vineland adaptive behavior scales: Classroom edition manual.* Circle Pines, MN: American Guidance Service.

Heber, R. (1959) A manual on terminology and classification in mental retardation. *American Journal of Mental Deficiency,* Monograph Supplement (Rev.). *56*

Heber, R. (1961). Modifications in the terminology and classification in mental retardation. *American Journal of Mental Deficiency, 65,* 499-500.

Holman, J., & Bruininks, R. (1985). Assessing and training adaptive behaviors. In K. Lakin & R. Bruininks (Eds.), *Strategies for achieving community integration of developmentally disabled citizens* (pp. 73-104). Baltimore: Paul H. Brookes.

Kamphaus, R. W. (1987). Conceptual and psychometric issues in the assessment of adaptive behavior. *Journal of Special Education, 21*(1), 27-35.

Kelly, T. (1927). *Interpretation of educational measurements.* Yonkers, NY: World Book.

MacMillan, D. L., Gresham, F. M., & Siperstein, G. N. (1992). Conceptual and psychometric concerns about the 1992 AAMR definition of mental retardation. *American Journal on Mental Retardation, 98,* 325-335.

MacMillan, D. L., Gresham, F. M., & Siperstein, G. N. (1995). Heightened concerns over the 1992 AAMR definition: Advocacy versus precision. *American Journal on Mental Retardation, 100,* 87-97.

McGrew, K., & Bruininks, R. (1989). Factor structure of adaptive behavior. *School Psychology Review, 18,* 64-81.

McGrew, K., & Bruininks, R. (1990). Defining adaptive and maladaptive behavior within a model of personal competence. *School Psychology Review, 19*, 53–73.

Nihira, K., Leland, H., & Lambert, N. (1993). *Examiner's manual, AAMR adaptive behavior scale-residential and community* (2nd ed.). Austin, TX: Pro-Ed.

Reschly, D. J. (1987). *Adaptive behavior in classification and programming with students who are handicapped*. St. Paul, MN: Minnesota Department of Education.

Schmidt, M., & Salvia, J. (1984). Adaptive behavior: A conceptual analysis. *Diagnostique, 9*, 117–125.

Sparrow, S., Balla, D., & Cicchetti, D. (1984a). *Interview edition, expanded form manual, Vineland adaptive behavior scales*. Circle Pines, MN: American Guidance Service.

Sparrow, S., Balla, D., & Cicchetti, D. (1984b). *Interview edition, survey form manual, Vineland adaptive behavior scales*. Circle Pines, MN: American Guidance Service.

Zigler, E., Balla, D., & Hadapp, R. (1984). On the definition and classification of mental retardation. *American Journal of Mental Deficiency, 89*, 215–230.

23

Inclusive Education and the Least Restrictive Environment (LRE)

Shirley McDonald
University of Illinois at Chicago

Robert Constable
Loyola University, Chicago

William Holley
School District 135

- ◆ The Least Restrictive Environment (LRE) and Inclusion
- ◆ Continuum of Alternative Placements
- ◆ Types of Integration
- ◆ Full Inclusion and the Regular Education Initiative
- ◆ What Do General Education Teachers Need for LRE?
- ◆ Prereferral Consultation: The Problem-Solving Team
- ◆ The Process of Making Placement Decisions: The IEP Team
- ◆ The Social Worker's Role in the Development and Maintenance of the LRE
- ◆ Preparations for Inclusion of a New Student
- ◆ Transition Planning

The policy that children with disabilities are to be educated with children without disabilities demands from the social worker a full range of skills: assessment, teamwork, consultation, planning, and intervention skills. Assessment for the least restrictive environment (LRE) demands an understanding, arrived at within the team, of the range of possibilities available to a pupil in the educational environment. These questions become the focus of the assessment: What are the pupil's general needs? What are her learning needs? What educational resources can she deal with and use? What responsibilities fall to the team, the school, and the family? What joint planning needs to emerge from this discussion? What process should take place within and between all of these to maintain the pupil in the least restrictive environment? The least restrictive environment may be a normalized environment, but it may be more stressful, and without appropriate supports it could be beyond her capabilities. The social worker consults with others, as a team member, and intervenes wherever it is necessary as a clinician or a case manager. The goal is that over time the pupil becomes able to adapt dynamically to an education environment and to learning tasks. The practice concepts are complex and fluid. They involve a sequence of the unfolding transactions of a pupil with a broader learning and family environment. The tasks inherent to integration and inclusion provide a natural focus for a school social worker. They are a good example of the processes of assessment, planning, and teamwork outlined in previous chapters.

THE LEAST RESTRICTIVE ENVIRONMENT (LRE) AND INCLUSION

To carry out the tasks just outlined, it is most important to develop a clear understanding of terms and definitions. The law defines LRE as:

> To the maximum extent appropriate, children with disabilities . . . are educated with children who are nondisabled, and that special classes, separate schooling, or other removal of children with disabilities from the regular education environment occurs only if the nature or severity of the disability is such that education in regular classes with the use of supplementary aids and services cannot be achieved satisfactorily. (20 U.S.C. 1412[a][5]; 34 C.F.R. 300.550)

The word *inclusion* is not to be found anywhere in the Individuals with Disabilities Education Act (IDEA) legal mandate. However, the principle of inclusion, the basis for various state (SEA) mandates for inclusion, can be found in two places. In IDEA, it can be found in a presumption that the child with disabilities should participate, to the maximum extent appropriate, in the general education curriculum. Reflecting this presumption, IDEA requires the individualized educational program (IEP) to explain the extent, if any, to which the child will not participate with children without disabilities in regular classes and in extracurricular and other nonacademic activities (20 U.S.C. 1414). This definition is developed further in a classic statement by Turnbull and Turnbull (1998) that the schools must include the student in the general education program and may not remove a student from it unless the student cannot benefit from being in that program, even after the provision of supplementary aids and services and necessary related services.

The use of the term *benefit* can create a problem. A pupil may derive benefit from something that may not be geared to his particular needs, that is, it may not be the most appropriate for him. He might derive more benefit from a more appropriate setting, or more appropriate objectives or learning tasks. This open-ended use of language creates the need for discussion among the team and with the parents and a systematic determination of what is most appropriate. This also can create confusion. The presumption of the law, however, is that, unless another environment can be justified as more appropriate, the general education environment, with supplementary aids and services, if needed, is the preferred site of learning.

CONTINUUM OF ALTERNATIVE PLACEMENTS

The concept of a *continuum of alternative placements* provides language to differentiate levels of restrictiveness. Federal regulations mandate that a continuum of alternative placements be available to children with disabilities. The following continuum is drawn from the law (20 U.S.C.1412[a]5), federal regulations (34 C.F.R.300.26), and the Illinois Administrative Code (23 Ill. Admin. Code Ch.I, 226.300). The alternative placements range on a continuum from the least to the most restrictive:

- ◆ *Instruction in regular classes.* The child receives basic educational experience through instruction in regular classes. However, these experiences are modified through:
  a. Additional or specialized education from the teacher,
  b. Consultation to and with the teacher,
  c. Provision of special equipment, materials, and accommodations,
  d. Modification in the instructional program (e.g., multiage placement, grading),
  e. Modification of curriculum content or education methodology, and
  f. Other supplementary services, such as itinerant or resource services in conjunction with the regular class placement.
- ◆ *Instruction in special classes.* The child receives specially designed instruction through a special education class; the child is included in those parts of regular classes that are appropriate.
- ◆ *Instruction in special schools.* The child receives specially designed instruction in a special school; the child is included in those parts of regular classes that are appropriate.
- ◆ *Instruction in the home/hospital.* The child receives services at home or in a hospital or other setting because he is unable to attend school elsewhere due to a medical condition.
- ◆ *Instruction in state-operated or nonpublic programs.* The child is served in a state-operated or nonpublic facility because her disabilities are so profound or complex that no services offered by the public schools can meet her needs.

Supplementary services to make education with less restriction possible may include resource rooms for special instruction for children with learning disabilities, emotional disorders, speech and language difficulties; itinerant instruction; and so on. School social work is listed as one of the supplementary aids and services or related services that would make LRE possible.

TYPES OF INTEGRATION

Another set of concepts very useful in planning for LRE is that of *types of integration*. These concepts emerged in the early discussion of LRE, quickly became basic concepts, and have continued to be useful (Kaufman, Gottlieb, Agard, & Kucic, 1975). There are three types of possible integration of a pupil into an LRE: *temporal integration, instructional integration*, and *social integration*. Each expands possibilities and assists in planning to balance the LRE and the most appropriate education. Each rests on a careful assessment as discussed earlier. The assessment includes the student's ability to move from one setting to another, and the support system available in place to help the student in any transitions.

Temporal Integration

Temporal integration refers to the amount of *time* the student with disabilities spends with peers who are not disabled. The underlying assumption is that the greater the amount of time spent by students with disabilities with peers without disabilities, the more socially adaptive will be their social and instructional growth experience. Students with disabilities need time and opportunity for interaction with all students to acquire essential socialization skills. Time spent with peers without disabilities need not necessarily be formal instruction time. It may involve the lunchroom, recess, shared field trips, or other shared activities. Such programming also provides an opportunity for students without disabilities to relate informally and to form friendships with peers with disabilities. Temporal integration involves an informed estimate of how the groups of students will interact in informal situations. Some preparation may be necessary for both groups and some monitoring of the experience is often necessary.

Instructional Integration

Instructional integration refers to the extent to which a student with special needs is integrated into the general classroom instructional environment or the extent to which the general education curriculum is taught in the special education classroom. Three conditions of *compatibility* must exist for instructional integration to occur:

1. Compatibility between the student's needs and the learning opportunities available in the general classroom;
2. Compatibility between the student with challenging physical or emotional needs, learning characteristics, and educational needs, and the

general education classroom teacher's ability and willingness to modify instructional practices; and

3. Provision by general and special education personnel of an appropriate, coordinated, and well-articulated educational program. (Kaufman et al., 1975)

One of the tasks for the social worker helping to meet conditions for instructional integration is to consult regularly with the general education teacher regarding the pupil's essential needs so that these can be met within the learning environment. The social worker might also arrange for a volunteer parent, a classmate, or an older student to tutor the pupil. Perhaps a pupil needs a quiet place, requires an opportunity to talk, or could benefit from more direct interaction with classroom materials or classmates. The social worker may help the teacher determine how he will provide these opportunities within the classroom to benefit the pupil and others as well.

Social Integration

Social integration refers to the placement of children with disabilities in situations where informal relations and friendships with their peers without disabilities are possible. Social integration may involve psychological and physical closeness, interaction with peers, and assimilation or acceptance of students with disabilities in the general classroom (Kaufman et al., 1975). The social worker, having an understanding of group and interpersonal dynamics, has a particularly important role in assisting social integration.

FULL INCLUSION AND THE REGULAR EDUCATION INITIATIVE

In the decade following the implementation of the law, concern was mounting that special education identification and placement processes were failing to achieve the intended purposes. Research suggested that referral and placement processes were leading unduly to placement in more restrictive environments (Algozzine, Christenson, & Ysseldyke, 1982; Christenson, Ysseldyke, & Algozzine, 1982; Ysseldyke et al., 1983). In addition, a series of demonstration projects in adaptive education showed that many children with mild-to-moderate disabilities did better in regular education classes *adapted to their needs* than a control group of similar children in smaller special education classes (Wang & Birch, 1984a, b). The result of this research emerged in a new policy, the *regular education initiative* (REI). Madeleine Will, then assistant secretary to the Office of Special Education and Related Services, challenged the "pull out" approach and the idea that poor performance in education can be understood solely in terms of the deficiencies in the learning environment.

> This challenge is to take what we have learned from the special programs and begin to transfer this knowledge to the regular education classroom. . . . There is

increasing evidence that it is better academically, socially, and psychologically to educate mildly handicapped children with nonhandicapped children, preferably within the regular classroom. (Will, 1986, pp. 10–12)

Will was proposing revolutionary change in regular education: that it adapt itself to the individual needs of children, particularly those with disabilities. Will's original challenge focused on children with mild disabilities and provision of a range of educational options, or continuum of alternative placements. Although no definition for full inclusion is agreed on, it is generally understood as going one step further than integration. It is the practice of serving students in the general education classroom with appropriate in-class support regardless of their type or severity of disability (Roach, 1995). Some interpretations of full inclusion have extended this to returning all or most children in special education settings to general education classrooms (without necessary attention to modifications or support). The question of whether this is appropriate has caused a great deal of dispute in education circles.

Integration and Inclusion: Developing Concepts

By the mid-1990s clearer understandings of integration and inclusion were developing. Ferguson (1995) shifts the focus to the general education class itself, incorporating everyone and viewing diversity as the norm. Inclusion, she concludes, is a "new challenge to create schools where typical classrooms will include students with more and more kinds of differences. . . . The learning environment will be a constant conversation involving students, teachers, other school personnel, families, and community members, all working together" for the common goal of a successful educational experience for all (p. 288).

Inclusion is the process of meshing general and special education reform initiatives and strategies to achieve a unified system of public education that incorporates all children and youth as active, fully participating members of the school community. Inclusion views diversity as the norm and ensures a high quality education for each student by providing meaningful curriculum, effective teaching, and necessary supports for each student (Ferguson, 1995).

She points out that inclusion is not about eliminating a continuum of alternate placements and services. It is rather a balanced incorporation of the philosophy and benefits of inclusion along this continuum, while still accepting the benefits of more restrictive environments to allow for the specific needs of particular students with disabilities and their families. She further states that "every child should have the opportunity to learn in a variety of different places—in small groups and large, in classrooms, in hallways, in libraries, and in a wide variety of community locations" (Ferguson, 1995, p. 289). She believes that segregation of students without disabilities from peers who do have disabilities results in each being overly sheltered from the breadth of realities in the world (Ferguson, 1995).

The policy shift to general education moves the thrust of change to teachers and to students in the general education classroom. Because of these fundamental policy shifts, many students with mild to moderate disabling conditions could spend all or part of their school hours with students with no identified disabilities. The philosophy of including a variety of students in the general education classroom necessitates routinely adapting the environment of the school, the classroom, and teaching methods to meet the special needs of students with disabilities. Students in the general education classroom are involved as part of that environment.

Inclusion is not always welcomed, particularly if the teacher is unclear about how to manage the child with special needs or feels unsupported in what he tries to do. The general education teacher may be in a particularly difficult position. He may have little background, readiness, or even commitment to having a youngster in his class whose needs are so different. Teachers have been known to teach to a hypothetical average student in the classroom, to "split the difference," rather than individualize instruction for various ability levels. This practice runs specifically against IDEA mandates and is dysfunctional for the student with special needs. Even well-intentioned teachers may wish to spare a student with special needs embarrassment by avoiding any direct reference to discrepancies in a pupil's achievement from what others may be doing. In any case, maintaining appropriate interventions and active reinforcement for a student with special needs often adds programmatic and planning complications to the general education setting.

Research has pointed out that the process of referral and recommendation for placement almost invariably ended in a more restrictive placement (Algozzine et al., 1982; Christenson et al., 1982; Ysseldyke et al., 1983). By the time the team completed a more formal process, there was an investment in placement, the general education teacher would often have given up, and the prophecy of placement became self-fulfilling. Teachers could be intimidated by students who presented difficult problems and demanded time and energy. The process of placing a student in a more restrictive environment carried with it a somewhat perverse incentive to place.

Research on teachers' attitudes toward integration/inclusion explains some of this. It is estimated that, although about two-thirds of teachers believe in the general concept of integration, only 40 percent believe that it would be a realistic policy for all children (Scruggs & Mastropieri, 1996). Teachers tend to be more negative about integrating the child with more severe disabilities (Forlin, 1995; Ward, Center, & Bochner, 1994). They tend to be negative about the impact of children with emotional and behavioral problems on other children (Hastings & Oakford, 2003). However the actual experience of inclusion in their school made a difference (Villa, Thousand, Meyers, & Nevin, 1996) in their confidence (Leroy & Simpson, 1996) that they could teach these students. These repeated findings may be stable indicators of teachers' concerns (Avramidis & Norwich, 2002), which are nevertheless modifiable by experience and by supports within the school environment itself (Carrington: 1999; Janney, Snell, Beers, & Raynes, 1995).

WHAT DO GENERAL EDUCATION TEACHERS NEED FOR LRE?

Having these concerns in mind, Janney, a teacher, and her colleagues studied this question in an inclusion project in several rural and urban Virginia school districts. What do general education teachers need to successfully include students with moderate to severe disabilities in their classes? All reported that inclusion was very difficult for them. Several factors appeared to be particularly significant in the successful integration of these students:

1. Teachers need top-down administrative support, guidelines and technical support, as well as demonstrated appreciation for their efforts in implementing the guidelines.

2. Teachers need at the same time to be given freedom to individualize and create their own adaptations, to be allowed to take ownership of the process.

3. Teachers need hands-on support from "coaches" with personal experience in integrating disabled students in their classrooms. Getting to know these coaches, who would be available to provide hands-on support to them and the integrated students, is preferable as initial preparation than the more traditional, didactic type of presentation or workshop.

4. Once the students are integrated, the experience of working with and thus getting to know these students well is what makes the final overall response to the integrative experience universally positive. This is true even for teachers who feel that significant extra work is involved in making the inclusion or integration of these students successful. "It was more work, but worth it."

5. Finally, teachers need a sense that they are not alone in the endeavor, that they have supportive people to turn to, even to lean on. This helps teachers work through difficult adjustments, particularly the adjustment of sharing their classrooms with other professional personnel. (Janney et al., 1995, p. 437)

Consultation with the Teacher

The Janney research points out that general education teachers can adapt to children with special needs when appropriate supports are provided. Social work consultation with teachers and other professionals is a direct and efficient intervention for adapting the classroom environment to better meet the special needs of students with disabilities. The social worker needs to take time to develop an empathic, supportive, and trusting relationship with the teacher, and to become knowledgeable about the problems between the student with disabilities and the students without disabilities. The social worker needs to listen to the teacher's perception of the situation, to be aware of the teacher's strengths in order to support the strengths the teacher brings to the situation.

She needs to help the teacher deal with concerns about the pupil's needs and his ability to deal with the student and find a workable educational approach, while being aware of the total educational milieu within which the teacher is functioning.

Social workers must become knowledgeable about the educational process so that their unique skills and understanding of human interaction may be effectively applied in the context of each educational situation. School social workers are in a position to offer teachers additional skills and techniques that can assist them in classroom management and in dealing with individual problematic behavior.

PREREFERRAL CONSULTATION: THE PROBLEM-SOLVING TEAM

Including students with widely diverse needs in a single classroom is a big task. Teachers often cannot deal easily with the wide array of students' needs simultaneously. The social worker and other support personnel may help most effectively by becoming part of a teacher assistance or *problem-solving team*. Problem-solving teams have the same multidisciplinary membership as a team conducting a more formal assessment for placement, except that more experienced teachers are usually available as resources or may be members of the team. In any case, the social worker is usually a member. The first use of such a team is the meeting prior to an actual referral, when the teacher is feeling the pressure of the needs of a particular pupil and is not certain how to deal with them. Prereferral consultation (Graden, Casey, & Bonstrom, 1985; Graden, Casey, & Christenson, 1985) is a means of appropriately maintaining a student with mild to moderate disabilities in general education. Over the past decade, prereferral problem-solving teams, under various names, have developed in districts and in many cases have been promoted by state policy. The case of Tommy in chapter 26 is a good example of the consultation process with a problem-solving team that successfully maintained Tommy in the general education environment.

Such teams may also provide a variety of other individual and group interventions. For example, the social worker and speech pathologist may conduct social skills groups. The psychologist, teacher, and social worker may offer role-playing exercises and include students as participants. Any of these specialists may enhance classroom integration of the student with disabilities by adapting their interventions to current lessons. The social worker may use playtime, or other less structured activities, as a social group-learning experience in the classroom. Through this team approach the social worker and other specialists can provide students with activities and experiences that they can share or model with peers in the general classroom. Such support personnel can share their expertise with a wide array of other professionals, and these in turn can share what they learn with others (Stainback, Stainback, Courtnage, & Jabel, 1986; Welsh & Goldberg, 1979).

THE PROCESS OF MAKING PLACEMENT DECISIONS: THE IEP TEAM

The process of formal assessment and planning leading to placement in the least restrictive environment has been outlined in previous chapters. Once the IEP conference has generally determined which services the student will require to address the identified needs, the final decision of an IEP conference is where the student under consideration is to be placed. The placement decision must take into account two often opposing considerations: (1) What setting can best meet the student's educational needs, and (2) which setting offers the least restrictive environment while giving adequate support to the student's identified educational needs. Unless the pupil has a severe or "low-incidence" disability, many decisions do become a compromise between these considerations. The team would want to maintain the child in as normal a setting as possible, and with as normal a routine as possible, and at the same time pay special attention to needs that require either additional support, or a different, possibly unique accommodation. Both the presumption toward the general education environment and the continuum of alternative placements are crucial to this decision process. If the student is to experience an interruption or a change in his general education program, the less restrictive options that were considered, but not agreed on, must be formally documented. The team must justify why each was insufficient to meet the student's educational needs.

THE SOCIAL WORKER'S ROLE IN THE DEVELOPMENT AND MAINTENANCE OF THE LRE

There is a range of options and a variety of supports intended to accommodate students in the general education classroom and to assist teachers to adapt educational processes to a pupil's needs. The increased use of consultation skills and the development of a multidisciplinary team approach to complex and difficult situations are important. Some students who might benefit from special education services may be clustered into general education classrooms. Resource teachers may do cooperative teaching in general education or help classes develop cooperative learning strategies (Will, 1986).

PREPARATIONS FOR INCLUSION OF A NEW STUDENT

The school social worker may assist the teacher in planning the physical location of the students within the classroom. Using the social worker's knowledge of patterns of interaction, students may be regrouped to make the climate more conducive to learning for everyone. The social worker may be asked to work directly with all of the children in the classroom to help them accept the student with disabilities and to assist in the integration of that student into the group. The three basic formats the social worker may use are: (1) an educational format: films, bibliotherapy, or discussion of the specific disability; (2) an affective education approach to help students know and understand one another better so that they can function more comfortably as a group; and (3) a problem-solving approach through formal classroom discussion of problems that affect students. The social worker can enable the classroom teacher to develop the necessary skills to use these formats in the classroom by modeling and co-leading these groups with the teacher and then consulting regularly in a supportive educational role.

LRE implies a complex process of people working together to support the growth of a student and her best dynamic adaptation to education and learning tasks. The case of Terry is a good example of this process:

> Terry is a 15-year-old freshman student in a large, diverse high school. She has cognitive limitations and generally needs help in containing her high levels of anxiety experienced in school. She has developed a variety of symptoms including rituals, phobias, panic reactions, and negativism. She is fearful of people looking at her. When things go particularly badly, she is capable of a temper tantrum. She needs help walking through crowded hallways to get to her next class. Although she is working and making improvements in feeling comfortable in social settings, she will withdraw and shut down in unfamiliar settings with unfamiliar people. She is isolated from peers and has no friends. She would benefit from getting involved, with support and careful planning, in extracurricular activities. She loves swimming and enjoys art. She is on medication, and gradually learning to manage her anxiety. When she does get upset, she has learned how to cope by asking to take a break and then retreating to an isolated place in the room where she can cool off. She usually recoups within five minutes. Teachers and other students accept this. She needs help going from class to class. In the beginning, the social worker and teachers accompanied her unobtrusively. Gradually a few student aides have gotten involved with this. Later she may manage some of these passages on her own, but she is not there yet. With the exception of her general education social studies and art classes, she works in self-contained classrooms. There is a plan to expand her general education participation, as she feels more comfortable. The social worker works directly with her, coordinating with the family and her psychiatrist, and with her general and special education teachers. A large part of the work is a team effort to support her coping. This is gradually taking place. She is conscious of dealing with anxiety-producing situations in the halls and with other students and gradually getting better at it. Teachers and eventually students are becoming sensitive to her signals when she feels under unusual pressure and needs more time and support to compose herself. They are learning a great deal from Terry.

For the social worker, working with Terry's situation was a matter of consultation, planning, therapeutic roles, solving problems, and keeping the process moving in a good direction. She worked directly with Terry so that she was able to process what she was doing and begin to take control. As Terry gradually developed abilities to cope with anxiety, the social worker helped her to generalize and take credit for her learning.

TRANSITION PLANNING

When a student requires a change to a different program, whether more or less restrictive, the social worker's task as a member of the special education team is to plan for a smooth transition to the new program, and to provide for the necessary resources during this process. In planning this transition, it is essential to explore the student's and her family's reactions, concerns, and general feelings about the recommended program or programs. With this knowledge the social worker needs to work with other team members to identify alternative programs or environments appropriate to the student's adaptive and/or educational needs. Next, the social worker's support and understanding can be key factors in helping the student adjust satisfactorily to another educational setting. If a child is placed in a specialized setting, the social worker may continue to see her individually. Moreover, the social worker may work with new teachers to help them understand how a particular student functions and how to deal with the student's legitimate needs. It must be stressed frequently that follow-up services, sometimes referred to as bridging activities, are essential to the student, family, or teacher for a successful transition. Betty Welsh and Grace Goldberg developed an eight-step process for such transitions. Although each of the steps by itself is not new, it is their combined use that is significant. If the transition is to be successful, all eight steps need to be incorporated. Only the order can be changed. Otherwise, the vulnerable child has a high probability of not succeeding in the program that she is entering.

1. Assessing the pupil's psychosocial and educational gains, her strengths and weaknesses, and readiness for a new program;
2. Assessing available educational programs that could meet the needs of the pupil;
3. Involving the pupil in the recognition of the need for change, in the assessment process and in the preparation of the planned change;
4. Involving the parent in the assessment process and in the preparation for the change being considered;
5. Obtaining the commitment on the part of the receiving program to take the pupil and preparing the school personnel who will be involved in the new educational plan;
6. Making arrangements with the new teacher to reach out to the pupil so that she can feel welcome;
7. Being there when the actual move is made, so that it goes according to plan; and
8. Offering supportive consultation services to the pupil, family, and teacher after placement. (Welsh & Goldberg, 1979)

All children are unique and have special needs and their own ways of learning. The ultimate payoff for creating more flexible programming often is a more effective educational environment for everyone. The problem is that this new emphasis, together with larger class sizes, can also awaken confusion, uncertainty, fear, and anxiety among school personnel. The school social worker, who has traditionally dealt with socio-emotional factors that hinder or promote the process of education, has much to offer in helping educators learn to understand and adapt to this challenge. The social worker may consult with teachers and other team members about instructional adaptations, reassuring them of the positive payoffs inherent in creating more opportunities for all students through the increased diversity.

FINAL NOTES

Without teamwork that supports pupils and teachers in complex arrangements, LRE is not possible. There are dangers inherent in rapid movement of schools into an inclusion model, where more and more students with serious disabilities are brought into the general classroom without supportive planning. The possibility is that few, if any, of the preparations discussed in this chapter will occur. Students who are reentering the general education system with little or no support are at great risk of dropping out after falling far behind both academically and socially. Transitions into different settings and systems with the school are, of course, crucial tasks to school social work service delivery.

The students most at risk for failure are those having what are sometimes labeled as "invisible disabilities," such as having learning disabilities, emotional disorders, communication deficits, or even mild motor dysfunctions. Such students have previously experienced significant difficulties in the general education setting. These have led to their being evaluated and identified as needing special assistance. The students are understandably anxious about reentering the system where they experienced those difficulties. Such students, without a visible sign of their disability, are at greater risk of misunderstanding and thus may be held to different standards than a student who has a limp or hearing aid, signaling to all that they have an identifiable challenge.

As the social worker assesses a student's total milieu, it may become apparent that environmental factors cannot be restructured sufficiently in a given general education setting to meet the needs of a particular student. If the available resources of the general education classroom and teacher cannot be restructured sufficiently to meet the student's needs, continuing to retain the student in that general education classroom, though it would be the least restrictive environment, might adversely affect the student. An example might be a student with a hearing impairment. For this student in a general education classroom, the environment might not be sufficiently stimulating. Perhaps there is insufficient social interaction because there are too few pupils who are skilled in signing. An appropriate recommendation may be to provide an environment with more students with hearing impairments with whom, through signing, the target student can experience more social interaction. On the other hand, to have a mix of experiences through different classes, some with students with hearing impairments, some without students with hearing impairments, might be most helpful.

School social workers have a special opportunity to make the educational process more beneficial to students as awareness of the meaning of the least restrictive environment and school social work practice continues to evolve. School social workers have the skills. The challenge for school social workers is to contribute creatively and positively to the changes in general education that serve the best educational interests of all students. The rights of all students are served by including those with identified disabilities into the general education setting whenever possible.

References

Algozzine, B., Christenson, S., & Ysseldyke, J. E. (1982). Probabilities associated with the referral to placement process. *Teacher Education and Special Education, 5*(3), 19-23.

Avramidis, E., & Norwich, B. (2002) Teachers' attitudes toward integration/inclusion: A review of the literature. *European Journal of Special Needs Education, 17*(2), 129-147.

Carrington, S. (1999) Inclusion needs a different school culture. *Inclusive Education, 3*(3), 257-268.

Christenson, S., Ysseldyke, J., & Algozzine, B. (1982). Institutional constraints and external pressures affecting placement decisions. *Psychology in the Schools, 19*, 341-345.

Ferguson, D. (1995). The real challenge of inclusion. *Phi Delta Kappan, 77*(3), 281-287.

Forlin, C. (1995) Educators' beliefs about inclusive practices in Western Australia. *British Journal of Special Education, 22*, 179-185.

Graden, J. L., Casey, A., & Bonstrom, O. (1985). Implementing a prereferral intervention system: Part II. The model. *Exceptional Children, 51*(6), 487-496.

Graden, J. L., Casey, A., & Christenson, S. (1985). Implementing a prereferral intervention system: Part I. The model. *Exceptional Children, 51*(5), 377-384.

Hastings, R. P., & Oakford, S. (2003). Student teachers' attitudes toward the inclusion of children with special needs. *Educational Psychology, 23*(1), 87-95.

Janney, R. E., Snell, M. E., Beers, M. K., & Raynes, M. (1995). Integrating students with moderate and severe disabilities into the general education classes. *Exceptional Children, 61*(5), 425-439.

Kaufman, M. J., Gottlieb, J., Agard, J., & Kucic, M. B. (1975). Mainstreaming: Toward an explication of the construct. *Focus on Exceptional Children, 7*, 4.

Leroy, B., & Simpson, C. (1996). Improving student outcomes through inclusive education. *Support for Learning, 11*, 32-36.

Roach, V. (1995). Supporting inclusion. *Phi Delta Kappan, 77*(3), 295-299.

Scruggs, T. E., & Mastropieri, M. A. (1996). Teacher perceptions of mainstreaming/inclusion, 1958-1995: A research synthesis. *Exceptional Children, 63*, 59-74.

Stainback, W., Stainback, S., Courtnage, L., & Jabel, T. (1986). Facilitating mainstreaming by modifying the mainstream. *Exceptional Children, 52*(2), 144-152.

Turnbull, H. R., & Turnbull, A. P. (1998). *Free appropriate public education: The law and children with disabilities.* Denver: Love Publishing.

Villa, R., Thousand, J., Meyers, H., & Nevin, A. (1996). Teacher and administrator perceptions of heterogeneous education. *Exceptional Children, 63*, 29-45.

Wang, M., & Birch, J. (1984a). Comparison of a full time mainstreaming program and a resource room approach. *Exceptional Children, 51*, 33-40.

Wang, M., & Birch, J. (1984b). Effective special education in regular class. *Exceptional Children, 50,* 390–399.

Ward, J., Center, Y., & Bochner, S. (1994). A question of attitudes: Integrating children with disabilities into regular classrooms? *British Journal of Special Education, 21,* 34–39.

Welsh, B., & Goldberg, G. (1979). Insuring educational success for children-at-risk placed in new learning environments. *School Social Work Quarterly, 1*(4), 271–284.

Will, M. (1986). *Educating students with learning problems: A shared responsibility. A report to the secretary* [Monograph]. Washington, DC: U.S. Department of Education, Office of Rehabilitative Services.

Ysseldyke, J. E., Thurlow, M., Graden, J., Wesson, C., Algozzine, B., & Deno, S. (1983). Generalizations from five years of research on assessment and decision-making: The University of Minnesota Institute. *Exceptional Children, 4,* 75–93.

24

Setting Goals: The Individualized Education Program and the IFSP: Content, Process, and the School Social Worker's Role

Robert Constable

Loyola University, Chicago

Galen Thomas

Southern Illinois University

- The Individualized Education Program (IEP)
- The Process of Setting Goals and Objectives
- What is the IEP Team?
- Developing Agreements and Integrating Resources
- Involving Children in the IEP
- The Individualized Family Service Plan (IFSP)

The Individualized Education Program (IEP) and the Individualized Family Service Plan (IFSP) are formal planning instruments under the IDEA law.[1] In

---

1. H.R. 1350, PL 108-446 The Individuals with Disabilities Improvement Act of 2004 (IDEA 2004). As of our publication date, the federal regulations had not been issued. Changes in the IEP

the United States they are central to the school social worker's work with any child or infant with a disability. They are the chief documents for the child's right to a free, appropriate, public education. The IEP deals with children aged 5 through 21; the IFSP deals with infants and toddlers, from birth through 5 years of age, and their families. Although the family is important in both, the family is particularly important in the IFSP, where it is a principal agent in management and implementation of a plan that may use a variety of resources to meet the young child's educational needs. The greater the need and complexity of family involvement, the more important the social worker's role becomes.

The school social worker's role is, however, only one part of a broader assessment and planning process done by the multidisciplinary team, culminating in the IEP or the IFSP. The annual goals and intermediate objectives in the planning instruments are specifically related to assessment (including the social worker's CSA) done by the team. The statement of special education and/or related services necessary for the student to attain the goals is related to the goals and objectives and the assessment. This makes it individualized. The planned interventions, the "program" needed (special education and related services), become a civil right when they are defined in the IEP/IFSP. Social workers need to fit their assessment and planning processes into this broader team process, which then defines the civil right. The specific description and the justification for the school social work services needed as a part of this overall plan must come from this relationship.

THE INDIVIDUALIZED EDUCATION PROGRAM (IEP)

The IEP is the central management tool used to ensure the child with disabilities the right to a free, appropriate, public education. The IEP assembles recent evaluation, present decision making, and future expectations in one document. It is a synopsis of the service efforts of the IEP team. It reflects the assessment effort that has previously taken place and the areas of need identified by a team of qualified professionals and the parents of the child. It involves the people who have interest in the child's education and who attend the IEP staffing: the parents, differing members of the IEP team (e.g., the teacher, administrator, psychologist, and other specialized personnel) when appropriate, and the child.

The IEP goes beyond a simple report. It is the living record of an evaluative, decision-making, and planning process. The social worker's input into the decision-making process will be based in part on a social developmental study (SDS). The completed agreement reflects a complex evaluation and goal-setting

---

format are drawn from the wording of the law itself. Until regulations are issued at each state level and taken up by local school districts, there is a period of transition, but school personnel are already anticipating the changes and this book reflects the transition as well.

process, which has taken place among parents, school, and child. If signed and not contested, it is concrete evidence that consensus has been reached. The decision-making process aims for an agreement in seven crucial areas:

1. *The child's present level of academic achievement and functional performance.* The social work SDS has studied the relation between appropriate social and developmental tasks, present functional performance, and academic achievement. These establish measurable *baselines* in different areas upon which measurable goals and objectives can be constructed. The school social worker will mainly contribute to the child's IEP in the areas of functional performance (see sampler of developmental learning objectives in this chapter).

2. *How the child's disability affects the child's involvement and progress in the general education curriculum.* This begins to align the assessment with the general education curriculum and its district-wide assessment processes. When a child cannot participate in the regular assessment, there must be an appropriate alternate assessment, aligned to alternate achievement standards, selected by the team.

3. *Measurable annual goals and objectives.* Annual academic and functional goals, reflecting the baseline assessment, are geared both toward progress in the general education curriculum and toward meeting other needs coming from the disability. There needs to be a description of how the progress toward meeting the annual goals will be measured and when the reports will be provided. Objective criteria are components of the child's behavior that may be observed and measured. Such criteria may be used to compare the child's current performance with previous levels of performance or they may be compared with a classroom norm that is typical of children his or her age. The results of these comparisons indicate whether or not objectives are being achieved or whether new and different objectives may be in order (20 U.S.C. 1414[1]). When there is an alternate assessment, there is a need for measurable short-term objectives or benchmarks leading to the annual goals. Otherwise periodic progress reports are needed, using academic measures or possibly variations of goal attainment scaling described later in this chapter.

4. *The "program,"* that is, the special education and related services to be provided for or on behalf of the child. This includes *program modifications* to enable the child to make progress in general education and/or *supports* for school personnel. For school social workers direct individual or group work with the pupil can be a *related service.* Consultation on behalf of the pupil can be a *support* or involve a *program modification.*

5. *A statement of the extent to which the child will not participate with nondisabled children in the regular class, with or without support services.* This underlines the importance of the the least restrictive environment for the child with disabilities. The negative wording (*not participate*) is meant to bring the team to justify nonparticipation in a general education environment, rather

than assume an environment that is directly matched to the child's learning needs but is more restrictive. School social workers have important responsibilities assisting the team to develop this optimal match (see chapter 23).

6. *The projected dates for initiation of services, planned modifications, and the anticipated frequency, location, and duration of those services and modifications.*

7. *Beginning at age 16, goals of postsecondary transition to training, education, employment and, where appropriate, independent living skills, as well as the needed transition services to reach these goals* (IDEA 2004 H.R. 1350, PL 108-446 Sec. 614(d)(1)(A)(j) I-VIII; current regulations: 34 C.F.R. 300.346; 20 U.S.C. 1414 et seq).

Transition Services

Transition services mean a coordinated set of activities for a student, designed within an outcome-oriented process that promotes movement from school to postschool activities. The coordinated set of activities is based on the individual student's needs, taking into account the student's preferences and interests. It includes instruction, community experiences, the development of employment and post school adult living objectives, and, when appropriate, acquisition of daily living skills and a functional vocational evaluation. If a participating agency other than the educational agency fails to provide agreed-on services, the educational agency would reconvene the IEP team to identify alternative strategies to meet the transition objectives.

Although the law specifies an Individual Transition Plan (ITP) for pupils 16 or older with certain variations as the student grows older, the term *transition* has also been applied to all movement from one level to another. For example, as a 5-year-old child with severe disabilities moves from early childhood special education to kindergarten, an appropriate transition plan should be developed. Whenever there is a delicate transition from one environment to another, there needs to be planning, and the social worker probably should be involved. To do good transition planning, the school social worker needs a broad, ecological perspective on the relations of the student to the home, the school, and community resources. She needs to understand the possible process of transition, and the supports needed to make the transition successful.

Statement of the Needed Special Education and Related Services. All of the IEP assessment and planning has to result in a statement of needed special education and related services. This statement builds on the annual goals and intermediate objectives. Here the social work services do not stand on their own. They are justified as *related services* that assist the pupil to attain these academic and functional goals and benefit from education. The social work services need to be specific and related to the annual goals and short-term objectives or benchmarks. Global descriptors, such as "a unit of casework," are not adequate. Rather, "the social worker will spend an hour a week working with

_____ on attendance and motivation for achievement," or "in a group to help him develop social and friendship skills. This will take place for a half semester with continuance based on evaluation." The goals dictate the needed resources. If necessary resources are unavailable within the school, the school must contract with outside agencies, individuals, or other school districts to ensure their provision.

The IEP thus encapsulates the entire provision of special education and related services as well as the evaluation of effectiveness. It is ultimately a list of services to be provided to reach agreed-upon goals. Although the IEP cannot guarantee the child will actually reach these particular goals, it is an agreement on the school's part to provide or purchase (if it cannot directly provide) the special education and related services listed in the document. Thus the importance of listing the "program" and setting measurable goals for each of the program components.

The IEP process is often confused with the (assessment) process of developing a multifaceted nondiscriminatory evaluation and determining disability. The assessment process is described in chapters 17 and 19. The IEP is a goal-setting, planning document, based on this assessment.

The full potential of what school social work can offer to children cannot be achieved without some significant level of participation by the social worker in the IEP process. No social worker can expect to offer services to children with disabilities in the school without IEP involvement. The unique contribution of the social worker to the IEP process takes place in at least three major areas. The social worker (1) participates in the process of setting the goals and objectives, which govern intervention, (2) helps the multidisciplinary team to develop sufficient consensus among itself and with parents to proceed, and (3) is involved with case management and integration of school and outside agency resources.

THE PROCESS OF SETTING GOALS AND OBJECTIVES

Goals and objectives provide a way for educators and parents to track the child's progress in special education. They should not be confused with the goals and objectives that are normally found in daily, weekly, or monthly instructional plans. Otherwise, there could be hundreds of educational goals for one IEP. They should *signify*; they should be milestones for the pupil's expected progress. They should be measurable, even if "measurable" means the presence or absence of an observed behavior, such as making a friend. Such objectives for children with disabilities reflect the confluence of academic and functional (social) goals. The concept of education is broad and includes social skills, life skills, problem-solving skills, and developmental steps. For children with disabilities these are often the most important parts of their education. The education of the child with disabilities is in large part a preparation for his or her best level of social functioning outside of the school situation. Particularly for children with severe disabilities, a large part of this preparation has to do with the learning of life skills: those skills that promote appropriate independence, appropriate and satisfying interpersonal relationships, problem-solving skills, an appropriate self-image, and tolerance for unavoidable stress (see chapter 35). These are areas where social workers have particular expertise and can make a crucial contribution to the educational process. These general areas can be broken down into shared objectives, achieved through consultation with the teacher, direct intervention with the child and parents, and social work involvement in the classroom.

Functional Performance and Developmental Needs: Functional Behavior Objectives

As long as school social workers have been participating in the IEP, they have sought to develop frames of reference for the developmental goals and objectives that underly the academic content and fall within their areas of expertise. Some social workers may tend to think in terms of psychological disorders. While these deficit frameworks open up a useful literature, they do not translate well into the normalizing, strengths-based, learning and functional orientations that characterize education. The problem of translating developmental objectives into measurable learning objectives has challenged school social workers since the inception of IDEA. David Sanders (2002) recently related developmental needs and functional school performances. From his perspective, there are four basic categories of developmental needs that impede a student's functioning in school. These are:

1. *Motivation*—referring to the desire to achieve and develop within school expectations;
2. *Behavior*—referring to actions dysfunctional to one's own learning and development or the learning and development of others;
3. *Social skills*—referring to skills in relation to others, difficulties making friends, or problems fitting into groups positively;
4. *Self-image*—referring to difficulties in self-esteem or self-confidence.

Each need category implies underlying needs as well as presenting behavior. It is only after careful evaluation of the pertinent data that a confident decision can be made. In an example of aggressive and defiant behaviors, fighting might at first indicate that *behavior* would be the appropriate basic category. But aggressive behavior is often symptomatic of weak or nonexistent social skills, or of a profound and pervasive feeling of inferiority. In these cases either *social skills* or *self-image* would be the more appropriate category (Sanders, 2002). Table 24.1 provides a sampler of strengths-based, developmental learning, together with the way each item could be measured. The list is not exhaustive and in any case should be individualized to develop goals and objectives for each student's situation. To assist the student to achieve a goal or objective the social worker's "program" could range from direct, individual work, crisis work,

TABLE 24.1   Developmental Learning Objectives Sampler

Area of Learning	*Measurement*
I. Motivation	
A. Profile: Poor homework completion, weak organization skills, poor study skills	
1. Student will learn the importance of completing homework assignments and being prepared for class.	Tests (content based)
2. With an incentive plan, student will complete homework as assigned and be prepared for class.	Charting (contracting, incentive plans) Daily log (teacher's records, assignment notebooks)
3. Independently, student will complete homework as assigned and will be prepared for class (receive passing grades in (*x*) class, maintain credits to graduate with class).	Charting (contracting incentive plans) Daily log (teacher's gradebook) Other (midterm reports, report cards)
B. Profile: Off-task behavior	
1. Student will learn the importance of listening and being on task at school.	Tests (content based)
2. With an incentive plan, student will begin in-class assignments and (with appropriate cues from the teacher) will be on task for (*x*) minutes (until work is completed).	Charting (contracting, incentive plans) Observations (documented) Other (formal classroom observations)
3. Independently, student will be consistently and appropriately on task.	Charting (contracting, incentive plans) Observations (documented) Other (consultations, formal classroom observations)
C. Profile: Poor school attendance, truancy	
1. Student will learn the importance of daily school attendance.	Tests (content based)
2. With an incentive plan, with a behavior modification schedule, student will decrease school absences to less than one (two) per month.	Charting (contracting, incentive plans) Other (attendance records)
3. Independently, student will be at school each attendance day unless ill (excused, etc.).	Other (attendance records)
II. Behavior	
A. Profile: Disruptive Behavior	
1. With an incentive strategy, student will follow the behavior plan	Charting (contracting, incentive plans) Daily log (teacher's records)

specifically written as part of his
IEP.

2. Independently, student will follow
   the behavior plan specifically written as part of his IEP.

Charting (contracting, incentive plans)
Daily log (teacher's records, office
records)

B. Profile: Poor listening skills, not following directions

1. Student will learn why paying attention and following directions
   are important in the classroom
   (on the playground, in the cafeteria, etc.).

Tests (content based)

2. With an incentive plan, student
   will listen for and follow directions in the classroom with appropriate cues from the teacher).

Charting (contracting, incentive plans)
Observations (documented)
Other (consultations, formal classroom
observations)

3. Independently, student will listen
   for and follow directions.

Observations (documented)
Other (consultations, formal classroom
observations)

C. Profile: Chronic classroom misbehavior

1. Student will understand the importance of rule systems in school
   and will know the classroom
   (school, playground, cafeteria)
   rules and consequences of noncompliance.

Tests (content based)

2. Student will learn the purpose of
   time-out and will learn and practice correct time-out behavior.

Tests (content based)
Daily log (record of practice sessions)

3. With an incentive plan, student
   will take time-out correctly in the
   classroom in compliance to the
   classroom behavior plan.

Charting (schedules, contracting)
Daily log (teacher's behavior records)
Observations (documented)

4. Independently, with an incentive
   plan, student will accept and follow the classroom behavior plan
   (increase acceptable classroom
   behaviors, decrease classroom disruptions to (x) or less per (x)).

Charting (schedules, contracting)
Daily log (teacher's behavior records)
Observations (reports from teachers,
staff)
Other (office discipline records)

D. Profile: Bothering others, aggressive behaviors

1. Student will learn why every student should feel safe and be safe
   at school.

Tests (content based)

2. Student will learn to identify motivations and causes of aggressive
   behavior (teasing, baiting).

Tests (content based)

3. With a conflict resolution program, student will learn and practice a conflict resolution strategy

Tests (content based)
Daily log (record of practice sessions)

(assertive, nonaggressive problem-
solving techniques).

4. Independently, with an incentive
plan, student will decrease incidents of physical aggression at
school (in the classroom, in the
cafeteria, to less than (*x*) per (*x*)).

Charting (contracting, incentive plans)
Daily logs (teacher's behavior logs)
Other (office discipline records)

E. **Profile:** Accepting consequences, respecting authority

1. Student will understand cause and
effect relationships as they relate
to behavior and prescribed negative consequences.

Tests (content related)

2. Student will be able to explain
how his or her behavior precipi-
tates a prescribed negative consequence.

Tests (content related)
Observations (reports from staff)

3. Independently, student will cooperatively accept prescribed negative consequences of his or her
behavior.

Charting (contracting, incentive plans)
Observations (reports from staff)

4. Independently, student will accept
legitimate direction, criticism,
and/or negative consequences.

Observations (reports from staff)
Daily log (daily record of incidents)

III. **Social Skills**

A. **Profile:** Uncooperative, dysfunctional social behavior

1. Student will learn the importance
of cooperative social behavior.

Tests (content based)

2. Using a conflict resolution strategy, student will learn and practice a conflict resolution (problem-solving) strategy.

Tests (content based)
Daily log (record of practice sessions)

3. Independently (with an incentive
plan), student will decrease incidents of social conflict in the
classroom (school environment,
on the playground) to one (two)
or less per day (week).

Charting (contracting)
Daily log (teacher's behavior records)
Other (office discipline records)

B. **Profile:** Poor social skills, difficulties making friends

1. With group work intervention,
student will learn and practice
basic social skills (taking turns,
waiting politely, saying nice
things, sharing, respecting differences, accepting others, good
manners, controlling teasing and
name calling).

Tests (content based)
Daily log (content based)

2. Independently, student will use (increase) positive, cooperative interpersonal social skills in the classroom (on the playground, at school, that can be observed by (*x*)). — Observations (documented)

C. **Profile:** Anger control

1. Student will be able to identify telltale feelings and body signals when becoming angry. — Tests / Charting

2. Student will develop a understanding of reactions to and perceptions of anger. — Tests / Charting

3. Student will learn a self-talk (cool-down) technique to reduce angry feelings. — Tests (content based) / Charting

4. Independently, student will use a self-talk (cool-down) technique to reduce and control his or her anger. — Observations (documented)

IV. **Self-Esteem**

A. **Profile:** Poor self-esteem, elementary, intermediate

1. Student will successfully complete a copyrighted esteem-building curriculum. — Tests (content related)

2. Student will keep a personal journal and will enter one positive statement about self each (*x*). — Charting (entries) / Daily log (record of entries)

3. Independently, student will increase and maintain positive feelings of self-esteem. — Charting (self-evaluation) / Other (Piers–Harris base and intervals)

B. **Profile:** Poor self-esteem, intermediate, secondary

1. Student will recognize unique positive personal attributes. — Tests

2. Student will learn and practice personal goal-setting strategies. — Charting (contracting)

3. Student will experience success by setting and achieving realistic personal (educational, social) goals. — Charting (contracting, incentive plan)

4. Independently, student will increase and maintain positive feelings of self-esteem. — Charting (self-evaluation) / Other (Piers–Harris base and intervals)

C. **Profile:** Poor self-confidence

1. Student will recognize unique positive personal qualities and attributes. — Tests

  2. With an incentive plan, student will volunteer positive statements about self to (ask clarifying questions of) teacher (familiar staff) when asked (with prompts).

  Charting (contracting, incentive plans)
  Observations (documented)
  Daily log (record of occurrences)

  3. With an incentive plan, student will ask clarifying questions and/ or make appropriate declarative statements spontaneously in the classroom.

  Charting (contracting, incentive plans)
  Observations (documented)
  Daily log (record of occurrences)

  4. Independently, student will gain self-confidence, increasing participation in playground activities (joining a school club, starting a conversation with a familiar staff person, eating lunch with classmates (x) days of the week, applying for a job).

  Charting (self-evaluation)
  Observations (documented)
  Others (Piers–Harris base and intervals, consultations)

D. **Profile:** Poor hygiene and weak self-care skills

  1. Student will learn the importance of good grooming, appearance, and personal hygiene.

  Tests (content based)

  2. Independently, student will show increased healthful personal hygiene habits in the classroom (school, cafeteria) (that will be noticed by (x)).

  Observations (documented)

E. **Profile:** Drug use

  1. Student will learn the consequences of drug abuse.

  Tests

  2. Student will learn strategies for assertively refusing offers from others to participate in drug use.

  Tests

  3. Student will set healthful personal goals about drug and substance use.

  Charting (contracting)
  Other (consultations with student)

  4. Independently, student will abstain from harmful drug use.

  Other (consultations, medical, parental)

F. **Profile:** Gang involvement

  1. Student will identify social and emotional needs and how those needs are met through gang affiliations.

  Tests

  2. Student will identify potential dangers and hazards of gang affiliations.

  Tests

  3. Student will identify satisfying and healthy alternatives to gang affiliations.

  Observations (documented)

4. Independently, student will choose satisfying and healthy alternatives instead of gang affiliations.

Charting (contracting)
Observations (documented)
Daily log (record of specific behaviors)
Other (consultations with significant others)

---

group work, social skills groups, consultation, direct classroom intervention or modifications, parent consultation or coaching, or other interventions appropriate to the situation. These also translate readily into an assessment framework, such as the functional behavior assessment and a resulting intervention system, such as positive behavior interventions and support (PBIS), discussed in chapter 19.

Goal Attainment Scaling. Goal attainment scaling (GAS) is a popular way to provide an individualized, criterion-referenced approach to describing, measuring, and documenting changes in student performance (Roach & Elliott, 2005). Members of the team first identify target behaviors—behaviors of concern where desirable change is possible and that can be used as benchmarks of progress. These behaviors are defined in objective terms so that they can be understood and accurately paraphrased. Interventions are planned and a scale for measuring change is constructed. The scale could be developed from three to five descriptions of the possible outcomes, ranging from "least favorable" to "most favorable." Table 24.2 (Roach & Elliott, 2005) illustrates this process and shows at least ten different possible dimensions of change, ranging from "frequency" of an activity through "engagement" with a process. After the scale is developed with the team and the student, the intervention can be implemented and the resulting behaviors evaluated.

WHAT IS THE IEP TEAM?

The *IEP team* means a group of individuals composed of: (1) the parents of a child with a disability, (2) a regular education teacher of the child (if the child is, or may be, participating in the regular education environment), (3) at least one special education teacher (or provider) of the child, (4) a representative of the local educational agency who provides or supervises special education and who is knowledgeable about the general education curriculum, and (5) an individual who can interpret the instructional implications of evaluation results.

Parents, as part of the multidisciplinary team, must be included in the decision-making process that determines these resources. "Parents" may also include an individual who may have special knowledge or expertise regarding the child. Also, whenever appropriate, the pupil should be included. The emphasis on self-determination would seem to require participation whenever the student is going to be able to manage appropriately in the meeting. Recent reviews of best practices suggest preparation of the student for the meeting

TABLE 24.2   A Framework for Developing and Utilizing GAS Ratings

---

Step 1: Identify Concerns. Teacher(s) identify academic or social behavior strengths, performance problems, and acquisition problems by considering data on performance gathered via standardized assessments, observations, and/or work samples.

Step 2: Analyze Concerns. Teacher(s) identify a target behavior and define it in objective terms so it can be read and accurately paraphrased.

Step 3: Plan Instruction or Intervention. First, teacher(s) establish the instructional or intervention goal, defining the desired outcome in concrete terms. In many cases, the target behavior and desired outcome will be the same. After identifying the desired outcome, teacher(s) describe the general instruction or intervention strategy that will be used to achieve this goal.

Step 4: Constructing the Goal Attainment Scale. The basic elements of GAS are a 5-point scale ranging from +2 to -2 and descriptions of the target behavior and instructional support that correspond with the following conditions: Best Possible Outcome (+2), No Change in Behavior/Performance (0), and Worst Possible Outcome (-2). The following characteristics or dimensions may be helpful in developing descriptions for the different GAS rating points:

- Frequency (Never–Sometimes–Very Often–Almost Always–Always).
- Quality (Poor–Fair–Good–Excellent).
- Development (Not Present–Emerging–Developing–Accomplished–Exceeding).
- Usage (Unused–Inappropriate Use–Appropriate Use–Exceptional Use).
- Timeliness (Late–On Time–Early).
- Percent complete (0%–25%–50%–75%–100%).
- Accuracy (Totally Incorrect–Partially Correct–Totally Correct).
- Effort (Not Attempted–Minimal Effort–Acceptable Effort–Outstanding Effort).
- Amount of Support Needed (Totally Dependent–Extensive Assistance–Some Assistance–Limited Assistance–Independent).
- Engagement (None–Limited–Acceptable–Exceptional).

Step 5: Implement Instruction or Intervention.

Step 6: Evaluate Instruction or Intervention. Graph the GAS ratings (collected daily or weekly) of student progress.

From Goal attainment scaling: An efficient and effective approach to monitoring student progress. *Teaching exceptional children, 34*(1), p. 9.

when necessary. This preparation may involve some form of verbal rehearsal, role-playing, or the use of verbal, visual and/or physical prompts as part of this. In addition, student involvement in the meeting can be facilitated by avoiding jargon, using understandable language and vocabulary, and directing questions to the student (Test, Mason, Hughes, Konrad, Neale, & Wood, 2004).

DEVELOPING AGREEMENTS AND INTEGRATING RESOURCES

The attainment of IEP and transition plan goals, particularly with children having more serious disabilities, often demands coordination and integration of a variety of services outside the school as well as inside. Most social workers have developed problem-solving and consensus-building skills through their professional education. These skills are often crucial to the successful completion of the IEP process. Social workers are often most likely to have a holistic perspective on the child. The social worker is usually the only member of the multidisciplinary team who is in everyday contact with outside resources and whose educational preparation includes concepts of coordination among these services. Consequently, many school districts routinely use the social worker as a coordinator of the initial multidisciplinary team and in the later IEP staffing with the parents. The high level of professional specialization within the school and the different interests often represented by parent and school create the potential for conflict. Agreements, if reached, are frequently perceived as accommodations between weaker and stronger sets of interests. Children with disabilities receive services from a variety of agencies: medical services, respite care, child welfare, mental health, financial assistance, transportation, vocational education, and so on. In addition to formal agency services, they can receive a variety of help from neighbors, relatives, and informal groups in the community. These can often work against each other if they are not coordinated. The U.S. Department of Education lists the social worker as one of the three professionals (the others are counselor and psychologist) who might serve as coordinator or case manager of the IEP process for an individual child or all disabled children served by an agency. Case managers might: (1) coordinate the multidisciplinary evaluation, (2) collect and synthesize evaluation reports and other relevant information about a child that might be needed at the IEP meeting, (3) communicate with the parent, and (4) participate in or conduct the IEP meeting itself (U.S. Department of Education, 1981). Chapter 30 discusses case management and coordination in greater detail.

Hypothetical Case Study

Let us begin by following a simple referral for a case study evaluation of Devin, with the IEP process, and service sequence through each of the stages of the process. For purposes of our first illustration let us assume that Devin cannot participate in the district-wide general education assessment. Thus he will require annual goals and short-term objectives, as every child has required through the implementation of IDEA 2004.

We may break down the steps that should be followed to arrive at those goals and objectives in the school social worker's contribution to the IEP. The steps represent a way of clarifying our own goals and involvement in developing the IEP. The reader should keep in mind that this is a hypothetical case study and that the type and extent of the school social worker's involvement in a particular case will depend on the individual child's needs as determined by the IEP team. We may begin with the presenting problem:

The Presenting Problem. In order to be eligible for funding, the problem must relate to the categories of disabilities written into the regulations. However, the fact that the child fits into one of the categories, for example, hearing impaired, does not automatically make him a candidate for social work intervention. The inability to deal with stress, potential breakdown of social functioning, or needed improvement of social functioning are general reasons for referral to a social worker. The additional stress of a disability and the need for individualized environmental support systems are reasons that many exceptional children need social work help. The child with a particular disability may have difficulty coping with the educational and social skill demands of the school. He may need help in acquiring such skills and/or in dealing with experiences that are new.

> Devin is a 12-year-old with multiple physical disabilities who is borderline educable mentally disabled. He was referred because of his teacher's concern that his excessive demands for attention were impeding his learning process in several general education classes, particularly in gym.

The Problem as a Whole. The school social worker's conference with teacher and parents resulted in a picture of a boy whose performance in school has been quite uneven and whose ability to function adequately in school has been hampered by parental overprotectiveness and disagreement on the degree of independence he should be allowed. He is currently enrolled in both special and regular education classes with poor adjustment to some of these classes, overwhelming needs for attention from adults, and withdrawal from relations with other children. In the family, the parents have had difficulty agreeing on the tasks he should be involved in and on his expected level of self-care. Consequently, Devin's participation in the family and in care of himself is considerably less than his potential. The parents are in conflict about this, and his two brothers and a sister reflect this ambivalence in their relationships with him. The social worker's assessment draws some connections between Devin's role in the family, the parents' feelings, and the way Devin has played out some of these family role interactions in school behaviors, particularly with parentlike school figures and teachers. The statement also includes alternative plans for working with the family, Devin, and his teachers. The results of the social worker's assessment, combined with the information gathered by the other team members, will be used by the team in the evaluative conference and later to formulate the statement of present levels of educational functioning in the IEP.

The Problem as It Is Experienced in the Context of Education. The next step is to define the problem as it is being experienced in the classroom and in relation to the goals of education. At the risk of oversimplifying, we may provide several social parameters of the educational problem. One parameter is that of engagement or withdrawal from educational tasks appropriate to the child's capabilities. The child may either engage in the learning process with distracting, attention-getting, inappropriately aggressive behavior or may withdraw from the process, attempting to compensate in other ways for the withdrawal. A second parameter is that of engagement or withdrawal from relationships with other children. Pupils need to learn social skills appropriate to their own maturational level. The learning of these social skills influences the performance of educational tasks. Thus, there is a direct relation between the learning environment and the child's social maturation.

To follow our example, the school wishes to place Devin in a general education gym class. We can predict with some certainty that Devin will place high demands on the gym teacher and the other pupils. The parents, although accepting of the idea, might endanger the arrangement because of their own anxiety and worries about Devin. Failure in the gym class could generalize to several other classes where he has recently made some adjustment. There is particular concern with the gym class due to dressing, showers, and inherent physical competition. Any one of these factors might place Devin's use of what the school could offer him at risk. What we know about the problem allows us to predict with some degree of accuracy the chances of goal achievement within a behavior setting and some ability to generalize to the overall ecology of the school. This understanding allows us to move to the next stage, definition of the problem in behavioral terms.

The Problem as Behavior. The purpose of this stage is to state the school social worker's formulation of the problem in behavioral terms and to relate it to the educational goals established earlier. Behavioral terms are statements of a person's present functioning, or what Devin is presently doing. These terms establish a baseline for goals and objectives and must be specific.

Behavioral objectives risk fragmentation and meaninglessness if they do not flow from the process of problem definition discussed earlier. The school social worker may find himself in the position of choosing from a seemingly infinite range of behaviors for any child. Actually, a few well-chosen examples are much better, particularly if they may serve as indicators or "milestones" of the pupil's progress.

To go back to our example, Devin has difficulty dealing with a situation that seems competitive and draws attention to his poor functioning. Under stress he has tended to retreat into social relations with adults, from whom he demands high levels of attention. He is particularly uneasy with the dressing and showering aspects of gym. His parents' anxiety adds to the situation and reveals another set of needs. Teachers also can tend to overreact to the situation, increasing the chances of failure. To enumerate specific aspects of the problem:

1. Devin withdraws from situations involving physical competition. Without intervention, the pattern is expected to continue or increase in gym class.
2. Devin tends not to interact with peers in his general education classes.
3. Social interaction is limited with peers in special education.

4. Devin has no close friends.
5. Devin makes excessive demands on adults, especially teachers, but doesn't function in the classroom up to his own capacities without constant support from the teacher.
6. Devin is particularly self-conscious concerning dressing and showering aspects of gym.
7. His parents have tended to protect Devin from situations that demand independence or involve any risking of self. Devin's home patterns are related to his school patterns.
8. Teachers have tended toward either excessive protection or excessive expectations of independence with Devin.

Annual Goals, Objectives, and Resources

Finally, we may define goals and objectives. *Annual goals* are specific statements of the skills the student should be progressing toward within the framework of the school year. Annual goals evolve out of the assessment of the child's needs and abilities and should be an index of student progress. Although there are different formats that may serve as examples for a particular child's IEP, most would probably contain:

1. *The direction of change desired*—to increase, to decrease, to maintain.
2. *Deficit or excess*—the general area that is identified as needing special attention.
3. *Present level of performance*—what the child now does in deficit or in excess, expressed in measurable terms whenever possible.
4. *Expected level*—where the child realistically could be or what he could gain, with proper resources.
5. *Resources needed*—to accomplish the needed level of performance. Resources could be specialists, materials, situations, or methods required to bring about the desired change.

Measurable terms can be derived in some cases from counting performances, such as attendance, suspensions, grades, homework returned, test scores, extracurricular activities, referrals to the principal, time-outs, etc. They can be derived from performance (or nonperformance) of a particular targeted activity. Or experienced teachers (natural experts for the normal range for the age group who know the student best) may rate the student on a 1–10 scale on some quality in comparison with a normal range for the age group (How does the student get along with his peers, or come prepared to school, or exhibit healthy hygiene?) (Raines, 2002). Or, data can be gathered by observation of the pupil's on- and off-task behavior as in chapter 21. The measurement should obviously fit the purpose and the meaning of the objective as much as possible.

In Devin's case, there are three major annual goals. The components are listed in brackets.

Annual Goal 1: For Devin to increase [direction] positive social relations with peers in general education [deficit] from limited [from] to more informal [to] through interaction experiences in a group with the social worker and regular social work contacts with the parents and teacher [resources].

Annual Goal 2: For Devin to increase [direction] his independence in dressing for gym [deficit] from never dressing for gym to dressing at least two days per week.

Annual Goal 3: For Devin to maintain [direction] his current academic adjustment.

Note that the direction set in the second goal is maintenance of current functioning. Maintenance equates present and expected levels of functioning.

Short-Term Objectives

Pupils who cannot participate in the district-wide general education assessment will need to follow alternate assessments and will need short-term objectives as well as annual goals. *Short-term objectives* can be thought of as measurable intermediate steps toward achievement of each annual goal. These steps are benchmarks or major milestones through which progress toward the annual goals can be assessed (see Lignugaris-Kraft, Marchand-Martella, & Martella, 2001). They should specify the conditions under which the behavior is to be exhibited by the student in his class, in unstructured group tasks, the lunchroom, gymnasium, and so on. For the social worker, these can be indicators or changes in behavior and do not have to reflect every single objective that might be defined for that goal. For Devin, our hypothetical case example, some short-term objectives might be:

1. Devin's level of class participation and quality of assignment completion in his regular education classes will be maintained at his current level through January 15.
2. Devin will interact compatibly with general education peers in an unstructured group task by March 15.
3. Devin will interact comfortably and spontaneously with general education peers in an unstructured lunchroom situation by May 15.
4. Devin will form casual friendships with peers in general and special education by June 15.
5. Devin's distractibility and talking out in class will reduce by 50 percent by June 15.
6. Devin will be able to dress for gym without special arrangement by January 15.

The social worker often assists the team by developing the appropriate goals and objectives in their own area of the student's social functioning. These are worked out individually for every student. For general reference, David Sanders' sampler of developmental learning objectives has been included in this chapter (see table 24.1). School social workers have developed lists of areas of learning using various developmental and social skill formulas (see Micek et al., 1982; Huxtable, 2004; Sanders, 2002).

Resources

The list of services and persons responsible is essentially a *resource state-ment.*There may be external barriers to Devin's accomplishing these goals and objectives.[2] For example, teachers and parents may need help to avoid over-protecting Devin or some modifications in the gym program may be necessary. A list of the specific educational services required must be written into the IEP so that the goals and objectives can be implemented. Parents have a right to request that educational services that are included in the IEP but are not avail-able in the school be purchased by the school district for the child or other-wise be provided at no cost to the parents.[3] Examples of such services might include:

1. The social worker will see Devin once a week for a 45-minute period with a group of other children with disabilities who are also dealing with the stress and social skill demands of a general education class.The appropriateness of whether Devin should continue in the group will be reevaluated on or about January 15.

2. The social worker will monitor Devin's group progress and act as liaison between the IEP team and the family service agency working with Devin's fam-ily and will inform Devin's parents of progress.

3. The teacher will monitor Devin's achievement of these objectives, rein-forcing independent and peer-affiliative behavior.

For our second illustration, let us assume that Devin can participate in the regular assessment and requires annual goals and periodic progress reports, based on goal attainment scaling. In Devin's case a series of objectives should

---

2. See Federal Register, Education of Handicapped Children, Tuesday, August 23, 1977, 121a.552(d)."In selecting the least restrictive environment, consideration is given to any potentially harmful effect on the child or on the quality of services which he or she needs."While the concept of external barriers is not highlighted in the law, it is a traditional concept in dealing with persons with handicapping conditions. Lack of focus on such tangible or nontangible barriers would be in effect "blaming the victim" for a condition that he or she did not create.

3. A free appropriate public education is defined in the law as: special education and related ser-vices that a) have been provided at public expense, under public supervision and direction and without charge; b) meet the standards of the state educational agency; c) include an appropriate preschool, elementary, or secondary school education in the state involved; and d) are provided in conformity with the individualized education program (20 U.S.C. 1401[8]).

be established on a quarterly basis, since this is the typical frequency of report cards being sent to students in general education classes. Table 24.3 outlines reasonable objectives using a goal attainment scaling model.

Monitoring these goals will be a joint responsibility of the classroom teacher and the school social worker. Devin will share in the monitoring by carrying a card with him so the goals can be marked each period and reviewed with his teacher and the social worker to reinforce his progress.

INVOLVING CHILDREN IN THE IEP

It is a good practice to involve the school child in IEP plans. Sometimes these goals may seem abstract, and so a mechanism, such as the car-in-the-garage technique, developed by Fairbanks (1985), is useful. This technique involves the following steps:

1. The school social worker draws a rough sketch of a garage on a piece of paper, connects it to a road, indicates that the garage is to be the child's destina-

TABLE 24.3   Goal Attainment Scaling Model to Rank Objectives

Predicted Levels Of Attainment	Goal 1: Devin will interact appropriately with peers.	Goal 2: Devin will dress for gym without special accommodations.	Goal 3: Devin will maintain successful effort and grades in all classes.
Much less than expected −2	Significant conflicts with peers in regular and special classes involving more than six rule violations per day.	Refuses to dress even with accommodations.	Failing one or more classes.
Somewhat less than expected −1	At least four class rule violations per day.	At least three "no dress" gym days per week, even with accommodations.	Grades drop in one or more subjects.
Expected level 0	Devin will attend social skills class and participate appropriately, with no more than three rule violations per day.	Devin will dress for gym with accommodations and no more than two "no dress" days per week.	Devin will maintain grades in all classes.
Somewhat more than expected +1	Devin will transfer behavior learned in group and practice it with peers in special calluses.	With accommodations, Devin will dress every day for gym.	Devin will improve grades in two classes.
Much more than expected +2	Devin will interact comfortably with peers in regular and special classes.	Devin will dress for gym without accommodations.	Devin will improve grades in four classes.

tion, and asks the child to identify what should be placed in the garage as goals.

2. The child tells the school social worker what changes are desired, and the social worker or the child writes these goals inside the garage.

3. The child places one or more cars at various points along the road to the garage, symbolizing how far away from the goals and objectives he or she is. Sometimes the child leaves one or more cars off the road completely, indicating extreme lack of progress toward the goals represented by those cars.

4. The social worker asks the child for additional information about the cars and records the responses. The child's stated goals and objectives then become part of the IEP that is formally drafted at the planning team meeting.

5. The child draws new cars on the road as treatment progresses, relocating the cars on the road either closer or farther away from the garage.

6. The child places one or more cars inside the garage when particular objectives are attained and either establishes a new set of objectives or terminates treatment.

Figure 24.1 illustrates use of the technique in clarifying initial objectives for Mike, age 12, and Jerry, age 8, in a public school day treatment program. Following the clarification of objectives, the technique can be used to measure

FIGURE 24.1   Using the Car-in-the-Garage Technique to Clarify Objectives

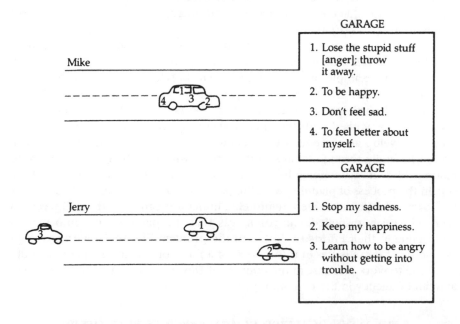

From Involving children in the IEP: The car-in-the-garage technique, by N. McDowell Fairbanks, 1987, *Social Work in Education, 9*(3).

progress and change objectives. In some cases, it can be used with a group because the technique becomes a visual and verbal metaphor for their accomplishments.

Behavioral Intervention Plans (BIP)

When disciplinary action is being considered, it is important to develop a functional behavior assessment of certain behaviors of concern of a child with a disability. The functional behavior assessment is the base for a behavioral intervention plan (both discussed in chapter 19). Thus the charts of functional behavior objectives, listed earlier in this chapter, are useful for assessment and treatment planning. Somewhat similar to the IEP in its construction and rationale, the behavioral intervention plan should focus on the behaviors of concern. It should have measurable goals and objectives and a clear description of how to increase positive behaviors rather than simply trying to reduce the undesirable ones. These measurable goals and objectives should clearly describe the desired improvement or remedy for the problem. The plan should include a description of the strategies that will be used to increase positive behavior and decrease undesirable behavior, including planned disciplinary procedures, if necessary. These should include strategies for generalizing and maintaining positive behavior outside of the educational situation. When this plan is developed, it should be monitored regularly, modified when necessary. It should be documented in a way that conveys to parents and others whether or not the student is making progress (Clark, 2001).

Where do parents fit into this picture? Chapters 26 and 27 outline how social workers relate their family focus to the goals of education (Welsh, 1985). Following the example of Devin, the problem in school was related to a long-established pattern of inconsistent expectations at home that caused Devin's self-care and participation in the family to be far below his capabilities. The social worker worked with the child and the parents and indirectly with siblings to develop an agreement on specific aspects of participation and contribution in family, through chores, helping with younger siblings, learning more responsibility in maintaining his room, choosing his clothes, and dressing himself. In the process of planning with the parents and with Devin, it became clear that parental differences were reinforcing immaturity, and that these differences were not easily dispelled. The result was that the parents went into marital counseling in their efforts to deal with the problem. The social worker identified some of these issues in the context of a focus on Devin. The parents could continue to work on these in the context of Devin, or begin marital counseling at a family agency in the community.

THE INDIVIDUALIZED FAMILY SERVICES PLAN (IFSP)

The individualized family services plan (IFSP) grows out of early intervention programs for infants and toddlers and the obvious necessity of family involvement with children from birth through two years of age, especially children with multiple disabilities. Many of the principles underlying the IEP are also applicable to the IFSP and need not be repeated. There are several differences, because the IFSP is more comprehensive than the IEP and takes in a wider universe. The focus of the IFSP is first of all on development, rather than a more static focus, appropriate to the older child. This is evaluated through a variety of means and instruments. In addition, a statement of the family's strengths and needs relating to enhancing the child's development is needed. A statement of the family's strengths and needs requires a family assessment and is best carried out by the school social worker. An agreement on goals, objectives, and tasks needs to emerge from this mutual assessment between social worker and family. In addition, the coping and adaptation of parents, siblings, and support systems in an extended family and friendship network need to be assessed.

The IFSP must contain:

1. A statement of the child's present levels of development (cognitive, speech/language, psychosocial, motor, and self-help);
2. A statement of the family's strengths and needs relating to enhancing the child's development;
3. The measurable outcome criteria, procedures, and timelines for determining progress;
4. The specific early intervention services necessary to meet the unique needs of the child and family, including the method, frequency, and intensity of service;
5. The projected dates for the initiation of service and the expected duration;
6. The name of the case manager;
7. Procedures for transition from early intervention into the preschool program.

The IFSP must be evaluated at least once a year and must be reviewed every six months or more, where appropriate.

The family is of crucial importance at the earliest stages of dealing with the possibility that a child has a disability. There is often a heavy involvement with the health-care system, and this is confusing at a time when parents are just beginning to bond with a child. Whose child is this, ours or the health-care system's, (or the school's)? The health-care system and the school actually have similar concerns with families. If either system seeks to displace the family, the result can be chaotic. When there are multiple specialists, parents often have a great deal of case management to do at a time when they are most uncertain of their role. They are often mourning the loss of the perfect child they had dreamed of, and thus the loss of their fondest hopes and expectations (Lachncy, 1982). The heavy caretaking demands can split even well-established marital relations into overadequate and enmeshed roles or underadequate and disengaged roles. These roles may follow conventional gender expectations. The resulting marital and family patterns are disruptive of other aspects of family living and may account for the higher rates of divorce, suicide, and child abuse among families of children with disabilities (Gallagher, Beckman, & Cross, 1983). Working with the parents while they are actively mourning their losses and when care patterns have not been completely solidified may prevent the most crippling effects of these disrupting patterns on the family and especially on the child with a disability. A certain amount of inactivity associated with being overwhelmed and with mourning, and the potential distortion of relationships inherent in heavy caregiving, demands often can be expected in these situations, and thus the risks should be assessed. The teaching role of parents can be distorted by the loss of hope implicit in a mourning process, and by the same relational distortions involved in the discussion of caregiving roles. Parents may be reluctant to accept help and may isolate themselves from other potential support systems in the process. Success in this process presupposes a good contact between the social worker and parents when the pressures and risks are discussed in a normalizing context.

Expected Outcomes

The IFSP, a statement of expected outcomes and an agreement on a type of partnership, can be used as the basis for the social worker's intervention with the child and the family. Based on the assessment and the particular contacts developed with the family, major expected outcomes now can be stated in a way that reinforces the primary roles of parents as educators as well as care givers and the appropriate assistance of the school in carrying out their mission. A key outcome will be the family's participation in the teaching and caregiving roles and ability to use the case management process. The outcomes are largely based on: (1) the assessments previously made of the child's present levels of development and (2) the new coping and adaptation patterns becoming established in the family. Although educational and medical specialists have an important role in setting achievable developmental outcomes, social workers should be involved in setting achievable family outcomes and showing their relation to developmental outcomes.

Service Coordination

The IFSP must contain the name of the service coordinator from the profession most immediately relevant to the infant's, toddler's, or family's needs who will be responsible for the implementation of the plan in coordination with other agencies or persons. She coordinates services to the family of an infant or toddler with a disability to assist in gaining access to early intervention services identified in the IFSP. Service coordination includes:

1. Coordinating assessments and participating in the development of the IFSP;

2. Assisting families in identifying available service providers;
3. Coordinating and monitoring the delivery of services, including coordinating the provision of early intervention services with other services that the child or family may need or is receiving, but that are not required under this part;
4. Facilitating the development of a transition plan to preschool services where appropriate. (*Federal Register* 52(222): 303.6)

The coordinator then assists parents in gaining access to these services. However, parents themselves should take responsibility as much as possible for the coordination roles (Garland, Woodruff, & Buck, 1988) or at least have a major role in the selection of a service coordinator. The social worker's role places him or her closest to the parents in carrying out service coordination responsibilities.

The final part of the IFSP is that of the child's transition from an early intervention program to the preschool program. Although this is frequently the domain of the educational specialists, the process and the timing of the entry of the child from a family context into a new program with new demands may be an area in which the school social worker needs to participate.

The family involvement projected in the IFSP need not be confined to infants and toddlers. When children present complex vulnerabilities and long-established patterns that inevitably affect the educational process, it is simply good practice to involve the parents in the work of the school. The IEP and the IFSP can be no better than the process of thinking, communicating, and decision making they represent. They certainly are accountability documents, but they also are vehicles for collaboration with parents and for coordination of resources and development of the working agreements necessary for complex goals to be achieved. The IFSP and the IEP are challenges for social workers in developing clarity about what they will be offering students, parents, and the school, while providing an opportunity to work systematically with all of the influences on the full educational process. It is an opportunity that we cannot afford to let pass.

References

Clark, J. (2001). *Functional behavior assessment and behavior intervention plans: Implementing the student discipline provisions of IDEA '97. NASW school social work hot topics.* Washington, DC: NASW Home Page: Retrieved from http://www.naswdc.org/sections/ssw/hottopics/schalark.htm

Fairbanks, N. M. (1985). Involving children in the IEP: The car-in-the-garage technique. *Social Work in Education, 7*(3), 171–182.

Gallagher, J. J., Beckman, P., & Cross, A. H. (1983). Families of handicapped children: Sources of stress and its alleviation. *Exceptional Children, 50*(1), 10–18.

Garland, C., Woodruff, G., & Buck, D. (1988). *Case management. Division for early childhood white paper.* Reston, VA: Council for Exceptional Children.

Huxtable, M. (2004). Defining measurable behavioral goals and objectives. *SSWAA Bell.* January, Northlake: Il: SSWAA (see also SSWAA@aol.com or www.sswaa.org). For a 26-

page list of behavioral goals and objectives in a PDF format from the Tuscon Unified
School District's Web site, see http://edweb.tusd.k12az.us/exced/forms03/Forms_pdf/
behavioralgoals_Obj_021027.pdf

Lachney, M. E. (1982). Understanding families of the handicapped: A critical factor in the parent-school relationship. In R. T. Constable & J. P. Flynn (Eds.), *School social work: Practice and research perspectives* (n.p.). Homewood, IL: Dorsey Press.

Lignugaris-Kraft, B., Marchand-Martella, N., & Martella, R. C. (2001). Strategies for writing better goals and short-term objectives or benchmarks. *Teaching Exceptional Children,* *34*(1), 52-8.

Micek, D., Barnes, J., Newman, C., Roelofs, M., Rosenbaum, M., & Sices, M., (1982). School social work objectives. In R. Constable & J. Flynn (Eds.), *School social work: Practice and research perspectives* (pp. 251-255). Homewood, IL: Dorsey Press.

Raines, J. C. (2002). Present levels of performance, goals and objectives: A best practice guide. *School Social Work Journal, 27*(1), 58-72.

Roach, A. T., & Elliott, S. N. (2005). Goal attainment scaling: An efficient and effective approach to monitoring student progress. *Teaching exceptional children, 37*(4), 8-16.

Sanders, D. (2002). Annual goals and short-term objectives for school social workers. In R. Constable, S. McDonald & J. Flynn (Eds.), *School social work: Practice, policy, and research perspectives* (pp. 279-288). Chicago: Lyceum.

Test, D. W., Mason, C., Hughes, C., Konrad, M., Neale, M., & Wood, W. (2004). Student involvement in individualized education program meetings. *Exceptional Children, 70*(4), 391-412.

U.S. Department of Education. (1981). *The case study evaluation.* Washington, DC: Author.

Welsh, B. L. (1985, March). *The individualized family plan (IFP): A social work component to the IEP.* Paper presented at the NASW School Social Work Conference, Philadelphia, PA.

Section Four

Practice Applications in the Schools

25

Developing and Defining the School Social Worker's Role

Robert Constable
Loyola University, Chicago

- ◆ Role Development
- ◆ Clinical Social Work in a School
- ◆ Units of Attention and School Social Work Role(s)

ROLE DEVELOPMENT

The role of a school social worker develops according to the assessment of the situation and the understandings reached within the team, with parents, and with students. The foundation skills of school social workers are focused on deciding (*with others*) what to do, who should do it, and with whom. These skills were discussed in Section III on assessment, multidisciplinary teaming, and consultation. The next set of skills concentrates on *role development*, that is, doing what has been decided. The school social worker helps pupils, parents, and the school to work with each other in ways that would best assist students in their tasks of learning and developing.

CLINICAL SOCIAL WORK IN A SCHOOL

To illustrate the function of the school social worker, we take a deliberately simplified example of social work services to a child, Jorge Oliverez, with a moderate disability in a regular educational setting.

Jorge is a 12-year-old Cuban American child with physical disabilities and explosive relations with others. He has just moved to a new school district and is beginning in Blake Junior High School. Jorge is the youngest child by 8 years of middle-aged parents. His previous school, Dorian Elementary, gave Jorge considerable attention but protected him from the effects that his hostile, demanding behavior had on others. His needs were perceived as overwhelming, and his demands for attention led to estrangement from other children. The problem tended to be reinforced by the parents, who, in their unqualified support for Jorge's demands, undercut any positive, socializing effects the school might have.

From the beginning, Jorge's new seventh-grade homeroom teacher, Mr. Beall, found Jorge's constant demands for attention difficult to deal with in an active classroom. He responded by ignoring Jorge in the hope that he would modify his behavior. Jorge responded with increased explosiveness and looked for support from other places. He found allies in his parents and his gym teacher. With the implicit approval of his parents, Jorge had not turned in an assignment in language arts for several weeks and was beginning to fail the subject despite nearly average ability. His classmates reacted to Jorge's behavior. The teacher felt that Jorge needed to learn to take consequences but tended to remove himself. The principal was informed that Jorge's parents had been using the situation to mobilize other parents of children with disabilities in a parents' organization around the real issue of district-wide neglect of programs for children with disabilities. Mr. Beall decided that, if the principal backed the parents, he in turn would file a union grievance. He took the step of referring Jorge for placement out of his current regular class into a special class that generally has children with more severe disabilities. The parents, although conflicted, were partially in agreement with the idea of placement. What would a social worker who had specific responsibility for conducting a social study do in this situation? How would a worker make recommendations regarding school placement and services to the multidisciplinary team?

We can map four components in this case: Jorge's actual behavior, the conditions behind Jorge's behavior, the impinging environment in the classroom, and the conditions behind the impinging environment (table 25.1). A social worker could conceivably work with Jorge, his family, or the teacher in program development in the school and in the community. At one point or another, the social worker would probably have some direct or indirect influence on all of these systems and could intervene selectively in a few of them, according to her assessment of the situation, her competence, and the time available.

UNITS OF ATTENTION AND SCHOOL SOCIAL WORK ROLE(S)

The locus of concern for the social worker may rest on Jorge, his family, Mr. Beall, or more broadly, children with disabilities as a group in school. One way to organize these complex choices for assessment and for intervention is to think of them as units of attention. A *unit of attention* is a chosen point of most effective change, a point or set of points in the system where, if change takes place, other positive changes will also become possible. For example, the social worker might work with the Oliverez parents and other parents of children with disabilities to promote greater awareness of the needs of children with dis-

TABLE 25.1   Transactions, Impingement, and Source Environments in the Case of Jorge

Source Environment (conditions behind behavior)	Transaction		Source Environment (conditions behind behavior)
	Coping Behavior	Classroom Impingement	
Jorge: Fearful; dependent; compensates by demands for attention; uses disability to control and manipulate adults around him	Irascible; inordinate demands for attention; isolate; physical limitations; turns in no work; "building a case" against teacher	**Homeroom teacher:** Ignores; has referred to special class placement	Likes independent children; feels should achieve at class level without special attention; resents Jorge's demands
Parents: Disability has had deep impact on own feelings of adequacy, feel guilty also; react by overprotection; but basically feel quite helpless and angry to have this responsibility	Alternate between high defensiveness and helplessness	**Peers:** Steal pencils; call him names	Don't understand Jorge's behavior or rejection of them; his disability bothers them
		Gym teacher: Sympathetic to Jorge; spends time with him	Had a minor disability that he overcame when he was young; has had special training to prepare for working with physically disabled; feels competitive with Jorge's homeroom teacher
		Principal: Concerned about image of school in community and with parents' organization; schools are being closed; tax revolt on	
		Parents' organization: Looking for test case to express concern about needs of children with disabilities	

abilities in the school district. The worker might use the strong connections in the Cuban American community as a resource. The worker might collaborate with school administrators to plan better services for children with disabilities. The worker might act as a consultant to Jorge's teacher, Mr. Beall, helping him come to a better understanding of Jorge and his relations with the other students in the class. The social worker might develop a close collaborative relationship between Jorge's homeroom teacher and gym teacher as a support system, without incurring the resentment of his homeroom teacher. The focus depends on the school social worker's assessment of the needs in the situation. The worker's competence in different areas, the time available, and the extent of development of the social work program in the school—in other words the realistic limitations and opportunities of the situation as perceived following a professional assessment—may affect the focus.

The School Program as a Unit of Attention

The first unit of attention of the school social worker is the school program offered to pupils. Here the school social worker may work with others in the school to develop programs for particular groups, such as pregnant adolescents or children being mainstreamed from special education programs, or for individual students. In one instance, the high school may be in crisis with the suicide of a well-known third-year student. The social worker is part of the crisis team, having helped prepare a general crisis plan, and will take part in working with different parts of the school community as it copes with the crisis. In another instance, the social worker may be assisting in the development of regular education classroom environments that appropriately accommodate certain children with special needs. He may be involved in transition planning for these children and consultation on placements. The social worker may design special group experiences to meet the needs of diverse populations, such as young parents, children of divorce, pregnant adolescents, eighth graders with developmental disabilities learning social skills, or teachers finding an appropriate role for themselves in dealing with children who tell them about abuse. The social worker may develop a mediation program to help the school find better and fairer ways for adolescents to deal with disputes and fights.

In individual circumstances, the social worker will work as a consultant to teachers. Many times, developing a program or consulting with teachers is enough to accomplish desired change. The change in the classroom affords the pupil an opportunity to accomplish learning and social developmental tasks. Sometimes nothing more is needed than consultation. Extending intervention to the parents or pupil would be unnecessary and therefore intrusive. On the other hand, when intervention with parents and/or pupil is necessary, it should be built initially on continuing consultation with the teachers and other resources in the school.

Jimmy B. is a 7-year-old boy with learning disabilities whose parents were going through a divorce. Jimmy was having great difficulty staying on task in class. He cried readily and was very dependent on adults in his environment. His classroom teacher, Ms. T., found him quite difficult and believed that he was simply avoiding the expectations of her class. His resource room teacher, Mr. G., saw more of what Jimmy could do in individual sessions but seemed to be protecting him from the expectations of Ms. T.'s class. The social worker, in consultation with both teachers and after observing Jimmy in class, saw a child who was withdrawing from learning tasks, probably because of generally slow development and inconsistent, sometimes conflicting school expectations. In cooperation with both teachers, the social worker facilitated an understanding of the tasks that could be expected of Jimmy in both classes. Both teachers developed a better understanding of the problems by sharing perspectives and by gaining a better understanding of the relation of his parents' divorce to Jimmy's efforts to concentrate. Both agreed on a program of support to encourage more mature functioning with gradually increased expectations of more independent functioning. The social worker agreed to contact the home, help the parents understand the educational goals, and solicit their help in supporting the new plan, especially when helping with Jimmy's homework.

The Family as a Unit of Attention

The second unit of attention is the family of the pupil. In harmony with the work begun by the teacher, the potential alliance of the school with the family may need to be developed through routine communication and consistent mutual understanding of what they should expect and what support Jimmy needs to take the next steps toward appropriate, developmental maturity. With many students, contact with the family and some ongoing work with teachers is enough to accomplish a goal. In any case, the family's involvement is usually necessary before going on to the next step.

In her contact with Jimmy's home, the social worker learned that his parents were at the point of separation. Mrs. B., a clerk, felt very close to Jimmy, who was her youngest child. She had always enjoyed his sweet and babyish qualities, whereas his father tended to have high expectations of him. This difference was a cause of marital difficulty. Mrs. B. had relied on Mr. B. to set limits and was having difficulty setting her own limits. The social worker had several contacts with Mrs. B. and one with both parents together. She helped them see some of the effects of their conflict on Jimmy and referred the couple to a family service agency for more extensive family counseling. Both parents became concerned about the extent to which Jimmy was reacting to their difficulties. Mrs. B. worked out an agreement so that she could be reached by phone away from her place of employment, and building on this, Mrs. B. was able to work more closely with the school regarding expectations of Jimmy. Mr. B. was willing to support this work. Both parents requested that the social worker observe Jimmy, and the social worker agreed to do this, provided she could remain in contact with them regarding developments at home and school. In her observations of Jimmy and in her contacts with the parents, the social worker noticed that Jimmy himself drew out either protectiveness or rejection from people around him in the same way he had experienced this division from his parents. This is common in children experiencing marital conflict in the home. She decided to develop a contract between the parents and the teachers to support their efforts to work together and set common rules and expectations.

Because of the parents' divisiveness over Jimmy, the worker was careful to see them together in a joint session. She had assessed the role of Jimmy in the couple's dynamics and did not want the contract between parents and teachers to accelerate the couple's division but to be a first step toward their getting help. She was careful to focus on Jimmy but knew that in working out details of the agreement with them, she was bringing them to a first step in dealing with their marital issues. Although the parents' differences in relation to Jimmy came out immediately in the joint session, the worker did not probe into the couple's relationship or attempt to do marital counseling. Within the concrete framework of an agreement with the school over Jimmy, she patiently guided them to an initial agreement that included ongoing communication between the social worker and the couple. The agreement set expectations of gradually more mature functioning on Jimmy's part but, with the worker being in touch with both parents, also allowed for some shifts in the couple's relationship with Jimmy. As the worker communicated with the parents over the ensuing months, she was able to help them differentiate their issues with each other from their parenting of Jimmy. Later, both were able to begin marital counseling in a community agency to which she had referred them.

In this example, the focus remained on Jimmy and how his parents could assist his maturation. The focus was safe enough for the parents to process many of their issues with each other, to differentiate Jimmy's needs from theirs, and eventually to get help with their marriage. The work of the school social worker with both parents needed to be as sophisticated as any family therapist. In Jimmy's case, the concrete focus on Jimmy's school difficulties provided a safe metaphor for the personal and family work that needed to be done. The worker was ready to assess the relation of the parents' dynamics as a couple to Jimmy's maturation and to school dynamics. She knew that when she intervened with the parents on Jimmy's behalf, they would inevitably have to deal in some way with their dynamics as a couple. She could help them maximize their new awareness of this situation. Essentially, she had translated knowledge of developmental and family dynamics to knowledge of school tasks. These tasks would be a context for Jimmy to work out some of his own issues, and for the parents to work out some of theirs.

Given the diversity of units of attention for the school social worker, what has centrality is: (1) the learning process of the student, Jimmy, and (2) the family and school worlds that surround Jimmy's learning process. These family and school worlds are often quite dysfunctional in relation to the child's attempts at active coping. To understand this more deeply, one must consider some paradoxes within the educational process itself. The action of the learner is inevitably central to this process. A whole environmental world—from parent through school secretary, janitor, school psychologist, social worker, teacher, and principal—waits to see whether and how Jimmy will engage. When necessary, the social worker moves among all the parts of this world to help it work for Jimmy, and to help find and share the best of himself to work with the environment and mature appropriately. The more the social worker can adapt methodology to the particular needs in the situation and use diverse approaches that help Jimmy make sense of his world and discover what he can offer to it, the better. However, ultimately Jimmy does the work, and multiplied by each student in the school, the educational process succeeds or fails on this. On the other hand, from Jimmy's perspective the learning process in school is a central developmental event. If he fails and denies its importance, even to himself, it is no less important an event. Buried in a thousand efforts to compensate in different ways by doing other things is the consciousness that he has failed in this social task. He will repeatedly try to succeed in his own way until he is discouraged and retreats in confusion. His surrounding world must help him find a match between "his own way" and the ways of the school, but the task for Jimmy and for the school demands flexibility, experimentation, and support for the process until some match is achieved. Educational tasks are so important and so central to the maturation of many children that there may be no more powerful way to help Jimmy grow. This will be particularly true if his family can participate in and support the process.

The Pupil as a Unit of Attention

The third unit of attention is the pupil. Whatever changes take place in the classroom environment and in what the school is able to offer, the pupil needs to use them and to deal with personal issues of change. Building on the sound base of a connection with home and school, the combination of small changes in home, school, and pupil is often much more powerful than an intensive focus on a single factor.

> Jimmy was willing to see the social worker after his parents discussed it with him. He enjoyed working with clay, making elaborate log houses and little people, but could get teary-eyed if the social worker made any association in the play sessions with home or with a mother or father. He eventually was able to talk about his feelings regarding school. The social worker was able to involve Jimmy in the contract with his teachers and his parents on assignments and expectations and reinforce improvements with him. She decided that she would go slowly with Jimmy, helping him deal with the positive changes in the classroom and home that she had been encouraging. When the mother was eventually able to develop a more realistic limit-setting relationship with him, he began to feel stress, but also the feeling that he was growing up. He initially met the teacher's expectations of independence in the same way, but his eventual positive response reinforced a changing relationship with both teacher and mother.

The Community as a Unit of Attention

A fourth unit of attention is the agencies and resources in the community. The community provides a variety of resources, such as child care, health care, employment, and so on, that may make it possible to achieve certain goals. In most cases, the social worker would have difficulty making the connection without first establishing a firm base with school, family, and pupil.

> Jimmy's parents requested marital counseling at a family service agency. The school social worker collaborated with the counselor they were seeing. Jimmy was clearly inappropriately involved with the marital issues, and only with considerable effort were his parents able to refocus their discussion. Both parents were concerned about Jimmy's reaction to their problems, but the school's work with Jimmy gave them insights that enabled them to get to issues more related to their actual marital problems.

In addition to helping people to use existing resources, frequently the school social worker is in a position to *develop* resources in the community. This is particularly possible when the school is used as the center in the community for developing family services (see chapter 9). The school social worker may also use informal resources, such as a student volunteer in a park system, to help an extremely isolated 13-year-old move into group game activities and eventually translate these gains into his relationships with others in school. A child with a severe disability is usually more vulnerable and depends on complex relations with systems external to the family, as well as the family itself, to meet her emergent needs. These external systems provide special education, physical and mental health services of different sorts, job training, transportation, and a variety of temporary or permanent care arrangements when family care is no longer adequate. The family of the child with disabilities is under considerable pressure and cannot really function without some assistance from the outside. The school social worker needs to negotiate networks of service agreements with the family and the appropriate providers. Considerable professional skill is necessary to keep such a network going, but these networks could make the difference between a child's remaining in the community and going to an institution.

Using first-hand accounts, let us consider a few examples of the process of working with different units of attention.

Tommy—Working Between Parents, Teachers, and Pupil

Tommy is a third grader who was initially referred for his out-of-control behavior. He is not on grade level, tends to disrupt the class, seldom finishes assignments, and steals and lies both in and out of class. He seldom tells the same story about an incident and has alienated himself from his classmates. He is a late reader and appears to have marginal learning disabilities in verbal and math skills. Tommy lives with his mother, stepfather, and his half-brother, aged 2. The parents, who work as orderlies in an extended-care facility, were married a year ago. Last year after his parents had punished him for something, Tommy reported to the school his parents were abusing him, and that his father had a drinking problem. The resulting referral to the child welfare agency (with no contact with the parents) was unfounded. Tommy admitted later that there had been no physical punishment. Tommy's parents responded to these accusations by refusing to meet, or have Tommy meet, with anyone from the school. Communications broke down, and Tommy's behavior worsened. At this point, it was referred to Julia Alvarez, the social worker. The teacher was determined to get Tommy into a class for the behaviorally disordered. The mother was very angry and reluctant to meet with anyone from the school. She saw the teacher (and the school) as an enemy, disrupting her marriage and undermining her authority with her son. She said that Tommy had the same problems at home, but that there had been no physical abuse and that her husband had stopped drinking. It took a great deal of work to regain the trust of the parents and help them to find alternate ways to deal with Tommy. Both parents agreed to form a united front in relation to Tommy. They made a plan where the stepfather agreed to walk Tommy back to school if he didn't bring homework home. Neither had a high school degree, and they felt hampered in helping him with his homework, but they did find a neighbor girl who would help him. Tommy agreed to go along with this plan.

In spite of these changes, the teacher was still determined to remove him from her class. The principal initially supported her in this. It was only with the involvement of the district-wide prereferral committee that the principal and teacher agreed to make an effort to work with the parents on this at all. Working between the teacher, Tommy's parents, and Tommy, it took Ms. Alvarez about a semester of constant work, together with Tommy's gradual, but evident improvement, for the teacher to change her attitude. For every step Tommy took, he sabotaged his progress the next moment. On the other hand, for the first time in his life Tommy was being exposed to consistent expectations and clear, appropriate consequences from everyone. Ms. Alvarez had to help the teacher overcome a tendency either to overreact to Tommy or to ignore him. She had to help the parents back up the teacher. She had to help Tommy adjust to the changes in class, and to accept his stepfather's, as well as his mother's, involvement with him. Later testing confirmed Tommy's borderline learning disabilities and now marginal behavior problems. Over the next three years, Tommy did improve gradually, and Ms. Alvarez continued to work with the parents, his teachers, and Tommy. When he went to junior high school, he didn't do badly. He came back to tell Ms. Alvarez how he was managing himself. His favorite subjects were shop and gym, and he was on the stage crew.

Cathy

With Cathy the focus was always on helping her manage her anxieties, but in the process John Atwood, the social worker, also worked over a period of four years at different times with her teachers, her parents, and a psychiatrist in the community.

On the first day of freshmen orientation at West Oakwood Senior High School, students were having a cookout, prepared by the administration and joined by faculty and staff. A senior girl came up to Mr. Atwood and asked for assistance with a girl in her group who was crying uncontrollably. At first, Cathy was almost unable to communicate, and he worried that she might hyperventilate from her sobbing. He was able to help her to calm herself. Later she stated that she was scared to death of being in this big school and away from her mother. Mr. Atwood helped her to stabilize, contacted the parents, and with their permission then met with Cathy to help her deal with her anxiety about the transition to West Oakwood. As part of this plan, he also wrote to Cathy's teachers that she was having difficulty with her transition, asking them for any input they might have and also letting them know he would be available. In the beginning, he would see Cathy before school started three days a week and then touched base with her before her study hall period to help get her through the second half of the day. He coordinated with the parents, with some of her teachers, and with the psychiatrist, who eventually evaluated her and prescribed medication. As she began to adjust, he would see her once a week to help her maintain her gains with monitoring by one of her teachers and occasional contact with her parents.

Cathy lives with her parents and younger brother and sister. Both of Cathy's parents work in the small family business they own. They are having marital problems, and the mother has been in therapy a year and a half. Her two younger siblings are state and national champion gymnasts, something her father is deeply involved with. Cathy is slightly overweight, feels awkward, neglected by her father and siblings, and closer to her mother. She has had panic attacks since sixth grade whenever she begins something new, such as going to summer camp. She had received help in a middle-school group addressing anxiety issues and was working with a counselor in the community. In Mr. Atwood's contacts with her, Cathy became increasingly worried about her attacks. She was afraid that something would happen to her father and mother when she was not with them. She recalled her father injuring his back at work, and getting the call just when she came home from school. As a freshman, she became more and more distraught and began to make comments about harming herself so that she would not have to come to school. When Mr. Atwood shared this with her parents, the family was initially reluctant to place Cathy on medication, but when Cathy started talking about harming herself, she was evaluated and placed on an antidepressant. Gradually Cathy showed signs of improvement and stabilized. He encouraged Cathy, who has always loved creative writing, to get involved with the school paper, and encouraged her parents to support her in this. Cathy gradually developed greater self-confidence and a few friends. The following year she did much better, and he dropped their contacts to check-ins every month. She had a difficult junior year when she had a very disappointing experience with a boy who was on the school paper with her. He saw her weekly for a while and stayed in occasional contact with her up to graduation. She came back to visit him once, looking for encouragement when she started at a local junior college.

Dealing with Sexual Harassment at Northwood Junior High School

The social worker first became aware of a big problem of peer sexual harassment in eighth-grade gym class when several girls told her about it with great embarrassment. It was going on mostly in the locker room and the showers, which were unmonitored. The gym teacher wasn't sure what constituted harassment and wasn't sure how to deal with it, if it was. He agreed to check into it. We developed an anonymous survey, which asked students whether they had experienced particular harassing behaviors (which were defined in the questionnaire) in school over the past year. When we received the returns, 75 percent of the boys and 85 percent of the girls had experienced sexual harassment in school. When they thought about these behaviors as harassment, they didn't like them. They had been uncertain whether this was just something to be expected in school. When the principal and the teachers saw the data, they were surprised. They also found themselves changing their thinking about harassment, and so did community members and parents when the issue was discussed. A policy was eventually developed that sexual harassment would not be tolerated. Later the social worker worked with the principal and faculty on ways to implement this policy. Students had to learn that the penalty for harassment was removal from school until it was clear that the harassment would stop. When this actually occurred, the social worker found herself working professionally with groups and individual victims on the meaning of what had happened to them. Students mediated some of the problems. She worked with perpetrators on the meaning of what they had done and on ways to rejoin the school community. This eventually created a profound change in the school.

In actual practice, the social worker will work with a variety of units of attention at the same time, and the focus of the social worker on these units of attention will also change over time. In the next chapter the case of Alan, his family, and his teachers, managed over a period of five years, is a classic example of clinical social work in a school. There were various permutations of units of attention over the years as Alan's family situation, teachers, and Alan himself changed. A paradox is that although over the years the worker actively shifted her role to fit the developing situation, most of the "work" was done by Alan, his family, and the school, as all of them shifted over time and in relation to each other. Their tasks in relation to each other were so compelling that the worker used this energy as the main tool for change, and so in fact, she did not need to be centralized at any time or to give an exhaustive amount of energy to the situation. With the situation and its dynamics accurately assessed, the principal actors did the work. The task of the social worker was to work with the principal actors, using a variety of intervention modalities, and to develop situations in which this work could be done most productively. Effectiveness did not come from the use of a single modality, but from matching modalities with the situation and the energies and capabilities of its participants. This approach to assessment and intervention is more complex, but undoubtedly more effective. As any team member will recognize, effective interventions are accomplished not by one member alone, possibly the school social worker, but by all the participants in the arena. Ineffective interventions are likewise a product of the participants in interaction and are not simply the fault of one team member.

School social workers will shape and hew their practice to meet the needs and possibilities of the actual situation, the school, and its community environment. As a result of this shaping and hewing, the practice of one social worker will emphasize resource development and teamwork facilitation; another will emphasize the traditional treatment model, and so on. Each becomes an adaptation to an environment of expectations and a professional decision on the worker's part about what is the most efficient, effective, and timely investment of self in service to a common social work commitment and perspective.

26

The Dynamics of Systems Involvement with Children in School: A Case Perspective

Helen S. Wolkow

Southwest Cook County,
Cooperative for Special Education

- ◆ Reason for Referral
- ◆ Case Study Findings
- ◆ Family History
- ◆ Educational Background and Evaluation
- ◆ Services Offered, Progress, and Results
- ◆ Current Progress

If we are to view students in their environment, then we must examine the many facets of that environment: academic, social, developmental, and emotional. It is often difficult for educators and administrators to recognize that all parts of that environment must be attended to if learning is to proceed effectively. If a student is having difficulty at home, or with peers, his or her academics almost invariably will suffer. Working with a student on emotional needs when there is also an academic problem is not enough. Working on academics when a student is emotionally upset is not enough. If we are to view the child as a whole, then we must attend to all of his or her needs so that he or she may develop and function at his or her optimum.

The following is an example of a case quite common to the caseload of the school social worker. It involves a child with whom the social worker worked over a period of six years (second through eighth grade), his parents, his teachers, the school administration, and outside agencies.

REASON FOR REFERRAL

Alan was referred for evaluation by his 2nd-grade classroom teacher toward the end of September, about five weeks after the start of school. He was a transfer student from another school district and was experiencing great difficulty with reading and spelling. He also had difficulty following directions and concentrating on his work, he was easily distracted, and he had poor fine-motor coordination and poor visual perception. Alan often would try to copy from his neighbors or just sit and not attempt to do his work. At times he would sit and suck his fingers. Teachers described him as shy and withdrawn.

The teacher presented the situation to the pupil personnel service team, and they agreed testing should be done. The parents were contacted and agreed to the evaluation. As part of this evaluation, or case study, I completed a Social Developmental Study. This provided us with some insight into possible etiology for some of his academic development and social difficulties.

CASE STUDY FINDINGS

Alan, a nice-looking, blond, blue-eyed White male, was age 7 at the time of our initial interview. When interviewed, he had a very quiet and shy manner, almost withdrawn. He spoke very softly, and at times it was difficult to understand what he said. A lot of his emotional energy seemed to be tied up with his parents' divorce process, which had started a year-and-a-half earlier. He felt school was rather difficult, especially reading, but math was okay. He believed his older brother had learned to read as a baby. Later I found out his older brother had been retained, had reading difficulties, and still seemed to be having some academic problems. He felt that his parents yelled a lot, both at him and his brother. He talked quite a bit about this, and many of his answers to my questions referred to this. He was able to say that he felt angry when he could not get his way.

FAMILY HISTORY

Alan, at the time of the evaluation, lived with his mother, his 10-year-old brother, and his 3-year-old sister. His mother and father had separated at the end of Alan's kindergarten year. Initially, the mother stayed home with the children during the day but went to her parents' home for the night when the father returned from work. The mother attended school at a local junior college at the time. The father works as an accountant and recently had become a born-again

Christian; the mother is Catholic and attends church on a weekly basis. The divorce became final the summer after Alan completed first grade. That summer, mother and children moved to the same mobile home park where her parents resided. This move placed them within our district boundaries. The park had many children in residence and was comprised mostly of working-class people. The family fit within the norms of that community. During this time, the father usually would take the children on weekends. He was most consistent in doing so, and both children and father seemed to enjoy the time very much. Both sets of grandparents were involved with Alan and supportive of the family situation. Alan often would visit a country cottage with the maternal grandparents, and he was quite fond of those times.

EDUCATIONAL BACKGROUND AND EVALUATION

Alan attended preschool a few days a week at age four and then kindergarten and first grade in a standard educational placement. He came to his present district at the beginning of second grade, and he was evaluated shortly after entry.

The assessment pointed out that his support systems were eroding and that his self-concept was rapidly deteriorating, along with his academic performance. To shore up this deterioration and to assist in rebuilding him to former levels of functioning, resources needed to be utilized within the educational system, within the family, and within the community. Coordination of resources would be essential, or there was the potential for systems to impact negatively on the efforts of the others, even when each support system is working within its individual sphere toward the best interests of the child. Such a case normally requires an extended period of time, both because of the amount of work indicated and the nature of the goals of the service delivery plan. This case extended over 6 years, during which this student was enrolled in the second through the eighth grade.

As a result of the evaluation, Alan was placed on a learning disabilities watch status, which meant that the learning disabilities specialist consulted with his classroom teacher weekly about possible interventions in the classroom for the perceived problems. In addition, Alan was placed with the reading specialist in a small group to see if this would strengthen his reading skills. The social worker was identified as the interim case manager because it was clear that case management was going to be crucial to Alan's case. As a case manager, I met jointly with the classroom teacher, learning disabilities specialist, and reading specialist to arrange mutual consultation. With regard to direct social work service, Alan needed help with divorce issues, self-esteem, socialization skills, and learning appropriate ways to express his needs. I explored the possibility of outside counseling with his parents. They did not agree to this, so I monitored him on a consultative basis until further direct work could be arranged.

It is important to look at the developmental stage Alan had been moving through to understand his sense of failure and defeat. Considering Erikson's model of developmental stages, Alan would be well within the stage described as industry versus inferiority (Erikson, 1963). If we look at Piaget's stages of cognitive development, he would be in the middle of the concrete operations stage (Campbell, 1976, p. 8). According to some developmental theorists, he has been in a stage of fear. The 5-year-old is fearful that his mother will not return home. Age 6 is also a fearful stage, in particular that something may happen to mother and she may not be there or may die (Ilg, Ames, & Baker, 1981). Alan had been wrestling with events in his life with which his cognitive abilities were not yet capable of dealing. Efforts to soothe himself or put events in perspective generally had met with failure. Thus, he was becoming increasingly overwhelmed and anxious, and as a result some regressive behavior was noted (finger sucking, passivity, and disengagement). Emotionally he had been challenged by events that went right to the core of his worst fears, both in terms of potential abandonment and of his sense of self-competence.

SERVICES OFFERED, PROGRESS, AND RESULTS

Alan's 2nd-grade teacher was highly structured and somewhat inflexible. She was not, initially, very encouraging with him, nor did she recognize his artistic and creative strengths and his good problem-solving skills. She found his slow pace of working, which was part of his perfectionistic need, difficult to relate to. This teacher was not particularly receptive to direct suggestions from me, so I had to develop some alternative strategies to implement through our already established consultation with the reading specialist. In these meetings, I explained what my goals were in my work with Alan and discussed some parallel goals that might be implemented by the reading specialist, and the classroom teacher was able to discuss her approach. She was able to draw on an approach that she had used with a similar student a few years back. In fact, the earlier situation was close enough to be useful, and she felt she could use the same approach with Alan. By seeing the similarities between students she was able to accept other suggestions.

At the end of February of second grade, Alan's classroom teacher went on maternity leave. Alan's new teacher was very warm, caring, and creative. She liked Alan and wanted suggestions on how to help him. The consultation meetings continued. We soon agreed that Alan needed more intensive academic support. We requested a new Individualized Educational Program conference to amend the findings of the original case conference. Alan was changed from the learning disabilities watch list to direct learning disabilities services and started with thirty to sixty minutes a week in a small group. In order to arrange this meeting in a timely manner, the school administration had to be consulted about Alan's high-priority status. Given this information, the special education director in particular put in extra effort to reschedule the team and the parents so we could meet within the following week.

A week after this meeting and Alan's being placed in the learning disabilities program, his teacher brought to my attention a picture Alan had drawn of himself with a noose around his neck. When I questioned him about it, he said he had just been kidding around but then did admit he had some very sad feelings. I told him that I wanted to check in with him every day for a while because his being this sad concerned me. I also told him I needed to talk to his mother and father because it was important that they also know about it. When I approached his mother regarding my concerns, she said that she felt it really was not serious and that in fact Alan seemed to be doing much better. His father felt it was serious and wanted Alan in outside counseling. I suggested to both that I continue to work with him until school was out in June and that then he should see an outside therapist. Both agreed. I felt that I needed to have another conference with his mother to support her awareness that in many ways Alan was doing much better, but that this new development was still something I hoped she would take seriously. She listened attentively, asked some very perceptive questions, and although she did not seem as convinced about the seriousness of Alan's situation as I had hoped, her attitude did seem to be much more open and cooperative.

Alan started to do much better after he started seeing the learning disabilities teacher. She continued to consult with me and the classroom teacher until the end of the year, and the classroom teacher began implementing similar strategies in the classroom to speed his progress. Likewise, he became more outgoing and started displaying improved social skills, first in our group and then in the classroom setting. When it was determined that he was starting to generalize the skills he was learning in our small group, I met with each of the personnel who worked with him to request that they encourage his fledgling efforts to become more assertive and outgoing. Most of them were indeed cooperative and actively helped him with this. They regularly reported to me informally. Retention still was considered at the end of the year because his academic progress was not as great as we had hoped, but the parents agreed that they wanted to wait to see how things would progress for him in third grade. I then went to the principal to encourage him to consider placing Alan with the more flexible and care giving 3rd-grade teachers. She said she would take my request into consideration when making class assignments.

When the school year was nearly ended, I contacted the mother and father about making arrangements for Alan to see an outside therapist and gave them some names I could recommend. I asked that when they had made arrangements, they give the therapist permission to call me regarding Alan's case, and that they give me permission to discuss the case with the new therapist. The mother was very uncomfortable about the whole arrangement, stating that Alan would not be comfortable talking with a stranger, just as she would not be. Because I felt that my relationship with the mother was fairly strong by this time, I encouraged her to at least meet with the people I had recommended; then, if she wished, she could call me to talk further about her concerns. She thanked me but did not act on this offer. In two weeks, just at the end of the school year, I received a call from the therapist whose named topped the list, who mentioned that the father had made the arrangements for the meeting, and only the father came. However, the therapist had called the mother, and she had agreed to cooperate in getting Alan to his appointments. At the beginning of third grade, I met with Alan and his parents separately after discussing his progress with his outside therapist. We all agreed that, following a few visits to assist in his adjustment to the new school year, direct social work service would not be indicated at this time.

Third grade generally went well for Alan. He made good academic progress. He was seen by the reading specialist and the learning disabilities specialist two times a week, with one other student. I had regular contact with his classroom teacher to make sure he was progressing both academically and socially. Initially, I discussed with her his previous struggles and alerted her to watch for signs of depression. I also helped her to institute a behavior modification plan for the whole class, focused on positive social interaction, as a way of keeping a handle on Alan's real social progress, aside from his teacher's impressions. Alan finished third grade on a positive note and was promoted to fourth grade.

Alan continued doing well in fourth grade. He had a male teacher whom he seemed to enjoy. The teacher noted that Alan improved greatly in his academic, organizational, and social skills after entering fourth grade. Alan improved several grade levels in reading, health, and social studies. Grades in other subject areas stayed the same or went up slightly. He became more organized and began writing his assignments down each day; his homework assignments were consistently completed daily. My work with his teacher that year was less intense than previously. I consulted with his teacher weekly for the first few weeks of school, giving him essentially the same background information as I had done for the 3rd-grade teacher, though not in such detail. This was followed by monthly check-ins, except when the occasional brief concern arose.

Alan became more involved in class discussions, although he still was shy about sharing experiences. One thing he did share, slowly, with each of us involved with him, was his mother's remarriage at the end of the summer. He was beginning to enjoy his stepfather, although he felt the stepfather sometimes was not confident when problems arose, but, as Alan suggested, perhaps this was because he had never had children before. I learned of this by asking Alan if he would like to come to talk with me a few times once I learned from his teacher of this new development. I also asked him for permission to contact his mother and stepfather to ask them if they would like to come in to talk to me about any issues surrounding their relationship with the children, especially with Alan. Surprisingly, they agreed and came in the following week. We decided to keep in contact throughout the rest of the year. I also agreed to start seeing Alan again in a small group of boys. He interacted with the other students, but he still needed work on social skills. At times he reacted in a negative way physically to others when annoyed; however, he eventually learned to walk away from those situations. I thus recommended that Alan return to therapy for the

summer months, given those latest developments, more to prevent backsr
than because of the former concerns regarding serious depression.

Alan became more comfortable with his academics and the school setting
He would have liked more friends. He enjoyed being with his stepfather and no
longer thought so much about the divorce. He visited with his father every week-
end and also became involved with outside activities, such as Boy Scouts. His
mother then started to work part-time in the office of one of the district schools.

Alan completed his middle and junior high school years successfully. He
was placed on a consult basis for LD/R services the last two years of junior high
and continued in the Chapter I reading program through sixth grade. Socially
he interacted well with others and was involved in the chess club. He was very
involved with the youth group at his father's church.

CURRENT PROGRESS

Alan is now a freshman in high school and doing well academically. He does
not seem to have many friends in the mobile home park but does have friends
in his father's neighborhood, which he visits regularly. He is still somewhat shy
and a "loner." Mother states he may move in with his father, after his junior year,
as did his oldest brother. The move will be prompted by the fact he would be
attending a much smaller and more personal high school in a small town setting. Alan continues to maintain the progress he made, academically, socially, and
emotionally—the progress begun when he first came to the attention of the
multidisciplinary team many years ago.

Alan is a good example of the importance of having several subsystems of the
larger educational system work together. Success never would have been
achieved by attacking only one component of this case. Alan needed to have his
academics attended to via the reading specialist, the learning disabilities specialist, and the homeroom teacher. He needed the social work component to
address his emotional and social needs, as well as to make his parents aware of
those needs. He needed the outside support of the therapist at the mental
health agency to carry on the therapeutic goals identified by the school when
school was not in session. He needed the cooperation of the administration and
staff to have these needs met appropriately and in a timely manner. Any of these
component parts without the others would have compromised the outcome,
with potentially serious results for Alan.

References

Campbell, S. F. (1976). *Piaget sampler* (pp. 8–11). New York: John Wiley & Sons.

Erikson, E. (1963). *Childhood and society*. New York: W. W. Norton.

Ilg, F. L., Ames, L. B., & Baker, S. M. (1981). *Child behavior* (revised edition from Gesell Institute of Human Development from Birth to Ten). New York: Barnes & Noble.

27

School Social Work Practice with Families

Robert Constable
Loyola University, Chicago

Herbert J. Walberg
University of Illinois at Chicago

- ◆ The School as a Community of Families
- ◆ The Necessary Arrangement of Relations Between Family and School
- ◆ Family Conditions, Family Risks, and Resilience
- ◆ The School Social Worker's Role with Families

Family, friends, work groups, and neighbors are the *mediating systems* that connect and stand between public and private life. This network of mediating systems allows each person to cope with the complexity of modern society. They help us relate to the necessary institutional worlds of modern life, such as schools, workplaces, and health-care organizations. Coping and adaptation are clearly related to one's access to and ability to call on and use such support systems. They supply the preconditions for our actions in a fully human sense.

Family, including the extended family, is the most important of the mediating systems. Although it is often protected in a variety of ways, family cannot be totally private. It needs assistance from relational and institutional communities and has obligations to these communities. When a society attempts to be composed of relatively privatized family units, close connections with their supportive surroundings, friends, extended family, and neighbors can deteriorate. The modern family often experiences some social isolation. Sometimes conflict, loss, family dissolution, even a physical move can cut off generational linkages. Families who lose access to support and to collective experience are often at risk. Losses can affect the family's own structural and functional adequacy; they can create social pathologies. Losses in the first generation can create progressive vulnerabilities in succeeding generations.

Families are essential to schools, and schools cannot accomplish their missions without connections with families. Since family is essential to the functioning and socialization of children, schools can forget only at their own risk that their clientele are members of families. It is no accident that the two most effective therapeutic programs dealing with youth violence and criminal behavior (National Institutes of Health, 2005), alcohol and drug abuse, and serious emotional disturbance are broadly based models, focused on the family and its surrounding systems as well as on the youth. Multisytemic Therapy (Sheidow, Hengeller, & Shoenwald, 2003) and Functional Family Therapy (Sexton & Alexander, 2003), have each in their own way succeeded in systematizing the broad approach social workers have always taken to families and their surrounding institutions with intensity of contact. Full-time masters-level multisystemic therapists will carry four to six families at any one time (Sheidow, Hengeller, & Shoenwald, 2003). Functional family therapists will work with perhaps twenty-six families over the period of a year (Sexton & Alexander, 2003). Both programs have shown their effectiveness with problems of youth violence through high quality randomized controlled trials (RCT) with effects sustained for at least one year postintervention and with at least one external RCT replicating the results (National Institutes of Health, 2005). The similarity of both practice models to what many school social workers have been doing, albeit on short rations and without elaborate research protocols, points out possible applications of this research to school intervention with families. Paradoxically, the popular foci on "scare tactics" directed toward the individual youth uniformly do not work. There are some indications that they may make the problem worse (National Institutes of Health, 2005, p. 11). The problems are clearly more complex and systemic; the route toward health goes through the family, the living, surrounding institutions, and the young person himself or herself.

When children have difficulty or special needs in school, the *relationship* of family to school often needs special attention. The school, as a complex community, so salient to development, can aggravate a youngster's vulnerabilities or can compensate somewhat for personal and/or family vulnerability. For example, it can provide alternate socializing relationships and demanding maturational experiences. More than simply working with the family or the youngster, working with this relationship is an important part of the school social worker's role. Some of the key functions of social workers in schools are to repair the mismatches between school and family and in situations of potential difficulty, to develop real partnership.

THE SCHOOL AS A COMMUNITY OF FAMILIES

From the origins of public education, schools in the United States have often operated in relative isolation from their constituent families. When schools saw students as individuals apart from families, they needed to protect their functions from "interference" from families. As long as this isolation of school from the family sphere has been taken for granted, the school social worker's role has historically been to span the boundaries between schools and families (Litwak & Meyer, 1966). It was when families were vulnerable or students had difficulty that this isolation became particularly counterproductive. School social workers and parents necessarily challenged these boundaries.

The alternative is to conceive of the school as a community of families, of teachers, parents, and others working in partnership with one another as socializers of children. The development of this supportive community is even more important when children, families, communities, and schools have special needs, where the connection between home and school is not easily developed, or where there is cultural or linguistic diversity. The social worker, who helps develop the community of teachers, parents, and others working in partnership (Nebo, 1963) may quietly assist in creating conditions where youngsters learn and resources for that learning are shared.

The cultural diversity of the contemporary U.S. school is now enormous. In urban areas there may be as many as thirty-five linguistic groups in a suburban, middle-class elementary school with a population of two hundred pupils. Pupil diversity is also family diversity. Where there is cultural difference between family and school, families may have ambitions for their children, but they are often fearful of involvement and participation. Schools may not be well connected with some of these diverse communities. Parents need help to participate in education and to build an effective school community.

Research and theory point out that resilience in children is promoted when the resources in the school, family, and community are united and dedicated to the healthy development and educational success of children (Christenson & Sheridan, 2001; Kelleghan, Sloane, Alvarez, & Bloom, 1993; Wang, Haertl, & Walberg, 1998). Recent research (Brooks-Gunn, 2005) suggests parents interact with their children along at least seven dimensions: they nurture them; they manage the home and provide a climate of language and communication; they set standards, expectations and discipline; they provide materials that children can use for learning and development; they monitor the child's behavior; and finally, they directly teach skills to survive and flourish in their environment. The climate of language, materials in the home and direct teaching of skills are aspects of parenting most linked with the child's school success. Reflecting these seven dimensions, Jeanne Brooks-Gunn (2004/2005; 2005) estimates that one-third to one-half of the variation in school outcomes between poor and not-poor children can be accounted for by differences in parenting.

The power of the parental relationship is central to the work of the school social worker, and it is beginning to be recognized as central to school reform. There is an explicit and expected link of families to schools in the national education goals pertaining to school readiness and parent participation (PL 103-

227). Special education has expected some use of partnership with parents for at least thirty years since the inception of IDEA in 1975. General education is moving in the direction of enhanced parental involvement and partnership as a matter of public policy in PL 107-110, the No Child Left Behind Act (NCLB).

Parent Participation

In the late 1960s Project Head Start, reflecting a general philosophy governing community action programs, was the first to initiate planned parent participation as an essential dimension of schooling. James Comer (1995), a psychiatrist, developed a model of education in disadvantaged communities, where parents were often initially perceived as "unmotivated" or "hard to reach." The model is built on parent participation as essential to the creation of an effective school community, and thus effective education. Social workers took the lead in activities that, over time, developed a community of parents involved in the schools (Schraft & Comer, 1979). There were three progressive levels of parent participation: (1) general activity geared to involving the majority of families, such as potluck dinners and fun fairs; (2) parents involved specifically in the daily life of the school, such as classroom assistants, as participants in workshops, or making materials for teachers; and (3) parents able to participate meaningfully in the decision-making process in the school. Parents might move from level to level, but Schraft and Comer cautioned against expecting involvement in the third level without much development of the first two levels over a relatively long period of time, that is, without a chance to develop a relationship with the school and its functions.

Adolfi-Morse (1982) applied these concepts to her work in a school for children with emotional disturbances in Fairfax County, Virginia. The school, which served a wide geographic area with many ethnic differences, is conceived of as a community of families. Events such as back-to-school night, potluck dinners, and parent-teacher organization meetings were used to reinforce this concept. Parents of children with disabilities, who may have been less involved than others, were often able to find important roles for themselves with their children as they were making the school-community work. Their involvement resulted in a change in their children's estimate of their own roles.

The states of Florida, Kentucky, and Tennessee have developed Family Resource Centers as part of their school reform. Schools in Kentucky sponsor these centers if at least 20 percent of pupils qualify for the federal free and reduced-price meals program (nine out of every ten schools in that state). These centers provide a range of programs, including family crisis counseling, referrals for health and other social services, preschool and after-school childcare. Evaluation results for these programs have been very positive (Southern Regional Education Board, 2001). As discussed in chapter 9 and chapter 30, these centers are now being developed in many other areas. They are a new and potentially very effective service delivery system for children, and school social workers will have very important roles in them.

Parent-Run Schools

Parent-run schools present exciting possibilities for a very different conception of education. Constable studied parent-run private schools in Milan, Italy. These were systematically organized networks of parents, normalizing and supporting the pitfalls and small triumphs of development. Children were admitted to the school on the condition that the parents agree to be partners with the school in the education of their child. The schools were keynoted by individual learning objectives for each student, parent involvement, and purposeful development of a protective and proactive school community. Developing these objectives was a shared process between the parents, the pupil, and the school. The objectives were much broader than merely "academic" objectives and were geared toward developmentally appropriate strengths and capacities of each child. Some children needed help in developing friendships; others needed to develop more consistent work habits. Each pupil (ages ranging from 6 through 19 in three schools) attended class but also worked with a tutor on individual goals geared to normal developmental stages. Teachers and tutors were trained to include the family in their picture of the child. When asked to describe a particular pupil, they would, without being asked, also describe the family situation. The effect of one child's changing and developing positive qualities was felt by classmates in many different ways, and this diffusion of one child's change through the student community was reinforced by peer friendship networks.

Parents were also encouraged to form friendship and resource networks with each other, overcoming a certain fear and reluctance. To do this a *coppia incaricata*, an experienced couple with a child at the same grade level, was specifically delegated to assist the family through their friendship and support. The couple's ability to be candid about their own struggles and about the normality of developmental crises helped other parents to be more secure in their roles. Teachers estimated parent involvement to be 90 percent. Both parents generally came to conferences and involved themselves in school meetings, as they had agreed to do. Allowing for growing pains, the emergent structure appeared to be working well and producing good results.

THE NECESSARY ARRANGEMENT OF RELATIONS BETWEEN FAMILY AND SCHOOL

There appears to be a necessary order in the relationship between family and schools. Families cannot educate their children in a complex modern society without the assistance of schools, and schools cannot educate without the cooperation of families (Walberg & Lai, 1999; Walberg, 1984). Each can prevent the other from accomplishing its proper function. This is particularly true for vulnerable children and families.

Families are the first educators of their children. When a family acts in its capacity to educate, these functions remain most important through the child's developing years. School functions exist to help the family carry out its prior functions in accordance with the needs and standards of society and the rights of members of the family. Children are in a recognized position of vulnerability and require protection from their environments. They have a right to receive adequate nurture and socialization whenever possible in their own families. The community, often represented by the school, is obligated to ensure that families have all the assistance—economic, social, educational, political, and cultural—that they need to face all their responsibilities in a human way. It is not for the school to take away from families the childrearing functions that families can perform on their own or in cooperative associations.

The relationship of the family unit to the school and the community can be encapsulated by three principles:

1. The family has primary functions in the care and socialization of its children. It has rights and responsibilities derived from this function that include the economic, social, educational, and cultural provision for the needs of its members. As such, the family is the basic social unit of society.

2. The school's primary functions are helping the family to accomplish its responsibilities and supplying certain cognitive instruction that the family cannot. The work of the family is always personal. Transactions *en famille* are expected to be based on affection and respect for the other person. Particular types of learning would be distorted if they excluded this dimension of affection and respect for the person *as a person*, as worthwhile in his or her own right. In families this personal dimension is experienced and learned in work, worship, gender roles, respect for others in social relations, and respect for one's developing sexuality. When affection and respect break down, the partnership of home and school can be developed through social work services that assist the family in developing or redeveloping the complex interactive relationships necessary for their children's survival and personal development.

3. A secondary function of the school (and in a broader sense, the community) is to monitor potential abridgment of rights of children as pupils and citizens when external conditions of society or internal conditions within the family make it impossible for the family to accomplish its primary function. This must be done, without inappropriately abridging the family's exercise of those functions it is able to accomplish.

These principles involve a balance between family and school, an order, and a defined relation between their respective functions. The increased awareness of the importance of effective families, the increasing numbers of vulnerable families, and the increasing school responsibility for the education of vulnerable children inevitably leads to the need for more integrated relationships between school and family. Recent data suggest many parents are spending less time with their children (Elias & Schwab, 2004). On the other hand, the development of school services closing the gap between family and school could pose a threat to family autonomy and effectiveness.

In the face of the weakness of the family and the complexity of the child's problems, schools may attempt to substitute for family functions. This never works well. It is legendary among school social workers to provide consultation to an intensely involved and otherwise effective special education teacher who feels the need to rescue a student from the parents. When services take over, rather than empower families to carry out their duties, the parent's response may be to become either less adequate or more angry. Defining a relationship of collaboration so that vulnerable children in vulnerable families are helped to make the most of what school has to offer demands skill. A balance is struck between the need for collaboration and the need to protect the rights of children to appropriate family nurture and socialization—to support the family in carrying out its responsibility.

FAMILY CONDITIONS, FAMILY RISKS, AND RESILIENCE

The conditions families and children experience often make a collaborative relationship difficult. This is particularly important for children with disabilities, whose high needs for caregiving, often felt in isolation from community support systems, add to the normal stresses encountered by all families. Severe family stresses and losses are ordinary experiences for many children. There may be few actual and continuing supports to buffer risk. Parents' energies may be "indentured" by demanding work roles or the priority need to survive. Even parents of children under age 6 predominantly balance the demands of participating in the workforce with child-care responsibilities (Children's Defense Fund, 1994; Hanson & Carta, 1995). Children of younger parents are at risk for cognitive, emotional, and physical difficulties (Smith, 1994). The unmarried teen birth rate increased by 119 percent between 1969 to 1991 (Children's Defense Fund, 1994) but has since leveled.

Research and practice experience with children with special needs point out a heightened need for parental involvement and participation in education. Paradoxically, the greater the child's difficulties, the greater the magnitude of disagreement between schools and parents (Victor, Halvorson, & Wampler, 1988). Thus the greater the difficulties, the greater the need for specialized attention of the school to the relationship with families. Partnership between family and school is particularly important when pupils show problems such as conduct disorders (Webster-Stratton, 1993), attention deficit hyperactivity disorder (ADHD) (August, Anderson, & Bloomquist, 1992), and difficulties in social interaction with others (Sheridan, Kratochwill, & Elliott, 1990). Nevertheless, families of children with disabilities, even after twenty years of mandated participation in school decision making, are still predominantly passive in response to this process (Fine, 1993; Harry, Allen, & McLaughlin, 1995). Often the school itself creates estrangement from families.

It is helpful to keep the strengths perspective in mind when working with families of children with disabilities. So much of testing, grading, and assessment focuses on the deficits of the child that this process is likely to create defensiveness or even despair in parents. A good deal of work is necessary on both sides. Both research and practice experience suggest that parents of children with disabilities, low-income parents, and people with cultural and other differences can become quite actively involved when their school has an inclusion policy that helps them to feel encouraged, supported, and valued (Lewis & Henderson, 1997; Schraft & Comer, 1979).

Poverty is associated with great risks for children. These risks are greater for single-parent families and persons with lower job skills. In addition, the gap between relatively well-off and poor people is increasing, with children the largest age group caught in poverty. Children born in poverty have their risks compounded: illness, family stress, lack of social support, and health and environmental risks (Hanson & Carta, 1995; Schorr, 1988). Further risks are experienced by children in families where there is substance abuse or violence (Hanson & Carta, 1995). On the other hand, resilient children seem to maintain cognitive skills, curiosity, enthusiasm, goal-setting behavior, and high self-esteem. They appear less vulnerable to some of these adverse environmental factors (Hanson & Carta, 1995). In some instances, family characteristics, such as rule setting, respect for individuality, and parental responsiveness, can "inoculate" children against adverse environmental factors (Bradley, Whiteside, Mundfrom, Casey, & Pope, 1994). Social support from the larger community or kinship group can also act as a buffer (Keltner, 1990). Usually resilient children will identify some significant adult in their environment who encouraged their positive growth. Such family or extended family arrangements, which can occur naturally and in spite of very difficult circumstances, can also be constructed and encouraged with the assistance of professionals, such as school social workers.

Family Processes and Family Resilience

There is an extensive literature on family process, family structure, and family intervention (Constable & Lee, 2004; Fine & Carlson, 1992). Every family must create for itself an environment of safety, belonging, and appropriate communication and socialization. These relational tasks involve the mutual construction of:

◆ A *safe* environment for each of their members, protecting dignity and often fragile and developing identities;

◆ A place where members can *belong*, that is, can be treated as unique persons of worth;

◆ Sufficient opportunities and models for effective *communication*, so that members can learn to communicate, respond to each other, and adapt to changes within the family and in its outside environment;

◆ Building on these prerequisites, each family needs to develop an environment where there is appropriate freedom, concern, respect, and care; capable of enabling members to make appropriate developmental choices, to be concerned about each other, to respect each other, and to be able to care for others appropriately. (Constable & Lee, 2004)

These interactive tasks uniquely organize family process. In their absence the effect on the younger members can be devastating. Since these complex, interactive tasks are related to the socializing mission of education, the school social worker often has the best and least intrusive access to them.

The concept of *family resilience*, developed by Froma Walsh (2003, 1999), extends the concepts of family processes, discussed above, to stressful situations. The resilient family forges transformation and growth from adverse circumstances (Walsh, 2003). In the midst of difficulty, the family is somehow able to develop its meanings, interact with its surroundings, adapt creatively to them, and preserve its own values. It manages to carry on as a family. Resilience is not a matter of a particular family structure, but of family process. When families are resilient, their members are able to communicate their needs and solve problems. Paradoxically, the effects of oppressive conditions may act on families in different ways, depending on external conditions and the family's own subjective processing of the situation. These conditions may act either to suppress the qualities that could lead to survival or stimulate them. According to Walsh, the resilient family is able to:

◆ Approach adversity as a challenge shared by the whole family;
◆ Normalize and contextualize distress;
◆ Use adversity to gain a sense of its own coherence;
◆ Make sense of how things have happened through causal or explanatory attributions;
◆ Have a hopeful and optimistic bias;
◆ Master the art of the possible;
◆ Draw upon spiritual resources;
◆ Develop flexibility and adaptability;
◆ Develop its internal connections;
◆ Use social and economic resources appropriately;
◆ Communicate clearly and openly with each other;
◆ Solve problems collaboratively.

The recognition of individual and family resilience connects with a large body of literature on family intervention and therapy and provides a conceptual map for a strengths-based approach. An ultimate test of the functional power of families is the way they continue their work even under stress. In spite of extreme stresses—slavery and subsequent discrimination, the Holocaust, deportation to Siberia, or refugee status—families have attempted to preserve as many of their human processes and functions as possible, often living a more human existence than conditions warranted.

THE SCHOOL SOCIAL WORKER'S ROLE WITH FAMILIES

Working with Pupil, Family, and School

The school is a powerful stage with opportunities for each student to play out the great developmental issues: separation-individuation, self-esteem, social relationships, language, imagination, emotions, assertiveness, achievement, competition, productive work, justice, and the discovery and use of one's self. The quality of a child's interaction with learning tasks and with others in school is usually a very accurate barometer of his or her broader developmental issues and the family situation. The normal tasks of adapting to school will draw the student's developmental energy. Accessing this developmental energy demands a professional approach to understanding and working with complex relationships but also makes school the best place for services to be delivered to children and families.

The key to family-school intervention comes from an understanding that family tasks and school tasks are intertwined and interdependent and that partnership in these tasks is possible. Families cannot really carry out socialization without schools and schools cannot succeed without families. These shared tasks place social workers uniquely on the inside of both, facilitating their complex relationship, without taking over the family's natural exercise of its own, appropriate functioning. This is particularly important where pupil or family vulnerability or school conditions might interfere with the effectiveness of their work. The school social work role demands a systems perspective applied to families and schools and the skills to work with each in a mutually reinforcing relationship in the interests of the student.

Schooling has different meanings for different families, defined by the family cultures and family histories. Family patterns relating to school are often handed down over generations. A history of disappointing relationships in one's family history may be difficult to overcome. Nineteenth-century Irish Americans had great difficulty with the schools and child welfare systems, to the point of developing their own alternative, religiously and culturally compatible systems. African Americans, in the wake of reconstruction, experienced prejudice and discrimination from all systems. They lacked the financial resources to develop alternate systems, except in religion and to some extent in child welfare. Only in the last decades of the twentieth century has this situation changed. Native Americans have long been in the same position, although in certain circumstances the tribe or band may act as a mediator. For Hispanics schooling is the means to "make it" in North American society, but there is often a considerable gap between these familistic cultures and an individualistic, Anglo-oriented educational experience. The school social worker often must advocate strongly to assist schools to adapt to the needs of their families, developing resources, helping them to fit with family needs, and removing obstacles that prevent families from using these resources and adapting education to cultural perceptions and histories.

Partnerships Between Home and School

Schools are beginning to recognize in policy and in practice that families are essential to their mission. Family partnership has become a major school policy objective. Bristol and Gallagher (1982), Walberg (1984), and Carter (Carter & CADRE, 2002) have suggested a number of different ways schools can develop effective partnerships with parents. Programs can be made more flexible, with individualized family plans, the establishment of meaningful parent roles, and the involvement of the father as well as the mother. Programs should focus on goals important to the family and should expect something of the parents. Parents often need help to see the importance of the often-small gains made. Meetings can be scheduled at times when parents are available. School personnel can be available who speak the native language of the parent, or translators can be present. School personnel can get involved with the community. Social workers can make home visits. The school social worker might help the parents develop their own support network of friends and relatives or assist them in building an expanded network. Associations of families of children with disabilities are especially important here. Parental involvement can be developed in a meaningful way through sharing power with families, not just asking parents to carry out an existing school agenda, raise money, or do volunteer work in the school (although each of these tasks has value). Often schools overtly state a commitment to parental involvement but want it only on their own terms. A true partnership exists when there is time to listen and respond to all voices. This takes time but is well worth the effort.

The Family Systems Perspective Applied to Schooling

The family systems perspective applied to schooling means that, to help children cope better with developmental needs and life circumstances, it probably would be ineffective to work with the child without working with the teacher, who can influence the school environment, and the parents, who can influence the home environment. It is important to begin with environmental changes, for from a systems perspective these may have the most rapid results. When changes in the child's real environments take place, the social worker can assist the child to change correspondingly. Even small changes taking place in the classroom environment, with the teacher, or in the home environment, with the parents, may be enough to give the child an opportunity to cope more effectively. Children who experience a small shift in the classroom or at home may see themselves differently.

We know from developmental research that children are for the most part responsive and flexible, that the child will inevitably be a part of these changes, and that they often do use well what opportunities they perceive (Fine & Carlson, 1992). On the other hand, to focus on the child alone, in the absence of a focus on school or family, would be to expect heroic changes in the child's patterns of behavior and in the multiple worlds the child inhabits. This focus alone is likely to be ineffective and an exercise in frustration. Small changes in the worlds that children inhabit, and corresponding changes in their relations to each other, create larger changes in the total environment supporting the child's learning to cope differently. When there are changes in classroom and family relations, working with the child individually, when necessary, becomes much less complicated. In addition, the social worker would be less prone to take on a role that teachers and/or parents should play, when both are already part of the team.

There are five foundational principles for school social work with families:

- ◆ *Understand Family Structure and Process.* This principle presupposes an understanding of family assessment and social work with families. Families have unique structures, which evolve out of their particular stories and cultures, but common processes, illustrated above. School social workers need to be able to identify these structures and processes to understand the context of meanings that family members and individual pupils bring with them, to work with them and to develop partnership (Constable & Lee, 2004).

- ◆ *Use a Strengths-Based Approach.* The diversity of family structures encountered in school social work and the individualistic approach often taken by school personnel could lead to misunderstandings and pathological labeling of families. The point where school social workers can work with families is at the point of their strengths, helping families to respond and compensate for parts that are breaking down and schools to support this process while it is taking place (Constable & Lee, 2004; Kral, 1992).

- ◆ *Develop Partnership.* Because parents are the first educators of their children, a workable home-school partnership needs to develop, characterized by communication, respect, general agreement on important issues, and reflexivity (appropriate responsiveness) in relation to the changing needs of the pupil. This is especially necessary when the pupil or the family is having difficulty or is under stress (Christenson & Sheridan, 2001; Fine & Carlson, 1992).

- ◆ *Use the School as a Holding System for Development While Changes Take Place.* Schools often provide some elements of relational stability, a natural "holding system," that pupils experiencing chaos and relational confusion at home are able to use. The school social worker can work between the pupil, the school, and the home to make this arrangement work.

◆ *Never Work with a Pupil without Some Connection with the Family.* No matter how limited the connection or how difficult the involvement, parents need to become your allies. Working with a student without the parents brings parents to work against you. Rarely will they lose this unnecessary competition.

Assessment and Intervention

To construct effective relationships between school and vulnerable families, the school social worker needs to have all the assessment and intervention abilities of a good family therapist. Assessment involves understanding the relationships, tasks, and expectations in the classroom and in the home, as well as the child's developmental progression and patterns of coping in the context of the small changes that lead to systemic shifts. Much of school social work intervention is working to assist parents and teachers to find different ways of responding to and working with the child's active coping strategies. Working between the worlds of home and school, the school social worker assists teachers and parents to discover their own personal repertoire of ways to assist the child's coping, often modifying their expectations of themselves in relation to the real needs of the child. When intervention with the child is necessary, the social worker can assist the child in relation to those changes and assist parents and teachers to respond to the child's present efforts at coping, and correspondingly the child's efforts to respond to the changing environment in new ways.

The skill of making a good assessment of the whole system in interaction, leading to the skill of assisting parents, teachers, and children to manage the interaction that is already taking place, is the basis for effective school social work practice. Social workers have not always understood their roles in terms of this balanced assessment and intervention between school, home, and pupil. In many cases there has tended to be an emphasis on one part or another, rather than on the relations between these parts. The paradox is that it takes less effort to focus on the whole, and then respectfully intervene where needed, than to exclude someone from the assessment and the joint effort and then attempt to compensate for what the excluded person might have offered.

In the assessment process, it is critical to maintain a focus on strengths. The strengths of families and children are the material that we have to build upon in order to reach our mutual goals. Thus every assessment interview with parents should include questions such as, "What is something that your child does very well?" or "What do you do that really works when you are helping your child?" or "What are some of your favorite things about your child?"

Choosing the Unit of Attention. School social work can be conceptualized taking two simultaneous directions: (1) helping family, school, and community work with one another and with the pupil, and (2) helping the pupil find his or her own resources and make use of what the family, school, and community have to offer. To accomplish this, the most important part of the role of the school social worker is choosing the unit of attention, that is, discovering where to focus and what to do to enable the best match to take place between pupil-family needs and school-community resources. The unit of attention should be the point of most effective change, a point or set of points in the systems where, if change takes place, other positive changes will also become possible. When this framework is used, each unit of attention makes its own special demands on the social worker. Choosing the most effective focus, in the context of the time available, is a complex professional task. However, it is by no means a random process. There is a logical progression to it, reflecting principles of efficiency and family partnership with the school.

Some Case Examples of School Social Work Practice with Families

With the focus on the education process, school social work services may continue at different levels of intensity throughout the school experience of a student. Instead of the intensity mainly carried by the therapist, as in the examples, cited earlier, of Multisystemic Therapy and Functional Family Therapy, there is a different type of intensity with a multitude of characters within the school community, maintained by the salience of school in every pupil's life. The total network of school relationships becomes a natural holding system. There is also a different way of approaching time. In an elementary school it would be possible for a school social worker to know and work with a child for up to nine years. The case of Alan in the previous chapter is a good example of the school social worker working over a number of years through every part of the student's relational system, through the home and through the school. While the home went through great changes, the school became a natural holding system, allowing Alan's development to stabilize as the home stabilized. The school social worker carried out a wide range of functions with different units of attention supporting the holding system, supporting the parents' better functioning, as well as supporting Alan's functioning and his developmental maturation. In the beginning Alan had great difficulty. His world, as he knew it, was falling apart. He could not deal with major changes in his family, his move from his old neighborhood, his learning disabilities, and the demands of schooling. When the school situation showed responsiveness and support, he began to let out his depression and suicidal ideation. Over seven years Alan showed considerable growth, while working steadily on the same problems. He was able to use the constancy and support of this system to avert possible deterioration. His family went through profound changes over four years—severe marital upset, separation, divorce, single parenthood with joint custody, and remarriage. While the school social worker's focus remained on Alan, she was also a resource for the changing family system. The social worker brought both parents and school into communication and support of Alan's best functioning. She helped the parents access outside helping resources for Alan. She worked with the complex family system and Alan in the context of the remarriage. Working between the worlds of family and school, the social worker helped the teacher, the parents, and Alan in different ways to develop this holding system, to support Alan's strengths, and—as Alan grew and matured—to help him to put things together. Alan's breakdown of school functioning—the massive breakdown of his ability to cope with educational and social tasks, his thoughts of dying, and his chronic sadness—were essentially concerns about himself and his family. And here Alan's developmental thrust to adapt to school became the key to the helping process. The parents expected to have some relationship with the school. They were open to the school social worker and the school at a time when they would not be open to any other resource. The social worker, from her position in the school, worked at different levels of intensity throughout Alan's elementary school experience, attempting to bring all the elements of the situation together. The focus on different units of attention varied according to the particular situation. At different times she provided consultation to everyone. She met with Alan according to Alan's current need, whether individually or in groups. She set the conditions for Alan and his family to find some resolution of this complicated situation. As a skilled clinician, she used a variety of modalities in the context of Alan's developmental tasks and the school to orchestrate a larger healing process.

The two following cases briefly illustrate practice of clinical social work in the school with families and students. As in Alan's case the school is used as a holding system for simultaneous work with the student and with the family. Given this basic temporal and organizing framework of school, which both adds a further ingredient and provides limits, a variety of different effective models of family therapy, such as the two cited earlier, can be drawn from to assist the social worker's understanding of the intervention process. Both cases below involved fragmented and fragile family systems and students whose reactions to these systems were evidence of their developmental risks. Both cases involved outreach to parents and home visits, an outreach that was geared to what the parent(s) could tolerate and what seemed appropriate in the situation. In both cases there was a remarkable healing process. For parent(s) and student the relationship with school, facilitated through the worker, provided the protection and the time (a holding system) necessary for a natural healing and maturing process to take place. For these early adolescents there is a close connection between the educational goals and developmental goals. The descriptions below contain brief outlines of the process.

> Lynda began seventh grade as a very anxious, educationally and socially limited 13-year-old with placement recommended to remedy the abuse she was experiencing. She had a mutually explosive, provocative, and destructive relationship with her mother, who was struggling with mental illness. In a rage the mother had once thrown a hot iron at Lynda and these explosions were becoming

the pattern in their relationship. Father was concerned about the situation but felt helpless and passive in the face of his wife. The family is Jewish, but isolated from any extended family system. When Lynda was in a self-contained class in her elementary school, the Alliance for Jewish Children (AJC) had made an extensive evaluation of Lynda and her home. They strongly recommended that Lynda be placed in a foster home. However there was no home available. Lynda was put on a waiting list and went on to junior high school. For any early adolescent it would be a great challenge to move from the relative safety and predictability of self-contained classes in a smaller elementary school to the multidepartmental, subject-oriented junior high school. Lynda would not cope with it as long as safety at home was the prerequisite need. The school social worker worked intensively over a period of two years with Lynda, with her teachers, and with her parents and collaborated with the AJC. Since the parents were unable to get to school, there were weekly home visits on the father's lunch hour. The structure provided by these weekly visits with both parents provided some safety. The parents gradually became responsive. Father became more appropriately involved with Lynda. Mother backed off from the intensity of some of their relationship, checking in with the worker when she felt prone to violence. Lynda became less anxious and provocative. Building on the safer relationships the family was constructing, the worker assisted both parents to move to a better connection with Lynda. At the same time she was assisting Lynda to use her school experience and what parents could offer her. Gradually feeling less stressed at home, Lynda responded to weekly meetings with the social worker and over the period of two years translated them into improved school and peer relations. She showed a good deal of creativity, particularly in art. Her grades, once failing, improved. She eventually came to the point of developing normal friendships with other pupils. At this point the social worker provided consultation to a volunteer group leader at the local YWCA. Lynda's membership in this group was an important developmental experience for her. With her graduation from junior high school Lynda was able to recognize and celebrate with her family the major steps she and they had taken.

Ed, a 12-year-old in a Swedish American family, lived in a world of his own. Although he was not psychotic, his relationships, patterns and perceptions were decidedly schizoid and often his fantasies simply took over. He had superior intelligence but never engaged with his sixth grade teacher or the class. Instead, he spent most of his time in fantasy, drawing spaceships and imagining himself on them. He had no social relationships at all and actively rejected any attempts on the part of classmates to make relationships. At one point he would spend free time mapping and exploring the town sewers. He lived with his grandparents and his mother in an emotionally impoverished environment. His mother had never married and was mainly invested in her work. Father was in prison. The mother related to Ed casually as an older sister but otherwise avoided him. The grandparents actively rejected Ed as an unwanted child. The social worker learned quickly in their first home visit that he could not ask much of her in relation to Ed. She would not come to the school ("too busy") and it was clear that she would reject implicit pressure to get more involved in a parental role with Ed. She did agree to work together in twice-yearly home visits with some phone follow-up. In their contacts he deliberately went slowly with her in a nondemanding, affirmative, strengths-building experience, always with its focus on her relationship with Ed. With Ed there was a three-year relationship of twice weekly, then weekly, and later biweekly contacts over the three year period. Ed made major gains in involvement with school and his friends. From his initial disconnectedness he developed better connectedness with his surroundings through his wonderful sense of humor and his art. The mother eventually felt free enough to make office contacts. She gradually became more effectively involved with her son. Between Ed's seventh and eighth grade this climaxed with an enjoyable auto trip through the West together. When Ed's father got out of prison the worker had some good sessions with him and with Ed as Ed got to know his father for the first time. The connection with school held everything together until both were able to find a better relationship. Ed's gains assisted the mother to find a connection with him. Her better connection helped Ed to take major developmental and social steps. As an ending gesture they celebrated his readiness for high school.

Respecting Relational Structure

In working with parents and children in the present family structure, the necessary power of the parent(s) in relation to their children, their concerns, their educational functions, and responsibilities need to be respected. In Alan's case multiple changes had made the parental hierarchy confused and dysfunctional. In Lynda's case the mother-daughter relationship was explosive and unsafe. In Ed's case the mother would have preferred not to take charge or invest much in their relationship and the power was unclear in the family unit. How does the social worker avoid taking over the process and thus displacing the parents? The temptation will be very strong for the social worker to enter a dysfunctional family as an "expert" and undercut the already tottering parental power. When the "expert" takes charge, both parents and child(ren) either move into further dysfunction and invest energy elsewhere or fight the agency and social worker in order to remain in control. It may be better for parents to fight with the agency and the worker, since moving into dysfunction is usually self-confirming and relationally circular. It eliminates the possibility of improvement.

Home Visits. Both of these cases involved home visits with parents. Normally an office interview at the school is preferable. It relates the parent(s) to the school, to their child's experience, and to his or her emerging developmental world. It is also an effective use of the school social worker's time. On the other hand, sometimes parents will not or cannot come to school for an interview, even to a school open house. A home visit becomes the only way to develop a connection and the basic mutual understandings and agreements to work together in the interests of the student. In Lynda's case her safety demanded a more intensive outreach and the social worker simply decided to use her lunchtime once a week for this. It appeared at the time to be the only effective way to help the parents to work on Linda's safety and their relationship with her. In Ed's case the combination of a home visit and phone contacts maintained a relationship that supported the mother's functioning while she supported his work with Ed. On the other hand, sometimes the neighborhood or the immediate circumstances preclude home visits. Sometimes a neutral spot, such as a community center, can be chosen. Social workers should avoid any situation where they are afraid or they sense danger. Parents for the most part do understand this and will usually go out of their way to facilitate an outreach of the social worker and make sure that everyone is safe. In chapter 28 we have included some practice-tested guidelines on personal safety, developed by the School Social Work Association of America. They are well worth reading.

It is also very important to involve the school principal with the fact that you are making these contacts in the community (without sharing particular details of these contacts). Such contacts are often new to schools. Schools are generally not accustomed to collaboration with parents other than on open house night or in the parents' organization. However, a more extensive involvement is often precisely what is needed in the situations social workers encounter, particularly in special education. Generally principals will support this if it is discussed with them. You are not practicing extramural family therapy. Rather you are taking the school into the community, developing a partnership with parents over your shared concerns and helping parents carry out their roles. Time spent with parents often pays enormous dividends, particularly with the overstressed, often single-parent, families of today. As in Ed's case, from a systems perspective a small change, even an attitude turned cooperative, makes other things possible.

School social workers will find an enormous range and variety of family structures in their school communities for which the task-oriented, family strengths, whole system approach, discussed here, will be equally effective. Alan's family went through a variety of structures—two parents, single parent, both spouses remarried. Ed's family was more complex—mother and grandparents in a confused power hierarchy, father in prison. The social worker found a different role with each part of the family system as the situation developed. In some Chicago schools up to 40 percent of parent figures may be substitute parents, usually foster parents. Foster children can have many problems with school, reflecting some of their losses, their uncertainty and ambivalence about their foster parents, while they still have contact with birth parents. With these uncertainties, the school remains an important holding system; and the foster parents and child must still carry out relational tasks. What is different is the difficulty of this because of the uncertainties. The social worker can work with foster parents, develop a collaborative relationship with the child welfare agency (discussed in chapter 32), as well as work with the pupil. The difference will be the need to understand the meanings of relational losses and new, but insecure, relationships being formed. In addition, there is always a need to coordinate with the child welfare agency.

In addition, many children in school are raised by kinship caregivers—a network of relatives, uncles, aunts, and grandparents who have taken responsibility for the child in the absence of a birthparent. The case of Danny in the next chapter, raised by a grandmother struggling with some incapacities, his parents out of the picture, and supported by a complex agency wraparound structure, is a good example of the situation of the kinship caregiver. Here the agencies provided support to help the grandmother to manage. In other cases there is a large family network. While each member of the network may be more or less available, it is the family network itself that with the school becomes the holding system. Here there is some similarity with working with tribal or clan arrangements, such as traditional Hmong society, where the clan system itself provides security and stability, and the leaders of the system and appointed index parent(s) (perhaps an aunt or grandparent) become the key people for the school to work with. It is important for the social worker to assess the system and its cultural understandings to work out what type of a partnership may be possible.

Social workers often work with parents in groups. Discussed in chapters 33, 34, and 35, the strength of any group of peers is its ability to normalize a situation everyone in the group is experiencing in one way or another, to support its members' confrontation of a problem they would have great difficulty facing alone. There are groups of parents around child-rearing issues using a variety of programs available. Parents with something in common, whether kindergartners, children with certain disabilities, or early adolescents; newly arrived parents in a school community; and parents undergoing divorce or grieving losses are among the many parents who can use a group as a vehicle for learning, support, and problem solving.

In addition groups are very useful in crises as well as in longer-term healing processes when a tragedy has taken place. There is a great deal to learn from the coping of others, particularly if this is the first time one has faced a particular situation. For mobile families the group often becomes a substitute family network where they can discuss concerns. For school social workers it is an effective and productive use of their time in a type of family education cum group therapy. For some school social workers facing a large number of parents in somewhat similar situations, groups are a major modality. Their needs assessment for the particular school will dictate their approach to the school community and their use of the limited amount of time available.

The Child with Disabilities and the Family

All families experience some stress; however, families of children with disabilities face special levels of stress, frequently related to increased childcare demands. The special needs of a child with a disability levy a heavy physical, financial, and emotional tax on the family. Most obvious are the financial burdens (Moore & McLaughlin, 1988). There are also needs for information, particularly medical and diagnostic information (Bailey, Blasco, & Simeonson, 1992; D'Amato & Yoshida, 1991). Moreover, parents must develop the skill to manage the specialized services needed. Otherwise, these services might seriously intrude on other aspects of the child's development, sense of mastery, self-esteem, and the family's ability to function independently. These families can experience increased divorce and suicide rates, a higher incidence of child abuse, increased financial difficulties, and a variety of emotional manifestations, such as depression, anger, guilt, and anxiety. Different types of disabling conditions may create secondary problems. Families of children with difficulty in communication (Frey, Greenberg, & Fewell, 1989), delay in developmental tasks, difficult temperament, need for constant supervision, or repetitive behavior patterns experience increased family stress. As the child develops physically and emotionally, increased age and caregiving demands can exacerbate the situation (Gallagher, Beckman, & Cross, 1983; Hanson & Hanline, 1990; Harris & McHale, 1989; McLindon, 1990).

Parents of children with serious permanent disabilities go through a mourning process that includes all the usual stages of anger, guilt, depression, and grief over loss of the "perfect child who never came." A realistic acceptance of the child may be reached. Yet chronic sorrow is often experienced in the day-to-day struggle to meet the needs of the child while maintaining personal self-esteem, integrity as a family, and a meaningful place in the community (Bernier, 1990; Bristol & Gallagher, 1982; Lachney, 1982; Olshansky, 1962; Turnbull & Turnbull, 1978). The initial grieving may return, continue, or intensify when the child is unable to accomplish developmental milestones adequately or at the prescribed times (Davis, 1987).

Coping with a Child with Special Needs. Intense and unrelieved involvement in caregiving for a child with special needs can put severe pressure on parents and siblings. If family members cannot adaptively share the caring role, the result is often rejection of the child or a split in the family into caregivers and noncaregivers, with the child empowered by the disability itself, and thus able to exploit the split. The effect of such increased and unresolved caregiving demands on spousal relations can be dramatic. Increased caregiving demands and perhaps excessive feelings of personal responsibility for a disability may cause parental roles to split into caregiving and noncaregiving specialties. One parent (often the mother) assumes the caregiving role to the (often voluntary) exclusion of the other parent. Without constructing shared responsibility together, the stress becomes overwhelming for the caregiver or can lead to other pathological relationship outcomes. The effect for parents of such over-adequate-underadequate role patterns is to seriously split and distort the spousal relationship. The distortion is often carried to the siblings, generating caregiving and noncaregiving specialists. Such families often need professional help to balance caregiving over the entire family and to use the support of other informal or formal caregiving systems in the community. For various reasons connected with feelings of personal responsibility, families of children with disabilities may have real difficulty accepting help from the outside and often suffer profound isolation at the time they most need workable social relations with friends, kin, and neighbors, as well as extended community resources. Such informal support can be a source of respite care, advice, information, and material assistance, as well as empathy and emotional support. This support can be a buffer against the stresses of child care (Beckman, 1991; Beckman & Pokorni, 1988), however, it still may not be sufficient to prevent parental dysfunction (Seybold, Flitz, & MacPhee, 1991).

Tavormina and associates noted four major parental styles of adapting to the realities of raising a child with disabilities:

1. One parent emotionally distances himself or herself from the child, leaving the care of the child entirely up to the other parent, and concentrates entirely on outside activities unrelated to the child, such as job and organizations.

2. The parents draw together in rejecting the child. The child in this type of family is most apt to be institutionalized, regardless of the severity of his or her disability.

3. The parents make the child the center of their universe, subordinating all of their own desires and pleasures to the service of the child.

4. The parents join in mutual support of the child, and of each other, but maintain a sense of their own identities and create a life as close to "normal" as possible. (as cited in Bristol & Gallagher, 1982)

The relations of such parents with institutions and organizations, such as schools, may become complicated. Despite an assumed community expectation that families be assisted in their functions, formal social support (from formal organizations: schools, social agencies, etc.) does not seem to have a significant effect in reducing stress in parents of young children with developmental delays (Beckman, 1991; Beckman & Pokorni, 1988). Indeed, parent-professional relations can be a source of additional stress (Gallagher et al., 1983). These paradoxical findings point out the problems of organizations or professionals attempting to supplant the parents. They challenge school social workers to assist families to construct appropriate relationships with formal resources. Families desperately need to benefit from these relationships, without distorting their own internal relationships.

Parenting a child with disabilities is a "24-hour, 7-day-a-week involvement," drawing considerable energy from other children and other responsibilities. When parents attempted to describe their experiences, they described great pressure from the child:

> Christine stated, "he'll do a lot of things purposely to get my attention, like break something or turn on the TV, turn off the TV or start yelling." Luz stated emphatically that Juan's behavior was about attention, "24 hours he wants my attention. And that's the problem. That's why he breaks things, writes on the walls, and everything. He just wants my attention."
>
> Carmen shared with us, "Everything is difficult. And then when you've got other kids and they've got homework and they've got to be at school in time and

everything. It's just hard to put everything together. . . .At that point I was working full time, but I couldn't do it because I had so many appointments with Arturo, so then I cut my hours to part-time. . . .We didn't know about it. It was a world we were thrust into when Arturo was born." (Fox, Vaughn, Wyatte, & Dunlap, 2002, p. 445)

Research points out that that the disability systemically affects every internal and external relationship, whether family relationships, physical circumstances, social networks, or daily routines and activities. There is a need for community and network resources, policy development, and an ecological approach to assessment, going well beyond the simple focus on child-in-school and certainly involving the home (Fox, Vaughn, Wyatte, & Dunlap, 2002*)*.

A Family with Severe Caregiving Demands

Many families of children with disabilities are at the point of breakdown, when the extreme caregiving demands of the child do not mesh with what family members see themselves as able to do. The school social worker works with both family and the pupil to help them to develop a workable environment. A child with severe disabilities, Betty Benson did better at school than at home. The mother wanted Betty placed. Placement was unavailable and the family's difficulties left the school in an unwanted position of offering the major consistent, developmentally appropriate relationships that Betty was experiencing.

Betty Benson is a 6-year-old with cerebral palsy who currently ambulates by rolling and crawling. She has a 7-year-old brother doing well in school. She shows "autistic-like" behavior but seems to have higher ability than her current diagnosis of profound developmental disability. Although her use of language at home is minimal, she follows directions in school and is able to indicate her need to use the toilet. She is expected to get a walker and orthopedic shoes from United Cerebral Palsy by the end of the year. At home her dominant activities are described by the parents as screaming, crying, grabbing, hitting, head banging, pulling her own hair out, and self-stimulating. The mother works in a factory, and the father is a janitorial worker. Mother is gone in the mornings, and the father in the afternoon and the evening. Grandmother watches the children sometimes during the day, and the family receives twenty-five hours a month of respite care. Mother is overwhelmed. She feels her only way to handle Betty is to give in to her demands to keep her from screaming and insists that the brother do the same. Father feels Betty's main problem is that she cannot walk, and this limits her contact with other children. Neither parent seems to have a clear idea of what can be expected from Betty in the future or how far she could advance in her ability to function normally.

Betty shares a classroom with five other students, a teacher, and an aide. She showed no behavior problems this year. Last year when the teacher used restraining techniques to manage her, she would scream, grab, and hit. This year the teacher is more nurturing. Betty appears happy and follows directions. When observed in class she quietly worked behind a screen, putting paint brushes together. She kept trying, even when it was difficult for her, and managed to have some success. The school would like the parents to use medication and behavior modification techniques at home, but they refused. Mother didn't feel that she could "change her own behavior." The parents did put Betty briefly on meds but discontinued them after a short trial. The school felt they should have waited longer for them to take effect. Mother and father are requesting a residential placement. The school administrator felt that Betty is currently placed in the least restrictive environment and is adequately served in their program. She feels the district should not pay for residential treatment because of home problems. In any case, she believes Betty would get more services from their school than from a residential placement. Both parents were surprised at how well Betty is doing in school this year. Father would like to know specifically how they are handling Betty in school, so they could do the same things with her at home. Mother was fearful that if Betty were doing well, it might endanger the possibility of placement.

Because she is doing well in school, there is no likelihood of the school (or the state) funding residential placement; everything now depends on the social worker working between family, school, and Betty. There needs to be a channel of ongoing communication with the school. As father indicates, it may be possible to help Betty generalize her gains made in school, thus relieving some of the pressure on the parents and brother. Mother feels desperate and hopeless and will need additional help. The parents need to be worked with at home together to explore rebalancing their roles and the support they might receive and provide each other in this stressful situation. They need to be able to mourn their situation and then to begin to see Betty as a real person, with real strengths. Some additional respite help might be possible. There is also the possibility of helping these very isolated parents connect with a group of parents of children with severe disabilities. As the social worker follows the situation over a period of time, the capabilities of the home to care for Betty could become more evident. In the meantime concrete supports for the parents, the possibility of a walker, orthopedic shoes for Betty, and most of all help and encouragement for the parents in management of Betty are important.

The case illustrations of Alan, Lynda, Ed, Betty, and their complex families are emblematic of clinical social work with pupils and families. A wide range of help was offered in a minimally intrusive way, using the child's and the family's own adaptive efforts to cope with the life tasks and family transitions. The ordinary "work" of a social institution, the school, the child, and the family was used to enhance the positive coping skills eventually developed in a remarkable healing process.

References

Adolfi-Morse, B. (1982). Implementing parent involvement and participation in the educational process and the school community. In R. T. Constable & J. P. Flynn (Eds.), *School social work: Practice and research perspectives* (pp. 231–234). Homewood, IL: Dorsey.

August, G. J., Anderson, D., & Bloomquist, M. L. (1992). Competence enhancement training for children: An integrated child, parent and school approach. In S. L. Christenson & J. C. Conoley (Eds.), *Home-school collaboration: Enhancing children's academic and social competence* (pp. 175–192). Silver Spring, MD: National Association of School Psychologists.

Bailey, D., Blasco, P., & Simeonson, R. (1992). Needs expressed by mothers and fathers of young children with disabilities. *American Journal on Mental Retardation, 97,* 1–10.

Beckman, P. (1991). Comparison of mother's and father's perceptions of the effect of young children, with and without disabilities. *American Journal of Mental Retardation, 95,* 585–595.

Beckman, P., & Pokorni, J. (1988). A longitudinal study of families of preterm infants: Changes in stress and support over the first two years. *Journal of Special Education, 22,* 55–65.

Bernier, J. (1990). Parental adjustment to a disabled child: a family system perspective. *Families in Society, 71,* 589–596.

Bradley, R. H., Whiteside, L., Mundfrom, D. J., Casey, P. H., & Pope, S. K. (1994). Early indicators of resilience and their relations to experiences in the home environments of low birthweight, premature children living in poverty. *Child Development, 65,* 346–360.

Bristol, M. M., & Gallagher, J. J. (1982). A family focus for intervention. In C. T. Ramey & P. L. Trohanis (Eds.), *Finding and educating high risk and handicapped infants* (pp. 137–161). Baltimore: University Park Press.

Brooks-Gunn, J. (2004/2005, Winter). A conversation with Jeanne Brooks-Gunn. In *Evaluating family involvement programs. The evaluation exchange, 10*(4), Harvard Family Research Project. Retrieved February 1, 2005, from http://www.gse.harvard.edu/hfrp/eval/issue28/qanda.html

Carter, S., & CADRE. (2004). *Educating our children together: A sourcebook for effective family-school-community partnerships.* Retrieved October 8, 2006, from http://www.directionservice.org/CADRE/EducatingOurChildren_01.cfm

Children's Defense Fund. (1994). *The state of America's children.* Washington, DC: Childrens' Defense Fund.

Christenson, S. L., & Sheridan, S. M. (2001). *Schools and families: Creating essential connections for learning.* New York: Guilford.

Comer, J. P. (1995). *School power: Implications of an intervention project.* New York: Free Press.

Constable, R., & Lee, D. (2004). *Social work with families: Content and process.* Chicago: Lyceum Books.

D'Amato, E., & Yoshida, R. (1991). Parental needs: An educational life cycle perspective. *Journal of Early Intervention, 15,* 246–254.

Davis, B. (1987). Disability and grief. *Social Casework, 68,* 352–357.

Elias, M., & Schwab, Y. (2004, October 20). What about parental involvement in parenting? *Education Week, 24*(8), 39, 41.

Fine, M. J. (1993). (Ap)parent involvement: Reflections on parents, power, and urban public schools. *Teachers' College Record, 94,* 682–711.

Fine, M. J., & Carlson, C. (1992). *The handbook of family-school intervention: A systems perspective.* Boston: Allyn & Bacon.

Fox, L., Vaughn, B. J., Wyatte, M. L., & Dunlap, P. G. (2002). "We can't expect other people to understand": Family perspectives on problem behavior. *Exceptional Children, 68*(4), 437–450.

Frey, K., Greenberg, M., & Fewell, R. (1989). Stress and coping among parents of handicapped children: A multidimensional approach. *American Journal on Mental Retardation, 95,* 240–249.

Gallagher, J. J., Beckman, P., & Cross, A. H. (1983). Families of handicapped children: Sources of stress and its alleviation. *Exceptional Children, 50*(1), 10–18.

Hanson, M. J., & Carta, J. J. (1995). Addressing the challenges of families with multiple risks. *Exceptional Children, 62*(3), 201–212.

Hanson, M. J., & Hanline, M. (1990). Parenting a child with a disability: A longitudinal study of parental stress and adaptation. *Journal of Early Intervention, 14,* 234–248.

Harris, V., & McHale, S. (1989). Family life problems, daily caregiving activities, and the psychological well-being of mothers of mentally retarded children. *American Journal on Mental Retardation, 94,* 231–239.

Harry, B., Allen, N., & McLaughlin, M. (1995). Communication vs. compliance: African-American parents' involvement in special education. *Exceptional Children, 61*(4), 364–377.

Kelleghan, T., Sloane, K., Alvarez, B., & Bloom, B. S. (1993). *The home environment and school learning.* San Francisco: Jossey-Bass.

Keltner, B. (1990). Family characteristics of preschool social competence among black children in a Head Start program. *Child Psychiatry and Human Development, 21*(2), 95–108.

Kral, R. (1992). Solution-focused brief therapy: Applications in the schools. In M. J. Fine & C. Carlson (Eds.), *The handbook of family-school intervention: A systems perspective.* Boston: Allyn & Bacon.

Lachney, M. E. (1982). Understanding families of the handicapped: A critical factor in the parent-school relationship. In R. T. Constable & J. P. Flynn (Eds.), *School social work: Practice and research perspectives* (pp. 234–241). Homewood, IL: Dorsey.

Lewis, A. C., & Henderson, A. T. (1997). *Urgent message: Families crucial to school reform.* Washington, DC: Center for Law and Education.

Litwak E., & Meyer, H. (1966, June). A balance theory of coordination between bureaucratic organizations and community primary groups. *Administrative Science Quarterly, 11,* 31–58.

McLindon, S. (1990). Mother's and father's reports of the effects of a young child with special needs on the family. *Journal of Early Intervention, 14,* 249–259.

Moore, J., & McLaughlin, J. (1988). Medical costs associated with children with disabilities or chronic illness. *Topics in Early Childhood Special Education, 8,* 98–105.

National Institutes of Health. (2005). Preventing violence and related health-risking social behaviors in adolescents October 13–15, 2004. *State-of-the-Science Conference Statement. Final Statement, January 18, 2005.* Washington, D.C.: National Institutes of Health. Retrieved February 24, 2005, from http://concensus.nih.gov/ta/023/Youth ViolenceFinalStatement011805.htm

Nebo, J. (1963). The school social worker as community organizer. *Social Work, 8,* 99–105.

Olshansky, S. (1962). Chronic sorrow: A response to having mentally defective children. *Social Casework, 43,* 190–192.

Schorr, L. B. (1988). *Within our reach.* New York: Doubleday.

Schraft, C. M., & Comer, J. P. (1979). Parent participation and urban schools. *School Social Work Quarterly, 1*(4), 309–326.

Sexton, T. L., & Alexander J. F. (2003). Functional family therapy: A mature clinical model for working with at-risk adolescents and their families. In T. L. Sexton, G. R. Weeks, & M. S. Robbins (Eds.), *Handbook of family therapy.* (pp. 323–350). New York: Brunner-Routledge.

Seybold, J., Flitz, J., & MacPhee, D. (1991). Relation of social support to the self-perceptions of mothers with delayed children. *Journal of Community Psychology, 19*, 29–36.

Sheidow, A. J., Hengeller, S. W., & Schoenwald, S. K. (2003). In T. L. Sexton, G. R. Weeks, & M. S. Robbins (Eds.), *Handbook of family therapy* (pp. 303–322). New York: Brunner-Routledge.

Sheridan, S. M., Kratochwill, T. R., & Elliott, S. N. (1990). Behavioral consultation with parents and teachers: Delivering treatment for socially withdrawn children at home and at school. *School Psychology Review, 19*, 33–52.

Smith, T. M. (1994). Adolescent pregnancy. In R. J. Simeonson (Ed.), *Risk, resilience, and prevention: Promoting the wellbeing of all children* (n.p.). Baltimore: Paul H. Brookes.

Southern Regional Education Board (SREB). (2001). *Helping families to help students: Kentucky's family resource and youth services centers*. Atlanta: Author.

Turnbull, A. P., & Turnbull, H. R. (1978). *Parents speak out: Views from the other side of the two-way mirror*. Columbus, OH: Merrill.

Walberg, H. J. (1984). Improving the productivity of America's schools. *Educational Leadership, 41*(8), 19–27.

Walberg, H. J., & Lai, J. (1999). Meta-analytic effects for policy. In G. J. Cizek (Ed.), *Handbook of educational policy* (pp. 418–454). San Diego, CA: Academic.

Walsh, F. (1999). *Strengthening family resilience*. New York: Guilford.

Walsh, F. (2003). Family resilience: A framework for clinical practice. *Family Process, 42*(1), 1–18.

Wang, M. C., Haertl, G. D., & Walberg, H. J. (1998). *Building educational resilience*. Bloomington, IN: Phi Delta Kappan Educational Foundation.

Webster-Stratton, C. (1993). Strategies for helping children with oppositional defiant and conduct disorders: The importance of home-school partnerships. *School Psychology Review, 22*, 437–457.

Victor, J. B., Halvorson, C. F., Jr., & Wampler, K. S. (1988). Family-school context: Parent and teacher agreement on temperament. *Journal of Consulting and Clinical Psychology, 56*, 573–577.

28

School Social Work Personal Safety Guidelines

School Social Work Association of America

- ◆ Personal Safety
- ◆ Guidelines When Providing Transportation Assistance on the Job

PERSONAL SAFETY

Incidents reported in local and national media have brought a heightened awareness of violence and the potential for victimization in school and community environments. School social work has a long history of conducting community outreach activities to students, families, and resource providers. Thus, personal safety issues are of increasing concern to school social workers and their administrators.

The School Social Work Association of America offers the following personal safety precautions as preventive measures to assist school social workers and other educational personnel in avoiding problems and increasing their awareness of actions promoting personal safety. Guidelines cannot be constructed to address every conceivable situation, therefore school social workers are urged to rely on individual and professional judgment as the best assurance for promoting personal safety in any situation

Before You Leave

◆ Always inform a responsible school employee, such as an administrator or secretary, of your destination(s) and anticipated time of return. Maintain and leave a readily accessible schedule including names, addresses, and telephone numbers (if available) where you can be reached.

◆ Leave a complete and detailed itinerary with your office.

◆ Confirm appointments ahead of time to remind the person you are about to visit.

◆ Obtain clear directions to your destination and keep current city and county maps in your car.

◆ Research and utilize the safest route. If you get lost, do not make it obvious. Be very discreet and careful when asking directions.

◆ Conduct visits with another school staff member when you have reason to believe that personal safety may be at risk.

◆ Arrange for the school to maintain your car license plate number and description it you use your vehicle for conducting community contacts.

◆ Carry a preprogrammed cellular telephone with you if at all possible and set your quick dial options to include 911.

◆ Request nearby police surveillance if you think a significant degree of risk may be present.

Walking

The immediate surroundings hold a wealth of obvious and subtle clues to an observant individual. Traveling on foot in a new or less frequented environment can, in and of itself, cause a person to feel less comfortable.

◆ Be actively aware of your surroundings.

◆ Always appear confident and purposeful.

◆ Carry keys and money in a pocket rather than in a purse or wallet.

◆ Ignore individual(s) who verbally harass you and immediately distance yourself from them.

◆ Turn around and make it obvious to anyone you sense following you that you are aware of their presence. Immediately move to a less isolated area where other people are present.

◆ Call your office to announce a safe arrival at each destination, if possible.

Driving

Traveling in a vehicle can provide a false sense of security especially when you are driving in a new or less frequented environment. It is even more important to practice safe driving habits under these conditions.

- ◆ Drive with the doors locked and the windows closed, whenever practical. Lock doors prior to leaving school property.
- ◆ Keep wallets, purse, and any other valuables out of view.
- ◆ Remain in your vehicle if someone "bumps" you from behind. Motion to the other driver to follow you to a police station.
- ◆ Park in open areas, routinely check for suspicious persons in the area before exiting your vehicle, and always lock all doors as you exit.
- ◆ Call your office to announce a safe arrival at each destination, if possible.
- ◆ Be prepared to unlock the driver's door by placing the car key firmly in your hand prior to returning to your vehicle .
- ◆ Look underneath your vehicle while approaching it. Walk around the exterior of your vehicle checking both the front and rear seats for intruders before entering. Lock the doors prior to departing.

Assessing Danger

School social workers are trained to be sensitive to and aware of the social dynamics of various social situations. Trust your instincts and apply this skill in unfamiliar or new situations.

- ◆ Avoid locations and buildings that appear unsafe. Those that are dark, isolated, and obstructed or where individuals are loitering and/or disorderly should not be entered.
- ◆ Avoid family-owned or neighborhood dogs. Ask the family to put their pet in another room or ask to keep the pet leashed.
- ◆ Identify yourself readily as a school employee conducting school business. Offer your school business card or identification card.
- ◆ Avoid moralizing, resorting to blame, and/or presenting ultimatums. State your purpose clearly. Always leave an "out" for the other individual(s).
- ◆ Share information in a respectful, sensitive manner. As a school employee, you are a guest in their environment. Remember that many individuals and families you work with are experiencing considerable emotional stress and that you may be relaying information which will increase their level of stress.
- ◆ When encountering a parent or other person who appears under the influence of alcohol or other drugs, advise the individual(s) that you will contact them at another time and leave your school business card and/or telephone number. Try to remain between the exit and the individual.
- ◆ Be especially cautious when contacting individuals who have a previous known history of violent or criminal behavior. Strongly consider interacting by telephone, in a public location (such as a mall, coffee shop, or place of employment), and/or asking another school staff person to accompany you. Where possible, sit between the client and the exit doorway.

◆ Do not enter a known drug house. When an emergency arises at school, such as a sick or injured student, school employees should attempt to conduct the necessary interactions/notifications by telephone. When telephone access is not available, the school system should have a policy delineating proper procedures to follow.

◆ Reschedule your business when you find yourself in a potentially unprofessional and/or compromising situation. For example, persons are not fully clothed or when confidentiality cannot be ensured.

◆ Listen and observe attentively when encountering an individual who states and/or indicates that you are unwelcome. Do not argue or insist on a visit.

Working with Agitated Persons

The following behaviors can help in calming a distraught and/or agitated individual during your interactions.

◆ Remain calm and observant. Attend to reducing your own fears and stay in control of your emotions.

◆ Be aware of your body language and personal space needs of the client. Agitated or potentially violent persons should not have their personal space threatened or violated. Even if your intentions are good, moving closer may raise the person's level of anxiety. Being closer than 2–3 feet, even in nonthreatening situations, is generally uncomfortable.

◆ Request the upset individual be seated or remain seated. Locate yourself between the person and the exit doorway, and at eye level with the agitated individual.

◆ Have your cell phone easily accessible in case you need to call 911.

◆ Speak clearly and directly regarding your intended reason for interacting with the agitated individual. Avoid language which could in any way be construed as argumentative, demanding, or demeaning. Do not touch the agitated individual.

◆ Speak clearly and respectfully, utilizing a low, calming tone of voice. Ask the distraught individual to speak clearly and at a normal pace so that he/she can be understood. Do not patronize the individual.

◆ When the level of agitation becomes personally threatening, focus the remainder of the interaction on the immediate problem. Alter your original agenda as needed.

◆ Listen attentively and respectfully, allowing the distressed individual to talk. Clearly communicate that your desire is to help the person solve problem(s) which are upsetting them.

◆ Terminate your interactions if the distraught individual remains in an agitated state or becomes increasingly agitated, uncooperative, verbally abusive, threatening, or displays a weapon. Exit promptly if any such circumstance arises and immediately report the situation to your supervisor and/or school security personnel, and local law enforcement when needed.

If You Are Victimized

Experience dictates that it is extremely unlikely that a school employee will be victimized while conducting official school business. In the unlikely event that you are victimized or threatened you should act quickly to do the following:

- ◆ Access emergency medical services when necessary.
- ◆ Report the incident to local low enforcement and your supervisor and/or school security personnel.
- ◆ Document the incident thoroughly, including the interactions, time, place, and individual(s) involved as soon as possible. Complete written documentation is essential for accurate recall and any potential law enforcement action.

GUIDELINES WHEN PROVIDING TRANSPORTATION ASSISTANCE ON THE JOB

At times, transporting students and/or families by car has been an expected and encouraged school social work service. Unfortunately in today's climate of litigation, transporting students can put the school social worker in jeopardy. SSWAA believes school social workers need to be aware of possible legal ramifications and make an informed decision before agreeing to transport students and/or families as a part of school employment. SSWAA recommends the following steps be taken by school social workers who provide occasional transportation assistance for students and others.

If providing transportation is expected on the job, then:

- ▶ Child and parent transportation expectations should be addressed in job descriptions and in collective bargaining agreements (when applicable). The purpose is to protect the school social worker.
- ▶ The LEA should provide liability insurance specifically covering employee transportation of students and others. School social workers should periodically review their district's policy.
- ▶ School social workers should contact their personal auto insurance carrier to determine the extent of liability coverage for accidents which may occur when providing transportation while on the job.
- ▶ If the school social worker has professional liability insurance through the employer or by individual purchase, a statement regarding transportation liability coverage should be obtained from that insurance provider.

If providing transportation is not expected on the job, then:

▶ School social workers should check with the employing LEA to find out if providing transportation violates any LEA rule, regulation, policy, or practice.

▶ School social workers should contact their personal auto insurance carrier to determine the extent of liability coverage for accidents which may occur when providing transportation while on the job.

29

Attendance and Truancy: Assessment, Prevention, and Intervention Strategies for School Social Workers

Erin Therese Gleason

Carol Rippey Massat
University of Illinois at Chicago

- ◆ Why Schools Need and Want to Prevent Truancy
- ◆ Risk Factors Associated with Truancy
- ◆ Multisystemic Assessment of Truancy Issues
- ◆ Intervention
- ◆ Case Examples

Compulsory school attendance laws became well established in all U.S. schools at the beginning of the twentieth century. These laws transformed the nature of U.S. schools from elitist institutions for the privileged to inclusive institutions that involved all children and teenagers. The government began to see education as necessary preparation for citizenship, a protection from premature involvement with employment, and an essential prerequisite to life success. All fifty states have laws requiring attendance, though states vary regarding details related to ages, vaccinations, acceptable equivalents of education, home schooling, sanctions, and other regulations. Compulsory attendance laws apply unless parents can demonstrate that their child is getting an education elsewhere that meets the same standards as those of the public school, such as through home schooling (Derezinski, 2004; Fischer & Sorenson, 1996). A 1972 Supreme Court ruling established another exception when it decided that Wisconsin could not require Amish parents to send their children to school beyond the eighth grade.

Though by 1918 all students were required by law to attend school, it was not until fifty years later that schools were desegregated, integrated, and mandated to offer an equal education through the historic 1954 *Brown v. Board of Education of Topeka, Kansas* court decision. In this decision, the Supreme Court ruled that education was essential to life success. The opportunity of an education, where the state had undertaken to provide it to any, was a right "which must be made available to all on equal terms." Inclusion of children with disabilities reflected the same principles. The movement toward inclusion continues.

From the beginning of the field of school social work in 1906, attendance has remained an issue of concern for the profession (Abbott & Breckinridge, 1917). Social workers, as attendance officers, studied the social ills of the community—poverty, ill health, and lack of secure family income, and their effects on attendance (Allen-Meares, 2004).

WHY SCHOOLS NEED AND WANT TO PREVENT TRUANCY

Law and education policies cause schools to want and need to prevent truancy and improve attendance (Allen-Meares, 2004; Council of Chief State School Officers [CCSSO], 2001). State financial aid to school districts is based, in part, on student attendance figures (Gehring, 2004). Regular school attendance has obvious links to factors such as academic achievement, graduation rates, and standardized test scores factors related to student success. In addition, the federal No Child Left Behind Act (NCLB) requires schools and districts to improve academic performance or face sanctions. Attendance rates are often a factor in determining adequate yearly progress, and if benchmarks are not met, schools may be closed (Gehring, 2004). Every state, locality, and school district has its own set of laws and guidelines regarding truancy. It is important for school social workers to understand these laws in order to best work with students, parents, and schools affected by truancy. Social workers may access truancy guidelines in their school district's handbook, the state board of education Web site, the professional literature, or public databases (Teasley, 2004).

RISK FACTORS ASSOCIATED WITH TRUANCY

Attendance and Academic Achievement

Attendance is clearly linked to student academic achievement. A number of studies have linked attendance to grade point averages in elementary school students (Heberling & Shaffer, 1995; Winkler, 1993; Yunker, 1967). Others have found a similar relationship among older students (Ackerman & Byock, 1989; Strickland, 1998). Roby (2004) found a positive relationship between attendance and student achievement in grades 4, 6, 9, and 12, with the relationship being the strongest in the ninth grade. Of course, many other factors influence academic achievement, and in some cases, a sense of failure in school or lack of hope may lead to absenteeism, rather than absenteeism causing academic failure. Whatever the direction of causality, if students are not in class, they do not have the opportunity to learn what is being offered. If school failure leads to absenteeism, then those absences will contribute to a vicious cycle of dwindling academic gains and reduced school engagement.

Attendance and Social Development

Truancy can interrupt students' social development by isolating them from peers and adults (McCluskey, Bynum, & Patchin, 2004). Previous friendships can dissipate, and students may be left with few opportunities to socialize (Mac-Donald & Marsh, 2004). If students eventually drop out of school, it may be more difficult for them to secure stable, well-paying jobs with potential for advancement because they lack skills or qualifications (McCluskey et al., 2004). Though truancy is rarely cited as a *direct* cause or effect of antisocial behaviors, it is significantly associated with a number of behaviors that may lead to negative personal outcomes (Teasley, 2004). For example, truancy has been found to be a better predictor than grade point average for all drug use behaviors among middle and high school students (Hallfors et al., 2002). Students who reported problems with alcohol or other drugs were three times more likely to be truant from school (Schroeder, 1993). Truancy has also been identified as an early warning sign of delinquent behavior ("Program keeps," 2001). In Arizona, 90 percent of the state's prison inmates had chronic truancy records ("Program keeps," 2001). Truancy has also been associated with drug use (Hallfors et al., 2002; Schroeder, 1993; Soldz, Huyser, & Dorsey, 2003), running away (Man, 2000), academic failure and school dropout (McCluskey et al., 2004), delinquency ("Program keeps," 2001), high school senior drinking and driving (O'Malley & Johnston, 1999), and smoking (Tomori et al., 2001).

Rational Choice

While truancy is associated with a number of negative outcomes, research suggests that truancy is not a unitary condition or personal deficit, but a student's solution to adapt to personal circumstances. Guare and Cooper (2003) argue that students, as rational decision-makers, are like clients or consumers, in that they decide whether to "buy" units of education or to reject them. Students perform a cost-benefit analysis based on factors such as the importance of the day's lesson related to grades, their excitement or boredom with the curriculum and pedagogy, and the punishment they might receive if they are caught skipping school. The law however defines this behavior as truancy and in this sense truancy, rather than simply an individual symptom, becomes a function of school officials' and the school community's definition of the situation (Carl, Pawlak, & Dorn, 1982) and willingness to enforce this definition. With this understanding, truancy intervention requires changing the circumstances rather than simply treating or punishing truant individuals.

MULTISYSTEMIC ASSESSMENT OF TRUANCY ISSUES

A comprehensive assessment is essential. Historically, truancy assessment has been approached from the sole angle of "what's wrong with the student or the parent," rather than understanding the impact of multiple systems (Harvey, 2003). There is no one approach that works best for all students, and the effectiveness of a given intervention depends on individual, family, or community needs (Lauchlan, 2003). Assessment should include an understanding of individual, family, peer, academic, school, socioeconomic, cultural and linguistic, and community issues that affect students' attendance behavior. It should include an evaluation of the risk factors that contribute to truancy, strengths, resources, and protective factors that work to prevent it (Teasley, 2004). Assessment could include interviews, reports from significant others, self-monitoring, and behavioral observations about social relationships, extracurricular activities, rational choice considerations, cultural and economic issues, mental health and health issues, academic ability and engagement, and both positive and negative attitudes about school.

Individual Assessment

On the individual level, school social workers should examine the functions that are served by nonattendance (Lauchlan, 2003). The social worker may choose to complete a formal functional behavior analysis (see chapter 19) to organize and document this information. A functional behavioral analysis identifies the antecedents and the consequences of behavior. Examples of antecedents that occur before skipping school are: staying up late the night before, an announcement of a test in class the day before, something more immediate, such as a panic attack on the way to school, or a frightening incident outside of the school doors. Safety issues in neighborhoods and gang turf concerns could make travel to school difficult or dangerous for some children. In some Chicago neighborhoods, children on the way to school have been shot, and parents have organized to form safety chains to escort children to school. The consequences of either attending or missing school also influence behavior. If students find that they experience rewards, such as enjoyable activities, or are able to avoid aversive activities, they may change their behavior. Contingency contracting and rewards are far more effective than punishment (Carl,

Pawlak, & Dorn, 1982), but they must be individualized. According to Kearney and Silverman (1990, in Laughlan, 2003), there are four main reasons for nonattendance by students.

♦ Students may be trying to avoid the experience of severe anxiety or fearfulness related to attending school. Examples include: fear of a school bathroom, fear of taking an exam, or anxiety about a certain class period.

♦ Students may be trying to avoid anxious or scary social situations. For example, they may be harassed by a bully, be socially isolated, or have problems with teachers. Students may be seeking attention or reducing a feeling of separation anxiety.

♦ Students may be staying home to take care of a sick or incapacitated parent or sibling, may get special attention at home, or may get attention for an illness that does not exist.

♦ Students may be enjoying a rewarding experience that nonattendance may bring. For example, students may get to spend time with their friends, watch TV, or sleep late.

Social and Psychological Issues. Given the developmental importance of peers in adolescent life, the social domain has an immense effect on student choices. Students may feel a sense of belonging to a subculture that protests formal education, or they may worry that they may be excluded from friendship groups if they do not skip school with friends (MacDonald & Marsh, 2004). Students may have difficulty standing up to peer pressure to skip school (Guare & Cooper, 2003). They may be victims of a range of bullying behavior from name-calling to persistent victimization They may have conflicts with or be embarrassed around peers or staff members. They may be socially isolated. Alternatively, students may have attachments to a wide or strong friendship group that supports a commitment to school (MacDonald & Marsh, 2004). In addition, students may feel particularly connected to certain school staff members. These relationships can act as protective factors for students.

Students with health and mental health problems are at significantly greater risk of academic failure and absenteeism (Needham, Crosnoe, & Muller, 2004). According to the U.S. Department of Education (2001), 50 percent of children with serious emotional disturbances will drop out of school, as compared to 30 percent of all children with disabilities. Chapter 31 discusses assessment and intervention issues with children with a range of mental health concerns.

School phobia or school refusal is one significant mental health–related cause of nonattendance. School phobia is correlated with a number of mental health conditions, including anxiety disorders, mood disorders, disruptive behavior disorders, learning disorders, and substance abuse. Criteria for diagnosing school refusal include:

1. Severe emotional distress about attending school; may include anxiety, temper tantrums, depression, or somatic symptoms.

2. Parents are aware of the absence; the child often tries to persuade parents to allow him or her to stay home.
3. There is an absence of significant antisocial behavior.
4. During school hours, child usually stays home because it is considered a safe and secure environment.
5. Child expresses willingness to do schoolwork and complies with completing work at home. (Fremont, 2003, p. 1555)

Cases of school phobia call for a referral for a multidimensional assessment that examines both physical and mental health (Rettig & Crawford, 2000). Treatment may include family sessions, medication, or cognitive behavioral interventions.

In all truancy situations, school social workers should gauge the prevalence of grief, loss, family transitions, stressors, teen pregnancy or parenting issues, abuse, and trauma. Experiences of loss and family transitions can be elicited by interviews with the child and the family in an unstructured format that permits children and their families to reveal sensitive information.

Academic Ability and Engagement. To fully understand causes for truancy, school social workers should assess students' academic abilities, engagement, and attitudes toward school. Teachers can provide this information as well as academic files, special education documents or plans, or standardized test scores. Do students see school as boring or pointless, or do they enjoy it? Do students feel intellectually challenged? Do they feel overwhelmed by academic expectations? What parts of the day do they look forward to or dread the most? What parts of the day are most calming or anxiety provoking? Some students may feel alienated in classes in which they cannot keep up (Passmore, 2003). Attitudes about school's relevance and instrumental value are important. In their qualitative study of eighty-eight young people in northeast England in 1999–2001, MacDonald and Marsh (2004) found that explanations for persistent truancy "related, in part, to powerful, (sub)cultural critiques of orthodox claims about the instrumental relevance of education" (p. 143).

Family Assessment and Intervention

Attendance is an issue that, perhaps more than any other, requires a balanced partnership between the family and the school. Constable and Lee (2004) note, "Families cannot educate their children in a complex modern society without the assistance of schools, and schools cannot educate without the cooperation of families" (p. 224). The home visit can serve to assess contextual factors, parent-child communication and interaction patterns (Lauchlan, 2003), understanding of truancy laws, and methods of discipline that may affect attendance (Teasley, 2004). Home visits are also a way of reaching out to families and creating a bridge between the home and the school. How engaged is the parent in the student's schooling? How do the parents feel about education and attendance? Children whose parents had positive school experiences tend to have more positive educational outcomes (Ferrer-Wreder, Stattin, Lorente, Tubman, & Adamson, 2004).

School Assessment

School and classroom climate are critical to engaging students in school. A welcoming, inviting, and warm climate is more likely to keep students engaged and attending than a chillier one. School policies, programs, climate, engagement, motivation, incentives, and interventions are all important. An understanding of whole-school class-cutting patterns is also useful. How many students arrive at school in the morning and then cut classes or cut the same periods, courses, or teachers regularly (Guare & Cooper, 2003)? School social workers should listen to school staff to understand how teachers' perceptions and teacher-student interactions influence attendance patterns (Lauchlan, 2003; see chapter 21).

Availability of Extracurricular Activities in the School. There is a positive relationship between extracurricular activities and academic achievement, including school attendance in the broader school population (Fletcher, Nickerson, & Wright, 2003; Jordan & Nettles, 2000), among economically disadvantaged, ethnically diverse students (Prelow & Loukas, 2003; Reis, Colbert, & Hebert, 2005), and foster children (Shin, 2003). These findings are important since a response to school nonattendance has been to restrict participation in extracurricular activities. Also, the current emphasis on test scores has led to threats to funding for school-based extracurricular activities. Extracurricular activities, sports, clubs, or other after-school programs may maintain connections to school, reconnect students to school, or provide a means of motivating students to maintain regular attendance.

Community Assessment

Assessment of community factors is critical to understanding truancy patterns. When the community gets behind the schools in attendance issues, the results can be impressive. One project called the Safety and Health through Action and Responsibility for Education (SHARE) developed grassroots assessment and intervention in its community (McMahon, Browning, & Rose-Colley, 2001) over four years. The project involved priority goal-setting, coordination of community services, door-to-door distribution/collection of a needs and assets survey (in which 70% of the population was interviewed), and community meetings. A task force to address the needs of at-risk students in the county was developed. It was made up of health-care providers, school district representatives, parents, clergy, social service agencies, and local government officials. The project resulted in a 75 percent decrease in truancy.

Many students encounter health, economic, or other environmental obstacles that affect their school attendance and achievement (McMahon et al.,

2001). Cultural and linguistic factors are important. What is the fit between the culture of the school and that of ethnic minority students (Teasley, 2004)? In 2001, 7.3 percent of White students between ages 16 and 24 dropped out, 10.9 percent of Black students dropped out, and 27.0 percent of Hispanic students dropped out (U.S. Department of Commerce, 2002). These data suggest that truancy programs may need to focus special efforts on engaging Black and Hispanic students.

In addition to cultural issues, economic issues such as homelessness and transitional housing may affect attendance. Homelessness is associated with high mobility of students, and high student mobility is associated with reduced academic achievement. Despite the McKinney Homeless Assistance Act, which requires schools to serve homeless students, schools often illegally fail to open their doors to students who cannot document a within-district address. Economic issues related to attendance should be raised. Do students usually go to college? Where do most students get jobs if they drop out of school? Do students' work schedules affect attendance? MacDonald and Marsh (2004) suggest that if there is a historical abundance of decent working-class jobs, then the importance of a traditional education may be undermined. Or if even high-achieving students can only get minimum wage jobs, then do students really believe school can help them succeed?

INTERVENTION

Strengths, protective factors, needs, and resources that were identified in the assessment process should clearly guide the choice of intervention program (Lauchlan, 2003). Interventions that affect multiple systems (individuals, peers, academics, families, communities) and have a strong research base are likely to have longer-lasting effects (Teasley, 2004). Students themselves should be involved in both individual and systemic change efforts (Guare & Cooper, 2003).

Broad Intervention Strategies

Punishment. Punishments, such as detention time, in-school suspension, additional assignments, prohibition of participation in extracurricular activities, removal of work-release privileges, lowered class participation grades (Wisconsin Legislative Audit Bureau [WLAB], 2000), and prohibition of driving (Viadero, 2004), are popular responses to truancy. Sanctions for parents have included fines, court proceedings, and prosecution. Such measures have little research backing (Judd, 2004). Courts often take too long to see attendance cases, so their interventions are not effective (Reid, 2003c). Critics of punitive measures for truancy argue that punishment unfairly puts schools in the police and prosecution business, assumes a deficit model and ignores environmental issues, and treats the symptoms rather than the causes of truancy (Guare &

Cooper, 2003). Punishment can act to further isolate students who are already isolated.

From Prevention to Intervention: Policy Development. Schools may respond to truancy through policy development, through programs that target school climate and school conditions, or through programs that focus on helping individual students who are truant. Prevention and policy development can impact a broader part of the problem than an initial focus on individual truants (Dupper & Evans, 1996; Ferrer-Wreder et al., 2004). Prevention and intervention programs should be integrated. Too often schools have fragmented services and distinct initiatives (Passmore, 2003). Reid (2004) writes, "What really matters is having an effective long-term attendance strategy in place which is consistent, facilitates monitoring, and acts both as a deterrent and, at the same time, in a positive, inclusive, and therapeutic manner" (p. 72). Carl, Pawlak, and Dorn's (1982) review of effective attendance policies and procedures found some agreement among researchers:

1. Parents should be alerted to their children's absenteeism.
2. Parent notification should begin at least with the third absence.
3. Parent and school cooperation in intervention is essential.
4. Consistent limits, enforcement, and record keeping on the part of administration and teachers are essential.

In high schools there has been some support for the use of a block schedule (1½-hour classes) rather than an hourly schedule in high schools to prevent students from skipping classes. Also, an open-campus policy that allows students to leave during their lunch period can contribute to truancy because students may be tardy or not return after lunch (WLAB, 2000).

School social workers can work to help create a positive school climate that may improve attendance (Guare & Cooper, 2003, p. 74). They can advocate for teaching methods that are participative, exciting, active, communal, collaborative, and meaning constructing (Guare & Cooper, 2003; LeCornu & Collins, 2004). Developing supportive learning environments that improve student self-confidence and combat social exclusion helps students to stay engaged. Knowing that teachers care about them is also crucially important to student engagement (Guare & Cooper, 2003; LeCornu & Collins, 2004). When a student is missing from class, teachers should ask, "Has anyone seen Cathy or Keith today?" (Guare & Cooper, 2003, p. 83). Students need to be consistently made aware that their attendance matters (Reid, 2003c). The most effective programs use contingency management. Recognizing and rewarding students for improved attendance may motivate students to attend school more regularly (Epstein & Sheldon, 2002). Schools should focus on improved and good attendance, not just perfect attendance (Colorado Foundation for Families and Children, n.d.).

Long-Term Strategic School-wide Prevention and Intervention. A whole-school strategic prevention approach, with evaluation over multiple years, may help reduce truancy (McCluskey et al., 2004; Reid, 2004). Such a plan is likely to work best when the idea is chosen and initiated from school staff out of a need-based response to a chronic attendance problem (Reid, 2003a). Since this type of approach is dependent on the consistent participation of all school staff members (Reid, 2003a), school social workers are in a good position to initiate, advocate for, and be key players in its development. Research has shown that the earlier the intervention, the more likely it is to prevent nonattendance (Reid, 2003c; Reid, 2004). Because 35 percent to 36 percent of all students' truancy and persistent attendance problems start in primary school, and the "trigger" point for truancy is normally between ages 7 and 13, it makes sense to intervene in these early years (Reid, 2003a; Reid, 2003b). Staff training, gradual and progressive growth, parent communication, ownership, and clear messages are also critically important to program success (Reid, 2004). The plan is dependent on consistently collecting data during elementary-school years and transferring it to secondary schools (Reid, 2004). This information allows for early identification and provides a baseline for evaluation (Reid, 2004).

One example of such a program, outlined by Reid (2004), involves identifying students for three groups based on level of risk factors related to truancy. The highest level of intervention is used for persistent nonattenders, a medium-level intervention is used for less serious cases of absence, and the lowest-level intervention is used for underachieving or at-risk students. The highest-level intervention utilizes a multidisciplinary team including social workers, teachers, special education supervisors, tutors, or other staff members. The team invites the parents and student in for a meeting, reviews relevant information, tries to determine the reasons for nonattendance, and develops an action plan. The medium-level intervention meets only with the student to make sure the student is well supported and to review if the student needs a different level of academic support. The lowest intervention tries to prevent potentially at-risk and underachieving students from deteriorating.

Specific Intervention Approaches

There are many different specific interventions that school social workers can use to address truancy problems with students. Some of these are outlined below:

Academic Adjustments. Students who have continuously failed at academic tasks have likely developed negative expectations and a sense of incompetence (Ferrer-Wreder et al., 2004). To return to school, they will need academic intervention with frequent opportunities to regain their sense of competence when they have opportunities to succeed and strengthen basic academic skills.

Mentoring and Tutoring Programs. Student mentoring and tutoring programs may decrease truancy by helping students to reconnect both academically and socially (cited in Teasley, 2004). In the Excellence in Cities program set up in 1998–1999, which covers fifty-eight urban areas in England, there was a 2.3 percent drop in truancy rates. The program involved

2,500 learning mentors and 1,000 learning support units, which gave help on site to students with behavior issues (Passmore, 2003). Successful tutoring programs make academic tasks more enjoyable; build confidence; provide support; show students that people care about them; reinforce cooperation, teamwork, and on-task behavior; and give students time to practice resilience skills such as planning, goal setting, self monitoring, and problem solving. Tutoring is especially appropriate for helping students who are at risk of academic failure. For peer-led programs to be successful, they need to have clear program aims and objectives, a good fit between project design and intervention efforts, adequate training of peer leaders, and well-specified interpersonal boundaries (Ferrer-Wreder et al., 2004).

Transitions Back to School. It is advisable to get the student to return to school as soon as possible, because the longer the student is out of school, the more difficult it may be to get him or her back (Lauchlan, 2003). School social workers should pay special attention to details related to helping chronically truant students return to school. To ensure a smooth transition, the school social worker should attempt to alleviate student concerns related to academics, peers, teachers, and other issues (Blagg, 1987; Reid, 2004).

Social Connections. To prevent truancy or reengage truant students, school social workers should help students to connect with a positive peer group and with school staff. By including students in social work groups, referring them to appropriate clubs or activities, or helping them make friends in other ways, social workers can help students to feel more comfortable and confident.

Buddy Systems. Reynolds (cited in Carl, Pawlak, & Dorn, 1982) describes a buddy system, used in combination with positive social and material reinforcement, which contributed to a marked improvement in attendance of thirty chronically truant junior high school students. Students who were reliable attenders and resided in the same vicinity as the truants or who had access to a telephone were voluntarily paired with their chronically absent counterparts. The buddies were instructed to make contact with each other daily, either by telephone or by meeting at the bus stop. A motivator party for the program's participants was held prior to the implementation of the buddy system. Throughout the following six weeks, the pair's mutual attendance was greeted with a smile sticker placed upon an attendance chart, which was maintained by a counselor aide. At the end of the six-week period all pairs demonstrating increased attendance were rewarded with music, picnics, and pizza parties.

Cognitive-Behavioral Interventions. For students who refuse school due to anxiety, cognitive behavioral techniques can be helpful. The school social worker can work with students on relaxation training, self-talk (replacing negative messages with positive ones), and exposure (incremental experience with the anxiety-provoking situation) (Lauchlan, 2003).

Student Education and Social Skills Training. Educating students about certain behaviors and lifestyle choices to help them make informed choices can be helpful, but only if it is one part of a more comprehensive program (Ferrer-Wreder et al., 2004). Because many students do not attend school due to anxiety or social difficulties, training students in social skills can be an appropriate truancy intervention (Lauchlan, 2003). School social workers can help students identify social situations that produce negative feelings and help them to practice how to cope in those situations (Lauchlan, 2003). Another approach to skill training is "life competence promotion" which involves teaching a broad set of skills that promote positive adaptation to life challenges. In order to change behavior, skill teaching should include a combination of generic skills and focused applications (i.e., role plays or real-life practice opportunities) (Ferrer-Wreder et al., 2004; see chapter 35).

Parent Partnerships. School social workers have an important role in promoting parent-school partnerships. These partnerships include general parent involvement in school, communication, and outreach. Schools may contact parents about truancy through meetings, letters, or phone calls. A strong effort to contact parents personally may act as a deterrent to truancy (WLAB, 2000). In addition, phone calls made by a person who knows the student or family well (i.e., homeroom teacher) may be more effective at preventing truancy than contact by an anonymous person or a phone recording (Colorado Foundation for Families and Children, n.d.). Reid (2004) emphasizes that the tone of the contact, including language and method of presentation used, is important. Schools need to get parents on their side to collaboratively solve truancy problems. If schools are defensive or punitive, parents are unlikely to want to collaborate (Reid, 2004). Giving parents the name and telephone number of an officially designated school staff member who can discuss attendance may also improve attendance (Epstein & Sheldon, 2002). School social workers can help ensure that communication efforts accommodate families who may have difficulty understanding the language, reading, or receiving mail. They must help parents understand truancy regulations, legalities, and potential consequences.

In their exploratory study, Epstein and Sheldon (2002) found that when school staff made home visits, they reported decreases in the percentage of students who were chronically absent. Constable (1970) did a study of home and school visitors in the Philadelphia schools working with chronic truants. He found that in a largely bureaucratized service, when the Home and School Visitor knew the student well enough to give a description of him or her, it significantly predicted a return to school after the home visits. Kearney and Albano (2000; in Lauchlan, 2003) suggest that home-school linked contracting may be used with students to outline clear expectations for attendance linked with rewards.

Parent Education and Training. Parent education is useful to make sure that parents understand their legal responsibilities to make children attend school (Reid, 2003c). Attendance and truancy policies should be clearly explained, written in a handbook, updated annually, and well publicized (Guare & Cooper, 2003; Reid, 2003c). Epstein and Sheldon (2002) found that workshops on attendance were associated with increases in average daily attendance, but they suggest that workshops be specifically related to attendance policies, procedures, and consequences. Parent education regarding reintegration strategies after a period of significant absence is also helpful (Reid, 2003c). Parent training related to truancy may also be useful in helping parents work together as a team, manage behavior, give clear expectations, and follow through with consequences (Lauchlan, 2003).

Programming. Certain programs may help students to stay in school. Alternative curricula, alternative schools, vocational/technical schools, and after-school programs may help some students to stay in school (Epstein & Sheldon, 2002; Reid, 2003c). Teen pregnancy or parenting accommodations may also be needed. Students who find it difficult to make progress in one school sometimes do better in a different learning environment (Reid, 2003c).

Student Engagement and Relevance. Educational relevance is critically linked to attendance (Reid, 2003c). Engaging students in relevant culturally appropriate (Guare & Cooper, 2003) participatory curricula through effective teaching methods is another way to combat truancy. School social workers can challenge practices, expectations, and discipline that have an adverse effect on culturally and economically diverse students. They can advocate for greater multiculturalism and diversity, and thus greater inclusion (Dupper & Evans, 1996; Teasley, 2004).

Community Involvement and Partnership Practices. Involving the community in partnership can help to increase daily attendance (Epstein & Sheldon, 2002). Houston, Texas, hosted a "reach out to dropouts day," a city effort in which 100 volunteers knocked on the doors of 800 students who hadn't shown up to school in the first two weeks of classes (Axtman, 2004). Truancy prevention and intervention should be integrated with existing programs, such as community-based Wraparound services that prevent out-of-school placement and Student Assistance Programs (SAPs) that address student drug and alcohol issues (Ferrer-Wreder et al., 2004; Maynard-Moody, 1994). Multiyear programs that integrate family and school initiatives and address a broad range of issues are more likely to produce significant behavioral change. In order to result in meaningful change, programs must be of sufficient duration and intensity, must be linked to structural changes, and must be reinforced by all staff (Ferrer-Wreder et al., 2004).

School-Police Partnerships. Innovative, nonpunitive school-police partnerships may help to improve attendance. In the Truant Recovery program implemented in Richmond, California, police agencies transport suspected truants to attendance offices and contact their parents/guardians for in-person meetings (White, Fyfe, Campbell, & Goldkamp, 2001). The program utilizes a Student Attendance Review Board that reviews habitual truancy cases, and a Suspension Alternative Class that allows for students suspended for truancy to remain in school. Here the teacher interacts with truants to discuss any underlying problems, arranges for the truants' homework to be brought in so he/she does not fall behind, and provides additional academic work. The primary aim of the program is "to return truants to school as soon as possible." Students who participated in the truant recovery program got into trouble less often and skipped school less often but continued to struggle academically (White et al., 2001).

CASE EXAMPLES

The following case examples are based on composite experiences with children and youth in school settings.

The high school is large, with 4,000 students, and few opportunities for students to be noticed. It had taken a punitive approach to absenteeism. More than ten absences results in failure of a class, and additional absences result in arrest and jailing of parents. The community is a lower-middle-class community with some opportunities for employment in fast food restaurants and retail stores. The library is small and little used. No community groups have taken up the issue of improving school attendance.

Tonya is a white 15-year-old from a working class family. In the past year, her attendance became a problem, so that, based on her high number of absences, she was in danger of school failure and disciplinary action. Ms. Fletcher, the school social worker, met with Tonya to discuss her absences. Tonya had little interest in school; rather she enjoyed spending time at the mall, watching TV, and seeing friends. She didn't like walking to school in the morning, especially in bad weather. She had few friends and no extracurricular activities at school, and she wasn't doing well her in classes. In a home visit with Tonya's parents, Ms. Fletcher met two hardworking, busy people who work long hours every day and, leaving for work quite early, were unable to ensure that Tonya got to school in the morning. They were concerned and wanted to work with the school to "get Tonya back on track." They had felt forced to write notes for her, since they had heard that they could be jailed if their daughter had too many unexcused absences. Both dropped out of high school before graduation, but they were employed and doing well. They wondered if Tonya would be better off working than in school.

Ms. Fletcher began by developing a working partnership with Tonya and her parents around her attendance. They developed a plan to take Tonya to a friend's house in the morning, so that another parent could drive Tonya to school. Ms. Fletcher intervened with Tonya's teachers and asked them all to greet her warmly, by name, whenever she was in class, and to note and appreciate her presence in class. Tonya was asked to report to the school social worker's office every morning that she was in school, when she received a sticker on a chart. After earning ten stickers, she got to go out to lunch at a fast-food restaurant of her choice with the school social worker. Ms. Fletcher and Tonya explored some of Tonya's interests and discovered that she enjoyed volleyball. She signed up for the volleyball team. Ms. Fletcher also reached out to the community, sought out key community stakeholders, and advocated for them to develop a community-based program to encourage school attendance. Tonya's attendance gradually improved, and her grades were better after one semester.

In this example, the school social worker engaged both the child and the family in school. Although there were obstacles to this engagement, the interventions attempted in the school did not require major time on the part of the teachers or the social worker, however, they did result in Tonya's reengagement in the school.

In the Hometown Schools, attendance problems often represent trends and patterns that need to be effectively addressed at a broader level through community-school-family partnerships.

The Hometown Schools are in a suburb of a major city. Mr. Blaine, school social worker, has noticed that in the middle school absences and tardies increased over the past year, while student grades decreased. There was no illness sweeping the school to explain this trend. Mr. Blaine brought together a task group to address the problem. It included school staff, the other school social worker, parents, two students, the principal, and the police liaison. The task group decided to conduct a needs assessment to evaluate the needs of the school and community and to identify strategies or programs that might improve student attendance. They involved key community leaders in the process. They found several models of strategies for improving attendance. They surveyed the community to determine which model would be the best fit for the community and decided to adopt a "Reach out to Dropouts" day and make it ongoing. They combined this with efforts to change the school climate to more fully engage students. They applied for a grant to fund more in-school services, including a Student Assistance program, to address drug, alcohol, and mental health needs of students. This developed into a community mentoring program for at-risk students. After one year, they had not yet received funding to implement all of their ideas, but a significant increase in attendance had taken place.

CONCLUSION

School districts have a compelling interest that students achieve academically, graduate, and perform well on standardized tests, all of which require regular attendance. Attendance is vital for students' social development and personal growth, future career opportunities, and economic survival. Attendance can also act as a protective factor to resist antisocial behaviors such as drug abuse, running away, and criminal activity. Finally, schools may face legal sanctions, get less financial aid from states, or have their schools closed if students do not attend.

School social workers should understand their distinct role on the multidisciplinary team. They are in a unique position to apply a comprehensive multisystemic, strengths-based approach to truancy issues. Their understanding of students in their environments needs to guide their interventions. Focused on risk and protective factors of individuals in their broader peer, family, and community environments, assessments may involve observations, interviews, team meetings, home visits, parent contact, questionnaires, policy review, academic review, or other actions. Punishment strategies, though prevalent, have little research support and can further isolate at-risk students. A variety of interventions have shown promise in preventing and intervening in truancy, including: academic adjustments; tutoring and mentoring; cognitive behavioral strategies; student education and skills training; parent partnerships, education, and training; policy changes; programming; student engagement strategies; strategic long-term whole-school approaches; and community partnerships.

References

Abbot, E., & Breckinridge, S. (1917). *Truancy and non-attendance in the Chicago schools: A study of the social aspects of compulsory education and child labor legislation of Illinois.* Chicago: University of Chicago Press.

Ackerman, S. P., & Byock, G. J. (1989). *Evaluation of the 1988 Freshman Summer Program and Transfer Summer Program, Phase II.* Los Angeles: University of Los Angeles.

Allen-Meares, P. (2004). *Social work services in schools* (4th ed.). Needham Heights, MA: Allyn and Bacon.

Axtman, K. (2004). Knock, knock: It's Houston's new truancy gambit. *Christian Science Monitor, 96*(194), 3.

Blagg, N. (1987). *School phobia and its intervention.* London: Croom Helm.

Brown v. Board of Education of Topeka, KS, 347 U.S. 483 (1954)

Carl, M. L., Pawlak, E. J., & Dorn, D. M. (1982). Research on truancy. In R. T. Constable, & J. P. Flynn (Eds.), *School social work: Practice and research perspectives.* Chicago: The Dorsey Press.

Colorado Foundation for Families and Children. (n.d.). 10 things a school can do to improve attendance. Retrieved February 28, 2005, from http://www.truancyprevention.org/attendance.html

Constable, R. (1970). *The home and school visitor and the recidivist, non-attendant school child: An exploration of certain dimensions of a relationship and their association with outcome.* Dissertation completed in partial fulfillment of the Doctor of Social Work degree, University of Pennsylvania. Ann Arbor, MI: University Microfilms.

Constable, R., & Lee, D. B. (2004). *Social work with families.* Chicago: Lyceum Books.

Council of Chief State School Officers [CCSSO]. (2001). *Key state education policies on K-12 education 2000.* Education Commission of the States "Clearinghouse Notes," August, 1997; California Department of Education, Safe Schools and Violence Prevention Office, School Attendance Review Boards. Retrieved February 16, 2005, from http://nces.ed.gov//programs/digest/d03/tables/dt151.asp

Derezinski, T. (2004). School attendance. In P. Allen-Meares (Ed.), *Social work services in schools* (4th ed., pp. 95-118). Boston: Allyn & Bacon.

Dupper, D. R., & Evans, S. (1996). From band-aids and putting out fires to prevention: School social work practice approaches for the new century. *Social Work in Education, 18*(3), 187-192.

Epstein, J. L., & Sheldon, S. B. (2002). Present and accounted for: Improving student attendance through family and community involvement. *Journal of Educational Research, 95*(5), 308-320.

Ferrer-Wreder, L., Stattin, H., Lorente, C. C., Tubman, J. G., & Adamson, L. (2004). *Successful prevention and youth development programs across borders*. New York: Kluwer Academic/Plenum Publishers.

Fischer, L., & Sorenson, G. P. (1996). *School law for counselors, psychologists, and social workers*. White Plains, NY: Longman.

Fletcher, A. C., Nickerson, P., & Wright, K. L. (2003). Structured leisure activities in middle childhood: Links to well-being. *Journal of Community Psychology, 31*(6), 641-659.

Fremont, W. P. (2003). School refusal in children and adolescents. *American Family Physician, 68*(8), 1555-1560.

Gehring, J. (2004). Districts tackling truancy with new zeal. *Education Week, 24*(4), 1-2.

Guare, R. E., & Cooper, B. S. (2003). *Truancy revisited: Students as school consumers.* Lanham, MD: Scarecrow Press, Inc.

Hallfors, D., Vevea, J. L., Iritani, B., Cho, H., Khatapoush, S., & Saxe, L. (2002). Truancy, grade point average, and sexual activity: A meta-analysis of risk indicators for youth substance abuse. *Journal of School Health, 72*(5), 205-211.

Harvey, A. D. (2003). Truancy again—and again. *Education Journal, 69*, 17.

Heberling, K., & Shaffer, D. V. (1995). School attendance and grade point averages of regular education and learning disabled students in elementary schools. *Research Report, 8.*

Jordan, W. J., & Nettles, S. M. (2000). How students invest their time outside of school: Effects on school-related outcomes. *Social Psychology of Education, 3*, 217-243.

Judd, J. (2004, April 2). Maths for mechanics might tempt truants. *The Times Educational Supplement*, p. 21.

Kearney, C. A., & Albano, A. M. (2000). *When children refuse school: A cognitive behavioral therapy approach*. Boulder, CO: Graywind.

Kearney, C., & Silverman, W. K. (1990). A preliminary analysis of a functional model of assessment and treatment for school refusal behavior. *Behavior Modification. 14*(3), 340-366.

Lauchlan, F. (2003). Responding to chronic non-attendance: A review of intervention approaches. *Educational Psychology in Practice, 19*(2), 133-146.

LeCornu, R., & Collins, J. (2004). Re-emphasizing the role of affect in learning and teaching. *Pastoral Care in Education, 22*(4), 27-33.

MacDonald, R., & Marsh, J. (2004). Missing school: Educational engagement, youth transitions, and social exclusion. *Youth & Society, 36*(2), 143-162.

McCluskey, C. P., Bynum, T. S., & Patchin, J. W. (2004). Reducing chronic absenteeism: An assessment of an early truancy initiative. *Crime & Delinquency, 50*(2), 214-234.

McMahon, B., Browning, S., & Rose-Colley, M. (2001). A school-community partnership for at-risk students in Pennsylvania. *Journal of School Health, 71*(2), 53-55.

Man, A. F. De. (2000). Predictors of adolescent running away behavior. *Social Behavior & Personality: An International Journal, 28*(3), 261-267.

Maynard-Moody, C. (1994). Wraparound services for at-risk youths in rural schools. *Social Work in Education, 16*(3), 187-192.

Needham, B. L., Crosnoe, R., & Muller, C. (2004). Academic failure in secondary school: The inter-related role of health problems and educational context. *Social Problems, 51*(4), 569-586.

O'Malley, P. M., & Johnston, L. D. (1999). Drinking and driving among U.S. high school seniors, 1984-1997. *American Journal of Public Health, 89*(5), 678-684.

Passmore, B. (2003, January 17). Playing the blame game with truants. *The Times Educational Supplement*, p. 24.

Prelow, H. M., & Loukas, A., (2003). The role of resource, protective, and risk factors on academic achievement-related outcomes of economically disadvantaged Latino youth. *Journal of Community Psychology, 31*(5), 513-529.

Program keeps truant students in school. (2001). *American City & Country, 116*(14), 74.

Reid, K. (2004). A long-term strategic approach to tackling truancy and absenteeism from schools: the SSTG scheme. *British Journal of Guidance & Counselling, 32*(1), 57-74.

Reid, K. (2003a). A strategic approach to tackling school absenteeism and truancy: The PSCC scheme. *Educational Studies, 29*(4), 351-371.

Reid, K. (2003b). Strategic approaches to tackling school absenteeism and truancy: The traffic lights (TL) scheme. *Educational Review, 55*(3), 305-321.

Reid, K. (2003c). The search for solutions to truancy and other forms of school absenteeism. *Pastoral Care in Education, 21*(1), 3-9.

Reis, S. M., Colbert, R. D., & Hebert, T. P. (2005). Understanding resilience in diverse, talented students in an urban high school. *Roeper Review, 27*(2), 110-121.

Rettig, M., & Crawford, J. (2000). Getting past the fear of going to school. *The Education Digest, 65*(9), 54-58.

Roby, D. E. (2004). Research on school attendance and school achievement: A study of Ohio schools. *Educational Research Quarterly, 28*(1), 3-14.

Schroeder, K. (1993). Student drug use. *Education Digest, 59*(4), 75.

Shin, S. H. (2003). Building evidence to promote educational competence of youth in foster care. *Child Welfare, 82*(5), 615-632.

Soldz, S., Huyser, D. J., & Dorsey, E. (2003). The cigar as a drug delivery device: Youth use of blunts. *Addiction, 98*(10), 1379-1386.

Strickland, V. P. (1998). Attendance and grade point average: A study. (Report No. SP 038 147). Chicago: Chicago Public Schools. (ERIC Document Reproduction Service No. ED423224)

Teasley, M. L. (2004). Absenteeism and truancy: Risk, protection, and best practice implications for school social workers. *Children & Schools, 26*(2), 117-128.

Tomori, M., Zalar, B., Kores Plesnicar, B., Ziherl, S., & Stergar, E. (2001). Smoking in relation to psychosocial risk factors in adolescents. *European Child & Adolescent Psychiatry, 10*(2), 143-150.

U.S. Department of Commerce, Bureau of the Census, Current Population Survey (CPS), unpublished tabulations; and U.S. Department of Education, National Center for Education Statistics. (2001). *Dropout rates in the United States, 2001.* Retrieved February 16, 2005, from http://nces.ed.gov/pubs2005/dropout2001/tab_fig.asp

U.S. Department of Education Office of Special Education Programs. (2001). *Twenty-third annual report to Congress on the implementation of the Individuals with Disabilities Education Act: Results.* Washington, DC: Author.

Viadero, D. (2004). Minnesota governor to link driver's licenses, truancy. *Education Week, 24*(3), 26.

White, M. D., Fyfe, J. F., Campbell, S. P., & Goldkamp, J. S. (2001). The school-police partnership: Identifying at-risk youth through a truant recovery program. *Evaluation Review, 25*(5), 507-532.

Winkler, D. F. (1993). *Working status and student performance.* Hickory, North Carolina: Lenoire College.

Wisconsin Legislative Audit Bureau [WLAB]. (2000). Truancy reduction efforts: A best practices review. *Journal of State Government, 73*(4), 13-15.

Yunker, J. A. (1967). Pre-high school group guidance for potential dropouts and non-college bound students. *Research Report, 39.*

30

Case Management, Coordination of Services, and Resource Development

Richard S. Kordesh

Bluehouse Institute, Inc.
Oak Park, IL

Robert Constable

Loyola University, Chicago

- ◆ The Continuing Challenges of Resource Development
- ◆ Interagency Agreements
- ◆ Case Management
- ◆ The Transagency Team in the Schools
- ◆ Emerging Roles in Resource Coordination
- ◆ Possible Future Scenarios for Social Workers as Resource Developers

Resource development and coordination roles remain essential and continuing aspects of school social work practice. These roles have become even more critical with the greater shared awareness of children's vulnerability, with the broadening scope of schools, and with school reform.

THE CONTINUING CHALLENGES OF RESOURCE DEVELOPMENT

From the very beginnings of practice, school social workers had to find resources, get clients connected with them, make sure they were providing appropriate services, work out difficulties between different service providers, and develop new services or fight for their accessibility. For example, as early as 1906 Louise Montgomery developed and coordinated resources at Hamline School and did case management.

The current mandate of the school for provision of special education and related services creates a situation in which the school is an even more important part of the network of services for children with disabilities. Schools are only now beginning to address the implications of their centrality in services for children with disabilities. There is an opportunity now for school social workers to reaffirm their historic commitment and to further develop long-standing skills. The movement to include youngsters with more severe disabilities in public education, especially infants and toddlers (see chapters 12 and 23), created a greater need for professionals who could do case management and develop complex support systems. The more severe the problem or the gap between home and school, the greater the need for complex and individually constructed supportive resource systems

There are a number of reasons for the importance of resource development and coordination of services for school social workers. First, the school and the family often cannot accomplish their own functions without specialized help from other agencies. These agencies might provide health services, counseling services, concrete assistance, respite care, summer camp, or other services necessary in modern society. School pupils may be involved with other systems in our society that have deeper claims on them, such as the juvenile justice system or the child welfare system. Second, the service delivery system is usually segmented, divided by special functions within health care, child welfare, vocational rehabilitation, educational systems, mental health, and so on, between a seemingly unlimited array of services, each with particular functions, missions, and rationales for helping. Even if these were integrated at the organizational level, it is still more important that service be integrated at the level of the case. Family and school, with a focus on the whole child and the environment, have concerns that can transcend segmentation. Both have natural roles in addressing the difficulty in accessing services for vulnerable children. The more vulnerable the child, the greater the need to coordinate services from different service providers and the greater the potential damage if something goes wrong. The more services needed, the greater the likelihood that something will go wrong, and thus the greater the need for a problem-solving professional to address the configuration and delivery of services. The school is central to the child, and the school social worker is directly in the middle as the person most likely to coordinate services and provide case management.

Resource development and coordination of services are recognized as crucial in working with diverse populations with profound and ongoing needs such as the elderly, children experiencing neglect or abuse, or persons with physical disabilities, developmental disabilities, or severe and persistent mental illnesses. Each area has developed a literature of its own regarding integration and coordination of services and case management. In schools, there have been particular concerns for young children with severe disabilities and older youngsters with disabilities nearing transition into the world of work. With both populations, some case management is mandated, but effective service cannot be provided to either of these populations without the larger structure of interagency agreements and the smaller structures of case management that appropriately involves the family and other resource persons in individual case plans.

The more vulnerable the pupil, the greater the needs for external services, the greater the difficulty in getting these services, and, finally, the greater the likelihood of family breakdown in the face of these difficulties. Difficulties are experienced both from the agency and from the family perspective. Often parents are not even aware of what resource systems exist. Access to resources is usually difficult and accompanied by multiple and conflicting behavioral demands. Children and parents often have multiple, complex involvements with these systems. Resource development and coordination are particularly important for the child with disabilities. These children often have difficulty and special needs in coping with other areas of their environment as well as school. The family's attempts to support the youngster and compensate for gaps in socialization and capability place it under pressure, particularly where the family is already under strain. Family units, such as single-parent households or households where both parents work, are particularly vulnerable. Whatever takes place in the family inevitably will affect what the pupil is able to do in school, and so it is artificial to draw a sharp boundary between what is educational and what is noneducational.

The social worker's investment of time in informing parents, removing barriers to obtaining services, and helping parents use services has a high payoff in the child's adjustment to a learning situation. The law firmly places the responsibility for the child's free appropriate public education on the school, but the actuality is more complex. If the network of family, informal support systems and formal community resources breaks down, the school is placed in the position of having to support more expensive and more restrictive alternatives for placement of the child with disabilities. The need for coordination and service integration is dictated by the belief that it is better that children with disabilities remain with their families, and by simple economics, which makes remaining at home a less expensive educational alternative. Given the scarcity of resources within school districts, the school faces the complex problem of bringing children and educational resources together in an appropriate environment and maintaining a support system. A commitment to vulnerable children places the school in the difficult position of having to interact with community agencies in complex planning efforts. Educators generally are unprepared for this task. The school social worker is frequently the only member of the school team whose orientation and general skill development includes interaction with community agencies, and so any coordination, if it is done at all, is and should be done by the school social worker.

Resources in the community can be divided into two groups. First, there are services available from formally constituted organizations, often purchased by either family or school, and, if not purchased, subject to complex eligibility determinations for entitlement. Second, there are informal, helping networks of neighbors, community people, relatives, members of church and civic groups, local merchants, and other schoolchildren who may be willing and able to help in a variety of ways. It would be unrealistic to assume that formal organizations by themselves will be able to meet the complex needs of children with disabilities and their families. The social worker may locate and help the family communicate with a variety of informal, helping networks that may exist in a community. Possible uses of such networks are almost limitless. The social worker will often maintain an ongoing consultative relationship with some network members so that they do not become disappointed or confused at the initial response of the child with disabilities or his or her family. The authors have used volunteers, police officers, and a wide variety of other persons in many ways to provide structure, an element of caring, and vitally needed help for the child with disabilities and her family.

New structures for collaboration are needed among public and private agencies having resources for children with disabilities, with particular focus on the family of students with disabilities. A mixture of hard services (programs and tangible resources) and soft services (counseling, access to psychological support, and information) that help people deal with stress is needed. Traditional services for children with disabilities have been quite segmented and competitive, with different agencies dealing with different aspects of the child with disabilities' needs. Either continuing this segmented system or giving the responsibility to the school alone would be grossly dysfunctional.

Because a variety of resources is being brought to bear on an individual child, the management problem is also quite different from the traditional model of educational administration. The traditional model involves a building, an administrative hierarchy, a faculty, a group of pupils, equipment more or less in one place, and transportation from home to school. With the decentralization of specialized personnel and equipment, the logistical problems faced by the school district or intermediate unit are complex. Proper use of resources both in and outside of school demands that services be coordinated over a large area, that services be integrated according to the needs of each child, and that there be accountability to ensure that the services promised in the individualized education program actually are delivered.

In Illinois, the assumption of increased responsibility by the schools in the wake of the Individuals with Disabilities Act (IDEA) seems to have led to a lessening of responsibility for these children by other state agencies, if there is a possibility of school support for these services. The response of the state education agency to this increased burden has been to develop a mandate for collaborative planning among agencies, each taking responsibility for its own area of service. Necessary services are in theory available at no cost to the parents.

Such a directive from the state level is necessary to conserve resources and to prevent unnecessary movement of children to more restrictive placements. The directive could not be implemented in the absence of structures on the local and regional level that develop the necessary interagency agreements. On the other hand, such fragile networks of interagency agreements are not workable without state support.

INTERAGENCY AGREEMENTS

As schools have become more central to service provision to children with severe disabilities, particularly the very young and those transitioning into the world of work, the demand for case management is accompanied by the need for interagency collaboration. Schools are only gradually seeing themselves as members of a larger community of services. Efficiency of service provision and indeed the effectiveness of any case management attempts will demand agreements reached beforehand among various agencies serving particular populations.

However, schools are not accustomed to thinking of themselves as parts of interagency networks coordinating services for their pupils. Some of the agencies demanding coordination and interagency agreement are large public agencies with complicated structures and difficult access: Some are small grass-roots operations. LaCour (1982) cites some of the difficulties in developing agreements:

◆ Lack of clarity on "first dollar" responsibility,
◆ Lack of coordination of agencies' priorities,
◆ Lack of coordination between state and local agencies,
◆ Failure to coordinate budgets with service mandates,
◆ Inconsistent service standards, and
◆ Conflicting views of constraints on confidentiality of information.

He suggests that efforts to overcome these barriers be based primarily on an understanding of pertinent law and regulations. With this understanding, the social worker needs to develop a network of informal connections to the leadership of the involved agencies. This task may not be so formidable when the school social worker is well connected with people in the school district administration, who often are in contact with their counterparts in the involved agencies. In addition, the social worker's parallel relation with these agencies at the direct practice level also affords entry into the organization and an understanding of how the service is working in specific cases. The social worker needs to know how the agency is working from the inside. This knowledge allows the social worker to identify the resources to be exchanged and point out the benefits of a resource exchange to the participating agencies. Building on reciprocity, an agreement can then be drafted.

For these networks to be viable, they have to include a commitment on the state level, the means to communicate at all levels, interagency agreements developed on the local or regional level, as well as practitioners equipped to implement and coordinate service agreements on the direct practice level. A good interagency agreement needs to be written in simple and clear language. It should contain sections that: (1) describe the reason for writing the agreement; (2) identify the responsibilities of each agency and the method for performing those responsibilities; (3) identify the standards each agency must meet when performing an activity; (4) describe the process of exchanging information on common clients; and (5) describe the method for modifying the agreement. The agreement should be flexible, focusing on the desired outcome rather than on the process of getting there. It should not jeopardize an agency's funding or turf. Instead, the agreement should seek to clarify these issues. Finally, and obviously, the mutual benefit should be evident, enhancing the opportunity for future agreement as well as the full implementation of the current agreement (LaCour, 1982).

CASE MANAGEMENT

The movement to services based on legal entitlement has taken place, not only in the schools, but also in most other agencies serving children with disabilities. To cope with the implications of this entitlement, laws have prescribed or agencies have developed case management approaches to the widened range of available services. These case management approaches have become instruments of compliance and management tools for ensuring that clients are getting what they are entitled to and have the opportunity to be active, rather than passive, consumers of services. The approaches to case management are fairly similar. Each involves an individualized plan founded on a databased assessment of needs. They are driven by specific objectives to be attained, placed in a time frame with a date for specific initiation and duration of services, and given expectations for evaluation and review and participation in setting objectives and deciding on appropriate resources. Table 30.1 illustrates

TABLE 30.1   Seven Case Management Approaches

Case Management Approach	Entitling Legislation or Framework
The Individualized Habilitation Plan	PL 94–103, for developmentally disabled
The Individualized Education Program	PL 105–17, for all children with disabilities
Individualized Written Rehabilitation Program	Rehabilitation Act of 1973
Individualized Service Plan	Title XVI, for children with disabilities eligible for social security income
Individualized Care Plan	For Title XIX Medicaid
Individualized Program Plan	Mandated by Joint Committee on Accreditation of Hospitals
Individualized Program Plan	Title XX, purchase of service

seven major case management approaches coming out of different enabling legislation or frameworks.

It is ironic that these different case management approaches could continue to segment services now under the grandiose label of a "plan." Such plans are worthwhile, but limited, instruments for ensuring appropriate service delivery. The next step would be to develop a single individualized plan that brings together all of the services needed by the client, with one focal case coordinator from one agency who would ensure the client's access to other services. Such an approach would need more support at higher policy-making levels than any one agency could provide and, on the other hand, would need to be closely related to the needs of the family. It should come out of a coordinating structure that is not attached to any one agency. Schools and school services would have to play a major role in the development of any service network addressed to families and children.

Case management is a commonly accepted approach in social work to the delivery of service to populations having ongoing or fairly complex needs, necessitating that different services work together. It is an approach that requires considerable skill, because the social worker is working simultaneously with pupil, parent, teacher, school, and a network of agencies. Indeed, from a systems perspective the combination of small changes in each sector often makes broader changes that no one sector—pupil, parent, teacher, school, or network—could ever accomplish on its own. Case management tasks described in the literature (Austin, 1983; Compher, 1984, Eriksen, 1981; Frankel & Gelman, 1998; Garland, Woodruff, & Buck, 1988; Kurtz, Bagarozzi, & Pollane, 1984) include the following:

1. Assessing client needs,
2. Developing service plans,
3. Coordinating service delivery,
4. Monitoring service delivery,
5. Evaluating services, and
6. Advocating on behalf of the needs and rights of the client(s).

To complete each step, the case manager needs to move beyond the confines of his or her agency or discipline. To coordinate the diverse segments of a service delivery system, the social worker needs to reach beyond the confines of agency and discipline and include other services with full respect for the differences they offer the totality. Two models of teamwork have emerged to meet the demands of case management: the transdisciplinary team and the transagency team.

Typically, the *transdisciplinary team*, composed of the family and professionals from a variety of disciplines, collaborates in assessment and program planning. One individual, chosen from among the team members, works in consultation with colleague specialists to carry out the individualized plan. Together with the family, the case manager integrates the information and skills of the entire team to work with the child and family on goals established, to ensure coordination and communication among providers, and to monitor services to make sure that services planned are actually provided. In the transdisciplinary model the case manager typically is both the primary provider and the service coordinator.

The *transagency team* provides an alternative structure for case management, bringing together not only the many disciplines working with a single agency but also a variety of agency representatives to assess needs and plan services. These are models in which the transagency team is created specifically for the purpose of a particular population, and the agencies represented on the team are determined by the nature of the program (Garland et al., 1988).

THE TRANSAGENCY TEAM IN THE SCHOOLS

Schools offer a natural setting for the coordination of services among agencies. Schools are the central public institution dealing with the normal needs of children; they are now central to children with disabilities and crucial to the development of mental health services. The transagency approach to services within school walls is a useful starting point for the development of more comprehensive models of service coordination and provision for children and families with complex needs. We developed such a structure in the Chicago south suburban area. The area is heterogeneous, with patches of severe poverty mixed with blue-collar and middle-class suburbia. There are large populations of black and Hispanic minorities and white ethnics of eastern or southern European background. The area has experienced considerable development over the past twenty years, development that had outstripped the capacities of the traditional service resources and provided the opportunity for a fairly innovative type of planning effort. A transagency committee was established, composed of the major public and private agencies that are resources to families of children with disabilities.

The transagency committee reaches agreements on individualized service plans and provides a means of communication around resource issues affecting children with disabilities. A major focus of the committee is to develop agreements on individualized service plans for particular situations of need. With participation of the client, family, or informal resource network, one particular agency is designated the focal agency, and a particular worker from that agency develops an agreement with the family about their overall goals and what resources they need to reach them. This agreement involves the client system, any appropriate informal support systems, and the committee. The social worker from the focal agency, who works with the client, family, or informal support system, needs to be sufficiently skilled to:

◆ Help the client and family define the problem, some resultant goals, and what resources, services, and supports are needed;

◆ Define with the family the supportive network available to the client;

◆ Involve the client, family, or informal resource network in decision making by working with them individually, coordinating with other sectors, and bringing them together when they are ready to come to an agreement;

◆ Identify formal resources needed, maintain a steady communication with the formal resource systems in the network, and carry out problem solving with these systems as questions arise;

◆ Help the client or family and members of the informal resource network relate to the formal agency resources as collaborators, without a feeling of loss of dignity or control and with the assumption that agency actions must be related to client need;

◆ Help clients to use the situation of receiving service to identify their own aspirations for change, to embark on a change process, to adapt to realities in the environment, and to change attitudes or accustomed ways of relating to others;

◆ In providing means of communication around issues of service development and planning among agencies working with a particular clientele, the committee focuses on gaps in services, situations where the client is at high risk, has needs involving a number of agencies, and requires coordination of services. It cannot represent any one agency if it is to carry out its function.

The social worker is the crucial link between planning processes. There is a duality in the social worker's role: the social worker has, on the one hand, a close relationship with an individual client and his or her family or informal support system and, on the other hand, a working relationship with formal agency resources through the committee. Except for the social worker, members of this particular committee generally do not have direct service responsibilities. They are to be far enough up the agency hierarchy to deal with potential resource commitments and close enough to practice and service delivery to communicate with the direct service level of the agency.

EMERGING ROLES IN RESOURCE COORDINATION

Wraparound Planning

Wraparound planning, now part of the lexicon of human service reform, is a method of resource development geared to particular cases of children presenting severe or complex need, particularly where there is the possibility of institutionalization if fragile and overloaded community resource systems and/or family fail. In general, the term refers to the involvement of multiple formal and informal resources in all phases of service delivery to particular clients. Often these clients, if not served by a more complex network of family, community, and social services, would face institutionalization (or are returning into the community from institutional settings).

Wraparound planning is a process that takes the interagency professional team another step toward comprehensiveness. It involves, when necessary, family members, friends, neighbors, pastors, or other significant persons in a client's life in problem definition, goal setting, implementation, and evaluation of services. It relates these informal resources to the formal social agency and school systems. It also stresses the importance of involving the client as part of the deliberation and "treatment" team. These emphases on comprehensiveness, the integration of formal and informal resources, and client empowerment all reflect the policy reforms discussed in chapter 9.

Wraparound creates a new avenue for the school social worker to engage in mobilization activities on behalf of children in school. The very commitment by a school to wraparound will usually trigger a more intensive outreach effort to families, friends, kin, and neighbors. Resource development activities for the school social worker, who participates in, or leads, a wraparound effort, will similarly begin with the formation of the child-family team. It continues through the assessment, planning, and implementation phases as the team identifies additional resources needed to "wrap around" the child, forming new supports for that child and bolstering the child's chances for school success.

To some school social workers, the components that define wraparound planning might not sound so new. Indeed, Louise Montgomery seems to have done a species of it in 1906. In essence the components do affirm many of the principles espoused in traditional, generalist models of social work practice. Wraparound planning is simply a good use of the natural position of the school in the life of the child and family. It is a response to the growing awareness of the need for community alternatives to institutionalization as well as a recognition of the continuing work, despite obstacles from community and school fragmentation, toward developing comprehensive, family-centered, ecologically based practice for vulnerable people in the community. Obstacles include policy fragmentation, overspecialization in treatment, services that neglect the family context, and a growing disassociation of clinical practice from community practice.

Eber, Nelson, and Miles (1997) described the uniqueness of the wraparound approach as it is utilized in a school-based setting for students with emotional and behavioral challenges:

> An important characteristic separating wraparound plans from other types of student plans is that they are driven by needs rather than by the parameters of programs currently available. In contrast to the traditional practice of evaluating student needs on the basis of available educational placements, existing program components and services are analyzed and employed according to their usefulness in meeting student needs. Services are not based on a categorical model (i.e., services are embedded in a program in which "eligible" students are placed), but are embedded or created on the basis of specific needs of the student, family, and teacher. The child and family team consists of persons who know the student best, and who can provide active support to the student, his or her teacher, and family. Extended family members, neighbors, family, friends, and mentors also are frequently participants in child and family teams. (pp. 547–549)

Eber illustrates wraparound planning as a process in table 30.2. The diverse perspectives recruited into the child and family team ensure that diverse domains of a student's life will be viewed as a whole. Specialists are challenged to open the boundaries of their own vision as well, working collaboratively to formulate strategies to resolve the difficulties students face academically as well as socially.

School-Based Family Empowerment as Resource Development

Although wraparound planning brings the school social worker into resource development, another trend that broadens the school social worker's resource development activities is multifaceted family empowerment projects in schools. As related in chapter 9, one type of project that increases the potential for school-based family empowerment is the family resource center in the school. Through school-based family resource centers, school social workers are able to mobilize a variety of assets for families. These assets help support families and bolster the productive roles families might play in the community. School-based or school-linked family resource centers have also become critical components of community revitalization strategies in impoverished neighborhoods. Although such centers represent innovations in school-based institutions, reshaping the service delivery system in impoverished communities, they are also grounded in classical social work principles (Dupper & Poertner, 1997).

Family Support America (FSA) (formerly the Family Resource Coalition of America) issued guidelines for practice that illustrate how intrinsically important resource development is to empowering families. Although phrased to pertain to community-based family support programs in schools and outside of schools, the principles reveal the practical opportunities for working with community assets that will emerge for school social workers. The FSA's principles for practice in schools (Family Support America, 2004) are as follows.

- ◆ Create a community of equal partners with parents, staff, and the community.
- ◆ Identify families' needs and use community resources to meet them.
- ◆ Build relationships with parents and create leadership opportunities within the school.
- ◆ Celebrate diversity and foster respect among people with cultural, religious, and other differences.
- ◆ Create "community schools" that offer a range of supports before, during, and after school.
- ◆ Involve parents in school governance and decision making.
- ◆ Make vital services accessible at school (for example, dental cleanings, skill building and childcare, parent-to-parent support groups).
- ◆ Empower parents to address community issues of concern and provide needed supports to affect change.

TABLE 30.2   Community-Based Wraparound Planning Steps

Step	Definition	Purpose
Issue identification	Prior to the team meeting, facilitator contacts key stakeholders, which include, at minimum, the parents, child, and significant others (e.g., agency providers, relatives, community mentors).	• Identifies issues that might affect outcomes of the plan, as well as concrete steps that must be taken immediately. • Identifies strengths of the child, parents, and others to use as a foundation for future planning. • Builds a sense of being listened to and heard by the persons most involved in the child's care. • Prepares facilitator to understand system and personal issues affecting the child's performance. • Develops knowledge of the situation as seen by the persons most involved in the child's care. • Allows the facilitator to understand points of agreement and disagreement between the parents and providers. • Allows the facilitator to develop immediate crisis response, if needed, prior to the first meeting.
Introductions and agenda setting	Facilitator allows participants to identify their roles and relationship to the student and sets expectations for the product to be developed in the meeting.	• Allows meeting participants to understand their relationship to the family. • Sets expectations against which the process can be measured (i.e., building practical support plan that will produce better outcomes for the child). • Begins to build a sense of team as well as communicating to the parents that they do have access to support in their care for the child. • Builds a sense of hope about the capacity for improved outcomes if all team members can agree on areas for improvement.

TABLE 30.2 Community-Based Wraparound Planning Steps—*(Continued)*

Step	Definition	Purpose
Strengths presentation	Facilitator presents a summary of family, student, and other participants' strengths as developed from conversations in the issue identification step.	• Begins to build appreciation across meeting participants relative to the family strengths as well as provider capacities. • Identifies strengths as the foundation for strategy and plan development. • Allows persons in attendance to move from the role of meeting participants to team members. • Builds an alliance between the parents and providers in appreciating each other's strengths. • Allows team members to commit to the possibilities of improved outcomes and creates a sense of commitment to the child. • Allows team members to see providers as both assets and as persons in need of support.
Goal setting and needs identification	Facilitator leads team through goal-setting exercise, focusing on present performance levels of a typical child. Information is presented and commented on by team members. When goals have been set, parents and significant others are asked where strategies need to be developed to bring the child's functioning level to the defined "typical" functional level.	• Allows team members to set realistic outcomes that are easily understandable to all team members. • Builds a framework in which team members can pinpoint areas of need as measured against the description of a typical child. • Builds an alliance between parents and providers as they begin to view their similarities in terms of needs statements. • Allows participants to voice expectations and feel "heard" by other team members.

Needs prioritization	Facilitator asks parents and providers to identify needs that must be addressed first. Prioritized needs are limited to no more than five per meeting. Other team members are asked if other areas are seen as needing to be addressed first.	• Allows the team to break the need for interventions into manageable parts. • Creates the expectation that other team members will provide support to the persons most closely involved with the child's daily life. • Solidifies the team's commitment to working together, creating interventions, and building a commitment to improved outcomes. • Strengthens alliance between parents and providers. • Expectations for future planning around other need areas often are set, in order to foster the expectation that when first priority needs are met, others will be added.
Strategy development	Facilitator leads the team through a brainstorming process in which strategies to meet identified needs are developed. Members are asked to be as specific as possible. Suggestions do not focus solely on linking traditional services or settings. The facilitator continually verifies with the parent whether the strategies suggested might be helpful for the child.	• Allows team members to create a plan that is tailored to the needs of the child as well as building team ownership of the action plan. • Sense of ownership is likely to pay off in terms of task completion and follow-through. • Allows team members to identify creative strategies that are tailored to the needs of the child rather than the programs or services currently in place. • Allows the team to specify target behaviors, potential reinforcement strategies, as well as support activities implemented by certain adults involved in the planning.
Securing team member commitments	After needs have been brainstormed and listed on a flip chart, team members are asked to commit to certain strategies.	• Builds a sense of public commitment to specific action steps by team members. • Allows the team to move toward self-management by requiring the facilitator to wait for their commitment. • Gives the team a sense of direction and response in building a student support plan.

TABLE 30.2 Community-Based Wraparound Planning Steps—*(Continued)*

Step	Definition	Purpose
Follow-up communication	As the plan is formalized, the facilitator identifies a communication plan by which team members can have contact with each other. Team members are encouraged to commit to contact other participants. The facilitator commits to contact stakeholders regarding the child's progress.	• Builds a sense of team functioning that is likely to occur between meetings. • Allows team members to build alliances and communication protocols apart from formal team meetings. • Creates an environment of volunteerism among team members when participants commit based on their ability to follow through rather than on their job descriptions. • Allows parents and other providers to feel supported and that help is nearby.
Process evaluation and closure	Facilitator checks with stakeholders regarding whether the plan developed will be helpful, whether the meeting was productive, and whether participants felt their ideas were heard. A follow-up meeting is scheduled within the next five weeks. Procedures for calling an emergency meeting are identified.	• Allows the team to gain ownership by evaluating the process. • Parents feel supported and heard in the teaming process. • Communicates a sense that help is available regarding day-to-day needs. • Allows the facilitator to set expectations regarding communication and crisis as well as establishing action steps to determining their efficacy.

◆ Provide strength-based child and family development training to staff, administrators, and parents.

Through family resource centers, school social workers find more support in reaching the families, neighbors, and agencies that can be helpful in working with their own students. It will be possible to engage in a different type of family practice. New opportunities for empowering families to wield more influence in the school and the community will continue to emerge. Schools may be taking on this broader community focus partly because of the presence of family resource centers in the schools, but even without family resource centers, the basic principles are similar.

The family is central to all of these processes, bringing together family and child with school and community resources. The case of Betty Benson in chapter 27 involves a family at an early stage of dealing with the complex needs of their 6-year-old child with profound developmental disabilities. Much of the focus of the social worker is on helping the parents to deal with the complex needs of their child, to divide tasks, to reframe their pictures of Betty and of themselves, and to support each other in the process. At the same time, the social worker is working with United Cerebral Palsy, a physician, a respite care provider, and eventually a group of parents of such children. The worker is working between the parents, as they begin to see and care for Betty in a different way, and the agencies as together they assist the parents to do this.

The following cases illustrate work with the family and agency systems of a ten-year-old boy in school and two young adults in transition out of school.

Danny is a 10-year-old African American boy with pervasive developmental disorder. In class he is disruptive; shows poor attention to tasks, even with assistance; has very poor academic performance; is aggressive with other children; and tends to isolate himself from them. They are afraid of him. Having come recently from living in Germany, his father in military service, he speaks a mixture of English and German, which isn't easily understood by others. According to his paternal grandmother, with whom he lives, he had been developing reasonably well in early childhood and walked and talked normally. Both parents have a history of severe drug and alcohol abuse. When he went to Germany, he experienced severe physical abuse by his mother, neglect by his father, and was heavily involved in the military social service program for children. Mother is in a residential substance abuse program. Father is still in the army. Danny is being raised by his grandmother. She has given up her twenty-year business to take care of him. The following agencies are involved with the case: (1) the State Child Protection Agency; (2) the State Department of Mental Health; (3) Adair School; (4) a Big Brother Program; (5) a Homemaker Services Agency; (6) karate lessons from a community volunteer; (7) in-home therapy from a contract therapist especially trained in pervasive developmental disorders; (8) tutoring twice a week.

The state child protection agency sponsors the wrap team through the school and pays for the services provided through its LANS (Local Area Network Services) program. Grandmother is overwhelmed with all the services involved.

The placement needs to be stabilized, particularly if mother returns. There are differences within the team about whether Danny should remain in this placement or be hospitalized. The main goal at the moment is that Danny maintain himself at school and that the home continue to provide appropriate parenting, belonging, and security for him. This is beginning to happen although the situation both at home and at school is very delicate. The team meets monthly, including grandmother, to discuss and work out issues.

The following two cases involve the transition out of school of young adults with severe disabilities:

Doris is an 18-year-old adolescent with severe psychological disturbance. Her reactivity to a symbiotic conflict with her mother and resultant self-destructive behavior has led to several hospitalizations. Whenever there is a possible separation from mother, she shows increased disturbance. The school had found itself reacting to the behavior and programming for Doris alone, rather than getting the mother and daughter into contact with help. Mother and daughter have now begun with a social worker in private practice. The school will now bring Doris into a one-hour-per-day class in ceramics with only the instructor present. If this can be established without incident, Doris will be involved with a pet zoo run by another agency. Because the situation between mother and daughter is potentially explosive, a shelter arrangement with a relative to be used in a crisis will be worked out. This would keep Doris in the community as long as possible. If the social worker is able to make further gains with the mother and Doris's school adjustment stabilizes, the next step is to develop a program with the Illinois Department of Vocational Rehabilitation. The state agency is involved in the plan and will give special consideration to Doris's needs.

Michael is a 21-year-old severe and barely stabilized diabetic, legally blind, who lives in a nursing home because his single, working parent was unable to care for him. He is about to graduate from his special education program because of his age. A plan is developed in the wrap team to make it possible for him to return home through utilization of public assistance, Medicaid, and homemaker and home health care services. Some further medical assessment is planned, and based on this assessment, some vocational assessment would be done. The social worker from the school will work with Michael and his mother, coordinating with other agencies, with the goal of passing on case management responsibilities to another agency when the two have solidified their own direction and connections with other services.

Although such cases present complex, chronic needs and will take work over a span of years, they are not particularly unusual. A combination of resources could prevent institutionalization or make movement from an institutionalized setting possible. Furthermore, none of the hard service provision, no matter how flexible, could have been effective or even possible without the soft services to parent and child that helped them deal with the situation and link their processes and needs with programs and resources. To make complex plans for families without their choice, involvement, and participation, indeed not to make the individual-in-family-unit the center of the decision process, is to court disaster and set up an unproductive struggle around power and control. And so, in addition to highly skilled family-oriented work, the social worker inevitably becomes an active member of the transagency team, a colleague, and a consultant.

POSSIBLE FUTURE SCENARIOS FOR SOCIAL WORKERS AS RESOURCE DEVELOPERS

Whatever the future holds for new school-based services, it certainly will continue to call for the many traditional resource development activities that social workers have conducted. School social workers will continue to serve as facilitators of school-community relations. Such activities will remain as varied as organizing services around particular children, building collaborations with agencies in the school, and monitoring the quality of service. Remedial, crisis-oriented, and preventive methods will endure as well. Moreover, negotiating, facilitating, drafting, and brokering interagency agreements will remain a resource development task of the school social worker. Fashioning such agreements will at times take place through the function of case management, at other times through participation as a member of an interagency team.

The future is not as certain with respect to school social work roles in the wraparound process. In fact, the future scope of wraparound in the school remains somewhat murky. Two scenarios seem possible. One scenario holds the lead role for the school social worker. Leading a wraparound team (or "wrap" team, as it is sometimes called) would engage the social worker in a more diversified, perhaps more strengths-based, model of case management for clients. A second scenario places the social worker into the wraparound as one of the resources on the team. As a member of a wraparound team, the school social worker might take more narrow roles, such as conducting social histories, negotiating referrals, or providing counseling as part of the wraparound's overall plan.

The expanded family support and empowerment programs that will grow in schools will also structure different possible scenarios for the resource development activities of school social workers. At a minimum, one might imagine school social workers conducting case management with some of the families present in the school in the family resource center. More broadly, one might envisage school social workers helping families form their own empowering associations, which could be either school-based or school-linked. Family empowerment associations will enable families to deliver more support to one another, exercise stronger roles as coteachers through tutoring and mentoring, and exercise more influence over school governance. In short, many experiments with family-based institutions in schools will take place. Some school social workers will likely lead in their design and formation.

From Louise Montgomery on, school social workers have had a long history of involvement with the community, developing community resources and doing a type of community organization work with education at the forefront of community activity and the school as a type of community center. Newer models of responsive, family-centered, school community services reinforce this trend. School reform, particularly in areas such as Chicago, has long focused on the development of a school community and local control. High-stakes testing is now pointing out areas of failing schools needing resources for development. There has been growing recognition that community organizing around education issues can be a viable strategy for educational improvement. Such "education organizing" would seek to develop the relationship between schools and their communities, particularly when the relationship is failing. Education organizing deals with the complexity of education policy and practice, the entrenchment of the status quo, the difficulty of developing strong, sustainable grassroots organizations, and many other challenges (Moore & Sandler, 2003).

New scenarios for resource development will arise because of the expanded community-building activities that are beginning to take place through schools. One entry point through which school social workers will participate in this trend will be the wraparound process. Or, it might be through an expansion of the interagency brokering roles school social workers have traditionally played. New school-based collaborations around violence prevention or dropout prevention might create leadership vacuums in school settings that school social workers would appropriately fill. The possibilities are not all clear, but it is clear that there will be new roles. These roles will carry forward traditional social work practices in schools into new institution and community-building initiatives.

Resource

The Family Support America Web site contains many resources and links that are useful for the family support and resource development activities of school social workers. Go to http://www.familysupportamerica.org

References

Austin, C. (1983). Case management in long-term care: Options and opportunities. *Health and Social Work, 8*(1), 16–30.

Compher, J. V. (1984). The case conference revisited: A systems view. *Child Welfare, 63*(5), 411–418.

Dupper, D., & Poertner, J. (1997). Public schools and the revitalization of impoverished communities: School-linked, family resource centers. *Social Work, 42*, 415–422.

Eber, L., Nelson, M. C., & Miles, P. (1997). School-based wraparound for students with emotional and behavioral challenges. *Exceptional Children, 63*(4), 539–555.

Eriksen, K. (1981). *Human services today* (2nd ed.). Reston, VA: Reston Publishing.

Family Support America. (2004). *Are schools ready for families: Case studies in school-family relationships*. Chicago, IL: Author.

Frankel, A., & Gelman, S. R. (1998). *Case management*. Chicago: Lyceum Books.

Garland, C., Woodruff, G., & Buck, D. (1988). *Case management*. Division for Early Childhood White Paper. Reston, VA: Council for Exceptional Children.

Kurtz, L. F., Bagarozzi, D. A., & Pollane, L. P. (1984). Case management in mental health. *Health and Social Work, 9*, 201–211.

LaCour, J. A. (1982). Interagency agreement: A rational response to an irrational system. *Exceptional Children, 49*(3), 265–267.

Moore, R. B., & Sandler, S. (2003). *Supporting the education organizing movement: An exchange between intermediaries.* Justice Matters Institute, 1375 Sutter Street, San Francisco, CA 94109. Retrieved December 1, 2003, from http://www.justicematters.org

31

Mental Health and School Social Work

Helene Moses

Eric D. Ornstein

Carol Rippey Massat
University of Illinois at Chicago

- ◆ Mental Health Policies and School Social Work
- ◆ Children's Mental Health and Academic Achievement
- ◆ The Role of the School Social Worker in Mental Health Services
- ◆ Assessment
- ◆ Disorders Commonly Encountered in Schools

Children often receive core mental health services in schools. Every school social worker needs to become familiar with the field of mental health, its research, assessment and interventions, its services and funding, confidentiality requirements, and state and federal policies related to the provision of mental health services to children. This chapter is an overview of mental health issues and services delivered in the schools. It reviews mental health policy, as well as assessment and intervention processes with selected disorders that may present themselves in the school setting.

School social workers encounter many children with mental disorders. According to the 1999 Surgeon General's Report, one in five American children has a mental disorder, with 5 percent to 9 percent of all children aged 9 to 17 having a serious emotional disturbance. Seventy-nine percent of children with such disorders do not receive treatment. The President's New Freedom Commission on Mental Health (2003) identified a disjointed, fragmented system of provision of mental health care with significant disparities in the availability of treatment. Services vary from state to state and from community to community.

The commission recommended that the mental health field and schools be partners in the provision of early mental health screening, assessment, and referral
to services:

> The mission of public schools is to educate all students. However, children with
> serious emotional disturbances have the highest rates of school failure. Fifty per-
> cent of these students drop out of high school, compared to 30% of all students
> with disabilities. Schools are where children spend most of each day. While
> schools are primarily concerned with education, mental health is essential to
> learning as well as to social and emotional development. Because of this
> important interplay between emotional health and school success, schools must
> be partners in the mental health care of our children. Schools are in a key position
> to identify mental health problems early and to provide a link to appropriate ser-
> vices. (p. 58)

It is notable that the mission of public schools is to educate all students.
However, students who are members of vulnerable populations and who are
also affected by mental illness face obstacles beyond those of the general population. Racial and ethnic minorities students are at greater risk for poverty. Both
poverty and its related stressors can exacerbate mental health issues and create
obstacles to the receipt of needed services. African American and Latino families
are less likely to use mental health services (Miranda, Azocar, Organista, Munoz,
& Lieberman, 1996). It is critical to reduce these barriers to mental health services. Children who live in circumstances of persistent poverty are at the greatest risk of negative mental health outcomes (Brooks-Gunn & Duncan, 1997).

Gay and lesbian students also have special mental health needs and risks.
They are frequent victims of violence and harassment in school and at home
(Morrow, 1993), which may lead to symptoms of post-traumatic stress disorder
(Thompson & Massat, in press).

MENTAL HEALTH POLICIES AND SCHOOL SOCIAL WORK

There is a long history of state involvement in mental health services. Federal involvement, contemplated from the days of Dorothea Dix, limited itself
mainly to veterans' services until the National Mental Health Act of 1946. This
act established the National Institute of Mental Health (NIMH) to promote
research about mental disease, to encourage training of personnel, and to
establish state mental health authorities to develop mental health programs.
In the 1950s both federal and state mental health programs broadened, leading
to the Community Mental Health Act of 1963. This act was a major support for
the movement to deinstitutionalize those suffering from mental illness. It
funded construction and staffing of comprehensive community mental health
centers throughout the country, and promised to provide inpatient care, outpatient care, partial hospitalization, twenty-four-hour emergency care, and consultation and education for twenty years. The act also encouraged diagnostic
and rehabilitative services, precare and aftercare, training, research, and evalu-

ation. Social work was identified as one of the four core disciplines for carrying out the purposes of the act. Deinstitutionalization of the mentally ill was further encouraged in the 1960s with the beginning discoveries of effective psychotropic medications, an area of continued growth and development since that time. In the 1970s it was recognized that the needs of persons with mental illnesses were not being adequately met by community mental health centers. NIMH developed the Community Support Program. The program asked states to plan and develop coordinated, comprehensive systems of community-based care that included outreach, referral, housing, mental health treatment, crisis intervention, social and vocational rehabilitation, family and community support assistance and education, coordination/development of natural support systems, protection and advocacy, and service coordination. There was a heavy emphasis on case management. The Omnibus Budget Reconciliation Act (1981) established the Alcohol Drug Abuse and Mental Health Administration (ADAMHA), which in 1992 became the Substance Abuse and Mental Health Service Administration (SAMHSA), a non-NIMH federal center for mental health services. The Comprehensive Mental Health Service Act (1986) required states to plan and implement comprehensive, community-based programs of care for the seriously mentally ill in order to receive block grant funds. The Comprehensive Children's Mental Health Services Program is administered by SAMHSA through the U.S. Department of Health and Human Services. The program, first authorized in 1992, offers grants to states, territories, Indian tribes, and communities to develop systems of care for children with mental health needs. These services are required to involve families, be need driven, collaborative, community based, and culturally responsive. Federal initiatives to promote safe schools are related to school mental health issues. The Safe and Drug-Free Schools and Communities Program (SDFSC) is intended to reduce drug, alcohol, and tobacco use and violence through prevention, early intervention, referral, and education in elementary and secondary schools. This program began in 1986 with the Drug-Free Schools and Community Act (20 U.S.C. 4601). It was reauthorized in 1994 as the Safe and Drug-Free Schools Act (20 U.S.C. 7101). The Principles of Effectiveness were established in 1998. These programs required schools to conduct needs assessments regarding drugs and violence, establish measurable goals, implement research-based approaches, and assess progress. The legislation was most recently reauthorized as part of the No Child Left Behind Act (NCLB), which imposed new accountability requirements. The State Incentive Transformation Grants (SIG) program is intended to support state efforts to develop collaborative plans to meet the currently unmet mental health needs of children and adults. These grants will be given to states that have formed commissions to transform public mental health systems into efficient, integrated systems of care. Other relevant federal legislation and programs include the Garrett Lee Smith Memorial Act (PL 108-355), which supplied funding for suicide prevention, a national suicide hotline, and a national resource center on suicide prevention. The focus on state control of the actual design of mental health services is characteristic of all of these policies. Each state has its own system of mental health services and policies that apply to school social work.

CHILDREN'S MENTAL HEALTH AND ACADEMIC ACHIEVEMENT

Since children's mental health has a demonstrable impact on their academic achievement, school social workers must be aware of these issues and partner with families, communities, and the mental health service system According to the U.S. Department of Education (2001), many students with serious emotional disturbances drop out of school. It is estimated that 12 percent to 30 percent of children have serious emotional disorders that will ultimately cause severe academic difficulty (Institute of Medicine, 1994; Kazdin, 1993; U.S. Department of Education, 1994). Other research has found that children with positive early psychosocial development have higher achievement test scores later on in school (Teo, Carlson, & Mathieu, 1996), and that mental health has a direct impact on children's grade point averages (Gutman, Sameroff, & Cole, 2003). Ialong, Edelsohn, and Kellam (2001) found that first graders' reports of depressed mood and feelings were associated with poor academic functioning later on, later need for mental health services, suicidal ideation, and major depressive disorder.

However, our mental health service system has created numerous barriers to mental health treatment for children. Flisher et al. (1997) found that lack of health insurance, economic disadvantage, and other factors posed significant barriers for children who require mental health services. Since minority children are overrepresented among those who are poor, this adds to the risk of minority children, who are less likely to receive needed mental health services. Kataoka, Zhang, and Wells (2002) found that nearly 80 percent of children needing mental health services did not receive them, and that Latinos and the uninsured were at particularly high risk for unmet mental health needs.

THE ROLE OF THE SCHOOL SOCIAL WORKER
IN MENTAL HEALTH SERVICES

The nationwide problems in the provision of mental health services to children place a greater burden on school social workers, who may be the first—and perhaps the only—social service providers to children and youth. Often the school social worker has far greater natural access to parents and children than any other community service. The role of the school social worker varies widely, even within school districts. In most cases school social workers are responsible for providing services to children who have conduct or emotional disorders that impede their academic functioning. In some settings, school social workers are responsible for providing extensive therapy in schools. However, in most situations, ongoing family work and medication management are delivered outside of the school setting. Here the most critical role of the school social worker is consultation, teamwork, and short-term support as well as referral and linkage to community services. If community services are unresponsive, however, school social workers find themselves doing much more. A few schools offer psychiatric services and medication management. When children are receiving services outside of the school, the school social worker must identify issues of concern, understand effective work with children experiencing mental health disorders, support children's work in school, and assist students who are making a transition from hospitalization.

Both intervention in the school and collaboration with service providers outside of the school are critical in preventing costly outcomes for children with serious emotional disturbances. Therapeutic schools and out-of-state care are costly for the school district and often costly for children. If effective services can be provided in the community, these more restrictive alternatives may be avoided. Children placed in residential treatment or therapeutic schools may need such an environment, but there is an emotional cost to the child when they lack normative school socialization. The student may feel isolated from the community and may lose out on critical social and networking opportunities.

ASSESSMENT

The first clinical role of social workers is *assessment*. Their assessment is part of a larger assessment process done with the multidisciplinary team and outside professionals. They are the bridge between outside professionals, school administration and teaching staff. They attend staffings in hospitals when a student has a psychiatric hospitalization. They help to develop transition plans to ease the student's return to school from the hospital, and it is their job to translate medical jargon into functional information for the students, teachers, and allied staff. School social workers help multidisciplinary teams to gain a holistic picture of the student. A mental health concern is only one aspect of the pupil-in-school, and the school social worker emphasizes student strengths and aspirations. The school social worker sensitizes the team to the student's cultural, familial, and spiritual needs and shows how these factors interface with the student's mental health issues and learning needs.

The school social worker needs to be skilled in making differential decisions as a member of a team, whether in the school or outside. Some students can be well served in the school environment through social skills groups, individual counseling, and crisis intervention. Other students require referral to outside providers for psychiatric evaluation, long-term mental health care, and family counseling. In schools and communities with few resources, school social workers are sometimes the only mental health professional that the student will ever see. School social workers must prioritize and determine which students have the most pressing need and which interventions will be most efficient and effective. Those students at risk for suicide, child endangerment and abuse, or criminal justice involvement require partnership with outside resources. These partnerships, discussed in chapter 30, often involve outside professionals who have a limited understanding of school social work with who it is necessary to develop a common language and a mutual process of learning and sharing.

Use of DSM-IV-TR

One common language of mental health professionals is the *Diagnostic and Statistical Manual IV Text Revision* (DSM-IV-TR; APA, 2000), which is the major classification and assessment tool used by the mental health system. DSM-IV-TR is a multiaxial system consisting of five axes. Axis I lists clinical syndromes, such as schizophrenia, mood disorders, anxiety disorders, and substance abuse. V Codes and behavioral and situational problems are also coded on Axis I. Axis II lists developmental disorders such as mental retardation and personality disorders. Axis III lists physical health conditions or disorders. Axis IV lists psychosocial and environmental problems such as poverty, housing problems, and issues of loss. Axis V is a global assessment of a person's functioning and adjustment currently and within the past year. The student is rated from 0 to 100, based on social, psychological, and school functioning.

Changes are frequent in this system, and the topic cannot be covered briefly. Many manuals can assist school social workers to understand and utilize the DSM-IV-TR (House, 2002; Morrison, 2001; Pomeroy & Wambach, 2003).

There are advantages and limitations in using the DSM-IV-TR diagnostic system (Shea, 1997). On the one hand, DSM-IV-TR provides a common language across disciplines to discuss students' mental health issues, and this can assist in effective treatment planning and service delivery. An accurate diagnosis can lead to determining the most evidence-based intervention and the appropriate medication regimen. The multiaxial system encourages social workers to understand students' mental health problems within the context of multiple interacting systems. It allows social workers to consider a wide array of possible interventions (Shea, 1997). On the other hand, diagnoses are labels and can be abused. People may be more prone to use diagnoses as stereotypical explanations of human behavior rather than seeing each person as an individual. There is a realistic danger that clients can become stuck with an inappropriate diagnosis. A DSM diagnosis needs to be viewed as an evolving process that is always subject to reexamination and revision. Diagnoses can have ramifications in terms of the student's culture, family, and social situations. For instance, a peer group may scapegoat the student due to a lack of understanding of the meaning of a diagnosis. Finally, the DSM-IV-TR does not address the etiology of the mental disorders that it describes; nor does it directly address issues of management of the disorder (Shea 1997).

DISORDERS COMMONLY ENCOUNTERED IN SCHOOLS

Attention Deficit Hyperactivity Disorder (ADHD). Attention deficit hyperactivity disorder is the most commonly identified problem for students in a school setting (Costello-Wells, McFarland, Reed, & Walton, 2000). It is most apparent in the school setting and problematic not only for the student but also for peers, teachers, and parents. It is marked by a student's lack of attention, often combined with hyperactive behavior and impulsivity. To be diagnosed, symptoms must be present before the age of 7, although the actual diagnosis might not come until an older age (APA, 2000). The disorder is more often noted in boys and can remain an impairment throughout adolescence and adulthood (APA, 2000). Some of its behavioral manifestations include: poor time management, incomplete or superficially written assignments, poor problem solving strategies for learning, and poor recall (Sattler, 1998). Diagnosis of this disorder is difficult. In families and classrooms with a high threshold or tolerance for ADHD, symptoms in these children can often be overlooked. On the other hand, sometimes normally active children are inappropriately diagnosed and treated for a disorder where none exists (Sattler, 1998). ADHD has many co-occurring conditions such as learning disabilities, oppositional defiant disorder, and mood disorders. These co-occurring conditions further complicate a student's ability to learn and pose significant challenges to social workers and teachers as they attempt to accommodate the student's learning needs.

The case of a 3rd-grade student, Tommy, in chapter 20 outlines a social worker's assessment of the situation, involving learning problems, anxiety and ADHD, consultation with the teacher, and work with outside medical resources, with the family, and with Tommy, whose enuresis, triggered by classroom situations, is disturbing to the teacher. In addition to working with the family and coordinating medication, school social workers can also work with teachers to develop effective behavior strategies and classroom management techniques that will allow for optimal student learning. In some cases, students will need specific classroom accommodations. These accommodations might include; shortened assignments, breaking tasks into smaller parts, peer tutoring, untimed tests, and taking breaks. Students might need to have their desks placed in the quietest part of the room to avoid overstimulation and distractions (Silver 1999). School social workers will need to educate students with ADHD about this disorder and how it is impacting their learning, social relationships, and school adjustment (Silver, 1999). Students may also require social skills interventions. Some students will be best served in a group and others will require individual counseling. Research suggests that best practice interventions for ADHD include: parent education, behavior modification both at home and in the school, and stimulant medications (Sattler, 1999).

Mood Disorders

Depression. Only recently has attention been focused on the study of depression in children and adolescents. It is currently thought that children and teenagers can and do experience depression, although it may manifest itself differently in young people than in adults. Diagnosis of depression in children requires a significant change in mood and functioning that persists over time (Sattler, 1999). The cause of this depression is not fully understood, although it is thought to have both biological and psychosocial origins. Depression is diagnosed in females almost five times more often than in males (Sattler, 1999). Depressed children and adolescents may experience loss of interest in activities, feelings of helplessness and hopelessness, and disturbances in sleep and appetite (Johnson, Rasbury, & Siegel 1997). Although adults might become withdrawn and lethargic when experiencing depression, children and adolescents tend to exhibit high degrees of irritability and agitation. The symptoms of adolescent depression tend to be similar to those of adults and include: an inability to experience pleasure, low self-esteem, fatigue, boredom, aggressive behavior, somatic complaints, and irritability. Sometimes depressed teenagers express their symptoms behaviorally. They may run away from home, engage in low-level criminal behavior such as stealing or shoplifting, or engage in conflict with peers and authority figures. They may experience an increase in suicidal ideation or behavior. Diagnosis of depression in children can be difficult because they are in a constant state of developmental flux, and typical children and adolescents experience fluctuations in mood and affect. Students are rarely referred to the school social worker for obvious symptoms of depression, but rather for abrupt behavioral changes or acting out at home or in the classroom. Students with moderate or severe depression often experience disruptions in their ability to learn. Teachers may mistakenly assume that a student's low energy, impaired concentration, or defiance is a result of a behavior disorder when the student may be suffering from an underlying depressive disorder.

Some psychosocial or environmental factors that contribute to a student's depression can include family neglect or abuse, or victimization by peers. Some children and adolescents experience depression resulting from the fear that they cannot or are not living up to parental expectations. Students who are vulnerable to depression may come to school without proper problem-solving and self-regulatory skills and are often overwhelmed by stressors that other children might be able to manage. Major life stressors such as the loss of a parent, pregnancy, moves, divorce, or remarriage can also trigger depressive reactions in children and adolescents (Sattler, 1999). The cases of Jimmy in chapter 25 and Alan in chapter 26 both involve working with young children showing depression, learning disabilities, and reactions to a major life stressor (parental divorce), as well as with their teachers, their families, and community mental health resources.

Bipolar Disorder. Sometimes the first episode of depression for children and adolescents can turn out to be what will later be diagnosed as bipolar disorder. Some estimates suggest that that nearly half of the children who develop major depression before puberty subsequently experience mania by age 20. The Child & Adolescent Bipolar Foundation (2001) identifies bipolar disorder as a treatable neurobiological brain disorder characterized by severe fluctuations of mood and activity level. The manic phase of bipolar disorder in children can include periods of crankiness, insomnia, hyperactivity, expansive mood, and racing thoughts. The depressed phase in children with bipolar disorder is not distinguishable from the symptoms of childhood depression discussed above. Some children experience rapid cycling where in the morning they appear depressed and by afternoon they are displaying a full-blown manic episode and their behavior becomes unmanageable. Scientists believe that a predisposition to the disorder is inherited and can be triggered by trauma, or it may occur with no identifiable cause (The Child & Adolescent Bipolar Foundation, 2001).

Diagnosis of this disorder is controversial and difficult to make. It can often be confused with unipolar depression, attention deficit disorder, or oppositional defiant disorder. This would have significant consequences with regard to appropriate medication and treatment planning. For instance, if there has been a misdiagnosis and the child is prescribed medication such as Ritalin for ADHD, instead of correcting the problem the medication can exacerbate the child's condition and may trigger a manic episode (Parmelee, 1996).

At school, students with bipolar disorder might be viewed as creative and verbally skilled but would have difficulty with organization, and problem solving. They might appear very distracted and inattentive. School expectations in the early years—learning to follow rules, taking turns, and completing tasks—place stress on these students by demanding that they perform in areas where they have deficits. In later school years, the hormonal changes of puberty can further exacerbate the symptoms of bipolar disorder. Most adolescents experience moodiness and powerful emotions; for those students with bipolar disorder these fluctuations are more extreme and may lead to risky or dangerous behavior. Teenagers with bipolar disorder are at an increased risk for suicidal behavior and substance abuse (Kluger & Song, 2002).

Best practice for treating students with mood disorders is a multimodal approach involving counseling, medication, and other psychosocial interventions. The primary aim of treatment is to shorten the period of the mood disorder and decrease the negative consequences of episodes of illness. Students need to be encouraged to continue to be active in school and with their studies even when they are still feeling badly inside. Adding structure to his/her day will help stabilize the student's mood. Positive reinforcement needs to be implemented to assist students in completing tasks of daily living such as getting ready for and going to school, completing assignments and staying at school for the whole day (Parmelee, 1996). Recent studies suggest that a focus on cognitive and behavioral skills is effective in treating students with mood disorders (Johnson, Rasbury, & Siegel 1997). Group treatment can have an especially important role in work with these students. Groups can reduce a student's sense of isolation and differentness and students can also learn social skills from their peers. In the group they can hear about successful recovery and this might increase their own compliance with medication and/or counseling.

Pervasive Developmental Disorders (PDD)

With the trend toward inclusion in the last decade more and more students with a pervasive developmental disorder (PDD) are attending local public schools. This has posed many opportunities and challenges for students, school social workers, and staff. PDD is an umbrella term that includes a heterogeneous group of conditions. PDDs are characterized by impaired social interactions, communication deficits, and stereotypical behaviors such as: rocking, head banging, and echolalia (Johnson, Rasbury, & Siegel, 1997). Impairments in these areas can be so severe that they require multiple interventions and services to allow these students to participate in the educational process. It is important to state that the term *pervasive* does not imply that there are no areas of normal functioning. These students can have significant strengths and talents in some areas that can include musical or artistic ability.

Autism. Students with autism can range from being mentally retarded and having no communication or social skills to having some speech and the ability to be trained to improve social interaction. These students are often not aware of the existence of other people and rarely give eye contact or demonstrate a need for closeness. This disorder is often diagnosed during infancy or the preschool years and can be lifelong in duration. The most common presenting concern that brings these children to a professional's attention is the failure to acquire language at the expected age (Parmelee, 1996).

Asperger's Disorder. Students with Asperger's disorder are different from students with autism because they do possess some communication skills and have average or above average intellect. The main deficit for students with Asperger's is in the area of social skill development. These students have trouble with nonverbal behaviors such as maintaining eye contact or maintaining appropriate physical boundaries with others (Johnson, Rasbury, & Siegel, 1997). Children with this disorder frequently have slowed motor skill development and can be clumsy and awkward. Students with Asperger's can become consumed with highly personalized interests that don't require other peer involvement. Examples of this might be collecting many facts about baseball or trains to the exclusion of other interests or relationships. Many students with Asperger's do want to connect with others but they lack knowledge and skills about how to make these connections.

The cases of Betty Benson in chapter 27 and Danny in chapter 30 both involve working with pupils with PDD, with their families, and with community resources. The role of the school social worker with children having PDD begins in early intervention programs before the child starts kindergarten. These students will require early intervention by an interdisciplinary team of school professionals. School social workers would be a bridge between the school, the teacher, and the family, part of a team that would assess eligibility for special education services and identify areas for growth and development. For many families when a diagnosis such as PDD is made, the families experience shock, grief, and denial. For many years parents were "blamed" for their child's autistic symptoms. As a result an adversarial relationship could develop between families and the medical or education system on which they depended. In Betty Benson's case the parents were defensive even without the school's reinforcement. It is now well understood that pervasive developmental disorders are neurological conditions, and that parents have not caused the problem but rather are integral parts of the team that will attempt to remediate the student's deficits. In order for parents to function in collaboration with the school, the social worker needs to establish a strong and supportive alliance that acknowledges parent's feelings and aspirations for their child. The school social worker can provide social skill groups and other behavioral interventions as part of the treatment team. They will be responsible for a thorough case study evaluation and for developing IEP goals for social work service.

Best practice interventions would focus on fostering normal development and helping students to compensate for their developmental deficits. The social worker's role is in the domain of social and emotional development. The goal of the work will be to increase the pleasure that a child can experience when engaging in social connections with peers and adults. These students will need repetitive training in areas such as greeting skills, personal hygiene, and appropriate classroom behaviors. They may need to be taught how to play with others and to become more aware of social nuance. If students are engaging in self-injurious or aggressive behaviors they will need behavior modification to reduce the frequency of these disruptive occurrences.

Conduct Disorders

Behavior problems are the reason why most children are referred for mental health services (Parmelee, 1996). Most children who have a behavior problem do not go on to develop a diagnosable disturbance of conduct. Some will go on to develop disturbances that get worse over time and cause multiple problems with relationships, undermining their adult functioning. Johnson, Rasbury, and Siegel (1997) describe children with conduct disorders who exhibit behaviors that bring them into conflict with their environment. These behaviors can include: tantruming, stubbornness, defiance, disobedience, and spitefulness. Children with more severe behavior problems can become aggressive with people or animals; destroy property, set fires, steal, lie, run away, and ultimately become involved with the juvenile justice system. According to DSM-IV-TR (APA, 2000) disruptive behavior disorders can be divided into two categories: conduct disorder and oppositional defiant disorder. Features of a conduct disorder involve a repetitive pattern of behavior where the rights of others are violated and/or societal norms are broken. Oppositional defiant disorder (ODD) is defined as a pattern of defiant, disobedient, and hostile behavior directed toward authority figures (APA, 2000). Disruptive behavior disorders are often associated with a number of co-occurring conditions including ADHD, substance abuse, and mood disorders (House, 2002).

Students with conduct or behavior disorders in the school setting take up significant amounts of time from school social workers, teachers, and administrators. Not only is learning impeded for those children whose behavior is disordered, but their behavior may also have a negative impact on the learning of other children in the classroom. Students with conduct disorders are often the school bullies, can be involved in gang activity, and are openly defiant to school authority. Teachers bring these students to the social worker's attention, hoping that behavior plans can be put in place or that the student can be identified as needing special education services. Animosity often develops between school staff and parents because of frequent phone calls home with concerns about noncompliant behavior. Some parents withdraw from school meetings and activities because of feelings of shame or helplessness. These disconnects between home and school leave more room for student misbehavior and manipulation. When communication has broken down, these students are vulnerable and may fall through the cracks. School shootings and random violence are worst-case scenarios. In recent years, many schools have taken on the challenge of teaching moral values and character development as a school-wide strategy to address the issues that contribute to disruptive school behavior.

The cases of Steve in chapter 17 and Jorge and Tommy in chapter 25 illustrate conduct disorders mixed with cultural and developmental factors and learning problems. It is important to learn the meaning or function of a student's disruptive behavior. A functional assessment (see chapter 19) includes a detailed description of behavioral antecedents and consequences, frequency, duration, intensity, location, and the function of the behavior. Additional information needs to be collected regarding the child's history including age of onset of the problematic behaviors, symptoms that might suggest a difficult temperament, and whether the child's problematic behavior has occurred alone or in the presence of others, within the family, or in the community. Children should receive a medical assessment to find out whether there has been a head injury or central nervous system or auditory processing difficulties. Any past involvement with the legal system should be documented. Awareness of any family history of mental illness, substance abuse, or abuse or neglect will assist in the treatment planning process (Sattler, 1998).

An outcome of a careful assessment will include appropriate interventions designed to target disruptive behaviors. The most effective approach needs to be multisystemic and focused on cognitive and behavioral skills. Specific techniques may include brainstorming and problem-solving strategies, role-playing, behavioral rehearsal, as well as teaching various self-soothing techniques such as progressive muscle relaxation and positive imagery (Parmelee, 1996). Increasing structure throughout the school day is critical for these children. Parent and teacher education is important, with the focus on assisting them to respond to provocative behavior appropriately. They need to provide consistent, positive reinforcement for prosocial behaviors and predictable and natural consequences for negative or antisocial behaviors.

Anxiety Disorders

DSM-IV-TR (APA, 2000) describes ten different types of anxiety disorders in childhood. The most common disorders include: separation anxiety, panic disorder, social phobia, obsessive-compulsive disorder, and post-traumatic stress disorder. Anxiety disorders are considered internalizing disorders, which means that they are directed toward self and the symptoms primarily involve excessive inhibition of behavior (Sattler, 1998). Symptoms of anxiety involve avoidant or escape behaviors. The subjective experience often involves a sense of dread, despair, and impending doom. Physical symptoms can include: rapid heartbeat, sweating, difficulty breathing, and impaired speech and coordination. Intense anxiety is an aversive experience, and phobic behaviors often result from avoiding the anxiety producing stimuli. Anxiety problems can be conceptualized as exaggerated fear responses in situations where the fear is no longer functional. For example a child who encounters a strange dog in his neighborhood and feels frightened is normal. A child with an anxiety disorder would no longer be able to feel at ease in the same area of the neighborhood even though the dog was no longer present (House, 2002). Separation anxiety and post-traumatic stress disorder will be described in more detail because of their prevalence among school-aged children and the impact they have on learning.

Separation Anxiety. Children with separation anxiety disorder show obvious distress when separating from their parents (Johnson, Rasbury, & Siegel, 1997). These children often refuse to go to school and may be mislabeled as school phobic. The fear for these students is not of going to school per se but instead is a fear of leaving their parents. These children may have physical symptoms such as nausea, headaches, and stomach aches. They may describe fears of getting lost or kidnapped and nightmares are a common experience. Separation anxiety is frequently the reason why families initially seek help for their children. More girls are diagnosed with this disorder than boys, and onset is usually between the age of 9 and 11. One third of these children have co-occurring depression and later may go on to have other features of anxiety (Parmelee, 1996; see Chapter 37).

Post-traumatic stress disorder is also classified as an anxiety disorder in DSM-IV-TR (APA, 2000). The central feature for children with post-traumatic stress disorder (PTSD) is the experience of a severe trauma such as witnessing a murder, being kidnapped, or living through a natural disaster, followed by the recurrent intrusive recollection of the trauma, avoidance of trauma-related stimuli, and hyperarousal (Parmelee, 1996). This is more fully discussed in chapter 37, Crisis Intervention.

Students with anxiety disorders present many challenges in the school setting. In the early years, getting to school can be difficult and taking risks in the learning process can be slowed. In later years, separation anxiety that is stopping students from attending school can lead to chronic truancy or dropping out of high school entirely. Even when these students attend school on a regular basis they are often so anxious and preoccupied with managing their fears that they are unavailable for learning. They may be slow to make friends, unable to establish trusting relationships with teachers or social workers, and unwilling to try new activities. When severely anxious students perceive the outside world as dangerous and anticipate impending doom, they may respond with rigidity, and inflexibility in dealing with the everyday demands of school. Their reactions may include: temper tantrums, aggressive outbursts, and petulant withdrawal. These behaviors are attempts to maintain sameness and predictability in the school.

The cases of Tommy in chapter 20, Devin in chapter 24, and Cathy in chapter 25 are good examples of students of different ages struggling with anxiety, together with the school social worker's response. Tommy's enuresis was triggered by anxiety in his class and to some extent by the teacher's concerns; Devin was fearful about competition and interpersonal relationships and about dressing and showering for gym. Cathy reacted to transitions with panic attacks in high school. In each case there was careful assessment of the problem and interpersonal triggers. Work took place with teachers, family, community resources, and with the student. Creating a school culture that helps children feel safe and form stable and reliable attachments to adults and peers can be a factor that mitigates student anxiety reactions. In all three cases there was considerable work developing a safe environment with attachments. Effective interventions with individual children may include contingency management techniques where desired behaviors are shaped through positive reinforcement for nonphobic responses and behavioral interventions such as systematic desensitization and progressive muscle relaxation techniques. Cognitive interventions involve helping the student become aware of the irrationality of her catastrophic thinking. Students can learn to replace these thoughts with more adaptive, more realistic positive thinking (Johnson, Rasbury, & Siegel 1997; Parmelee, 1996).

Suicidality

Almost 5,000 young people between the ages of 15 and 24 commit suicide every year. Suicide is the third leading cause of death among adolescents and the second leading cause of death for college age youth (Brown University, 2003).

School social workers are frequently the first adults who become aware that a student is experiencing suicidal ideation. This can be one of the most anxiety provoking and troubling issues in school social work practice. Sometimes students reveal these thoughts to the social worker as in the case of Alan in chapter 26; sometimes a student's friend comes to the social worker; and there are times when a student or teacher passes on a suicide note to the social worker. Many times parents are unaware of their children's suicidal feelings. When they are aware, they can be at a loss about what to do and will frequently turn to the school social worker for support and direction.

Students with a diagnosed mental illness are at greater risk for suicide than other students (Parmelee, 1996). The pain of depression, anxiety, or bipolar disorder can be accompanied by hopelessness, isolation, and despair. These negative feelings can trigger both suicidal ideation and behavior. Students who feel alone and are not part of a social support structure at home or at school are particularly vulnerable to suicidal feelings. Because adolescents are impulsive and may not have a developed a vision for their future, they can idealize suicide and see it as a solution to their problems without any thought to the consequences of their self-destructive behavior (Cooper & Lesser, 2005).

Some students who voice suicidal feelings are actually crying out for help and wish for an adult to rescue them from their agony. If a student reveals suicidal feelings, asking the simple question "Who would find you?" allows the student who is struggling with suicidal ideation to verbalize their pain and reveal the source of the interpersonal conflicts that are triggering their suicidal ideation (Holman, 1997). It is a common myth that discussing suicidal ideation will promote suicidal behavior. Rather the opposite is true. When a student can verbalize these thoughts they are less likely to act them out.

Other students may present to the school social worker as having chronic suicidal feelings and may make significant demands on school personnel for their time and attention. Although these students may not always require hospitalization, they are at risk and need ongoing services to manage the emotional disregulation that they experience. When a student poses a threat of self-harming it is necessary to breach confidentially and inform parents, outside service providers, and school administration.

A major goal of work with this student population is to teach them cognitive and behavioral skills to help them to manage their painful emotions (Linehan, 1993). School social workers need to develop clinical judgment and skills that enable them to evaluate the level of a student's lethality and the possible need for hospitalization and/or other services. An interview protocol can include: determining the frequency and duration of suicidal ideation, the specificity of the suicidal plan, and the extent of action already taken in carrying out the plan (Shea, 1998). Shea recommends a chronological assessment of suicide events (the CASE approach). The school social worker needs to explore the presenting suicidal ideation or events, the degree of the student's suicidal ideation within the last two to six weeks, any past suicidal ideation or events, and current ideation or intent. By breaking up the interview into four discrete time frames, the worker can be more confident that she has captured a complete picture of the student's suicide risk (Shea, 2002). Obtaining information from collateral sources, such as parents, family members, and friends, is a critical step in assessing lethality. It is wise to get another opinion about the student's risk through a referral for a psychiatric assessment. However, hospitalization is not a magical solution to a student's acute suicidal crisis. In this age of managed care, students who are hospitalized often return to school in a few days. Sometimes the hospitalization is so brief that the suicidal ideation is not fully resolved. In many cases the underlying issues or problems that lead to the crisis will continue to need to be addressed.

Safety contracts have been a popular and often used tool during risk assessment. However research has not shown that safety contracts in themselves are effective deterrents (Shea, 2002). They can be appropriately used as part of an assessment to further explore the student's ambivalence about living or dying.

Suicide Risk with Gay and Lesbian Youth. Gay and lesbian youth may be two to three times more likely to kill themselves than heterosexual youths and constitute 30 percent of all adolescent suicides (McBee, Rogers, & James, 1997). The negative reactions of family and society and internalized homophobia appear to sometimes lead to a pervasive sense of hopelessness and despair in this population. Hetrick and Martin (as cited in Morrow, 1993) reported that one-third of their adolescent gay and lesbian clients had suffered violence because of their sexual orientation. Of those who reported suffering violence, nearly half of the violence (49%) was inflicted by family members. Uribe and Harbeck (1992) in their description of a program to assist gay and lesbian youth write:

> Although most in this early group were very intelligent, few were performing at the level of their native capacity. Many were involved in self-destructive behavior, including substance abuse and attempting suicide, and were on the verge of dropping out of school. They felt they existed in a box, with no adults to talk to, no traditional support structures to lean on for help in sorting out problems, and no young people like themselves. In effect, they felt stranded in an environment that shunned their very existence. (pp. 51–52)

Alcohol and substance use compounds risks for gay and lesbian youth. Gibson (1989) reported that substance abuse is up to three times greater among gay and lesbian youth than other youth, and Blumenthal (1988) found that completed suicide was rare if substances were not involved.

CONCLUSION

This chapter discussed mental health issues commonly encountered by school social workers and has focused on related policies, research, assessment, and intervention. Using real case examples from other chapters, we see school social workers helping to develop supportive and responsive environments and to assist students to find better ways of coping and learning. In each case school became a place to grow, to test out new relationships, and to find healing. No other setting could provide this level of access to vulnerable children over the developmental span. Over a period of four years Cathy (chapter 25) learned she could deal with her crippling anxieties and that the environment was not as bad as she imagined. She eventually was able to deal effectively with painful personal crises and with junior college. Over seven years Alan (chapter 26) dealt with his depression, suicidal ideation, learning problems, interpersonal difficulties, and relationship shifts with his family to graduate ready for high school. In each case, the school social worker used a wide variety of interventions—environmental modifications, consultation with teachers, family, group, and individual work—helping Alan and Cathy to develop appropriately and healthily. While the social worker orchestrated things, the central reality was not the social worker, but the natural process of the student putting his and her energies into the commonly expected tasks of learning and coping with school, and in this finding health. There was collaboration, orchestrated by the social worker, between the school and mental health resources in the community. Such collaboration, including wraparound planning, is discussed in chapter 20 and chapter 30.

There are other possibilities for a more coordinated and seamless service delivery. An emerging model for provision of mental health services involves partnering between community agencies and schools to bring into the school additional social workers, psychiatrists, and other mental health professionals to provide longer term or more intensive therapeutic services. In this model, the school district contracts with one or more agencies to come into the school to provide services. Grant funding may be used to support these services.

The full-service school, discussed in chapter 9, offers mental health services to students and community members in the school setting as one of an array of on-site services. Full-service schools may include vaccination and health clinics, family planning services, drug and alcohol treatment, as well as mental health services (Gruman, Weist, & Sarles, 2002).

School social workers are in the best position to draw upon the resources around them to establish community-school partnerships, family-school interventions, and school-wide interventions, as well as individual and group interventions, in caring for mental health needs of children.

Internet resources for ADHD:

Children and Adults with Attention Deficit Disorder www.chadd.org
National Attention Deficit Disorder Association www.add.org

Internet resources for mood disorders:

Depression and Bipolar Support Alliance www.dbsalliance.org
Child and Adolescent Bipolar Foundation www.bpkids.org
All About Depression www.allaboutdepression.com

Internet resources for PDD:

Center for the Study of Autism www.autism.org
Online Asperger Syndrome Information and Support www.udel.edu/bkirby/asperger

Internet resources for conduct disorders:

Conduct Disorders.com http://www.conductdisorders.com/
Teens with Problems www.teenswithproblems.com/conduct_disorder

Internet resources for anxiety disorders:

Anxiety Disorders Association of America www.adaa.org

Internet resources for suicide:

American Association of Suicidology www.suicidology.org
Training Institute for Suicide Assessment and Clinical Interviewing
www.suicideassessment.com

References

American Psychiatric Association. (2000). *Diagnostic and statistical manual of mental disorders: Text revision* (4th ed.). Washington, DC: Author.

Blumenthal, S. J. (1988). Suicide: A guide to risk factors, assessment, and treatment of suicidal patients. *Medical Clinics in North America, 72*, 937–971.

Brooks-Gunn, J., & Duncan, G. J. (1997). The effects of poverty on children. *Future of Children, 7*(2), 55–71.

Brown University. (2004). Teen suicide. *Brown University Child & Adolescent Behavior Letter, 20*(8), 2.

Child & Adolescent Bipolar Foundation. (2001). *Early-onset bipolar disorder fact sheet.* Retrieved February 27, 2005, from http://www.bpkids.org

Cooper, M. G, & Lesser, J. G. (2005). *Clinical social work practice: An integrated approach.* Boston: Allyn & Bacon.

Costello-Wells, B., McFarland, Reed, J., Walton, K. (2003). School-based mental health clinics. *Journal of Child and Adolescent Psychiatric Nursing, 16*, 60–71.

Flisher, A. J., Kramer, R. A., Grosser, R. C., Alegria, M., Bird, H. R., Bourdon, K. H., et al. (1997). Correlates of unmet need for mental health services by children and adolescents. *Psychological Medicine, 27*(5), 1145–1154.

Gibson, P. (1989). Gay male and lesbian youth suicide. In U.S. Department of Health and Human Services (Ed.), *Report of Secretary's Task Force on Youth Suicide* (pp. 11–142). Washington, DC: U.S. Department of Health and Human Services.

Gurman, H. S., Weist, M.D., & Sarles, R. M. (Eds.). (2002). *Providing mental health services to youth where they are.* New York: Brunner-Routeledge.

Gutman, L. M., Sameroff, A. J., & Cole, R. (2003) Academic growth curve trajectories from 1st grade to 12th grade: Effects of multiple social risk factors and preschool child factors. *Developmental Psychology, 39*(4), 777–790.

Holman, W. D. (1997). "Who would find you?": A question for working with suicidal children and adolescents. *Child and Adolescent Social Work Journal, 14*, 134.

House, A. E., (2002). *DSM-IV diagnosis in the schools.* New York: Guilford.

Ialong, N. S., Edelsohn, G., & Kellam, S. G. (2001). A further look at the prognostic power of young children's reports of depressed mood and feelings. *Child Development, 72*(3), 736–747.

Institute of Medicine. (1994). *Reducing risks for mental disorders: Frontiers for preventive intervention research.* Washington, DC: National Academy Press.

Johnson, J. H., Rasbury, W. C., & Siegel, L. J. (1997). *Approaches to child treatment* (2nd ed.). Needham Heights, MA: Allyn & Bacon.

Kataoka, S. H., Zhang, L., & Wells, K. B. (2002). Unmet need for mental health care among U.S. children: Variation by ethnicity and insurance status. *American Journal of Psychiatry, 159*(9), 1548-1555.

Kazdin, A. E. (1993). Adolescent mental health: Prevention and treatment programs. *American Psychologist, 48*, 127-141.

Kluger, J., Song, S., Cray, D., Ressner, J., Dequine, J., Sattley, M, et al. (2002). Young and bipolar. *Time, 160*(8), 38-48.

Linehan, M. M. (1993). *Skills training manual for treating borderline personality disorder.* New York: Guilford.

McBee, S. M., & Rogers, J. R. (1997). Identifying risk factors for gay and lesbian suicidal behavior: Implications for mental health counselors. *Journal of Mental Health Counseling, 19*(2), 1-8.

Miranda, J., Azocar, F., Organista, K. C., Munoz, R. F., et al. (1996). Recruiting and retaining low-income Latinos in psychotherapy research. *Journal of Consulting & Clinical Psychology, 64*(5), 868-874.

Morrison, J. (2001). *DSM-IV made easy.* New York: Guilford.

Morrow, D. (1993). Social work with gay and lesbian adolescents. *Social Work, 38*(6), 655-660.

North Carolina Public Schools. (2005). *School social work.* Retrieved February 24, 2005, from http://www.ncpublicschools.org

Parmelee, D. X. (1996). *Child and adolescent psychiatry.* St. Louis, MO: Mosby-Yearbook.

Pomeroy, E., & Wambach, K. (2003). *The clinical assessment workbook.* Pacific Grove, CA: Brooks/Cole.

President's New Freedom Commission on Mental Health. (2003). *Achieving the promise: Transforming mental health care in America. Final report.* (DHHS Publication No. SMA 03-3832). Rockville, MD: Department of Health and Human Services.

Sattler, J. M. (1998). *Clinical and forensic interviewing of children and families.* San Diego, CA: Sattler.

Shea, S. C. (1991). The practical use of DSM-III-R. In M. Hersen & S. M. Turner (Eds.), *Adult psychopathology and diagnosis* (pp. 23-43). New York: Wiley & Sons.

Shea, S. C. (1998). *Psychiatric interviewing: The art of understanding.* Philadelphia: W. B. Saunders.

Shea, S. C. (2002). *The practical art of suicide assessment.* Hoboken, NJ: John Wiley & Sons.

Silver, L. B. (1999). *Attention-deficit/hyperactivity disorder* (2nd ed.). Washington, DC: American Psychiatric Press.

Surgeon General's Report. (1999). Mental health: A report of the surgeon general. Retrieved February 27, 2005, from http://www.surgeongeneral.gov/library/mentalhealth/home.html

Teo, A., Carlson, E., & Mathieu, P. J. (1996). A prospective longitudinal study of psychosocial predictors of achievement. *Journal of School Psychology, 34*, 285-306.

Thompson, T., & Massat, C. R. (in press). Experiences of violence, post-traumatic stress, academic achievement and behavior problems of urban African Americans. *Child and Adolescent Social Work Journal.*

United States Department of Education. (1994). *To assure a free appropriate public education of all children with disabilities: Sixteenth annual report to Congress on the implementation of the Individuals with Disabilities Education Act.* Washington, DC: Author.

United States Department of Education Office of Special Programs. (2001). *Twenty-third annual report to Congress on the implementation of the Individuals with Disabilities Education Act: Results.* Washington, DC: Author.

Uribe, V., & Harbeck, K. M. (1992). Project 10 addresses needs of gay and lesbian youth. *Education Digest, 58*(2), 50-55.

32

School Social Work Collaboration with the Child Welfare System

Sandra J. Altshuler

Eastern Washington University

- ◆ Mandated Reporters
- ◆ School Performance
- ◆ Social and Emotional Needs
- ◆ Best Practice Recommendations

Schools have a wide range of connections with the child welfare system, having in common the care and well-being of children involved with the child welfare system. Some of these children are still living with their own parents or family; others are at risk of child abuse or neglect; others live in foster care homes or group homes or are returning from the child welfare system, including from institutional care. This chapter focuses on the complexity of the relationship between schools and the child welfare system, and the ways that school social workers may strengthen collaboration with child welfare agencies and workers. Despite the fact that the majority of children living in foster care attend public schools, school social workers are not always aware of the extensive needs of these students. In fact, public child welfare systems and public educational systems have traditionally had difficulty working collaboratively with each other (Altshuler, 2003). Child welfare systems tend to focus on achieving safety and permanency whereas educational systems tend to focus specifically on academic success. Educational systems may be unprepared to deal with the vast array of needs that students living in foster care present, while child welfare systems may be unprepared to deal with the academic needs of their clientele.

Few mechanisms exist to support successful collaboration. One unfortunate result is that the children ostensibly being served by both systems often end up receiving inadequate services from either system, while neither system works collaboratively with the other (Zetlin, Weinberg, & Kimm, 2003; Zetlin, Weinberg, & Luderer, 2004). Children in foster care are often the most vulnerable children in the school system, because they are struggling with personal, familial, and educational challenges that other students may not need to confront.

The number of students living in foster care has been growing exponentially for the past twenty years, with over one-half million children living in out-of-home placements (U.S. Department of Health and Human Services, 2003). Many of these children are at risk for school failure based upon their low socioeconomic status ("SES"), minority status, and special education needs. In fact, the majority of children in foster care come from poor, minority families, with African American children being the single largest overrepresented ethnic group in the foster care population (Mech, 1983; Tate, 2001; Zetlin & Weinberg, 2004). A large majority of all children living in foster care also attend public schools; school social workers are in a unique position to address the needs of these students in collaboration with child welfare systems.

School social workers can intervene at the macro, meso, and micro levels of the environment. More specifically, school social workers can work to collaborate with agencies from the child welfare system on behalf of these vulnerable students; to ensure that these students experience schools as safe and appropriate havens and to provide appropriate, individualized services for these students. This chapter discusses current research that has demonstrated the educational problems that children in foster care have experienced and applies that knowledge to explore implications for practice for school social workers to address the needs of these highly vulnerable children.

MANDATED REPORTERS

School social workers, and all professionals working in a public school system, are legally defined as "mandated reporters" of suspected child abuse and neglect. This means that all legitimate suspicions of abuse and neglect must be reported to the child abuse hotline, or professionals risk losing their licenses. A "legitimate suspicion" is one in which school social workers have some reason to suspect abuse or neglect has occurred. School social workers or teachers, however, do not need to assess the validity of their suspicions; indeed, they should not even attempt to do so. Rather, after documenting the details that explain their suspicions, they should immediately report their concerns by calling the local, state, or federally available child abuse hotline. As mandated reporters, school social workers or teachers will be required to identify themselves and their professional positions but can request that the family not be informed of the identity of the reporter. They cannot, however, remain anonymous in their reporting.

Once school social workers or teachers have filed a report, they will receive a report number and the name of the person with whom they spoke and include that information in their ongoing documentation. Depending on the circumstances, the investigating child protection worker may then contact the reporting professional to arrange for an immediate interview with the child at the school. Usually the school social worker will eventually be notified of the outcome of the investigation, but, unfortunately, this does not necessarily occur, or it may take more time than expected. The implications of being mandated reporters will demand a good deal of assistance by the school social worker in the form of consultation and workshops for teachers and other school personnel, who may be less familiar or less equipped to deal with these requirements.

SCHOOL PERFORMANCE

Concerns about the school performance of students living in foster care have arisen over the past twenty-five years, because these students change schools often, usually in mid-year, and have consistently demonstrated lowered achievement and academic performance in school. Researchers have assessed the educational performance of children in nonrelated foster care (placed with a family to whom the child is not related), kinship foster care (placed with a blood relative), and group home care.[1] The results from these studies all indicated that students in foster care demonstrate significantly lower achievement and lower performance in school, compared to normed expectations. The conclusions were based primarily upon standardized achievement tests, school cumulative records, teacher assessments, or parent ratings. Compared with other students in similar classes, students living in foster care consistently perform and are placed below age-appropriate grade levels, demonstrate inappropriate school-related behaviors more frequently, have poorer attendance records, change schools more frequently, and have higher retention rates (Benedict, Zuravin, & Stallings, 1996; Berrick, Barth & Needell, 1994; Canning, 1974; Dubowitz, Feigelman, Harrington, Starr, Zuravin, & Sawyer, 1994; Fanshel & Shinn, 1978; Fox & Arcuri, 1980; Goerge, VanVoorhis, Grant, Casey, & Robinson, 1992; Heath, Colton, & Aldgate, 1994; Iglehart, 1994; Runyan & Gould, 1985; Sawyer & Dubowitz, 1994; Smucker, Kauffman, & Ball, 1996; Wolkind & Rutter, 1973).

Students living in foster care demonstrate a variety of academic difficulties, including weaker cognitive abilities (Fanshel & Shinn, 1978; Fox & Arcuri, 1980)

---

1. More restrictive placements, such as institutional care, are not discussed in this chapter because these children do not usually attend public schools.

and poorer academic performance and classroom achievement (Heath et al., 1994; Iglehart, 1994; Runyan & Gould, 1985; Sawyer & Dubowitz, 1994). These difficulties lead many of these students to experience grade retentions and placement below age-appropriate grade levels (Berrick et al., 1994; Benedict et al., 1996; Canning, 1974; Sawyer & Dubowitz, 1994; Smucker et al., 1996).

Students living in foster care demonstrate behavioral problems in school settings that range from aggressive, demanding, immature, and attention-seeking behaviors to withdrawn, anxious, and over-compliant behaviors (Canning, 1974; Fanshel & Shinn, 1978; Smucker et al., 1996; Wolkind & Rutter, 1973; Zima et al., 2000). They have higher rates of absenteeism and tardiness than their classroom peers (Benedict et al., 1996; Canning, 1974; Runyan & Gould, 1985) and lower levels of school engagement or participation in extracurricular activities (Kortenkamp & Ehrle, 2002). They change schools more frequently and drop out in significantly higher numbers than students not living in foster care (Cook, 1994; Eckenrode, Rowe, Laird, & Brathwaite, 1995). These attendance difficulties also contribute to poor academic performance and behavioral problems.

Students living in foster care receive special education services at higher rates than children in the general population (U.S. Department of Health and Human Services, Administration for Children & Families, 2003a; Zetlin & Weinberg, 2004). The two primary disabling conditions identified for a majority of children placed in foster care and special education are related either to a learning disability or to a serious emotional disturbance (Berrick et al., 1994; Goerge et al., 1992). Interestingly, Goerge and his colleagues speculate that children in foster care are actually being underidentified for emotional disturbances, given that research has demonstrated the extensive mental health needs of these children (see DHHS, ACF, 2003b; Clausen, Landsverk, Ganger, Chadwick, & Litrownik, 1998; Stein, Evans, Mazumdar, & Rae-Grant, 1996).

Poor educational functioning while in care has led to poorer outcomes of adult functioning. Retrospective reports from adults who had been placed in foster care as children indicate that they experienced significant school difficulties while growing up in foster care and regret not receiving extra help to succeed academically (Benedict et al., 1996; Blome, 1997; Courtney, Piliavin, Grogan-Kaylor, & Nesmith, 2001; Festinger, 1983). Benedict and her colleagues (1996) highlighted school failure and retention, behavioral problems, and attendance problems as some of the most significant difficulties experienced by these former foster children. Former foster children who had not graduated from high school were less likely than those who did graduate to be employed, maintain stable housing, have strong leisure interests, feel satisfied with their lives (Pilling, as cited in Jackson, 1988), or have higher levels of self-sufficiency, including the ability to maintain stable housing and full-time employment (Cheung & Heath, 1994; Stein, 1994). Studies of adult functioning after foster care have demonstrated the importance of academic success for employment, self-sufficiency, and self-esteem (Aldgate, Heath, Colton, & Simm, 1993; Benedict & Zuravin, 1996; Courtney et al., 2001; Kerman, Wildfire, & Barth, 2002).

SOCIAL AND EMOTIONAL NEEDS

The vast majority of children living in foster care have experienced physical or sexual abuse, neglect, and in all cases, some type of separation from parents. A great deal of literature has convincingly documented that these experiences significantly increase the risk of these children developing serious emotional, behavioral, or developmental problems, as well as attachment disorders (see DHHS, ACF, 2003b; Clausen, Landsverk, Ganger, Chadwick, & Litrownik, 1998; Halfon, Berkowitz, & Klee, 1992; Hughes, 1999; Manly, Kim, Rogosch, & Cicchetti, 2001; McIntyre & Keesler, 1986; Orme & Buehler, 2001; Pilowsky, 1995; Stein et al., 1996).

In one of the first national longitudinal studies examining the characteristics and needs of children and families involved in the child welfare system, initial findings show that the children in the study scored below general population norms on virtually every developmental measure. In other words, children involved in child welfare—albeit similar to those living in poverty—demonstrate lower cognitive abilities and language development, and higher levels of behavioral problems, yet only about 25 percent of them received at least one specialty service to address those problems (DHHS, ACF, 2003a). The authors of this study point out that these children most lack social skills and daily living skills.

Other studies have assessed the emotional difficulties of children living in foster care with standardized measures of child behavior (e.g., the Achenbach Child Behavior Checklist [CBCL]) or based upon diagnostic criteria for psychological disturbances (e.g., the American Psychiatric Association's Diagnostic and Statistical Manual [DSM]). Children in foster care consistently demonstrate clinically high levels of externalizing and internalizing behavioral problems, as evidenced on the CBCL, and in the DSM (Clausen et al., 1998; Heflinger, Simpkins, & Combs-Orme, 2000), with prevalence of psychiatric disorders comparable to those of children who receive services of mental health settings (Stein et al., 1996).

BEST PRACTICE RECOMMENDATIONS

School social workers need to be mindful of the myriad of potential consequences that result from children traumatized by having been abused, neglected, and/or separated from their primary caregiving parent. It is difficult, however, to generalize the exact behavioral manifestations of such trauma, so school social workers must anticipate the presence of a wide range of problems, not all of which are predictable based upon the child's previous history. What is predictable is knowing that these students are struggling with emotional challenges on a daily basis: a profound change in their living situation; the knowledge that they have been removed from their primary caregiver; the uncertainties they feel about their parents and their future living arrangements; and the difficulty in overcoming the actual experiences of abuse or neglect at the hands of their loved ones. Often children in foster care must also struggle with the added challenges of low SES and minority status and the tendency to change schools frequently due to changes in placements. It is easy to understand why the challenges at school may not be the top priority for these children, as they struggle to give meaning to the recent upheavals in their lives. Nonetheless, school social workers can support these students by ensuring that the schools they attend are a safe haven from these concerns, offering a stable, consistent, accepting, and predictable environment in which they can thrive.

Using Bronfenbrenner's ecological systems theory (1986) and social work's person-in-environment perspective, school social workers are in a strong and unique position to help support the educational functioning of students living in foster care. At the macro level, they must begin to increase collaborative efforts with the public child welfare system. At the meso level, school social workers must constantly work to improve the school environment to ensure a welcoming and safe place for these, and all, students. And, at the micro level, school social workers can ensure that these students have an adequate classroom placement, that their teachers can relate to their needs to develop a functional role in their classroom, and that they are receiving interventions appropriate to their individualized needs.

Macro: Increase Collaboration with Public Child Welfare

Increase Trust. There is a tendency for educators and child welfare workers not to understand or trust each other to carry out their professional duties toward students in foster care (Altshuler, 2003). Child welfare workers may be concerned that school systems would not follow through on educating students living in foster care. They may believe that schools simply do not want students in foster care—especially those with behavioral problems—in their schools and are therefore uncommitted to working with them. They may believe that schools do not maintain high academic expectations for students in foster care or do not act promptly on academic concerns. On the other hand, these beliefs may be symptomatic of the child welfare worker not having the time, the energy, or even the knowledge to engage with the education system. Despite the importance of the school, child welfare workers are sometimes unmotivated to prioritize school collaboration over other issues such as achieving safety and permanence for children. Unfortunately, this allows educators and school social workers to believe that child welfare workers are unreliable, uncaring, and uninvolved. Educators often complain about the child welfare workers' "obvious lack of caring" toward students (Altshuler, 2003). As a result, successful collaboration remains difficult to achieve and the child who needs the joint services of the school social worker and the child welfare worker may become lost in a "sea of professional adversity" (Altshuler, 1997).

School social workers and child welfare workers must begin to alleviate that sea of adversity by earning the trust of each other. School social workers could initiate contact with the local child protective agency to discuss how the two systems can best support and complement each other's work. In addition, they should contact the specific child welfare workers responsible for children currently placed in foster care in their school to discuss each child's unique educational needs. They may be pleasantly surprised at child welfare workers' responsiveness to these efforts, ultimately supporting the vulnerable children for whom they are all responsible.

Improve Communication to Increase Information-Sharing. Historically, educational systems and public child welfare systems are perceived by the other as uncommunicative and unhelpful. Professionals in each system may appear to place the responsibility for communicating upon the professionals in the other system, creating a lack of information sharing. Currently, while educators generally understand the legal and policy constraints faced by child welfare workers, they nonetheless often feel that child welfare workers deliberately withhold vital information from them. Conversely, while child welfare workers generally understand the justification for school systems to know about the educational needs of the students, they often feel that educators expect them to divulge confidential, nonessential information (Altshuler, 2003). In actuality, the schools, through their testing and their proximity to the pupil, have a great deal of information on the child's current functioning and capabilities.

Clear guidelines for sharing confidential information (see chapters 7 and 30) need to be developed within and across both systems, to increase the flow of needed information provided in a timely manner. With clear and consistent guidelines, school social workers can exchange vital, timely information with child welfare workers more freely or can understand, based upon written policy, when they cannot. Since the concerns they share have to do with the child's current functioning, the issue of history is less important, except in relation to what the child has told them already. More complex issues arise when the child is suddenly removed from the home and from the school as well.

Improve Professional Relationships. With an increased flow in communication, the professionals in both systems have an opportunity to build stronger relationships with each other. Once school social workers are aware of a student's foster care status, it is their responsibility to initiate and maintain ongoing contact with the student's child welfare worker. This would include inviting the child welfare worker to meetings, informing child welfare workers about available in-school programs (e.g., tutoring, mentoring), and asking about specific problems or issues of which the school should be aware.

School social workers can provide workshops and training opportunities for the local child welfare workers about educational policies and laws, especially those related to special education and accommodations for disabilities.

Child welfare workers often do not attend school meetings because they do not understand the complexity of schools today and feel unable to provide professional input (Altshuler, 2003). Teaching child welfare workers about the processes and practices of multidisciplinary conferences, the educational language and acronyms, and the importance of alerting the school promptly about a child's special educational or disability needs can help improve collaborative relationships. Secondarily, it may also increase the frequency with which child welfare workers attend meetings and initiate contacts with school social workers.

Some governing bodies have successfully legislated the necessity for interagency collaboration between child welfare and public education. The Foster Youth Services Program was enacted in 1981 in California (Ayasse, 1995) and the Manchester Teaching Service was implemented in Great Britain in 1989 (Walker, 1994). Both programs are designed to increase the collaboration between child welfare and education and both employ independent social workers to accomplish their goals. However, school social workers should not wait for legislated mandates before taking other proactive steps to increase the collaborative efforts between the two systems.

In summary, collaboration at the macro level requires a balancing of the diverse roles of school social worker and child welfare worker. Clarifying the distinct roles of school social workers and child welfare workers is the first step in developing collaboration. The school social worker has the advantage of weekly or even daily contact with the child. This degree of contact may be difficult or impossible for the child welfare worker. The school social worker has easy access to family caregivers for the child, without the constraints of the power relationship that exists between the child welfare system and families. On the other hand, the child welfare worker has access to the courts, to decision-making power, and to family history that are inaccessible to the school social worker. Each role has differing strengths and opportunities. By working together, a synergy can be created that will benefit children and families.

The collaboration between schools and the child welfare system goes far beyond the collaboration between an individual school social worker and an individual child welfare worker. It is important for schools as systems to develop collaborative partnerships with agencies serving children and families, and, specifically, with the child welfare system. Such partnerships are described in greater detail in chapter 30, which focuses on coordination of services and resource development, particularly on the development of wraparound systems, to develop a holding environment and prevent institutionalization.

Meso: Improve the School Environment

Create a Safe and Welcoming Environment. Foster care status can significantly impact both how the students perform in school and how teachers react to them (Altshuler, 2003). As noted earlier in this chapter, school success understandably can become less of a priority for children who have experienced abuse, neglect, and/or separation from their primary caregivers. Nonetheless, it is crucial to ensure that students in foster care are treated with sensitivity to their unique circumstances, and to their potentially more urgent needs. This would include maintaining consistent structure and expectations for both behavioral and academic performance. In addition, school social workers should be at the forefront in implementing multicultural and diversity education for the entire school system to improve the educational climate for diverse students (Dupper & Evans, 1996).

Foster parents also need a warm and welcoming educational environment that values them. Despite the knowledge that parent participation in school has a beneficial effect on student achievement, the public education system has not always reached out to foster parents to participate in the educational system (Kurtz, 1988; Kurtz & Barth, 1989). They may be ignored or only superficially included in multidisciplinary and special education planning meetings, school functions, and the PTA. Often foster parents may be uncertain of their role, the school uncertain of how long the child may remain with them, and the agency uncertain of the school. Foster parents often do not have the history of working with the school that other parents have. Because of their overall uncertainty, foster parents may remain on the sidelines unless the school and/or the child welfare agency encourages them to get involved with the school. This situation can be exacerbated if the foster parents are ethnically, culturally, or socioeconomically different from the majority of the school (Outland-Mitchell & Anderson, 1992; Pine & Hilliard, 1990), and no professional person addresses these issues.

School social workers and child welfare workers together must take a leadership role to change this. They can solicit the foster parents' opinions regarding how the school can best meet the children's educational needs through home visits, phone calls, or face-to-face meetings. They can also carry out their role as advocates by joining the parents and caregivers at meetings with teachers and administrators, and ensuring that their solicited opinions are heard and valued.

School social workers and/or other team members may offer sessions for all parents, including foster parents, about educational policies and laws, especially those related to special education and accommodations for disabilities. Teaching foster parents about the processes and practices of multidisciplinary conferences, the educational language, and the importance of alerting the school promptly about a child's special educational or disability needs can help empower the parents to advocate more effectively for the children in their care.

Teach the Educators. Just as school social workers can provide workshops for child welfare workers, school social workers must do the same for their teachers and administrators. Teachers need some information on the specific issues faced by students living in foster care, and how those issues may be manifested academically, behaviorally, emotionally, and developmentally. However, since children do respond differently in different environments, and the previous environment was undoubtedly stressful, there is a danger of stereotyping the pupil's behavior. To protect against stereotyping a specific child, the child welfare agency needs current information on how the student is doing.

School social workers can provide educators with an overview of some of the challenges faced by child welfare workers and foster parents, to strengthen the collaboration between the parties. Workshops can be offered either at the beginning of the school year, or periodically throughout the year, as specific issues and challenges arise. Individual contacts about particular issues are of paramount importance. It is important for teachers to know that students in foster care not only want to be treated equally to other students but also want their teachers to be sensitive to their unique needs.

Ensure Support Within the School. Across the country, there is wide variation in the extent of supportive and social services provided within any school. Programs such as tutoring, mentoring, social skills, and peer counseling in schools have all demonstrated their effectiveness in helping at-risk students (Bein, 1999; Durlak, 1995). Like other at-risk students, those living in foster care may also benefit from such services. For example, there has been some promising research showing that mentoring programs specific for meeting the needs of children in foster care can enhance their educational success, if implemented well (Altshuler, 2001; Rhodes, Haight, & Briggs, 1999). In-school mentors could be particularly beneficial for students who change schools mid-year, by offering an ability to provide specific direction for students in negotiating the demands of that specific school.

Advocate to Maintain Students in Their Home School. The frequent disruptions in placements negatively impact students' ability to establish a connection with a home school and have serious detrimental effects on the students' ability to succeed educationally. Keeping the student in the same school, regardless of his/her movement within the foster care system, requires a tremendous commitment on the part of school systems, particularly since transportation, policy, and financial issues are often involved. However, if all school systems were to make such a commitment, students in foster care would indeed experience a "home" at school, as a safe haven from which they will not be wrenched, especially through no fault of their own.

Micro: Provide Appropriate Interventions

Address Concrete Needs. Both school social workers and child welfare workers often overlook the importance of ensuring that family systems have the requisite concrete needs for optimal functioning that are often outside the purview of their own systems. Concrete assistance is particularly important for children in foster care, and especially those living in kinship care. Kinship foster parents are more likely to have lower incomes, be single female heads of households, and live in publicly subsidized housing than other parents, including nonrelated foster parents (Berrick et al., 1994; Dubowitz, Feigelman, & Zuravin, 1993; Le Prohn, 1994). Without adequate finances, food, shelter, or clothing, it is very difficult for foster families to support their children's educational needs. School social workers and child welfare workers can enhance the possibilities of success of these children by acting as advocates in securing needed economic supports and other concrete services for their families.

Be More Proactive in Anticipating Student Needs. Based on the extensive knowledge researchers have provided, there is no doubt that virtually every student in foster care may have some type of special need in order to succeed academically. Therefore, school social workers must be more proactive in anticipating such needs. Certainly, all of the meso-level interventions discussed in the earlier section would be effective, but assessments for each individual student are crucial as well. School social workers need to advocate at the local child welfare agency to ensure a policy of immediate notification whenever a student in foster care begins to attend that school. Upon notification, the school social worker or the child welfare worker should organize joint meetings involving, at a minimum, the classroom teacher, the school administrator, and the foster parents to develop a collaborative approach. The student, too, should be involved, unless age or developmental functioning prohibits appropriate participation. The purpose of the meeting would be to create a clearly delineated plan for individualizing each student's needs, and specifying who is responsible for what activities (e.g., what is the child welfare worker going to do, what is the teacher going to do, and what are the foster parents and pupil going to do, etc.). If these meetings were held routinely, it is likely that collaborative efforts between the professionals in both systems would be enhanced and students in foster care would be less likely to slip through any educational cracks.

Counseling and Consultation. Group counseling can be helpful for students in foster care, particularly for those who have not yet established friendships among classmates. Group counseling normalizes the fostering experiences for students and allows them to rely on peer support in a meaningful way (Altshuler, 1999). It can also help students learn the norms and expectations of a new school system.

Individual consultation with teachers regarding specific student needs can also support the educational functioning of children living in foster care. For example, school social workers can arrange a behavioral management plan for attendance, tardiness, or behavioral problems. By providing consultation to teachers, school social workers can target specific behavioral or emotional problems of students in their classes, to ensure their unique needs are being met.

CONCLUSION

Children in foster care are often the most vulnerable children in the school system. They are struggling with personal, familial, and educational challenges that other students may not need to confront. School social workers must play a critical role in creating a safe and supportive haven for children in foster care. School social workers are in a unique position to support the academic success of these students at all systems levels, by increasing collaboration with the child welfare system, by ensuring a welcoming school environment for diverse students and foster parents, and by providing direct, individualized services. Although school social workers are not always in a position to prevent children from the consequences of abuse or neglect, they are certainly in a pivotal position to advocate for them in the school system, so that children in foster care do not suffer further harm by lacking the educational skills they may need to succeed in life's challenges.

While education may not be the top priority for these students, their foster parents, or child welfare workers, it is crucial for school social workers to support their school functioning. Not only has academic success consistently predicted successful adult functioning, but school itself is a potential anchor for a child whose life has been uprooted. The stability and security of a familiar school system can help these children weather the storm of foster care placement, but only if the key participants involved make an active commitment to truly working in the best interests of the child with whom they work.

References

Aldgate, J., Heath, A., Colton, M., & Simm, M. (1993). Social work and the education of children in foster care. *Adoption and Fostering, 17*(3), 25-34.

Altshuler, S. J. (1997). A reveille for school social workers: Children in foster care need our help! *Social Work in Education, 19*, 121-127.

Altshuler, S. J. (1999). The educational needs of children in foster care: The perceptions of teachers and students. *School Social Work Journal, 23*(2), 1-12.

Altshuler, S. J. (2001). When is mentoring not helpful for students living in foster care? *School Social Work Journal, 26*(1), 15-29.

Altshuler, S. J. (2003). From barriers to successful collaboration: Public schools and child welfare working together. *Social Work, 48*(1), 52-63.

Altshuler, S. J., & Kopels, S. L. (2003). Advocating in schools for children with disabilities: What's the new I.D.E.A.? *Social Work, 48*(3), 320-329.

Ayasse, R. H. (1995). Addressing the needs of foster children: The Foster Youth Services Program. *Social Work in Education, 17*, 207-216.

Bein, A. M. (1999). School social worker involvement in mentoring programs. *Social Work in Education, 21*, 120-128.

Benedict, M. I., & Zuravin, S. (1996). *Foster children grown up: Social, educational, economic and personal outcomes. Final report.* (DHHS, ACF, Children's Bureau, Grant No. 90-CW-1076). Washington, DC: Clearinghouse on Child Abuse and Neglect.

Benedict, M. I., Zuravin, S., & Stallings, R. Y. (1996). Adult functioning of children who lived in kin versus nonrelative family foster homes. *Child Welfare, 75*, 529-549.

Berrick, J. D., Barth, R. P., & Needell, B. (1994). A comparison of kinship foster homes and foster family homes: Implications for kinship foster care as family preservation. *Children and Youth Services Review, 16*, 33-63.

Blome, W. (1997). What happens to foster kids: Educational experiences of a random sample of foster care youth and a matched group of non-foster care youth. *Child and Adolescent Social Work, 14*, 41-53.

Bronfenbrenner, U. (1986). Ecology of the family as a context for human development: Research perspectives. *Developmental Psychology, 22*(6), 723-742.

Canning, R. (1974). School experiences of foster children. *Child Welfare, 53*, 582-586.

Cheung, S. Y., & Heath, A. (1994). After care: The education and occupation of adults who have been in care. *Oxford Review of Education, 20*, 361-374.

Clausen, J. M., Landsverk, J., Ganger, W., Chadwick, D., & Litrownik, A. (1998). Mental health problems of children in foster care. *Journal of Child and Family Studies, 7*, 283-296.

Cook, R. J. (1994). Are we helping foster care youth prepare for their future? *Children and Youth Services Review, 16*, 213-229.

Courtney, M., Piliavin, I., Grogan-Kaylor, A., & Nesmith, A. (2001). Foster youth transitions to adulthood: A longitudinal view of youth leaving care. *Child Welfare, 80*, 685-716.

Dubowitz, H., Feigelman, S., Harrington, D., Starr, R., Zuravin, S., & Sawyer, R. (1994). Children in kinship care: How do they fare? *Children and Youth Services Review, 16*, 85-106.

Dubowitz, H., Feigelman, S., & Zuravin, S. (1993). A profile of kinship care. *Child Welfare, 72*, 153-69.

Dupper, D. R., & Evans, S. (1996). From Band-Aids and putting out fires to prevention: School social work practice approaches for the new century. *Social Work in Education, 18*, 187-192.

Durlak, J. A. (1995). *School-based prevention programs for children and adolescents.* Thousand Oaks, CA: Sage.

Eckenrode, J., Rowe, E., Laird, M., & Brathwaite, J. (1995). Mobility as a mediator of the effects of child maltreatment on academic performance. *Child Development, 66*, 1130-1142.

Fanshel, D., & Shinn, E. B. (1978). *Children in foster care.* New York: Columbia University Press.

Festinger, T. (1983). *No one ever asked us . . . a postscript to foster care.* New York: Columbia University Press.

Fox, M., & Arcuri, K. (1980). Cognitive and academic functioning in foster children. *Child Welfare, 59*, 491-496.

Goerge, R. M., VanVoorhis, J., Grant, S., Casey, K., & Robinson, M. (1992). Special-education experiences of foster children: An empirical study. *Child Welfare, 71*, 419-437.

Halfon, N., Berkowitz, G., & Klee, L. (1992). Mental health service utilization by children in foster care in California. *Pediatrics, 89*, 1238-1244.

Heath, A. F., Colton, M. J., & Aldgate, J. (1994). Failure to escape: A longitudinal study of foster children's educational attainment. *British Journal of Social Work, 24*, 241-260.

Heflinger, C. A., Simpkins, C. G., & Combs-Orme, T. (2000). Using the CBCL to determine the clinical status of children in state custody. *Children and Youth Services Review, 21*, 55-73.

Hughes, D. A. (1999). Adopting children with attachment problems. *Child Welfare, 78*, 541-560.

Iglehart, A. (1994). Kinship foster care: placement, service and outcome issues. *Children and Youth Services Review, 16*, 107-122.

Jackson, S. (1988). Education and children in care. *Adoption and Fostering, 12*(4), 6-10.

Kerman, B., Wildfire, J., & Barth, R. P. (2002). Outcomes for young adults who experienced foster care. *Children and Youth Services Review, 24*, 79-104.

Kortenkamp, K., & Ehrle, J. (2002). *The well-being of children involved with the child welfare system: A national overview.* Assessing the New Federalism Policy Brief, Series B, No. B-43. Washington, DC: Urban Institute.

Kurtz, P. D. (1988). Social work services to parents: Essential to pupils at risk. *Urban Education, 22*(4), 444-457.

Kurtz, P. D., & Barth, R. P. (1989). Parent involvement: Cornerstone of school social work practice. *Social Work, 34*, 407–413.

Le Prohn, N. (1994). The role of the kinship foster parent: A comparison of the role conceptions of relative and non-relative foster parents. *Children and Youth Services Review, 16*, 65–84.

Manly, J. T., Kim, J. E., Rogosch, F. A., & Cicchetti, D. (2001). Dimensions of child maltreatment and children's adjustment: Contributions of developmental timing and subtype. *Development and Psychopathology, 13*(4), 759–782.

McIntyre, A. E., & Keesler, T. Y. (1986). Psychological disorders among foster children. *Journal of Clinical Child Psychology, 15*, 297–303.

Mech, E. V. (1983). Out-of-home placement rates. *Social Services Review, 57*, 657–667.

Orme, J. G., & Buehler, C. (2001). Foster family characteristics and behavioral and emotional problems of foster children: A narrative review. *Family Relations, 50*(1), 3–15.

Outland-Mitchell, C., & Anderson, R. J. (1992). Involving parents of at-risk children in the educational process: A literature review. *School Social Work Journal, 17*, 17–24.

Pilowsky, D. (1995). Psychopathology among children placed in family foster care. *Psychiatric Services, 46*, 906–910.

Pine, G. J., & Hilliard, A. G. (1990). Rx for racism: Imperatives for America's schools. *Phi Delta Kappan, 71*, 593–600.

Rhodes, J. E., Haight, W. L., & Briggs, E. C. (1999). The influence of mentoring on the peer relationships of foster youth in relative and nonrelative care. *Journal of Research on Adolescence, 9*(2), 185–201.

Runyan, D. K., & Gould, C. L. (1985). Foster care for child maltreatment. II. Impact on school performance. *Pediatrics, 76*, 841–47.

Sawyer, R. J., & Dubowitz, H. (1994). School performance of children in kinship care. *Child Abuse and Neglect, 18*, 587–597.

Smucker, K. S., Kauffman, J. M., & Ball, D. W. (1996). School-related problems of special education foster-care students with emotional or behavioral disorders: A comparison to other groups. *Journal of Emotional and Behavioral Disorders, 4*(1), 30–39.

Stein, M. (1994). Leaving care, education and career trajectories. *Oxford Review of Education, 20*, 361–374.

Stein, E., Evans, B., Mazumdar, R., & Rae-Grant, N. (1996). The mental health of children in foster care: A comparison with community and clinical samples. *Canadian Journal of Psychiatry, 41*, 385–391.

Tate, S. C. (2001). The academic experiences of African American males in an urban Midwest foster care system. *Journal of Social Studies Research, 25*(2), 36–46.

U.S. Department of Health and Human Services, Administration for Children and Families, Children's Bureau. (2003, March). *The AFCARS report—Preliminary FY2001 estimates as of* (Vol. 8, pp. 1–7). Washington, DC: U.S. Government Printing Office. Available from http://www.acf.hhs.gov/programs/cb/publications/afcars.

U.S. Department of Health and Human Services, Administration for Children and Families. (2003a). *National survey of child and adolescent well-being, one year in foster care; Executive summary*. Retrieved April 4, 2005, from http://www.acf.hhs.gov/programs/opre/abuse_neglect/nscaw/reports/exesum_nscaw/exsum_nscaw.pdf

U.S. Department of Health and Human Services, Administration for Children and Families. (2003b). *National survey of child and adolescent well-being, one year in foster care; Wave 1 data analysis report*. Retrieved April 4, 2005, from http://www.acf.hhs.gov/programs/opre/abuse_neglect/nscaw/reports/nscaw_oyfc/oyfc_report.pdf

Walker, T. G. (1994). Educating children in the public care: A strategic approach. *Oxford Review of Education, 20,* 339-47.

Weinberg, L. A., Weinberg, C., & Shea, N. M. (1997). Advocacy's role in identifying dysfunction in agencies serving abused and neglected children. *Child Maltreatment, 2,* 212-225.

Wolkind, S., & Rutter, M. (1973). Children who have been "in care": An epidemiological study. *Journal of Child Psychology and Psychiatry, 14,* 97-105.

Zetlin, A. G., & Weinberg, L. A. (2004). Understanding the plight of foster youth and improving their educational opportunities. *Child Abuse & Neglect, 28,* 917-923.

Zetlin, A. G., Weinberg, L. A., & Kimm, C. (2003). Are the educational needs of children in foster care being addressed? *Children & Schools, 25,* 105-119.

Zetlin, A. G., Weinberg, L. A., & Luderer, J. (2004). Problems and solutions to improving education services for children in foster care. *Preventing School Failure, 45*(1), 1-7.

Zima, B. T., Bussing, R., Freeman, S., Yang, X., Belin, T. R., & Forness, S. R. (2000). Behavior problems, academic skill delays and school failure among school-aged children in foster care: Their relationship to placement characteristics. *Journal of Child and Family Studies, 9*(1), 87-103.

33

Perspectives on Groups for School Social Workers

Edward J. Pawlak
Western Michigan University

Danielle Wozniak
University of Connecticut

Michele McGowen
Disability Resource Center of Southwest Michigan

- ◆ Examples of School-Based Groups from the Literature
- ◆ Counseling Groups in Schools—Unique Opportunities and Challenges
- ◆ When to Use Groups in Schools
- ◆ Group Structure
- ◆ Normative Structure

Schools can be viewed as organizations consisting of small groups. Groups can be administrative or programmatic task groups. These can be curriculum committees, an individual education program (IEP) team, a PTA executive committee, and a crisis management team that deals with student fights or the death of a student. Educational program groups can be the student council, the Spanish Language Club, and the Chemistry Club. Social and recreational clubs can be a hiking and skiing club. There are athletic program groups. Counseling groups could be a children-of-divorce support group, a bereavement support group, peer relations, self-esteem, and problem-solving enhancement groups. There are natural groups, such as gangs, cliques, or friendship groups of students or teachers. This chapter concentrates on counseling groups, because these are the groups that school social workers are most likely to form and serve. We begin our discussion with an overview of the literature on the use of counseling groups in schools to inform readers about the variations in practice among school social workers. We then turn our attention to the unique opportunities and challenges in the use of counseling groups in schools. Although school social workers are more likely to work with counseling groups, and some task and natural groups, the other types of groups are likely to be engaged as practitioners work in behalf of their student clients. Practitioners must be able to assess and understand the structures of all these school groups if they are to be effective practitioners. Thus, we end our discussion with an examination of frameworks that are useful in analyzing group and normative structure and demonstrate their application to groups in schools.

EXAMPLES OF SCHOOL-BASED GROUPS FROM THE LITERATURE

Several journals, primarily *Social Work in Education*, were reviewed for articles on the use of groups in schools. The selections reported here reveal that school social workers engage in group work that is rich, varied, and designed to address a wide range of human needs.

Groups for Students Dealing with Substance Abuse Issues

A psychoeducational group approach was used with school children from drug-involved families living in economically depressed, inner-city neighborhoods in Philadelphia (Dore, Nelson-Zlupko, & Kaufmann, 1999). Demar (1997) used a social-cognitive group intervention with fifty-seven 3rd-, 4th-, and 5th-grade students to focus on substance abuse prevention. Beaudoin (1991) established an aftercare support group for students returning to school from in-patient substance abuse treatment. The group was designed to provide peer support to recovering students and a place to learn new coping strategies as they encounter situations where old responses are expected of them. McElligatt (1986) described an after-school group in secondary schools providing a forum for students concerned about parental substance abuse.

Groups for Students with ADHD

A support group for teenagers with attention deficit hyperactivity disorder (ADHD) focused on self-esteem, feelings, behavior change, communication, conflict, friendship, anger, and problem solving (Timmer, 1995). A 2-year follow-up with approximately half the parents of these teens found that the students had graduated or were going to graduate and had improved behavior and compliance with community rules.

Groups Addressing Racial and Cultural Issues

Culturally grounded group interventions were used with adolescent Native American students in a Southwestern school district. Participants strengthened their cultural identity, improved their self-esteem, increased their interpersonal skills, and used the group as a means of expressing legitimate concerns about unfair treatment in the school without fear of reprisal (Marsiglia, Cross, & Mitchell-Enos, 1998). Student forum groups were used by McGary (1987) in a high school that was experiencing interracial violence. Most of the group participants were considered high risk for behavioral deficits and poor achievement. The six groups, generally comprising students of similar racial backgrounds, set goals related to stopping the violence in the school and addressing racial issues that had surfaced. In the year and a half that forum groups were in place, interracial fighting stopped, there was student-initiated elimination of institutionalized racist practices, and standardized test scores increased, especially for minorities. In addition, positive responses to postforum survey questions increased significantly (e.g., "I feel safe in school" and "Adults in this school are willing to help me with my personal problems"). Congress and Lynn (1994) managed a group for urban elementary school immigrants to help them adjust to life in the United States.

Groups Addressing Socialization and Peer Interaction Skills

Abrams (2000) developed a conflict resolution group for boys who were disruptive in class, oppositional, and who taunted and fought with peers. The two Latino and two Bosnian boys were in the same fourth grade made up entirely of children who speak English as a second language. Lee and Lee (1989) successfully used group work to help educable students with mental retardation learn age-appropriate behaviors, become more expressive, and feel better about themselves. Students were able to transfer these new behaviors to situations outside the group. Owen and Anlauf-Sabatino (1989) worked with 1st- and 2nd-grade children displaying cognitive developmental delay, withdrawn behaviors, or aggression. Each group focused on only one of these issues. The first group worked on strengthening deficient cognitive skills to improve classroom behavior, and the other two groups worked on verbalizing feelings to problem-solve and become aware of the effects of their behavior socially and academically.

Groups for Students Who Are Parents

Bennett and Morgan (1988) suggested using groups to teach adolescent mothers effective interaction skills with their infants, reinforce feelings of competence, and lessen anxious and helpless feelings through peer influence. A group for adolescent fathers was designed to provide support, parenting education, and motivation to stay in school (Anthony & Smith, 1994). Seven of the eight fathers in the program completed the school year, and the average GPA for the group improved from 2.07 to 2.17.

Groups for the Parents of Students

Greif (1993) formed a school-based drop-in support group for African American parents in an urban neighborhood depicted as unsafe. The group served as a medium for discussing parenting concerns and providing mutual support and coaching related to the difficulties of raising children. Vayle (1992) established a group for mothers from multicultural families who had recently immigrated to the United States. These mothers provided a support network that enabled them to be effective advocates for their children as their families made the often difficult transition to U.S. culture. Gonzalez-Ramos (1990) used school-based groups for recent immigrants, specifically Hispanic families who underutilize other traditional mental health services. In a study conducted with Puerto Rican mothers, Gonzalez-Ramos found that they overwhelmingly chose the school as the place they would prefer to go for help with their children's problems.

Groups for Students Whose Families Are Experiencing Divorce

Admunson-Beckmann and Lucas (1989) used groups for children of divorce to address children's feelings of isolation, loss, anger, guilt, and helplessness. The groups also provided a support network, and opportunities to share feelings with children in similar circumstances and rehearse new coping skills. Mervis (1989) involved children's groups in the production of a video on coping with divorce. The children videotaped themselves or puppets and then invited parents to watch the "premiere." Strauss and McGann (1987) developed a support group for children coping with divorce that included a parent group that met several times concurrently with the children's group. Teachers and parents reported an increase in communication between the home and school, and some parents reported children were more able to discuss issues about the divorce than they were before participation in the group.

Groups for Trauma-Related Recovery

Pope, Campbell, and Kurtz (1992) discussed two groups formed in a school after nine students were held as hostages by a student with a gun. One group was for middle school students exhibiting symptoms of post-traumatic stress disorder (PTSD) who requested help from the counselor, and a high school support group was created for the former hostages. The group helped the middle school students return to a precrisis level of functioning. The students in the group for hostages, however, achieved an even higher than precrisis level of functioning.

Groups for Students at Risk of Dropping Out

Charney (1993) used groups in a dropout prevention program for low achievers (GPA less than 2.0) in the second to sixth grades. These groups helped students learn to handle behavior problems that impeded their academic progress by incorporating students with GPAs of 3.0 or above as role models within the group. At termination, 30 percent of the underachieving students had attained a "C" average, and another 37 percent improved in smaller increments. Balsanek (1986) used short-term groups with 7th- and 8th-grade males who had failed at least two subjects during the preceding grading period but had achievement test scores showing above-average scholastic ability. All participants improved at least one letter grade in the subsequent marking period, and most improved by two or more letter grades. The participants also displayed increased peer collaboration behaviors and verbalized many positive self-comments. Carley (1994) created a group for marginalized, hostile high school students at risk for dropping out. Interested staff were also asked to participate, and they and the students were asked to metaphorically re-create the story of how they wished to be perceived at school. Reputations could be rewritten to include new possibilities that shift beyond hostility or authoritarianism. Teachers reported changes in students' attitudes and that they were easier to deal with. There was also an increase in rapport with administrators.

Groups Addressing Stress, Grief, and Loss Issues

A solution-focused, mutual aid group was developed for five 4th- and 5th-grade Hispanic children who were experiencing the impact of parental incarceration and were exhibiting trauma-reactive behavior (Springer, Lynch, & Rubin, 2000). Fisher (1989) used "magic circle" groups in a school with 4th-grade students whose teachers had miscarriages within one week of each other. The groups were formed to let the students explore their feelings and fears about death and loss. The farm crisis of the 1980s led Staudt (1987) to form a group for children to deal with the fear, loss, and change associated with the ways the crisis affected their families and the community. Bloomfield and Holzman (1988) formed a group for children whose families had recently relocated to the community to help the children adjust to their new environment and to cope with the change and losses incurred by moving.

COUNSELING GROUPS IN SCHOOLS— UNIQUE OPPORTUNITIES AND CHALLENGES

Forming Counseling Groups

School settings provide social workers with unique advantages while forming counseling groups. These advantages emanate from both the organizational structure of schools and the school social worker's intervention process. For example, practitioners can observe the behavior of prospective group members in structured settings, such as physical education, English, and music classes, and in unstructured situations, such as lunch and recess. Observations made in both of these settings provide an empirical basis for deciding the composition of counseling groups to include members with complementary characteristics and to avoid imbalances, for example, too many acting-out members. When the composition of the group is decided, the appropriate school officials and teachers must be informed. Parents of prospective members must be provided with an explanation of the purpose of the group, the reason for referral, and confidentiality policies. These explanations serve as the basis for obtaining written, informed, parental consent for their child's participation in the group.

School social workers can also gather information about a student's behavior from several different sources (e.g., teachers in different classes, custodians, food service workers) to find out with which people and in which settings the student does well or poorly. Their observations often yield information that is essential for an accurate assessment and an effective treatment plan. For example, personal observations and information received from teachers are helpful in assessing students' strengths and areas in need of development, as well as understanding how various problems are manifested or exacerbated. This information is useful in guiding group composition and focusing content during group counseling sessions. Information gleaned from observations can be reflected back to the student in the context of the therapeutic relationship and incorporated in a student's self-assessment of his or her own difficulties and strengths. For example, students who have low self-esteem, poor impulse control, and poor peer relations might be expected to have a more difficult time in unstructured situations like recess or lunchtime. Teachers' complaints about the student might include classroom disruption and management issues. However, on closer inspection, the student's difficulties might be limited to unstructured classroom activities exacerbated by arguments and fights occurring during recess. Intervention for that student might include both group counseling and work with teachers to restructure the child's day, alleviating many unstructured activities until the student has gained greater proficiency and comfort with them.

Collaboration with School Personnel

Another advantage to counseling groups in schools is that teachers, social workers, school administrators, and parents can participate in the therapeutic process together. The African proverb, "It takes a whole village to raise a child," is particularly applicable to school-based counseling or support groups. Groups are most effective when the school social worker has the support and understanding of teachers and administrators. School social workers must enlist the direct help of classroom teachers, guidance counselors, parents, and administrators and consider them an intricate part of the therapeutic process. Such collaboration can be achieved by establishing and maintaining good communication between teachers and social workers, and by educating personnel about what constitutes helpful exchange. One way to begin this process is to ask teachers what kind of information or feedback they would find helpful and to tell teachers what kind of information school social workers find useful. This is a good time to educate professionals about what practitioners and student group members are expected to keep confidential about group discussions. The requirements and opportunities for collaboration abound, and we discuss them in the context of other issues that school social workers must address in their use of counseling groups in schools.

"What the heck goes on in those groups anyway?" The importance of educating school personnel about group process deserves attention. What do school social workers do with students? What do students work on? How? If the group has a curriculum, it should be shared with teachers. This can be done individually or as an in-service training presentation at a staff meeting. Preemptively educating school personnel about group processes eliminates unprofessional communication. For example, complaints about student behavior or inquiries about "what was discussed in group" can be recontextualized from deviant, bad, or troublesome to behavior that is amenable to intervention and improvement. Strong teacher-social worker communication also helps school personnel own some aspects of the problem, to become invested in the solution, and thus to work with school social workers and the students toward problem resolution. In this respect, intervention is a shared process and not simply a "pull-out" program where the social worker meets students at the classroom door, conducts a group session, and returns them forty-five minutes later magically "fixed" or at least "made better."

Good teacher-social worker communication around therapeutic intervention issues begins with careful explanation of what the group is, what school social workers hope to attain, the benefits to students, and behaviors (either improvements or potential problems) school personnel can and should watch for. Practitioners should regularly ask for feedback from teachers regarding student behavior and progress and provide information to teachers about the issues the group is working on. This can be done in general terms without breaking the confidence of group members. For example, teachers might be told that "this week the divorce support group is talking about how they first learned about their parents' divorce, and how the students felt it affected them. This is an exercise requiring introspection and looking directly at a painful time in their lives. Sara may be quieter than usual, more sensitive, more prone to tears, or intolerant of frustration right after the group meeting." Through a therapeutic alliance, teachers can spot potential problems arising in the classroom and bring them to the school social worker's attention immediately. Informed teachers can also support group counseling efforts with follow-up classroom activities. For example, if the group is working on issues of self- or impulse control, an informed teacher can acknowledge times when students participating in the group show improvement. Teachers also can structure student activities to provide "moments of success."

Good communication is also important when a social worker informs teachers that what looks like fun and play is really a developmentally appropriate way of tackling some tough or sensitive problems. Practitioners must share their vision of the therapeutic process and help teachers understand and appreciate the social worker's role in counseling groups. Perhaps most important, the exchange provides opportunities to discuss the ways in which troublesome or challenging life experiences—that initially appear unrelated to academic achievement or performance—are intricately related to students' ability to benefit from their education and function in the school environment. That is to say, a strong teacher-social worker alliance helps teachers and social workers explore the relationship between life crises and a child's school performance. Many school social workers report that most teachers involved in such a discussion see a life crisis (e.g., divorce) as one that would affect a child's ability to concentrate in school, complete assignments, or interact successfully with peers. Many teachers who interact with children of divorce believe these children can benefit from intervention by the school social worker and state affirmatively that such children are in need of intervention. By understanding the nature of trauma inherent to a divorce, and the resulting sense of isolation and depression, teachers favor using the school setting to run divorce support groups.

Sometimes parents and teachers have difficulty understanding the treatment focus of some groups, especially when meetings involve participation in activities. When counseling groups are viewed as social or recreational groups, some parents want siblings to join the group, or teachers withhold a student's participation in a group meeting to discipline him for disruptive, unruly classroom behavior. These moments should be seized to interpret the counseling focus of group meetings and the relationship of the service to school problems and performance. Teachers can be helped to understand that students with emotional impairments often do not have fun during group activities. Those critical group incidents are therapeutic moments to be seized to work on important issues in a developmentally appropriate context. One school social worker described an outing to a public pool, in which five 10-year-old students spent as much time out of as in the water. He and the lifeguard had to issue many time-outs and restrictions for safety and rule violations, which were also connected to related problems in the school setting.

Group counseling in schools provides members with access to services and school social workers with reasonable assurances that students will be present at group meetings and on time. However, when students are released from class to attend group meetings, and the discussion or activity becomes turbulent, the conflicts may carry over into the classroom upon the student's return. This situation creates management problems for teachers and increases their skepticism about the merits of in-school, on-school-time counseling groups. Sometimes group meetings can be scheduled at the end of the school day or after school. However, strong teacher-social worker communication can either quickly resolve problems that carry over into the classroom or prevent them from occurring.

The role of school administrators should not be overlooked. Principals, vice principals, and housemasters are regularly in the position of doling out punishments or consequences to students who are not complying with school rules. However, many are eager to expand their role and their interaction with children. Involving administrators in therapeutic conferences, and keeping them informed of group activities and goals, enables them to interact with students positively. For example, students who are working in a group on impulse control in unstructured settings can be "caught being good" by informed administrators. Students who are often sent to the principal's office because of misbehavior can be sent to the principal's office for rewards, positive feedback, and praise. As allies, school administrators can often help the social worker with administrative or scheduling impediments to group counseling. For example, socialization groups ideally can be lunchtime groups, unless prospective student group members eat lunch on different shifts. Administrative understanding and support can make an insurmountable structural problem one that is easily corrected.

"You want to pull my kid out of class and put him in a group for bad kids?" Parents vary in their responses to recommendations that their children might benefit from participation in an in-school therapeutic group. Some parents fear that their children will get behind in their work or will be stigmatized and teased by other students. Another response of a few parents is that "my child doesn't have problems." Often parents' denial is a part of the overall problem experienced by a child and the school community. Other parents are relieved to know that help is finally available, and they no longer have to deal with difficult social and emotional problems alone. Helping all parents in working through their feelings is an important predictor of a child's successful participation in school-based group counseling. To reassure parents and gain their support, communication is essential about group purposes, the benefits to students, protection of confidentiality, and measures to ensure that group participation will not cause them to fall behind academically.

"How do you make sure no one talks about what we talk about?" Confidentiality requires special consideration, especially when it may be virtually impossible to maintain, as students are released from class to participate in counseling group sessions. The importance of confidentiality to students should be addressed directly with them in the group context. When confidentiality of membership is important to some students, they will want to develop strategies for maintaining it, or at least reduce the obviousness of their participation. For other students, public knowledge of their group participation will be inconsequential or an occasion for pride.

Confidentiality of discussions that take place during group meetings must be pursued but cannot be ensured. Some members may not be vigilant about confidentiality as they disclose their group experience to peer confidants or inquisitive fellow students. Student peers can be empathic, supportive, and understanding, but they can also be cruel. Breaches of confidentiality may have serious social and psychological consequences for members whose disclosures have been revealed. Affected students could be tormented, taunted, teased, shunned, or the object of whispered conversations. Members of student counseling groups sometimes "feel paranoid" that "others know" and devote energy to image and identity management, damage control, and obsess with public-presentation-of-self issues, even when confidentiality is maintained.

Group members should be told that confidentiality is a condition of participation. Groups may want to deal directly with their fears or concerns that confidentiality will not be maintained, or with how they hope to be their own enforcers. In one group of second-grade girls who were working on self-esteem and peer relationship issues, the group identified one girl whom they feared would not keep their confidence. This quickly became a group issue. The girl acknowledged that she sometimes used group information as a way to gain friendships with children outside the group. In a controlled setting, the group showed their disapproval with this friendship-gaining strategy and helped her devise alternative strategies to making and keeping friends, as well as group strategies to help her maintain confidentiality. These activities were ultimately in service of the group's general goals, which were to strengthen peer relationships and problem-solving skills. Thus, potential problems may be important therapeutic issues and become a beneficial part of the therapeutic process. Finally, however, if confidentiality remains an issue or is continually breached, school social workers in collaboration with relevant others should evaluate whether some student problems are best treated in individual counseling sessions.

"I don't wanna be in your group." Stigma associated with membership in particular counseling groups may contribute to student resistance or refusal to participate. For example, one student who was being interviewed by a school social worker for possible inclusion in an after-school activity group asked, "Is this a group for crazies?" The social worker led the student into an exploration of the characteristics and behavior of other students who were being invited to join the group. The student said that a couple of kids were "crazy," and she explained what she meant by saying "they act up, and they're wild." She didn't want to be in a group with crazies. However, she also recognized that "one boy was sad, another acted like a queer," still another "did not have many friends, "and some "don't stick with their work." The school social worker then suggested that the student's initial characterization—"a group for crazies"—was inappropriate and asked her to reframe her perception of the group. She responded by saying, "It's a do-better group." This student figured out how she would explain her membership to inquiring peers. However, others may not be so insightful and clever. Thus, school social workers should help student members of counseling groups formulate a way of explaining membership in a counseling group and managing identities associated with such affiliation. Sometimes stereotypes of counseling groups develop because many referrals are understandably students who are behavioral management problems in the classroom. On the other hand, developmentally, adolescents tend to be self-conscious and wary of being singled-out or made different. Calling a student out of class to engage in individual counseling is often an embarrassment. Group intervention allows students not to feel singled out, but to feel included and supported in a peer setting.

WHEN TO USE GROUPS IN SCHOOLS

The Case of a Bereavement Support Group

When should one consider forming a group? How do issues of context, which is the unique social and structural environment of schools, pose impediments and provide unique supports for forming a group? What other issues are important to consider? The following is an analysis of important considerations revolving around the formation of a bereavement support group by a school social worker. These considerations include case management issues, group themes, the students' developmental issues, how to evaluate sound intervention strategy, how to set group goals, and how to think about the benefits of a group to students with whom practitioners are working.

Case Management. One of the authors was a school social worker in a high school of approximately 800 students with 2 school psychologists and 8 guidance counselors. The staff was regularly faced with a serious problem—caseloads were extremely high. Often the need to contact students and their families to begin intervention was urgent because problems faced by adolescents are seldom those that can wait three weeks for an appointment. Traditional models of intervention, such as individual counseling or even home visits and family counseling, were not always feasible. As we began to think and talk about alternative, yet effective interventions, we began to think about the context in which we were providing service. Most students placed themselves in groups and spent most of their waking hours living in intentionally created groups. Individual counseling, although essential for some students, had traditionally been the preferred and only mode of treatment selected by mental health professionals in the schools. Yet, this was neither effective nor possible given our high caseloads. Based on case management constraints we began to think about the feasibility of groups.

Group Themes. At the high school, we regularly had team meetings with all social service personnel to discuss the students who had been referred to us by teachers, parents, administrators, or guidance counselors. In discussing how to best serve the needs of students who had been referred for social work or psychological services, we began to look at the common issues each student was dealing with. We were startled to find fourteen students who had been referred to us over the previous two months had lost a parent. We were even more startled to find after talking to each student's guidance counselors and teachers that each was described in very similar terms. Each was truant from school. Each had often spent most of each day in the nurse's office complaining of somatic illness. Each was involved to a greater degree than other students in substance abuse, mostly alcohol abuse. Each was emotionally withdrawn and depressed, had poor or tumultuous peer relationships, and was often described as a "loner." With this information we began to think about a group. We weren't concerned about how to form a group or even if we should. Rather we conceived of formed and natural groups as concepts to think with, and thus to change the way we thought about our students, their troubles, and our approach to them. Common problems or life themes, or even difficulty with similar developmental tasks, made students at our high school little more than aggregates, or "collections of people who share a common circumstance or condition" (Longres, 1995, p. 319). However, thinking about students' shared concerns and shared developmental tasks became one way to think about ways in which peers could potentially be brought together to form groups. These groups could help, support, and strengthen each other. From this perspective, support groups, problem-solving groups, and issue-directed therapy groups made sense, not only because they allowed us to provide services to larger numbers of students, but because group counseling represented a sound intervention strategy for particular groups of students.

Thus, we began to think about forming a group based on themes that were relevant to students. To the fourteen who had lost a parent, loss and bereavement were the hallmarks of their existence. We began to gather information about the students who would be invited to participate in the bereavement support group. We also shared with teachers our idea about forming the group, especially because we knew that to get fourteen high school students released from class once a week was going to take cooperation. Teachers reported that each student's academic performance, ability to concentrate, and attendance was an issue. Many teachers expressed frustration with these students' lack of communication and their academic failure. Because for many of these students their loss was not in the recent past, teachers needed to understand that without effective intervention students' feelings of bereavement would not just go away. Because teachers saw that we were addressing the "root causes" or etiology of academic and adjustment problems, they were supportive of our efforts, pledging their willingness to release students from class and help them make up missed work. Contextualizing the student's alienating, depressed, or antisocial behaviors in terms of life trauma that could be resolved or worked with had an impact on how teachers defined and then related to their students. We found that no longer were students "blamed" for their high absenteeism or failure to turn in work on time. Instead, teachers were more inclined to take an empathic approach to students, to extend additional help and support, and work with students and with group coleaders. The changed response from school personnel had the benefit of reducing student alienation and hostility and created an atmosphere in which students could reengage in the academic process. Students who were overwhelmed emotionally by feelings of depression relating to their loss felt support and empathy from their teachers. Thus, students began to look at school as "not a total failure" and began to engage more in their work. This pattern continued as students progressed through the group, dealing in a supportive context with the painful issues of death, loss, and unresolved, and for the most part, unabating grief.

Therapeutic Goals

Although part of evaluating whether a group is a sound intervention strategy includes an analysis of the setting and the potential issues students are facing, another component has to do with the therapeutic issues and goals. From this perspective, the most salient question becomes, based on your knowledge of students' issues and needs, and sound intervention strategies, does it make sense therapeutically to place students in a group to deal with their issues? For example, in the bereavement support group, one reaction to a dramatic life event is to feel a sense of isolation from others and a sense of alienation from familiar settings and friends. Based on our review of the literature and our assessment of students' needs, a small group designed to reduce isolation and increase support was deemed beneficial. Other groups with similar goals might include alcoholism support groups, groups dealing with gay and lesbian sexual identity, and groups for students who have experienced sexual abuse.

Developmental Issues

A third consideration was developmental issues. We began by asking, developmentally, where are these students functioning? What are the important issues in their lives? Are those issues amenable to processing in a group? Can group work ease the processes by which students work through developmental issues? For the adolescents coming together to form a bereavement support group, constructing a sense of identity was one task with which they struggled. Another was to gain a sense of identity concerning a peer group. The social class and ethnic composition of the bereavement support group was primarily Anglo American, working- and middle-class males and females, generally from two-parent families. Establishing identity for these students was at times a tumultuous process and was often enacted through challenging parental rules, talking back to their parents, pushing boundaries, and creating distance between themselves and their parents in favor of peers. Parents and adolescents in the general community commonly described their relationships with each other as conflicted, problematic, and painful. In the course of these experiences, fourteen of these students lost a parent. From a developmental perspective, one aspect of each teenager's story was to talk about the argument, the disagreement, the battle he or she was in the middle of when his or her parent died. Students talked about their sense of regret, shame, and guilt. Sharing these feelings in a group normalized their experiences and reduced their anxiety and isolation by placing them within a context of developmental issues shared by other students.

Developmental issues are related to other questions: How do individuals arrange themselves and what issues are most salient to them? Do these issues influence the way they group themselves? These questions often point to identity concerns or to a sense of goals and purpose. For example, students who identify themselves as "Hispanic" in a predominantly Anglo American high school may be a part of a natural friendship network whose purpose is to support each other and share interests and activities based on a common sense of culture, family, values, and life ways. In this case, the way in which students see themselves has a direct relationship to the way in which they are also grouping themselves. In this case, friendship networks can be supported, enhanced, and often used to form the foundation for treatment, education, or task groups. For example, Hispanic friendship networks can be used to increase Hispanic pride, to educate Anglo American students about Hispanic culture, and help Hispanic students to find a comfortable place in a predominantly Anglo American setting. Students in the adolescent bereavement group did not naturally form a group. Yet, individually, an important part of their "identity" was as persons who had lost a parent. Thus, bringing these students together with others who identified themselves in a similar way makes sense, because such a group composition helps them form friendship networks with students who shared a similar experience.

GROUP STRUCTURE

Group structure refers to stable patterns of interaction among group members at a point in time (Johnson & Johnson, 1997). School social workers must discern these patterns in groups to understand and influence them. Group structure may be assessed in terms of formal structure—relationships among positions, and informal structure—relationships among individuals. We turn to a discussion of different types of formal and informal group structure, and then we explore their relevance and application to school social work.

Formal Structure: Relationship among Positions

Relationships among positions may be classified according to formal authority/leadership, communication, tasks, and mobility. Formal authority/leadership structure refers to group hierarchical positions that have been legitimated by members or officials. Examples of such structure include chairperson, president, vice president, coordinator; teams elect captains or cocaptains; counseling groups may rotate the roles of convener or facilitator among members. Communication structure refers to required or expected patterns of exchange of information, viewpoints, or feelings between group members. Examples of such structure include committee deliberations regulated by parliamentary procedure, rules regarding timely advance notice of group meetings and circulation of the agenda, procedures governing recording and circulation of minutes of meetings, who is supposed to be informed about what, and who is supposed to send information to whom. Even counseling groups establish formal communication patterns when members agree to decision making by consensus in selecting topics to be explored. Task structure refers to the legitimated distribution of the group's work among members. Examples of such structure include treasurer, recorder, corresponding secretary, membership secretary, faculty advisor to the student council, and representative to the IEP team. Counseling groups may rotate initiation of self-disclosure and first respondent among group members (note this is an example of both task and communication structure). Mobility structure refers to the patterns of movement in and out of group positions. Examples of such structure include term limits on occupancy in a group position; rules that govern eligibility for group positions (e.g., only seniors who were group members during their junior year may serve as president); and rules about succession (the vice chair is the chair-elect).

This framework can be used in several ways as school social workers approach or work with groups in schools. For example, before attempts are made to help a social isolate join a hiking group, practitioners would be wise to learn about the group's leadership and authority structure, and the role of faculty advisor. The student may have to be coached about the appropriate ways of approaching student leaders and faculty advisors. Sometimes cliques dominate the leadership structure of educational program, recreational, or social groups, and some students never have an opportunity to be in leadership or task roles. To alter these patterns, the mobility structure of groups must be understood. School social workers may have to help school administrators, staff, teachers, students, or parents understand the formal structures of groups to help them learn how to maneuver them. In working with IEP teams, the group's task and communication structure must be understood if school social workers are to understand their roles and effective ways to influence members on behalf of students. As one begins to understand group structure, one can figure out who should be approached in what ways to accomplish particular objectives. Furthermore, school social workers cannot influence what they cannot see and understand. The framework for assessing formal structure serves as a lens to discern prescribed patterns of group interaction.

Informal Structure: Relations among Individuals

Relations among individuals may be classified according to power, communication, task, affection, and status. Power structure refers to relationships based on ability to influence and affect the decisions or behavior of others. There are four types of power: referent, expertise, reward, and coercive (French & Raven, 1968). Referent power refers to the influence members have because they are liked. Expertise power refers to influence members have because they have knowledge and skill that is valued by others, such as knowledge of math, or skill in photography. Reward power refers to influence members have because they positively reinforce others and are supportive. Coercive power refers to influence members have because they can impose their ideas on others, gain compliance, or require particular behaviors through psychological or physical force. Communication structure refers to the nature (e.g., hostile, friendly, attentive) and frequency of exchanges among members, who talks to whom, and communication roles members play in groups (e.g., listener, initiator). Task structure refers to the roles of members in carrying out the work of the group (e.g., who volunteers to do what?). Affectional structure refers to patterns of social acceptance and rejection, and preferences members have for each other. Status refers to the location of members on a hierarchical scale according to dimensions that are important to the group (e.g., physical strength, intelligence, sense of humor, ability to get along with others) (Johnson & Johnson, 1997).

This framework can be used in several ways as school social workers approach or work with various groups in schools. For example, although school task groups may have formal leaders, other members may have substantial power because they have expertise or are well liked. Both formal and informal leaders have to be considered as practitioners attempt to influence the group. In counseling and natural groups, practitioners must assess the types and distribution of power and then strive to harness, redirect, or change the group's power structure, if they intend to use the group as a means of influence. An assessment of communication structure in counseling groups is important because members are often referred to the school social worker for their troublesome patterns of communication.

Discussion

Within and between both types of group structure, members are likely to occupy several positions. For example, members of the formal task structure might also be members of the formal leadership structure. Some members are likely to be a part of the informal affectional and informal power structure. Members who are part of the informal affectional structure may also be members of the formal authority structure. Both types of group structure may affect the members' feelings toward each other, their attraction to the group, their commitment to group purposes, conflict, and the potential of the group as a means of influence on members. Effective social work in schools requires practitioners to discern and assess the structures and processes of small groups that might have a bearing on their clients' school adjustment and performance. The results of such assessments must be used to modify group structure and guide group processes. Such modification is essential to influence group and individual goal achievement, whether these pertain to behavioral change in a student, unruly school behavior of a clique, or modification of decision making by an IEP team.

Group structure can be viewed as a factor that can affect members' behavior through alterations of the dimensions identified previously. For example, by altering the task structure of the group, practitioners might change a member's group status. By modifying group mobility structure, practitioners might alter leadership opportunities and the confidence and self-esteem of some members. Group structure can also be viewed as a factor that can be affected by group composition (e.g., removal of a bully from the group), auspices (e.g., groups with or without a faculty advisor), program activities (e.g., competitive vs. cooperative activities), physical setting (e.g., off-campus vs. on-campus group meetings), and in-group and out-of-group interventions by the school social worker.

NORMATIVE STRUCTURE

Norms can be set formally or informally. Formal norms are prescribed standards of behavior that have prescribed consequences for failures in compliance (e.g., standards of conduct when school groups make field trips). Informal norms are also standards of behavior, but they are regulated by shared feelings of approval or disapproval among group members (e.g., group members' approval of taking turns or disapproval of horseplay that disrupts a group meeting) (Johnson & Johnson, 1997).

Among students, group norms have powerful influences on imitation, compliance, conformity, the ability to exercise independence, and respect for one's own and others' individuality. Discussions about norms are inevitable in group counseling in schools. For example, normative discussions are likely about relations with teachers, school officials, fellow students, parents, law enforcement personnel, and others. Among junior and high school students in some counseling groups, normative discussions are likely about respect, race relations, use of substances, dating, and sexual activity. Norms about levels of effort to be expended on schoolwork and after-school employment are also topical. Violations of school norms are often reasons for referral to the school social worker and the focus of individual and group counseling discussions. Group norms also have powerful influences on teachers, school officials, and parents. For example, these groups make normative judgments that may be convergent or divergent about student discipline, parental involvement, teacher commitment, and equal opportunities for participation in school activities.

Group normative structure can be assessed in several ways:
- The scope of behavior that is approved or disapproved,
- The intensity of the group's feeling about norms,
- The degree of agreement about norms among members,
- Peer pressure for conformity,
- Reference groups, and
- Congruence of group norms with those of relevant others in the group's life space (Johnson & Johnson, 1997; Radin & Feld, 1985).

School social workers can involve members from all types of groups in assessing their norms, the consequences of compliance and noncompliance, and conformity and nonconformity. Members might explore methods of coping with pressures for conformity with questionable norms. Alternative normative reference groups might be presented to group members.

CONCLUSION

A final consideration when thinking about groups in schools is what course of action would be most beneficial to the group of individuals with whom you are working? In the case of students, this might be how you can best enhance the problem-solving skills of a class of special education students who are struggling to learn self-control and impulse control. When working with naturally formed faculty groups, such as all the third grade teachers at a particular school, the question might be how do you help them coalesce into a task group that can effectively address curriculum changes to meet the increasingly culturally diverse needs of students? When you begin to think about the formed and natural groups that exist in schools rather than thinking about how can I make individuals function better, the question becomes, how can I help these groups of individuals meet their goals? This approach is one that automatically requires the social worker to examine the social and cultural context within which individuals live and work, as well as to integrate into an intervention strategy the culture of a particular group. Thinking with group concepts also broadens the definition of school social work. Practice shifts away from the social worker as only a provider of treatment to individuals who are in some way functionally impaired or having problems. The focus on functional impairment reproduces the individual psychopathology model of intervention, and this may have a limited place in contemporary school social work. Practice in groups also shifts toward a model of intervention that is inclusive and strengths based. Social work is defined as services that can enhance the functioning and cooperation among people who see themselves as connected through either the experience of interdependence, through a working structure, through a common identity, or through the delimitation of boundaries. In this respect, social work services are provided to various systems within the organization of the school and thus enhance the overall functioning of the school community.

References

Abrams, B. (2000). Finding common ground in a conflict resolution group for boys. *Social Work with Groups, 23*(1), 55–69.

Admunson-Beckman, K., & Lucas, A. R. (1989). Gaining a foothold in the aftermath of divorce. *Social Work in Education, 12*(1), 5–15.

Anthony, I., & Smith, D. L. (1994). Adolescent fathers: A positive acknowledgment in the school setting. *Social Work in Education, 16*(3), 179–184.

Balsanek, J. A. (1986). Group intervention for underachievers in the intermediate school. *Social Work in Education, 9*(1), 26–32.

Beaudoin, E. (1991). Assessment and intervention with chemically dependent students. *Social Work in Education, 13*(2), 78–89.

Bennett, T., & Morgan, R. L. (1988). Teaching interaction skills to adolescent mothers. *Social Work in Education, 10*(3), 143–151.

Bloomfield, K. M., & Holzman, R. (1988). Helping today's nomads: A collaborative program to assist mobile children and their families. *Social Work in Education, 10*(3), 183–197.

Carley, G. (1994). Shifting alienated student-authority relationships in a high school. *Social Work in Education, 16*(4), 221–230.

Charney, H. (1993). Project achievement: A six-year study of a dropout prevention program in bilingual schools. *Social Work in Education, 15*(2), 113–117.

Congress, E. P., & Lynn, M. (1994). Group work programs in public schools: Ethical dilemmas and cultural diversity. *Social Work in Education, 16*(2), 107–114.

Demar, J. (1997). A school-based group intervention to strengthen personal and social competencies in latency-age children. *Social Work, 19*(4), 219–230.

Dore, M. M., Nelson-Zlupko, L., & Kaufmann, E. (1999). "Friends in need": Designing and implementing a psychoeducational group for school children from drug-involved families. *Social Work, 44*(2), 179–190.

Fisher, H. A. (1989). Magic circle: Group therapy for children. *Social Work in Education, 11*(4), 260-265.

French, J. R. P., & Raven, B. (1968). The bases of social power. In D. Cartwright & A. Zander (Eds.), *Group dynamics* (3rd ed., pp. 215–235). New York: Harper & Row.

Gonzalez-Ramos, G. (1990). Examining the myth of Hispanic families' resistance to treatment: Using the school as a site for services. *Social Work in Education, 12*(4), 261–274.

Greif, G. L. (1993). A school-based support group for urban African American parents. *Social Work in Education, 15*(3), 133–139.

Johnson, D. W., & Johnson, F. P. (1997). *Joining together* (6th ed.). Boston: Allyn & Bacon.

Lee, B., & Lee, S. (1989). Group therapy as a process to strengthen the independence of students with mental retardation. *Social Work in Education, 11*(2), 123–132.

Longres, J. S. (1995). *Human behavior and social environment.* Itasca, IL: Peacock.

Marsiglia, F. F., Cross, S., & Mitchell-Enos, V. (1998). Culturally grounded group work with adolescent American Indian students. *Social Work with Groups, 21*(1/2), 89–102.

McElligatt, K. (1986). Identifying and treating children of alcoholic parents. *Social Work in Education, 9*(1), 55–70.

McGary, R. (1987). Student forums addressing racial conflict in a high school. *Social Work in Education, 9*(3), 159–168.

Mervis, B. A. (1989). Shaggy dog stories: A video project for children of divorce. *Social Work in Education, 12*(1), 16–26.

Owen, M. C., & Anlauf-Sabatino, C. (1989). Effects of cognitive development on classroom behavior: A model assessment and intervention program. *Social Work in Education, 11*(2), 77–87.

Pope, L. A., Campbell, M., & Kurtz, P. D. (1992). Hostage crisis, school-based interdisciplinary approach to posttraumatic stress disorder. *Social Work in Education, 14*(4), 227–223.

Radin, R., & Feld, S. (1985). Social psychology for group practice. In M. Sundel, P. Glasser, R. Sarri, & R. Vinter (Eds.), *Individual change through small groups* (pp. 50–69). New York: The Free Press.

Springer, D. W., Lynch, C., & Rubin, A. (2000). Effects of a solution-focused mutual aid group for Hispanic children of incarcerated parents. *Child and Adolescent Social Work Journal, 17*(6), 431–442.

Staudt, M. (1987). Helping rural school children cope with the farm crisis. *Social Work in Education, 9*(4), 222-229.

Strauss, J. B., & McGann, J. (1987). Building a network for children of divorce. *Social Work in Education, 9*(2), 96-105.

Timmer, D. F. (1995). Group support for teenagers with attention deficit hyperactivity disorder. *Social Work in Education, 17*(3), 194-198.

Vayle, M. R. (1992). International Women's Group: A bridge to belonging. *Social Work in Education, 14*(1), 7-14.

34

The No-Fault School: Understanding Groups— Understanding Schools

Joy Johnson*

University of Illinois at Chicago

- ◆ What Makes Groups Work
- ◆ An Ideal School
- ◆ The Value of Diversity
- ◆ A Challenge
- ◆ The Problem-Solving Process: Your Ally

Schools can be seen as complex organizations composed of groups. The education process takes place when loosely organized and often isolated groups of teachers interact with groups (called classes) of students within an administrative hierarchy. Surrounding these school-based groups are a wide variety of community organizations and families. Formal education clearly takes place in a multitiered social environment. The student is learning social skills concurrently with the academic content, and these skills are essential to satisfactory progress. To learn to function successfully in a setting almost entirely dominated by various group structures, essential learning must occur in the areas of communication, cooperation, consensus decision making, and democratic organizational structure in addition to the academic regimen.

This chapter examines the nature of group life in the education experience to discover how to use it constructively to create a more effective learning environment. Defining this experience adds another conceptual dimension to edu-

*Revised and edited in collaboration with Shirley McDonald.

cation from a social work perspective, and looking at the group process may assist in clarifying appropriate social work roles in these processes.

WHAT MAKES GROUPS WORK

I have consulted in numerous school systems with teachers, administrators, and pupil-personnel team members about group issues. Usually I have been asked to assist with a group that was floundering. As I studied "what went wrong," I saw a pattern emerge that elucidated some of the factors that appear crucial to group performance. My thought was that if I could isolate the elements that were destructive, I might be able to formulate a conceptual structure of what makes groups work. Continuing in my attempt to move from what went wrong to how to make groups go right, I found my consultation moving from a problem-solving focus to a preventive one. For the past several years, I have been testing these formulations against actual groups—classroom and therapeutic, natural and formed—and have been able to find several consistent criteria for what it takes to make groups become cohesive, well-functioning units.

Perhaps the most important element in creating a positive group experience is the merging of purposes of why that group exists. The multiple goals of the various group members, of the group leader, and of the sponsoring school must be compatible. If these goals do not somehow mesh together, the group is doomed before it starts. That does not mean that the goals have to be the same, but they must be able to coexist. In one teachers' association there were some teachers who were power hungry, who needed to be recognized, who needed to be valued, and who very much wanted to take a strong leadership role to satisfy their personal needs. Although some teachers in that association looked for group cohesion and closeness with one another, others were interested in getting more pleasant working surroundings and higher salaries. These sets of goals, although very different, are compatible. They can exist together. One group may say to another, "Okay, you can have the power. We will help you feel important and significant if you also will keep our interests in mind."

Group composition is another important part of what makes groups work. Who are the members? How is the group composed? In a classroom group, the composition frequently is arbitrary, and you have little control. Understanding how the membership fits together is very important in any event. When you form groups yourself, either for therapeutic purposes or for task completion, you will want to think about some group process issues that will help you form efficient and compatible groups.

There are certain combinations of people that seem to work well together and others that do not. Before you compose a group you need to be aware of some general guidelines of composition. As you select your members, try to make sure that all of the basic maintenance roles are included—nurturer, subject changer, enabler, and leader. A group will not work well if everyone in the group tends to fulfill the same role. If you have a group of all leaders with no followers, that group is likely to be in a power struggle from beginning to end. If, on the other hand, you have a group of people who nurture a great deal but are not particularly strong leaders, people may feel good about each other but never get the task done.

There are some other basic issues with respect to composition for constructive group process. One is to try to avoid too many extremes; another is to try to avoid putting only one person from a particular category in a group. Let me explain what I mean. If I had a choice, I would never put just one poor child in a group of affluent children, nor just one Black child in a group of White children, nor one girl in a group of boys, nor one child with slight mental retardation in a group of bright children. When one group member is quite different from the others, regardless of what the difference is, that person tends to be a built-in scapegoat and may get picked on or act out for the others. Whether you are composing a classroom, a therapeutic group, or a faculty committee, if you have a choice, try to find enough people who are representative of the various maintenance roles that are needed to form a helpful group and try to avoid setting up a situation that may inherently create one or more scapegoats.

There is another "golden rule" for forming a group in a school. Avoid putting people with similar problems together. This is true regardless of the type of group—whether it is a faculty committee or a therapeutic group of young people in a junior high school. If you put people with similar problems together, they will tend to integrate that problem as a group norm. Groups with members who have a variety of coping mechanisms greatly enrich the opportunities for members to view a variety of alternative behaviors. I was a member of a committee composed of people who all dealt with their frustrations by blaming the administration. We sat around and complained, and nobody did anything to make it better. There was a dramatic change in that committee when we invited two people who were doers rather than complainers. They said, "Yes, you are right, it is intolerable, and what are we going to do about it?" This new, more active approach made all the difference in the world to the functioning of the committee.

Four Essential Qualities

Another consideration regarding what makes groups work is the issue of why, and when, people want to belong to a group. What are some of the qualities essential to voluntary participation in any group? What entices someone to decide to participate in group interaction? As I have studied groups, it has become clear that the qualities necessary for an individual to want to participate in a group are the very same qualities needed in a classroom for students to want to learn. These qualities are many and varied, and some differ from community to community and from person to person. Every socioeconomic and ethnic group represented in the schools with which I have worked has different expectations of the groups within their subculture and differing values for their members. However, there are four qualities that consistently are required for someone to want to participate in a group. The way these qualities are acted out may differ greatly, but the qualities themselves are universal.

Safety. For anyone to want to participate, the group needs to be a safe place. By that I mean emotionally and physically safe for everyone present. In a school where knives and guns are prevalent, it may not be physically safe to set foot in the classroom, or the school at all, and peoples' fears greatly inhibit learning. On the other hand, the fear within a classroom that is not emotionally safe also strongly inhibits learning and group participation. In any unsafe group, the goal moves from participation to survival, and the energies and efforts of the participants are focused to that end—survival. Many a teacher has said to me, "My only goal is to survive the rest of the school year." There are many reasons why a classroom or school may not be a safe place, emotionally or physically or both. This chapter attempts to help everyone who comes in contact with groups assist in making those groups safe.

You may think I am putting too much emphasis on the quality of safety, because adults do not need that much safety, especially emotional safety. You may feel that adults can take care of themselves. And yet I wonder what it would be like if you and I were sitting across from each other in a group session, I had encouraged you to be open, and then the first time you asked a question, I ridiculed you. Perhaps I could have said, "Boy, that was the dumbest question I have ever heard! Any more stupid questions?" That interaction might have caused you to get your dander up and fight back and say, "Hey, you can't talk like that to me!" My hunch is that you would do as I would have done— shut up and say to myself, "I better keep my mouth shut in this group; it is not safe to open it." Then, if I had a chance, I would probably leave at the first opportunity.

Another interesting dynamic about group safety is that if the group is not safe for everyone it is safe for no one. If I put you down, not only would the group feel unsafe for you, but for the other group members as well. They might think, "Forget it, I'm not going to take a risk either." This dynamic occurs in classrooms, faculty meetings, and groups of all kinds in schools. Time after time I have known safety to be a core issue.

Safety, or the lack of safety, passes not only from the teacher, leader, or facilitator to the group member but also exists among the members themselves. If a bully in a group makes it unsafe for another member and if that is allowed to continue, the group becomes unsafe for everyone there, including the bully. If group members feel safe with one another, they protect one another from attack, from the leader or other sources. As a leader, therapist, teacher, or principal, whatever your role is in the school system, you need to help the school to be a safe place.

Something for You. Another dimension that makes one want to participate in a group is that the group provides something for all the members. If I am going to risk myself in my learning, in talking about myself, or in my teaching, there must be something in it for me. One of the first things that most people ask, whether they consciously think about it or not, is, "What's in it for me? What do I get for making this investment?" In some classrooms what students get is teacher or parent approval or higher grades, and these certainly are of value. But there are additional things students can get out of learning. You may want to do some thinking about how you (being who you are) can help students make an investment in their learning. How can they get something back for themselves in addition to grades and approval? One of my prime goals as a teacher is to help each student find something that he or she can get excited about in whatever it is that I am teaching. This makes the learning itself inherently useful instead of merely a source of external recognition or rewards. I have what I call the "selfish approach" to learning and teaching. Everybody, including the teacher, ought to get something out of every learning experience.

That may be somewhat idealistic; there are courses, and some parts of most courses, that are not going to be exciting. Some material you have to learn just because you have to know it, and some content that is exciting to some students is boring to others. But, it is to be hoped, this is the exception to the rule. When the prevailing focus of a teacher is on motivating and exciting students about their learning, the more boring learning tasks do not loom as large. Other groups are also faced with unpleasant tasks at times, but you should not expect any member of a committee, any member of a therapeutic group, any member of a class, or anybody playing on the playground to participate constructively in the group unless there is something they get back for themselves; that is normal, natural, necessary, and, I think, kind of nice.

Something to Contribute. Every person in every group should feel he or she has something to contribute. It is not enough to just take; a group member must feel that he or she has something to give. I vividly remember meeting with some high school students who had been in a treatment group for the majority of their junior year. As we reviewed at the end of the year what it was that made the group so successful in the eyes of the members, a consistent response (which each gave in his or her own way) was, "When I joined this group, I felt pretty crummy about myself, but when I found that I could be helpful to other people—could give advice and support when other people were hurting—I knew I wasn't as bad as I thought I was." This ability to give to other people turned out to be one of the prime curative factors in that group.

This is not necessarily the case in every group nor for all people. Many of you have had members in your group or class who did not seem to want to give. One teacher described two such students: "They don't want to give. They just think about themselves. They don't care about anybody else!" It is very difficult to work with people who appear to have this attitude, but it is important to find creative ways to help them to give, for them and for you. I worked with a group of delinquents who "ripped off" everybody and everything in sight and whose negative feelings about themselves and others led to their pretending they did not care about anything. When they were hired to manage a shelter for injured animals, this antagonistic attitude turned to one of deep concern. Discovery of their ability to give lessened their need to act out.

We have a responsibility as school personnel to see not only that our group participants get something for themselves, but also that everybody contributes something. Sometimes this is harder than seeing that everyone gets something, but it is even more important.

Someone Cares. A final important quality is that every member in a group has to know that somebody cares whether he or she is there or not. As one teacher said, "There's nothing worse than being gone for a week with the flu and nobody noticing that you were gone." All of us need warm, caring relationships, both on and off the job, in and out of the classroom, whether we are teachers, administrators, or students. One of the things that makes it so hard for the young person in a classroom who is being made a scapegoat is that he feels that no one cares, and therefore he makes little investment in trying to get people to like him. Besides that, he probably does not like himself much either. My experience is that when caring can come through, when I am able to show a person who has no friends that I care, if indeed I do, then he has reason to think that he might be likable after all and may begin to care about himself, even just a little.

Striking a Balance

No group or class can always have all four qualities at one time. No class or group can always be safe, always have something in it for everyone, always help everybody contribute, and always help everyone feel cared for and significant. I have found, however, that when those qualities usually are present and the group is constructively functioning, during those rocky times when one or more qualities is missing, one of the others temporarily makes up the loss. In my own group treatment there were times when it was pretty scary, when it was not safe. At those times the caring that I experienced from the other members made that lack of safety temporarily manageable. Everyone has, at one time or another, sat through a boring, difficult lecture or class where there was absolutely nothing in it for you, but still you were required to be there. Perhaps you were able to tolerate it because you were sitting next to somebody you cared about with whom you exchanged complaining notes. I have gotten through many a faculty meeting or dull committee meeting by sitting with somebody I like.

Other Applications

Although this discussion has been related mostly to the classroom, the same dynamics are easily transferable to any other group within a school. I wonder how many PTA presidents have thought of dealing with their dwindling attendance by asking all members to come to one meeting to discuss how to make it a more viable experience for everyone? How many principals, when things begin to go sour in the faculty, give the faculty the task of making it better for themselves? To do this, a principal runs the risk of getting honest feedback from the faculty about things he might be doing that get in the way of positive group functioning. (One of the problems of asking people what they think is that they might tell you.) My experience in a variety of settings shows that insistence on mutual assumption of responsibility and decision making is very important.

Your response to this discussion may well be, "It sounds very nice but what if it doesn't work? And what about the time that I get so angry I don't want to be rational?" These are good questions. You may want to find new ways to get yourself out of a bind you are in as well as try to stay out of the bind in the first place. As a teacher, I have my classes trained. If I temporarily lose control of myself or my feelings or become irresponsible or irrational, the students not only let me know it, but they help me out. Even second graders can say, "Hey, Mrs. Johnson, you're yelling again." That can be a signal to me to take a look at what I am upset about. By sharing this with my class, I can then help them see what it is they are doing that gets me so angry. Then we can discuss what we can do about it to have a better day together.

A school is a system in which every individual who walks in the door ought to feel valued as a worthwhile human being. Too often, instead, people (students and faculty alike) feel that they are insignificant members of a huge bureaucracy. The groups of which you are a part contribute greatly to these positive and negative feelings. Your understanding of the dynamics and meaning of the things that happen in these groups is a key to making your life in school more satisfying.

Think about your school for a moment. Think of the number of groups that you are a part of, the number of different subgroups that you belong to, and think about what it does to you to be a part of these groups. Are there some groups in which you feel significant and valued? Are there others in which you feel frustrated and angry most of the time? When you close the door to your office, do you feel that the young people are expectant and excited about working with you? Or do you feel hostility as you close the door, both from you and from them? When you sit down in the faculty lunchroom, do you always sit with the same group of people? Do they make you feel valued and cared about? Are they people whom you trust? Can you take risks with them? Can you tell them where you "blew it" and still feel okay about yourself?

Now take a step back and look at your school as a whole. Which groups are functioning well? Which are having difficulty? What is it like to be in a faculty meeting in your school? A committee meeting? A curriculum planning meeting? A pupil-personnel staffing? How are these groups functioning? What would you change if you could?

As you become more tuned into group dynamics, you will discover your power to help facilitate better group interaction. Every member of a group affects what is going on, whether he or she knows it or not. If you choose, you can play a conscious part in helping any group you are in to function in a more productive and satisfying way. You may also choose, as often as you like, to stay out of the group process and not try to help it function better. You may decide to protect yourself and avoid the pain of trying to interact. Or perhaps you do not know what would be most helpful. Whatever the reason, you have a choice once you understand what is happening within a group.

AN IDEAL SCHOOL

Knowing that it is an impossible one, let me share with you my dream of an ideal school. This dream has evolved over the course of ten years of consulting in different school districts and seeing some schools that function very well and others where the conflict and constant crises took so much time and energy that there was not much left over for teaching. My ideal school is a place where everyone's goal is to provide an environment in which growth and learning can take place, and where everyone who enters is respected for the contribution that he or she can make toward that goal. It is a school where people feel valued and significant and assume responsibility for helping others feel important. In the same way that I have advocated that school people work with students in cooperative ways, in this ideal school the principal respects the faculty, expects them to participate in the decision-making process, and freely shares with them his mistakes as well as his strengths. There is a mutual agreement that faculty will understand and support the principal's attempts to be a good administrator, in the same way they expect him to work with them regarding their strengths and weaknesses as teachers. If something goes amiss in this school, the parties involved meet together to figure out what went wrong and how they can work together to make it right.

The No-Fault School

This ideal school operates on what I would call a no-fault basis. The vast majority of schools I have visited are fault schools. In a fault school when something goes wrong, the important thing is to find somebody to blame. If there is a problem in the classroom, you try to find someone on whom to pin it. If you cannot find someone to blame, it might mean that there is something wrong with you, that it is your fault. Or perhaps the incident occurred because the principal did not give you enough support, so it is really her fault. This need to find fault, which is prevalent in many schools, is the essence of destructiveness when it comes to working cooperatively to provide a safe learning milieu.

In one high school where I was consulting, an incident occurred in which the fault finding progressed right down the line. A student made a remark that made the teacher extremely angry, and he threw the student out of class. Because he was so angry, the teacher immediately sent a "referral" down to the office requesting disciplinary action for that student. After class, the student came to the teacher, apologized for his behavior, and asked to be readmitted. Because this was a fault system, the teacher was in a bind. If he readmitted the student and withdrew the referral, he would be admitting that he had acted precipitously. Knowing how the vice principal had responded in the past to similar situations, he was afraid that she would judge him harshly. On the other hand, the teacher felt the student was genuinely sorry and deserved another chance. Not knowing what else to do, he let the student return to class and yet, feeling very guilty, allowed the referral to stand. The vice principal felt a responsibility to punish the young man in order to support the teacher, even though she felt the teacher was wrong. When I talked with the vice principal later about the incident and expressed my concern that the young person had been disciplined after the student and the teacher had already resolved the issue, she said, "Well, we have our eye on that teacher, and he may not have his contract renewed at the end of the year, but we have to support him in the meantime, even at the expense of the student."

It seems as if everybody lost and nobody won. Because the school environment did not permit mistakes, everybody got punished and everything that occurred was blamed on someone else. I wonder what might have happened if that same situation had taken place in a different school with a supportive environment? If the teacher had felt valued, he might not have lost control as quickly as he did over the insolence of the student. But if he had lost control and sent the referral prematurely, a supportive school system would have permitted him to go to the vice principal and say, "That student really got to me, but I don't think I want to continue with the referral. I'd like to work it out with him myself." That would have ended that administrative involvement and then he could have sat down with the student and talked about what had made him so angry. Instead of being punished, the student would have had to take responsibility for his own behavior and make plans to change the way he treated the teacher.

There is something about punishment that is positive and negative at the same time. On the one hand, particularly in a junior high school, some children need to have rules to test, to push against. For these situations, providing some form of repercussion may be helpful. On the other hand, punishment lets children "off the hook," and they may feel they do not have to assume responsibility for their behavior as long as they are willing to take the consequences.

I was amused one day when I walked into a junior high school and found a very angry principal walking up and down the hall among fifteen children who were sitting on the floor, writing fifty times each "I will not be tardy again." She had said that for every minute they were late they would have to write that sentence ten times. I found some young people outside plotting together about how many times they were willing to write that statement, so that they could be that many minutes late to school. One girl came in ten minutes late. She had written "I will not be tardy again" a hundred times at home so that she would have an extra ten minutes to finish watching a television show before she came to school. For her it was worth it.

You may think that behaving in this way is childish and irresponsible, and you may be right. But how many of us park in an illegal parking place because we are in a hurry, and it is worth paying the fine to have the convenience? I am not sure, but I think that kind of response to punishment is natural.

The School as a System—The Faculty as a Group

Because the tardiness in the junior high school in the previous example was getting increasingly out of hand, I suggested to the principal that she inform the students that the punishment system was no longer in effect, and they would have to start coming to school on time. I also suggested that she ask each teacher to discuss with his or her class how frustrating it was to teachers when the students straggled in and to ask the students to assume responsibility for seeing that this did not continue to happen. With a great deal of skepticism, the principal agreed to try removing the punishment for students who were late and asked them to see that they came to school on time. Obviously, I would not have included this example if it had not worked so well. Within three days, instead of having fifteen students tardy, there were two or three with some very legitimate excuses, and peer pressure from class members helped these students get to school on time in the future. The fault system of schools, although it is a natural part of many bureaucracies, is not conducive to creating responsibility for behavior.

My ideal no-fault school is one where people share the excitement, planning, and responsibility. Students and faculty are free to make mistakes, and the expectation of the group members is that when someone makes a mistake, others will try to help, rather than sit back and blame. This attitude starts with the administration, and the sharing process of administrators and faculty needs to be two-way. A principal ought to be free to help faculty members who make errors in judgment and at the same time expect the staff to assist him if he gets into difficulty.

There are constructive ways to develop this mutual support system within a faculty group. An outside consultant is very helpful, but not essential. Principals or other administrators or school social workers can implement this process themselves. The no-fault system starts with the assumption that everybody who comes into the school is entitled to have a good day. Then the question is, what are some of the things that can help this come about? One principal asked this question on the first faculty institute day. In small groups the faculty was requested to draw up several sets of goals. One set included broad school goals. Another set of goals was for the faculty—what would make school a good place for them? Another set involved goals for the students—what is it that we want our students to learn? As the administrator helped the faculty outline these goals, she tried to ensure that the four essential qualities for voluntary participation (safety, something for them, something to contribute, and someone caring) were all included, not only that day but in the future goal setting. These are just as important and significant for faculty and administration as for students. After she helped the faculty outline some basic goals and they decided what type of environment they wished the school to provide, they moved toward a plan of implementation by posing several questions:

1. What can we do together to develop these qualities?
2. What role do we want the principal to play?
3. What can each of us do to facilitate the desired outcome?
4. Knowing that it is going to take some time and that there is much that must be undone and begun, where should we start?

As these questions were discussed, the faculty developed a commitment to work toward a no-fault approach—a freedom to make mistakes as long as you learn from them—and a general agreement that faculty, staff, and students can support one another. This required some reworking of the old group norms that had operated in the faculty and had prohibited the openness just discussed.

Many faculties have norms, such as "Always be polite, even if you don't mean it," or "Never show a colleague how you really feel." These norms usually develop in a fault school where much of the complaining and arguing goes on behind people's backs. I can go into a school and in about thirty minutes tell you whether it is a fault or no-fault school. One of my prime diagnostic sources is the faculty lounge. In the faculty lounge I can see whether people are listening to one another, showing mutual concern, offering suggestions to teachers with problems, or whether it is a place where a great deal of nonproductive complaining and griping occurs with nobody offering any suggestions or attempting to make anything better. In the latter situation, if a teacher does something to make another teacher angry, the problem is rarely dealt with openly. The offended teacher usually goes to someone else to complain. How the faculty handles disagreements with one another and with the administration is an important indicator of their ability to function cooperatively as a group.

I am not saying that all faculty members have to like one another, socialize together, or be comrades and confidants. That is neither possible nor desirable. There will always be subgroups of people who like each other better than other people, and who trust each other more than the rest of the faculty; however, it is extremely important that these natural social friendships do not interfere with an overall atmosphere of mutual acceptance in the school.

The Ladder Concept. Once you feel you can make a mistake and still be valued as a teacher, you may want to think about developing the "ladder concept" in your school. The ladder concept gives each person in the school an imaginary ladder that can be used to help colleagues get down if they get stuck "up a tree." I believe that working with human beings is an extremely emotion-laden endeavor and that it is not possible to be a good teacher without sometimes having emotions take over. The times when I temporarily lose control of myself are the times when I would love to have somebody there with a ladder to help me get down out of the tree. That person must be someone who is not caught up in the incident and who cares enough about me to see that I do not get myself further out on the limb than I already am.

A 4th-grade teacher was out of control, temporarily, in his fury at a girl in his class. This girl, Sara, had been irritating, insolent, and difficult to work with from the first day of school. The teacher, Mr. S., had tried everything he could to reach Sara.

Sara not only seemed to be unreachable, but also able to make Mr. S. feel inadequate. Sara's message was, "I'm not responding because you are not a good teacher," and there was a part of Mr. S. that believed this, although the girl was wrong. The last straw came one day when Sara was late from recess, and Mr. S. looked up as she came in and asked her why she was late. Sara's defensive response was, "There was no reason to come to class—nothing interesting ever happens here." The teacher lost control, took Sara out in the hall, and started screaming at her. This strong emotional response was a very honest and natural one under the circumstances. How many teachers could have taken this all year without at some point letting it get to them?

A teacher who had been nearby realized that Mr. S. was temporarily out of control and that he needed a ladder to get down out of his tree before he said or did something he would regret. Because this was a no-fault school, the teacher who was not upset was able to extricate Mr. S. from the situation by going in and saying, "It looks like Sara has really gotten to you. Why don't you let me take her off your hands for a while?" This removed Sara from the wrath of Mr. S. and gave each of them a chance to calm down. The helping teacher, the one with the ladder, walked off with Sara and without having to punish her or bawl her out was able to calmly comment, "You really made Mr. S. furious. Is that what you wanted to do?" She then talked for a few minutes with Sara about what her goal was in relation to that teacher. After their talk, Sara came and sat in her classroom for a while until Mr. S. sent word that he was ready to have the girl return.

This approach differs vastly from one where a teacher, trying to be supportive by not interfering, lets another teacher go on until real damage is done; or a colleague attacks the child in a false need to protect the angry teacher. The ladder concept is possible only when faculty members agree that these outbursts are normal and natural and act as helping agents rather than judges. The ladder concept can also work among students in a classroom. Children can learn to help one another, but the tone must be set within the faculty. The guideline is: the person who is in control is the one responsible for helping make the situation better. As faculty members master this approach, they can educate their students to do the same thing—to carry ladders to help both students and teachers down from "trees" when they begin to do something that could be destructive to themselves or somebody else.

Conflict Management. Even in an ideal school there will, of course, be conflicts. Some of these conflicts occur among subgroups; some of them may be theoretical in nature, others may be much more practical. Some conflict is healthy for a school and a good exchange of ideas and suggestions can be helpful. If conflicts are resolved in a supportive way, or there is consensus (or even agreement not to reach consensus), the school can exist with its conflicts without real difficulty. If, on the other hand, the conflicts are driven underground and acted out rather than talked out, there may be real problems with communication. If one conflict cannot be discussed openly, it is difficult for any conflict to be resolved. But because working in schools is emotionally laden, it is not unusual for a faculty not to want to have to deal with conflict. I talked with a teacher who said, "I just can't stand any more hassles. When two faculty members begin to argue, I want to get up and leave." I can certainly understand how she feels, and yet if a norm develops in that school that it is not acceptable to air differences, then the disagreements will be handled covertly, which will create another problem.

One district in which I consult has two high schools, each of which resolved the same conflict in a different way. The issue was whether or not to have a "smoking room" for students. Faculty differed greatly on the issue of students smoking in school. Some felt that smoking was dangerous and that to allow it was setting a bad example and was extremely destructive for students. Others felt that some young people were going to smoke anyway and rather than drive it into the washrooms, they would like to provide a smoking area on the condition that the students agreed (and kept the agreement) to confine all smoking to that one area. One of the reasons that this was a loaded issue was because there was conflict among the faculty themselves about whether or not they should smoke in school. Some teachers complained, "We can't even go into the teachers' lounge because the smoke is so heavy we have trouble breathing!" Others said, "Smoking is part of life and we ought to accept it."

In one of the two schools an agreement was reached that was satisfactory to everybody—something that everyone could live with—even though there were parts of the agreement that nobody liked. In the other school, a decision was made based on strong opinions that were expressed by a few vocal faculty members. Three-fourths of the faculty did not really agree; they were hesitant to challenge the other faculty, so they gave in rather than fight for their own beliefs. If I am pushed into acquiescing to a rule with which I really disagree, the likelihood that I will enforce it actively is not very great. Even though I know I should, I tend not to. In the school where the faculty really worked together to find a solution with which everybody in the school could live, all of the faculty supported the decision. In the other school, the solution worked only sporadically. Some faculty closed their eyes when they found children smoking, and others became extremely rigid. There was no cooperative enforcement of the policy that had been developed in that school.

Now, exploration of the question of permitting smoking in school or any-where else could easily fill another whole book. The point here is that the way the decision was made and the willingness and ability of the faculty to support it were inalterably intertwined.

THE VALUE OF DIVERSITY

This leads to the whole issue of how a school can accept and use differ-ences among faculty to strengthen the program. One of the things that is excit-ing to me about some faculties is their diversity. I would hate to be in a school where everybody was the same and where norms were developed that said that we should all operate in the same mold. In my ideal school each faculty member would have some strengths and concerns of his or her own that would be known to and respected by other faculty members. Each faculty member would be free to develop his or her program, to utilize strengths, and to fit concerns within the broad overall curriculum and school goals. There would be a minimum of expectations for faculty members to act in the same manner. Of course fundamental school rules and state laws are mandates that all teachers have to enforce, but there are many rules that can differ from class to class. There is no reason why every classroom should have the same rules; in fact, there are contraindications for that structure. Insisting that all teachers follow the same rules inhibits their freedom to teach in ways that are com-fortable to them. Students know when a person is enforcing a rule in which he or she does not believe, and it can create mistrust in some students. On the other hand, students are able to adapt to different rules in different classrooms. They are not only aware of, but also responsive to, contrasting requirements of teachers.

One 7th-grade teacher said, "I know there is nothing wrong with chewing gum, but there is something about seeing all those young people with their mouths going all the time that drives me up a wall. I just can't stand it." Once she felt free enough to have her own particular bias, she was able to say to her students, "It may not make sense to you, but gum chewing is so annoying to me that when I see it I can't teach. I think more about your mouths going than I do about the subject, so in my class you can't chew gum." Of course, the stu-dents' immediate response was, "But Mr. Jones lets us chew gum in his class!" This teacher, fortunately, felt comfortable enough with herself, and Mr. Jones, to say, "Marvelous! I'm delighted that Mr. Jones lets you chew gum in his class. Chew all the gum you want there, but not here." It is this acceptance of your-self and your own expectations and desires in a no-fault school that frees you to set different rules for behavior in your classroom than there are in others. That is perfectly all right. What is not okay is for you to try to get all teachers to outlaw gum chewing because it is offensive to you. That is where schools run into difficulty. There are certain behaviors that some faculty expect from their students but others do not, and faculty members ought to have permission from one another as well as from the administration to formulate with their classes their own rules, based on the needs of the faculty member and desires of the students.

A CHALLENGE

Take a step back now and think about your school. What goes on in the teachers' lounge? What expectations do faculty have of one another and of the principal? What kind of support system exists? Do you have a desire to get away from backbiting and work toward mutual support? Is it possible for disagreements to be aired between the people who disagreed rather than pushed underground? These are all important questions and challenges. Take a look at your faculty as a group. How do you relate to one another, and how does the administration relate to you?

Such an analysis may seem like an overwhelming and insurmountable task. You might begin by asking yourself, "If I could walk into school tomorrow and have one thing different in the way the faculty relates to one another and to the administration, what would it be?" If you could only have one change, where would you start? Now think about whether you can go to school tomorrow and begin to effect that one change.

THE PROBLEM-SOLVING PROCESS: YOUR ALLY

One of the principles of "human education" is that children, teachers, principals, and school social workers are important human beings. Each is unique, special, and very human. Many schools give permission to children to be human, including the right to err. How many schools, however, see the teacher as having the right to make mistakes? One teacher bitterly stated, "I spend all day accepting both the strengths and weaknesses of the children in my class. I teach them, nurture them, value them, and help them learn from their mistakes. When is someone going to care about me? Why can't I make mistakes as the children do? I'm human too!"

Teachers do make mistakes, of course, as do administrators, psychologists, social workers, consultants, and all other people. The very human qualities that cause errors are the same ones that make teachers so responsive to the children. The ability to become involved with the children you serve is a great strength, and yet it leaves you vulnerable to being hurt, to letting your feelings get in the way, to err.

The problem-solving process is not for anyone who is perfect. It was designed to be used by those of us who make more mistakes than we choose to admit. Basically, it is an approach to problem resolution to use when difficulties occur between you and any other person or group of people within the school. The process assumes that most real problems are two-way, that both you and the other party are responsible. This means that you also have the power to use this process to change the way things are, to resolve the problem in some way or another.

Define the Problem

The first step in the problem-solving process is to define the various parts of the problem as you perceive them. What is wrong? What happened? How did it happen? How do you feel about what happened? What did it do to you as a person to have had this experience? You need to try to get in touch not only with the content of the problem and the process of how it happened, but also with your personal response to it. Then you can move beyond that to questions about the other people involved. What do you think happened to them personally? How do they feel?

One teacher kept a whole class after school because they had become "smart alecky" and defiant. Usually she could handle such an occurrence and settle the children down without becoming punitive. But this particular day she was feeling rotten physically, she had had a disagreement with her husband before school, and the material that she had carefully ordered for her lesson plan had not arrived. The combination of all of these aggravations, plus the obnoxious behavior of some of the children in the class, made her feel furious, sorry for herself, frustrated, and helpless. She was certainly entitled to those feelings. Her affective response was very real and relevant to the situation. But she felt bad about the way she had blamed and punished the children and asked me to help her understand what had happened. This incident had brought out a side of her that she did not like very much.

Sometimes keeping children after school can be helpful, but in this instance the teacher perceived it as her attempt to get even because the children had made her feel bad. When I encouraged her to take a look at the problem in its entirety, supporting her feelings both from within and without the classroom as being important, we were then able to move to another question. How could she help the children understand what had happened and regain a nonpunitive attitude in the classroom?

Accept Your Feelings and Fantasies

The second step of the problem-solving process is to accept your feelings and allow yourself to imagine what you would like to do. When the teacher was so angry, for instance, what would she have liked to do? Clearly, in this case, a part of the teacher wanted to get even because the pupils had hurt her feelings. Her desire to get even was perfectly natural. Many teachers, when they have been hurt, have vivid fantasies of methods of retaliation and relish them! Having fantasies is usually harmless yet potentially very helpful—it is what you do that matters.

I would like to digress a moment to talk about the tremendous therapeutic value for people within a school system of permitting themselves to have wild fantasies about ways to cope with disquieting situations. Fantasies do not cost anything, do not hurt, and can help a teacher experience his or her own legitimate feelings. Perhaps the teacher in the prior illustration, had she allowed herself, would have fantasized some wicked way to get even with those demons in her class. One teacher used to enjoy fantasizing hanging pupils from the coat hooks in the closet. She never actually did this, but the fantasy helped her through some rough times with difficult children. Do not be afraid to have negative fantasies as well as positive ones and to allow yourself to experience your feelings.

Stop

Once you know what the problem is, once you know how you feel about it and have allowed yourself a fantasy, stop. Just stop. This is the third step in the problem-solving process. That pause gives you a chance to regain your equilibrium. Then, without giving up the relevance of your feelings, try to move beyond them and think about what it is that you would really like to have happen. What kind of rapport would you like to have with those young people? What kind of a relationship do you really want with your faculty if you are a principal? And in that stopping process, when your feelings are very evident and appreciated (but put aside for a few moments), you can set specific goals for what you would like to have happen next.

A word of caution. The goals you set must be limited enough so that they are attainable if you act in a different way. You cannot take a child who makes you furious when he continues to say how much he hates school and have as your goal to make him love school. This obviously is not realistic. But you may very well be able to take a small piece of that unrealistic goal and say, "Okay, if he hates school and I want him to like it, I'd like to start with finding out if we can have one good experience together in the classroom. Can we have a good day, or a good lesson, any one time that both of us would enjoy to set the tone for other things to come?"

Develop a Plan of Action

After you have set your limited goal, you then need to move to the fourth step, which is to develop a plan of action to attain that goal. Ask yourself, "If my goal is to help this youngster have a positive experience with me and for me to enjoy him, what are some of the things I can do to help that come about?" This is the time when you may want to pick up those feelings that you put aside in the "stop" phase and consider whether there is some way to use those feelings in a way to achieve your goal. Your plan of action should include helping the other people involved understand some of the things they did that upset you and what you can do to improve things together.

You, for example, in your anger and frustration at the boy who hates school might take him aside and share your frustration with him. Without blaming him, you can let him know that you are frustrated and that you know he must be too. Together you can develop a plan to try something new. Is it possible to have a good morning tomorrow? What could each of us do to enjoy our morning? This conversation might lead to some partialized, workable goals, agreeable to both student and teacher. The teacher who is so angry with his class that he becomes punitive may be able to use his anger in a helpful way. He might tell the class how angry he is, not blaming them, but as a way to get them involved. He can then ask them how they feel. What would they like to be different? After this mutual sharing of feelings, the students and teacher can put together what each of them can do to change the situation, or be ready for it if it begins to happen again.

Develop a Built-In Contingency Plan

The fifth step in the problem-solving process is what I call the "escape hatch." Suppose you get in touch with your feelings, you stop, you set a goal, you make a plan of action, and it falls flat. That is always a risk, so your next step is to ask, prior to putting your plan of action to work, "What if . . .?" What if the plan does not work? What if the child does not respond? What if I cannot control my feelings? In this way you build in a contingency plan, which you can hold in reserve for use as necessary (as you would take a spare tire on an auto trip in case you need it).

Even if your plan of action does not work out the way you had originally intended, this contingency plan is a means by which most of your problem solving can be in some way successful. You will find as you begin to use this model that, in most instances, some of its methods work and some do not, and your contingency plan may help you cope with any negative outcomes.

Postpone Action

This problem-solving model works best when you are aware enough of your own feelings that you can creatively and spontaneously go through the process, which may take anywhere from thirty seconds to thirty minutes. There will be times, however, when your feelings are too intense, when you have been hurt too deeply, when you care too much to use this framework at the time. You may be too angry to care what the child thinks at that moment. You may be too hurt by another teacher to be able to understand how she feels. These are the times when the process needs to be put aside for a while. At these moments, the best and most helpful thing you can do is to acknowledge to yourself and to the people you are working with that you feel too intensely to make a decision right now about anything. That temporary inability to act is okay. In fact, when you feel that intensely, it is best not to act until things are in better perspective for you.

One faculty member, who had been called filthy names by a group of angry students, felt she had to act. She had tried very hard to reach these young people, and their abusive language hurt and upset her so much that she knew that to talk with them at that point would not be helpful to her or to the students. Instead, she said, "Kids, right now my feelings are so strong that I can't talk to you without saying some things I might be sorry I said. You've hurt me deeply, and we need to take a look at this and see what we're going to do about it. But I can't do it now. Come back after school, all four of you, and let's all sit down and see if we can figure out together what happened and how we can keep this from happening again. I don't like being hurt and I don't think you do either."

Not even that amount of objectivity showed a great deal of ability on the part of the teacher to share her feelings in a helpful way. Many of us cannot even say that much. We may just have to say, "Go away right now, I can't talk to you. Come back after school." Or, "I'll talk to you tomorrow." There are many ways a teacher or principal can create "cooling off time." Sometimes it helps to ask the group of young people to write down what they think happened, using the time that they are writing as space to recoup, to get in touch with your feelings, and to get back into the problem-solving process.

Evaluate the Process

It is an impossible task to understand all of the things that go on in groups and also keep in touch with your own feelings and desires to be able to always use yourself in a helping way. Indeed, if you must succeed to feel good about your interventions, if they must work out the way you planned, then you may be frequently disappointed. In my own work in the schools with faculty and administrators, I have discovered that for this problem-solving approach to work, I have to change the way I evaluate myself. I used to evaluate my decisions and actions based on how successful I was at getting the outcome I desired. If noise was a problem in my class, I evaluated my success as a teacher by how quiet I was able to get the children to be. I do not do that anymore. Now I evaluate myself, not by the specific outcome, but by how much I am able to help the students in my class and myself find some common goal that all of us can support. This plan may not be the same as one I might develop on my own, but it is usually more successful because it was created by all of us together. I must, then, change my usual investment from the end result to the process by which the result takes place.

There are times, of course, when the end result becomes crucial and the process much less important. These are times when safety is involved, when prompt obedience and response are needed, or when the outcome is particularly important to the teacher or principal. If you are primarily a process person who lets your staff, students, or therapeutic group participate in the problem-solving process, the times that you have to say, "This is what it must be, you must follow me now," the group members will usually do so because they know you would not ask if it was not important. Because in the past they have not needed to act out against your authority, they probably will not need to now.

A further dimension involves how I evaluate myself overall in my role in school. As always, my prime measure is what people learn in an objective sense. But in other ways, I find I have to evaluate myself differently than I used to. I no longer can judge myself as a teacher by how perfect I am and how few mistakes I make. Instead, I evaluate myself based on how responsive I was to the class or to the staff. How well was I able to hear their point of view? How able was I to facilitate the respect for each other's rights, both theirs and mine? If I got into a power struggle, how quickly was I able to perceive that I was in a conflict with a student or students or other staff? How able was I to accept my piece of the power struggle? How willing was I to be flexible so that it could be resolved? All of these questions are relevant to successful use of the problem-solving process in your work within a school system.

The roles of the school social worker, the teacher, the principal, the school secretary, the janitor, and the librarian are all different, but they all work together for and through one another to make the education process work, each contributing in his or her own unique way. When they do act, it is no longer a single role, but a cooperative effort whose success or failure will not be dependent so much on the talents of every person, but on their ability to interact and to work with each other. This is the quality about schools that is most often missed and, when missed, can lead to the breakdown of parts of, or all of, the process. The holistic perspective of the social worker can often make a more positive interaction possible and develop a living environment that can allow what each person has to offer to be nurtured and supported.

35

*Social Skills Training in School Settings: Some Practical Considerations**

Craig Winston LeCroy
Arizona State University

- ◆ The Development of Social Skills Programs in the Schools
- ◆ Group Format and the Social Skills Training Method
- ◆ Guidelines for Practitioners
- ◆ Social Skills Training Illustrated
- ◆ Classroom Social Skills Approaches

School is the major socializing institution for children. In school, children develop social behavior as well as learn academic skills. Although schools focus on children's educational and cognitive skills and capabilities, they recognize an important but neglected area of concern—the healthy social development of children. The National Mental Health Association Commission on the Prevention of Mental-Emotional Disabilities recommended, "programs should be developed in schools (preschool through high school) that incorporate validated mental health strategies and competence building as an integral part of the curriculum" (as cited in Long, 1986, p. 828). In general, the public supports a broader educational agenda that includes enhancing children's social and emotional competence (Rose & Gallup, 2000).

In addition to academics, schools should promote children's healthy social development. Without proper social skills, children face numerous negative consequences later in life. In fact, there are well-researched links between poor

---

*Lisa Wooton was a co-author of a similar chapter in the previous edition.

social skills in childhood and difficulties in later life such as psychiatric disorders, externalizing problems, and internalizing problems. Self-regulation skills (e.g., being able to communicate thoughts and needs, being sensitive to others, and following instructions) are critical to school readiness (Blair, 2002). Teachers most often cite the self-regulation of pupils as more important than academic skills because it is easier to help a child catch up academically when he or she has the expected and needed self-regulation capabilities.

In general, research has supported the efficacy of social skills training; it is perhaps the most promising new treatment model developed for working with children and adolescents. Offering social skills programs in schools can facilitate the socialization and academic education of children. Lela Costin (1969) argued more than thirty years ago that social workers should apply group work methods more broadly in school settings. Social skills groups can equip children with prosocial skills to help them replace aggressive or withdrawn behaviors with appropriate coping strategies. For example, interpersonal skills can be taught to enhance communication with peers, parents, and authority figures. Self-regulation skills can be taught to enhance classroom processes such as taking turns and following instructions. Numerous opportunities exist for the implementation of various skill-based programs that can help facilitate the successful socialization of children and adolescents in our schools. School social workers can play an important role in the design and implementation of social skill programs that: (1) enhance children's ability to learn and interact successfully with others, and (2) enable teachers to focus on and better accomplish educational goals.

THE DEVELOPMENT OF SOCIAL SKILLS PROGRAMS IN THE SCHOOLS

Clinical observation and research have found a relationship between poor peer relationships and later psychological difficulties (Hartup & Abecassis, 2002). In fact, disturbances in peer relationships are among the best predictors of psychiatric, social, and school problems. Research strongly suggests that social competence is essential for healthy normal development. Child developmentalists stress that it is through a child's interactions with peers that many of life's necessary behaviors are acquired. For example, children learn sexual socialization, control of aggression, expression of emotion, and caring both from their families and through interaction with peers. When children fail to acquire such social skills, they are beset by problems such as inappropriate expression of anger, friendship difficulties, and an inability to resist peer pressure. It is this understanding that has led to the present focus on changing children's interpersonal behavior with peers. Because many problem behaviors of young people develop in a social context, the teaching of social skills in the classroom, or in small-group sessions outside of the school, is one of the most promising approaches in remediating children's social difficulties.

Defining and Conceptualizing Social Skills

Social skills can be defined as a complex set of skills that facilitate successful interactions between peers, parents, teachers, and other adults. *Social* refers to interactions between people; *skills* refers to making appropriate discriminations—deciding what would be the most effective response and using the verbal and nonverbal behaviors that facilitate interaction. The conceptualization of social skills as training suggests that problem behaviors can be viewed as remediable deficits in a child's response repertoire (King & Kirschenbaum, 1992; LeCroy, 2002). This perspective focuses on building prosocial responses as opposed to eliminating excessive antisocial responses. Children learn new options in coping with problem situations. Learning how to respond effectively to new situations produces more positive consequences than using behaviors that may have been used in similar situations in the past. This model focuses on the teaching of skills and competencies for day-to-day living rather than on understanding and eliminating defects. This model is an optimistic view of children and is implemented in an educative-remedial framework.

A classic social skills training study by Oden and Asher (1977) sought to improve the social skills and peer relationships of third- and fourth-grade children who were identified as not well liked by their peers. The social skills program taught the following four skills: participation, cooperation, communication, and validation/support. The intervention consisted of a five-week program whereby each skill was (1) described verbally, (2) explained with examples, (3) practiced using behavior rehearsal, and (4) refined through feedback, coaching, and review of progress. This study found that the children increased their social skills and that they had improved significantly more than a group of elementary schoolchildren who did not participate in the program. Particularly impressive was the finding at one-year follow-up that the children showed gains in how their classmates rated them on play and peer acceptance.

GROUP FORMAT AND THE SOCIAL SKILLS TRAINING METHOD

Social skills training is usually conducted in a group format. The group format provides support and a reinforcing context for learning new responses and appropriate behaviors in a variety of social situations. The group is a natural context for social skills training because of the peer interactions that take place as the group members work together. In addition, the group allows for extensive use of modeling and feedback, and these are critical components of successful skills training. However, it is important to note that not all children do well in group settings, and on some occasions certain children experience negative effects from working in groups. In these situations, social skills are best taught on a one-to-one basis.

Practical Considerations in Conducting Social Skills Groups

Group Composition. Conducting group prevention and intervention services is an efficient use of a school social worker's time, because several students can be seen at one time. However, groups must be recruited and constructed with certain key factors in mind. First, recruitment for social skills training groups will depend on the goals of the particular program. It may be necessary to limit the number of participants involved, in which case procedures must be used to help identify students most likely to benefit from the program. This screening process can be accomplished by administering assessment devices, identifying students who meet specified risk criteria, conducting pregroup interviews, or designing a referral system for teachers and other professionals to use to refer children directly to the group. On the other hand, limiting groups only to children who meet certain risk criteria may not be best in some groups. Often including participants who do not have social skills difficulties but are highly socially competent can have positive implications. Because some groups will contain children who act out antisocially, a higher degree of poor social skill modeling could initially take place. By including high functioning children in an antisocial group, the opportunity for prosocial modeling increases. Moreover, it may be less difficult to maintain order (Merrell & Gimpel, 1998). In addition, because the social skills group affects parental roles, a collaborative relationship and permission for entry into the group needs to be developed with the parents.

Finally, group composition will be influenced by factors such as how well the group participants know one another, how heterogeneous the group is, how large the group is, the age and developmental level of the participants, and their gender. LeCroy (1994) noted that too much intergroup familiarity can lead to problems with control; a preponderance of good friends in a single group may be counterproductive. Another important consideration in constructing groups is group size and ratio of group leaders to participants. For this to happen it is important that all members of a group have the time and attention they need to practice skills and receive important feedback; social skills groups should have between six and ten members; and there should be a low leader-to-participant ratio. Two group leaders are recommended, especially if the group has as many as ten participants. Merrell and Gimpel (1998) proposed the members in the group should not vary in age by more than two or three years, and depending on the developmental level of the group, the level of structure and language used may need to be altered. It is not difficult to recognize the need for language and interventions to be age and developmentally appropriate. Presenting social skills that require a high level of cognitive ability will not be effective for group members who are either too young or who are functioning at a lower developmental level than the skill requires. For certain purposes, mixed-gender groups may provide a realistic context for interaction and increase the possibilities of generalization of particular skills.

Developing Program Goals. The first step in the development of a successful social skills training program is to identify the goals of the program based on the needs and strengths of the target population. A program goal, for example, might be for withdrawn children to be able to initiate positive social interactions. Once the goals of the program are clearly defined, the next step is to select the specific skills that are to be taught. Then you may help the group get ready for the skills by discussing with them the details of the skills as well as when, where, and why this skill could or should be used.

Selecting Skills. Research has been helpful in identifying skills by studying behaviors that contribute to healthy social functioning in children and adolescents. Depending on the type of problem to be addressed, a number of different skills may be appropriate. Skills for withdrawn and isolated children include greeting others, joining in ongoing activities, managing a conversation, and sharing/cooperation around things (e.g., toys) and ideas (King & Kirschenbaum, 1992; Weiss & Harris, 2001).

As a specific example, Barth (1996) elaborated assertiveness skills needed for preventing teen pregnancy, including problem solving and refusing unacceptable demands. The basic principles are: (1) to break the preferred behavior down into a number of skills and (2) assist the group in practicing them, while (3) the members support each other's efforts. Skills for children with disabilities include classroom skills, coping skills, and skills that enable children to get along with others and make friends (Cartledge & Milburn, 1995).

It is important to remember each member's developmental level of communication, motor skills, and cognition. This is especially important when working with children who have disabilities (Nevil, Beatty, & Moxley, 1997; Weiss & Harris, 2001).

Refining Selected Skills. The process of social skills training requires continual attention to refining each skill that is to be taught. After identifying the broad social skills, it is important to divide each broad skill into its component parts so that they can be more easily learned. For example, LeCroy (1994) breaks down the skill "beginning a conversation" into six component parts (see also Cartledge & Milburn, 1995; Elias & Tobias, 1996):

1. Look the person in the eye and demonstrate appropriate body language.
2. Greet the person, saying one's own name.
3. Ask an open-ended question about the person. Listen attentively for the response.
4. Make a statement to follow up on the person's response.
5. Ask another open-ended question about the person. Listen attentively to the response.
6. Make another statement about the conversation.

Depending on the program, the same basic skill, such as starting a conversation, may be broken down differently. The important thing to remember is that social skills are more complex than they appear on the surface. Elias and Tobias (1996) break down "engaging in conversation" into the following subskills:

1. Deciding whom to talk to;
2. Thinking of something to say or a topic to talk about;
3. Approaching the chosen person in a nonthreatening manner and at an appropriate time;
4. Staying at a comfortable distance and making appropriate eye contact;
5. Active listening;
6. Taking turns and timing your comments;
7. Keeping the conversation going;
8. Asking relevant questions;
9. Assessing the other person's interest in what you are saying;
10. Modifying your statements relative to the other person's responses;
11. Ending the conversation;
12. Assessing whether you want to talk to that person again;
13. Planning future contact.

Major Skill Areas for Healthy Development

There are five major social skill areas that children and adolescents need for healthy development (Merrell & Gimpel, 1998). The following is a list of major skill areas and the most important skills within those areas. Each specific skill can be further broken down into subskills:

Peer Relationship Skills

1. Compliments, praises, or applauds peers;
2. Offers help or assistance to peers when needed;
3. Invites peers to play or interact;
4. Participates in discussions; talks with peers for extended periods;
5. Stands up for rights of peers; defends a peer in trouble;
6. Is sought out by peers to join activities; everyone likes to be with him or her;
7. Has skills or abilities admired by peers; participates skillfully with peers;
8. Skillfully initiates or joins conversations with peers;
9. Is sensitive to feelings of peers;
10. Has good leadership skills; assumes leadership role in peer activities;
11. Makes friends easily; has many friends;
12. Has sense of humor; shares laughter with peers.

Self-Management Skills

1. Remains calm when problems arise; controls temper when angry;
2. Follows rules; accepts imposed limits;

3. Compromises with others when appropriate; compromises in conflicts;
4. Receives criticism well; accepts criticism from others;
5. Responds to teasing by ignoring peers; responds appropriately to teasing;
6. Cooperates with others in a variety of situations.

Academic Skills

1. Accomplishes tasks or assignments independently; display independent study skills;
2. Completes individual seatwork and assigned tasks;
3. Listens to and carries out teacher directions;
4. Produces work of acceptable quality for ability level; works up to potential;
5. Uses free time appropriately;
6. Is personally well organized;
7. Appropriately asks for assistance as needed; asks questions;
8. Ignores peer distractions while working; functions well despite distractions.

Compliance Skills

1. Follows instructions and directions;
2. Follows rules;
3. Appropriately uses free time;
4. Shares toys, materials, and belongings;
5. Responds appropriately to constructive criticism or when corrected;
6. Finishes assignments, completes tasks;
7. Puts toys, work, or property away.

Assertion Skills

1. Initiates conversations with others;
2. Acknowledges compliments;
3. Invites peers to play; invites others;
4. Says and does nice things for self; is self-confident;
5. Makes friends;
6. Questions unfair rules;
7. Introduces self to new people;
8. Appears confident with opposite sex;
9. Expresses feelings when wronged;
10. Appropriately joins ongoing activity/group.

Constructing Realistic Social Situations

It is important to construct realistic social situations that demand the use of social skills being taught, and that the social situations and skills be determined empirically. Okamoto, LeCroy, Dustman, Hohmann-Marriott, and Kulis, (2004) constructed problematic or difficult situations that American Indian youth encounter involving drug and alcohol. The process involved conducting a series of focus groups and recording the typical kinds of situations that American Indian youth typically face when confronted with situations that involve substance use. These "difficult" situations were then put into a survey and American Indian youth were asked to rate each situation in terms of frequency and difficulty. At the end of this process there is a list of common and difficult situations with "social" validity (in this case cultural validity) that can be used for skills training. For example, in this study we found that many of the difficult situations for American Indian youth revolved around family interactions and social gatherings. When conducting substance abuse prevention groups with this population, we include these exact situations and help young people learn appropriate skills for handling these situations.

Similarly, MacNeil, and LeCroy (1997) constructed problematic situations that youth with emotional disturbances in residential settings were likely to encounter, elicited responses to these situations, and then had the responses rated for effectiveness. This gives a clear indication of the types of situations that are problematic for such youth and the responses considered appropriate in those situations. However, due to the uniqueness of each interpersonal interaction, most practitioners must develop their own problematic situations or elicit them from the group during social skills training. For example, a substance abuse prevention program could address the following problem situation:

> You ride to a party with someone you've been dating for about six months. The party is at someone's house; their parents are gone for the weekend. There is a lot of beer and dope, and your date has had too much to drink. Your date says, "Hey, where's my keys—let's get going."

This situation ends with a stimulus for applying the skills of resisting peer pressure. An effective response to this situation would include the steps involved in resisting peer pressure: name the trouble, say *no* quickly, suggest alternatives, and leave the situation.

An example that could be modeled to teach responses to verbally provoking statements could include the following social situation:

> You are a new student at school. Your parents bought you some new clothes and shoes for your first day at your new school. Your shoes do not look like the shoes most of the other children are wearing. On the playground one of the students, Ron, begins teasing you about your "funny-looking" shoes. (Cartledge & Milburn, 1995)

Possible responses to this situation could be verbalizing that Ron is intentionally trying to provoke you, that Ron will likely continue to tease you if you respond at all, or that pretending Ron's statements are not provoking may encourage Ron to stop teasing you.

Social skills programs must be sensitive to racial and ethnic considerations. Cultural differences are often also differences in communication. Practitioners must be aware of differing familial and cultural goals when determining social skills goals. Due to the diversity of cultures in the United States, deciding on one specific set of U.S. values or other such standards is virtually impossible. Thus, the goals that are targeted in social skills groups must be culturally sensitive and depend on the major cultural values of the participants in the program (Meyer, Park, Grenot-Scheyer, Schwartz, & Harry, 1998). The selection of social skills must be tailored to become an effective social interaction in a variety of cultures. If we remain sensitive to these issues, social skills training can help promote successful interactions in a variety of circumstances. A standardized social skills program, for example, may not work for a Native American child living on a reservation or a Mexican American child who speaks Spanish. In such families, the value of interdependence instead of independence is pertinent. It is possible that the goal of a social skills program for high school students in special education classes would be to foster a child's ability to live as an independent member of society. However, it is also possible those students come from a culture that does not value independence from the family.

GUIDELINES FOR PRACTITIONERS

After program goals are defined and skills are selected, there is a sequential process for teaching social skills. The following seven basic steps delineate the process that leaders can follow (based on LeCroy, 1994; see also Merrell & Gimpel, 1998). These guidelines were developed for social skills groups with middle school and high school students. Social skills groups with younger children would use modified guidelines (see King & Kirschenbaum, 1992). Table 35.1 presents these steps and outlines the process for teaching social skills. In each step there is a request for group member involvement because it is critical that group leaders involve the participants actively in the skill training. In addition, such requests keep the group interesting and fun for the group members.

1. *Present the social skill being taught.* The first step for the group leader is to present the skill. The leader solicits an explanation of the skill, for example, "Can anyone tell me what it means to resist peer pressure?" After group members have answered this question, the leader emphasizes the rationale for using the skill. For example, "You would use this skill when you're in a situation where you don't want to do something that your friends want you to do; you should be able to say *no* in a way that helps your friends to be able to accept your refusal." The leader then requests that group members voice additional reasons for learning the skill.

2. *Discuss the social skill.* The leader presents the specific skill steps that constitute the social skill. For example, the skill steps for resisting peer pressure are good nonverbal communication (including eye contact, posture, and voice

TABLE 35.1 Steps in Teaching Social Skills Training

1. Present the social skill being taught.
   A. Solicit an explanation of the skill.
   B. Get group members to provide rationales for the skill.
2. Discuss the social skill.
   A. List the skill steps.
   B. Get group members to give examples of using the skill.
3. Present a problem situation and model the skill.
   A. Evaluate the performance.
   B. Get group members to discuss the model.
4. Set the stage for role playing the skill.
   A. Select the group members for role playing.
   B. Get group members to observe the role play.
5. Have group members rehearse the skill.
   A. Provide coaching if necessary.
   B. Get group members to provide feedback on verbal and nonverbal elements.
6. Practice using complex skill situations.
   A. Teach accessory skills, for example, problem solving.
   B. Get group members to discuss situations and provide feedback.
7. Train for generalization and maintenance.
   A. Encourage practice of skills outside the group.
   B. Get group members to bring in their problem situations.

volume), saying *no* early in the interaction, suggesting an alternative activity, and leaving the situation if there is continued pressure. Leaders then ask group members to state examples of times they used the skill, or examples of times they could have used the skill but chose not to.

3. *Present a problem situation and model the skill.* The leader presents a problem situation. For example, the following is a problem situation for resisting peer pressure.

> After seeing a movie, your friends suggest that you go with them to the mall. It's 10:45 and you are supposed to be home by 11:00. It's important that you get home by 11:00 or you won't be able to go out next weekend.

The group leader chooses members to role play this situation and then models the skills. Group members evaluate the model's performance. Did the model follow all the skill steps? Was his or her performance successful? The group leader may choose another group member to model if the leader believes he or she already has the requisite skills. Another alternative is to present videotaped models to the group. This has the advantage of following the recommendation by researchers that the models be similar to trainees in age, sex, and social characteristics.

4. *Set the stage for role playing the skill.* For this step the group leader needs to construct the social circumstances for the role play. Leaders select

group members for the role play and give them their parts. The leader reviews with the role players how to act out their roles. Group members not in the role play observe the process. It is sometimes helpful if group members not in the role play are given specific instructions for their observations. For example, one member may observe the use of nonverbal skills; another member may be instructed to observe when *no* is said in the interaction.

5. *Have group members rehearse the skill.* Rehearsal or guided practice of the skill is an important part of effective social skills training. Group leaders and group members provide instructions or coaching before and during the role play and provide praise and feedback for improvement. Following a role-play rehearsal the leader will usually give instructions for improvement, model the suggested improvements, or coach the person to incorporate the feedback in the subsequent role play. Often the group member doing the role play will practice the skills in the situation several times to refine the skills and incorporate feedback offered by the group. The role plays continue until the trainee's behavior becomes more and more similar to that of the model. It is important that "overlearning" take place, so the group leader should encourage many examples of effective skill demonstration followed by praise. Group members should be taught how to give effective feedback before the rehearsals. Throughout the teaching process the group leader can model desired responses. For example, after a role play the leader can respond first and model feedback that starts with a positive statement.

6. *Practice using complex skill situations.* The next-to-last phase deals with more difficult and complex skill situations. Complex situations can be developed by extending the interactions and roles in the problem situations. Another possible and relevant way to construct complex social situations is to ask group members to describe a situation in their own lives or in the lives of their friends that relates to the skill the group is working on. Most social skills groups also incorporate the teaching of problem-solving abilities. Problem solving is a general approach to helping young people gather information about a problematic situation, generate a large number of potential solutions, evaluate the consequences of various solutions, and outline plans for the implementation of a particular solution. Group leaders can identify appropriate problem situations and lead members through the seven steps. Problem-solving training is important because it prepares young people to make adjustments as needed in particular situations. It is a general skill with large-scale application (for a more complete discussion on the use of problem-solving approaches, see Elias & Clabby, 1992; Rose, 1998).

7. *Train for generalization and maintenance.* The success of the social skills program depends on the extent to which the skills young people learn transfer to their day-to-day lives. Practitioners must always be planning for ways to maximize the generalization of skills learned and promote their continued use after training. There are several principles that help facilitate the generalization and maintenance of skills. The first is the use of overlearning. The more overlearning that takes place, the greater likelihood of later transfer of skills.

Therefore, it is important that group leaders insist on mastery of the skills. Another important principle of generalization is to vary the stimuli as skills are learned. To accomplish this, practitioners can use a variety of models, problem situations, role-play actors, and trainers. The different styles and behaviors of the people used produce a broader context in which to apply the skills learned. Perhaps most important is to require that young people use the skills in their real-life settings. Group leaders should assign and monitor homework to encourage transfer of learning. This may include the use of written contracts to do certain tasks outside of the group. Group members should be asked to bring to the group examples of problem situations where the social skills can be applied. Last, practitioners should attempt to develop external support for the skills learned. One approach to this is to set up a buddy system whereby group members work together to perform the skills learned outside the group (for examples see Rose, 1998).

SOCIAL SKILLS TRAINING ILLUSTRATED

This methodology may be applied to a whole range of problem areas. Social skills training is being applied to many different child and adolescent populations, including delinquents, children with behavior disorders, and children with developmental delays, and it is used extensively in prevention programs. As such, skills are reinforced for children in the general school population. Table 35.2 illustrates some common focus areas for social skills training in the schools, along with general skills to be developed and resources for more specific information about these focus areas.

Although the examples in table 35.2 examine particular aspects of social skills training interventions, many practitioners use multiproblem social skills training in groups with children experiencing a variety of problems. For example, groups could include children with such problems as acting-out behavior, withdrawn behavior, fear, and so forth.

In groups designed for prevention purposes, the goal is to promote positive prosocial alternative behaviors (LeCroy, 1994; 2001; LeCroy & Rose, 1986). Such programs may be tailored to meet the needs of specific populations. Although social skills training will likely be the major component of the treatment, other treatment procedures also can be used; for example, a social skills training program may be enhanced by the addition of a psychoeducational component. A specific example of the development of one such prevention program follows.

A Prevention Program for Early Adolescent Girls

A social skills training psychoeducational prevention program called *Go Grrrls* (LeCroy & Daley, 2001) was developed specifically for early adolescent

TABLE 35.2   Problem Behaviors and Related Social Skills Training

Type of Program and Resources	*Social Skills Focus*
Aggressive behavior Bierman & Greenberg, 1996 Frindler & Guttman, 1994 Olweus, 1996 Larson, Lochman, & Lochman, 2001 Waterman & Walker, 2001	*Skills to work on* 1. Recognizing interactions likely to lead to problems; 2. Learning responses to negative communications; 3. Learning to request a behavior change.
Depression Clarke, Lewinsohn, &, Hops, 2001 Mufson, Moreau, Weissman, & Klerman, 1993	*Skills to work on* 1. Conversation skills; 2. Planning social activities; 3. Making friends; 4. Increasing pleasant activities; 5. Reducing negative cognitions.
Anxiety or withdrawn, isolated behavior Gottman, 1983 Hops, Walker, & Greenwood, 1979 Kearney & Albano, 2000 Kendall, Choudhury, Hudson, & Webb, 2002 Dowd & Tierney, 1992 Weiss & Harris, 2001	*Skills to work on* 1. Greeting others; 2. Joining in ongoing activities; 3. Starting a conversation; 4. Sharing things and ideas.
Substance abuse prevention Botvin, 1996 Hohman & Buchik, 1994 Henggeler, Clingempeel, Brondino, & Pickrel, 2002	*Skills to work on* 1. Identifying problem situations; 2. Learning effective refusal skills; 3. Making friends with non-using peers; 4. Learning general problem-solving techniques.
Teen pregnancy prevention Barth, 1996 Jermmott & Jermmott, 1992 Wang et al., 2000	*Skills to work on* 1. Identifying risky situations; 2. Refusing unreasonable demands; 3. Learning new interpersonal responses; 4. Learning problem-solving techniques.
Peer mediation for interpersonal conflict Begun, 1995 Schrumpf, Crawford, & Usadel, 1991	*Skills to work on* 1. Learning communication skills; 2. Focusing on common interests; 3. Creating options; 4. Writing an agreement.
Children with cognitive and other disabilities Sargent, 1991 Walker, Todis, Holmes, & Horton, 1988 Weiss & Harris, 2001	*Skills to work on* 1. Gaining teacher attention; 2. Following classroom rules; 3. Being organized; 4. Drinking from the water fountain appropriately (and other skills appropriate for this population).

girls. Program goals were identified through empirical investigation of problems common to this population and through direct interaction with middle-school girls. In response to these identified problems, a group of "core" social skills— for example, assertiveness skills and basic conversational skills—is presented and taught during the first half of a twelve-session program. Participants are then asked to build on core skills by applying them to more specific situations, such as substance abuse refusal, during the latter half of the program.

Identifying a Problem Area and Selecting Appropriate Skills. Consider the following information:

♦ A national survey by the American Association of University Women revealed that both boys and girls believed that teachers encourage more assertive behavior in boys and that, overall, boys received the majority of their teachers' attention (Orenstein, 1994).

♦ Girls are beginning to experiment with alcohol, tobacco, and other drugs at earlier ages than ever before, and teen pregnancy rates in the United States are among the highest of the Western industrialized countries (Resnick et al., 1997).

♦ At all grade levels, girls have lower self-esteem than boys, and this difference increases by 30 percent from sixth to seventh grade. Girls who make the transition from grade schools to middle schools show the most severe drops in self-esteem (Simmons & Blyth, 1987).

One potential conceptualization of this "cluster" of information would be that girls could resist these problems better if they were equipped with the social skills to augment their assertiveness and ability to form new friendships during the middle school transition period. Thus, two important program goals for the *Go Grrrls* program are to equip girls with assertiveness skills, and with the skills necessary to build healthy peer relationships.

Building a Solid Foundation of Skills. We have already discussed the importance of overlearning in social skills training. The *Go Grrrls* program is designed to increase the odds of participants' overlearning by selecting key skills girls need to learn and building participants' confidence and mastery of these skills over several sessions. For the focus area of *assertiveness*, the *Go Grrrls* program provides three sessions that help girls to learn this skill. In one of the early group meetings, girls are introduced to the general concept of assertiveness and are given practice using this skill. In two later sessions, girls are given additional practice using assertiveness skills in the context of refusing substances and unwanted sexual advances. As the program progresses, girls are able to combine several of the core social skills they learned in early sessions to help them deal with more specific problem areas in the later curriculum. For example, by the time participants reach the curriculum section dealing with substance abuse, they have already completed sessions on the core social skills of assertiveness and starting conversations. They can draw from both of these areas in learning to effectively deal with peer pressure to use drugs. Table 35.3 illustrates how social skills may be combined in a complementary fashion to

TABLE 35.3   *Go Grrrls* Skill Building

Go Grrrls Program Goal	Related Social Skills Training
Core skill: Assertiveness Goal: To teach girls to act assertively rather than passively or aggressively. Rationale: Teaching basic assertiveness skills to girls will help them speak up in classrooms and withstand peer pressure and will serve as a foundation for learning more specific refusal skills.	1. Discuss the skill of assertiveness. 2. Group leaders demonstrate assertive, passive, and aggressive responses to sample situations. 3. Group members practice identifying assertive behavior. 4. Group members practice assertiveness skills. 5. Group leaders and other members provide feedback. Sample scenario: You are in science class, and the boy you are partners with tells you that he wants to mix the chemicals and you can be the secretary. What do you do?
Core skill: Making and keeping friends Goal: To equip girls with the tools they need to establish and maintain healthy peer relationships. Rationale: Disturbances in peer relationships are among the best predictors of psychiatric, social, and school problems. Teaching friendship skills can reduce these problems.	1. Discuss the components of a successful conversation, including the beginning, middle, and end. 2. Group leaders demonstrate both ineffective and effective conversational skills. 3. Group members practice identifying effective conversational skills such as making eye contact and asking questions of the other person. 4. Group members practice conversation skills in role-play situations. 5. Group leaders and other members provide feedback. Sample scenario: It is your first day of junior high and you don't know anyone in your homeroom. Start a conversation with the girl who sits next to you.
Specific skill: Avoiding substance abuse Goal: To teach girls coping strategies and skills they may use to avoid using alcohol, tobacco, and other drugs. Rationale: More girls are using drugs, and at earlier ages, than ever before. Early drug use may place girls at risk for serious health and psychological problems.	1. Discuss the reasons why some girls use drugs. (Reasons may include: They don't know how to say no, they don't have friends and get lonely, etc.) 2. Discuss reasons why some girls don't use drugs. 3. Group members practice refusing drugs in role-play situations. They build on the core skill of assertiveness learned earlier. 4. Group members list coping strategies they can use instead of turning to drugs. They build on the core skill of starting conversations, by recognizing that they can build healthy friendships with non-using friends to help them stay drug free.

help participants build strengths. Research studies (LeCroy, 2004) have found this program produced significant outcomes in comparison to a control group of participants who did not receive the program.

CLASSROOM SOCIAL SKILLS APPROACHES

Although few evidence-based interventions have been developed specifically for teaching social skills in the classroom, such efforts are gaining greater appeal in order to target a large number of students that could benefit from such interventions (see Webster-Stratton & Taylor, 2001, for an exception). Practitioners can take many of the same methods as used in teaching child management skills to parents and apply them in classroom settings with teachers. Studies have found that modifying teacher-child interactions can have an impact on child engagement and behavior (Howes, 2000). Such classroom-based interventions are more typically established with younger children. Teachers are taught skills in promoting positive social behavior using attention, praise, and encouragement (Webster-Stratton & Taylor, 2001).

Additionally, teachers can be taught the specific skills of helping improve students' self-regulation. Research is documenting that self-regulation and its component parts (working memory, executive attention, and emotional regulation) can be harnessed to improve children's mental health and social functioning (Buckner, Mezzacappa, & Beardslee, 2003). This may be accomplished by guiding students in tasks that require higher order cognitive skills to successfully negotiate or using situations that heighten negative emotional arousal and require higher order reasoning and executive function skills to successfully resolve. Many researchers believe promoting self-regulation offers advanced benefits for students. The National Research Council's (2000, p. 3) report, *From Neurons to Neighborhoods: The Science of Early Childhood Development*, states that "the growth of self-regulation is a cornerstone of early childhood development that cuts across all domains of behavior."

SUMMARY

As school social workers work toward the goal of enhancing the socialization process of children, methods for promoting social competence, such as social skills training, have much to offer. Social workers can make an important contribution to children, families, and schools through preventive and remedial approaches like those described in this chapter. As we have seen, children's social behavior is a critical aspect of successful adaptation in society. The school represents an ideal place for children to learn and practice social behavior. It provides the needed multipeer context and offers multiple opportunities for newly learned behaviors to be generalized to other situations and circumstances.

Social skills training provides a clear methodology for providing remedial and preventive services to children. This direct approach to working with children has been applied in numerous problem areas and with many child behavior problems. It is straightforward in application and has been adapted so that social workers, teachers, and peer helpers can successfully apply the methodology. Although we have emphasized the group application, social skills training also can be applied in individual or classroom settings.

References

Barth, R. P. (1996). *Reducing the risk: Building skills to prevent pregnancy, STD and HIV* (3rd ed.). Santa Cruz, CA: ETR Associates.

Begun, R. W. (1995). *Ready-to-use social skills lessons & activities for grades 4-6.* West Nyack, NY: Center for Applied Research in Education.

Bierman, K. L., & Greenberg, M. T. (1996). Social skills training in the fast track. In R. D. Peters & R. J. McMahon (Eds.), *Preventing childhood disorders, substance abuse, and delinquency* (pp. 65-89). Thousand Oaks, CA: Sage.

Blair, C. (2002). School readiness: Integrating cognition and emotion in a neurobiological conceptualization of children's functioning at school entry. *American Psychologist, 57,* 111-127.

Botvin, G. J. (2000). *Life skills training: Promoting health and personal development.* New York: Princeton Health.

Buckner, J. C., Mezzacappa, E., & Beardslee, W. R. (2003). Characteristics of resilient youths living in poverty: The role of self-regulatory processes. *Development and Psychopathology, 15,* 139-162.

Cartledge, C., & Milburn, J. F. (1995). *Teaching social skills to children and youth: Innovative approaches* (3rd ed.). Boston: Allyn & Bacon.

Clarke, G. N., Lewinsohn, P. M., & Hops, H. (2001). *Instructor's manual for the Adolescent Coping with Depression course.* Retrieved January 20, 2005, from http://www.kpchr. org/public/acwd/acwdl.html

Costin, L. B. (1969). An analysis of the tasks of school social work. *Social Service Review, 43,* 247-285.

Dowd, T., & Tierney, J. (1992). *Teaching social skills to youth: A curriculum for child-care providers.* Boys Town, NE: The Boys Town Press.

Elias, M. J., & Clabby, J. F. (1992). *Building social problem-solving skills.* San Francisco: Jossey-Bass.

Elias, M. J., & Tobias, S. E. (1996). *Social problem solving: Interventions in the schools.* New York: Guilford.

Feindler, E. L., & Guttman, J. (1994). Cognitive-behavioral anger control training. In C. LeCroy (Ed.), *Handbook of child and adolescent treatment manuals* (n.p.). New York: Lexington.

Gottman, J. M. (1983). How children become friends. *Monographs of the Society for Research in Child Development, 48,* 410-423.

Hartup, W. W., & Abecassis, M. (2002). Friends and enemies. In P. K. Smith & C. H. Hart (Eds.), *Blackwell handbook of childhood social development* (pp. 285-306). Malden, MA: Blackwell.

Henggeler, S. W., Clingempeel, W. G., Brondino, M. J., & Pickrel, S. G. (2002). Four-year follow-up of multisystemic therapy with substance-abusing and substance-dependent juvenile offenders. *Journal of the American Academy of Child and Adolescent Psychiatry, 41*(7), 868-874.

Hohman, M., & Buchik, G. (1994). Adolescent relapse prevention. In C. LeCroy (Ed.). *Handbook of child and adolescent treatment manuals* (pp. 200–239). New York: Lexington.

Hops, H., Walker, H. M., & Greenwood, C. R. (1979). PEERS: A program for remediating social withdrawal in school. In L. A. Hamerlynch (Ed.), *Behavior systems for the developmentally disabled: I. School and family environments* (pp. 224–241). New York: Brunner/Mazel.

Howes, C. (2000). Social-emotional classroom climate in child care, child-teacher relationships, and children's second-grade peer relations. *Social Development, 9,* 191–204.

Jermmott, L. S., & Jermmott, J. B., III. (1992). Increasing condom-use intentions among sexually active inner-city adolescent women: Effects of an AIDS prevention program. *Nursing Research, 41,* 273–278.

Kearney, C. A., & Albano, A. (2000). *When children refuse school: A cognitive-behavioral therapy approach therapist guide.* New York: Academic Press.

Kendall, P. C., Choudhury, M., Hudson, J., & Webb, A. (2002). *The C.A.T. project workbook for the cognitive-behavioral treatment of anxious adolescents.* Ardmore, PA: Workbook Publishing.

King, C. A., & Kirschenbaum, D. S. (1992). *Helping young children develop social skills.* Pacific Grove, CA: Brooks/Cole.

Larson, J., Lochman, J. E., & Lochman, J. (2001). *Helping school children cope with anger: A cognitive-behavioral intervention.* New York: Guilford.

LeCroy, C. W. (1994). Social skills training. In C. LeCroy (Ed.), *Handbook of child and adolescent treatment manuals* (pp. 126–169). New York: Lexington.

LeCroy, C. W. (2001). Promoting social competence in youth. In H. E. Briggs & K. Corcoran (Eds.), *Social work practice: Treating common problems.* Chicago: Lyceum Books.

LeCroy, C. W. (2002). Child therapy and social skills. In A. R. Roberts & G. J. Greene (Eds.), *Social work desk reference* (pp. 406–412). New York: Oxford University Press.

LeCroy, C. W. (2004). Experimental evaluation of the 'Go Grrrls' preventive intervention for early adolescent girls. *Journal of Primary Prevention, 25,* 457–473.

LeCroy, C. W., & Daley, J. (2001). *Empowering adolescent girls: Examining the present and building skills for the future with the Go Grrrls program.* New York: W. W. Norton.

LeCroy, C. W., & Rose, S. D. (1986). Evaluation of preventive interventions for promoting social competence in adolescents. *Social Work Research and Abstracts, 22,* 8–17.

Long, B. B. (1986). The prevention of mental-emotional disabilities: A report from a National Mental Health Association Commission. *American Psychologist, 41,* 825–829.

MacNeil, G., & LeCroy, C. W. (1997). Promoting social competence among severely emotionally disturbed youth: Development of a social competence inventory. *Residential Treatment for Children, 15,* 63–78.

Merrell, K. W., & Gimpel, G. A. (1998). *Social skills of children and adolescents: Conceptualization, assessment, treatment.* Mahwah, NJ: Lawrence Erlbaum Associates.

Meyer, L. H., Park, H., Grenot-Scheyer, M., Schwartz, I. S., & Harry, B. (1998). *Making friends: The influences of culture and development.* Baltimore: Paul H. Brookes.

Mufson, L., Moreau, D., Weissman, M. M., & Klerman, G. L. (1993). *Interpersonal psychotherapy for depressed adolescents.* New York: Guilford.

National Research Council. (2000). *From neurons to neighborhoods: The science of early childhood development.* Washington, DC: National Academy Press.

Nevil, N. F., Beatty, M. L., & Moxley, D. P. (1997). *Socialization games for persons with disabilities: Structured group activities for social and interpersonal development.* Springfield, IL: Charles C. Thomas.

Oden, S. L., & Asher, S. R. (1977). Coaching low accepted children in social skills: A follow-tip sociometric assessment. *Child Development, 48,* 496–506.

Okamoto, S. K., LeCroy, C. W., Dustman, P., Hohmann-Marriott, B., & Kulis, S. (2004). An ecological assessment of drug-related problem situations for American Indian adolescents in the southwest. *Journal of Social Work Practice in the Addictions, 4,* 47-64.

Olweus, D. (1996). Bullying at school: Knowledge base and an effective intervention program. *Annals of the New York Academy of Sciences, 794,* 265–276.

Orenstein, P. (1994). *School girls.* New York: Doubleday.

Resnick, M. D., Bearman, P. S., Blum, R. W., Bauman, K. E., Harris, K. M., Jones, J., et al. (1997). Protecting adolescents from harm: Findings from the National Longitudinal Study on Adolescent Health. *Journal of the American Medical Association, 278,* 823–832.

Rose, L. C., & Gallup, A. M. (2000). *The 32nd Annual Phi Delta Kappa/Gallup poll of the public's attitudes towards the public schools.* Retrieved July 10, 2002, from http://www.pdkintl.org/kappan/kpol0009.htm

Rose, S. D. (1998). *Group therapy with troubled youth.* Thousand Oaks, CA: Sage.

Sargent, L. R. (1991). *Social skills for school and community: Systematic instruction for children and youth with cognitive delays.* Reston, VA: Division on Mental Retardation, Council for Exceptional Children.

Schrumpf, F., Crawford, D., & Usadel, H. C. (1991). *Peer mediation: Conflict resolution in the schools.* Champaign, IL: Research Press.

Simmons, R. C., & Blyth., D. A. (1987). *Moving into adolescence: The impact of pubertal change and school context.* Hawthorne, NJ: Aldine.

Walker, H. M., Todis, B., Holmes, D., & Horton, G. (1988). *The ACCESS program.* Austin, TX: Pro-Ed.

Wang, L. I., Davis, M., Robin, L., Collins, J., Coyle, K., & Baumler, E. (2000). Economic evaluation of safer choices: A school-based human immunodefiency virus, other sexually transmitted diseases, and pregnancy prevention program. *Archives of Pediatric Adolescent Medicine, 154,* 1017–1024.

Waterman, J., & Walker, E. (2001). *Helping at-risk students.* New York: Guilford.

Webster-Stratton, C., & Taylor, T. (2001). Nipping early risk factors in the bud: Preventing substance abuse, delinquency, and violence in adolescence through interventions targeted at young children (0–8 years). *Prevention Science, 2,* 165–192.

Weiss, M. J., & Harris, S. L. (2001). *Reaching out, joining in: Teaching social skills to young children with autism.* New York: Woodbine House.

36

Interpersonal Violence in Schools: Developing Safe and Responsive School Communities

Shirley McDonald
University of Illinois at Chicago

Susan Fineran
Boston University

Robert Constable
Loyola University, Chicago

Anthony Moriarty
Olympia Fields, IL

- ◆ A Context for School Policy and Practice
- ◆ Bullying, Harassment, and Intimidation: Pathways to Assessment and Intervention
- ◆ Peer Sexual Harassment
- ◆ Administrative Responses to Bullying and Sexual Harassment
- ◆ The Violence Prevention and Response Plan
- ◆ School Social Work Practice with Interpersonal Violence and Intimidation

Concerns have emerged throughout the world that schools are not as safe as they once were believed to be. Bullying, intimidation, or personal denigration, including sexual harassment, while different, are parts of a continuum of interpersonal violence, which, if unchecked, can seriously impair the educational process. Such interactions frequently result in psychological as well as educational damage to students, if not addressed quickly and effectively. Such behaviors and responses to them, if anticipated and prepared for, will not disrupt a normal, sustained climate of civility in the school. This prepared response must, of course, focus on both victims and perpetrators.

The climate of civility is dependent on awareness and anticipation of the problem and is likely to be supported by state mandates. Responsive school communities need an awareness and understanding of emergent best practices. For the school social worker, as a member of the response team, the dynamics of the problem in their particular school community need to be "mapped" (Astor, Meyer, Benbenishty, Marachi, & Rosemond 2004; 2005; see also discussion of needs assessment in chapter 15). Sophisticated policy and practice interventions, focused on the problems of interpersonal violence, have been emerging with solid research backing (Astor et al., 2004; 2005; Dwyer, Osher, & Warger, 1998; National Institutes of Health, 2005).

These effective interventions rely upon changing the whole school. School social workers have the background knowledge and skills to help guide this change, but school administrators are often the ones with the power to carry them out. To bring about effective school change, the school community should first address the problem through mandates and policies that set the context for change. Effective, efficient, and economical policies and practices involve a commitment from everyone in the school to change a school culture that once permitted interpersonal violence and intimidation. Effective change involves complicated processes. The school cannot just develop new policies and send a memo to inform staff and students of the rules. Unspoken norms and unwritten rules of behavior underlie interpersonal violence in schools. Changing these underlying elements of a school culture requires deliberate and purposeful actions, beginning with school leadership and carried out by the entire school community. Only through these complex processes can interpersonal violence in schools be reduced or prevented.

This chapter is the first of three dealing with the school social worker's role in situations of potential interpersonal violence. It is focused on problems of bullying and peer sexual harassment, the school community policy matrix, and the consequent school social work role. As a culmination and a test of the school social work practice model in this book, the discussion of safety can be linked to all the other chapters in the book. School social workers have important roles in the school's early and appropriate response to crises and threats to safety. Through needs assessments, mediation, conflict resolution systems, and safety and crisis plans, the school social worker takes part with others in the formulation of school policies and development of programs. In the context of school policies that demand safe, nonthreatening, nonharmful behavior in the school, school social workers work with victims and perpetrators of interpersonal violence and their families. Centrally involved in the school community, they are often the first to know about a problem. They have been trained to interpret the meanings of interpersonal behavior and to work with others to find respectful solutions. In so doing they draw on their skills of collaboration, consultation, individual, group, and family intervention, social skills education, crisis intervention, conflict resolution, and development of mediation systems. While they need assistance themselves, victims of harassment are not the sole point of intervention. Because harassed students are often different from adolescent cultural and gender stereotypes, the school social worker will need to work with others to change the entire school culture in which harassment of girls, gay or lesbian students, or racial or ethnic minorities may have been condoned or ignored.

A CONTEXT FOR SCHOOL POLICY AND PRACTICE

Concerns about safety and the school's response to interpersonal violence, threats, and tragedy have been present in local school districts for several decades. The explosion of the space shuttle, *Challenger*, in front of millions of watching students brought a focus on crisis planning in schools. By the end of the decade of the 1980s it was considered best practice to have a crisis plan that would prepare for a wide variety of possible occurrences causing normal decision-making protocols and procedures of the school to break down, leaving students to perceive the school as unsafe. Crisis planning might deal with a school bus accident, an intruder in the building, gang violence, a student with meningitis, the suicide of a student or teacher, a car running out of control onto the school grounds, weapons in school, or other threatening conditions, including tornadoes, hurricanes, or other severe weather.

At the same time as these concerns were developing, school reform brought with it a focus on academics, on discipline (Grant, 1981, 1985; Rutter, Maugham, Mortimore, & Ousten, 1979), and on *effective schools*. Research points out that despite all sorts of differences, such as income level or educational philosophy, effective schools have certain common characteristics. Where there is strong instructional leadership, a safe and orderly climate, a school-wide emphasis on basic skills, high teacher expectations for student achievement, and continuous assessment of student progress, students have better achievement (Finn, 1984; Purkey & Smith, 1983). The effective schools movement was fueled by a burgeoning literature, including the identification at the federal level of best practices in implementing school effectiveness (Kyle, 1985). School social workers, their own focus broadening to teamwork relationships and consultation, have had an important role in making schools more effective. School social workers, trained to anticipate, prevent, or ameliorate problem situations, often avert potential crises. The concern for safety is an indispensable part of school effectiveness. Without safety, nothing else matters. When concerns for school safety mounted, the effective schools construct became particularly useful in developing an effective response. As part of efforts to construct a safe and responsive school environment, nonviolent resolution of differences, and planning for crises would become normal and accepted practices in schools.

Violence in schools has come from the inside, from students, bullying, harassing, intimidating, or causing physical harm to other students and from outside with violence spilling over into schools. The responses of school communities to a spectrum of possible interpersonal violence are conditioned by a new awareness of the seriousness of its effects. This awareness has changed school policies and practices, and the practice of the school social worker. It is now expected of everyone that one's participation in the school community should not include being harmful to others, that schools are safe places, and that safety and crisis plans are in place to ensure a high level of safety.

Recent court decisions (*Davis v. Monroe County Board of Education*, 1996; *Nabozny v. Podlesny*, 1996) have created what amounts to a right to an education without peer harassment. Schools and school personnel who knowingly fail to respond to harmful conditions are made responsible and can be held legally liable. In a discussion of the harassment of gay or lesbian students, Hunter and Schaecher (1995) point out "Teachers and administrators bear responsibility for (the students') lack of learning ... because students are forced to concentrate on surviving in the school system, rather than on their studies" (p. 1058).

There is an emergent body of policy and practice at the federal, state, and local level as well as a strong research base both for effective prevention and effective intervention. Schools are expected to respond quickly to safety concerns. However, an effective response cannot be a rigid one. Zero-tolerance policies, initially focused on firearms and later extended to drugs, have not in themselves been successful (Astor et al., 2005; National Institutes of Health, 2005). Rigid enforcement of such policies, for example, the failure to distinguish plastic squirt guns from the real thing, is not an appropriate response. In such situations students are likely to hold the school administration in contempt, thus undercutting the supportive school environment necessary to reduce the likelihood of violent behavior (Black, 2004; Mulvey & Cauffman, 2001).

The Federal Policy Context

Federal initiatives to promote safe schools began in 1986 with the Drug-Free Schools and Community Act (20 U.S.C 4601), reauthorized in 1994 as the Safe and Drug-Free Schools and Communities Act (20 U.S.C. 7101), and again reauthorized in PL 107-110, the No Child Left Behind Act (NCLB). By 1998 schools were required to conduct needs assessments regarding drugs and violence, establish measurable goals, implement research-based approaches, and assess progress (see discussion in chapter 15).

In 1998 the Departments of Education and Justice (Dwyer, Osher, Warger, et al., 1998), and then in 2005 the National Institutes of Health (NIH), developed publications that analyzed the problem of adolescent violence and recommended best practices to respond to the problems. The NIH (2005) report, *Preventing Violence and Related Health-Risking Social Behaviors in Adolescents*, was produced by an independent panel of experts, reviewing systematically the existing evidence on the prevention and treatment of adolescent violence (National Institutes of Health, 2005). Problems of adolescent violence were seen as a *continuum* of risk factors, which could predict the possibility of violent outcomes. Interventions that can be shown to reduce the prevalence of the risk are likely to reduce the possibility that the outcome (violence) itself would take place. Competent parenting skills such as monitoring, consistent discipline, and supportiveness could reduce the likelihood of children engaging in more violent, antisocial behaviors. Pointing out that family, neighborhood, and community were key factors in protecting against or generating antisocial behavior, the report went on to discuss two effective programs dealing with youth at high risk for violence, and their families. These were functional family therapy (Sexton & Alexander, 2003) and multisystemic therapy (Sheidow, Henggeler, & Schoenwald, 2003). Both are community- and family-based prevention and intervention programs, and both are compatible with how social workers work with families (Constable & Lee, 2004; also see chapter 27). Positive results (reductions in recidivism, violent crime arrests, and out-of-home placements of children) were sustained in both programs over four years, using external replications and random clinical trials (RCTs). Six other similar programs, including brief, strategic family therapy, were also found to be effective, although only using internal RCTs. These programs are geared to foster competence and skill development. Core components of effective programs strengthen:

◆ Parent effectiveness (communication style, behavior management, goal setting, problem solving, and monitoring),
◆ Individual coping on the part of the child/adolescent (impulse control, anger management, decreased risk taking, communication skills),
◆ Academic achievement (school readiness, organization skills, good learning habits, reading),
◆ Peer relations (conversational and other social skills), and
◆ The social climate of schools (classroom and playground management, parent-teacher collaboration).

These appear to be most effective when adapted to differing developmental levels of their clientele and the differing circumstances of ethnic communities. Many of the interventions were long term, often lasting a year and sometimes much longer. They worked intensively with their clientele and involved multimodal and multicontextual approaches. Therapists often had low caseloads (4–6) and were available to the family, when needed. Other programs that were coercive, that limited themselves to scare tactics, lectures, and toughness strategies, were unsuccessful.

Applications to Schools: Early Warning, Timely Response. In the fall of 1998 the federal Departments of Education and of Justice, by presidential request, jointly disseminated a research-based, best practices manual on safety in schools. The manual, *Early Warning, Timely Response: A Guide to Safe Schools* (Dwyer, Osher, & Hoffman, 2000; Dwyer, Osher, Warger, et al., 1998), shifted the focus from the problems of interpersonal violence in themselves to the school as a responsive, normative environment. It was sent to every school and district in the nation. The development of best practice manuals had become a way of influencing discussion and models for dealing with a national concern without passing laws. The issues clarified by the guide quickly became the basis for further discussion of safe schools, and for further development of policy and practice.

The guide broadens the focus on violence and shifts the focus to the school as an orderly, responsive, normative environment. The term *violence* includes a broad range of troubling behaviors and emotions shown by students: serious aggression, physical attacks, suicide, dangerous use of drugs, and other dangerous interpersonal behaviors (Dwyer, Osher, Warger, et al., 1998). Near homicidal violence is rare in schools, but there are early warning signs for behaviors that could lead to violence. The focus therefore must be broadened to unsafe relationships and situations in the school. Children who become violent to self and others often are those who already feel themselves rejected and psychologically victimized (Guerra, Huessman, Tolan, Van Acker, & Eron, 1995). Children who exhibit aggressive behavior, if not provided support, may continue a progressive developmental pattern toward severe aggression or violence (Dwyer, Osher, Warger, et al., 1998; Olweus, 1980; Walker, Colvin, & Ramsey, 1995). Meaningful connections with an adult however can reduce the possibilities for violence (Dwyer, Osher, Warger, et al., 1998). The report goes on to list a number of research-based behavioral warning signs of potential violence. These are of particular concern if an increase in these indicators is observed. They are:

- ◆ Social withdrawal,
- ◆ Isolation, rejection by peers,
- ◆ Feelings of being a victim,
- ◆ Lowered interest in school and reduced academic performance,
- ◆ Becoming a victim of violence,
- ◆ Patterns of uncontrolled anger,
- ◆ Intimidating and bullying behaviors,
- ◆ History of violent and aggressive behavior,
- ◆ Intolerance of differences and prejudicial attitudes,
- ◆ Gang affiliation,
- ◆ Use of firearms,
- ◆ Making serious threats of violence, and
- ◆ Limited access to supportive adults.

The implication of the discussion is that to lessen the possibility of serious violent episodes, there needs to be both a focus on vulnerable students and the creation and maintenance of civility within the school community.

The guide (Dwyer, Osher, Warger et al., 1998) recommends a multilayered approach to prevention and intervention. Programs such as Positive Behavioral Intervention Systems (PBIS) and Peace Builders are examples of programs that are school-wide and aimed at just such issues. The concept of a *responsive*, rather than reactive, school shifts the focus from individual students to civility in the school, and from reactive intervention to prevention. Within the school and in the school community there is a team approach. Policies protect the right all students have to attend safe schools. The *safe school* model draws from and extends the effective schools research discussed earlier. The focus shifts to the school community. The entire school community makes a commitment to behaving responsibly. There are high expectations and support for socially appropriate behavior. Schools reinforce positive behavior and highlight sanctions against aggressive behavior. All staff, parents, students, and community members develop an awareness of problem behavior, what they can do to counteract it, and how they can reinforce and reward positive behavior (Dwyer, Osher, Warger, et al., 1998). The school community by setting clear standards helps individual students to function effectively within a more actively safe, responsive, normative environment.

The responsive school community employs a three-tiered approach toward the creation of a safe environment:

- ◆ *Primary prevention* provides instructional and psychosocial supports so that all students succeed academically and behaviorally and learn cultural competence and respect for diversity. Elementary schools teach students to solve problems and stop and think before acting. The expected long-term effect of this intervention would be the reduction of harassing behaviors in high school (Batsche & Knoff, 1994).
- ◆ *Early intervention* involves more intensive intervention for students at risk for troubling outcomes. An example would be providing a program that provides a long-term, reliable, and positive relationship with an adult mentor. Responsive schools can provide an opportunity that allows children to feel safe in discussing their personal concerns about friends, intimidation, and stress. Responsive schools can help children feel respected and comfortable with being themselves, whether or not they fit the mold of the average student.
- ◆ *Targeted intervention* provides individualized and intensive support for students with the highest level of need (Dwyer, Osher, & Hoffman, 2000).

Planning that includes training for the entire school to become appropriately responsive is necessary. Schools develop prevention plans, response teams, and safety plans. Similar to crisis teams, the core prevention and response team consists of an administrator, a pupil services representative, teacher and parent representatives, a school board member, and others from the school community. An effective written violence prevention plan includes discussion of early warning signs of problems, effective prevention practices the school community is undertaking, and intervention strategies. These strategies must include early interventions for students at risk and more intensive, individualized interventions for students with severe behavioral problems or mental health needs. A part of the violence prevention plan is a crisis intervention plan that includes multiple contingency plans to be used in the aftermath of a crisis (Dwyer, Osher, Warger, et al., 1998).

School responsiveness involves the entire school community. Prevention often is a process of developing and changing the basic school culture. One example is Johnson's discussion of the no-fault school in chapter 34. Mark Mattaini (2001a) and the Peace Power working group (2001b) have developed systematic, evidence-based strategies for schools to construct alternative organizational cultures of nonviolence and noncoercive action. The PEACEPOWER and Peace-Builders programs, inculcating proven strategies and certain Native American customs and beliefs, institutionalize practices within the school of:

1. *Systematic recognition of contributions and successes.* Among the practices would be recognition notes, recognition circles, group incentives and celebrations of success.
2. *Development of a culture of acting with respect.* Among the practices would be "put-ups, not put-downs," respectful discipline procedures, bullying prevention programs, and empathy training.
3. *Building community through shared power.* Among the practices would be councils and working groups to improve school climate, service projects and service learning, family-school partnership programs and family-school governance structures.
4. *Making peace.* Among the practices would be conferencing to resolve school conflicts and discipline issues, peer mediation and healing circles. (Mattaini, 2001a, p. 442–443)

Ron Astor's review of effective school-wide intervention programs reveals seven general characteristics, which can be individualized through needs assessment to the particular situation of a school community (Astor et al., 2005; 2004). Such programs:

- ◆ Raise the awareness and responsibility of students, teachers and parents regarding the types of violence in their schools;
- ◆ Create clear guidelines and rules for the school community;
- ◆ Target the various social systems in the school and clearly communicate to the entire school community procedures to be followed before, during and after violent events;
- ◆ Focus on getting school staff, students and parents involved in the program;
- ◆ Fit easily into the normal flow and mission of the school;

- Use faculty, staff and parents in the school setting to plan, implement and sustain the program;
- Increase monitoring and supervision in nonclassroom areas. (Astor et al., 2005)

Such approaches are aimed at building appropriate connections with families, with peers, and within the school community (Smith & Sandhu, 2004). They are absolutely compatible with the NIH findings on effective practice with problems of youth violence and fit very well into the approaches to school social work practice discussed elsewhere in this book.

The State Policy Response to the Need for Safe Schools

The federal policy initiative was accompanied by considerable activity at state education agency (SEA) policy levels in support of it. State laws, policies, and SEA consultants introduced a similar model for practice and policy at the local (LEA) school-community level. The Illinois law, the Safe and Responsive Schools Act, cited earlier as an example, can best be understood in the light of the national discussion of best practices and policy development. The school community, including parents, develops discipline policy. The focus for concern is broadened from bullying to all students at risk for aggressive behavior: Discussion of early intervention should take the three-tiered approach while avoiding an imposition of primary prevention responsibilities on all school districts:

> The school board, in consultation with the parent-teacher advisory committee and other community-based organizations, must include provisions in the student discipline policy to *address students who have demonstrated behaviors that put them at risk for aggressive behavior*, including without limitation, bullying, as defined in the policy. These provisions must include *procedures for notifying* parents or legal guardians, and *early intervention procedures* based upon available community-based and district resources. (Illinois Safe and Responsive Schools Act, author's italics)

BULLYING, HARRASSMENT, AND INTIMIDATION: PATHWAYS TO ASSESSMENT AND INTERVENTION

Bullying, intimidation, and sexual harassment can be seen as a continuum of related problems. Many schools have developed active measures to establish a climate of civility because of increasing concerns regarding the impact of these issues (Kauffman & Burback, 1997). Experience as victim or perpetrator can negatively affect a student's life through adulthood if no intervention is available. Many students, both boys and girls, report school performance difficulties due to such harassment. These may take the form of significant tardiness and truancy, decreased quality of schoolwork with resultant lower grades, dropping classes, and avoidance of or loss of friends (AAUW, 1992, 1993, 2001).

Defining Bullying

Definitions of bullying and intimidation are essential to a discussion of the harmfulness and unacceptable nature of these behaviors and to eventually develop a climate of civility:

> Bullying and/or intimidation of others, includes any aggressive or negative gesture, or written, verbal, or physical act that *places another student in reasonable fear of harm* to his or her person or property, or that has the effect of *insulting or demeaning* any student in such a way as to *disrupt* or *interfere* with *the school's educational mission*, or the education of any student. Bullying most often will occur when a student *asserts physical or psychological power over*, or is *cruel* to, another student perceived to be weaker. Such behavior may include but is not limited to pushing, hitting, threatening, name-calling, or other physical or verbal conduct of a belittling or browbeating nature. (Zuehl, Dillon, Schilling, & Oltmanns, 2002, n.p., author's italics)

The Prevalence of Bullying and Intimidation

Among 150,000 Norwegian and Swedish students ages 7 to 16, about 15 percent reported being involved in bully-victim problems occurring once a week or more frequently (Olweus, Limber, & Mihalic, 1999). Despite what appear to be lower rates than the United States, these percentages, together with several student suicides, caused considerable concern about bullying in Scandinavia and became the basis for the development of bullying prevention programs there. The problem is also of great concern in Japanese and Korean schools. Bullying rates among North American students seem to be related to age. In addition, as cultural definitions of bullying vary, so also does the literature on prevalence. However, there is some agreement that bullying peaks in middle school (Haynie et al., 2001; Nansel et al., 2001) and declines as children mature in high school. Nansel et al. (2001) concluded in their analysis of 15,686 students that bullying occurs with greater frequency among middle school students. Haynie et al. (2001) found 31 percent of middle-school students are victims, while Roland (2000) found only 5 percent of middle-school students are victims. Smith, Madsen, and Moody (1999), studying students ages 5 to 14, concluded that the numbers of younger children reporting being bullied are inflated by the level of understanding of these children of what it actually means to be bullied. As their concept of bullying matures, the frequency of reporting seems to decline. Or it may be that, given the pupil's perceptual organization of her world, the importance of certain bully-victim issues peaks during the middle-school developmental years. For individuals who bully, the behavior appears to be a precursor to sexual harassment and other forms of escalating interpersonal violence (Stein, 1995). High schools have a higher incidence of peer sexual harassment complaints. Most prevention work regarding school violence, including sexual harassment, has been targeted toward high school students.

There have been many attempts in the literature to define the developmental problems that lead to bullying behavior. These conclusions read like a litany of psychopathology symptoms, leading one to infer that bullying is symptomatic of emotional maladjustment. Bullies have more psychiatric symptoms than others (Kumpulainen, Raesaenen, & Henttonen, 1999). Nansel et al. (2001) stated that these youth suffer from insecurity, anxiety, depression, loneliness, unhappiness, physical and mental symptoms, and low self-esteem. Curtner-Smith (2000) suggested that bullying is learned from influential role models in the social environment of the child. Bullying is a significant indicator of risk for mental disorders in adolescence (Kaltiana-Heino, Pilla, Ruan, Simmons-Morton, & Scheidt, 2000). Physical discipline at home contributes to the prediction of bullying (Smith & Myron-Wilson, 1998; Smith & Shu, 2000). Bullying in the home predicts bullying outside the home (Duncan, 1999). Children from larger families are more likely to bully (Eslea & Smith, 2000).

Victims. Although the literature portrays a dim view of bullies, the picture is worse for the victims of bullying. A history of being victimized (being teased, hearing rumors spread about oneself, being or feeling deliberately excluded, experiencing violence or threats of violence) is associated with subsequent development of anxiety and depression in adolescents (Bond, Carlin, Thomas, Rubin, & Patton, 2001). Victims have a lower level of social acceptance than their peers (Haynie et al., 2001). They have more serious mental health problems and fewer support systems than others (Rigby, 2000). Rigby also found that victims of bullying have relatively poor physical health, perhaps suggesting that the trauma of victimization may become somaticized. Moreover, these victims often have experienced parental maltreatment, both emotional and physical (Duncan, 1999). Nansel et al. (2001) found victims more anxious, depressed, lonely, unhappy, and lacking in social skills. Finally, victimization is related to a greater incidence of suicidal ideation in young people (Carney, 2000; Rigby & Slee, 1999).

Victims of bullying do not always respond by suffering in silence. There is increasing concern about how these victims may express their frustrations and act them out in the school setting. McGee and DeBernardo (1999) studied sixteen students who committed homicide in the schools and found fourteen of them to be bully victims. These students chose to retaliate against the school, perhaps in a generalized rage against the school for not providing some protection to them. School was a dangerous place for them, but also a required place. Their dilemma resulted in retaliatory violence.

Victim-Perpetrator Identity. Although schools want to offer support to students affected by bullying, the realities of a victim-perpetrator relationship complicate the situation enormously. Many student perpetrators also report being victims, and similarly, victims report being perpetrators. This fact poses clinical and policy dilemmas. It would be easy to say that social workers need to provide support groups for victims or perpetrators, and in many circumstances this would be appropriate. However, some students who are victims may be retaliating or perpetrating in self-defense, and other students who are perpetrating may find themselves being victimized.

Furthermore, the focus on the victim-perpetrator relationship alone has the effect of shifting the focus away from the normative culture of the school, which may implicitly permit, or even demand, interpersonal violence and retaliation. The relationship can best be understood in the light of a culture of violence and retaliation. Nisbett (1993) suggested that Southern cultures in the United States place a high value on the use of aggression and violence as a means to uphold one's honor. He concluded that a cultural base of support underlies the finding that substantially higher homicide rates exist for White Southern males, especially in rural areas. The findings suggest that bullying rates reflect a climate of support within the school and in the family.

One of the main complaints from students experiencing bullying is that it occurs in front of school personnel who do nothing to stop it, and in these cases inaction supports interpersonal violence (AAUW, 1993, 2001; Stein, Marshall, & Tropp, 1993; Permanent Commission [Connecticut] on the Status of Women [PCSW], 1995). Teachers may be hesitant to intervene unless they are sure that consequences for the behavior are in place and will be enforced. A more direct course, recommended in the best practices guide (Dwyer, Osher, & Warger et al., 1999), is for anyone in the school community who is present when students are being harassed or intimidated, to intervene. Social workers would work closely with teachers and support them in providing immediate intervention when they observe bullying. Students are encouraged to move away from their role as "participant observer," to band together and warn or report their peers when they see harassment. As civil rights attorney Catherine McKinnon (1979) suggested, the unnamed should not be taken for the nonexistent. Students and teachers should be encouraged to name this behavior and not accept it as "normal adolescent behavior."

Differential Assessment of Students Who Bully. To develop effective intervention plans, school social workers must develop a broader assessment, disaggregating bullies and victims of bullying into situational, relational, and diagnostic categories. It is essential to take relevant developmental dynamics into consideration to be effective in responding to incidents of bullying. The task is more complex than what is normally addressed in school policy statements and administrative procedures.

A number of studies make a distinction between the bullies who are impulsive as a condition of an attention deficit disorder, and those who are more calculating. Arsenio and Lemerise (2001) argued that there are hot-blooded and cold-blooded bullies, concluding that the intervention and treatment strategies for school social workers should be differentiated on the basis of this differential assessment. Many bullies, especially younger students, might be acting out, driven by attention deficit hyperactivity disorder (ADHD) behavior patterns. The bullying aspect of these behaviors may be a symptom of ADHD (Wolke, Woods, Blomfield, & Karstadt, 2000). These children are referred to by Arsenio and Lemerise (2001) as the hot-blooded bullies. For behaviors that are manifested because of a lack of impulse control, the behavior should diminish as better strategies for developing impulse control are learned through routine interventions for ADHD. Treating this type of student strictly as a behavior problem (i.e., without taking ADHD into account) may have serious counterproductive consequences.

There are also a number of studies that conclude that the bully may be a student who is very competent socially. They seem socially skilled, have a high level of self-esteem, and give the impression of being more aloof and detached emotionally from others. These are identified by Arsenio and Lemerise (2001) as the cold-blooded bullies, and they are the most challenging to work with. These bullies exploit other students in the pursuit of their own needs and do so with a sense of justification (Smith & Shu, 2000) and thus feel no need to change their behavioral patterns. Sutton, Smith, and Swettenham (1999) concluded that such bullies are likely to be cold, manipulative, and highly skilled in social situations. They also have significantly higher levels of self-esteem than their classmates (Salmivalli, Kaukiainen, Kaistaniemi, & Kirsti, 1999). Perry (1997) has long argued that childhood experiences can lead to the child becoming cold-blooded. The latter group is of particular concern because these children may pose a higher risk to the safety of other children. Failure to deal with this type of bully as a discipline problem will likely encourage further bullying behavior. The first task of any intervention with this category of bully is the need to develop some motivation for change. The second task is to get the family involved in the intervention plan (Hoover & Oliver, 1996).

Bully-Seeking Behavior. Some authors have suggested that a small number of victims of harassment may be meeting their own emotional needs through the role of victim (Mahady-Wilton, Craig, & Pepler, 2000; Schwartz, Proctor, & Chien, 2001). Students who have not found a viable role for themselves in the school may find that the only role available is that of victim. In some cases, the victim behavior may be learned through experiences of child maltreatment. In other cases, the behavior is learned in social settings, the victim preferring to be abused rather than forgotten. With the attention as a reinforcer, they may bait bullies or potential bullies, preferring the bullying experience to that of being ignored. The need for attention is sufficiently strong that attention from bullying is anticipated as a positive outcome. Such a child may be capable of drawing students who may be generally able to control themselves in such situations into bullying behaviors. A student who has learned such a pattern may be at risk of developing a significant, persistent dysfunctional approach to solving perceived social problems, or developing a lack of positive and meaningful social involvement. They receive involvement and support mainly by being a victim. Such a student is in need of immediate intervention with an extensive therapeutic component and long-term planning. The therapeutic challenge for the social worker is to help clarify the student's experiences and the student's responses to those experiences, which have led the child to adopt the bully-seeking behaviors.

Outcomes for Children who Bully. The long-term prediction for bullies is not good. Baldry and Farrington (2000) concluded bullying is a good predictor of juvenile delinquency. Colvin, Tobin, Beard, Hagan, and Sprague (1998) see bullying predilection as a strong predictor of later community violence. The most striking conclusions have been drawn from the work of Olweus (1993) who found that former bullies were four times more likely to engage in criminal behavior. At the age of 24, 60 percent of former bullies in his study had one or more criminal convictions, and 35 percent of this sample had three or more convictions. Clearly, bullying is learned early in life, and it remains the solution of choice for these early learners for a long time. It is also evident that we must seek earlier identification and treatment of these children if there is to be hope in solving this problem in our schools.

PEER SEXUAL HARASSMENT

Although bullying behavior has been a concern for a long time, peer sexual harassment in school has only recently been identified and studied. Responding to a study of the high school experience, many Minnesota students identified sexual harassment as the "norm" in their schools.

> There have been numerous reports of sexual assaults and rapes on school grounds and in school buildings. In an environment that condones sexual harassment, everyone is a victim, not just those who are direct targets of the harassment. All students come to see school as an unsafe place, hostile and intimidating. They may alter their own behaviors in an attempt to decrease their sense of vulnerability. (Strauss & Espeland, 1992, p. 7)

The research basis for the AAUW report, *Hostile Hallways*, was first conducted in 1993 and repeated in 2001. Both studies listed fourteen types of sexual harassment. They asked 1,600 high school students in 1993 and 2,064 students in 2001 if someone had done any of these things to them:

◆ Made sexual comments, jokes, gestures, or looks;
◆ Showed, gave, or left you sexual pictures, photographs, illustrations, messages, or notes;
◆ Wrote sexual messages or graffiti about you on bathroom walls, in locker rooms, etc.;
◆ Spread sexual rumors about you;
◆ Said you were gay or lesbian;
◆ Spied on you as you dressed or showered at school;
◆ Flashed or mooned you;
◆ Touched, grabbed, or pinched you in a sexual way;
◆ Pulled at your clothing in a sexual way;
◆ Blocked your way or cornered you in a sexual way;
◆ Forced you to kiss him or her;
◆ Forced you to do something sexual, other than kissing.

In the AAUW study, four out of five students reported being sexually harassed and of those harassed, 85 percent stated it was by a peer. The 1993 study was the first to document a high level of sexual harassment experienced by boys as well as girls. In the 2001 study, 83 percent of the girls and 79 percent of the boys reported being sexually harassed by a current or former student at school. Most of the previous literature on peer sexual harassment had indicated that over 90 percent of the time males are the perpetrators of sexual harassment against females (Langelan, 1993; Stein et al., 1993; Strauss & Espeland, 1992). Fifty-seven percent of all boys and 50 percent of all girls surveyed in the 2001 study admitted that they have sexually harassed someone in the school setting. Of the students in the 1993 AAUW study who said that they had sexually harassed someone in the school setting, 94 percent claimed they themselves had been harassed (98% of girls and 92% of boys). The fact that 81 percent of students report being harassed by peers and 54 percent report harassing other students leaves a minority of students experiencing a secondary education free from the stresses of peer sexual harassment. The problem needs to be approached from a systemic perspective, as well as involving individual students.

Stein et al. (1993) and the Wellesley College Center for Research on Women conducted a survey, in conjunction with the National Organization for Women (NOW) Legal Defense and Education Fund, which was published in *Seventeen* Magazine in September of 1992. This endeavor resulted in the 1993 report *Secrets in Public: Sexual Harassment in Our Schools*. The girls' responses provided detailed information regarding their personal experience of sexual harassment. The most common forms of sexual harassment the girls experienced were sexual comments, gestures or looks, and being touched, pinched, or grabbed. Thirty-nine percent of the girls reported they experienced these behaviors every day. Ninety-seven percent of the harassers were identified as male peers and one percent were female (Stein et al., 1993). Another study conducted by Roscoe, Strouse, and Goodwin (1994) focused on students in a middle school. The students were asked about their experience of and acceptance of sexually harassing behaviors. Forty-three percent of the students experienced peer sexual harassment (50% of females and 37% of males). Results also documented that both boys and girls were highly unaccepting of sexual harassment behaviors.

Additional findings from the AAUW (2001) and PCSW (1995) studies found that students who experience sexual harassment reported more school absence, lowered concentration, and less participation in class. These studies also reported physical symptoms that included sleep disturbance and appetite changes. Students reported feeling angry, upset, and threatened by sexual harassment, all of which contributed to lowered self-esteem and confidence (Fineran & Bennett, 1999; PCSW, 1995; Strauss & Espeland, 1992; Stein et al., 1993).

A 1995 study in a public high school conducted by the Connecticut Permanent Commission on the Status of Women (PCSW) found that 35 percent of events of sexual harassment were perpetrated by a schoolmate the student knew casually. Nine percent were perpetrated by a schoolmate the student did not know. Twelve percent were perpetrated by students who were boyfriends or girlfriends. Fifty percent of the boys and 75 percent of the girls reported being upset by the experience of sexual harassment at school. The victims reported that 75 percent of the perpetrators were male and 25 percent were female. Fineran and Bennett (1999) surveyed high school students reflecting a high minority population. Eighty-four percent of the students experienced peer sexual harassment (87% of females and 79% of males), and 75 percent reported perpetrating sexual harassment. Boys perpetrated sexual harassment twice as often as girls. Sixty percent of harassing events were perpetrated by a schoolmate the student knew casually, 15 percent by a schoolmate the student did not know, and 25 percent by students in dating or ex-dating relationships. A related issue of dating violence surfaced in these surveys. The number of students in dating or ex-dating relationships who identify themselves as being sexually harassed indicates that dating violence among high school students continues to be an area requiring proactive education and intervention (Bergman, 1992; Fineran & Bennett, 1998, 1999; Molidar, 1995; O'Keefe, Brockopp, & Chew, 1986).

A certain amount of sexual harassment is same-sex harassment. In the AAUW (2001) study 18 percent of girls reported being sexually harassed by other girls, while 45 percent of the boys reported being harassed by other boys. Overall, 16 percent of the students admitted targeting students of the same sex. The negative implications of this become clearer when related to the AAUW (1993) findings. Eighty-six percent of all students surveyed stated that being labeled as "gay" or "lesbian" created the most distress for them. For boys, this finding in particular was severe. The report stated "no other type of harassment, including actual physical abuse, provoked a reaction this strong among boys" (p. 20). Trigg and Wittenstrom in their 1996 study of peer sexual harassment indicate that, "boys were most disturbed by behaviors that threatened their masculinity, such as being called homosexual or being sexually harassed by other boys" (p. 59). They found that the only harassing behavior that boys experienced at a higher rate than girls was being called gay.

In a study of 712 high school students Fineran (2001, 2002) found that sexual minority students experienced sexual harassment more frequently than heterosexual students. Sexual minority students and heterosexual girls reported being significantly more upset and threatened by peer sexual harassment victimization. In addition, sexual minority students identified unfamiliar male schoolmates as primary perpetrators and were physically assaulted more frequently than heterosexual students.

Additionally, Shakeshaft et al. (1995) in their research on peer harassment found that adolescent girls and boys are harassed in different ways, but the central issue for both was whether they conformed to gender stereotypes. They found that three types of students reported more harassment than did others:

girls viewed by peers as being physically well developed and pretty, girls who were considered unattractive and not dressing stylishly, and boys who did not fit a stereotypic macho male image.

Legal Issues in Sexual Harassment

Recent court decisions have indicated that schools and school personnel who knowingly fail to respond to harmful conditions, such as peer sexual harassment, are made responsible and can be legally liable. This amounts to a right to a safe school environment and is a strong motivator for schools to respond appropriately to needs for safety. In *Nabozny v. Podlesny* (1996) a gay male student was harassed for four years, called names, struck, spat on, and subjected to a mock rape. The school's response was the equivalent of "boys will be boys." He brought suit under the equal protection clause, prevailed, and received substantial damages. The court ruled that the school was unjustified in allowing its students to assault another student based on sexual orientation. In addition, the school would be obligated to intervene were he a female student. He was entitled to an equivalent level of protection. Other same sex harassment cases that have been litigated (*Sauk Rapids-Rice(MN) School District #47*, 1993; *Seamons v. Snow*, 1994) buttress this protection.

In other cases, Title IX of the Education Amendments Act of 1972 has been used when the school knowingly failed to respond to sexual harassment complaints (*Davis v. Monroe County Board of Education*, 1996). Title IX requires that an institution receiving federal funds provide an environment free of discrimination. It prohibits sexual harassment in education and directs education institutions to maintain a grievance procedure that allows for resolution of sex discrimination, including sexual harassment. In another pathway to protection an employer or school system can be responsible when they knowingly allow a "hostile environment." This would take place when the harassing behavior of anyone in the workplace (or school) causes the workplace to become hostile, intimidating, or offensive, and unreasonably interferes with employee or student work (Langelan, 1993). Employers are responsible for the actions of their employees in regard to sexual harassment. Schools are responsible for the actions of both their employees and their students. Thus, a person experiencing sexual harassment while the school turns a blind eye could file a grievance under Title IX with the school system, file a complaint with one's regional Office of Civil Rights of the U.S. Department of Education, or sue in court for damages.

School Policy and Implementation

Policies will not work unless they reverberate with the culture of the school. A culture of violence, intimidation, and retaliation needs to be changed. This is a most complex and difficult task. Many schools have developed sexual harassment policies and procedures that legislate behavior and are more reactive than proactive. This approach places the burden directly on the student to file a complaint and face the response. Stein (1995) pointed out that arbitrary rules can be problematic. One school district banned all physical touching due to numerous complaints from female students about being sexually assaulted by a football player. Lee, Croninger, Linn, and Chen (1996) pointed out that it is difficult to think that a policy of punishing the perpetrator and protecting the victim will be effective in eliminating (peer) sexual harassment in schools. The victim-perpetrator model breaks down when the majority of students are both perpetrator and victim (AAUW, 1993; Fineran & Bennett, 1998). Using the school as a courthouse with a jury of one's peers may also be questionable (Stein, 1995). Blaming the victim by "popular vote" can have perverse effects. A popular student accused of sexual harassment could paradoxically gain status as a victim, whereas the student who points the finger becomes the accuser and is blamed for provoking the behavior.

Some policy approaches to the problem are bound to be ineffective because they do not address the basic issues, which are issues of moral and ethical solidarity. Denial of the existence of the problem, or its suppression, will not work. Neither will purely formal changes in the school's discipline code or grievance procedures. What Lee et al. (1996) identified as the ethical approach has a much broader and deeper focus. Shared values and ethical or moral concepts that bind members together as a community are most important. From Lee et al.'s (1996) perspective, sexual harassment is a sign of the failure of existing organizations to instill ethical coherence and integrity in their members. The schools need to take responsibility for teaching the basic tenets of respect for others, for self, and for a moral community. Lee et al. (1996) supported a cultural theory approach utilizing the ethical dimensions where "more discussion of basic democratic values" is encouraged and "moral and ethical questions are hotly debated" (p. 409). Stein and Sjostrom (1994) believed that sexual harassment needs to be considered "a matter of social injustice" and schools should promote democratic principles.

ADMINISTRATIVE RESPONSES TO BULLYING AND SEXUAL HARASSMENT

The School as a Normative Environment

The school social worker works closely with the school administrator and others on discipline policies, safety plans, crisis plans, and frequently on other administrative issues in the school community. Effective schools research suggests that effective education occurs when, among other things, there is a normative agreement among teachers, parents, and administrators on the content and process of education (Finn, 1984; Kyle, 1985; Purkey & Smith, 1983). Key norms focus on the school as not being a hostile or hurtful environment. Such an environment challenges even the most gifted student's ability to learn. A toxic atmosphere for students hinders the school from carrying out its mission to educate. When students do not feel protected in the school environment, they develop a sense of the school as unsafe. This overrides other messages including those about the primary importance of education. The education of students is at risk, and for many their development as individuals is potentially harmed.

Characteristics of Safe and Responsive Schools. The federal best practices manual (Dwyer, Osher, Warger, et al., 1998) identified thirteen research-based characteristics of schools that foster learning, safety, and socially appropriate behaviors. Effective prevention, intervention, and crisis response strategies operate best in school communities that:

- ◆ Focus on academic achievement;
- ◆ Involve families in meaningful ways;
- ◆ Develop links to the community;
- ◆ Emphasize positive relationships among students and staff;
- ◆ Discuss safety issues openly;
- ◆ Treat students with equal respect;
- ◆ Create ways for students to share their concerns;
- ◆ Help children feel safe in expressing their feelings;
- ◆ Have in place a system for referring children who are suspected of being neglected or abused;
- ◆ Offer extended day programs for children;
- ◆ Promote good citizenship and character;
- ◆ Identify problems and assess progress toward solutions;
- ◆ Support students in making the transition to adult life and the workplace. (Dwyer, Osher, Warger, et al., 1998, p. 6)

Each of these qualities of the safe and responsive school community can also be seen as a set of collaborative tasks for members of the community to construct a safe and responsive environment. Although the school administrator carries primary responsibility for what goes on in the building, the social worker, working in the thick of the issues where the school is most vulnerable, will most likely be heavily involved in the school's efforts to institute all of these.

The Discipline Plan. In the context of current education, none of these qualities happens by accident. They are subject to planning. The best practices manual (Dwyer, Osher, Warger, et al., 1998) identifies three types of written plans that the school community would use to establish a safe environment. The first is an appropriate *discipline plan*. Rules need to be clear, broad based, and fair. Disciplinary procedures need to be developed collectively by members of the total educational community. They need to be communicated clearly to all parties and followed consistently by everyone. In particular, the disciplinary policy should include a code of conduct, specific rules, and consequences that can accommodate student differences on a case-by-case basis when necessary. Negative consequences need to be combined with positive strategies for teaching socially appropriate behaviors. It should include antiharassment and antiviolence policies and due process rights. The school community should participate in the development of these rules and thus have ownership. Peer mediation and conflict resolution would provide student-controlled means of working out some problems and promote a climate of nonviolence. A zero-tolerance statement for illegal possession of weapons, alcohol, or drugs is necessary, as well as services and supports for students who have been suspended and/or expelled (Dwyer, Osher, & Hoffman, 2000).

THE VIOLENCE PREVENTION AND RESPONSE PLAN

The second and the third plans are the *safety plan* and the *crisis plan*, now combined in the school-wide *violence prevention and response plan*. These plans are developed by a core prevention and response team, of which the social worker will most likely be a member. The team should oversee the preparation and implementation of the plans and ensure that every member of the school community takes ownership. An effective safety plan is a long-term and everyday response to the need for safety. It includes a discussion of early warning signs of potentially violent behavior, prevention practices, and intervention strategies adopted by the school community.

A crisis response plan needs to reference a wide range of possibilities. Crises, discussed in the next chapter, can be natural disasters, tragic accidents, suicides, intruders, gang and other violence spilling over into school, contagious diseases, or losses of members of the school community. Crises have the potential to overwhelm and shut down the school decision-making process, when it is most needed, and shatter any belief that school is a safe place. They have long-term effects on education and children's development. Responses call for immediate planned action, good communication, and differentiation of roles of members of a crisis team and others. Team members and others need to divide responsibilities in advance. Some will deal with individual students and teachers in crisis; others with a victim's family and the community, others with community resources, agencies, police, hospitals, or the news media. The school social worker has an important role on the team. The crisis plan spells out contingencies and responses as much as possible, even to the point of advance checklists of things to do and people to contact. The team not only plans what to do when violence strikes, but it also ensures that students and staff know what to do. Students and staff feel secure when there is a well-conceived plan. Everyone understands what to do or whom to ask for instructions. Of course, no one can fully anticipate a particular crisis, but developing some common understandings paves the way to working effectively as a team and a functional school community if something does happen. Once a plan, however well conceived, is formulated, it needs to be kept up to date. Team members and circumstances change every school year. Moreover, beyond an immediate response to a crisis, it is important to take into account the long-term healing that often needs to take place when something tragic or threatening happens (Dwyer, Osher, & Warger, 1998).

Administrative Challenges. Given the evidence, one can safely conclude that few, if any, schools exist without problems in the general area of interpersonal violence, which includes bullying and peer sexual harassment and other forms of violence. On the other hand, the mantra of many superintendents and school board members to their principals is that "good administrators do not have problem children in their schools." If an administrator has problems in her school, it is often interpreted that she is not getting the job done, and that it is time to look for a more qualified administrator. The principal is thus encouraged to give the impression that the school is free of such vexing problems or to minimize them. However, an effective administrator is, first and foremost, honest. She must have the courage and support of others to stand up to the sweeping problems of denial that adversely impact many schools.

The first step in developing an effective intervention program may be to develop an anonymous student and teacher survey (needs assessment) of the nature and incidence of the problem in the district and in each school (Olweus, 2001). A survey gives a better picture of the problem as experienced in different schools and among different age groups and confronts denial that such a problem exists at all. The next step is for the school board to develop parallel policies that prohibit peer sexual harassment and bullying. Implementation guidelines for these policies need to be included in the administrative procedures and in the student handbook. Budget priorities should reflect a commitment to doing something about an identified problem. A cadre of staff needs to be identified and developed to provide the leadership for a school-wide commitment to work on the problem of interpersonal violence. Staff development and staff awareness training are key to an effective anti-harassment policy. Despite a predictable concern that some teachers may not see the problem's relation to education, effective teaching and learning cannot occur in a hostile environment.

When policies are developed, the next challenge is their consistent enforcement. Zero tolerance, as a policy, needs to be a reasonable, consistent, and fair response to acts of student misconduct in the school. Such a policy does not mean a rigid reaction to all infringements as equally punishable. A plastic, yellow dinosaur-shaped squirt gun is not a weapon, though it may be inappropriate at school. Even-handed enforcement and proportionality form the essence of a good zero-tolerance policy. Many schools in trouble have good rules; what is lacking is agreement on reasonable enforcement. All staff must come to agreement that a real act of misbehavior, observed but ignored, is an act affirmed. If there is a clear set of rules governing peer harassment in the school, they will be most effective with a total commitment to their being uniformly and fairly enforced.

Disciplining of staff is a very difficult administrative responsibility. Administration is responsible for getting all staff on board. There should be no tolerance of any staff person who ignores the responsibility to follow policies and procedures in place for curbing interpersonal violence. Compliance is no longer an option; it is the law. However, staff need sufficient training and skill development to intervene appropriately and effectively in bullying and harassing behavior. In-service education and consultation on emergent situations are particularly important. Much harassing behavior may well be overlooked because staff simply does not know what to do.

With policies in place, training developed and carried out, and agreement reached regarding consistent interventions, a final, important piece is to get the broader community involved. Parents, as well as students and staff, should have some say in the process. The more broad-based participation the social worker and others can develop, the greater the resulting ownership and support for the program will be.

Once the program is in place a confidential reporting system must be developed and refined, and an administrator must be assigned to the role of compliance officer. All complaints go through this system and must be taken seriously and in confidence. Although it is beyond the scope of this chapter to address training for the compliance officer, this position is a necessary piece of the program and most state boards of education, and in some cases regional educational offices, can provide this service.

Finally, the greatest challenge to the school administrator may well be that of developing a creative strategy to reduce repeated and continuous intimidation and harassment once it has been identified. In cases such as these, involving serious behavior problems, traditional school discipline, including suspension, detention, and other punitive measures will not work well. An effective intervention must primarily seek to prevent recurrence of any misbehavior. One approach that has met with considerable success is the Confluence model developed at Homewood-Flossmoor Community High School (Moriarty, 2002). Rather than responding to events with rigid and punitive policies and procedures, this approach focuses on teaching new behaviors and using individually developed curriculum materials as a prerequisite for suspended students to return to a regular school program. This program provides the opportunity for the school social worker to play an active role working with the behavior of students who harass and intimidate.

SCHOOL SOCIAL WORK PRACTICE WITH INTERPERSONAL VIOLENCE AND INTIMIDATION

Effective best practices for professionals working with problems of interpersonal violence emphasize: (1) the development of a responsive school community, (2) development of capacities of school team members and teachers, (3) functional assessment of dangerous conditions, (4) positive interaction training, and (5) early, coordinated, multifaceted intervention with students in need (Dwyer, Osher, & Warger, 1998). Building on the determination of the school community that it be a safe place for vulnerable young people, the school district needs to develop policies that recognize the problem and put the resources of the district behind the effort to create a safe environment for each school. This demands a mapping of the safety problem in that particular school community and using that information to develop an appropriate response of the school community to a potentially violent situation (Astor et al., 2004). School social workers can then find a variety of roles for themselves within this broader commitment of the school: These may include

- ◆ Contributing to school policy development;
- ◆ Developing conflict resolution, mediation, and grievance procedures;
- ◆ Making functional assessments of contexts that incite violence;
- ◆ Consulting with teachers and administrators;
- ◆ Developing the capacity of staff, and others as appropriate to intervene effectively in potential conflict situations;
- ◆ Working with groups in school and in the community;
- ◆ Working with victims and perpetrators of interpersonal violence;
- ◆ Coordinating services in the community and resources in the school;
- ◆ Developing responsive referral and intervention systems;
- ◆ Intervening in the situation as early as possible. (Dwyer, Osher, & Warger, 1998)

School Policy Development

No further approach to these problems is possible without explicit policies, and so the first direction for the social worker is to assist in the development of school district policies. As a normative community, each school's effectiveness rests on recognizing problems of serious interpersonal violence and preventing these problems from taking over the school and damaging students. To be successful, the school needs to develop and carry out clear expectations. Rather than approaching this from a negative perspective, the school must affirm that a basic principle underlying membership in the school community is that *persons respect each other, their rights, and their dignity*. Respect for others and trust is the key to inclusion in the school community. This principle, mandated by federal law applying to firearms, can be applied to other acts that endanger others and undermine education. The social worker, who is often the member of the school community most aware of interpersonal violence and its effects, can consult and assist in the development and implementation of school policies. School social workers can provide consultation to administrators and to the board of education on the development of such policies. When students place others at risk, the school must administratively decide what process is necessary for them to be included. Perpetrators need to demonstrate their readiness to return without creating further danger in the environment. Teachers need the support of policy, as do social workers.

Teamwork, Consultation, and Program Development

Identifying and setting consequences for interpersonal violence will create the need for conflict resolution, mediation, and grievance procedures. Mediation procedures reinforce norms that apply to everyone. They avoid making faculty alone responsible for norm development. They are crucial for a whole-school approach to the development of civility. School social workers currently are creating and coordinating mediation programs that enable the maintenance of a respectful and civil environment. By implication these programs reinforce norms of respect for others. The school social worker's role in the development of these policies and practices is described throughout the book. Assisting teachers in dealing with situations of interpersonal violence in their classrooms, gym, hallways, and other school settings demands a more developed consultative role, together with some possible group facilitation of teachers' problem-solving efforts.

Direct Intervention. School social workers can work with students individually or in groups that have become involved in bullying or harassment incidents. They may develop positive interaction or social skills groups. They may work with victims to help them deal with their loss of self-efficacy and allay the certain damage. Such victims may need help to restore their normal, but damaged, assertiveness and feelings about their gender and emergent sexuality. Social workers may work with perpetrators to develop the skills to return to a civil and respectful environment. Social workers may deal with groups to help the group feel safe again or may help teachers to do this.

CONCLUSIONS

For most pupils, especially adolescents, the school experience is critical to their personal development and readiness to become part of the adult world. Peer sexual harassment, intimidation, and bullying of any kind interferes with and inhibits this important developmental process. Social workers who are able to clearly identify the problems associated with peer sexual harassment and bullying strengthen their positions as advocates for improved school environments. They assess hostile school environments as a serious social problem with negative mental health and legal ramifications. In the past, peer harassment has been viewed as just "teasing" or "good natured fun." This "typical behavior" needs to be reframed as behavior that hurts everyone in the educational setting and perpetuates discrimination against students who are vulnerable or who do not fit the current social model for appearance or behavior.

References

American Association of University Women Educational Foundation. (1992). *How schools shortchange girls.* Washington, DC: Wellesley College Center for Research on Women.

American Association of University Women Educational Foundation. (1993). *Hostile hallways: The AAUW survey on sexual harassment in America's schools* (Research Rep. No. 923012). Washington, DC: Harris/Scholastic Research.

American Association of University Women Educational Foundation. (2001). *Hostile hallways: Bullying, teasing and sexual harassment in school.* Washington, DC: Author.

Arsenio, W. F., & Lemerise, E. A. (2001). Varieties of childhood bullying: Values, emotion processes, and social competence. *Social Development, 10*(1), 59-73.

Astor, R. A., Benbenishty, R., & Meyer, H. A. (2004) Monitoring and mapping student victimization in schools. *Theory into Practice, 43*(1), 39-49.

Astor, R. A., Meyer, H. A., Benbenishty, R., Marachi, R., & Rosemond, M. (2005). School safety interventions: Best practices and programs. *Children in Schools, 27*(1), 17-32.

Baldry, A. C., & Farrington, D. P. (2000). Bullies and delinquents: Personal characteristics and parental styles. *Journal of Community and Applied Social Psychology, 10*(1), 17-31.

Batsche, G. M., & Knoff, H. M. (1994). Bullies and their victims: Understanding a pervasive problem in the schools. *School Psychology Review, 23*, 165-74.

Bergman, L. (1992). Dating violence among high school students. *Social Work, 37*, 21-27.

Black, S. (2004) Beyond zero tolerance: Schools don't need extreme policies to be safe and secure. *American School Board Journal.* Retrieved September 14, 2004, from http://www.asbj.com/current/research.html

Bond, L., Carlin, J. B., Thomas, L., Rubin, K., & Patton, G. (2001). Does bullying cause emotional problems? A prospective study of young teenagers. *British Medical Journal, 323*, 480-484.

Carney, J. V. (2000). Bullied to death: Perceptions of peer abuse and suicidal behavior during adolescence. *School Psychology International, 21*(2), 213-223.

Colvin, G, Tobin, T., Beard, K., Hagan, S., & Sprague, J. (1998). The school bully: Assessing the problem, developing interventions, and future research directions. *Journal of Behavioral Education, 8*(3), 293-319.

Constable, R. T., & Lee, D. B. (2004). *Social work with families: Content and process.* Chicago: Lyceum Books.

Curtner-Smith, M. E. (2000). Mechanisms by which family processes contribute to school-age boy's bullying. *Child Study Journal, 30*(3), 169-186.

Davis v. Monroe County Board of Education, 74 F. 3rd 1186 (11th cir. 1996).

Drug-Free Schools and Community Act (20 U.S.C 4601).

Duncan, R. D. (1999). Peer and sibling aggression: An investigation of intra- and extra-familial bullying. *Journal of Interpersonal Violence, 14*(8), 871-886.

Dwyer, K., Osher, D., & Hoffman, C. C. (2000). Creating responsive schools: contextualizing early warning, timely response. *Exceptional Children, 66*(3), 347-365.

Dwyer, K., Osher, D., & Warger, C. (1998). *Early warning, timely response: A guide to safe schools.* Washington, DC: U.S. Department of Education. Available at http://www.air.dc.org/cecp/guide

Dwyer, K., Osher, D., Warger, C., Bear, G., Haynes, N., Knoff, H., et al. (1998). *Early warning, timely response: A guide to safe schools: The referenced edition.* Washington, DC: American Institutes for Research.

Eslea, M., & Smith, P. K. (2000). Pupil and parent attitudes toward bullying in primary schools. *European Journal of Psychology of Education, 15*(2), 207-219.

Fineran, S. (2001). Sexual minority students and peer sexual harassment in high school. *Journal of School Social Work, 11*(2), 50-69.

Fineran, S. (2002). Sexual harassment between same-sex peers: The intersection of mental health, homophobia, and sexual violence in schools. *Social Work, 47*(1), 65–74.

Fineran, S., & Bennett, L. W. (1998). Teenage peer sexual harassment: Implications for social work practice in education. *Social Work, 43*, 55–64.

Fineran, S., & Bennett, L. W. (1999). Gender and power issues of peer sexual harassment among teenagers. *Journal of Interpersonal Violence, 14*, 626–641.

Finn, C. E., Jr. (1984). Toward strategic independence: Nine commandments for enhancing school effectiveness. *Phi Delta Kappan, 66*(8), 513–524.

Grant, G. (1981). The character of education and the education of character. *Daedalus, 110*(3), 135–149.

Grant, G. (1985). Schools that make an imprint: Creating a strong, positive ethos. In J. H. Bunzel (Ed.), *Challenges in American schools: The case for standards and values* (pp. 127–143). New York: Oxford University Press.

Guerra, N. G., Huessman, L. R., Tolan, P. H., Van Acker, R., & Eron, L. D. (1995). Stressful events and individual beliefs as correlates of economic disadvantage and aggression among urban children. *Journal of Counseling and Clinical Psychology, 63*, 518–528.

Haynie, D. L., Hansel, T., Eitel, P., Crump, A. D., Saylor, K., Yu, K., et al. (2001). Bullies, victims, and bully/victims: Distinct groups of at-risk youth. *Journal of Early Adolescence, 21*(1), 29–49.

Hoover, J. H., & Oliver, R. (1996). *The bullying prevention handbook: A guide for principals, teachers and counselors.* Bloomington, IN: National Educational Service Press.

Hunter, J., & Schaecher, R. (1995). Gay and lesbian adolescents. In R. L. Edwards (Ed.), *Encyclopedia of social work* (19th ed., pp. 1055–1063). Washington, DC: National Association of Social Workers Press.

Illinois Safe and Responsive Schools Act, PA 92-0260. 105 ILCS 5/10-20.14: Student Discipline Policies.

Kaltaina-Heino, R., Pilla, M., Ruan, W. J., Simmons-Morton, B., & Scheidt, P. (2000). Bullying at school: An indicator of adolescents at risk for mental disorders. *Journal of Adolescence, 23*(6), 661–674.

Kauffman, J. M., & Burback, H. J. (1997). On creating a climate of classroom civility. *Phi Delta Kappan, 79*(4), 320–325.

Kumpulainen, K., Raesaenen, E., & Henttonen, I. (1999). Children involved in bullying: Psychological disturbance and the persistence of the involvement. *Child Abuse and Neglect, 23*(12), 1253–1262.

Kyle, F. (Ed.). (1985). *Reaching for excellence: An effective schools sourcebook.* Washington, DC: U.S. Government Printing Office.

Langelan, M. J. (1993). *Back off.* New York: Simon & Schuster.

Lee, V. E., Croninger, R. G., Linn, E., & Chen, X. (1996). The culture of sexual harassment in secondary schools. *American Educational Research Journal, 33*(2), 383–417.

MacKinnon, C. A. (1979). *Sexual harassment of working women.* New Haven, CT: Yale University Press.

Mahady-Wilton, M. M., Craig, W. M., & Pepler, D. J. (2000). Emotional regulation and displays in classrooms victims of bullying: Characteristic expressions of affect, coping styles and relevant contextual factors. *Social Development, 9*(2), 226–245.

McGee, J., & DeBernardo, C. R. (1999, May/June). The classroom avenger: A behavioral profile of school shootings. *The Forensic Examiner, 8*, 16–18.

Mattaini, M. (2001a). Constructing cultures of non-violence: The Peace Power! strategy. *Education and Treatment of Children, 24*(4), 430–447.

Mattaini, M. (2001b). *Peace Power for adolescents: Strategies for a culture of non-violence.* Washington, DC: National Association of Social Workers.

Molidar, C. E. (1995). Gender differences of psychological abuse in high school dating relationships. *Child & Adolescent Social Work Journal, 12,* 119-134.

Moriarty, A. R. (2002). *Managing kids: Direct answers for tricky issues.* CASE/CCBD Mini-library series on safe, effective and drug free schools. Arlington, VA: Council for Exceptional Children Press

Mulvey, E. P., & Cauffman, E. (2001). The inherent limits of predicting school violence. *American Psychologist, 56,* 797-802.

Nabozny v. Podlesny, 92 F 3d 446 (7th cir. 1996).

Nansel, T. R., Overpeck, M., Pilla, R. S., Ruan, W. J., Simmons-Morton, B., & Scheidt, P. (2001). Bullying behaviors among US youth: Prevalence and association with psychosocial adjustment. *Journal of the American Medical Association, 285*(16), 2094-2100.

National Institutes of Health. (2005, January 18). *State of the Science Conference Statement: Preventing violence and related health-risking social behaviors in adolescents (October 13-15, 2004),* Retrieved February 24, 2005, from http://consensus.nih.gov

Nisbett, R. E. (1993). Violence and U.S. regional culture. *American Psychologist, 48*(4), 441-449.

No Child Left Behind Act of 2001, PL 107-110.

O'Keefe, N. K., Brockopp, K., & Chew, E. (1986). Teen dating violence. *Social Work, 31,* 465-468.

Olweus, D. (1980). Familial and temperamental determinants in aggressive behavior in adolescent boys: A causal analysis. *Developmental Psychology, 16,* 644-660.

Olweus, D. (1993). *Bullying at school: What we know and what we can do.* Cambridge, MA: Blackwell Press.

Olweus, D. (2001). Peer harassment: A critical analysis and some important issues. In J. Juvonen & S. Graham (Eds.), *Peer harassment in school: The plight of the vulnerable and victimized* (pp. 3-20). New York: Guilford.

Olweus, D., Limber, S., & Mihalic, S. F. (1999). *Blueprints for violence protection, book nine: Bullying prevention program.* Boulder, CO: Center for the Study and Prevention of Violence.

Permanent Commission (Connecticut) on the Status of Women (PCSW). (1995). *In our own backyard: Sexual harassment in Connecticut's public high schools.* Hartford, CT: Author

Perry, B. D. (1997). *Maltreated children: Experience, brain development and the next generation.* New York: Norton Press.

Purkey, S. C., & Smith, M. S. (1983). Effective schools: A review. *The Elementary School Journal, 83*(4), 427-452.

Rigby, K. (2000). Effects of peer victimization in schools and perceived social support on adolescent well-being. *Journal of Adolescence, 23*(1), 57-68.

Rigby, K., & Slee, P. (1999). Suicidal ideation among adolescent school children, involvement in bully-victim problems, and perceived social support. *Suicide and Life-Threatening Behavior, 29*(2), 119-130.

Roland, E. (2000). Bullying in school: Three national innovations in Norwegian schools in fifteen years. *Aggressive Behavior, 26*(1), 135-143.

Roscoe, B., Strouse, J. S., & Goodwin, M. P. (1994). Sexual harassment: Early adolescents' self-reports of experiences and acceptance. *Adolescence, 29*(115), 515-523.

Rutter, M., Maugham, B., Mortimore, P., & Ousten, J. (1979). *Fifteen thousand hours: Secondary schools and their effects on children*. Cambridge, MA: Harvard University Press.

Safe and Drug-Free Schools and Communities Act, 20 U.S.C. 7101.

Salmivalli, C., Kaukiainen, A., Kaistaniemi, L., & Kirsti, M. J. (1999). Self-evaluated self-esteem, peer-evaluated self-esteem, and defensive egotism as predictors of adolescents' participation in bullying situations. *Personality and Social Psychology Bulletin, 25*(10), 1268-1278.

Sauk Rapids-Rice (MN) School District #47, MN, no. 05-93-1142. Office for Civil Rights, U.S. Department for Education, Chicago, IL (June 23, 1993).

Schwartz, D., Proctor, L. J., & Chien, D. H. (2001). The aggressive victim of bullying: Emotional and behavioral dysregulation as a pathway to victimization by peers. In J. Juvonen & S. Graham (Eds.), *Peer harassment in school: The plight of the vulnerable and victimized* (pp. 147-174). New York: Guilford.

Seamons v. Snow, 864 F. Supp. 1111 (D. Utah, 1994).

Sexton, T. L., & Alexander, J. F. (2003) Functional family therapy: A mature clinical model for working with at-risk adolescents and their families. In T. L Sexton, G. R. Weeks, & M. S Robbins (Eds), *Handbook of family therapy* (pp. 323-350). New York, Brunner-Routledge.

Shakeshaft, C., Barber, E., Hergenrother, M. A., Johnson, Y. M., Mandel, L., & Sawyer, J. (1995). Peer harassment in schools. *Journal for a Just and Caring Education, 1*(1), 30-44.

Sheidow, A. J., Henggeler, S. W., & Schoenwals, S. K. (2003). Multisystemic therapy. In T. L Sexton, G. R Weeks, & M. S Robbins (Eds.), *Handbook of family therapy* (pp. 303-322). New York: Brunner-Routledge.

Smith, D. C., & Sandhu, D. S. (2004). Toward a positive perspective on violence protection in schools: Building connections. *Journal of counseling and development, 82*, 287-293.

Smith, P. K., & Myron-Wilson, R. (1998). Parenting and school bullying. *Clinical Child Psychology and Psychiatry, 3*(3), 405-417.

Smith, P. K., & Shu, S. (2000). What good schools can do about bullying: Findings from a survey in English schools after a decade of research and action. *Childhood: A Global Journal of Child Research, 7*(2), 193-212.

Smith, P. K., Madsen, K. C., & Moody, J. C. (1999). What causes the age decline in reports of being bullied at school? Towards a developmental analysis of risks of being bullied. *Educational Research, 41*(3), 267-285.

Stein, N. (1995). Sexual harassment in K-12 schools: The public performance of gendered violence. *The Harvard Educational Review, Special Issue on Violence and Youth, 65*(2), 145-162.

Stein, N., Marshall, N. L., & Tropp, L. R. (1993). *Secrets in public: Sexual harassment in our schools*. Wellesley, MA: Wellesley College Center for Research on Women.

Stein, N., & Sjostrom, L. (1994). *Flirting or hurting? A teachers guide on student to student sexual harassment in schools*. Washington, DC: National Education Association.

Strauss, S., & Espeland, P. (1992). *Sexual harassment and teens*. Minneapolis, MN: Free Spirit Publishing.

Sutton, J., Smith, P. K., & Swettenham, J. (1999). Social cognition and bullying: Social inadequacy or skilled manipulation? *British Journal of Developmental Psychology, 17*(3), 435-450.

Title IX, Education Amendments of 1972. *Federal Register*, Part II Department of Education. *45*, 30955-30965.

Trigg, M., & Wittenstrom, K. (1996). That's the way the world goes: Sexual harassment and New Jersey teenagers. (Special Issue: Sexual Harassment). *Initiatives, 57*(2), 55-65.

Walker, H. M., Colvin, G., & Ramsey, E. (1995). *Antisocial behavior in school: Strategies and best practices*. Pacific Grove, CA: Brooks/Cole.

Wolke, D., Woods, S., Blomfield, L., & Karstadt, L. (2000). The association between direct and relational bullying and behavior problems among primary school children. *Journal of Child Psychology & Psychiatry & Related Disciplines, 41*(8), 989-1002.

Zuehl, J. J., Dillon, E., Schilling, J. L., & Oltmanns, J. K. (2002, January 26). Student discipline issues. In Franczek & P. C. Sullivan (Eds.), *Attorneys at Law eighth annual school law conference*. Unpublished paper.

37

School-Based Crisis Intervention for Traumatic Events

Jay Callahan
Loyola University, Chicago

- ◆ Social Work Involvement
- ◆ Definitions
- ◆ Type I versus Type II Trauma
- ◆ Common Post-Traumatic Reactions
- ◆ Predictors of Distress
- ◆ Trauma Versus Grief
- ◆ Definitions of Crisis and Crisis Intervention
- ◆ Crisis Team and Levels of Crisis
- ◆ Crisis Plan
- ◆ On-Scene Interventions
- ◆ Team Activation
- ◆ Teachers Meeting
- ◆ Notification of Students
- ◆ Support Services
- ◆ Scope of School Response
- ◆ Screening of Victims
- ◆ Critical Incident Stress Debriefing
- ◆ Ongoing Support Groups
- ◆ Consultation and Assistance to Faculty
- ◆ Ongoing Tracking and Review
- ◆ Media
- ◆ Community Meeting
- ◆ Rumor Control Mechanisms
- ◆ Reducing Suicide Contagion
- ◆ Community Healing

In the aftermath of the terrorist attacks of September 11, 2001, the psychological impact of traumatic events has become all too clear to many people throughout the world. The emotional consequences of these events spread far beyond New York and Washington, and people across the country experienced intrusive images, anxiety, and fear that the attacks would happen again.

The twenty-first century brought another dramatic example of the emotional consequences of trauma in the tsunami that struck south Asia at Christmas, 2004. The World Health Organization issued a statement expressing concern for the "millions of children" who were expected to have "psychological scars" from the disaster, which killed over 157,000 people (Huuhtanen, 2005). These devastating incidents, one human-caused and the other an act of nature, are overwhelming in their scope and impact. Other incidents, not so large or dramatic, are also emotionally devastating to victims and survivors. Some of these traumatic incidents took place in schools:

◆ In a small Arkansas town in March 1998, two schoolboys dressed in fatigues hid in the woods near their middle school, armed with several semiautomatic rifles. The boys, ages 11 and 13, set off a false fire alarm and then fired twenty-seven shots at students and teachers who came out on the playground. They killed four young girls and a teacher and wounded ten others (Bragg, 1998).

◆ Early one morning in the mid-1990s, in a small town west of Chicago, a substitute school bus driver drove across a pair of railroad tracks and stopped for a red light. Distracted by the noise of the engine and the students in the bus, she was unaware that the rear of the bus was extending over the railroad tracks. A commuter train plowed into the bus, killing five high school students and injuring thirty others. Virtually everyone in their high school was traumatized (Washburn & Gibson, 1995).

◆ In the late 1980s in a small town in southeastern Michigan, during the summer a 10-year-old boy committed suicide by hanging. Just after school began in the fall, a 12-year-old girl from the same neighborhood also committed suicide, also by hanging. The middle school in that neighborhood was thrown into crisis. Friends and acquaintances of the second suicide victim attempted to cope with her death, while faculty, parents, and administrators feared that additional suicides would occur (Callahan, 1996).

Thus it has become quite clear that schools are not immune to the traumatic events that occur in all facets of our society and, indeed, the entire world. Traumatic events take place in schools, on the way to and from schools, and in the communities to which schools belong. Many of these situations precipitate crises for schools and their surrounding communities. In this chapter we will discuss traumatic events and the crises that they often cause, as well as crisis intervention techniques to respond to these traumatic situations.

SOCIAL WORK INVOLVEMENT

In all of these cases, and in many others, school social workers have been central to the interventions that have followed these traumatic events. As individual professionals, and as members of school crisis teams, social workers are frequently leaders in providing crisis intervention to traumatized schools, faculty, and students. By virtue of training and education, social workers are often better prepared to respond appropriately than other school professionals. However, this is not to imply that all school social workers have an adequate background in crisis intervention and responding to traumatic stress; indeed, the purpose of this chapter is to outline this advanced level of training. Nonetheless, social workers are ideally suited to provide crisis intervention activities in the aftermath of a traumatic event.

DEFINITIONS

Traumatic events are extraordinary situations that are likely to evoke significant distress in many people. Such events involve the threat of death or serious physical injury. They include homicide, suicide, or accidental death; specific examples include gang-related violence, the abrupt heart attack and death of a teacher, and an auto accident in which students are seriously injured. A traumatic stressor is defined by the American Psychiatric Association as an event in which

> the person experienced, witnessed, or was confronted with an event or events that involved actual or threatened death or serious injury, or a threat to the physical integrity of self or others [and] the person's response involved intense fear, helplessness, or horror. (American Psychiatric Association [APA], 1994, p. 431)

Traumatic stressors include both individual events as well as certain ongoing or chronic circumstances. Other terms that are synonymous with traumatic stressor are psychic trauma, psychological trauma, and emotional trauma.

It has only been in the past twenty years that empirical studies of children's and adolescents' responses to traumatic stressors have been carried out. Prior to the early 1980s, a few psychoanalytic case studies existed, but little research was done. In 1980, the American Psychiatric Association's DSM-III was published (APA, 1980), which included a new category entitled post-traumatic stress disorder (PTSD). Although the impetus for this inclusion was the experience of Vietnam veterans, it soon became evident that other traumatic events and stressors also could lead to PTSD. Moreover, it was also evident that children and adolescents frequently experienced a variety of traumatic events and exhibited reactions that could be understood, not as manifestations of previous psychopathology, but as responses to the trauma (Pynoos & Nader, 1988; Terr, 1991). PTSD was conceptualized as a syndrome of persistent reactions following a traumatic stressor that was fairly similar among children, adolescents, and adults. A new disorder, acute stress disorder (ASD) was included in the DSM-IV in 1994. ASD is essentially PTSD in the short term—that is, less than one month; PTSD can only be diagnosed when the symptoms have persisted for one month or more. In this chapter we will not focus on diagnosable disorders, but rather on the spectrum of post-traumatic reactions and phenomena in general, which will be labeled traumatic stress. Even though traumatic events are defined as extraordinary situations that are likely to evoke significant distress in a large proportion of the population, victims can exhibit a wide range of reactions. Even in highly stressful events, reactions range from mild to severe. As traumatic stress reactions become better understood, it is evident that many individuals experience only mild, transient responses (Bonanno, 2004).

TYPE I VERSUS TYPE II TRAUMA

Traumatic stressors can take many forms. One helpful distinction is between acute, "single-blow" traumatic events and multiple or long-standing traumas (Terr, 1991). Type II traumas are multiple or continuous and occur in a context of physical or psychological captivity. Multiple or long-standing traumas for adults include experiencing combat, concentration camps or being a prisoner of war, or the victim of political torture. Among children and adolescents, prolonged childhood physical and sexual abuse are the primary examples. Crisis intervention, such as the activities that are described in this chapter, is not appropriate for Type II traumas. In these situations, the full nature of the trauma is frequently not evident to authorities and individuals in a position to intervene until months or years of abuse have passed. After such continued trauma, much more extensive treatment is required than the relatively brief interventions described here for Type I individual traumas.

Type I traumas that affect a school community include suicides, homicides, and sudden accidental deaths of faculty members; transportation accidents; significant violence occurring in the school; and disasters in the surrounding community, such as tornadoes, hurricanes, earthquakes, and wildfires. Rare but overwhelming events include hostage situations and sniper attacks on school grounds. Occasional national disasters, such as assassinations and the explosions of the *Challenger* and *Columbia* space shuttles, can also have a powerful impact on a school community.

COMMON POST-TRAUMATIC REACTIONS

Although many social workers may think of the word *post-traumatic* as shorthand for post-traumatic stress disorder, the word means "after a trauma." Therefore, in discussing common post-traumatic reactions, no implication is intended that these are symptoms of PTSD. Post-traumatic reactions occur on a continuum, as noted earlier, and span many different aspects of human functioning; only in the most severe cases is it appropriate to assign a diagnostic label. Recent research has also focused on the positive side of this equation—that many people experience highly stressful events and do not develop post-traumatic symptoms. In fact, the evidence suggests that, at least in some instances, the majority of people exposed to a traumatic stressor will experience only mild and transient symptoms (Kessler, Sonnega, Bromet, Hughes, & Nelson, 1995). It appears that in our tendency to focus on helping people who are harmed, we have overlooked the fact that many individuals are resilient in the face of traumatic events (Bonanno, 2004; Bonanno, Wortman, et al., 2002). In fact, at least in some cases, stress can lead to adaptive and constructive psychological growth. Receiving appropriate support and intervention is frequently crucial in producing these positive outcomes. However, it is also true that many people are able to handle traumatic stress in their own way and with their own natural support systems.

Among those who are harmed, PTSD is not the only consequence. The negative sequelae of trauma include depression, maladaptive alcohol and drug use, somatic symptoms, such as headaches and muscle aches, and various manifestations of anxiety. The most common post-traumatic symptoms can be conceptualized as occurring in four major categories. These four clusters of reactions are: (1) intrusive thoughts and images that are frequently reexperienced; (2) purposeful avoidance of places, people, and situations that remind the individual of the traumatic stressor; (3) dissociative phenomena; and (4) increased anxiety and autonomic arousal. These are described next, along with some consideration of the different reactions of children and adolescents. Adolescents' reactions tend to resemble adult reactions in most ways.

Reexperiencing

Reexperiencing phenomena include intrusive thoughts about the event that occur unbidden, and usually unwanted, and are relatively resistant to conscious control. Adults and adolescents may experience "flashbacks," in which they visualize the trauma and feel as if it is happening again. Children do not seem to experience flashbacks in the same way, although they may visualize images or hear sounds briefly (Pynoos & Nader, 1988). "Flashbulb memories" are so traumatic and dramatic that the individual retains the image like a flash photograph. Powerful and painful images of this kind that accompanied the explosion of the *Challenger* have been described among children of Concord, New Hampshire, who attended the school in which Christa McAuliffe taught (Terr et al., 1996). Dreams and nightmares are common, and children often incorporate trauma themes into their play (Terr, 1991).

Purposeful Avoidance

The second cluster of symptoms consists of conscious and purposeful avoidance of situations, places, and people that remind a victim of the traumatic event. Adolescents as well as children are reluctant to return to places where traumas occur, including school or home. In the aftermath of a sniper shooting at a school in Los Angeles, daily absenteeism increased to a peak of 268 per day from its normal level of 64 and remained elevated for a month (Pynoos et al., 1987). In addition, some individuals consciously avoid talking about the event, so as not to stir up strong feelings that may be overwhelming; such avoidance has been termed affect avoidance. Because children often have even more difficulty tolerating strong feelings than adults do, affect avoidance may be particularly persistent in children.

Dissociation

The third cluster of symptoms refers to mild to moderate kinds of dissociation. Usually these experiences are described as "emotional shock" or "numbing of responsiveness." In this instance individuals report a variety of experiences such as "It didn't seem real" or "I couldn't believe it was actually happening." Dissociation is the structured separation of normally integrated functions of memory, emotion, consciousness, and identity (Spiegel & Cardena, 1991). Dissociation of memory is the common experience of being unable to remember all the details of a traumatic event afterwards, or of having "patchy amnesia." Dissociation of emotion is the frequent experience of feeling numb or of feeling nothing immediately after a trauma. Dissociation of consciousness is the feeling of unreality or disbelief that many individuals have during and after a traumatic event. Finally, dissociation of identity is the extreme separation of an individual's personality into several partial personalities. This extreme form sometimes occurs in the aftermath of chronic and severe sexual and physical abuse and has previously been labeled multiple personality disorder.

Dissociation has received renewed attention in recent years, and it has become increasingly clear that not only is dissociation a frequent consequence of a trauma, it is a marker or indicator of distress. The common conception of emotional numbing, or feeling of unreality, for example, is that it is a protective mechanism in the aftermath of a traumatic event that shields the individual from the full realization of the horror that has taken place. However, recent research has overwhelmingly demonstrated that individuals who make frequent use of dissociation fare poorest in the long run (Griffin, Resick, & Mechanic, 1997; Marmar et al., 1994; Marmar, Weiss, Metzler, Ronfeldt, & Foreman, 1996). During the occurrence of an emotional trauma, victims frequently experience dissociation of consciousness, in which the passage of time seems altered (usually slowed down), the world seems unreal, the event seems to not really be happening, and similar phenomena. Dissociation at the time of the trauma is termed peritraumatic dissociation, and a variety of studies have shown that victims who experience peritraumatic dissociation have the highest probability of developing PTSD (Griffin et al., 1997; Marmar et al., 1994, 1996).

Hyperarousal and Anxiety

The fourth symptom cluster is that of hyperarousal or heightened anxiety. In the aftermath of a traumatic stressor, people very frequently report difficulty sleeping, an increased startle reflex, jumpiness or a sense of being "keyed up," and anxiety in general. One particular aspect of this anxiety is fear of recurrence of the trauma; it is as if one occurrence, no matter how rare, suggests that the event could happen again. Similarly, the experience of being exposed to one trauma opens up the possibility of other traumas happening as well. For example, individuals of all ages who lose a family member or friend to sudden illness worry that others may die in car accidents.

Guilt is another common reaction and can have many referents. Frequently individuals who have been present when others were killed or injured feel guilty that they were not able to prevent or lessen the loss, or that there is no discernible reason that they survived while others died.

PREDICTORS OF DISTRESS

Because there are many different types of post-traumatic reactions, the general term distress is used here to indicate the severity of possible symptoms. Although a traumatic event is distressing to almost everyone, some people react more intensely than others, as noted above. Recent research has sought to clarify the factors that are associated with the severity of response. Across virtually all studies, for adults, adolescents, and children, the amount of exposure to the trauma is the single most powerful predictor of the intensity of the post-traumatic reaction. A helpful example, empirically validated, was presented by Pynoos et al. (1987). Near the end of a school day, a sniper opened fire on a school playground in Los Angeles from a nearby apartment building window, killing one child and one adult and wounding thirteen others. He was found to have committed suicide when the police broke into his apartment. A group of 159 children were studied, and exposure to the gunfire was found to be the strongest predictor of distress. Children who were actually on the playground, who saw others being shot and heard the gunfire, were most severely affected. Children who were still in school at the time, and who were kept in their classrooms by their teachers, who feared an assault on the school, were next most affected. Children who had already gone home for the day were less affected. Finally, children who were "off track" in their twelve-month school schedule, who were not attending school that month, were least affected. The degree of exposure to the violence and the threat of death were the most powerful variables.

However, other variables have been shown to make significant differences in the severity of distress. The meaning of the event to the individual is perhaps one of the most important (Webb, 1994). In the Los Angeles situation, a twelve-month follow-up found that the children who were in the school building during the sniper attack, who feared that armed men would storm the school and kill students and teachers, had reappraised their risk. That is, in the days following the event it became evident that the gunman acted alone, that he shot from an apartment window across the street, and that the fear of an armed assault on the school was groundless. Consequently, many of the children revised their appraisal of risk and altered the meaning of the event to them, now concluding that they were never in any danger. As a result, their level of distress decreased markedly, whereas the children who were on the playground continued to have high levels of anxiety and other post-traumatic reactions a year later (Nader, Pynoos, Fairbanks, & Frederick, 1990).

Traditionally, theories of stress have included the concept of appraisal (Lazarus & Folkman, 1984). That is, the meaning that the individual attaches to the event is paramount in predicting and understanding his or her response. Controlling for the amount of loss of life and property damage, natural disasters are usually less distressing than human-caused accidents, and accidents are less distressing than incidents caused by human malevolence. These distinctions are thought to be due to most people's attributions that conscious human intent to harm others, such as the 9/11 terrorist attacks, are considered more preventable and less understandable than a human-caused accident, such as many airplane crashes, which are frequently due to pilot error. Human error is thought to be preventable in theory, but most people realize that it is impossible to prevent 100 percent of accidents. Finally, natural weather disasters are considered inevitable/not preventable; they simply happen.

Another aspect of meaning is the possible violation of basic assumptions about life and the world. According to Janoff-Bulman (1985) and other theorists, adolescents and adults from all Western cultures share a small number of common, unstated, but deeply believed assumptions. One primary assumption is that the world is predictable, which gives rise to long-standing searches to find an understandable meaning. Survivors of trauma struggle to understand why it happened to them. Many people believe "everything happens for a reason" and that a victim "must have done something to have this happen to him," or they ask "What did I do to deserve this?" Of course, children may draw a variety of personal and malignant meanings from an event, partly due to cognitive immaturity.

Malignant meanings that individuals attach to events lead to higher levels of distress. Individuals who are able to find benevolent or positive meanings in events fare better. Furthermore, there appears to be a natural inclination to try to find some positive meaning in the aftermath of a trauma, and eventually many people find satisfaction in having survived, in having done the best they could under the circumstances, and similar conclusions.

Other factors that affect the outcome include prior trauma. As noted earlier, in the past theorists suggested that repeated trauma may provide a kind of inoculation against the destructive effects of additional trauma. However, recent research has indicated that multiple or continued trauma is harmful. For example, Vietnam veterans who were physically abused as children were more likely, given a certain amount of exposure to combat, to develop PTSD than those who were not (Pynoos & Nader, 1988; Schlenger et al., 1992). Clearly, this suggests that children and adolescents who have been victims of prior trauma are more likely to be severely affected by current trauma than those who have not. Family discord or a personal history of depression or other emotional problems are also associated with more negative outcomes. Conversely, individuals with stable backgrounds and psychologically healthy families frequently possess the personal qualities of resilience or hardiness that enable them to withstand very stressful events.

Finally, social support plays an important role in shielding an individual from the most severe impact of traumatic stress. Numerous studies of stress, both normative and traumatic, have demonstrated that people with supportive family and friends cope with trauma better than those without. Especially important may be the initial response of significant others—the homecoming of Vietnam veterans and the initial response of the spouse of a woman who has been sexually assaulted (Johnson et al., 1997). In a trauma that affects a school, supportive and positive responses of teachers and staff to traumatized children are crucial.

TRAUMA VERSUS GRIEF

Death or the threat of death has a central role in many, perhaps most, of these traumatic situations. School social workers and other mental health professionals tend to conceptualize students' and teachers' reactions to death as grief or bereavement. However, such a conception is incomplete. Grief is the reaction to the death of a significant other, but post-traumatic reactions are a separate aspect and involve a variety of other symptoms and cognitive phenomena, which will be described next. Recent research suggests, in fact, that when both are present, post-traumatic reactions must be attended to first, before the grieving process can proceed (Nader, 1997). Almost all deaths of young people, as well as unexpected deaths of adults, involve trauma as well as grief. Many of these deaths are by suicide, homicide, or sudden accidents, and many involve violence; these events evoke trauma responses as well as grief reactions.

DEFINITIONS OF CRISIS AND CRISIS INTERVENTION

A crisis is a period of psychological disequilibrium during which a person's normal coping mechanisms are insufficient to solve a problem or master a situation (Callahan, 1994). A state of crisis necessarily persists for at least a few days, up to perhaps six weeks, during which the individual usually feels tense, anxious, depressed, and frequently overwhelmed. However, the disequilibrium and tension of the crisis state cannot last indefinitely; individuals naturally reach a new equilibrium. However, depending on a variety of factors, including the type and appropriateness of help received, this new equilibrium may be at a lower level of functioning than the person's previous level. Individuals may enter a state of crisis in reaction to a variety of precipitating events, including many that may be thought of as normative or common. For example, parental divorce may precipitate a crisis for many children and adolescents. Although traumatic in the ordinary sense of the word, a divorce is not a traumatic stressor in the sense that we have been describing here, that is, involving the threat of death or serious physical injury.

Many crises are precipitated by traumatic stressors. In fact, in particularly severe events, many people experience a state of crisis. This does not mean that they necessarily qualify for a diagnosis of ASD, but it does mean they are significantly distressed, do not function at their normal levels, and are in danger of ongoing dysfunction—which may eventually justify a diagnosis of ASD or PTSD—if appropriate help is not received in a timely fashion.

In a similar way, a system may be thought of as being in a state of crisis when many of its members experience tension, anxiety, and depression and when the system as a whole does not function at its normal level and in its normal fashion. A school as a whole may experience a crisis after a traumatic event, and its continued health and ability to function effectively may depend on receiving appropriate help in a timely fashion.

CRISIS TEAM AND LEVELS OF CRISIS

The school social worker is often one of the primary professionals who can offer this help. In fact, a team of professionals is necessary to offer intervention to a school in crisis, and usually this team is designated the *crisis team* or the *traumatic event response team*. The remainder of this chapter consists of guidelines on responding to traumatic events, along with suggestions on how to decrease the possibility of cluster or contagious suicide when the original event is a student suicide.

It is helpful to conceptualize a variety of levels of severity, usually corresponding to the nature and breadth of impact of the event itself. A common typology defines three levels of crisis:

- ◆ *Level I*—a personal tragedy for one individual or a threatening incident primarily affecting a student, teacher, or administrator at one site. Examples are the death of a parent or family member, the serious illness of a student or faculty member, a suicide threat in school, or a student bringing a weapon to school.
- ◆ *Level II*—a major personal crisis or a major threatening incident at a single school, or a major disaster elsewhere that affects students and teachers. Examples include the death of a student or teacher while not in school, an accident with severe injuries, a student abduction, or gang violence.

◆ *Level III*—a disaster or threatened disaster that directly affects one or more schools. Examples include a tornado or flood; the taking of hostages or sniper fire at a school; an air crash, explosion, or fire at or near the school; cluster suicides; or a death at a school.

A graded series of interventions should be planned, corresponding to the level of crisis. A Level I crisis can often be responded to by one or two school social workers or other school mental health or health professionals and may not require the active intervention of a larger team. In contrast, a Level II or Level III crisis clearly requires a crisis team, made up of at least six to eight individuals, and may require additional help from other schools or the community (Dallas Public Schools, 1997; Smith, 1997).

CRISIS PLAN

Each school, and each school district, should have a carefully designed and periodically updated crisis plan. Such a plan would indicate a variety of activities, described next. Annual in-services for all faculty and staff should be provided, so that the plan is not simply filed and forgotten. In many schools, a school social worker is the director or leader of the crisis team; in any case the school social worker usually has an important role in the development of the crisis plan. Members of the crisis team usually include the school nurse, the school psychologist, and several volunteer teachers who are interested. A Level I crisis can usually be managed by just a few members of the team. Six to eight members on the crisis team is enough to provide most of the leadership and actual coverage in a Level II crisis. With a Level III crisis, outside help will always be necessary. It is always advisable to include at least one school social worker or other school mental health professional from another school in the same district, or an outside mental health consultant. In certain crises in which the members of the crisis team are personally affected, or in which teachers need particular attention, the use of a consultant or professional from outside eliminates the undesirable situation in which the school social worker needs to provide personal support and intervention to faculty members who are his or her peers during regular school days. Such dual relationships should be avoided if at all possible.

ON-SCENE INTERVENTIONS

The vast majority of social work interventions for school crises take place in the aftermath of the traumatic event, that is, after the event itself is over. *Postvention* is another term for these responses, which indicates the timing of the activities, relative to prevention and intervention activities (American Association of Suicidology, 1997). Rarely does the event last long enough or occur in a place close enough for school personnel, including the school social worker, to become actively involved while the event is still unfolding. In the case of the sniper who fired at children on a school playground described earlier, teachers and other school personnel were involved in the traumatic situation itself. In fact, several hours passed after the gunfire stopped before it became clear that the sniper had killed himself and that it was safe to leave the school building. In other cases, such as fires or suspected fires, parents may arrive at the school and congregate on the playground or in the parking lot, and it may appear that some kind of intervention by the social worker is indicated.

During the event, no psychological interventions should be attempted. The only activities that are appropriate in this kind of situation are keeping order, providing information, and responding to rumors. Occasionally, social workers have attempted to engage parents or students in discussions of their feelings and thoughts at the time of an incident, before it is resolved. Such attempts are ill advised. Until the safety of everyone concerned is assured, parents and students are in a psychologically vulnerable state and are primarily experiencing fear, anxiety, and a sense of vulnerability. It is not appropriate to engage them in a discussion of these fears and anxieties when the outcome is unknown. In such situations parents and students have not explicitly or even implicitly agreed to such a discussion. Providing information about support activities that will be scheduled for the near future is appropriate, as are periodic informational updates and rumor control. The only possible exception would be to provide informal support on a one-to-one basis with an individual who is already obviously upset.

TEAM ACTIVATION

Many traumatic events, fortunately, take place away from school. As soon as knowledge of such an event becomes known to anyone on a school staff, the crisis team and the principal should be notified. If the school social worker is the leader of or a member of the crisis team, it may be her responsibility to coordinate a meeting of the crisis team either late on that same day, if staff are still at school, or early the next morning. Most school crisis teams meet early in the morning prior to school, and before a special teachers' meeting that itself is scheduled for thirty or forty-five minutes prior to the opening of school. In the crisis team meeting, the current situation and the crisis plan are reviewed, and a general approach to the current crisis is outlined. If no representative of administration is on the team, close communication with administration must be established and maintained.

As part of team activation, the principal of the school or superintendent of the school district should confirm the details of the event. Most often this entails talking to the police, or a hospital, or the medical examiner, or the family of the individuals affected by the traumatic event. Although most of the details of these situations may be confidential, authorities usually understand that the event will have a powerful impact on the school and that accurate information is essential in order to plan an effective response. Confirming the names of the deceased, for example, is often the central issue in a traumatic death.

With Level II and Level III crises, crisis team members need to spend most if not all of their time for at least several days responding to the traumatic event. Teachers who are team members will need to be replaced by substitute teachers, and school social workers will rarely be able to carry out many of their regular responsibilities.

TEACHERS MEETING

Using a "phone-fan-out" system or other emergency notification system, teachers are notified as soon as possible about the crisis situation and are asked to attend a special meeting. This special meeting is usually held thirty to forty-five minutes before school begins the next morning. At this meeting, the principal usually briefs the faculty on the nature of the event and then turns the meeting over to the crisis team leader. The team leader describes the range of reactions expected from students, notes interventions and activities to be held over the next few days, and provides an opportunity for faculty to ask questions. If possible, an expert in the specifics of the traumatic event can be brought in to provide more detailed information. However, the range of reactions to almost all traumatic events is similar enough that general knowledge of the nature of traumatic stress is usually sufficient. In addition, a later voluntary meeting or other opportunity for faculty to talk with the crisis team and each other is essential. Faculty and staff cannot effectively help students if they are themselves distracted and preoccupied by their own reactions to the tragedy.

It is strongly recommended that information about the event be communicated to students through a prepared statement written by the crisis team and read to first-period classes by each teacher. Therefore, the written statement is prepared and duplicated by the crisis team in advance and distributed to the faculty at the early morning meeting. The written statement should include only information that has been confirmed definitely. Distributing a vague and generic announcement is not useful; by the time school has begun, many students will know more details about what happened than most of the faculty, and if the school does not appear knowledgeable, the crisis team and the faculty in general will lose credibility. If the death is a suicide and the family has indicated that they do not want this fact to be announced, the school should gently suggest to the family that little is gained by trying to conceal the manner of death and that the school must abide by the ruling of the medical examiner or coroner. If the medical examiner or coroner does not provide a definitive decision (in some cases, a decision with regard to mode of death is not available for some weeks), the statement should simply indicate that no ruling has yet been reached.

NOTIFICATION OF STUDENTS

As noted previously, notification of students should take place in a personal manner, with teachers reading the statement previously prepared by the crisis team and administration. Announcements over the public address system are impersonal and inevitably poorly received, whereas classroom-by-classroom notification by teachers is usually appreciated by students. Inevitably, time for discussion must be provided immediately, and little normal work will be accomplished. In a Level II crisis, there are usually some students and some classes that are not intensely affected by the event, and discussion can be brief. In cases where students knew the victims well, much more time will be needed. If a student or students have died, a member of the crisis team should attend each of the deceased student's classes throughout the day and assist the teacher in structuring the discussion.

SUPPORT SERVICES

Throughout the first few days of a Level II or Level III crisis, a school drop-in center or centers should be established. These centers are easily accessible offices or rooms where students are encouraged to go if they feel the need to talk about the traumatic event or other related concerns. Drop-in centers should be staffed by members of the crisis team, with extra assistance if needed. Group or individual discussions should be conducted. Some experts in the field of traumatic stress have recommended that individual sessions be emphasized (Leenaars & Wenckstern, 1999), but the consensus of the field is that group sessions are preferable and more practical, given the limitations of time and staff.

In a Level II crisis, students are typically permitted to leave their regular classes without an excuse to go to these drop-in centers for the first two or three days. After two to three days, school should begin to move back toward business as usual. Many students will not be intensely affected and deserve to have their education continue with as few interruptions as possible. In a Level III crisis, return to normalcy may take considerably longer. Limiting the availability of the drop-in centers is also appropriate given some students' tendency to become emotionally involved in the trauma in a melodramatic fashion. Such students seem to be "seduced" by intense feelings and seem to unconsciously desire to continue the crisis state's emotional intensity as long as possible (Callahan, 1996). In addition, it is possible that some students will simply take advantage of the opportunity to miss class and to do something else that appears to be more interesting, whether they really need to or not.

SCOPE OF SCHOOL RESPONSE

For some time, the consensus of experts has been that opportunities for discussion, processing of trauma, and grief work should be made available to as many students as possible. The reasoning was that it is impossible to really know, after a given traumatic incident, who is affected and who is not. There-fore, it was considered important to cast a wide net, so that students who might find it awkward to come forward on their own, or those who are confused about their own responses, would still receive help.

Recently, however, many experts in the field of traumatic stress have adopted a different philosophy. This new consensus is that we should not try to provide interventions to everyone but rather devise a screening system to iden-tify those most strongly affected. Our limited resources can then be utilized to assist these individuals. This new philosophy is highlighted in the recent report of an NIMH consensus conference on severe traumatic events ("mass violence") (National Institute of Mental Health, 2002), which states:

◆ A sensible working principle in the immediate post-incident phase is to expect normal recovery;

◆ Effective early intervention following mass violence can be facilitated by careful screening and needs assessment for individuals, groups, and popula-tions;

◆ Follow-up should be offered to individuals and groups at high risk of developing adjustment difficulties following exposure to mass violence, includ-ing those: (1) who have acute stress disorder or other clinically significant symp-toms stemming from the trauma; (2) who are bereaved; (3) who have a preex-isting psychiatric condition; (4) who require medical or surgical attention; and (5) whose exposure to the incident is particularly intense and of long duration.

Thus in schools this means that widespread support or grief groups should not be made available to everyone, but only to those who manifest some indi-cations of difficulties.

SCREENING OF VICTIMS

The new NIMH approach described above recommends *screening* of vic-tims and survivors. In a school setting when a death has occurred, the friends and close classmates of the deceased would obviously be included. In addition, screening for other affected individuals can be done fairly unobtrusively by requesting that teachers observe students for signs of distress and communicate the names of those students to the crisis team. In addition, any student who is frequently absent after the event, or who evidences other indirect indicators of distress, should be followed up. Certainly help should be provided to any stu-dent who requests it.

CRITICAL INCIDENT STRESS DEBRIEFING

In previous editions of this chapter, the author recommended a crisis inter-vention technique called critical incident stress debriefing (CISD), a structured one-session group discussion (Bell, 1995; Mitchell & Bray, 1990; Mitchell &

Everly, 1995). In recent years a controversy has developed about the usefulness of CISD, centered on its originators' claim that it forestalls the later development of post-traumatic stress disorder. The bulk of the empirical evidence now suggests that CISD does not prevent the development of PTSD, and some studies seem to suggest that participation in CISD, especially mandated or involuntary participation, interferes with some individuals' natural recovery processes.

In addition, for most individuals who do need assistance, a "one-shot" group meeting is frequently insufficient. Ongoing individual or group support and treatment is usually necessary.

ONGOING SUPPORT GROUPS

Multiple-session group discussions or support groups should be arranged with all naturally occurring groups who were strongly affected by the traumatic incident. Homogenous groups are preferable. For example, one group might be made up of the close friends of any students who died, with a separate group of peers from classes. A third group might be composed of an athletic or extracurricular group of which those students were a member. In all cases, participation should be voluntary. (Students who request help but who are uncomfortable in groups should be seen individually.)

Support groups are ideal for helping students cope with a traumatic event. A typical group might meet a six times on a weekly basis, with a stable and fixed membership. The group leader should be a social worker or other school mental health professional who is experienced in group process. Support groups are not therapy groups: the material discussed is at a conscious level; the leader does not interpret hidden feelings or unconscious motivations. Support groups should be held at a time and place where there will be no interruptions, and the content of the group must be kept confidential (although the usual exceptions apply). Because support groups usually continue for six weeks or so, there is often a rich opportunity to more fully process the traumatic material. In addition, because support groups normally include the students most affected by the trauma, the social worker can observe how well or poorly individuals are processing and coping with the incident. The social worker is in a unique position to recommend additional individual help if necessary.

CONSULTATION AND ASSISTANCE TO FACULTY

As noted previously, in many situations faculty members are deeply affected and distressed themselves. A meeting, debriefing, or other structured discussion with faculty is an important aspect of crisis team functioning, although it is frequently overlooked. This session should be conducted by a school social worker or other mental health professional from outside the school in question, or an outside community professional, so that the teachers are not put into a position of talking about their personal emotional reactions with the school social worker they work with as a peer on a daily basis.

The school social worker and crisis team can also assist teachers in small ways. For example, some teachers are so distressed that they have difficulty reading the prepared statement to their first-period classes in the immediate aftermath of the traumatic event. A crisis team member could accompany them to class, read the announcement, and cofacilitate the ensuing discussion.

ONGOING TRACKING AND REVIEW

As the first few days of the crisis unfold, periodic feedback needs to be established, so that the crisis team and the social worker can make corrections as needed. A combined teachers' and crisis team meeting after school on day 2 or 3 is quite helpful; the experience up to that point can be reviewed, and changes can be made if necessary. It may be time to suspend the drop-in centers, for example, or it may be decided to continue them for another day. Specific students who are particularly distressed can be discussed, and in some cases, plans can be made for the social worker to speak to those students individually or call their parents. If faculty are still distressed themselves, their difficulties can be addressed individually.

MEDIA

Especially in a Level III crisis, print and electronic media may be present at the school and demand information, access to witnesses, or statements from children. One member of the crisis team, or one member of the administration, should be designated the media representative, and everyone else should refuse to comment. Students should be informed that they are not obligated to speak to media personnel and that in fact the school suggests that they do not. Media representatives can be quite persistent and will often cite the illusory "public's right to know," which has no legal standing at the time of a crisis. For example, during a Level II crisis in a midwestern middle school in which five members of one family were killed in a fire, TV reporters (with cameras and microphones) walked uninvited into the school that the remaining child attended and attempted to interview his classmates. They refused to leave the building until directed to by the police and then set up their cameras on the sidewalk, just off school property (P. Reese, school psychologist, personal communication, 1990).

The media representative should provide information and answer questions concerning the school's response to the traumatic event. No information about the actual event—what happened, who was injured, who was killed— should be provided; this information should properly be obtained from the family, or from legal authorities. The media representative should be straightforward and nondefensive, even in response to what might be perceived as provocative questions. The most effective way to respond to media inquiries is to provide the information that the school wants to provide, regardless of the question asked.

COMMUNITY MEETING

Within a few days of the traumatic incident, a community meeting for parents and others should be held. This meeting should normally take place in the school auditorium on a weekday evening, and the principal should lead it. Representatives of the crisis team should also attend. They will frequently be called on to explain the details of the school's response to the traumatic event. Community members and parents can be confrontative and demanding at community meetings, and staff speaking to them must be prepared for this. If the community turnout is large, as it may be for a Level III crisis, it is helpful to present some information in a large group, but then to break down into small discussion groups. These would be each led by a crisis team member or teacher who is knowledgeable about traumatic stress and the school's response. If the community includes groups whose native languages are not English, it is helpful to have one or more group facilitators who are fluent in those languages.

RUMOR CONTROL MECHANISMS

Throughout the period of crisis, numerous rumors will be circulated among students, parents, and the community in general. Frequently these rumors represent peoples' fears about additional trauma, or their attempts to find a "cause." For example, in the aftermath of an adolescent suicide, and especially following two suicides, rumors of additional "suicide pacts" are extremely common, even though actual suicide pacts are quite rare (Gibbons, Clark, & Fawcett, 1990). Similarly, after an accidental death, whatever the circumstances, rumors may circulate that the driver was drunk, or that this student was walking on that road because she had been thrown out of her parents' house, or that that student was secretly a gang member.

Various procedures to attempt to defuse and debunk these rumors can be useful. Foremost among these is answering questions frankly from students and parents as they arise, and explaining that there is no basis in fact to a particular rumor. Making announcements to large groups or to the media that a particular rumor is untrue is often not effective; in this era, a denial of a rumor that some people have not yet heard is, unfortunately a very effective way of promoting that rumor. On the other hand, debunking rumors when meeting with small groups of students or parents is usually effective.

REDUCING SUICIDE CONTAGION

When the traumatic event is a student suicide, which is usually a Level II crisis, school officials and community members are frequently concerned about the possibility of suicide "clusters." This is the phenomenon of one suicide lead-ing to other "copycat" suicides, and it has been observed in groups such as schools and hospitals. After one suicide, especially of a well-known or popular student, additional suicides are a possibility, although the number of actual sui-cide clusters in the United States has been fairly small (Davidson, Rosenberg, Mercy, Franklin, & Simmons, 1989; Gibbons et al., 1990).

The only research that has demonstrated the contagious nature of suicide has been carried out using the United States as a whole, following heavily pub-licized suicides of famous people. Only on such a large scale can a statistically significant increase be convincingly demonstrated. In these situations, some celebrity suicides have been shown to result in an increase in suicide over a three- to four-week period, primarily among adolescents and young adults (Phillips, Lesyna, & Paight, 1992).

Other studies have focused on specific cases with small numbers of sub-jects. One well-conducted study of specific individuals followed fifty-eight friends and acquaintances of ten different suicides for a six-month period. These friends and acquaintances had no more thoughts of suicide or suicidal behavior than a control group but did have significantly higher rates of depression, which may have represented complicated grief (Brent et al., 1992). These same researchers also studied twenty-eight high school students who witnessed another student committing suicide on a school bus, after accidentally shooting another student while taking out his gun. In this report, the witnesses did not develop suicidal behavior themselves but did develop post-traumatic symptoms (Brent et al., 1992). These studies suggest that after an adolescent suicide, grief, depression, and trauma are much more likely to occur than additional suicides.

Nonetheless, the prospect of cluster suicides is anxiety provoking (Centers for Disease Control, 1988). In fact, when a traumatic event is a completed sui-cide, the goals of a school's crisis intervention program are frequently not only to assist students to process the trauma but also to forestall additional suicides. Many of the crisis intervention activities already described are also useful in reducing suicide risk, in that they provide arenas for students to voice their con-cerns and feelings and give and receive support. These activities also provide opportunities for the crisis team members and the faculty to observe students for signs of unusual distress, and therefore for intervention. However, above and beyond these standard activities, there are a number of other steps that can be taken to lessen the possibility of contagion.

Perhaps most important is undermining the tendency of students to iden-tify with the deceased suicide victim. Although cluster suicides are not well understood, it appears that the primary mechanism of the contagion is identifi-cation and imitation in someone already experiencing suicidal impulses. Ado-lescents are prone to perceive the world in rather judgmental and rigid cate-gories and frequently see themselves and their friends as heroes and heroines attempting to combat an evil and corrupt adult society. Thus a teen suicide is often viewed as a defiant gesture by a heroic individual who was beaten down by powerful but destructive adult forces. The story of Romeo and Juliet exemplifies this concept, and adolescents' tendency to view a suicide as a romantic tragedy (Smith, 1988) could set the stage for a possible cluster suicide.

The key to prevention, therefore, is to undermine the atmosphere of romantic tragedy. One clear way to do this is to portray the deceased student, in all announcements and especially in small-group and individual discussions, as a troubled or depressed or substance-dependent isolated young person who made a bad decision. This portrayal must of course be done with sensitivity and tact and must remain sympathetic, but it will counter students' tendency to idolize and make heroic what is almost always a result, in part, of psychopathology.

Other activities can also help prevent additional suicides. Any student with a history of serious depression, previous suicide attempts, or suicide in the family must be sought out and interviewed individually by a member of the crisis team. Many of these students may benefit from a debriefing or support group, even if they do not belong to any of the naturally occurring groups for whom sessions will have already been planned. Alternatively, many of these students may need to be referred to a community mental health professional for traditional outpatient treatment.

A confidential list of students thought to be at risk for suicidal behavior should be prepared and maintained by the crisis team or school social worker. In addition to students with histories of suicidal behavior, the close friends of the victim should be considered at risk, along with any other students who appear to be strongly affected. Every student on this list should be interviewed privately by a mental health professional experienced at suicide risk assessment, and in any instances in which more than trivial risk exists, parents should be contacted and asked to come to the school and arrange suitable community treatment, outpatient or inpatient, with the assistance of school staff.

Although it may seem counterintuitive, the resumption of business as usual in a school is also an antidote to possible suicide contagion. The structure of the school routine is comforting and helpful to most students (and faculty). A long-lasting crisis atmosphere in which usual classes or programming is canceled or altered can easily contribute to an atmosphere of romantic tragedy and artificially elevated melodrama. A more detailed discussion of reducing suicide contagion may be obtained in the author's case study of a postvention program that appeared to inadvertently worsen the situation (Callahan, 1996).

COMMUNITY HEALING

In recent years, memorials, rituals, and anniversary ceremonies have arisen as a way to help groups and communities continue to heal in the aftermath of a traumatic event. Especially in the case of major events, these rituals help victims and survivors integrate the event into the context of their lives. Perhaps counterintuitively, occasions to look back and remember seem to help victims and survivors move on with their lives. One recent example was the 10th anniversary of the bombing of the Oklahoma City federal building. In April 2004 a week-long series of activities was held, including tree plantings, public lectures, a national symposium on terrorism, an evening candlelight service, and a day of remembrance.

CONCLUSION

Traumatic events lead to crises in many schools and for many students, but it must be remembered that a crisis manifests both "danger" and "opportunity" (Slaikeu, 1990). The danger in a crisis, of course, is that an individual will be unable to cope effectively with the traumatic stress involved and that the lack of resolution will result in long-term distress and a reduced ability to function. This long-term psychopathology typically takes the form of PTSD, major depression, alcohol or drug dependence, or some other disorder. On the other hand, the opportunity is due to the uncharacteristic openness that individuals exhibit while experiencing a crisis. During a crisis, people are much more open to considering and trying out alternative coping techniques than they are at any other time, since (by definition) their customary coping mechanisms have not worked to resolve the current situation (Golan, 1978). Thus, with appropriate assistance, such as that provided by an effective school crisis team, an individual may work through a crisis and adapt new coping techniques. These could be self-reflection, realizing the value of talking with friends and family about important and personal matters, the ability to tolerate strong feelings, adoption of a more adaptive world view, and the like. When a crisis leads an individual to adopt these or other new coping techniques, that individual becomes stronger, more capable, and more resilient than before the crisis. Many survivors of traumatic events feel "if I survived that, I can survive anything." This sense of confidence and mastery is especially important for children and adolescents, who may otherwise begin to perceive themselves as generally helpless and prone to victimization. The growth that students can build out of tragedy is one of the most gratifying processes that a school social worker can experience.

References

American Association of Suicidology. (1997). *Suicide postvention guidelines* (2nd ed.). Washington, DC: Author.

American Psychiatric Association. (1980). *Diagnostic and statistical manual of mental disorders* (3rd ed.). Washington, DC: Author.

American Psychiatric Association. (1994). *Diagnostic and statistical manual of mental disorders* (4th ed.). Washington, DC: Author.

Bell, J. L. (1995). Traumatic event debriefing: Service delivery designs and the role of social work. *Social Work, 40*, 36–43.

Bonanno, G. A. (2004). Loss, trauma, and human resilience. Have we underestimated the human capacity to thrive after extremely aversive events? *American Psychologist, 59*(1), 20–28.

Bonanno, G.A., Wortman, C. B., Lehman, D. R., Tweed, R. G., Haring, M., Sonnega, J., Carr, D., & Nesse, R. M. (2002). Resilience to loss and chronic grief: A prospective study from preloss to 18-months postloss. *Journal of Personality and Social Psychology, 83*(5), 1150-1164.

Bragg, R. (1998, March 26). Arkansas boys held as prosecutors weigh options. *New York Times*, pp. A1, A20.

Brent, D. A., Perper, J., Moritz, G., Allman, C., Friend, A., Schweers, J., et al. (1992). Psychiatric effects of exposure to suicide among friends and acquaintances of adolescent suicide victims. *Journal of the American Academy of Child and Adolescent Psychiatry, 31*, 629-640.

Callahan, J. (1994). Defining crisis and emergency. *Crisis, 15*, 164-171.

Callahan, J. (1996). Negative effects of a school suicide postvention program: A case example. *Crisis, 17*, 108-115.

Centers for Disease Control. (1988). CDC recommendations for a community plan for the prevention and containment of suicide clusters. *Morbidity and Mortality Weekly Report, 37*(Suppl. S-6), 1-12.

Dallas Public Schools. (1997). *Crisis management plan: Resource manual.* Dallas, TX: Author.

Davidson, L. E., Rosenberg, M. L., Mercy, J. A., Franklin, J., & Simmons, J. T. (1989). An epidemiologic study of risk factors in two teenage suicide clusters. *Journal of the American Medical Association, 262*, 2687-2692.

Gibbons, R. D., Clark, D. C., & Fawcett, J. (1990). A statistical method for evaluating suicide clusters and implementing cluster surveillance. *American Journal of Epidemiology 132*(Supp. 1), S183-S191.

Golan, N. (1978). *Treatment in crisis situations.* New York: The Free Press.

Griffin, M. G., Resick, P. A., & Mechanic, M. B. (1997). Objective assessment of peritraumatic dissociation: Psychophysiological indicators. *American Journal of Psychiatry, 154*, 1081-1088.

Huuhtanen, M. (2005, January 14). *WHO fears psychological tsunami damage.* Retrieved January 14, 2005, from http://www.comcast.net/News/healthwellness//xml/1500_Health_medical/b20e

Janoff-Bulman, R. (1985). The aftermath of victimization. Rebuilding shattered assumptions. In C. R. Figley (Ed.), *Trauma and its wake* (Vol. 1, pp. 15-35). New York: Brunner/Mazel.

Johnson, D. R., Lubin, H., Rosenheck, R., Fontana, A., Southwick, S., & Charney, D. (1997). The impact of the homecoming reception on the development of posttraumatic stress disorder: The West Haven Homecoming Stress Scale (WHHSS). *Journal of Traumatic Stress, 10*, 259-277.

Kessler, R. C., Sonnega, A., Bromet, E., Hughes, M., & Nelson, C. B. (1995). Posttraumatic stress disorder in the National Comorbidity Survey. *Archives of General Psychiatry, 52*, 1048-1060.

Lazarus, R., & Folkman, S. (1984). *Stress, appraisal, and coping.* New York: Springer.

Leenaars, A. A., & Wenckstern, S. (1999). Principals of postvention: Applications to suicide and trauma in schools. *Death Studies, 22*(4), 357-391.

Marmar, C. R., Weiss, D. S., Metzler, T. J., Ronfeldt, H. M., & Foreman, C. (1996). Stress responses of emergency services personnel to the Loma Prieta earthquake Interstate 880 freeway collapse and control traumatic incidents. *Journal of Traumatic Stress, 9*, 63-85.

Marmar, C. R., Weiss, D. S., Schlenger, W. E., Fairbank, J. A., Jordan, B. K., Kulka, R. A., et al. (1994). Peritraumatic dissociation and posttraumatic stress disorder in male Vietnam theater veterans. *American Journal of Psychiatry, 151*, 902-907.

Mitchell, J.T., & Bray, G. P. (1990). *Emergency services stress.* Englewood Cliffs, NJ: Prentice Hall.

Mitchell, J.T., & Everly, G. S. (1995). *Critical incident stress debriefing: An operations manual for the prevention of traumatic stress among emergency services and disaster workers* (2nd ed.). Ellicott City, MD: Chevron.

Nader, K. O. (1997). Childhood traumatic loss: The interaction of trauma and grief. In C. R. Figley, B. E. Bride, & N. Mazza (Eds.), *Death and trauma* (pp. 17–41). Washington, DC: Taylor & Francis.

Nader, K., Pynoos, R., Fairbanks, L., & Frederick, C. (1990). Children's PTSD reactions one year after a sniper attack at their school. *American Journal of Psychiatry, 147,* 1526–1530.

National Institute of Mental Health. (2002). *Mental health and mass violence: Evidence-based early psychological intervention for victims/survivors of mass violence. A workshop to reach consensus on best practices.* (NIH Publication No. 02-5138), Washington, DC: U.S. Government Printing Office.

Phillips, D. P., Lesyna, K., & Paight, D.J. (1992). Suicide and the media. In R.W. Maris, A. L. Berman, J.T. Maltsberger, & R. I. Yufit (Eds.), *Assessment and prediction of suicide* (pp. 499–519). New York: Guilford.

Pynoos, R. S., & Nader, K. (1988). Psychological first aid and treatment approach to children exposed to community violence: Research implications. *Journal of Traumatic Stress, 1,* 445–473.

Pynoos, R. S., Frederick, C., Nader, K., Arroyo, W., Steinberg, A., Eth, S., et al. (1987). Life threat and posttraumatic stress in school-age children. *Archives of General Psychiatry, 44,* 1057–1063.

Schlenger, W. E., Kulka, R. A., Fairbank, J.A., Hough, R. L., Jordan, B. K., Marmar, C. R., et al. (1992). The prevalence of posttraumatic stress disorder in the Vietnam generation: A multimethod, multisource assessment of psychiatric disorder. *Journal of Traumatic Stress, 5,* 333–363.

Slaikeu, K.A. (1990). *Crisis intervention: A handbook for practice and research* (2nd ed.) Boston: Allyn & Bacon.

Smith, J. (1997). *School crisis management manual: Guidelines for administrators.* Holmes Beach, FL: Learning Publications.

Smith, K. (1988, October). *One town's experience with teen suicide.* Presentation at the annual meeting of the Michigan Association of Suicidology, Lansing, MI.

Spiegel, D., & Cardena, E. (1991). Disintegrated experience: The dissociative disorders revisited. *Journal of Abnormal Psychology, 100,* 366–378.

Terr, L. C. (1991). Childhood traumas: An outline and overview. *American Journal of Psychiatry, 148,* 10–20.

Terr, L. C., Block, D.A., Michel, B.A., Shi, H., Reinhardt, J.A., & Metayer, S. (1996). Children's memories in the wake of the *Challenger. American Journal of Psychiatry, 153,* 618–625.

Washburn, G., & Gibson, R. (1995, October 26). Ride to school ends in tragedy. *Chicago Tribune,* p. 1.

Webb, N. B. (1994). School-based assessment and crisis intervention with kindergarten children following the New York World Trade Center bombing. *Crisis Interventions, 1,* 47–59.

38

Mediation as a Form of Peer-Based Conflict Resolution

Shirley McDonald
University of Illinois at Chicago

Anthony Moriarty
Olympia Fields, IL
Culture and Conflict

The skills of conflict resolution have become recognized as core social skills. These skills are now viewed as fundamental for effective participation in ordinary day-to-day negotiations between people, and for negotiating those episodes in our lives that threaten to create major disruptions.

Conflict resolution programs such as mediation are geared toward individual students and constellations of students, but they imply a larger commitment of the school community to become safe and responsive. While mediation alone cannot prevent school violence (Astor, Meyer, Benbenishty, Marachi, & Rosemond, 2005), mediation programs are not only very popular but can be effective instruments in a broader program to make the school community safe and responsive (Mattaini, 2001).

Students can become disenchanted with and alienated from the decision-making and governing processes that are in common use in schools (Rappoport, 1989).They may experience an inability to develop a sense of self-determination or to achieve self-responsibility, two powerful motivators for adolescents. If social workers are to play a significant role in helping schools to become more effective, they must participate in developing channels for school support systems that empower students to develop this sense of self-determination (Germain, 1988). Conflict resolution training and peer mediation are two resources for such empowerment.

Students become increasingly vulnerable to a variety of problems, such as anxiety, stress, a sense of personal inadequacy, and low self-esteem, when they are blocked from developing autonomy and self-determination. Such alienated students are at risk of becoming involved in conflict and can be disruptive to the educational process. Social workers can counter this alienation with strategies that reconnect and empower students in a positive manner. Conflict resolution skills are such a tool. For elementary and high school students, these skills play a major role in confirming their sense of social competence. Some students seem to possess these skills naturally, but nearly all need training and additional practice to be able to use them appropriately and effectively (Moriarty & McDonald, 1991).

The formal process of conflict resolution builds on the fundamental practice skills of social work. Because such skills are already part of our professional repertoire, the preparation required for teaching these skills is only the time required to learn the process of conflict resolution. This chapter discusses a variety of methods for resolving conflicts, both formally and informally, and the skills necessary to achieve such resolutions.Attention will be given to issues of training special student populations to become proficient in both the skills and the process. Such school programs already in place are widely recognized as having a positive impact on individual student's lives, as well as a positive impact on the climate of the school (South Suburban Peer Network, 1993). When these skills are learned and modeled by teachers, administrators, parents, and community members, the process and skills learned are significantly reinforced, thereby producing family and community benefits.

CULTURE AND CONFLICT

How conflicts are handled in any society depends on community cultural norms, as well as individual perceptions of threats to personal safety in case of unsatisfactory resolution of the conflict (Combs & Snygg, 1959). For example, in many Eastern cultures a third person is used as a go-between.Thus, the disputants need never directly acknowledge to each other that there is a difficulty and may continue civil behavior as negotiations over the difficulty are in process (Sue & Sue, 1990). The person acting as go-between will be selected because of a reputation for possessing skills of fairness, clear communication, and creative problem solving, all of which contribute to the potential for obtaining a mutually agreeable solution. Peace may be preserved, and the disputants can discard the previous concerns without directly acknowledging their feelings about the problem to the other. Although the skills needed for an effective go-between in such cultures closely mirror the skills that describe an effective mediator in Western culture, the potential for problems with such a process may occur if the go-between is not perceived as fair, or does not communicate well in a particular dispute. In these cases, the outcome may or may not bode well for the concerned parties. Because the reason for using a go-between is to resolve a dispute without the parties confronting each other directly, they are of course not able to hear the discussion with the go-between and the other disputant. The problem is that without this knowledge a process of checks and balances for correcting possible misinformation may be lacking. In Western society there is perceived honor in directly confronting one's accusers or provocateurs, and there is no recourse to a go-between as there would be in many Eastern societies. A combination of these two cultural patterns for solving conflict could draw on the best attributes of each.

Day-to-day attitudes toward conflict in most Western societies tend to be those of avoidance, despite the perceived honor of confronting one's foes or potential foes. This avoidance takes many forms. Some of these, as already discussed, have cultural roots, and some are socially driven, but all seem to have the common theme of desiring painless resolution of the dispute. Unfortunately, once it is clear that a controversy will not dissipate or dissolve, there seem to be very few alternatives but to stand one's ground and defend it, aggressively if needed (Fisher, Ury, & Patton, 1991). Alternatively, one can avoid the difficulty for the immediate present then stand firm against any challenges if the dispute does not dissipate. In either case one can be drawn into a confrontation that may be hurtful to both parties and to order and peace within the particular social context.

Conflict and Emotional Expression

Real feelings often are not easily expressed in our society, at least publicly. By revealing emotions one may be perceived as being overly sensitive, insecure, unsure, vulnerable, or manipulative. The interpretation of the expression of emotion is dependent on the relationship between the person displaying the emotion and the interpreter of the experience. The potential is great for misunderstanding and may leave the person showing emotion vulnerable to another's interpretation. Unfortunately, emotional displays are often discounted, apologized for, and perceived to be a weakness. Such negative interpretation is portrayed routinely in the media. The lesson learned most often is to withhold expression of feelings until one is in the safety of one's own space. For a child this is likely to be his or her home, room, or special secret hideaway.

An alternative reaction is to overreact aggressively early in the dispute's development as a warning that further incidents or perceived threats will not be taken lightly. This behavior can have the effect of rapid escalation of the emotional reaction to the dispute. The disputants may revert to physical aggression. Children and adolescents, unless they are taught alternatives, can be particularly prone to physical aggression. In any case, the decision to warn of potential confrontation, or not to warn, has its own cultural and personal pressures. We continue to struggle with honest expression of feelings versus a sense of extreme vulnerability when emotional expression is experienced. This reluctance to reveal negative reactions to others' behaviors exacerbates the difficulty of confronting others when their perceived actions cause discomfort. As school social workers, we routinely help students become more comfortable with their emotions and the productive expression of emotional responses. This skill must be achieved before a student is likely to profit from the process of conflict resolution.

SKILL BUILDING FOR RESOLUTION

A number of discrete skills are critical in learning the process of conflict resolution. Students need to be supported in demonstrating empathy for others' emotional responses. There is also a great need to explore mutually advantageous ways to defuse aggressive responses and to resolve underlying problems before such potential conflicts escalate to physical assault. Finally, the social worker must incorporate teaching, coaching, reinforcing, and supporting of students in their ongoing use of conflict resolution skills.

A crucially important skill for a person in conflict is to learn to identify his or her feelings, and at the same time to be able to have sufficient empathic sensitivity to others' feelings through attention to their words, facial expression, tone of voice, body posture, and body language. Mutual ability to interpret emotional expression allows accurate communication to occur (Fast, 1970), and this is a skill fundamental to effective conflict resolution.

Once students show competence in the communication of feelings, the next step is expressing accurately how one feels, and communicating such feelings with nonpejorative language, such as "I messages" (Gordon, 1975). This gives the disputant the proper language and format to describe how she feels when the other disputant behaves in certain ways. This process has three parts:

1. State the behavior that affects you.
2. State the feeling that this behavior creates in you.
3. State the effect of the behavior on you (your feeling reaction).

For example:

1. Problem behavior: ignore me
2. Feeling created: worry
3. Effect: afraid you don't like me anymore

Using this formula, the following I message might be created: "When you ignore me I feel worried because I am concerned that you may not like me anymore." This nonaccusing language may allow enough communication to occur so each disputant may experience how the other is feeling.

Not all people have natural listening skills, certainly not all young people. Unfortunately, these are seldom taught or even effectively modeled. The cliche "Just because you said it, does not mean she heard it" is testament to the ability to hear words without comprehending the intended meaning. The child's game of telephone where a circle of children attempt to pass a message successfully around the circle without the message being changed is a second illustration of social awareness that messages are frequently distorted. Often the results are funny, and seldom does the message stay intact around the circle. Therefore, real listening skills need to involve dialogue designed to "check out" the meaning of what was stated, such as "Can you be more specific," "Can you say that in another way," or the client-centered reflective listening response, "Let me tell you what I think I just heard you say, correct me if I am wrong."

Staying with one subject is also difficult for some children, whether distracted by something said previously, or by their own thoughts. Teaching phrases such as "How does that relate to" (what the original subject was) may be helpful to reconnect the dialogue to the stated problem to be solved. At the same time, validating the student's new area of concern is critical also, so that he does not feel belittled or marginalized. This can be dealt with by teaching children to give assurances that they will return to the new topic once the current topic is resolved.

Role playing is another aid in the development of good listening skills, once the skill has been taught and modeled by the instructor. Making up scenarios for role plays can be an enjoyable and useful exercise and personalizes the activity for the students. For younger children the use of puppets may be helpful to begin a dialogue leading to role playing. Self-talk, that is, unexpressed thoughts about what is occurring or being said, can be good, neutral, or negative. However, self-talk can be an impediment to successful conflict resolution, especially if the participant is anxious. Keeping the dialogue focused on the subject is essential to the process, and staying on task can be confounded by emotionality. It will be helpful to coach children to avoid negative self-talk, that is, to avoid statements one thinks silently, such as, "I'm getting nervous" or "I hope he still (likes me) (doesn't get angrier) (doesn't tell my friends), etc." To counteract negative self-talk, children can be encouraged to repeat phrases to themselves, such as "Keep it up" or "Did I make that point clearly?" Being their own coaches through the use of positive, constructive self-talk statements is another powerful skill that will serve them well throughout their lives.

PROCESS OF CONFLICT RESOLUTION

The actual process of conflict resolution has several components: (1) identification of the problem in specific language, (2) brainstorming possible solutions, (3) agreeing on a solution, and (4) confirming intent to make the resolution work.

First, the student needs to learn to identify problems. They must specify problems, avoid general terms and "fuzzy" language (Moriarty, 1992), and then prioritize the problems according to the level of seriousness or, in some cases, according to the level of likelihood of the problem being resolved. Again, this skill will serve the student in many arenas. To acquire this skill at a useful level students need to be able to:

1. State the present problem as specifically as possible and then
2. Identify the most troublesome parts of the problem.

At this point, it is important to help each disputant put in words what they feel they want to achieve from an agreement, if they are able to reach one. This is crucial if each disputant is going to be able to accept the outcome as fair. This process usually involves several components:

- The student needs to reconfirm her desire for a solution
- She wishes this solution to occur within a problem-solving process, and
- The process may involve compromising on some points.

3. Next, it is important for the student to determine what his position is regarding the ideal resolution of the problem, and then, what the bottom line is, that is, *what is not negotiable* (Fisher et al., 1991). The student must learn that it is better to argue from a bargaining position that has some maneuverability.

4. The next skill that students find difficult is focusing on the important issues, that is, not getting sidetracked. When people get into arguments, they normally have a sense of being threatened, and when this threat becomes too great, it is very common for the disputant to divert the argument by introducing extraneous information or additional complaints not directly related to the argument. Role plays are probably the most effective tool to demonstrate and practice the skill of staying with core concerns.

5. Control of emotions is a skill that needs to be emphasized during the actual resolution process. It can be difficult, especially for younger students, but coaching students as they practice can quickly help them see how much emotional control may often operate to their advantage if the real goal is resolution of the dispute.

Special Student Populations

One fundamental reason for diverting arguments or at least getting off the subject is the fear of being exposed, either for faulty thinking, or overemotionalism. These threats are often intensely felt by students who struggle in school because of developmental delays, learning disabilities, attention deficit disorder, or emotional disturbances/behavior disorders. Such children are already accustomed to being ridiculed for not succeeding, often in cognitive areas. For many, overemotionalism is a persistent struggle as they attempt to become empowered in the school setting, and among their peers. They need extra support in learning to sort out the important from the unimportant and to stay with the main theme of the dispute. These students sometimes retain linear thinking processes longer than their age mates who are not so disabled, and thus extra support in brainstorming for solutions may be necessary. This is not to say that such populations cannot benefit from conflict resolution training; in fact, the opposite is true, and these students have some amazing assets and insights into the process, making them good candidates for such training.

Other students who need extra support are those struggling with poor self-concepts and general problem-solving skills, sometimes identified as *at-risk* students. These students tend to cave in quickly to any challenge and are more likely to have difficulty staving off emotional responses that overwhelm their ability to think through problems clearly. However, the skills of conflict resolution can enhance their sense of competence once they have successfully mastered them, and their ability to identify their bottom-line needs in a dispute may be valuable to help them understand their rightful position in social encounters.

Problem-Solving Process

Finally, students need a *formalized process of problem solving* to keep them on track to the end point of reaching an agreement. Problem solving is both a natural and a formal process. Most people go through a process of looking at a few options before making even small day-to-day decisions. This process may be barely conscious. A few options are considered and all but one ruled out. This becomes this person's decision about taking action or beginning an activity. This process works well if conflicting emotions are not significantly involved, or if the stakes are not very high. However, as the outcome of a decision increases in importance, the process becomes more important, and emotions are more likely to come into play, complicating the ability to think clearly and creatively. In addition, the extent of an individual's routine use of formal operations in thinking patterns may further determine the goodness of fit of the resolution to the problem. Teaching a formal method of problem solving will certainly enhance the quality of life of students who receive such training, by giving them tools to use when they find themselves under pressure. Such skills will be retained throughout their lives.

These are the steps to the problem-solving process:

1. Identify the specific problem needing resolution;
2. Brainstorm potential solutions without criticizing any suggestions, including some that may initially seem frivolous—all ideas are acceptable;
3. Discuss the positives and negatives of each possible solution that may have some potential;

4. Agree on one solution that has the most potential for satisfying both parties to the dispute, and that has the greatest potential of succeeding;

5. Agree on a time line for trying the solution, even if it does not seem to be working very well at first. Stay with the proposed solution to give it a chance for success;

6. Evaluate whether the solution is meeting the needs of each disputant in resolving the identified and agreed-on problem, or whether some modifications need to be made or a new solution proposed.

Once the potential solution has been agreed upon, the disputants and anyone helping to guide them through the process should congratulate each other on a successful outcome of the dispute. Older students will often shake hands as a sign of agreement. There should also be an understanding about not talking about the disagreement with outside parties, so that the privacy of all is respected (confidentiality).

Adapting the Process to Your Setting

Schools use conflict resolution in a variety of ways, but the process previously outlined is essentially the same. The details are often quite different. Some school districts have instituted system-wide training in conflict resolution skills but have no formal program, such as a trained team of mediators or conflict resolvers. Other districts do some training with all students but also train a cadre of students who are available in more difficult situations. This is especially important when emotions are running high, or when there seems to be an imbalance in power. In these situations care is required to ensure that each party to the dispute is respectful to the other. These specially trained students are often identified as a team and have regular meetings. Younger students may wear special vests on playgrounds and in lunchrooms, or during special functions where students are not being closely supervised. Other schools have students identified in each classroom who are the designated conflict resolvers and who may hold such dispute resolution sessions in the classroom, ideally in an area somewhat removed from the rest of the class. Other schools do not train all students but rely on a cadre or team of conflict resolvers or mediators to deal with identified problems. In such schools there is likely to be a set policy regarding which types of problems are appropriate for referral to such specially trained teams. In all cases, the school must have a means to oversee the referral process so that conflict resolvers and mediators are at all times protected from serious problems or risks.

Any plan for using a formal conflict resolution program in schools needs administrative sanction and support, as well as occasional morale boosts in terms of recognition for a job well done. Any faculty or staff may choose to sponsor such efforts. The only real requirement for such sponsorship is that the adult be invested in conflict resolution and dedicated to the program.

Teaching children such life skills serves them well when they are students and later as adults. The school climate is enhanced when students resolve their own personal problems, and a language of respect is developed when people in the school disagree. Thus, conflict need not be avoided as a personal threat and something dangerous, but conflict becomes an opportunity for positive change when the skills are at hand to resolve the conflict in a creative and lasting way.

PEER MEDIATION

There are many formats within which mediation can occur. Some are relatively structured and formal, especially those developed to intervene and, it is hoped, prevent legal confrontations, as in special education disputes (Gallant, 1982), or those developed for neighborhood or community disputes (Neighborhood Justice Center of Atlanta, Inc., 1982). Peer mediation in the format discussed here has been adapted to reflect the school milieu, the relative and unique skills of student mediators, and the types of disputes identified as amenable to the more formal student-to-student peer mediation process. However, there does not seem to be a significant difference in the experience of, or the quality of, outcome of less-structured formats of conflict resolution. Mediation is inherently democratic in its process and effectively balances the concerns for the needs of students with the needs of the institution.

Peer mediation is an effective model that provides a relatively structured format for addressing problems that have a disruptive and negative effect on students' daily lives. Students, able to resolve disagreements with dignity, are more able to pursue meaningful activity in school and are less likely to experience feelings of estrangement or alienation from the school culture and the school system. We have found that students who experience a personal sense of empowerment tend to demonstrate a greater capacity to assume responsibility for their own behavior and welfare than those who do not feel empowered.

Peer Mediation: Keeping Students in School

Peer mediation can help keep students in school by defusing the potential escalation of disagreements. If students are suspended and sent home, they are at increased risk for more serious problems. When not in school, they generally are without supervision either at home or in the community, while likely being angry with the school and cut off from social interaction with their peers. The dropout rate for students who have been suspended significantly exceeds the rate of the general school population (National School Safety Center, 1988). Some authors believe that peer mediation in schools may be the most positive and effective means of intervention with students at risk for more serious problems (Wheelock, 1988). The process of mediation conveys a belief that students are indeed competent and therefore have the capacity and potential to resolve their own problems. Peer mediation significantly deters the serious side effects of alternative punitive interventions found in most school discipline codes.

Schools as Change Agents

Schools vary in their receptivity to change. The organizational characteristics of the institution affect the degree to which a peer mediation program will function congruently within the school community. Systems such as schools, or school districts, in general are *open* or *closed*, depending largely on the administrative ability to accept change. In a closed system, a rule infraction is dealt with according to a predetermined procedure and without a process of organizational reflection about possible change. In a more open system, rule infractions have prescribed consequences, but they also serve as indicators of the effectiveness of the school's relationship with its students and the overall educational process. Consequently, in an open system, although infractions require a response, the school sees itself as capable of change and adaptation to enable each individual student to better cope with the causes and circumstances of infractions. Mediation probably cannot function in an entirely closed school system. It requires a degree of flexibility and openness to creative problem solving. It also depends on a school philosophy that reflects a belief that everything that goes on between students in a school can be used for growth.

Peer Mediation as an Educational Support

Peer mediation empowers students but does not discard reasonable controls. A principle long recognized is that an individual's interpersonal conflicts are best resolved in a dialogue with his or her peers. Our judicial system is based on the principle that peers can make fair judgments on disputed questions. Students from the intermediate grades on up are at the developmental stage where they are interested in and value approval and/or sanction from their peers. When interpersonal disputes arise that appear to be unresolvable to the disputants, a growth-inducing settlement using peer mediation is likely to have a more positive long-term effect than a mandated solution imposed by an adult authority figure.

Peer mediation teaches the art of compromise, effective listening, judicious inquiry, rational thinking, and a skillful focus on areas of mutual concern and benefit. Consequently, both the students who are trained as mediators and those who avail themselves of the process actively engage in a fundamentally democratic activity. In conflict resolution vernacular, the basic goal of mediation is to arrive at a *win-win* outcome rather than the traditional *win-lose* outcome of more closed styles of dispute resolution (Fisher et al., 1991). This process has proved to be an effective face-saving opportunity for students who find themselves caught in a web of peer conflict.

SELECTION CRITERIA FOR MEDIATORS

Mediation training does not require the teaching of entirely new skills. It is an inherently efficient process because it redirects talents demonstrated by students. This is true especially of the talents developed in peer relationships. Mediation training builds on these demonstrated talents to develop the necessary elements of the mediation process. These skills are defined, identified, and sanctioned by the school as valuable and important. They are put to work for the greater good of the school community and the mediators themselves.

Identifying potential student mediators is a process that relies heavily on recognizing leadership traits and specific personal qualities. The students selected should be those who are sought out by others in times of personal difficulty, rather than those who have identified leadership characteristics resulting from academic, athletic, or social talent. Students who are able to serve effectively as mediators are found in every strata of student populations. They may not be well known to each other because they are the effective leaders of their separate social groups. Effective mediators do not emerge more frequently from any one particular type of group in the school.

These students readily learn the fundamental interpersonal communication skills essential to the mediation process. Once students are selected for mediation training, the process of refining these preexisting skills begins. Indigenous leadership skills are shaped, and a degree of structure is imposed on them. Thus, it is clear that teaching new skills is not a major focus of training. Training tailors skills students have brought with them to the job of conflict resolution.

DEVELOPMENT OF A MEDIATION PROGRAM

An example of a training program is the effort that began in the spring of 1988 to develop such a program at Rich East High School in Park Forest, Illinois. The program is still functioning. This effort has met with an impressive degree of acceptance by the students and success in resolving interpersonal conflicts between students. The project was initiated in a two-day workshop for the students selected to serve as mediators. This training program described an approach to mediation that was a combination of several existing models.

The Selection Process

The first step in developing this specific model was a decision to proceed with the training program. Once this took place, students needed to be selected. It was important that students selected to be mediators should have clout with their peers. Such clout in a school has two relevant definitions: First, it means influence or pull; and second, it implies power or muscle. Deans and counselors were asked to recommend students they believed were sufficiently influential and whom they believed possessed clout. Surprisingly, the deans and the counselors largely recommended the same students, despite the seemingly vague definition of this criterion. All ten of the original nominees agreed to participate in the project. This level of agreement was a surprise to the project planners, who expected some students to decline to participate. However, the level of participation correlates with the characteristics of the students selected. When the general concept of the program was explained, all the students appeared to recognize the program to be a valuable contribution to the school, as well as an opportunity for personal growth.

This group of students defied generalization. They were dissimilar in every category except that of age. Race, gender, grade-point average, extracurricular participation, and regular and special education defined no common characteristics. Some had problems themselves that had brought them to the deans' offices earlier in high school. Others were relatively unknown to the administrative staff. It soon was clear that students with identifiable clout came from a wide range of social and educational strata in the high school.

The Orientation Process

This group of fledgling mediators was given an orientation to the process of mediation and a series of structured steps to follow in the actual mediation process. Emphasis was placed on creating the proper atmosphere, personal demeanor, the structuring of the physical setting, and the preliminary remarks made by the mediators. Ensuring confidence and respect in the process by starting out with a well-delivered opening statement was seen as critical to the success of the experience. Consequently, time was spent helping each student develop the opening statement, make introductions, establish ground rules, and explain the process of mediation and rules of decorum. It also was essential that these content areas be explained in language compatible with each mediator's personal style.

Opening Statements. Several elements are necessary in an appropriate opening statement. First, mediators need to structure a win-win environment. The disputants are told clearly that no one comes out of mediation a loser. This stimulates student interest and also lets them know early on that they are being provided a face-saving opportunity. Second, the principle of confidentiality is defined, and its application to the mediation process is clearly established. Third, it is emphasized during the training sessions that a commitment to neutrality needs to be made clear in the opening statement. This is important for two reasons. The students in dispute need to know that the mediators are not going to take sides. It is also important for the protection of the mediators to reinforce the fact that mediators will not have any involvement with disputants outside the mediation session, at least in regard to the issue in dispute. Mediators must make it very clear that they will have no involvement with the problem or its solution outside of the mediation session, including any follow-up.

Finally, rules of order are introduced in the opening statement. The mediator requires appropriate decorum and specifically states what is and what is not appropriate behavior. In the pilot project, the mediators quickly realized that full control of the mediation session is most effectively accomplished by insisting that all conversation be directed to and through the mediator. This style, although allowing each of the disputants to listen to the other's story, establishes equality and fairness in the disputants' opportunities to present their positions and helps prevent interruptions.

Interpersonal Skills

Disputes brought to mediation often are not thoroughly understood by the disputants. Mediation trainers need to discuss the concepts of *secondary* or *hidden agendas*. These ideas were readily grasped by the mediators, as were double-bind messages, reflective listening skills, and the general techniques of good therapeutic style, including the withholding of judgment, neutrality, the use of I messages, and confidentiality. The students' affinity for these concepts seemed to be a natural by-product of their preexisting leadership abilities.

The skill-building component of the training focused on sharpening communication skills to serve the specific goals of the mediation process. The most effective mediators are those who are especially good at the use of reflective statements and those able to quickly ferret out hidden agendas. Reflective statements convey to the disputants that their issues are understood; the discovery of hidden agendas brings into focus why the disputants are clinging to their conflictual issues. The process transcends the angry and rigid presenting of positions and guides the students to their real agendas. In short, the mediators are learning basic techniques essential to good therapeutic intervention, and they come to appreciate and respect the power of good communication skills.

Issues Brought to the Table

Problems presented may involve interpersonal relationships, space violations, and possession of property. Some issues are relatively minor, others potentially catastrophic. The significant point is that the students in dispute are themselves involved in developing the agreement that resolves the dispute. A follow-up component is intended to monitor students' compliance with the terms of the agreement, but this must be done by someone on staff, and not a mediator. Once the dispute is settled and the agreement written and signed by all, and congratulations given for a job well done, the mediators' work is done, other than to continue to maintain confidentiality indefinitely.

PEER MEDIATION AND SCHOOL SOCIAL WORK

The philosophy and process of mediation are compatible with the same tenets in social work. The only distinguishing characteristics of mediation that

separate it from the fundamentals of social work practice are the relative for-
mality of the process and the degree of personal distance maintained by the
mediators, as opposed to that of the usual social worker's more empathic
response level. Moreover, the practical restrictions placed on mediators regarding their involvement in cases after the mediation is completed differ from
good social work practice, where follow-up of cases may be indicated. Disputants, whether successful or not, are given directions for finding support
from appropriate school personnel, should they feel the need for further follow-
up. The process of mediation serves to facilitate system change and effectively
enables students to acquire more self-responsibility and competent independence within a complex system, a goal highly compatible with good social work
practice.

The implementation of a program of student mediation in a secondary
school has several benefits that affect the operation of the school and the effectiveness of the social worker in the school setting. First, it is congruent with the
goals of social work in general. A program of student mediation is an effective
vehicle for the promotion of mental health issues. Social workers are under an
ongoing pressure to reach more students, and mediation helps to achieve this
outreach goal.

Second, mediation also serves to increase general awareness in the school
of the social worker's availability and effectiveness in program development.
Such awareness is a prerequisite to encouragement of appropriate referrals of
students for whom early interventions may be appropriate.

Third, the position of the social worker can be enhanced by the implementation of a mediation program. The social worker's role becomes more
effective when a position of relative indispensability is developed in the school
system. Mediation is on the forefront of innovations compatible with a systems
approach to school management, and school administrators, seeing their social
worker developing effective programming in terms of both cost and public relations, may consider such services essential to the effective administration of
their school.

Fourth, the skills learned during mediation training, as well as the experience of mediation itself, have excellent carry-over value to other life situations
involving dispute resolution. Peer mediators, as well as many of the disputants
who have been through a mediated settlement, do not leave these skills at
school. They have reported finding them useful in dealing with problems at
home and in the community, and using them regularly and, as they report, effectively in off-campus settings.

Fifth, mediation is proactive. It promotes intervention and problem solving
before the school requires disciplinary sanctions. Consequently, a mediation
program reduces suspensions, enhances student morale, and contributes to the
overall positive operation of the school system.

Sixth and finally, mediators provide a significant service to the school. Mediation is serious business; the school runs better because of it. Mediators have a
powerful experience in having their personal levels of self-esteem enhanced

because they feel important to the school. Being important and doing an important job raises self-esteem as effectively as any activity the school can provide.

EVALUATION

The usual measures to chart effectiveness of mediation programs have focused on one of three measures: (1) satisfaction of training as evaluated by the students who have been trained; (2) satisfaction ratings by disputants as they report back, usually a week or so after the conflict has been resolved (Moriarty, Mansfield, & Leverence, 1992); and (3) school impact studies measuring recidivism rates of individual students (whether the original identified problem has resurfaced, or not), or a global school profile regarding reduction of violent incidents and/or reduction in the number of disciplinary actions such as suspension rates (Tolson, McDonald, & Moriarty, 1991). Each of these evaluations measures only part of the total impact of an established conflict resolution program. While mediation alone cannot make the school safe or responsive (Astor et al., 2005), it demands an orderly context and a commitment to safety, respect, and fairness on the part of the whole school community. We have observed an appreciable positive effect on students' lives, their self-esteem, and on the climate of the school. Students have been doing an important job. Graduating students who have developed mediation skills go out to make a real contribution to the community.

References

Astor, R. A., Meyer, H. A., Benbenishty, R., Marachi, R. ,& Rosemond, M. (2005) School safety interventions: Best practices and programs. *Children in Schools, 27*(1), 17–32.

Combs, A., & Snygg, D. (1959). *Individual behavior: A perceptual approach to behavior*. New York: Harper & Row.

Fast, J. (1970). *Body language.* New York: Pocket Books.

Fisher, R., Ury, W., & Patton, B. (1991). *Getting to yes.* New York: Penguin Books.

Gallant, C. B. (1982). *Mediation in special education disputes.* Silver Spring, MD: National Association of Social Workers.

Germain, C. B. (1988). School as a living environment within the community. *Social Work in Education, 10*(4), 260–276.

Gordon, T. (1975). *Parental effectiveness training.* New York: Bantam Books.

Mattaini, M. A. (2001). Constructing cultures of non-violence: The Peace-Power strategy. *Education & Treatment of Children, 24*, 430–448.

Moriarty, A. (1992). *Training guide.* (Mimeograph). Park Forest, IL: Author.

Moriarty, A., Mansfield, V., & Leverence, W. M. (1992). Student satisfaction and peer-based mediation. *School Social Work Journal, 16*(2), 32–35.

Moriarty, A., & McDonald, S. (1991). Theoretical dimensions of school-based mediation. *Social Work in Education, 13*(3), 176–184.

National School Safety Center. (1988). *Increasing student attendance.* NSSC resource paper. Malibu, CA: Pepperdine University Press.

Neighborhood Justice Center of Atlanta, Inc. (1982). *Dispute resolution in education: The NJCA mediation model.* Atlanta, GA: Author.

Rappoport, L. (1989). Entering the sacred: Prologue to a theory of transcendent consciousness. *Theoretical and Philosophical Psychology, 9*(1), 12–19.

South Suburban Peer Network. (1993). Susan Tantillo & Frank DuBois. Steering Committee Coordinators, Homewood-Flossmoor High School, Flossmoor, IL. Organized 1993.

Sue, D. W., & Sue, D. (1990). *Counseling the culturally different* (2nd ed.). New York: John Wiley and Sons.

Tolson, E., McDonald, S., & Moriarty, A. (1992). Peer mediation among high school students: A test of effectiveness. *Social Work in Education, 14*(2), 86–93.

Wheelock, A. (1988). Strengthening dropout prevention: The role of school mediation programs. *The Fourth R, 16,* n.p.

Index

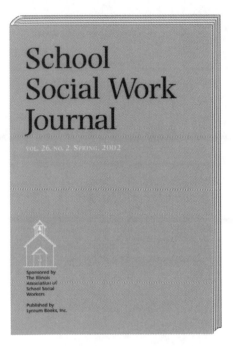